THE REFORMATION WORLD

———◆–■–◆———

The Reformation was a pivotal event which permanently fractured Western Christianity, creating competing Catholic and Protestant churches, which, for a century or more, fought ruthlessly for supremacy.

It divided nations, communities, even families; it undermined the worship traditions of the medieval church; it created new forms of congregation and multiple competing sects. In the second half of the sixteenth century it led to two decades of bitter civil conflicts which undermined the very fabric of Europe's new nation states.

This volume of thirty specially commissioned essays offers a complete survey of the impact of the Reformation right across Europe. Contributions consider not only well known case studies - Germany, England and France - but also countries which have barely featured in previous syntheses: Scandinavia, Italy (home to a fascinating but ultimately failed attempt at evangelical reform), Spain and Eastern Europe. The extensive introduction considers the church before the Reformation, no longer regarded as a tottering edifice ripe for destruction, but a lively and vigorous institution which enjoyed widespread popular support.

While illuminating structural, political and theological change, the book gives refreshing attention to the Reformation 'experienced' in people's lives right across the continent. Issues of architecture, art, music, family life and popular culture are considered, along with a broad ranging account of the late medieval church.

Richly illustrated, *The Reformation World* brings together the foremost experts in the field, in an incisive new survey which offers a fundamental reappraisal of one of the seminal events of the Early Modern Period.

Andrew Pettegree is Professor of Modern History at the University of St Andrews, and Director of the St Andrews Reformation Studies Institute. He is author of several books including *The Early Reformation in Europe* (Cambridge University Press, 1992), *Emden and the Dutch Revolt: Exile and Development of Reformed Protestantism* (Oxford University Press, 1992), and he co-edited *Calvinism in Europe, 1540-1620* (Cambridge University Press, 1994) with Alastair Duke and Gillian Lewis.

THE REFORMATION
WORLD

Edited by
Andrew Pettegree

London and New York

First published 2000
by Routledge
11 New Fetter Lane, London EC4P 4EE

Simultaneously published in the USA and Canada
by Routledge
29 West 35th Street, New York, NY 10001

First published in paperback 2002

Routledge is an imprint of the Taylor & Francis Group

Typeset in Garamond by Taylor & Francis Books Ltd
Printed and bound in Great Britain by TJ International Ltd, Padstow, Cornwall

British Library Cataloguing in Publication Data
A catalogue record for this book is available from the British Library

Library of Congress Cataloging-in-Publication Data
The Reformation world / edited by Andrew Pettegree.
p.   cm.
Includes bibliographical references and index.
1. Reformation. 2.Europe–Church history–16th century.
I. Pettegree, Andrew
BR305.2.P48   2000   99-35295
274′.06–dc21   CIP

ISBN 0–415–16357–9 (Hbk)
ISBN 0–415–26859–1 (Pbk)

CONTENTS

— Contents —

— Contents —

ILLUSTRATIONS

CONTRIBUTORS

Andrew Pettegree is Professor of Modern History at the University of St Andrews, and Director of the St Andrews Reformation Studies Institute.

David Bagchi is Lecturer in the Department of Theology at the University of Hull.

David Coleman is Professor of History at the Eastern Kentucky University.

C. Scott Dixon is a Lecturer in the Institute for European Studies at the Queen's University, Belfast.

Bruce Gordon is Lecturer in History at the University of St Andrews.

Michael F. Graham is Professor of History at the University of Akron, Ohio.

Ole Peter Grell is a Lecturer in European History at the Open University.

Sigrun Haude is Professor of History in the Department of History, University of Cincinnati.

Francis Higman recently retired as Director of the Institut de l'Histoire de la Réformation in Geneva.

Trevor Johnston is a Lecturer in the Faculty of Humanities at the University of the West of England, Bristol.

Susan C. Karant-Nunn is Associate Director of the Division for Late Mediæval and Reformation Studies at the University of Arizona.

Karin Maag is Director of the H. Henry Meeter Center for Calvin Research at Calvin College, Grand Rapids, Michigan.

Guido Marnef is a Lecturer in the Faculteit der Geschiedenis of the Universiteit Antwerpen.

Raymond A. Mentzer is Professor of History at Montana State University.

Charlotte Methuen is Wissenschaftlichen Assistentin in the Evangelisch-

Theologische Fakultät of Bochum University.

Graeme Murdock is Lecturer in the School of History at the University of Birmingham.

William G. Naphy is a Lecturer in History at the University of Aberdeen.

Bodo Nischan is Professor of History in the East Carolina University.

Helen Parish is a lecturer in History at the University of Reading.

Jonathan A. Reid is a postdoctoral research fellow of the St Andrews Reformation Studies Institute.

Richard Rex is a University Lecturer in the Faculty of Divinity and a Fellow of Queens' College, Cambridge.

Andrew Spicer is a member of the history department at Stonyhurst College.

James M. Stayer is Professor of History at the Queen's University, Kingston, Ontario.

R.N. Swanson is Senior Lecturer in History at the University of Birmingham.

Mark Taplin, now an officer of the Scottish Parliament in Edinburgh, recently completed a doctoral dissertation in the St Andrews Reformation Studies Institute.

Margo Todd is Professor of History at Vanderbilt University.

Carl Truman is a Lecturer in Theology at the University of Aberdeen.

ACKNOWLEDGEMENTS

For the editor of a collaborative project the first and largest debt is bound to be to his contributors. A project of this size and complexity imposes an especial need for disciplined adherence to schedules and house style, and it is a great pleasure to be able to acknowledge here the exemplary professionalism of all of those who have contributed to this volume. As a result this book has been far less time in the making than many smaller projects in which I have been involved. Two contributors were forced through ill health to withdraw at a late stage in the project. I am especially grateful to my colleague Bruce Gordon for stepping in to fill one of these vacancies (Italy); the other, a planned piece on Poland, proved impossible to reassign. I also acknowledge with great gratitude the helpfulness and courtesy of those libraries and collections that provided prints for illustrations, often waiving their usual fees. In this connection a special debt is due to two partner institutions of the St Andrews Reformation Studies Institute – the Lutherhalle, Wittenberg, and the H. Henry Meeter Center for Calvin Research in Grand Rapids – and to the Ashmolean Museum, Oxford. These and other obligations are acknowledged in the photo credits, below. The Head of Special Collections of the University Library at St Andrews, Christine Gascoigne, was especially helpful and the project owes a great deal to her and her staff. The St Andrews School of History Research Fund provided financial support for the research which underpins my own contributions, and this I acknowledge with gratitude. Finally, I am sure the good friends who have contributed to this book will forgive me if I dedicate our collective effort to my wife and children, Jane, Megan and Sophie, who in their different ways have made the years while this book was taking shape a magical time.

Andrew Pettegree
April 1999

CREDITS FOR ILLUSTRATIONS

—•◦•—

Photographs are courtesy of:

Bildarchiv Photo Marburg (27.4, 27.5), Colmar, Musée d'Unterlinden (30.1), Copenhagen, National Gallery (15.1), Copenhagen, Royal Library (27.6), Edinburgh, Royal Commission on Ancient and Historical Monuments (27.7), Edinburgh, Historic Scotland (27.8), Glasgow, Burrell Collection (2.3), Glasgow, Stirling Maxwell Collection (20.2), Goshen College, Mennonite Historical Library (14.1), Grand Rapids, H. Henry Meeter Center for Calvin Research (7.6, 18.1, 26.3), London, British Library (6.1, 6.2, 21.1, 21.2), London, Wallace Collection (27.3), Montauban, Bibliothèque Municipale (25.10), North Newton, KS, Kaufman Museum (14.1), Nuremberg, Nationalmuseum (2.2), Oxford, Ashmolean Museum (25.2, 25.4, 25.9, 30.2), Oxford, Bodleian Library (13.1, 13.2), Paris, Bibliothèque Nationale (27.1, 27.2), Rome, Biblioteca Casabatense (2.1), St Andrews University Library (7.3, 7.4, 12.1, 12.2, 19.1, 23.2, 25.3, 26.2), Wittenberg, Lucas-Cranach-Stiftung (25.5), Wittenberg, Lutherhalle (3.1, 4.1, 5.1, 5.2, 5.4, 7.1, 7.2, 24.1, 25.1, 25.6, 25.7, 26.1), Wittenberg Stadtkirche (25.8), Wolfenbüttel, Herzog August Bibliothek (8.2, 22.1, 22.2, 22.3, 28.1, 28.2, 28.3)

Maps are courtesy of:

Cambridge, Cambridge University Press (10.1), Ian Johnston (11.1), Oxford, Oxford University Press (20.1), Michael Graham (23.1)

Every effort has been made to obtain permission to reproduce copyright material. If any proper acknowledgement has not been made, we would invite copyright holders to inform us of the oversight.

XV

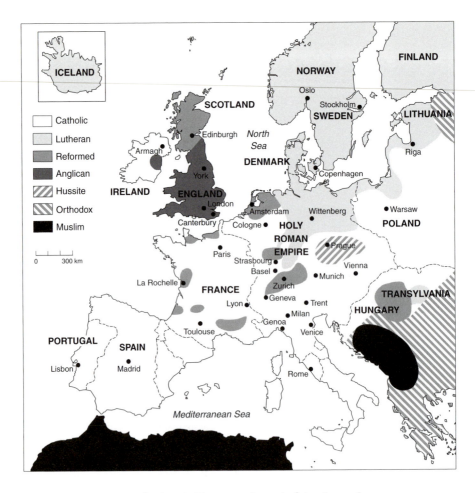

Figure 0.1 Religious confessions in Europe at the end of the sixteenth century

CHAPTER ONE

INTRODUCTION

The changing face of Reformation history

Andrew Pettegree

No two generations write history in the same manner. As society changes, so do the preoccupations of scholars, students and those engaged at the coal-face of historical investigation. This is not merely a matter of fashion or taste. Different times also offer different opportunities. To compare history-writing with only twenty years ago is to realize that we have lived through a time of very rapid change, both in terms of the technology of scholarship and the social and political circumstances that affect history-writing – more than we sometimes recognize. In technological terms, the way we work has in recent years been revolutionized both by general access to cheap, convenient computer facilities and by the dissemination of source materials through commercial microfilm or digitization. Through such advances historians working on geographically distant cultures can now access a vastly increased array of relevant source materials. But there is also much more that we can do and many more places that we can freely go to in the pursuit of our studies. Most pertinently to our field, the global political change of the last decade has led to the opening up of many previously closed archives, notably in Eastern Europe since 1989, following the disintegration of the Soviet bloc.

It may not be immediately obvious why these changes should impact so forcibly on the history of the Reformation. This was, certainly, a cataclysmic eruption in the history of European society, but one that occurred 400 years ago. In fact there have been few fields of history where historians have so radically adjusted their approach to the subject in the space of a generation. Their terms of reference, intellectual preoccupations, the geographical scope of their enquiries – all these have changed out of all recognition. The modern approach or, indeed, variety of approaches which now characterize the study of the subject are reflected in the essays which follow in this volume. But it may be helpful if by way of introduction one pauses to consider precisely in what respects this collection differs from what might have been offered in a survey study of the Reformation a generation ago.

Thirty-five years ago the distinguished English historian Geoffrey Elton published a new survey of the Reformation period, *Reformation Europe*. Elton was then one of Britain's leading scholars and this is one of his most successful projects. It contains all of the bravura qualities which mark out Elton's writing: crisp, pacey

1

narrative, fine and clear judgements on issues and people. In its way, it too was an important milestone in the writing of the subject, published just as Reformation history was emerging from a confessional strait-jacket which previously impeded its accession into the mainstream of history. In this previous age the history of Protestantism had been almost exclusively written by Protestants, while Catholic history remained largely in the hands of members of the Catholic religious orders. Elton's book symbolized the successful secularization of the subject. By placing the history of the Reformation in what was in effect a political narrative-context, he drew it out of the ghetto of church history and into the mainstream of history courses. It was an enormously successful book and one that has been a staple of school and university courses since.

Nevertheless, reading Elton's narrative now (and it has conveniently been republished recently after several years out of print) is to be very forcibly reminded of how different is Elton's perception of the Reformation world from our own. In this, Elton does not differ from other general histories of that time; it is just that the subject has changed out of all recognition since those times. When Elton wrote, the Reformation world was a much smaller place. Elton presented the great drama of the Reformation through the conflict of two men, Martin Luther and Charles V. Their actions and decisions are central to his narrative; to a very large extent they made the Reformation. Even as a convenient shorthand, this now seems a misleading presentation. It is indeed impossible to ignore the importance of these great personalities and we can be thankful that an attempt to write Luther out of the Reformation narrative (a fashion that flourished fleetingly in the 1970s) has now been abandoned. But even without going to this extreme, historians now recognize much more fully the importance of the huge movements of social change which accompanied, and to some extent preceded, the Reformation disputes.

Our understanding of these events is really the fruit of a new wave of archival studies begun in the 1970s. The descent into the archives by a new generation of scholars has since that time yielded a rich harvest of studies of particular localities, exploring how the preaching and writing of the reformers impacted upon local conditions and local political circumstances. Research of this type has transformed our understanding of the Reformation movement in Germany, but also over a longer span the Reformations in France and the Netherlands (Chapters 19 and 20). The article on Calvin and Geneva in this volume (Chapter 18) is a splendid example of the sort of radical reinterpretative work that is possible if one looks beyond the best-known published sources – in this case Calvin's letters and writings – to what may be discovered from local town archives. The first generation of these new local studies were almost all devoted to the towns and cities, identified by most modern scholars as the principal engines of evangelical activity. But the role of the ruling princes cannot be ignored. In this volume, chapters on the German princes (Chapter 9) and the Reformation in Scandinavia – a classic 'princely' Reformation (Chapter 15) – help restore the balance.

Another major difference of the modern era is our approach to the outcome of the Reformation movement. When Elton wrote, there is no doubt that he regarded the Reformation as in general terms a force for progress. The mediæval church was universally acknowledged to be a deeply flawed institution, in urgent

CHAPTER TWO

THE PRE-REFORMATION CHURCH

R.N. Swanson

The origins of the Protestant Reformation remain one of history's great conundrums. The question Catholics put to the early Protestants – 'Where was your church before Luther?' – continues to tax historians. Just what caused the massive and sudden shift in opinion in the 1520s that fractured the apparent consensus of the preceding years is still debated and unresolved. Peter Blickle speaks for many other historians when he admits:

> I do not know what motives drove people from the Roman Church and to the reformers, nor does anyone else know it. Why did people around 1515 want to see the Body of Christ in the Eucharist, but around 1525 demand to hear the Word of God? No one has produced a plausible answer to this question, much less an adequate one. On this point I admit to being as ignorant as anyone else.[1]

Yet there is *an* answer – which is not *the* answer – to the Catholics' question: before Luther's secession, his church was part of the Catholic church. By definition, the Reformation was an internal transformation, not an external assault; the division of a unit, not a conquest. The state of the late mediæval western church therefore needs some consideration as the prelude to the onset of Reformation.

THE MEDIÆVAL CATHOLIC WORLD

To talk of 'the church' in the singular carries overtones of a monolithic and rigid body, in organization and belief. Such implications must be rejected immediately: although the church proclaimed itself 'one, holy, catholic and apostolic', it embraced a wide and constantly changing variety of religious and spiritual standpoints. United by the broadly shared definitions of the faith and under the organizational headship of the papacy, the actuality of religion differed considerably from region to region, and even within regions, between different bodies, perhaps right down to the atomized spirituality of the individual Christian. Catholicism was (almost) all-embracing: diversity without adversity was the norm, although there were some limits (which themselves varied over time and space) to what was considered acceptable and tolerable.

At first sight, the late mediæval church was in a strong position. Admittedly, the Turkish advance threatened its position in the eastern Mediterranean, but that had not totally eliminated a Catholic presence in the conquered territories, or prevented access to the Holy Land itself by western pilgrims. Still, the Genoese colonies on the Black Sea coast, the islands of the eastern Mediterranean and the Frankish states established in Greece after the Latin Conquest of Constantinople in 1204, were being picked off – a process emphasized in 1522 by the fall of Rhodes and the end of Hospitaller rule there. The Turks threatened Catholic Hungary, even Italy: they captured Otranto in 1480 and, although soon expelled, the threat remained. To some this seemingly unstoppable Turkish advance was but one sign of the imminent Apocalypse.

In contrast to the eastern gloom, in the west the Christian capture of Granada in 1492 was a Catholic triumph, completing the political Christian take-over of the Iberian peninsula. Islam would soon be officially eradicated in Spain (although the problem of crypto-Muslims, the Moriscos, persisted during the sixteenth century). The year 1492 also saw the official expulsion of the remaining Jews from Castile and Aragon, further affirming Catholic triumph. Catholicism was also expanding beyond the Pillars of Hercules: faith followed the flag, accompanying the conquistadors to America. It was also taking root in Africa, the King of Kongo being converted under Portuguese influence. However, Spanish attempts to fan out into Morocco were to be thwarted.

In Catholicism's core territories, western Europe, the established ecclesiastical structures continued to function. All was not, however, static; after all, Lithuania's conversion had occurred only in 1386. The structures had to change in response to a changing world, and the late Middle Ages were certainly a time of change. In the aftermath of the Black Death of 1348–50, radical social and economic changes affected ecclesiastical revenues, the distribution of population and spiritual concerns. Other problems arose from the theoretical challenges inherent in conciliarism (Chapter 3), the jurisdictional claims of increasingly assertive secular rulers and the intellectual challenge of humanism (Chapter 4).

ROME

At the head of this church was the papacy. In theory, papal powers were as extensive as ever: the pope was the Vicar of Christ, the direct link between the terrestrial Church Militant and the God it worshipped. Christ's identification of St Peter as the rock on which the church would be built and the grant to him of the Power of the Keys, the authority to bind and loose on earth and in heaven (as recorded in the Gospel of Matthew, 16:18–19, and duly to be inscribed around the dome of the new St Peter's basilica), remained the papacy's fundamental title-deed. Acceptance of this scriptural foundation for papal power made it virtually unchallengeable: Lorenzo Valla's exposure of the Donation of Constantine (whereby Constantine the Great supposedly transferred the governance of the whole western Roman Empire to Pope Silvester I) as a forgery was a pinprick, not a radical challenge. As monarch, the pope claimed to direct the church, with an active role in defining its spirituality and overseeing its mission. That mission, from a papal perspective, was to bring the world to Christ and to papally led Catholicism. The aspiration was seemingly flaunted, acknowledged and validated in 1493, when Pope Alexander VI literally divided the world into spheres of influence for the nascent Portuguese and Spanish Empires, a division confirmed (with minor adjustments) by the Treaty of Tordesillas in 1494.

Ostensibly, the fifteenth century saw papal power recover from the major traumas of the Great Schism (1378–1417) and the clashes of the Council of Basle (1431–49). Elected as pope of a reunited church in 1417, Martin V returned the papacy to Rome and began repairing the damage caused by years of division. The old rhetoric of papalism was retained, but the fifteenth-century papacy increasingly assumed the characteristics of a localized principality. The popes usually resided in or near Rome (although Eugenius IV spent a decade in Florence after a revolt in 1433). Nicholas V (1447–55) began a great rebuilding to make the city a fitting capital for the universal church, as well as for the papal states. His plans envisaged the renewal of the basilica of St Peter itself. Indeed, that work began in his pontificate, but did not really take off until the reign of Julius II (1503–13). The new Rome was to be a Renaissance capital of a Renaissance principality, the papacy's commitment to the new intellectual ethos being demonstrated in 1475 when Sixtus IV established the Vatican Library, appointing Bartolomeo Palatina as its first Prefect.

The papacy remained the church's core institution, its international administrative heart; but politically it turned in on itself. As territorial princes, the popes developed their fiscal resources and defended their lands (both being increasingly necessary as income from outside Italy diminished). They became embroiled in defensive actions against other Italian states and in aggressive campaigns to impose their authority on local tyrants. Cesare Borgia's wars suppressed several of these petty rulers, but the task continued into the sixteenth century. The papacy was also exposed to the ambitions of greater princes: straddling Italy, its territories were constantly a corridor. In the early 1400s, Ladislas of Naples hoped to march through northwards; at the end of the century Charles VIII of France traversed them *en route* to conquering the Neapolitan realm.

Finance was always an issue, as the papacy became more dependent on local resources and short-term expedients like the sale of offices. The discovery of alum mines at Tolfa in 1462 offered a short period of relief: this being the only abundant source of alum in western Europe, the popes sought to exploit its importance for the cloth industry by establishing a monopoly enforced by spiritual sanctions. It could not be maintained.

The papacy's political identification with its Italian territories was accentuated by the greater role of Italians and Italian at the papal court. From the 1400s cardinals were no longer required to reside at the curia, which led to a reduction of the non-Italian presence in the College. This made Rome even more a focus for Italian dynastic and political factionalism, encouraging papal nepotism almost for self-preservation. Conversely, the process decentralized the church by allowing cardinals to extend their influence in their own local (and national) churches, maintaining only loose contacts with Rome. The process would culminate in the legatine powers granted to cardinals as quasi-popes in the early 1500s, Wolsey being the most obvious example.

As the curial cardinals became as a group more tight-knit and Italian, so they asserted increasingly oligarchic claims to a share in the church's central government: extending their own power, they sought to hem in the pope. At conclaves they tried to bind candidates for the papacy to pre-election pacts, but all such arrangements were frustrated: the *papabile* were quite happy to buy votes with promises, but determined once elected to prevent any reduction in their powers and authority. Family interest and political faction further fed tensions and rivalries between popes and individual cardinals.

The practical issues affecting the papacy were compounded by the changed ecclesiological context facing Martin V and his successors. The Great Schism of 1378–1417 was not just a disputed succession: it challenged the papacy's ideological foundations, bequeathing uncertainties which could not be easily eradicated. The concepts of papal supremacy and plenitude of power became themselves part of the problem manifested in the schism, impeding the search for reunion: how could there be two legitimate successors to St Peter, each enjoying all the authority of a Vicar of Christ?

The election of Martin V in November 1417 restored a papacy, but also highlighted an irreconcilable tension within the church. The restored papacy desired by Martin and his successors had a rival: now the concept of accountability in *Haec sancta* and *Frequens* threatened the monarchical interpretation of the Petrine Commission. The inevitable clash occurred at the Council of Basle, which met from 1431–49, in a brutal battle for control of the church, played out between papalists supporting monarchical authority and conciliarists insisting on papal subjection to the council. Pope Eugenius IV responded to the conciliarist challenge by assembling a rival gathering at Ferrara (later moved to Florence) – technically this was a continuation of Basle, Eugenius having merely decreed a change of location. In 1439 the papal gathering achieved the long-held aspiration of reunion with the Greeks and other eastern churches (or so it thought), giving the pope a significant propaganda bonus. Eugenius also turned to the secular princes for support by pointing to the mob rule of Basle.

Starved of political support and funding the assembly at Basle duly withered, but conciliarism was not annihilated as a threat to papal authority and continued to haunt successive popes throughout the period. In 1509, Louis XII of France supported cardinals in rebellion against Julius II who tried to hold another council at Pisa (although political considerations duly changed his mind later on). The papal view was not that councils were abhorrent *per se*, but that they should meet under papal auspices and papal control, as was to apply to the Fifth Lateran Council, assembled in 1512. Yet despite papal attempts to undermine conciliarism, the Pisan popes of 1409–15 were considered legitimate, which implicitly legitimated the conciliarist stance: the second Borgia pontiff accordingly continued the numbering from the first Pisan pope, to reign as Alexander VI (1492–1503).

NATIONAL CHURCHES

To confine attention to the church's highest ranks gives a skewed picture of the church as a whole. For all the drama, intrigue and even debauchery of the Renaissance papacy, most Catholics would be unaware of what was happening at the curia – and perhaps had little real interest. This raises the question of the papacy's real place in the late mediæval church as a whole. The emerging local role of non-resident cardinals points to a key feature of the pre-Reformation church, a decentralizing process usually labelled as the emergence of national churches.

For the papacy, decentralization was a two-edged process. Inexorably, power drifted to the localities, primarily into the hands of lay rulers seeking to construct their own sovereignties and eliminate the incursions of rival jurisdictions – those associated with the church being easily the most significant and intrusive of these. Rulers particularly wanted greater control of ecclesiastical matters in three key spheres, each of which affected the autonomy of the church in their domains and in turn had implications for the reality of papal authority.

The first key area was church appointments: rulers (and laity in general) sought a malleable local hierarchy, ideally composed of their own subjects, so that they could exploit such patronage for their own ends. Here papal rights, especially those of provision (the power to appoint directly to benefices), were challenged head-on; although only when considered prejudicial to local (or princely) interests. The debate over Gallican liberties in France frequently focused on papal power to appoint to prelacies. In the fourteenth century, England had enacted the Statutes of Provisors, which effectively ended the practice of clerics running to Rome for jobs. Yet every English bishop was still a papal appointee, because papal provision circumvented the rights of local electors, allowing the royal government to nominate, the pope to appoint and the cathedral chapter to be ignored. Pragmatism usually won the day: kings willingly compromised in their own interests. England provides the best demonstration of this, with several Italians being appointed as absentee bishops at royal request under Henry VII and Henry VIII, to secure support and advocates at the papal curia.

Money was the second main area of contention in a bullion-hungry period. The illusion of the papacy sucking funds to Rome at the expense of the regions through taxes and other demands was one hard to eliminate. The conciliar reform programmes had particularly railed against annates, the payment of first fruits to the papacy by those appointed to certain benefices. Yet Rome's ability to bleed the localities was limited and its powers to tax the church as a whole were negligible by 1500. Nevertheless, rulers still complained about the drain. Some of this was subterfuge: what they wanted was not the elimination of the charges, but their own cut. A considerable share of 'papal' exactions actually stayed in local pockets, clerical and lay. In Germany, for instance, Eugenius IV had bought support by allowing the princes to collect papal taxes. In England, unknown amounts annually collected as 'Peter's Pence' stayed in the purses of churchwardens, archdeacons, bishops and others, and only some £200 was paid to the papal collector. When papal agents sold indulgences to fund the rebuilding of St Peter's in Rome, Henry VII arranged to take a cut of the proceeds – again an unknown amount.

Last, there were clashes over jurisdiction. The curia remained, in theory, the ultimate court for all of Christendom, with cognizance of everything which might be dealt with in a lesser church court. Local church courts also exercised extensive spiritual jurisdiction, which often impinged on secular matters. Lay rulers, with their own law courts and their own jurisdictional claims, resented such interference, were reluctant to see such cases elude their oversight and did not like the possibility of appeal to an external authority. The lawyers in their courts were even less entranced by such prospects and wanted to increase their own business. Hence the struggle, aiming usually not to challenge matters at Rome itself, but to create structures and impose laws which precluded cases going to Rome. This was part of a general struggle against any jurisdictional autonomy perceived to undermine local sovereignty and was not specifically anti-papal, or exclusively between sovereigns and popes: local ecclesiastical jurisdictional privileges and the use of spiritual weapons to enforce them were a frequent source of conflict, notably in some of the German cities. However, conflict was not universal: priorities varied. In Italy, for instance, the rulers of the principalities and city states often extended control over their local church, but exploited papal proximity for partisan or family purposes. This situation was epitomized in the osmotic relationship constructed between the Medici and Rome. For the Medici it proved its value when Clement VII's control of the papacy provided the springboard for the family's return to Florence in 1531 from exile; returning not as mere citizens, but as sovereign dukes.

As the papacy's monarchical control was eroded, its role within the church became more uncertain. The reformers' rejection of papal supremacy in the sixteenth century encourages a search for earlier antipathy and an assumption that support for the papacy declined over the late mediæval period to a state at best of indifference. Whether this really happened is hard to say. Certainly the papacy had few vocal supporters – but the real need for them has yet to be demonstrated. While individual popes had detractors and the curia itself faced criticism for corruption and exploitation, few openly challenged the papacy's existence. A Catholic church without the Vicar of Christ was inconceivable. The determination to resolve the Great Schism, to re-establish a single united headship of the church, attests the positive acceptance of the papacy at least by the political and ecclesiastical hierarchs of the early fifteenth century. At lower levels there is similarly no real evidence of rejection among the orthodox. The pope was regularly prayed for as part of the liturgy. The papacy still played a part in many lives: granting dispensations for marriages within the prohibited degrees, or to facilitate clerical careers; confirming the statutes of new foundations; granting spiritual privileges to religious orders and other groups which were then marketed across Europe. Admittedly, most people's awareness of the papacy was limited and distance encouraged neither affection nor attachment – although Rome retained its spiritual significance as a pilgrimage centre, encouraged by the proclamation of jubilees offering extraordinary indulgences. The papacy was possibly appreciated more as a utilitarian administrative mechanism than for its religious significance, treated with ignorance and indifference until its powers had to be invoked for particular reasons and it suddenly became useful.

As the ties between Rome and the local churches eased (but were definitely not abandoned), so lay rulers stepped into the gap to develop the administrative autonomy of the churches in their lands, often in collusion with local prelates. The process of 'nationalization' of the late mediæval church can easily be exaggerated by examining administrative structures at the expense of the spiritual entity. There was decentralization and a shift in the balance of control; but it must be kept in perspective. The Pragmatic Sanction of Bourges, promulgated by Charles VII of France in 1437, was a clear declaration of French ecclesiastical autonomy, affirming Gallican liberties and adopting the reforming decrees of the Council of Basle. But it did not abandon Eugenius IV as pope. Resented by later pontiffs, but taken as a fundamental statement of French ecclesiastical rights by the Parlement of Paris, the Pragmatic Sanction was a bone of contention between popes and kings throughout the period. Yet at no stage did the French kings deny papal spiritual authority or their own status as Catholics. While the rulers exerted ever increasing control over their local churches, they continued to recognize the theory of papal prerogatives and to exploit them for their own ends. Decentralization often required an acknowledgement of papal power in name at least, the arrangements being couched in diplomatic language and in treaty form as a concordat. The words would be those of a papal privilege, a delegation of authority or a negotiated settlement (whose terms might not all be implemented); the reality would be a shift in power from pope to prince. So, in 1434, the Concordat of Redon strengthened ducal power over the church in Brittany, but fully acknowledged papal authority. Of course there was ambiguity, advantageous to both pope and prince. The Franco–papal agreement of 1472 was for the pope the concession to Louis XI of a temporary privilege; for Louis within his lands a formal prerogative enactment for the national church (although he also excused the concordat's imperfect implementation to the pope by claiming that his good intentions were being obstructed by the Paris Parlement). The demands of politics – for both princes and popes – meant that the relationships were constantly under negotiation, dependent on the advantage to be gained fom the particular context.

LOCAL RELIGION

Alongside its role as an international institution, the church also had to function in the localities, at the levels of province, diocese and parish. The shift of focus to examine this more localized (and, perhaps, more 'religious') church points attention towards a very different type of church, although one equally liable to provoke contention in matters of status and privilege, and one often criticized for the personal failings of the clergy, its exploitation of economic power and the misuse of endowments to fund personal and family advance.

The parish remained the basic building block of the diocesan church, with the fifteenth and early sixteenth centuries being a time of considerable change. The economic and social shifts induced by the changing population patterns following the Black Death and other disasters (including the Hundred Years War in France and the Hussite Wars in Bohemia) undermined the established parochial structure, especially as the source of funds to provide clerical incomes and maintain church

buildings. Numerous parishes had to be merged because their revenues (and populations) were now insufficient to justify two churches and to sustain the appropriate
number of clergy. In contrast, there were also numerous attempts by expanding
settlements to secure their own parochial identity by breaking away from their
official mother church. Despite legal problems and vested interests, such attempts
were often successful, at least to some extent. Across Europe newly rising settlements gained their own churches and their own clergy. This could take some time.
The German village of Balgach had a newly built chapel in 1424, but not until
1521 did it gain formal parochial separation from its mother church of Marbach.
In England, the inhabitants of Ditchford Friary in Warwickshire struggled for
some forty years before successfully seceding from the parish of Great Wolford.

The late mediæval parish often epitomizes Catholicism at its most active and
vital. Churchwardens' accounts show extensive lay participation in parochial administration and funding, which also gave the laity effective control over a considerable
number of clerical careers. The accounts provide evidence for participation in
fund-raising, for investment in liturgical necessities, for the provision and maintenance of lights and images, and a host of other activities which establish the parish
church and its religious regime as a central element in parochial life. This evidence
is augmented by that supplied by wills and by the records of devotional guilds and
fraternities which were founded in such numbers that they have been called 'the
most characteristic expressions of late medieval Christianity'.[2] One of the most
important points demonstrated by this accumulated evidence is precisely the
laity's growing control over clerical lives. Their opportunities to provide employment were expanded by the use of clerics as private chaplains, as chantry priests to
pray for souls (both on short-term contracts and in perpetuity) and as fraternity or
guild chaplains. As well as paying the piper, the laity increasingly called the tune,
demonstrating a growing awareness of the demands of the Christian religion and
appreciation of the ideal state appropriate for a priest, together with a real concern
to ensure that the clergy they employed met the required standards. This expansion of the laity's role in the church has a significance which cannot be
underestimated. How far it also reflected a fundamental shift in concepts of
authority and control is less easy to determine.

THE RELIGIOUS ORDERS

If, at the local level, the parishes show increasing vitality and the diocesan structures were at the worst ticking over, the state and fate of the religious orders are
less clear. Just how they were perceived is open to question: it has recently been
suggested that traditional gentry support in England was declining, as the religious houses were considered less relevant to the contemporary world in general
and specifically to their patronal families (where these survived). Minor houses
were frequently dissolved, even by bishops, and their endowments transferred to
other uses (in England, frequently to endow university colleges). Yet even in
England all was not bleak. The Carthusians in particular attracted support, and
were a formative spiritual influence. Henry V's foundations at Sheen and Syon
were a devotional powerhouse throughout the period. There were signs of reform

and revivification, with effective use of visitation powers and demands for change. Even the Observant movement took shallow root, with the establishment of a few Franciscan houses – but that was the only order whose Observant branch moved into England.

On the continent, the religious orders faced similar dilemmas. Individual houses might well atrophy, with several striking cases among the Italian Benedictines; but the Observant movement, affecting most of the main orders, encouraged renewed vitality by insisting on obedience to the orders' original rules, and showed a determination to uphold old ideals. Moreover, especially among the Augustinians (as heirs to the Netherlandish *devotio moderna* of the fourteenth century), there were a number of new foundations, rather than just the take-over of old houses. However, the Observants' claims did cause tensions within the orders, which were of accumulating significance and bitterness. Two interpretations of the same rule could not easily co-exist and the separatist urge was hard to resist: the Franciscans were to be formally divided in 1517, when Pope Leo X recognized the existence of the Capuchins.

Of the regular orders, the friars probably had most impact on contemporary society. Mendicants were among the leading preachers of the day, characterized by Bernardino of Siena (d. 1444), Antoninus of Florence (d. 1459) and Savonarola in Florence. The first two became saints, the last was burnt as a heretic in 1498 after unleashing extraordinary religious enthusiasm in Florence. All attracted massive audiences and had a considerable impact. As well as preaching, the mendicants retained their intellectual vigour – a vigour duly displayed by Martin Luther, and by several of his adherents and detractors.

BELIEF AND PRACTICE

At all levels, the church operated as a spiritual and theological entity. That was its prime function: to emphasize the administrative and institutional is too overlook Catholicism's main imperative, which was to offer the hope of salvation and assist the search for its attainment. Precisely here the tendency to see Christianity and the church in monolithic terms obstructs understanding. While there were core statements of the faith in the creeds, and a common spiritual and ethical culture based on the seven sacraments, the Ten Commandments and shared views on sin and virtue, beyond those essential elements the religion was extremely flexible and variable. 'Catholicism' was no single, unified, coherent body of dogma or devotion; to treat it as such is a gross misrepresentation.

The reality was often regional and fragmented. This was most obvious in the varieties of spirituality, as local practices differed to reflect different traditions and needs. It was also manifested in liturgy: although the basic elements of the services might be shared, liturgies differed institutionally between the various religious orders and geographically between dioceses and ecclesiastical provinces. There might be increasing standardization (as in the liturgical imperialism of the Sarum rite in late mediæval England, encouraged by the spread of printing), but regional and local differences persisted, most visibly in the calendar and the local commemoration of saints.

Even theologies were regionalized. The proliferation of theological faculties in late mediæval universities and the maintenance of their separate *studia* by the mendicant orders, permitted the development of distinct theological strands and allegiances. These were competitive – as with the tension between the *via antiqua*, based on Thomas Aquinas, and the *via moderna*, which owed more to William of Ockham – but the adversity could be contained.

As important as the fragmentation is the cumulative nature of the Catholic religion: the past was rarely explicitly rejected, might always be revived. The fifteenth century saw a major revival in interest in twelfth-century theology; the early sixteenth century witnessed a revival of the Patristic writers. Even in a manuscript culture, these old ideas were simultaneously as valid as those of contemporary thinkers; printing also made them all simultaneously available.

Attempts to comprehend the nature of pre-Reformation religion must face the problems inherent in this cumulative character, especially in spirituality. That covers a wide spectrum of activities, from what might now be considered gross superstition to the most intense mysticism. Among historians, this range has provoked attempts to identify specific types of religious culture, setting 'elite' against 'popular' or 'learned' against 'lewd', with occasional blanket denials that pre-Reformation Europe was really 'Christian' at all. Whatever the modern judgement, on their own terms the people of pre-Reformation Europe were Christian, even if some of them displayed the most abysmal ignorance when actually questioned about their supposed beliefs. Distinctions between 'elite' and 'popular' or 'learned' and 'lewd' may have some practical validity, but still rest on insecure foundations. There were gradations in spirituality; but divisions cannot be forcefully applied or rigidly maintained.

The tensions varied. The intricacies of a Latinate learned theology were not universally accessible; but a vernacularized theology which may have been originally Latin was more widely diffused. The learned could dismiss some popular activities as superstitions – as with the constant attempts to control the sacred landscape by curtailing pilgrimages to allegedly holy wells and other places; but they also exploited such behaviour in other cases. (Disputes among the learned over the cult of the Precious Blood at Wilsnack also show that they were not immune to similar tensions.) Meanwhile, those for whom the Latinate theology was inaccessible might condemn its verbosity and remoteness, as an alienation from God. While the learned theologized, the unlearned believed and prayed. Their spirituality was validated by others among the learned, who encouraged an active vernacular spiritual regime, centred on the need to live as a Christian, regardless of theological debates. The Spanish Franciscan Francisco de Osuna, writing in 1527, decried an over-dependence on learning, urging a meditative and mystical approach to the divine and criticizing those who 'place all their learning in talking to God as though they were talking to Lorenzo Valla or someone else who could accuse them of speaking bad Latin.'[3] His and others' comments show that much of the contemporary debate about status and learning was generally confined to the literate classes.

The spirituality itself combined a bewildering array of elements. At one extreme was the quasi-magical exploitation of the sacramentals, the sanctified objects regularly used as talismans. In this world church bells were rung as protection against thunderstorms; the candles blessed on the Feast of the Purification of the Virgin (2 February) were preserved at home as protective forces; insects which threatened crops were formally anathematized. Here specific prayers functioned as incantations against the malefic forces abounding in the world. At the other extreme was the intense spirituality of anchorites and recluses, who abandoned human society (but not a dependence on that society for material support and adherents) to devote themselves to God. In between lay a vast array of practices, lifestyles and devotions too varied and localized to catalogue. Saints influenced this world; the sacramental round – centring on the mass and penance – provided the basic structure of religious action; a charitable impulse supposedly directed all human action. Ideally this was a world of mutual dependence, a relationship most forcefully demonstrated in the links between the living and the dead evinced in the doctrine of purgatory. Central to it all was Christ and Christocentric devotions became increasingly significant in the later Middle Ages.

Commemoration of and meditation on Christ's death were important elements of late mediæval spirituality, but a concentration on Christ's death was not enough. His life also had to be relived. The full implications of late mediæval Catholicism are summarized in one German manuscript illustration, showing the approach to Christ in three distinct stages: *imitatio*, by following his actions; *conformatio*, by sharing in his emotional experiences, and *devotio*, reaching the foot of the Cross and gaining immediate access to the Passion itself (see Figure 2.1). The purpose of this is clear in an adjacent deathbed scene, where the merits of the Passion outweigh the penalty of sin and the machinations of the Devil to secure redemption.

Like the theology, the spirituality was cumulative, as tradition was added to tradition, devotions increased and accretions accrued. It was relatively easy to add to the store, rather more difficult to rationalize and reduce, let alone control. Inertia was an effective weapon against some additions: new cults often withered from lack of support and, in a manuscript culture, production factors limited availability of texts. Spirituality could also be controlled, to some extent. Formal opposition might nip a devotion in the bud or at least prevent its extension. Pilgrimage to a stream at Plaigne in southern France credited with healing qualities was quashed by the local ecclesiastical authorities in 1443; several other spontaneous attempts to create a sacral landscape faced equal condemnation. At Plaigne, the strength of popular devotion and play of vested interests could not ensure continuity. Elsewhere, the hierarchs might join the sacralizing process or have to concede to popular demand and ratify a cult. At Wilsnack, popular devotion carried the day: the cult survived, despite some clerical opposition to the cult of the Precious Blood in the early 1400s, and the reservations of Nicholas of Cusa during his legatine visitation of 1451. Vested interests were also important: the cult's financial benefits secured support from local ecclesiastics; Pope Nicholas V's need for German support after the Council of Basle gave those local authorities leverage against Nicholas of Cusa's reservations.

The cumulative nature of spirituality encouraged regionalism, making it possible to speak of Catholicism*s* rather than Catholicism, a range of regionalized spiritual discourses which, contained under the overall umbrella of the papally

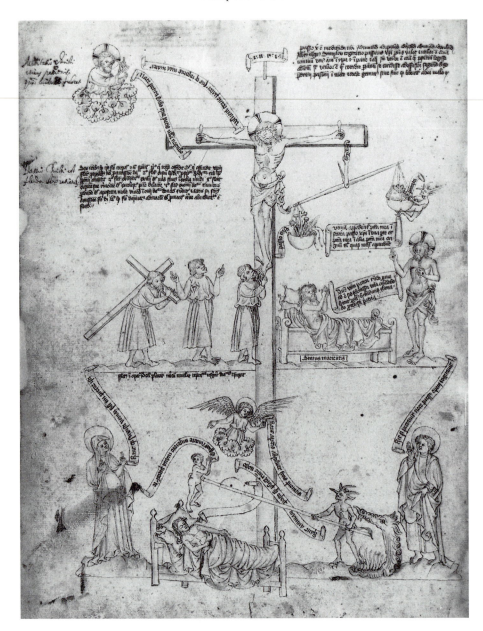

Figure 2.1 The Passion and the pattern of the Christian life and death. This complex fifteenth-century German illustration offers a meditative focus for analysis of Christian life and death. At the foot of Christ's Cross, a soul appeals to Mary for aid to evade the Devil's hook. In the centre, on the left, three figures depict different relationships with the crucified Christ: *imitatio* in carrying the cross, *conformatio* in sharing the pain of the five wounds and *devotio* in worship. To the right, a dying Christian appeals to Christ while in the balance above him the *arma Christi*, the instruments of the Passion, outweigh the penitent's sins. (Rome, Biblioteca Casabatense)

headed church, retained distinct and distinctive characteristics. The precise importance (and, indeed, character) of this regionalism remains relatively untested, partly
because it is obscured by the looming shadow of Reformation. Attempts to find
the roots of Reformation in these regionalized Catholic spiritualities may also
distort the picture. The significance of the regionalization needs to be considered
in terms of Catholicism and its manifold manifestations, rather than simply as a
seedbed for the sixteenth-century changes.

The main difficulty is to establish the regional identities and to differentiate
the layers of the overall spiritual pyramid. Ultimately, each individual was responsible for their own salvation and had to construct an appropriate devotional and
spiritual regime within the context of a family, a parish and the many other
aspects of life which affected devotional behaviour. Local will-making traditions,
the varying catchment areas of cults, access to differing cycles of prayer, would all
make their mark. All, also, were changeable, over time and space, as new cults
emerged to satisfy new demands or supplant old devotions, as new devotional texts
circulated, as new charitable practices came into vogue – and, of course, as old
cults died, as old devotions decayed, as old practices were abandoned. Yet as well
as fluctuation and centrifugalism, there was continuity and coherence. Fragments
became building blocks, as horizons lifted above the personal, parochial and
national, and individuals acknowledged a role in the wider church, perhaps most
evident in the continued vitality of international pilgrimages and financial contributions to international fund-raising campaigns.

One critical factor in late mediæval spiritual developments was the rise of
printing, with all its implications. Before the Reformation (and, indeed, during
and after it), Catholic works were a mainstay of the presses. Works of canon law, of
scholastic theology, sermons, devotional manuals and much more poured from the
presses, as did an array of ephemera ranging from illustrated woodblocks to indulgences and miracle books, all of which encouraged popular devotionalism. The key
transition may have been not the fact of printing, but the sudden accessibility of
material in the vernacular. Certainly, from the 1490s, the production of devotional
and instructional works in local tongues shows a striking increase – often these
were translated from Latin, but were now made more widely accessible. This has
several implications. An international learned Latin culture could still be maintained in print, with communication made more widespread and rapid by the ease
of reproduction. The availability and stability of printed texts possibly facilitated
international debate among the learned, and revived old texts and writers. Vernacular
texts could draw on this international culture in translation, but the regionalization
inherent in vernaculars also reinforced local spiritualities. Nevertheless, the proliferation of texts, especially instruction manuals and devotional works, made widespread
domestic devotionalism a realistic possibility.

The trends in late mediæval spirituality were too many and varied to be
summarized effectively, and point in several directions. This was a time of mysticism
and heightened Christocentric spirituality, focused especially on the Passion. Among
other feasts, the fifteenth century saw the formal establishment of those of the Five
Wounds, of the Holy Name and of the Transfiguration. Local adoption was a slow
process: English parochial visitation reports often record that the appropriate texts

had not been obtained, sometimes decades after the formal promulgation. At the same time, the religion sometimes appears sordidly mundane and mechanistic, concerned with a quantification of spiritual works which is sometimes condemned as semi-Pelagian, and with a dependence on the quasi-magical power of sacraments and sacramentals which seems little short of pagan.

Two particular aspects stand out in late mediæval spirituality: the concern about purgatory and an emphasis on the mass. Each stimulated and encouraged further concerns, affecting many areas of religious and devotional life.

Purgatory is unavoidably tied to the role of death in Christian existence. However, death was only a part of the equation which included purgatory, for the ultimate concern was with salvation. Death marked the point when humans lost control over that search for salvation, in itself an awesome prospect in a religion where justification was usually perceived as tied to works. In life it was possible to work towards salvation (although theologically faith was also needed), the main directives for a good Christian life being summarized in Christ's two Great Commandments. They were given more detail – and perhaps became more daunting – by elaboration beyond those commandments in a wide range of catechetical material dealing with the Seven Deadly Sins, the Ten Commandments, assorted Virtues and the role of the sacraments (especially confession). The requirements of a Christian life also directed attention to relationships with other humans: if there was a universal ideal driving force in late mediæval religion, it was the imperative of *caritas*, 'charity'. As a state of mind and demonstration of concern for others, this was more than mere action out of a sense of impersonal obligation or a search to salve a conscience.

At the same time, late mediæval Western culture has been viewed as a 'guilt culture', which may be right in part. If there was a sense of guilt, which might manifest itself in despair at a deathbed, purgatory offered hope and the prospect of release from guilt. Despair – hopelessness – induced by awareness of past misdeeds or an over-scrupulous conscience was considered the most dangerous state in which to approach death and worried the writers of fifteenth-century instruction manuals written to aid the dying. Deathbed overconfidence as a form of pride was equally dangerous. Although a 'third way' after death, neither the immediate and utter condemnation of hell nor the immediate and utter bliss of heaven, purgatory was not a middle way. It was where the debt of satisfaction due to God for unremitted and unexpunged sin was annihilated through suffering, through pains physically as great as those of hell, but which would end once the debt had been cancelled. Once that was done, admission to heaven was assured. The key point at death was not to be so bad as to merit hell, for admission to purgatory guaranteed salvation.

If purgatory guaranteed heaven (at a price), then a speedy transit through was much to be desired and, if possible, secured in advance. This concern stimulated many of the post-mortem commemorations which are prominent in pre-Reformation religion: the foundation of chantries (their endurance depending on the wealth of the commissioner), of obits and anniversaries, trentals, doles and charitable distributions, and (in some countries) the astonishing proliferation of masses for souls. Testators (whether anxious to expunge their sins or hopeful of a speedy progression to heaven) demanded that clerics and laity pray for their souls, leaving appropriate bequests. English and French wills might well stipulate 1,000 masses and more, to be said within surprisingly short periods (Italian and Spanish wills show less dependence on post-mortem masses for salvation).

The emphasis on the mass was a second major component of late mediæval spirituality. Theologically, the celebration retained a sacrificial focus. Each enactment was a re-enactment of Christ's Passion; when the priest consecrated the bread and wine and thereby converted the elements into the actual Body and Blood of Christ (the process of transubstantiation), he re-sacrificed the Son to the Father (although, theologically, this was not an additional sacrifice, but the same as that made on the Cross). It was the action which mattered: usually the laity were spectators rather than communicants, usually performing their own routines of prayer and praise in response to the verbal and choreographic cues of the priest's rite. Communion was only required once a year, at Easter (after the mandatory annual confession); but more frequent communion was not unknown, especially among devout women.

As an action, a sacrifice, the mass was quantifiable and potent. People might well attend several a day; they would commission votive masses to secure good weather or improved health, among other intentions. It was considered particularly efficacious for relief of the souls in purgatory, to secure their speedy release. At the heart of the ceremony was a small circle of consecrated bread, the host, which became the Body of Christ. It was adored at the elevation during the mass, reserved as a relic (especially in the host shrines which appeared across Europe) and commemorated in the Feast of Corpus Christi, which was one of the main feasts of the Christian year.

The sacramental heart of Catholicism, especially the mass and confession, had significant implications for priestly status. Only a priest could consecrate a eucharist; only a priest could grant absolution. Such powers put the priest in a Christ-like position, as intermediary between God and man. At the same time, idealistic lay expectations and aspirations for the qualities demanded of a priest were intense. The obligations of priestly status and the uncertain ability of mere humans to live up to the ethical and personal standards demanded by their flocks made priesthood itself a contentious issue during these years. This was not necessarily voiced as anticlericalism, despite being vocal criticism. It was rather a case both of trying to cut priesthood down to size by making it less elevated and remote, and of insisting that clerics live up to the standards demanded of them. In this sense laymen, by complaining about abuses and demanding their abolition, actually wanted clerics to be more rather than less 'clerical'. Priests' inability to meet those demands, while an increasingly sophisticated laity gained more control over clerical careers and was able to debate theology as effectively as clerics, established a major tension at the heart of the religion.

Other notable elements in spirituality included the continuing and expanding devotion to Mary, demonstrated by the rise of the rosary in the fifteenth century. The new pattern of prayer originated in Germany and spread widely, duly exploiting the new technology of print. The association of the rosary with confraternities – albeit confraternities which demanded no fees and held no meetings, being bound together solely by prayer – increased its appeal; the addition of indulgences compounded the process. Yet this particular devotion of the rosary remained, at the time, confined mainly to Germany: the Hail Mary was a basic prayer of the Catholic church, but was not usually recited in the structured sequences of the rosary.

The indulgences conferred on prayers of the rosary highlight a final major ingredient in late mediæval religion. Indulgences and letters of pardon were vital components of the search to avoid the pains of purgatory, their sheer ubiquity being often overlooked. Arguably they were one of the most significant and adaptable aspects of contemporary Catholicism. Although their distribution is sometimes derided as mercenary exploitation (as it occasionally was at the time), most indulgences were not actually bought, but earned by action. This was often devotional, as a reward for attending sermons, visiting specific churches at set feasts and for saying certain prayers (including prayers for nominated souls). Other acts were more obviously charitable, like aiding the poor and those who had suffered calamity (among them Greeks who had fled west after the Fall of Constantinople in 1453), contributions to maintain roads and bridges, and funding of churches. The pardons offered were generally small, usually reckoned in periods of forty days rather than years (although papal plenary indulgences gave full remission and the mathematics of multiple grants easily increased the pardons available). Alongside the official grants was a range of spurious indulgences, nevertheless treated as valid, which were linked to certain devotional acts. Praying before a depiction of Christ as Man of Sorrows or an image of the Mass of St Gregory could earn some 26,000 years of pardon for repeating a few Our Fathers, Creeds and Hail Marys, according to the inscriptions (see Figure 2.2).

The range of interests involved in indulgence distribution illustrates the integration of the church's local, national and international levels. During the late 1400s and early 1500s, the diocese of York was toured by numerous questors or pardoners. The beneficiaries included the fabric funds of York Minster and its sister minsters of Ripon, Beverley and Southwell, and the London hospitals of St Anthony of Vienna, St Thomas of Acon and St Mary, Bethlehem. Other national bodies like the Order of St Lazarus of Jerusalem, the Jesus gild under St Paul's Cathedral in London, the hospital or guild of Holy Trinity, Walsoken, and the fraternity of St Mary Roncesvalles, at Charing Cross, also benefited. Occasional licences were granted to collectors for St Anne at Lincoln, St Cross at Colchester, St Roche at Exeter, St James at New Shoreham, the Hospital of the Holy Sepulchre and St Katherine at Lincoln, and Bardsey Abbey in Wales. International collections were represented in questorial licences issued on behalf of the hospital of St Thomas the Martyr at Rome, a licence in 1517 to relieve the recent devastation of Durazzo, and one for the monastery of St Katherine, Sinai. There were probably also several very local Yorkshire causes, individual and parochial, which could offer indulgences, but these remain unrecorded.

MEDIÆVAL CRITICS

The varieties of religious experience available in the late Middle Ages produced competition among their proponents and advocates. Rivalry was part of the

Figure 2.2 Passion and devotion: the Mass of St Gregory. According to tradition, on one occasion when Gregory I was celebrating Mass, at the moment of consecration the elements turned into the physical body of the risen Christ, a miracle which proved transubstantiation. The inscription offers an indulgence of 14,000 years for reciting three Our Fathers and three Hail Marys in devotion, with repentance of sins. (Nuremberg, Germanisches Nationalmuseum)

liveliness of contemporary religion: cults had to be encouraged lest they collapse; those who would be saints had to denigrate their rivals; differing philosophies and theologies competed for support. To some, Bernardino of Siena's advocacy of the cult of the Name of Jesus demonstrated his sanctity and piety; to others his constant display of Christ's monogram (JHS) and call for its veneration was a form of idolatry. For their adherents, Spanish *beatas* (devout prophetesses and healers) were inspired by God; to their detractors (sometimes rival *beatas*) they were Satanic influences.

Such competition bred uncertainty and awareness of gaps. These problems, exacerbated by the fluid borderlines and defining limits of Catholicism, are reflected in the appearance of dissent and nonconformity during the pre-Reformation century. This was not necessarily expressed – or condemned – as heresy: sometimes a local version of Catholicism might raise official concern by seeming to stray too far beyond the completely acceptable. Dissent was certainly not uncommon. The Waldensians persisted in Germany and Central Europe (and, as the Vaudois, in the Alpine regions of southern France and northern Italy, a stronghold for their beliefs in the late 1400s and early 1500s). Originating in the late 1100s, they survived despite persecution and the attentions of the Inquisition. In Italy, occasional trials of Fraticelli suggested that that heresy – derived from extremist adherence to Franciscan poverty, mingled with the apocalypticism of the late-twelfth-century seer, Joachim of Fiore – had also survived. Other movements were of more recent origins: in England, the Lollards; in Bohemia and parts of Poland, the Hussites and their offshoot, the Moravian Brethren.

Lollardy, associated in its origins with the thought of John Wyclif (d.1384), remains a movement of uncertainty and debate. Challenging sacramentalism and sacerdotalism, its formal identity remains elusive, but it clearly articulated many of the tensions surrounding late mediæval religion. Its coherence and continuity as a movement remain unclear from the available evidence; it is also possible that some aspects were more widespread than hitherto suspected. Traditionally, Lollardy after about 1414 has often been dismissed as an undercurrent among the lower orders; but gentry involvement may have evaded detection. Lollardy – or what was considered Lollardy – continued as a thorn in the side of the English church until the Reformation.

Hussitism (named after the Prague academic Jan Hus, burnt at Constance in June 1415) had affinities to both Lollardy and Waldensianism. Although the Hussites provoked the Bohemian revolution and civil wars of 1419–36, and had several crusades called against them, they were eventually reconciled with the Catholic church. The adoption of Utraquism (which allowed lay communion in both bread and wine, rather than the host alone) made the lay chalice the movement's identifying and focal element, and in some ways marginalized its cerebral challenge to Catholicism. The search for reconciliation focused on matters of discipline rather than doctrine, so reducing the apparent scale of differences between moderate Hussitism and Catholicism. In the *Compactata* of 1436, which reintegrated the Hussites into the church, communion in both kinds was conceded, with some of Hussitism's institutional reformist aspects; the intellectual and doctrinal elements were virtually ignored. Here the acceptance of diversity did not end adversity: later popes struggled unsuccessfully to eradicate the lay chalice, while the Moravian Brethren emerged in the mid-fifteenth century as a continuing Hussite group. Nevertheless, Hussitism became a controlled diversity – confined to Bohemia, its adherents struggling to sustain continuity within the permitted structures against a hostile Catholic hierarchy, it could neither challenge nor threaten the church as a whole.

Dissent and nonconformity also erupted in other forms. Spain witnessed a particular variant when the coerced conversion of Jews created a class of *conversos* or New Christians, who faced increasing hostility in the fifteenth century and were feared as a fifth column whose continued links to Jews and Judaism might undermine Catholic orthodoxy. Often scapegoats for evolutions within Spanish Catholicism, fears about their activities lay behind the establishment of the Spanish Inquisition in 1478 and the expulsion of the Jews from Castile in 1492.

The attacks on the *conversos* reflected the hierarchy's fears about the continuing problem of unsupervised spiritual activity. Christianity's intellectual demands had always caused problems, and still did. Individuals might well have difficulty in accepting particular beliefs, and thereby incur criticism and suspicion. Among academics, for instance, questions of free will and predestination and of the derivation of grace, or rival philosophies which produced incompatible theologies, were a constant irritant. Also important were uncertainties about the religion's authoritative foundations, and a growing tension between an insistence on scriptural foundations (which would invalidate all accretions which could not be proved from the Bible) and a willingness to accept the authority of the church in defining the tradition, even if building on scriptural foundations. This tension became ever more insistent as increasing literacy and the greater availability of vernacular Bibles reduced clerical control over the interpretation of scripture and allowed untaught individuals to assert their own reading of the Bible against the authority of the church. In almost every country intellectuals were challenged – from Lorenzo Valla in Italy, to Pedro de Osma in Castile, to the unfortunate Bishop Reginald Pecock in England (whose attempts to refute Lollardy backfired, causing him to be charged with heresy and deposed from the bishopric of Chichester in 1458). Among the wider populace, a 'common-sense' approach to religion (perhaps rooted in an awareness of discrepancies between the physical facts of the world and the spiritual interpretations of the church) could also generate doubts, but these would only have to be taken seriously if made public.

In the response to uncertainty, it was important that Catholicism's cumulative tradition was also one of precedents, which included the acknowledged heresies. Novelty could always be tested against heretical precedent and was sometimes found wanting. The articles condemned at Blackfriars in 1382 acknowledged such precedents to define the Wycliffite heresy (although Wyclif was not named in them); Luther was likewise reviled as a second Wyclif or Hus, implicitly a mere follower and reviver rather than innovator. Mystics were particularly problematic, with their determination to negate their own wills in submission to the divine. Such self-denial could lead to claims that they were incapable of sin, generating heresy charges which revived the fictitious Heresy of the Free Spirit. That heresy may have been a figment of inquisitors' imaginations in the early fourteenth century, but it still provided a precedent to be cited against enthusiasts. Charges of reviving Free Spiritism were, for instance, levelled against the *alumbrados* in early sixteenth-century Spain.

The ecclesiastical hierarchy's concern about unorthodoxy – whether represented by unauthorized holy sites or by heresy – also extended to matters diabolical. The growing sense in the later fifteenth century that the world was drawing to a close encouraged a wave of apocalyptic and Messianic expectation, which foretold the imminent appearance of Antichrist and the final confrontation between Christ and Satan. Alongside there grew a fear of diabolical influences, sorcery and witchcraft. The appearance in 1486 of the *Malleus maleficarum* as the key handbook for the hunt against witches and sorcerers marks a watershed: a world in which the Devil was an active and potent force, and had his human accomplices, was dangerous indeed. It became even more dangerous when tensions within Christianity could be explained as diabolically inspired, setting people on opposite sides of a confessional divide to lambast each other with diatribes and accusations of diabolical intent.

CONCLUSION

Despite the widespread apocalyptic sentiment evident around 1500, it could not have been anticipated at that point that, within a few decades, profound convulsions would tear the Catholic communion apart, as Europe moved relentlessly from an age of confession to one of confessionalism. Although the church faced problems and acknowledged them, none seemed to constitute major threats to its continuity as a unit. However, the demands and variety of late mediæval Catholicism, the centrifugal tendencies of regionalized and personalized religion, the overloading in the demands made of the laity (whether ethical, spiritual or financial) and the competitiveness between types of devotional activity, may mean that by 1500 Catholicism was becoming in some ways 'top-heavy'. The increasing burden of ritual and commemoration, the feverish devotion exhibited at pilgrimage sites, the moral and psychological demands made of clergy and laity, may have been approaching breaking point. In some places the financial demands made on the living to fund prayers for the dead were possibly reaching the point where they were considered not beneficial, but oppressive. Nevertheless, a double standard operated: people perhaps resented having to pay for ancestors, and even more for people to whom they felt no real obligation who had imposed rent charges on their properties; but they had few reservations about burdening their own descendants and successors in similar fashion. Old traditions and religious practices may have seemed of decreasing validity in some areas, but still lingered.

Despite the extensive evidence available on late mediæval Catholicism, its evolutionary direction at the start of the sixteenth century remains unclear. The existence of tensions, very real tensions, cannot be denied and the voices complaining against clerical malpractice and exploitation, and calling for reform, do seem more shrill and insistent. But such demands were not novel and could be replicated from almost every preceding century. In any case, these reformers aimed to transform the system, not to smash it. Moreover, whatever the complaints about

Figure 2.3 Fox preaching to sheep. In this English stained-glass panel of the fifteenth century, traditional jibes at the ravenous clergy are wittily expressed. Note the indulgence in the fox's paw. (Glasgow, Burrell Collection)

institutional arrangements and personal defects, there is little evidence of antipathy to Catholicism as such: among the populace the religion remained vital, its manifestations often exuberant, even flamboyant. In their search for personal salvation, in their involvement in collaborative effort at the level of the parish, or in devotional guilds and confraternities, in their participation in pilgrimages and acquisition of indulgences, there is little sign of any decline in people's commitment or investment – often the reverse. Even if devotionalism was in some places at fever pitch and close to breaking point, it might not have to break to resolve the tensions. Whatever the status accorded to the papacy, in 1500 Catholicism was still united under the pope. In 1500 Catholicism could still for the most part accommodate diversity without adversity. That situation would not last much longer.

NOTES

1 Peter Blickle, from a conference paper delivered at Washington in September 1992, quoted in S. Seidel Menchi, 'Italy', in B. Scribner, R. Porter and M. Teich (eds) *The Reformation in National Context* (Cambridge, 1994), p. 196, n. 9.
2 J. Bossy, *Christianity in the West, 1400–1700* (Oxford, 1985), p. 58.

3   Quoted in Alastair Hamilton, *Heresy and Mysticism in Sixteenth-Century Spain: The Alumbrados* (Cambridge, 1992), p. 15.

FURTHER READING

Work on the late mediæval church has proliferated in recent years, with a constant stream of studies of specific issues and localities. Suitable wide-ranging material in English nevertheless remains relatively scarce. A useful broad survey which does deal with the late mediæval church on its own terms is Francis Oakley, *The Western Church in the Later Middle Ages* (Ithaca and London, 1979), covering the period from around 1309. Issues of doctrinal development and uncertainty are considered in Alister McGrath, *The Intellectual Origins of the European Reformation* (Oxford and Cambridge, MA, 1987). For the spiritual evolutions, R.N. Swanson, *Religion and Devotion in Europe, c.1215–c.1515* (Cambridge, 1995), offers a general overview. Eamon Duffy, *The Stripping of the Altars: Traditional Religion in England, 1400–1580* (New Haven, CT, and London, 1992), provides a magisterial depiction of pre-Reformation pious practice in its first half; while Miri Rubin, *Corpus Christi: The Eucharist in Late Medieval Culture* (Cambridge, 1991), focuses on that particular devotion in its manifold manifestations. A. Eljenholm Nicholas, *Seeable Signs: The Iconography of the Seven Sacraments, 1350–1544* (Woodbridge, 1994), is mainly concerned with England, but gives a useful analysis of sacraments and their artistic representation. Also worth looking at for considerations of devotional behaviour are Jeffrey F. Hamburger, *Nuns as Artists: The Visual Culture of a Medieval Convent* (Berkeley, 1997), and A. Winston-Allen, *Stories of the Rose: The Making of the Rosary in the Middle Ages* (University Park, PA, 1997). Henk van Os, *The Art of Devotion in the Late Middle Ages in Europe, 1300–1500* (Princeton, NJ, 1994), covers a lot of ground with excellent illustrations. One particular devotional movement is treated in great depth by R.R. Post, *The Modern Devotion: Confrontation with Reformation and Humanism* (Leiden, 1968). Problems of moral discipline are considered in Thomas N. Tentler, *Sin and Confession on the Eve of the Reformation* (Princeton, NJ, 1977), which also demonstrates the effect of the accumulative tradition within the church. Preaching is usefully addressed from a regional perspective in Larissa J. Taylor, *Soldiers of Christ: Preaching in Late Medieval and Early Modern France* (New York and Oxford, 1992). Relations between 'church' and 'state' are covered in J.A.F. Thomson, *Popes and Princes, 1417–1517: Politics and Polity in the Late Medieval Church* (London, 1980). The church's integration into its social setting is largely a matter of regional histories, for example R.N. Swanson, *Church and Society in Late Medieval England* (Oxford, 1989), and D. Hay, *The Church in Italy in the Fifteenth Century* (Cambridge, 1977). Significant insight into parish life is provided by Beat Kümin, *The Shaping of a Community: The Rise and Reformation of the English Parish, c.1400–1560* (St Andrews Studies in Reformation History, Aldershot, 1997). A magisterial discussion of Lollardy as a dissenting movement developing its own doctrines is Anne Hudson, *The Premature Reformation: Wycliffite Texts and Lollard History* (Oxford, 1982).

CONCILIARISM IN LATE MEDIÆVAL EUROPE

Bruce Gordon

CONCILIARISM AS A RESPONSE TO SCHISM

Thus let the holy Universal Council restore and reform the Church Universal according to the ancient laws. Let it limit the misused papal power contained in the *Decretum* and the Decretals, and the pretended power in the Sext and the Clementines, not to mention other papal constitutions. For Christ gave to Peter no other power than that of binding and loosing – of binding by means of penance and of loosing sins. He did not empower him to bestow benefices, to possess kingdoms, castles, and cities, nor to deprive emperors and kings [of their authority]. If Christ had in such a way conferred power on Peter, then Peter himself or Paul (which is not right to say) gravely sinned or erred in that they did not deprive the Emperor Nero of his imperial power, whom they knew to be the worst and most savage persecutor of the Christians.[1]

In his attack upon the venality of the papacy, Dietrich of Niem drew upon a biblical text which deeply divided the late mediæval church. What did Christ mean when he said to Peter 'Truly I tell you, whatever you bind on earth will be bound in heaven, and whatever you loose on earth will be loosed in heaven' (Matt. 18.8)? The problem was twofold. Dietrich argued that the binding and loosing was a spiritual rather than temporal power, and he thereby rejected the worldly powers which had accrued to the papal monarchy. More fundamentally for the late mediæval church, however, was the question, who is the 'you' to whom Christ was speaking? Was the authority he was granting being passed to Peter alone or to the whole church through Peter as its representative?

These questions were laid upon the church by events in the fourteenth century: the Avignon papacy (1305–77) and the Great Schism (1378–1415). The scandal caused by the papacy led many churchmen of Europe to consider very carefully the nature of the church. The emergence of conciliarism – the idea that the whole church is represented in a General Council of the Church and that this council is superior to the papacy – was a direct response to the need to resolve the crisis at the head of the church. Conciliarism embraced the idea that authority resided in the body and was only delegated to the head by the consent of that body. This notion was derived from a variety of sources: scripture, canon law, history and the corporate nature of many late mediæval institutions (i.e. universities). As a coherent movement its time was brief, ending with the dissolution of the Council of Basle in 1447, but conciliarism was closely interwoven with late mediæval politics and ideas of church reform, and it continued to animate the thoughts of Catholic and Protestant thinkers through the early modern period.

The events which led to the rise of the conciliar movement in the fourteenth century centred around the papal election of 1378, the year after the papacy had returned to Rome from Avignon. The French cardinals found that the new Italian pope, Urban VI, had a rather austere view of his office and duties, and nothing but scorn for the luxurious life to which all had grown accustomed in Avignon. Seeking a more agreeable successor to Peter, thirteen cardinals withdrew to Anagni to elect Robert of Geneva as Pope Clement VII. Once again the papacy had passed into French hands, as Clement returned to Avignon, and there were two popes. This new crisis must be seen against the backdrop of the Hundred Years' War raging between England and France. Not surprisingly Europe divided its loyalty to the papacy along English and French lines, with Scotland, Savoy, Spain and Portugal recognizing Clement. England supported Urban and the Holy Roman Empire remained divided.

Clement was a relative of King Charles V of France, and there was considerable royal pressure on French churchmen and laity alike to recognize the new pope. The primary object of this royal campaign of persuasion was the University of Paris, which harboured strong doubts about Clement's claim, preferring a conciliar solution to the dual papacy. At the University of Paris there were many distinguished German masters, men like Conrad of Gelnhausen and Henry of Langenstein. The principal weapon in the armouries of the warring popes was patronage of benefices, and Clement and Urban zealously used this system to reward and punish their respective supporters and enemies. Clement took revenge upon German support for Urban by attacking Gelnhausen and Langenstein, thus inadvertently driving these men into the conciliar camp. Like many churchmen scandalized by renewed division within the church, the academics believed that a General Council of the Church could and should settle the opposing claims. Yet, as John Morrall has argued,

> throughout the 1380s the only solution which official circles in either obedience would consider was the unconditional submission of the rival obedience. This could only be achieved by force alone and the rival pontiffs were only too ready with lavish promises of territorial gains to encourage their secular supporters to seek this solution.[2]

In 1394 the masters of the University of Paris declared themselves in favour of a *via cessionis* – an abdication by both popes. The death of Clement in the same year seemed to bring this goal within sight until it became clear that his successor, Benedict XIII, was equally determined to cling to office. The ending of the schism became the stated goal of the French monarchy in 1395 when the king summoned a national council which voted overwhelmingly to work to heal the divide. The situation in France became even more fraught in 1398 when a synod of bishops, clergy and University representatives voted to withdraw obedience to Benedict XIII.

In the end it was a group of cardinals who grasped the nettle. These leading churchmen were motivated by a genuine sense that it fell to them to act. Under the leadership of Cardinal Baldassare Cossa members of the Sacred College from both obediences agreed to meet in Pisa. When Cardinal Uguccione, Archbishop of Bordeaux, appeared before King Henry IV and the three estates of the English kingdom, he represented the cardinals when he pleaded that to do anything less than convoke a General Council supported by Christian princes would transgress the vows made by each cardinal 'to pursue the business of union by way of resignation or any other reasonable way'.[3] Mammon, however, also inspired the deeds of these cardinals, for the schism was bad for business. By the late mediæval period the holders of ecclesiastical office were extremely mindful of the financial worth of their possessions. The schism, by dividing the cardinals into two camps, was having the effect of halving the income of the church. This propelled many of the cardinals to set aside their partisan differences and agree to meet with their rivals.

In taking matters into their own hands the cardinals were cognizant of the fact that they were on uncertain ground. There had always been a latent tension between the powers of councils and the papacy. From the twelfth century, with the great revival of Roman law in the West, the church had essentially embraced monarchy as its form of government, developing strong central government with powers of legislation and taxation. The *Decretum* of the canonist Gratian which appeared in 1140 was a foundation stone of the papal monarchy. Subsequent commentators on this text, known as the 'decretalists', made use of it to develop their concept of the papal monarchy. In so doing they used the language of Roman law to articulate the powers they believed to adhere in the office of Peter. The Roman pontiff became, in the language of Roman law, a 'prince', with virtually unbridled powers. A thirteenth-century text in this tradition read:

> The pope is the successor of Peter and the vicar of Jesus Christ, holding the place on earth not of mere man, but of God ... whence he rules and judges all ... the pope has the plenitude of power to which he is called ... so long as he does not go against the faith he can say and do whatever he pleases in all things. ... No one can say to him 'Why do you do this?' ... What pleases him has the force of law ... he can abolish any law ... he has no superior ... he is set over all and he can be judged by no one.[4]

Against this bold assertion of papal absolutism it must be noted that the canonists also recognized the right of the community to defend itself against a corrupt or heretical pope; church history would not permit the decretalists to ignore the fact that there had been unworthy successors to St Peter. Therefore one also finds in the writings of twelfth- and thirteenth-century legal scholars a conception of how the truth is to be found in the body as well as the head. The commentator Huguccio wrote in the 1180s:

Although the Roman pope has sometimes erred this does not mean that the Roman church has, which is understood to be not he alone but all the faithful, for the Church is the aggregate of the faithful; if it does not exist at Rome it exists in the regions of Gaul, or wherever the faithful are ... for it was said to Peter and in the person of Peter to the Universal Church 'that your faith shall not fail'.[5]

The great period of canon law had bequeathed to the late mediæval world an ambiguous legacy which lay dormant until roused by the schism in 1378. Faced by a divided papacy, who in the church, it was asked, had the authority to act? While the papacy held its course conciliarism remained a theoretical point; the events of the late fourteenth century, however, forced churchmen to turn in desperation to the only available option: a General Council.

PISA

The importance of the Council of Pisa in 1409 lay not in what it achieved – very little – but in its articulation of conciliarist principles. The first hurdle over which the cardinals had to pass was the vexed question of how a council might be summoned without the consent of the pope. When, in the early years of the schism, men such as James Orsini, Peter Corsini and Simon de Borsano first floated the idea of a council, they were deterred by uncertainty concerning the legitimacy of a non-papal council. Although the prevailing wisdom in the fourteenth century remained that only a pope could summon a council of the church, there had been some dissenting voices. William of Ockham (d.1349) provided a definition of a council which proved influential on subsequent conciliar thought. Ockham maintained that a council could be convoked without papal consent in times of crisis, but his thinking did not extend to an assertion of conciliar superiority.

The most important conciliar thinkers of the Pisan period were Pierre D'Ailly (1350–1420) and his friend and disciple, Jean Gerson (1363–1429). Both men were deeply implicated in the events of the period. D'Ailly, as chancellor of the University of Paris, was widely believed to be the natural successor to Clement VII. Gerson was D'Ailly's successor as chancellor, and both men devoted themselves to the ending of the schism. Whilst recognizing that there was little ground in canon law for a council to be summoned other than by papal initiative, they maintained that the primary goal of such a council was reform of the church 'in head and members'. Tradition, Gerson argued in a sermon entitled *Propositio facta coram Anglicis*, is no impediment to action; the council of the church must move to restore unity and to achieve this end it should employ the measures it deems necessary. Gerson's arguments were based on his conception of the church, which 'derives its efficacy and strength from the Divine seed, which like life-giving blood is diffused through the ecclesiastical body and implanted firmly and inseparably there.'[6]

Gerson, like all subsequent fifteenth-century conciliarists, adamantly defended the relationship between hierarchy and authority in the church: the Holy Spirit dwells in the body of the visible church, sanctioning its decrees and labours. The crucial distinction which he made was between the office, which was divine, and its incumbent, who manifestly was not. As he argued in the text *De Auferibilitate Papae ab Ecclesia*, Christ is the real head of the church, which he never abandons, and he continually infuses his grace into the body through the Holy Spirit. This inpouring of grace is manifested in the outward hierarchy of the church. Following the tradition of canon law, Gerson and the other conciliarists spoke of the church in terms of a body with a head and limbs. The sacraments of the church are what vivify that body and sustain it in its various functions. The body, therefore, remains holy even if its members are not.

It is crucial to understand that none of the conciliarists wished to deny the divine origins of papal supremacy, but rather, in light of the ghastly situation at the beginning of the fifteenth century, to limit it. This was the aim of their interpretation of the relation of the head (pope) to body (church). In a council of the church the various levels are represented, so that the council speaks the mind of the church. If a council finds a pope in error, or if the pope refuses to accept the arguments of the council, the council is empowered to force its decision upon him. As Morrall has commented, the real argument upon which Gerson relied was that in cases of necessity the ordinary letter of the law can be overruled.[7] Cardinals electing the pope act as representatives of the whole church, in whom final authority resides. When the election is completed the body still retains that authority even though it has chosen a head. The pope might occupy the highest rung on the ecclesiastical ladder, and for that he must be duly respected, but he is not greater than the whole body of the church, in whom resides the authority of Christ. That body of the church, as represented by a council, must impose limitations on the pope and, when necessary, act against him. Gerson cited the extreme cases in which a council might have to act in this respect: vacancy, madness, heresy or a disputed election.

The cardinals meeting in Pisa in 1409 withdrew their allegiance to Benedict and Gregory and elected as pope the Archbishop of Milan, Peter Filargi, who took the name Alexander V. Filargi was a Greek and therefore acceptable to both the English and French, though his two rivals retained powerful backers, Gregory in northern Italy and Germany, and Benedict in the Spanish kingdoms. Alexander, however, proved a less than enthusiastic reformer and the hopes placed in him were disappointed. He shied away from any serious reform programme, claiming that another council of the church should be summoned. The Council of Pisa was closed, but Alexander did not live to see the next meeting of the church. He died in 1410. The council which had been summoned to end the schism had only succeeded in giving the church a third pope.

THE CHURCH RESTORED: THE COUNCILS OF PISA AND CONSTANCE

In the years following the Council of Pisa there was a rhapsodic chorus calling for reform within the church. The primary issue of the divided papacy overshadowed the need, recognized by virtually all churchmen, for reform at every level. If the church was generally thought of as a body, then it had an open wound which festered: the abuse of the benefice system. Throughout Europe, simony – the buying and selling of ecclesiastical privileges, pardons and offices – was rife. The church was disfigured by an obscene distribution of its wealth as, on the one hand, the common people were increasingly made to pay for the services of the church, whilst, on the other, ecclesiastical offices became sinecures for leading families.

As the church continued to be riven by internecine warfare over the papacy, storm clouds gathered in the east. Jan Hus was appointed to the Bethlehem Chapel in Prague in 1402 to hold vernacular sermons before congregations of 3,000 people. He preached in Czech in a crescendo against clerical abuse and, most directly, against simony. In the period between 1402–10, precisely the time of the Pisan Council, Hus's views became increasingly radical, leading to his excommunication. His incendiary preaching cast in relief the failings of the hierarchical church. This emphasis on church reform was transformed in character by a rising tide of Bohemian nationalism which quickly baptized Hus a hero. This would only grow in the wake of Hus's execution at the Council of Constance. The whole issue of the Hussites cast a pall over the ecclesiastical debates of the fifteenth century. The determination of the papacy to quash these heretics was without question, but the strength of the movement enabled it to defy emperor and pope. Like the growing threat of the Ottoman Empire in the east, the Hussites emerged as one of the defining issues in the power politics of the late mediæval church.

As with every other ecclesiastical event of significance in the fifteenth century, the Council of Constance was made possible by the intervention of powerful secular interests. Sigismund became Holy Roman Emperor in 1411 following the deposition of his brother Wenzel. By the late mediæval period the emperors theoretically ruled over a vast expanse of Europe, but in truth they were rather pallid figures. Long exiled from the Italian heart of the empire, the Holy Roman Emperors found that the growing power of the German princes in the north had stripped them of real authority anywhere but in their own territorial lands. Sigismund longed to restore the glory of the empire and he saw his chance in the papal scandal. John XXIII, successor to Alexander V, was primarily concerned with restoring papal authority in Italy. His contribution to ending the schism was to wage war on his rival Gregory, and he even managed to capture Rome. John, however, was being bullied by Ladislas of Naples and he sought aid from Sigismund, who proved quite obliging. The emperor's terms were clear: aid would be forthcoming on condition that the pope summoned a council. When Ladislas died in August 1414, the pope – desirous only of returning to Rome to consolidate his power – reneged on his promise to attend the council. It was the determination of the cardinals to end the schism which forced the pope to attend.[8] Careful negotiations conducted by Cardinal Francesco Zabarella (1360–1417) between the emperor and the cardinalate brought about the Council of Constance.

In the end John XXIII did come to Constance and even preached at the opening session. His promise to abdicate if his rivals did likewise caused Emperor Sigismund to throw himself at his feet and for a Te Deum to be sung. John was, however, a marked man. The conciliar leaders wanted rid of this truculent pope who possessed few if any of the spiritual qualities to lead a renewal of the church.

The council, which opened in 1414, was organized by nations (Italian, French, English, German and, from 1416, Spanish) rather than by ecclesiastical rank in a shrewd ploy to limit the strength of the various popes. If a vote had simply been by show of hands then the domination of the Italian prelates, who generally favoured John, would have secured an undesirable result. With voting carried out by nations, John had little chance of survival.

The crucial role played by Sigismund in the rise of the conciliar movement was not limited to summoning the council in 1414. The following year, John XXIII, after his initial offer of resignation began to plot with Sigismund's rival, the Habsburg Frederick of Austria. When his mendacity came to light, John – dressed as a common soldier – bolted to the nearby Swiss city of Schaffhausen, imploring his supporters among the cardinalate to leave the council. This was a defining moment, a test of conciliar strength. The council at Constance now had to decide whether it would proceed against the pope. Many of the cardinals favoured dissolving the council, but Sigismund held firm, demonstrating his support by appearing at a plenary session on 26 March 1415 in full imperial regalia. This was also Jean Gerson's great moment as he preached to the council in the midst of the crisis. The sermon was a clear declaration of conciliar principles. A legitimately summoned council does not need a pope, to whom he referred as 'secondary head' from whom the church could be divorced. A General Council of the Church is:

> a gathering together, made by legitimate authority, in any place, of every hierarchical estate of the entire Catholic Church, no faithful person who requires audience being excluded, for the purpose of the salutary treatment and arrangement of those things which relate to the right ordering of the Church in faith and morals.[9]

The sermon concluded with an affirmation of conciliar principle: 'The Church has no efficacious means for its general reformation, unless a continual meeting of General Councils be decreed, together with the assembling of provincial councils.'[10]

The sermon galvanized the cardinals against John, resulting in his deposition in May 1415. Gregory XII sportingly offered his resignation in July, leaving only the recalcitrant Benedict XIII. Again Sigismund played a key role by travelling to Aragon to negotiate Benedict's abdication. The negotiations were successful in that Ferdinand of Aragon ordered the withdrawal of support for Benedict within his lands. This effectively pulled the rug from underneath the last of the three popes, clearing the way for an election. Sigismund's efforts on behalf of the council, however, proved a mixed blessing. During the course of his Aragonese negotiations Sigismund abandoned neutrality in the war between France and England, openly declaring himself an ally of the English. This poisoned the waters of the Council of Constance. The French nation at the council, outraged by the emperor's actions, allied with the Italian curialists, a conjunction which resulted in the election of Martin V in 1417. The council had succeeded in restoring unity throughout the Christian West through the ending of schism, but the means by which this was achieved – the striking of deals between the papacy and secular governments – would ultimately defeat the conciliar movement.

The ill will generated by John's irascible conduct enabled the council fathers at Constance to seize the initiative and issue a cogent statement of conciliar theory. This well-known canon *Haec Sancta* was issued at the Council's fifth session on 6 April 1415:

> This holy synod of Constance ... declares that, being lawfully assembled in the Holy Spirit, constituting a General Council and representing the catholic Church, it derives power directly from Christ, and to it everyone, of whatever rank or dignity including the pope, is subject in those things which pertain to the faith, the ending of the schism and the reformation of the Church in head and members. It further declares that anyone, of whatever condition, rank or dignity, including the pope, who contumaciously neglects to obey the orders, canons, regulations or directions made or to be made by this holy Council or by any other lawfully assembled Council on or related to the aforesaid matters, shall (unless he comes to his senses) be subjected to condign penitence and duly punished, even by recourse to other legal sanctions if need arise.[11]

In many respects *Haec Sancta* was the most important statement of fifteenth-century conciliarism and its influence would be felt throughout the following century. It underpinned all subsequent conciliar activity and thought. *Haec Sancta* was an extraordinarily controversial document: many among the conciliarists did not support it without reservation, for the cardinals hoped that they, rather than the council, would in the end be the final authority within the church. The canon *Haec Sancta* was followed by the decrees *Frequens* in October 1417. Whereas the first determined the superiority of councils, the second bound the newly restored papacy to the regular holding of those councils:

> General Councils shall meet frequently in the future. The next will be held in five years' time, the second seven years after that, and thereafter they will be celebrated every ten years. These intervals may be shortened by the pope, in case of necessity and with the assent of the cardinals, but under no circumstances may they be lengthened. A month before the end of a Council the pope, with the agreement of the Council, shall determine the meeting place of the next Council; if this is not done by the pope the Council shall itself determine the place.[12]

The Council of Constance did make some progress on the central problems afflicting the church at the beginning of the fifteenth century: it resolved the papal schism, removed some of the worst financial abuses within the church, reformed the operation of the curia and fostered reforms within the Franciscan and Benedictine orders, giving rise to the Observant movements. These achievements, however, must be weighed against those areas in which the council failed to act. The most prominent issue left unresolved was annates, which were such an important part of papal income. Annates, or first fruits, were a tax paid to the pope on the first year of revenue from a benefice. Payment of this tax generated anti-

Roman sentiment across Europe and throughout the fifteenth century the princes of Europe sought to keep that money within their lands. Likewise, the council did nothing about simony. The council was powerless to meet the challenge posed by the laity to the church. Across Europe, though notably in the empire, the church was dominated by noble families who had a firm grip on church offices that they held in their gift. Ecclesiastical titles and, more importantly, moneys were conferred upon sons who were semi-literate, violent and oppressive.

The situation among the clergy was hardly much better. Pluralism, simony and concubinage were commonplace, while the destruction of the benefice system meant that in many areas church offices had been so denuded that no one was willing to fill them. None of these problems was merely a symptom of a corrupt church; they reflected the deeper nature of European society in the early fifteenth century. Feudal structures still shaped a society struggling to recover from the Black Death. The problem of pluralism, for example, was that it was deeply rooted in the economic and demographical landscape of late mediæval Europe. The revenues from benefices in some areas were so meagre that pluralism was the only means of survival.

The Council of Constance has been described by historians as bringing unity without reform. The council did not manage to determine its longer-term relationship with the papacy. The Constance conciliarists believed they were acting in extraordinary times; in the decrees *Haec Sancta* and *Frequens* they had established that councils should form a prominent part of the church. But the council fathers had not resolved the older contradiction between conciliar and papal forms of sovereignty. There was an assumption that council and pope would work together, but in what form was never made clear. Constance had healed the schism but could not mask the reality that there were still two visions of the church contesting supremacy. Although Martin V cooperated with the council at first, the depth of the problem would be brought into relief by renewed warfare between the Renaissance papacy and the General Council of the Church.

With the end of the Council of Constance the inevitable conflict between the papacy and the conciliarists began to take shape. Martin V, who owed his election to the work of the council, despised the principles of conciliarism and by no means accepted the idea that popes were subject to councils. He was a highly talented man who did much to restore papal fortunes in the areas of finance, administration and foreign policy. His adherence to *Frequens* was scrupulous, though desultory; a council was summoned at Pavia in 1423, but it was poorly attended, riven by factions and visited by plague. The debates at Pavia suggested that despite the triumph at Constance there were many leading churchmen who were unsure about the principle of conciliar superiority. What had been done *in extremis* was not necessarily good for the church in normal times. Martin V demonstrated his lack of enthusiasm for the council by staying far away, preferring to shift it to Siena during the summer. The council eventually petered out in the spring of 1424, having achieved little more than deciding that the next council should be held in Basle in 1431.

— *Chapter Three* —

THE COUNCIL OF BASLE: THE CHURCH DIVIDES

By the opening of the Council of Basle in September of 1431 the situation was quite different. Martin V had died in that year to be replaced by the Venetian Eugenius IV, an even more virulent opponent of conciliarism. The effect of *Haec Sancta* and *Frequens* was to turn the papacy into a limited monarchy rather than an absolute sovereign. There was to be a written constitution by which the popes had to abide and there was even to be a General Council of the Church to which appeals against papal policies could be made. As Denys Hay has written,

> The curious mixture of spiritual and temporal sanctions by which popes ruled not only the Church at large, but their own Papal State, was thus threatened with dissolution and the pope as prince was stripped of his most valuable diplomatic weapons.[13]

The restoration of the Renaissance papacy in the fifteenth century was directly connected to the resumption of control over the Papal State in the middle of Italy. Acting as any other Renaissance prince would, the popes – beginning with Martin V – sought to consolidate their authority in their lands through centralizing government, a more efficient collection of taxes and military prowess. The evisceration of the papal office envisaged by the conciliarists would certainly have destroyed the papacy as an institution and Eugenius understood this all too well. He made it a primary objective, therefore, to frustrate the Council of Basle.

The Council of Basle acted as a weather-vane in the swirling winds of the mid-fifteenth century. Distant events, particularly in the east, did much to mould the fate of the council. The Hussite wars were going very badly: four crusades by church and empire had failed miserably to bring the heretical Bohemians to heel. In August 1431 Cardinal Cesarini left Nuremberg, accompanied to the gates of the city by Emperor Sigismund himself, leading an army of imperial troops against the Hussite leader Prokop the Great. As the imperial soldiers entered the forest near Domazlice they heard the chilling strains of the Hussite chorale 'You Warriors of God'.[14] The soldiers fled in fear, only to be cut down by the Hussite cavalry. The rout did not end until what was left of the imperial army staggered back to Nuremberg. The cardinal managed to survive the carnage, but lost his mantel, gold cross and the papal bull which named him as legate for the crusade. Cesarini, despite this humiliation, urged Eugenius to recognize the council in order to keep a line of communication to the Hussites, whose power in the east could not be ignored. The willingness to negotiate expressed by the council towards the Hussites accounts for the support offered the council by Emperor Sigismund, who greatly desired the Bohemian crown.

Another shadow which lay across the council at Basle was the growing Ottoman threat in the east. The Byzantine Empire, feeling Turkish pressure and desperate for support from the West, had signalled a willingness to resolve the schism between the eastern and western churches which had existed since the eleventh century. The readiness of the Greeks to attend a council in Bologna was cited by Eugenius in his bull *Quoniam alto* (18 December 1431) as grounds for transferring the council from Basle to more favourable territory. Eugenius' own difficulties on the Italian peninsula, where powerful Roman families such as the Colonna had become sworn enemies, left him in a weak position to combat Basle. Thus during the crucial opening years 1431–2 the council was able to resist papal opposition.

The Council of Basle had a different structure from Constance, which had been organized by nations. At Basle there were four deputations each concerned with a particular theme (faith, peace, reform and general business).[15] Each of the deputations consisted of equal numbers from the nations (France, Italy, Spain and Germany – there was no English nation) and contained clergy of different ranks. The complex nature of the council is evident from the manner in which the deputations were structured. If there was agreement among the deputations on an issue, it could be put to a plenary session of the council, an event carried out with great liturgical ceremony in the Basle cathedral. The most remarkable aspect of the council was the breadth of its membership, which was dominated by the lower clergy and not bishops. In asserting its superiority the Council of Basle had its own chancery, courts of law and curial organization. The complexity of its constitution and decision-making process enables us to understand why it so quickly became prisoner to competing interests.

Under the leadership of Cardinal Cesarini the early years of the Council of Basle consisted of bold statements of conciliar superiority. *Haec Sancta* and *Frequens* were reasserted against arguments from canon law brought forward by Eugenius' supporters. Pope Martin V, weeks before his death, appointed Cesarini to the presidency of the council. Cesarini attempted to marry fidelity to the papacy with respect for the integrity of conciliarism, but he could not resist the growing radical nature of the council as the fathers responded to papal opposition. A further step in the radicalization of the conciliar movement took place in 1434 when Eugenius attempted to assert control over the council by appointing three legates to Basle who were to be joint presidents with Cesarini. The council rejected these legates, arguing that it alone was competent to appoint its leaders. This incident was important in marking a further development of conciliar thought.

At Constance the guiding principle was that power was divided between pope and council, with the council acting in an emergency. At Basle the unfettered power of the council was declared. The Council of Basle, unlike Constance, became distinctly anti-papal; in the minds of the Basle fathers there was to be no reconciliation with Eugenius. Thus their own path forward was a radical one. As Anthony Black has observed, 'It was a conscious attempt to transfer the central government of the Church from the Roman papacy to an [itinerant] council.'[16]

It was during the fraught years of 1433–4 that the greatest intellectual achievement of the conciliar period appeared: *De concordantia catholica* of Nicholas of Cusa.[17] The work was not merely a theoretical treatise, it was the last and most impressive expression of that group of men, including Cesarini and Aeneas Sylvius Piccolomini (later Pope Pius II), who believed in the ultimate harmony of papal and conciliar views of the church. Nicholas asserted the principle of conciliar superiority over the pope, but in a rather complex manner:

Hence just as Peter was prince of the apostles, the Roman pontiff is prince of the bishops since the bishops succeed the apostles. There is almost an infinite number of writings of the saints on this. This rulership is over all men in the Church of the believers, for he is the captain of that army, as Emperor Leo wrote to Theodosius: 'The most blessed bishop of the city of Rome to whom antiquity gave the priestly rule over all has the power of judgement in matters of faith.' … However a matter of faith is not always defined by the arbitrary will of the Roman pontiff alone for he could be a heretic – on which more will be said below. Indeed in decisions on matters of faith which is why he possesses the primacy, he is subject to the Council of the Catholic Church.[18]

Cusa's delicate balancing of papal and conciliar powers reflected his concern for the growing divide between the two, evident in the early 1530s. The conflict offended Cusa's guiding principle – the belief which underlies the whole of the *Concordantia catholica* – that the divine will is made manifest in the world through concord and consent. Nicholas of Cusa picked at the deep quarry of neoplatonic thought in formulating his view that the hierarchies of this world are a reflection of the divine hierarchies. The restoration of the church, in his view, lay in restoring harmony to the earthly hierarchies by bringing them in line with their celestial forms. The church is a 'hierarchy of corporations', each with its chosen representatives. Local churches would come together to form provincial synods, provinces would form national synods and all the provinces would constitute a General Council.[19] Each would retain its own integrity, but through the power of representation confer certain powers on individuals. In Cusa's words, the pope is given power for the 'edification' of the church; pope and council should, ideally, work together, but if they find themselves in conflict then the judgement of the council is to be preferred.[20]

During this difficult period the council was involved in protracted negotiations with the Hussites and by 1434 there were signs of real progress. For the Hussites the central issue was communion in both kinds (bread and chalice). Eugenius refused to have anything to do with the Bohemian heretics while the council was involved in negotiations with them, but during this period the council once again received crucial support from Emperor Sigismund, who was in Basle for seven months during 1433–4. The emperor had much in common with the conciliar fathers: a hatred of schism, a need to reconcile the Hussites and a sense of the urgency of church reform.[21]

In the period following the emperor's departure the council seemed to make progress on much of its agenda. The situation was, no doubt, aided by the difficulties faced by Eugenius at home. On 29 May 1434 the people of Rome had risen in revolt against the pope, forcing him to flee to Florence. It was during this time that the leader of the Basle council, Cardinal Cesarini, undertook a programme of reform. The zeal of the Basle fathers was impressive: a requirement of regular diocesan and provincial synods, the extirpation of heresy and simony, the regulation of clerical immorality, the residency of monks and improving the quality of preaching.[22] Clerical celibacy was affirmed and bishops were ordered to search the houses of priests suspected of having concubines. In the summer of 1435 the council proposed the reform of worship, dictating that priests should sing the entire Creed and Lord's Prayer at mass, that secret prayers should be audible and that spectacles, dances and other forms of festivals be banned from churches and cemeteries. The council also turned its attention to the Sacred College, limiting the number of cardinals to twenty-four, with each to have degrees in theology or law. The size of the houses of the cardinalate was also to be limited. Under Cesarini, reform legislation continued to recognize papal primacy, though popes were bound to defend the decisions of Constance and Basle. The papacy was to govern Rome and the Papal States with care, and to appoint cardinals free from the stain of nepotism. The most contentious of the Basle reforms, however, was the abolition of annates in 1435. On 3 June 1435 the council approved a decree prohibiting the payment for provisions, holy orders or any other form of office under the pretext of annates or 'first fruits'.[23]

Eugenius, whose fortunes had rallied in 1435, launched a bitter attack on this decision on annates. In 1437 he issued the bull *Doctoris gentium* which attacked the Council at Basle directly and transferred it to Ferrara. The issue in the background was the negotiations with the Greeks. Cesarini had led the council's talks with the delegates from the east, but it became increasingly apparent that the Byzantine church leaders had little interest in dealing with truculent churchmen in northern Europe. In November 1437 the Byzantine emperor, the patriarchs and bishops sailed from Constantinople to Italy in ships provided by the pope. This was a great triumph for Eugenius and did much to undermine the prestige of the council. It was this issue which played an important role in the desertion of Cardinals Cesarini and Cusa to the papal camp in 1437. To compound the problems of the fathers at Basle, the peace made with the Hussites in 1436 diminished the Holy Roman Emperor's interest in the council.

The year 1437 brought the decisive break between the council and Pope Eugenius IV. The pope had moved the council to Ferrara and then to Florence, thus renewing schism within the church. The departure of many leading moderates left the council in more radical hands. The council, however, still had powerful backers, most decisively the French monarchy. In 1438 the French church adopted the reforming legislation of Basle in the Pragmatic Sanction of Bourges. French influence at the council was manifest in growing anti-papalism. With the departure of Cesarini in 1437 the most important voices at Basle belonged to Niccolo de 'Tudeschi (Panormitanus), Archbishop of Palermo, and Juan de Segovia. In the heated debates with the radical conciliarists which led to the deposition of Eugenius IV in 1439, Tudeschi had attempted to persuade the council not to take this drastic step. But once the council elected another pope, Felix V, he returned to Basle to receive a cardinal's hat from the anti-pope. Segovia, on the other hand, had led the forces seeking to depose the pope. He was an advocate of unbridled conciliar supremacy and a tireless worker on behalf of the council in seeking support among secular rulers.

The deposition of Eugenius IV in 1439 by the council was a serious miscalculation. In the same year the pope, at the Council of Florence, achieved what appeared to be an ending of the schism between the Greek and Latin churches. The conciliarists – who had failed in their negotiations with the Greeks – offered only a new schism in reply, and following the success of the pope their voices were starting to sound rather shrill. Europe was so traumatized by the memories of the schism ended at Constance that the horror of a new one was too much to bear. One by one, Eugenius came to terms with the rulers of Europe, systematically depriving the council of any support. Only in Germany was there much enthusiasm for Pope Felix V, but even there the electors and princes had been won away from the conciliar cause. The early years of the 1440s brought a bitter harvest for those remaining in Basle, full of recriminations. Dwindling political support was matched by increasingly ferocious rivalries within the city walls. Even the Pope Felix V had very poor relations with the council and he had abandoned the city before the final session in 1443, resigning his office in 1449. A small rump of conciliar fathers moved to Lausanne where the Basle council was officially closed and Nicholas V, who succeeded Eugenius IV in 1447, was elected pope.

CONCILIARISM AFTER THE AGE OF COUNCILS

The rather pathetic end of the Council of Basle closed what many historians would regard as the 'classic age' of conciliarism. Indeed, never again would a council so rigorously challenge the authority of the papacy. This was, however, by no means the end of the story. The defeat of the conciliar movement was a complex historical event. Certainly the revivification of the papacy was a major factor, but that does not tell the whole story. The rise of the Renaissance papacy was itself a pyrrhic victory, for despite its triumph over the Council of Basle its authority was confined to the Italian peninsula. For most churchmen and politicians there was a desperate need to establish authority. The theological world of scholasticism had disintegrated into the rival schools of nominalism and realism; virtually the whole of Europe was engulfed in war; Constantinople had finally fallen in 1453, and plague continued to take a heavy toll. Conciliarism had arisen out of crisis and churchmen had been prepared to break with tradition in order to solve a terrible problem, but in the end they were more comfortable with a notion of sovereignty in which power was firmly in the hands of one person. The radical positions taken at Basle in its last ten years, beginning with the deposition of a legitimately elected pope, evoked too many dark memories to retain support. Conciliarism became associated with schism. The conciliarism of the fifteenth century certainly reflected the corporate nature of late mediæval European society, with its universities, guilds and estates, but it never articulated a clear sense of how it was to take a permanent place in the polity of the church. In the social, religious and intellectual worlds of the fifteenth century one senses anxiety and the search for certainty, and to this conciliarism, as a political movement, had no answer. The triumphant papacy did what it could to kill this dying bird: Pius II (Aeneas Piccolomini) issued the bull *Execrabilis* in 1460 which condemned the appeal from papal policies to future General Councils. This was then followed by the decree *Pastor aeternus* in which papal supremacy was clearly asserted.

But all was not finished. While there were not many who argued strict principles of conciliar supremacy, the language of a council became inseparable from the overwhelming desire to reform the church. In purely theoretical terms the truest disciples of conciliar thought remained at the University of Paris. Conciliarism was a foundation of Gallicanism. In January 1497 King Charles VIII of France asked the theological faculty at Paris whether the decree *Frequens* was still valid, and the answer was an unequivocal yes. The University of Paris repeatedly defended the decrees of Constance and Basle, and ferociously attacked the *Summa de ecclesia* of Juan de Torquemada, the primary defence of absolute papal power from its publication in 1453 until the Council of Trent. The French kings found the conciliar legislation extremely useful in shoring up their control of the church.

In the empire, conciliarism retained supporters, principally in the universities. Emperor Frederick III, however, who needed any ally he could find, was an avowed supporter of the papacy, while the German princes, whose instincts were to support the councils, lost interest following the endless bickering. They too found Rome willing to make deals which gave them what they wanted, control over their church properties and revenues. Nevertheless, the idea of reform had a strong hold on all leading figures within the empire. Perhaps in Germany more than in anywhere else in Europe the disintegration of the local church was evident. The corrosion of parochial life, abetted by the virtual monopoly on higher church offices held by noble families, had created a situation that many regarded as intolerable. One finds in the plethora of reform literature that appeared in the second half of the fifteenth century repeated calls for the summoning of a reforming council, but these fell on stony soil. The reform of the church was closely connected to the restoration of the empire and all could nod in assent to this noble goal, but there was no structural means to bring it about. There was a good deal of anti-papal sentiment, given expression in the *Gravamina der deutschen Nation* of 1456 in which the Germans demanded a degree of independence similar to the French, but the fragmented nature of the empire precluded the possibility of an effective council. No one, least of all the emperor, had the force to pull together the myriad of territorial princes and cities. The language of conciliarism was employed in the attempt to rescue a desperate situation in the empire, to bring about much-needed reform, rather than to make any point about the superiority of a General Council.

In England, Spain and Italy there were individual voices raised in favour of conciliarism, but they did not find receptive audiences. England's virtual independence from Rome rendered the conciliar debate rather pointless, while in Spain the war against the Moriscos, seen very much as a religious crusade, had little place for the conciliar debate. In Italy the stranglehold of the mendicants on teaching positions in the theological faculties ensured that conciliar thought was given meagre attention. On the whole the great Italian conciliarists – Zabarella, Tudeschi, Pontano, among others – had been jurists, not theologians.

Another confrontation, however, did bring conciliarism back to the fore of European affairs. Pope Julius II was declared suspended in April 1512 by a small gathering of cardinals at Pisa under French leadership. The Council of Pisa reasserted the validity of the fifteenth-century conciliar decrees. Emperor Maximilian I and King Louis XII had been attempting to force Julius to hold a reform council, but their fragile alliance did not hold and in the end only France supported the Pisan endeavour, which has become known as a *conciliabulum*. Nevertheless, Julius summoned a council to Rome in May 1512, known as the Fifth Lateran Council. The French attempt at a council had flopped, with Louis XII referring to it as a 'bad joke'. By 1515 his successor, Francis I, was negotiating a concordat with Pope Leo X in which recognition of papal supremacy was given in return for royal control over 600 benefices in France. The Concordat of Bologna, promulgated in Rome in 1516, confirmed growing royal control over the French church, but it did so in such a way as seriously to damage the conciliar threat within France.

The intellectual attack on the Council of Pisa was delegated by Julius to the Dominican theologian Cardinal Cajetan. In October 1511 the brilliant Cajetan published his *De comparatione auctoritatis papae et concilii* in which he rejected the principles of conciliarism, including the notion that cardinals have the power to convoke a council in an emergency.[24] The responses to this text came principally from Paris, from the pens of Jacques Almain and John Mair. Almain's work bears witness to the continuity of conciliar thought into the sixteenth century. He did not reject the papacy as the highest office in the church, but argued, in classic conciliarist terms, that Christ's commission of binding and loosing to Peter was given to the body of the whole church. That body was represented by a General Council which was superior to the pope, whose office was for the good of the church. Pure conciliar theory, therefore, was still alive, but mostly in France and actively in the service of Gallican aspirations.

The Fifth Lateran Council, which ran from 1512 until 1517, was a remarkable event. Julius II, as part of his election capitulary signed in 1503, had promised to hold a General Council, but fear of latent conciliarism, not only in France but also within his own curia, deterred him from acting. His priority was the assertion of his role of supreme ruler of the Papal State, an act which required the destruction of Cesare Borgia. In the north, French troops presented the greatest threat to papal power. Julius formed a 'Holy League' against France, but the resulting war left both Louis XII and the pope looking for peace. The instability of the situation in Italy caused by the animosity of Julius towards the French dictated the course of religious affairs.

Against this background the conciliar fathers met in the Lateran halls to put forward a penumbra of reform plans. There was an urgent sense that the hand of God was upon the church, ready to punish it for its failure to reform itself. The Turks were a constant reminder of divine disfavour. While there was no recourse to the fifteenth-century conciliar decrees, it was believed that the council held the best prospects for saving the church before divine judgement was pronounced. The fundamental concept of reform current at the council was that of restoration. The church was not debated in its structural form, as it had been at Constance and Basle, nor was theology treated in any detail. The primary issue was a return to the observance of church law. As Nelson Minnich has commented, this view of reform revealed the hold of Roman legal thought – with its emphasis on a restoration of justice – on the church at its highest level.[25] The council issued a range of reforming legislation, but virtually all of it consisted of decrees of former councils, previous canons and laws. At the centre of the council's mentality was a strict adherence to tradition, a return to a golden past when the church was faithful to its laws. Exemplary conduct and the enforcement of church law were understood

Figure 3.1 A Society of Orders. From Petrarch, *Glücksbuch*, 1520. (Wittenberg, Lutherhalle)

as the means to reform the head and body of the church. There was no discussion of how the head and the body were related; the Fifth Lateran Council was strictly controlled by the papacy.

The popes did not have to face down another council in the sixteenth century, but conciliarism continued to haunt the ecclesiastical corridors of Europe. In France the University of Paris continued to defend its ideals with vigour. Throughout the empire after 1517 the solution to the religious question was thought to lie with a General Council of the Church: indeed this was the hope of both Martin Luther and Charles V. Protestant writers such as John Calvin made extensive use of conciliar arguments, especially in their interpretation of Matthew 18, without being themselves conciliarists in the strict sense. The English Reformation, with its break from Rome, saw the deployment of conciliar arguments to justify the actions of Henry VIII. Within the Catholic church, the popes remained nervous of a council and in the end the Council of Trent was forced upon them. Even at this great gathering of the Catholic church conciliarism was present. As Francis Oakley has recently commented, the failure of the church to promulgate any doctrine on the nature of the church harks back to the difficulties of the previous century and a half.[26]

Historians have recognized that conciliarism had two distinct elements: the concept of the superiority of a General Council over the papacy and the belief that the reform of the church required the summoning of a council. From the period of the Great Schism through to the collapse of the Council of Basle the two went hand in hand. As Basle grew more radical the two became uncoupled, with many zealous reformers turning their faces against expressions of conciliar superiority. Pure conciliar thought survived into the early modern period, but mostly as an aspect of Gallicanism and as a polemical tool for opponents of papal monarchy. The idea of a reforming council, however, had a much more robust hold on ecclesiastical and secular minds of the Reformation Age. Although the Protestant reformers made use of conciliarist writers, it would be incorrect to see these fifteenth-century figures as forerunners of Protestantism. From Ockham through to Almain there was never any doubt that the authority of the church inhered in its hierarchy; at issue was the distribution of this authority. Nevertheless the conciliarism of the late mediæval world spawned a profound spiritual, moral and intellectual examination of what it meant to be the Body of Christ, and the fruits of those reflections fed the thought of many sixteenth-century churchmen.

NOTES

1 Dietrich of Niem, *Ways of Uniting and Reforming the Church* (1410). Quoted from Matthew Spinka (ed.), *Patterns of Reform from Wyclif to Erasmus* (London, 1953), p. 161.
2 John B. Morrall, *Gerson and the Great Schism* (Manchester, 1960), p. 3.
3 E.F. Jacob, *Essays in the Conciliar Epoch* (Manchester, 1943, repr. 1963), p. 4.
4 Quoted from Brian Tierney, *Religion, Law and the Growth of Constitutional Thought, 1150–1650* (Cambridge, 1982), p. 14.
5 Ibid., p. 15.
6 Quoted from Morrall, *Gerson*, p. 80.
7 Ibid., p. 81.
8 Jacob, *Essays*, p. 6.

9 The sermon was entitled, *Ambulate dum lucem habetis* ('Walk in the light while you have light'). Quoted from Morrall, *Gerson*, p. 96.
10 Ibid., p. 97.
11 Quoted from Denys Hay and W.K. Smith (eds), *Aeneas Sylvius Piccolominus, De Gestis Concilii Basiliensis Commentariorum Libri II* (Oxford, 1967), pp. xiii–iv.
12 Ibid., p. xv.
13 Ibid., p. xvi.
14 This account is taken from Gerald Christianson, *Cesarini: The Conciliar Cardinal. The Basel Years, 1431–1438* (St Otrilien, 1979), pp. 23–5.
15 The account of the structure of the Council of Basle is largely from Hay and Smith, *Aeneas Sylvius*, pp. xv–xvi.
16 Anthony Black, *Council and Commune. The Conciliar Movement and the Council of Basle* (London, 1979), p. 56.
17 The work is available in an excellent modern translation with commentary and notes. Paul E. Sigmund (ed.), *Nicholas of Cusa, The Catholic Concordance* (Cambridge, 1991).
18 Ibid., pp. 42–3.
19 Tierney, *Religion, Law and the Growth of Constitutional Thought*, p. 69.
20 Ibid., p. 20.
21 Christianson, *Cesarini*, p. 123.
22 Ibid, p. 133.
23 Ibid., p. 139.
24 Francis Oakley, 'Almain and Major: Conciliar Theory on the Eve of the Reformation', *American Historical Review* 70 (1965), p. 674.
25 Nelson H. Minnich, *The Fifth Lateran Council (1512–17)* (Aldershot, 1993), p. 234.
26 See his article 'Conciliarism' in Hans J. Hillerbrand (ed.), *The Oxford Encyclopedia of the Reformation* (4 vols; New York, 1996), vol. 1, p. 396.

FURTHER READING

The most comprehensive treatment of the conciliar period remains volume one of Herbert Jedin, *A History of the Council of Trent*, trans. E. Graf (London, 1957). A very fine overview of the mediæval church which gives a good summary of the fifteenth-century councils is John A.F. Thomson, *The Western Church in the Middle Ages* (London, 1998). Also Francis Oakley, *The Western Church in the Later Middle Ages* (Ithaca, 1979). See also the stimulating essay, Scott Hendrix, 'In Quest of the Vera Ecclesia: The Crisis of Late Medieval Ecclesiology', *Viator* 7 (1976), pp. 347–78. On conciliar theory the standard work remains Brian Tierney, *Foundations of the Conciliar Theory: The Contribution of the Medieval Canonists from Gratian to the Great Schism* (repr. Cambridge, 1968) and *Church Law and Constitutional Thought in the Middle Ages* (London, 1979). James A. Brundage, *Medieval Canon Law* (London, 1995), is helpful in explaining the legal background. On the schism and conciliar thought: Walter Ullmann, *The Origins of the Great Schism: A Study in Fourteenth-Century Ecclesiastical History* (London, 1948); Francis Oakley, *The Political Thought of Pierre D'Ailly: The Voluntarist Tradition* (New Haven, CT, 1964); John Morrall, *Gerson and the Great Schism* (Manchester, 1960); Louis Pascoe, *Jean Gerson: Principles of Church Reform* (Leiden, 1973); C.M.D. Crowder, *Unity, Heresy and Reform, 1378–1460: The Conciliar Response to the Great Schism* (London, 1977). On the Council of Constance the most important new work is Phillip H. Stump, *The Reforms of the Council of Constance (1414–1418)* (Leiden, 1994). Other work of interest on the subject includes John MacGowan, *Pierre D'Ailly and the Council of Constance* (Washington, 1936); Thomas Morrissey, 'Cardinal Franciscus Zabarella (1360–1417) as a Canonist and the Crisis of His Age: Schism and the Council of Constance', *Zeitschrift für Kirchengeschichte* 96 (1985), 196–208, also his 'The Decree Haec Sancta and Cardinal Zabarella: His Role in Its Formulation and Interpretation', *Annuarium historiae conciliorum* 10 (1978), pp. 145–76, and 'The Emperor-Elect Sigismund, Cardinal Zabarella and the Council of Constance', *Catholic Historical Review* 69

(1983), pp. 353–70. On the revival of the papacy, see Peter Partner, *The Papal State under Martin V: The Administration and Government of the Temporal Power in the Early Fifteenth Century* (London, 1958). On the Council of Basle, the most important work remains that by Anthony Black, *Council and Commune. The Conciliar Movement and the Fifteenth-Century Heritage* (London, 1979) and *Monarchy and Community: Political Ideas in the Later Conciliar Controversy, 1430–1450* (London, 1970). The best treatment of the political defeat of the council is found in Joachim W. Stieber, *Pope Eugenius IV, the Council of Basel and the Secular and Ecclesiastical Authorities in the Empire. The Conflict over Supreme Authority and Power in the Church* (Leiden, 1978). Also highly recommended is Gerald Christianson, *Cesarini: The Conciliar Cardinal. The Basel Years, 1431–1438* (St Ottilien, 1979). A fascinating account of the council is found in *Aeneas Sylvius Piccolominus, De Gestis Concilii Basiliensis Commentariorum Libri II*, ed. and trans. Denys Hay and W.K. Smith (Oxford, 1967). On Nicholas of Cusa, see James E. Biechler, 'Nicholas of Cusa and the End of the Conciliar Movement: A Humanist Crisis of Identity', *Church History* 44 (1975), pp. 5–21; Morimichi Watanabe, *The Political Ideas of Nicholas of Cusa with Special Reference to His 'De Concordantia Catholica'* (Geneva, 1963). On post-Basle conciliarism, see J.H. Burns, 'Conciliarism, Papalism and Power, 1511–1518', in Diana Wood (ed.), *The Church and Sovereignty: Essays in Honour of Michael Wilks* (London, 1991), pp. 409–28; also his *Lordship, Kinship and Empire: The Idea of Monarchy 1400–1525* (Oxford, 1992). J.H. Burns and Mark Goldie (eds), *The Cambridge History of Political Thought, 1450–1700* (Cambridge, 1991) provides useful material on post-Basle conciliarism. The texts of Cajetan, Almain and Mair are found in J.H Burns and Thomas M. Izbicki (eds), *Conciliarism and Papalism* (Cambridge, 1997), and also Francis Oakley, *Natural Law, Conciliarism and Consent in the Late Middle Ages: Studies in Ecclesiastical and Intellectual History* (London, 1984). Nelson H. Minnich, *The Fifth Lateran Council (1512–17)* (Aldershot, 1993), contains a collection of his essays. R.J. Schoeck, 'The Fifth Lateran Council: Its Partial Success and Its Larger Failure', in G.F. Lytle (ed.), *Reform and Authority in the Medieval and Reformation Church* (Washington, 1981), pp. 99–126. On Julius II there is a fine biography which provides a lucid account of political events, Christina Shaw, *Julius II: The Warrior Pope* (Oxford, 1993).

CHAPTER FOUR

HUMANISM

————◆◆◆————

Richard Rex

Humanism, as used of the world of the Reformation, denotes a phenomenon which was part intellectual fashion and part educational curriculum. At one end it meant a world of high scholarship, where figures such as Desiderius Erasmus and Guillaume Budé rubbed shoulders with printers like Aldo Manuzio of Venice and Johannes Froben of Basle, or with patrons like Pope Leo X or King Francis I. At the other it meant the humdrum world of the English grammar school, the Jesuit college or the Protestant academy, where teenage boys pored over Latin and Greek grammars to acquire that acquaintance with the culture of classical antiquity which was in effect to constitute a Western education until the later nineteenth century.

Although the spectrum was wide and often colourful, spanning Catholic and Protestant Europe (and in some respects bridging the doctrinal gulf between them, providing them with a common language), humanism was an exclusive and elitist movement. It was accessible only to that small minority of men (as also to a very small minority of women) who received a classical education. Indeed, humanism was a classical education. The beneficiaries of this education were, it is true, a varied bunch. The *crème de la crème* might go on to become university professors or renowned authors: Scaliger, Lipsius, Casaubon, Kircher. More commonly, the abler and better-connected students would occupy public office in church or state: Thomas More, William Cecil, Pierto Bembo, Jakob Sturm. Others would find employment as lawyers, clergymen, secretaries, civic officials and schoolmasters. Others still, the offspring of civic patriarchs, landed gentry and minor nobility, or even of merchants and yeomen, would take their intellectual baggage back to a life of estate management or trading, in due course sending their own sons down the same path and turning up, like their fathers before them, to see a classical or neoclassical drama performed at the school and to nod knowingly as some Latin or Greek tag rang a distant bell in the memory. Yet beyond these social elites the vast bulk of the population of Europe was entirely innocent of the direct impact of humanism. It shaped to varying degrees the religious and cultural universes they inhabited, but most people lacked the equipment to detect this influence, however great it may have been.

THE HARDWARE AND SOFTWARE OF HUMANISM

Humanism was not a word which writers at the time used to describe this field of academic endeavour. They used terms like humanities, *litterae humaniores*, *bonae litterae* (*belles lettres*, 'good letters') or simply literature (and certainly not 'new learning'). Many of those terms are still current in one form or another and their modern usage still betrays their Renaissance ancestry. For the core activity at the heart of the complex we call humanism was the study of the language and literature of the classical world: in short, of Latin and Greek. The fact that, as in the Middle Ages, Latin remained an international language of diplomacy and scholarship gave it far more prominence than Greek. But one of the most obvious differences between mediæval and Renaissance education was precisely that the latter aspired to add a working knowledge of Greek to the standard curriculum, and to a large extent succeeded in doing so (however useless the attainment might later have been to most of its recipients).

If the core activity of Renaissance humanism was the study of Latin and Greek, its goal was the pursuit of eloquence. The educational programme of humanism was intended to produce orators, men whose skill in the art of rhetoric equipped them to debate and to persuade. Humanism was above all practical. The continuities of the Renaissance with the mediæval past have, rightly, been observed by scholars such as Paul Oskar Kristeller, who has traced the roots of the Renaissance concern with rhetoric back to the *ars dictaminis* of the mediæval Italian communes. Yet while the notaries and secretaries who were trained in the *ars dictaminis* certainly shared the aspirations of later humanists to the acquisition of skills in writing and speaking, and even their huge respect for Cicero as the prince of orators, they laboured under severe disadvantages, most notably in the limited source material available for them to work on, and in the absence of any understanding of the social and political context in which classical oratory had operated.

Humanists were convinced of the relevance of classical learning to contemporary life. Traditional mediæval respect for the intellectual achievement of classical culture was transformed in the Renaissance into a desire to retrieve that achievement – preserved in classical literature – through a recovery of the full knowledge of classical languages, and thus to recreate the glories of the ancient world. This sense of relevance could be very specific. Hans Baron emphasized – some say exaggerated – the importance of Florence's defence of its republican liberty against the ambitions of the princes of Milan – tyrants in Florentine eyes – as a motive for the recovery of the classical past. Nevertheless, the republicanism of Cicero's rhetoric and philosophy offered a valuable model for Florentine propaganda in a war which was fought as much by pamphlets, speeches and letters as by arms. But republicanism was not the only model the ancient world offered. Critics of Baron have pointed to the Milanese appropriation of the rhetoric of principate and imperialism available from a later period of Roman history. Most commentators would now agree that the similarities between civic humanism on the one hand and princely or courtly humanism on the other were more significant than the differences. Both sought to apply the lessons of antiquity to their own time and both insisted that education had to be justified by its utility in promoting the common good – the *res publica*.

One of the most influential aspects of Renaissance humanism was its new evaluation of the classical heritage. The classical heritage had not been in any way disprized during the Middle Ages. Despite the undercurrents of fideism and antiintellectualism which surfaced throughout that era (and beyond), mediæval culture had looked back in awe at the Roman past. And in a peculiar way this lived on in the claims of the papacy, the Holy Roman Empire and, indeed, the Byzantine Empire to embody *Romanitas* (the essence, as it were, of being Roman). What the Renaissance added was precisely a sense that the classical heritage was past and needed to be recovered. The very concept of the Middle Ages, which we still find helpful, was itself a product of this new realization that there was a historical gulf between ancient Rome and their own times. The concept of the Renaissance is a product of the same realization. Although the themes of rebirth and renewal (*renovatio*) were, as Walter Ullmann argued, deeply Christian and continually recurred in political and cultural contexts throughout the Middle Ages (not least in the Reformation), the sense of the rebirth and retrieval of ancient culture in the fifteenth and sixteenth centuries has its distinctive elements as well as its continuities with the mediæval past. The huge respect for the classical past evident throughout the Renaissance period was itself a mediæval legacy. Yet the way in which that past was approached and appropriated was entirely novel.

The privileging of the classical past and the awareness of the decline of classical culture in what were now seen as the Middle Ages played their part in the vociferous humanist critique of mediæval academic life and style which arose in the fifteenth century and intensified in the sixteenth. Humanists sneered at the 'barbarous' style of the scholastics. The polysyllabic jargon of scholastic logic and philosophy, the highly unclassical grammar of late mediæval Latin, and its almost total innocence of rhetorical sophistication left it beneath contempt. But the critique of scholasticism went deeper. Humanists saw scholasticism, with its emphasis on dialectic, as pointlessly speculative and wildly irrelevant. The myth that mediæval theologians argued about how many angels could dance on the head of a pin originated in the prolonged humanist assault on scholasticism. The stylistic critique, then, was also a methodological critique.

The Renaissance sense of the past can be best summed up in the words historicity and anachronism. The humanist sense of the past as past alerted scholars to the problem of anachronism and thus enabled them to detect spurious and forged documents. The most notorious instance of this, and one with special relevance to the Reformation, was Lorenzo Valla's decisive exposure of the Donation of Constantine, the mediæval document which purported to be a charter of endowment from the Emperor Constantine to Pope Silvester bestowing upon him jurisdiction over much of the western Mediterranean empire. It served in the high Middle Ages both as a charter for papal claims to temporal rule in Italy and as useful support for its more grandiose aspirations to a universal temporal jurisdiction. It had been questioned before, usually by experts in Roman law who spotted its defects as a putative legal instrument within the parameters of that legal system. But it took Valla, the maverick genius of fifteenth-century Italian humanism, to combine legal and philological criticisms in an overwhelming assault upon its authenticity. Valla's work had little immediate impact, but through the printing press and the Reformation, it was to play an important role in sixteenth-century debates on the papacy. Martin Luther published an edition of it in pursuance of his own campaign against the pope, while an English translation was published in 1534 with the approval of Henry VIII's chief minister, Thomas Cromwell, at exactly the moment when the English king was repudiating papal jurisdiction.

The reappropriation of classical culture depended primarily on access to its literary texts (although the use of what we would call archaeological evidence to flesh out the texts also originated in this era). These had been preserved through the Middle Ages thanks to the efforts of monastic scribes – to whom the scholars of the Renaissance were at best grudging in their thanks – in religious houses from the British Isles to the Balkans, from Scandinavia to Sicily. The discovery of these hidden treasures had begun in the fourteenth century, when Petrarch came across various works of Cicero, including his letters to Atticus and Brutus. Fresh discoveries followed thick and fast in the late fourteenth and even more the early fifteenth centuries as the pioneer humanists of Florence and Rome systematically hunted for new texts in the course of their travels on diplomatic or ecclesiastical business. Poggio Bracciolini found a complete version of Quintilian's *Institutio oratoria* at St Gallen in 1416, along with several of Cicero's speeches, while three other fundamental rhetorical works of Cicero turned up in 1421, when the *Orator*, the *De oratore* and the *Brutus* were found by Gerardo Landriani at Lodi. These particular finds were crucial to the development of Renaissance rhetorical culture. Like many intellectual trends, the search for manuscripts was technologically and socially conditioned. The introduction of paper in the later Middle Ages meant that writing materials were more widely available: though still expensive, paper was considerably cheaper than parchment. The copying of texts therefore proliferated in the fourteenth and fifteenth centuries. Many of the major manuscript discoveries resulted, as Jacob Burckhardt observed, from the enthusiasm of a new kind of book collector, of men like Niccolò Niccoli, Cardinal Bessarion or Pope Nicholas V, whose personal collections came to form the basis of some of Italy's great libraries (such as the Biblioteca Marciana at Venice and the Biblioteca Vaticana at Rome). The invention of printing itself was a response to the new demand for copies fostered by the increased availability of paper.

Although humanist scholarship originated in Italy and printing originated in southern Germany, it was not long before the intellectual technique consummated a fruitful marriage with the new technology. It was print, obviously, that brought about the diffusion of the classical texts on which the propagation of humanist skills had to depend. Print also generated the demand for accurate and reliable texts, as the replication of a particular recension made readers more aware of the variants evident in their own manuscripts and thus of the tendency to textual corruption and variation inherent in manuscript culture. This in turn fostered the development of the techniques of textual criticism which were among the enduring achievements of the Renaissance. The landmarks of humanism were in the early phases the discoveries of manuscripts; but from the late fifteenth century the landmarks were editions of books: the Aldine Greek classics, Erasmus's *Adages*, the *Encomium moriae*, the *Novum Instrumentum*, Agricola's *De inventione dialectica*, *Utopia*, Budé's *De asse*, the *Epistolae obscurorum virorum* and the Complutensian

Polyglot. The centres of humanist scholarship in this, perhaps its Golden Age, were not so much the universities as the printing shops of Venice, Antwerp, Lyon, Paris, Basle, Cologne, Strasbourg and elsewhere. This meant, as Lisa Jardine has shown, that the great humanist centres were inevitably the great commercial centres, the only places which could accumulate and mobilize the huge capital needed to finance the mass production of books. Books required expensive raw materials (paper), sophisticated tools (moveable type) and highly skilled labour (scribes, editors, compositors and readers). Only with the diffusion of this bulk of scholarship did the universities outside such commercial centres, such as Louvain, Heidelberg and Padua, recover their intellectual leadership later in the sixteenth century. Erasmus spent most of his career in printing shops. But Scaliger spent most of his in universities.

Just as printing soon came to Italy, it did not take long for humanism to leave its cradle in the peninsula. There were many channels of transmission. Italians travelling abroad on church business were one. Poggio Braccionlini reached England in the reign of Henry VI and sowed the seeds of humanist interests in the mind of Duke Humphrey of Gloucester, while Pier Paolo Vergerio spent over a quarter of a century at the Hungarian court, inspiring King Matthias Corvinus to found his renowned library. Aeneas Sylvius Piccolomini, having risen in the service of the antipope Felix V, was recruited to the service of Emperor Frederick III in Vienna in 1442 and brought humanism to prominence at the imperial court. Much later, it was still possible for papal agents like Pietro Carmeliano and Polydore Vergil to go native and put their humanist attainments at the disposal of the Tudor kings. Political connections could be vital. Thanks to the dynastic union between the kingdoms of Naples and Aragon, humanists employed at the court of Naples (where Valla did much of his work) under Alfonso V made their way to Barcelona when Alfonso's successor took the court back to Spain. The Italian wars undertaken by the kings of France from 1494 added great impetus to the advance of humanism in France, as Italian humanists were lured by the patronage of the Valois court. Foreign students who came to study law or perhaps medicine in the Italian universities often took humanist texts and ideas back home with them, as did Antonio de Nebrija, the leading humanist of fifteenth-century Spain. Indeed, foreign students were soon coming to Italy expressly to drink at the font of the renewed humanities. The German scholars Johann Regiomontanus and Peter Luder were putting their studies in Italy to good use at the Universities of Vienna and Heidelberg in the 1450s. Englishmen such as William Grocyn and John Colet and Frenchmen such as Robert Gaguin and Jacques Lefèvre d'Etaples were making the pilgrimage south in the late fifteenth century, and even in the 1520s Reginald Pole and Richard Morison were completing their studies in Padua. Finally, Italian scholars sensitive to the rising demand for the humanities north of the Alps also helped spread the movement. Lorenzo Guglielmo Traversagni of Savona was teaching classical rhetoric at the Universities of Vienna, Paris, Oxford and Cambridge in the latter half of the fifteenth century, while better-known humanists such as Filippo Beroaldo were active in France, and Italian teachers introduced 'good letters' to Louvain in 1478. By 1500 humanism was well established throughout most of western Europe. Here and there in the universities it was prey to the hostile vested interests of scholasticism and occasionally of sheer obscurantism, but its triumph in the grammar-school curriculum was rapid and that gave it an almost unshakeable position among Europe's elites. The triumph of humanism is best summed up in the fact that it was possible for Erasmus to become an accomplished humanist by 1500 on the strength of an education acquired exclusively in the Netherlands and at Paris.

Humanism was not merely widely established. It was in itself an international movement, and its internationalism combined with its delight in discourse to produce one of its most distinctive features – the cultivation of communication by letter. Indeed, the humanist movement might even be viewed as a network held together by amicable correspondence. The learned communities of the Middle Ages were for the most part local, confined to a monastery or a university, secluded to a degree from the world. There was intercommunication, of course, particularly between universities, but it was often based more on the movement of persons than of information and it was certainly less widespread than it later became. It was Cicero's letters to his friends (the *familiares*) which established the model of the humanist as correspondent, and the example of St Jerome was almost as important. The Renaissance was a great age for textbooks and handbooks, so it is no surprise that manuals of letter-writing became a major new genre at this time. Erasmus, the exemplar *par excellence* of the epistolary phenomenon, himself composed an influential *De arte conscribendi epistolas* and, like many other humanists, was acutely aware of the possibility and desirability of preserving his own correspondence for posterity. He took great care over the collection and selection of his letters for publication. Luther's ideas spread so rapidly after 1517 not simply because of print but also because of the epistolary network which linked little learned coteries in towns, monasteries and universities with like-minded groups throughout Germany and Europe, a network which was the creation of the humanists. Of course, this network itself rested on a technological basis. It was the underlying network of messengers and agents established by the Italian banking houses in the fourteenth century to facilitate international trade which often carried these vital letters. These networks of correspondence were in due course to be supplanted, towards the end of the seventeenth century, by the learned journal as the primary vehicle for the transmission of new ideas. But if the learned journal was as representative of the Scientific Revolution and the Enlightenment as the elegant letter was of Renaissance humanism, it should not be forgotten that the journal itself, often the organ of a corresponding society, originated as a more efficient method of multiplying the audience for communications which long continued to be composed in epistolary form. And the letter itself remained something poised between means of communication and art form for as long as humanism remained the core of the European curriculum, until the later nineteenth century.

CHRISTIAN HUMANISM

It was inevitable that Renaissance humanism would have a significant impact on Christianity, particularly upon Christian theology. But while that impact used often to be seen by historians as hostile or confrontational, the secular rebelling against the sacred, the pagan reviving against the Christian, it has become increasingly clear from two or three generations of scholarship that many Christian intellectuals were eager to embrace humanist techniques and ideals. This was evident first of all in the characteristically Renaissance demand for texts, which – together with the revival of knowledge of Greek – stimulated new efforts in translation as well as in the search for Latin classics and patristics. The meagre Greek learning of the Latin Middle Ages was rapidly expanded in the fifteenth century, even for those who never themselves acquired familiarity with the language. The works of Aristotle, Euclid and Ptolemy, and one or two of Plato's dialogues, constituted almost the entire mediæval Latin knowledge of ancient Greece: a limited selection with a strongly technical bias. Knowledge of the Greek fathers of the church was even more limited in the mediæval Western church than knowledge of the Greek classics. A very early version of Eusebius was available, along with a small selection from the homilies of John Chrysostom. But the best-known work ascribed to Chrysostom was the *Opus imperfectum in Matthaeum*, which was actually a Latin work of the fifth century. It was the *Catena aurea* of Thomas Aquinas, a compilation of patristic texts arranged according to the order of the gospels, included citations from Chrysostom, Theophylact and Cyril, which gave the broadest introduction to the Greek fathers, but its renderings were often loose. Western ignorance of Greek combined with a certain suspicion towards the theological tradition of the East – which was by this time divided from the West by centuries of schism – to limit interest in the Greek fathers. One of the crucial contributions of humanism to Western theology was not merely to revive the study of Greek and thus make the Greek fathers accessible, but the gift of (relative) intellectual openness which enabled Western theologians to overcome their historical prejudice and actually read them. There is an obvious parallel here with the way in which humanism fostered an openness towards the pagan heritage of classical antiquity, notwithstanding the strong vein of fideistic hostility towards secular learning which ran through mediæval culture. In any case, the fifteenth century saw huge strides in the study of the Greek fathers, with manuscripts brought back to Italy in bundles from the declining Byzantine Empire, most notably in the baggage of Cardinal Bessarion and other delegates to the Council of Florence which, in the 1430s, achieved a short-lived reunion of the Western and Eastern churches. Still more importantly, there was a concerted effort to make these texts available to a wider audience through translation. The Carmelite friar Ambrogio Traversari, who translated almost all of Chrysostom, as well as Basil, Pseudo-Dionysius and Gregory Nazianzen, was the most productive of a series of translators who included Matteo Palmieri, Georgios Trapezuntios and Angelo Poliziano.

It should be noted that these translators were all in the humanist mainstream. Many of them were at least as deeply interested in secular as in Christian humanism. Traversari was a friend of Niccoli and Bruni, and was a central figure in the circles of Florentine humanism. Poliziano is better known as a commentator on the classical poets, Greek as well as Latin. Although there can be useful and specific meanings to the term Christian humanism, it cannot be emphasized too strongly that all humanists were Christians and had Christian interests. Niccoli himself had fifty Greek patristic manuscripts in his library – and discovered the very early Christian text, the *Shepherd* of Hermas – while Poggio collected the epistles of the Latin father Jerome in the 1430s. Even a mind as radical as Lorenzo Valla's remained thoroughly Christian. Valla is indeed a perfect example of the combination of sacred and secular interests typical of so many humanists. His notes on Livy and his enormously influential *Elegantiae latinae linguae* were the fruits of the same kind of labour as his notes on the New Testament and his debunking of the Donation of Constantine. However, Renaissance humanism unarguably stimulated some cultural developments of particular significance for Christian theologians. It not only brought knowledge of the Greek and the more obscure Latin fathers, but aroused widespread interest in the study of the canonical scriptures in their original tongues – Greek and Hebrew. Although it is only fair to note that Hebrew had been rather better served than Greek in mediæval western Europe (because of the presence of Jewish communities and occasional conversions from Judaism), it is also important to realize that is only since the Renaissance that Christian Europe has possessed a continuous tradition of Hebrew scholarship.

It was in fifteenth-century Italy that the Renaissance interest in Hebrew first surfaced, with Giannozzo Manetti who, adding Hebrew and Greek to his Latin, produced new translations of the New Testament and the Psalms. Only in the early sixteenth century, however, on the very eve of the Reformation, did Hebraic scholarship establish itself firmly, thanks largely to the German humanist Johann Reuchlin. Just as traditional suspicion of the Eastern Church had impeded the reception of Greek, so traditional anti-Semitism proved an even greater threat to the study of Hebrew. But humanists were mostly open at least in principle to the scholarly opportunities which Hebrew afforded. Indeed, the relative intellectual openness of humanism is perhaps its most remarkable characteristic in the early modern era. By the 1520s, the study of Hebrew as well as Greek was enshrined in educational foundations as far apart as Corpus Christi College, Oxford, St John's College, Cambridge, Busleiden's *Collegium Trilingue* at Louvain, and the new university at Alcalá de Henares. Humanists came out strongly in favour of the subject in the bitter controversy which broke out around this time in Germany (but attracted interest throughout Western Europe) over the study of Hebrew and Reuchlin's advocacy of it. As influential humanists lined up in support of Reuchlin, advocacy of the *tres linguae* (three languages, i.e. Latin, Hebrew and Greek) became a badge of intellectual respectability; opposition was stigmatized (not always unjustly) as obscurantism. The lines of battle were symbolically drawn by two published collections of letters, one fictitious and one entirely genuine. The *Epistolae obscurorum virorum* (an early masterpiece of printed satire) purported to be the infuriated and barbarously inarticulate correspondence of Reuchlin's opponents, while the *Epistolae illustrium virorum* was a collection of letters written to or in support of Reuchlin by leading humanist scholars from all over Europe.

The tools of philological criticism which a humanist education placed in the hands of its specialists had many uses in a specifically Christian context. Miracle stories, lives of saints and accounts of relics were easy prey, and not simply to the avowed enemies of the Roman Catholic church. The French humanist Jacques Lefèvre d'Etaples (also known as Faber) neatly disentangled the confusion between Mary Magdalene and Mary the sister of Martha and Lazarus, a confusion which stretched back over a millennium. His relationship with the Catholic church was ambivalent: he was condemned by the Sorbonne and died in exile at Strasbourg, but despite his sympathies with evangelical theology, he never openly broke with the traditional faith. Protestant reformers were sometimes delighted to make similarly acidic assaults upon traditional pieties, but increasingly tended to repudiate the cult of the saints by simply attacking its theology, disdainful of the details of particular lives. It was actually within the Catholic church that this legacy of humanism was to bear its greatest fruit in the herculean labours of the *Bollandistes*, the Jesuit scholars who cleansed the Augean stables of hagiography, purging accretions of myth and legend, and thereby significantly advancing the development of the historical sciences. But the critical mind was far from triumphant in the Catholic world. An episcopal attestation of the immemorial veneration of a relic was still considered an adequate guarantee of its sacred character. Such attestations would in our terms be regarded more as the authorization of a cult than as the authentication of a historical claim: but the distinction between these concepts was at best blurred. A similar blurring affected the official attitude of the church to the Vulgate Bible after humanist criticism began to call many of its readings into question.

Rhetoric, queen among the arts of Renaissance humanism, was also of especial importance for Christian scholars, most immediately in the art of preaching. Here, too, the humanist movement manifests continuities as well as contrasts with respect to the mediæval past. Preaching was an almost obsessive concern of the Western church from the thirteenth century onwards and was cultivated intensively by the orders of mendicant friars, most notably the Dominicans (whose official title was the Order of Preachers) and the Franciscans. The preaching manual (or *ars praedicandi*) is one of the commonest genres of later mediæval writing. And even before the arrival of print technology, thousands upon thousands of sermons survive, in manuscript, from the later mediæval church. The church did not need humanists to tell it of the importance of preaching. But, given the enormous interest in preaching, it is hardly surprising that the techniques of classical rhetoric, recovered by the humanists, were soon applied in this field. Indeed, many of the earliest humanists were clergymen who hoped to find in their studies the key to more effective communication of the gospel. Lorenzo Guglielmo Traversagni of Savona, a Franciscan who brought humanism with him to Paris and Cambridge in the 1470s and 1480s, saw in the pulpit the proper stage for the rhetorical skills he taught. John O'Malley and the late John D'Amico have shown us how the preachers of Renaissance Rome applied the classical concept of epideictic rhetoric (the rhetoric of praise and blame) in preaching contexts as various as the festival of a saint or the convening of a church council. Their style, too, became more classical and ornate – more systematically Ciceronian. Indeed, if one had to identify anywhere in early modern Europe that theology of glory to which Luther opposed his theology of the cross, it would surely be in the preaching of Renaissance Rome: triumphalist, papalist, complacent, the rhetoric of a calm bureaucracy oblivious of the storm about to break.

The impossibility of drawing a clear-cut distinction between humanism and Christian humanism is most effectively demonstrated by a consideration of the man who was at once the greatest humanist and the greatest Christian humanist of the early modern age: Desiderius Erasmus of Rotterdam. The difficulty in deciding whether he belongs to church history or cultural history testifies not only to the central importance of religious affairs in the culture of the sixteenth century, but also to his monumental achievements in both sacred and secular learning. Erasmus's books on Latin style (the *De copia* and *Ciceronianus*), letter-writing and civil behaviour, and his collections of adages and colloquies, not to mention his editions of classical authors such as Seneca, defined the humanism of his century. At the same time, the stream of publications which made up his scriptural programme, the *Novum Instrumentum* (see below), his annotations on the New Testament, his paraphrases of the Gospels and Epistles, together with a series of critical editions of the major patristic authors (Cyprian, Jerome, Lactantius, Ambrose, Athanasius, Chrysostom, Irenaeus, Augustine and, finally, his beloved Origen), would have guaranteed his place in history on their own. Erasmus himself was wont to use the term *philosophia Christi* to describe his holistic sense of the cooperation of human learning with divine revelation, of grace and nature, in the worship of God and service of humanity. Indeed, he would have found our anachronistic division of the sacred and the secular unacceptable. The *Adages* and *Colloquies* were read not only for their style but for their content, which included his critique of mechanistic and superstitious religious practice, his heartfelt pacifism, his moralism, his aspirations for social justice, his aversion from public disorder and his distaste for dogmatism and persecution.

THE ROLE OF HUMANISM IN THE REFORMATION

Erasmus's *Novum Instrumentum* – his edition of the Greek New Testament with a fresh Latin translation on facing pages – was indeed a landmark of European history. The publication of Jacques Lefèvre's *Quincuplex Psalter* in 1509 and his commentary on the epistles of Paul in 1513 had already whetted the appetite of theologians for scholarship of this kind. The *Quincuplex Psalter* presented, in five parallel columns, five Latin renderings of the Psalms: the Vetus Latina (that is, the old translation that preceded Jerome's) and Jerome's own version (both these versions in effect enjoyed Vulgate status, in that Jerome's version had never succeeded in driving the other out of circulation); the so-called Gallican Psalter, and mediæval attempts at literal renderings of the Septuagint and Hebrew Psalms. His Paul, although it gave merely the Vulgate Latin text, made regular and useful reference to the Greek text in the ample commentary which surrounded the text on the page. Lefèvre's scriptural works were widely read and used. Many copies were to be found in the libraries of scholars at Cambridge from the 1530s onwards and at Wittenberg Martin Luther had used Lefèvre's commentaries in delivering his own early lectures on the Psalms and Paul's epistles (1512–18). The phrase *sola fides* (faith alone), which became so central to Luther's understanding of St Paul's theology of justification, is first found in such a context in Lefèvre's notes on the Epistle to the Romans.

The *Novum Instrumentum*, however, made a still more dramatic impact than the earlier works of Lefèvre – not least because of Erasmus's international reputation and circle of acquaintance, which ensured a prompt and ready sale throughout academic Europe. (Lefèvre had never been as skilled as Erasmus at what today is called networking.) The significance of the *Novum Instrumentum* lay partly in simply making the Greek New Testament available for the first time to the theological community of the Latin West. But it lay more in the radical implications of the enterprise. Erasmus's Latin translation differed at times dramatically from the Vulgate, although the most famous departure – his substitution of *In principio erat sermo ...* ('In the beginning was the discourse ... ') for *In principio erat verbum ...* ('In the beginning was the word ... ') at the start of John's Gospel – was introduced only in the 1519 edition. This was in itself a perfectly respectable attempt to give a more exact sense of the Greek *logos*. Yet it was soon taken up as a symbolic bone of contention by those who regarded Erasmus's edition as an irreverent assault upon traditional values; which to some extent it was. To alter, even for a scholarly audience, the time-honoured verbal formulations of the Catholic church – especially with respect to a text which, as the 'last gospel', was read at the end of almost every mass – was to call into question the infallible tradition which that church claimed not simply to deliver but to embody. The widely held view of biblical inerrancy – according to which if even one iota of scripture could be shown to be false, the authority of the entire corpus would be undermined – was in effect being extended to tradition. The notion that the church had been setting a 'false' version of the scriptures before the people for centuries was one which many scholars were simply not prepared to entertain. Falsehood in such a fundamental matter, they argued, undermined the credibility of the entire institution. Of course, there had always been problems – and known problems – with the textual transmission of the Vulgate. Scholars were aware that scribal errors could creep into particular copies. Yet Erasmus's work went beyond the mere correction of the transmission of the text to the correction of the text itself, and for many this was a step too far.

The result was that the *Novum Instrumentum* brought storms of controversy down upon Erasmus's head. His scholarship and his motives were impugned in sermons and pamphlets as far as the book itself spread, in France, Spain, the Netherlands, Germany and England. Nevertheless, Erasmus had taken the elementary precaution of dedicating his epoch-making work to Pope Leo X and this, together with his excellent relations with Christian princes and respectable bishops across Europe, ensured that the charges of heresy soon hurtling towards him could do no real damage. Erasmus was perhaps fortunate, though, to have published the fruit of his labours before, rather than after, Luther had raised the theological temperature of Europe to an uncomfortable level. Fortunate, that is, unless one sees the *Novum Instrumentum* as a necessary cause of Luther's theological breakthrough. In fact Luther's reflections upon Paul were based on the Vulgate text and depended more on Lefèvre than on Erasmus at this stage. The *Novum Instrumentum* was not necessary for the development of Luther's doctrine, nor was there much consideration of the original Greek in the early lectures during which his Reformation theology evolved. However, the controversies surrounding Erasmus may have contributed to a livening of interest in theological debate which brought Luther's ideas before a wider audience than they might otherwise have reached.

Simplistic views of humanism as a cause of the Reformation and of humanists as almost guaranteed recruits for it are no longer so common as they once were, although they are occasionally still to be encountered. For a start, scholars have observed a distinct generation gap in humanist responses to the Reformation. The humanists of an older generation – Erasmus himself, Thomas More, Thomas Lupset, Guillaume Budé, Johann Reuchlin, Jodocus Clichtove, Johann Cochlaeus – for the most part stood aloof from or actively opposed the new doctrines (though exceptions can be found in figures such as Lefèvre and Konrad Pellican). It was the younger generation – men such as Melanchthon, Zwingli, Bullinger, Capito, Oecolampadius, Richard Morison, John Cheke and John Calvin – which was more open to novelty. This is hardly surprising, as age tends to immunize against innovation. Yet scholars have also noted that there were many important and unimportant humanists among the younger generation too who remained loyal to the old ways: men like Thomas Robertson, the Oxford grammarian; George Witzel, one of the earliest converts from Lutheranism back to Catholicism, and John Seton, the Cambridge dialectician. Reforming sympathies were hardly any more apparent among the humanists of Spain and Portugal than among their populations in general, and Italian humanists often sought to combine evangelical theology with ecclesiastical loyalty or at least conformity. If for no other reason than their readier access to the world of new ideas, humanists doubtless were more likely than others to espouse the doctrines of the Reformation. Yet humanism alone was a hardly a sufficient cause of conversion in individual cases, any more than it was a sufficient cause of the Reformation in general.

This is not to deny, though, that humanist scholarship played an important part in the Reformation. The study of rhetoric affected reading as well as writing. It fostered an approach to texts which was radically different from that typical of the Middle Ages. Essentially, it encouraged consideration of the text as an organized whole rather than as an assemblage of information. Of course, this contrast – like so many of those drawn between the Middle Ages and the Renaissance – is unduly schematic. There were scholastics who could view a text as a whole (one thinks of Thomas Aquinas on Romans) just as there were humanists for whom texts were in practice little more than arsenals of adages, figures of speech and off-the-peg opinions. Yet the rough and ready contrast remains useful. No scholastic commentary on Romans reads like Philip Melanchthon's exposition of 1519, which inevitably reflects the massive influence of his theological mentor, Martin Luther, in presenting Paul's epistle as an organized account of justification by faith alone. Equally remarkable, though, is the way Melanchthon combines evangelical theology with humanist rhetorical analysis, presenting the epistle as one organized on the principles of a classical oration. The real assimilation of humanist concepts and techniques by a scholar of his capacity was bound to produce this kind of holistic and contextual analysis, just as a training in scholastic dialectic tended to foster an approach to texts as compilations of propositions for insertion at appropriate points in lengthy chains of syllogistic reasoning. The basic textbook of mediæval Catholic theology, after all, was Peter Lombard's four Books of Sentences – a handbook of extracts from the scriptures and the fathers arranged in topical order for easy reference and study. Sentences, one might say, rather than books, were the raw material of mediæval theology. Here, too, the contrast can be exaggerated. Melanchthon himself compiled a book which, from a certain angle, looks very like the Lombard's. His *Loci communes* (or 'Commonplaces'), initially published in 1521, was also a collection of extracts, arranged this time under headings which reflected his evangelical concerns. But, as the title indicates, the collection was designed more for the preacher than the scholar. The commonplace book was the recommended research tool of the humanist. Humanists were meant to compile such books for themselves, on the basis of their own reading. Ready-made examples by masters of the art, such as Melanchthon's *Loci communes* or Erasmus's *Adages*, were more aids to their labours than substitutes for them.

Even Melanchthon's rhetorical and dialectical textbooks are stuffed with examples dripping with highly evangelical theological significance. They must have done much to spread the new doctrines among the rising generations. But the potential which humanism had to influence theological debate is best illustrated by a comparison between the fourteenth-century scholastic John Wyclif and the sixteenth-century humanist Huldrych Zwingli in their attempts to provide an alternative account of the eucharist in place of the Catholic doctrine of transubstantiation. They had much in common. Both were schooled in the Aristotelian metaphysics of substance and accident, within whose terms the doctrine of transubstantiation was formulated. And both felt that the Thomist doctrine of the conversion of the substance (inner reality) of bread into the substance of Christ's body without any accompanying conversion of the accidents (the observable phenomena) of the bread was, in Aristotelian terms, nonsense. What both needed to do, however, to break the hold of the doctrine was to formulate an adequate alternative interpretation of Christ's apparently clear words: 'This is my body'. Wyclif sought to do this by excogitating a new category of being or presence – habitudinal presence – which was worked out with a subtlety that only he seems ever to have mastered. It is hardly surprising that few even among the Lollards (his English followers) seem to have understood his tortuous dialectic.

The humanist substitution of rhetoric for dialectic at the core of the curriculum enabled sixteenth-century Reformers to cut the Gordian knot. The literal sense of scripture was as important to scholastic theologians as to their later Protestant counterparts. But the advent of Renaissance rhetoric enabled the literal sense to take more effective account of figurative speech – a concept with which Wyclif had been profoundly uncomfortable. Once rhetoric could be invoked to account for figures of speech ('Turn the other cheek', 'if thy hand offend thee, cut it off'), it could be applied equally easily to statements like 'This is my body'. Zwingli invoked the rhetorical figure of *catachresis* (abuse) to explain that 'is' was being 'abused' to mean 'signifies'. Another Protestant humanist, Oecolampadius, preferred to invoke the figure of metonymy (the substitution of cause for effect, effect for cause or sign for signified) to explain that 'my body' in this case meant 'sign of my body'. Wyclif had aspired to a biblicism akin to that of the later Protestant reformers. But without the sophisticated analytical tools provided by Renaissance rhetoric, his biblicism was too easily tied up in dialectical knots by the skilled debaters of the late mediæval church.

But perhaps the most useful contribution which humanism made to the

1526.

VIVENTIS·POTVIT·DVRERIVS·ORA·PHILIPPI
MENTEM·NON·POTVIT·PINGERE·DOCTA
MANVS

Figure 4.1 Albrecht Dürer, *Philip Melanchthon*, 1526. The development of Melanchthon's theology reflected the continuing influence of his humanist training. (Wittenberg, Lutherhalle)

Reformation was extrinsic, in the credibility which it could lend to the new ideas. Rhetorical concepts and philological arguments enabled Protestant theologians not only to produce alternative biblical theologies, but to present their findings with something of the sense of unarguable finality associated in the twentieth century with the appeal to science. Just as in the thirteenth century transubstantiation had appealed to the fashionable sciences of its day, namely dialectic and Aristotelian physics, so sixteenth-century figurative interpretations of the eucharistic words were able to deck themselves in the fashionable feathers of rhetoric, which was, for its practitioners, the science of words and language. The intellectual status of humanism helped bolster the authority of the new eucharistic doctrines of the Reformation.

CHRISTIAN PROBLEMS WITH RENAISSANCE HUMANISM

It was not only the fideistic tendencies in Christianity which experienced problems with Renaissance humanism. The retrieval of antique culture could take extreme forms and begin to look suspiciously like the resuscitation of paganism. The allegorical interpretation of pagan myth by the Florentine neoplatonists might have been harmless, even Christian, enough in their own eyes, but not in the eyes of an old-fashioned revivalist like Savonarola. Savonarola was hardly anti-intellectual: he was a talented scholastic. But the bonfires of vanities showed how far he was from sympathizing with the culture of humanism. And you did not have to be Savonarola to feel uncomfortable with the habit of some Italian preachers who, when composing in Latin, avoided the Christian theological vocabulary of incarnation, Trinity and penance because such words were not to be met with in the Ciceronian canon. Erasmus famously ridiculed such anachronistic pedantry in his dialogue *Ciceronianus* and pretty much laughed it out of vogue. And, in fact, most humanists remained Christians, though not necessarily devout ones. But the interest of humanists in an essentially pagan culture left them vulnerable to attack from Christian backwoodsmen.

The Catholic church had some obvious problems with humanism, even before the Reformation. The incipient rationalism of humanism could sit uncomfortably with the mystical and miraculous in the Catholic tradition. Witness the curl in John Colet's lip on being invited to kiss the dirty handkerchief of St Thomas at Canterbury, or even the ironic humour of Thomas More's defence of relics and images in his *Dialogue concerning Heresies*. The scholastics had been well aware that not everything taught by or in the name of the church enjoyed the same authority, but they did not always feel it appropriate to bring this truth before a general audience. Christian humanists, in their zeal to reform and raise standards, happily transgressed traditional taboos by poking fun at the more obvious or ludicrous extravagances of the cult of the saints. Some of those monks and friars who saw in this nothing more than impertinence and impiety might have felt themselves vindicated by the ease with which Protestant reformers took up the Christian humanist rhetoric of superstition and deployed it against the cult of the saints as a whole. The further temerity of the humanists in making their criticisms not in the traditional way – before an audience of clergy at a synod or council, in Latin – but in print, before an increasingly sophisticated and discerning lay audience, and often in the vernacular, represented another assault on taboo which some clerics were quick to resent. The Erasmian criticism of ecclesiastical abuse and excess soon came to be perceived in certain quarters as heresy. The literary subtleties and rhetorical strategies of such texts as the *Praise of Folly* and the *Colloquies* were interpreted as crude polemics against Catholic tradition.

The humanist focus upon the text also caused problems for the sixteenth-century Catholic church. Although no less an authority than Pope Leo X was to accept the dedication of Erasmus's *Novum Instrumentum* in 1516 and Catholic theologians such as Bishop John Fisher and Cardinal Cajetan were to endorse and avail themselves of his critical endeavours, there were others who found them harder to swallow. Humanism's focus upon the text could sit quite easily with the Protestant notion of *sola scriptura*, but a little less easily with the Catholic concept of tradition. And the pedagogical thrust of humanism tended towards a vernacular piety and a vernacular scripture-reading culture that smacked to the Catholic authorities too much of the Protestant Reformation. Hence the increasing suspicion with which the Catholic church came to view the textual criticism and translation of the scriptures in the sixteenth century. The Council of Trent did not, as is often suggested, stamp out either scriptural criticism or scripture-reading in the Catholic church. But its prescription of the Vulgate as the authentic text of scripture, normative for the Latin Church, and its introduction of wholesale theological censorship, showed that the conservative forces at Trent carried significantly more weight than their opponents. Significant scholarly work on the Bible was still possible in the Counter-Reformation church, not least in the preparation of new editions of the Vulgate and the Septuagint at Rome in the later sixteenth century. But the ill-specified assertion of the Vulgate's authenticity gave many hostages to fortune in the endless theological controversies during which Catholic polemicists found themselves struggling to justify particular Latin readings. Although those who wished to prohibit the vernacular Bible were unable to carry the day at Trent, the Counter-Reformation hierarchy displayed a marked reluctance to encourage lay Bible-reading. In those countries, mostly in northern Europe, where the vernacular Bible nevertheless did become accessible to the Catholic laity, this was not so much a pastoral initiative as a response to the aspirations of an educated laity and the perceived need to provide Catholic Bibles to stop the faithful reading Protestant ones.

Protestant problems with humanism have been every bit as evident as those of the Catholic church, although – as with the Catholic church – there has been no shortage of apologists to argue that these apparent problems were illusory. The most fundamental problem was theological in character. Mainstream Protestant theology denied the freedom of the human will, while humanists for the most part affirmed or assumed it. Of course, one can find humanists who denied free will, just as one can find humanists who preferred the contemplative to the active life. Lorenzo Valla made a forceful case for determinism decades before Luther. But the principle of free will was inscribed in the humanist educational programme. The moral agenda of humanism was universalist in principle, although in practice it was available only to the schooled elite. The thrust of reform by education was always potentially in conflict with the thrust of reform by faith alone. This pedagogical contradiction of Protestant humanism has been amply explored by Gerald Strauss, whose study of Lutheran catechesis has brought out the inherent irony of the inculcation by rote of a religious system founded on grace.

The tension between humanism and evangelical theology is perhaps most evident in the intellectual trajectory described by the greatest of the Protestant humanists, Philip Melanchthon. In the first flush of youthful enthusiasm for the teachings of his father-figure, Melanchthon briskly despatched free will and affirmed an unrelenting determinism in a few short paragraphs of his original *Loci communes* (1521), inviting readers to note how much more competently he had dealt with the matter than had predecessors like St Bernard. This airy dismissal of free will was accompanied by a contempt for Aristotelian ethics, which Luther had already repudiated before 1520 as in effect the codification of Pelagianism. Aristotle's assertion that you become just by doing just works was, after all, the exact opposite of Luther's claim that the person had to be made just by faith before there was even a possibility of performing just works.

Yet even before 1530 Melanchthon was moderating his line. The crisis of the Peasants' War in Germany had alerted all parties to the antinomian potential of the doctrine of justification by faith alone, and the survival of the Reformation depended crucially on negotiating this crisis. Aristotelian ethics and the apparatus of classical moral philosophy might be of no avail for salvation, but suddenly their social utility became all too apparent. As Sachiko Kusukawa has shown, Melanchthon reconstructed the humanities in the later 1520s in order to find room in the new theological system for traditional ethics. Ethical endeavour and education might not produce that true justice in the soul which was needed for salvation, but they could produce civil or political justice, that outward obedience and respect for law which, though it might simply mask hypocrisy and concupiscence, at least guaranteed the social order necessary for the fruitful preaching of the gospel. The new space for ethics was itself secured by admitting the freedom of the will in earthly or civil – as opposed to heavenly and spiritual – things. Arguably there was some inconsistency in seeing the human will as free in one domain while disabled in another. Yet the two positions could at least be justified with an appeal to experience in the first case and to scripture in the second.

As he grew older, Melanchthon's position on free will softened still further until, in the final version of his *Loci communes* (1559), he avoided all danger of inconsistency by postulating, in a fashion suggestively close to that of the Council of Trent, that there had to be some element of free human response (albeit under grace) to God's promise of salvation, if the difference in outcome between the elect and the reprobate was to be accounted for by anything other than an arbitrary whim of a tyrant God. Few Protestant theologians followed him this far, not least because even the minimal affirmation of free will used to vindicate God's justice jeopardizes that certainty of grace which rests on the elimination of the unreliable human contribution by the doctrine of justification by faith alone. Nevertheless, the strategies adopted for reconciling the humanities with divinity can mostly be located somewhere on the course Melanchthon plotted.

Humanism was in fact such a powerful social force that the Reformation had to make terms with it. The early fervour of Reformation in Wittenberg, during Luther's absence in hiding at the Wartburg, indicated one possible future: a fideistic and fundamentalist scripturalism which would cast aside all human sciences as trivial and a distraction from the business of salvation. It would have been simple to transform Luther's radical expulsion of Aristotle from the domain of theology into a radical expulsion of the humanities in general from the Christian polity. Such was the tendency of the Zwickau prophets, with their reliance upon the direct inspiration of God for the understanding of scripture. Even as quintessentially donnish a figure as Melanchthon was thrown off balance until the broader and brusquer sanity of Luther steadied him and dismissed the prophets and their like as fanatics. But the episode showed how justification by faith alone might lead to an anti-intellectualism akin to the antinomianism which its enemies claimed it entailed in the moral sphere. Both tendencies surfaced regularly in the assortment of religious movements which we call the Radical Reformation. Anti-intellectualism would have doomed the Reformation as effectively in the academic world as antinomianism would have done in the political world. But Luther knew when to temper radicalism with pragmatism and saw the dangers of anti-intellectualism in the stirs at Wittenberg as clearly as he saw the dangers of antinomianism in the Peasants' War. In short, the Reformation had to accommodate itself to the requirements of public order and education. The task of intellectual accommodation was carried out by Melanchthon. It was Luther's humanist lieutenant who produced a plausible account of the place of the humanities and of civic morality in a theological system which disprized human potential and damned human virtues. The magisterial Reformation had to accommodate the *magistri* of the now-humanist universities as well as the magistrates of courts and cities if it was to establish its place in respectable society.

Notwithstanding the problems which both sides found in certain aspects of humanism, its techniques could be detached from their would-be theoretical framework and made to function effectively enough by either party. Indeed, in a curious way humanism could function as a common idiom which allowed the two sides to make intellectual contact. Melanchthon's rhetorical textbooks not only circulated quite freely in Catholic institutions for many years, but (as O'Malley has shown) were then suitably censored and adjusted for continuing use – under new authorial names – in Catholic education. The ideas and methods of German Protestant humanists and the Jesuit rhetoricians cross-fertilized each other despite the theological divisions. It was Melanchthon who added a fourth genre of oratory – the *genus didacticum* (or *genus didascalicum*) – to the traditional three genres of classical rhetoric (forensic or judicial, epideictic or encomiastic and demonstrative) in order to make room for the Christian sermon, a form which in his view combined elements of the classical genres in a new way. His fourth genre became a commonplace of the Jesuit rhetorics and preaching handbooks of men like Cipriano de Soarez and Luis de Granada.

Humanism was also welcome to both the Catholic church and the magisterial Reformation because of its inherent social conservatism. This is a claim which seems counter-intuitive partly because of the progressive connotations which the term humanism bears in its twentieth-century context and partly also because of the mental association even of Renaissance humanism with concepts of social and moral progress. It might also seem contestable when faced with particular examples of socially challenging or even radical texts, such as Erasmus's pacifist *Complaint of Peace* and, above all, Thomas More's *Utopia*, as well as with the genuine republicanism of much civic humanism. And it is true that not all elements of humanism were conservative: the slogan *virtus vera nobilitas* ('virtue is the true nobility') challenged the assumptions of aristocratic society and the concept of the active life pursued in the service of the common good (*res publica*) was an equal challenge to the acquisitive and selfish motives which in fact drove much of public life. Yet these challenges achieved little. Throughout the era of humanism, European society remained thoroughly aristocratic and ruthlessly competitive. In fact, humanism was in many ways the perfect expression of an aristocratic and elitist culture. The complacent Ciceronianism of Renaissance Rome in the decades before the Reformation; the literature of the Siglo de Oro in Spain; the polished rhetoric of the Jesuit colleges in the century after 1550; the Tudor obsession with hierarchy and obedience; the courtly pulpit eloquence of Counter-Reformation France, Baroque Bavaria and Jacobean England; all these cultural forms sanctioned and glorified the existing order.

Of course humanists were to be found in subversive and rebellious contexts. But in these situations their humanism was accidental rather than essential. It was basic concerns of confessional, national or even provincial identity which fuelled the rebellions of early modern Europe. Humanists might serve such movements, as they served both sides in the French Wars of Religion. But when peace returned, the ideological resources of humanism were always at hand to bolster the cause of order – as in the France of Henry IV. The most effective challenge to any establishment policy in this era was the Spanish scholastic challenge to the conquest and colonization of the New World. It was the Castilian humanist Juan Gines de Sepúlveda who produced the starkest justification for the suppression of the indigenous cultures of America. The vast majority of humanist writers promoted a socially conservative and politically conformist message, summed up in the words 'order' and 'obedience'. Even when some humanist authors found themselves called upon to justify political resistance, they were obliged to draw heavily on the scholastic traditions of theology and Roman law for convincing materials. Humanists like Erasmus, More and Pole may have been committed to the international ideal of the Catholic church transcending national boundaries. As Erasmus remarked, the Rhine might divide French from Germans, but it ought not to divide Christians from Christians. But the vein of civic pride and service, of patriotism, which ran through Renaissance humanism meant that a narrower view was easier to adopt. Humanism readily subordinated itself to the vanities of kings.

Humanism began and ended as technique. Erasmus and his circle might have forged something more ideological out of it, but Reformation politics supervened and the tools of the humanist trade were available on every side. Christian humanism might possibly have become a new philosophical synthesis based on education, rhetoric, dialogue, criticism and ethics. But it may be that the metaphysical naivety of the Christian humanists made such a project incoherent. Perhaps, too, the Reformation emphasis on original sin and total depravity made more sense than the mild, moderate and moralistic optimism of the humanists in a Christian world racked by internecine conflict, overshadowed by the Turk, disorientated by the New World and feeling the first shocks of a prolonged economic slump accompanied by renewed bouts of epidemic disease. Doctrine and discipline, rather than love and liberty, were the watchwords of Reformation Europe – Catholic or Protestant.

FURTHER READING

Charles Nauert's recent survey *Humanism and the Culture of Renaissance Europe* (Cambridge, 1995) is the best place to start, while P.O. Kristeller's collections of essays *Renaissance Thought* (New York, 1961) and *Renaissance Thought II* (New York, 1965) remain a sound introduction to the intellectual components of humanism. On the importance of medieval ideas of *Romanitas* and *renovatio*, see W. Ullmann, *Medieval Foundations of Renaissance Humanism* (London, 1977). Hans Baron's thesis on the political conditioning of early civic humanism is presented in his monumental study, *The Crisis of the Early Italian Renaissance* (2 vols, Princeton, 1955), and criticized in J.E. Seigel, *Rhetoric and Philosophy in Renaissance Humanism* (Princeton, 1968). The technical achievements of the humanists are assessed in Rudolf Pfeiffer, *History of Classical Scholarship: From 1300 to 1850* (Oxford, 1976), while Charles Stinger, *Humanism and the Church Fathers* (Albany, NY, 1977), surveys the 'patristic Renaissance' which accompanied the classical Renaissance in fifteenth-century Italy. Easily the most informative general discussion of Renaissance rhetoric is found in Brian Vickers, *In Defence of Rhetoric* (Oxford, 1989), and this subject is pursued further in J.W. O'Malley, *Praise and Blame in Renaissance Rome* (Durham, NC, 1979), and J.F. D'Amico, *Renaissance Humanism in Papal Rome* (Baltimore, 1983). On humanism across Europe, see Roy Porter and Mikulás Teich (eds), *The Renaissance in National Context* (Cambridge, 1992), and Anthony Goodman and Angus MacKay (eds), *The Impact of Humanism on Western Europe* (London, 1990). The huge literature on Erasmus and Christian humanism is more often disappointing than not, but J.K. McConica's brief *Erasmus* (Oxford, 1991) stands out from the crowd. John R. Schneider provides a fine study of the interaction of Renaissance and Reformation in *Philip Melanchthon's Rhetorical Construal of Biblical Authority* (Lewiston, 1991). This topic is explored more deeply still in Sachiko Kusukawa, *The Transformation of Natural Philosophy: The Case of Philip Melanchthon* (Cambridge, 1995), and from a different angle in Gerald Strauss, *Luther's House of Learning* (Baltimore, 1978). There are many useful contributions across the whole field in Albert Rabil, Jr (ed.), *Renaissance Humanism: Foundations, Forms and Legacy* (3 vols; Philadelphia, 1988). Despite the baleful influence of nineteenth-century liberalism, nationalism and secularism, Jacob Burckhardt's *The Civilization of the Renaissance in Italy* (2nd edn, 1868) remains required reading. Wider aspects of Renaissance culture are, more recently, explored in Peter Burke's masterly *The Italian Renaissance* (revised edn; Cambridge, 1986) and Lisa Jardine's superb and illuminating *Worldly Goods* (London, 1996).

PART II

LUTHER AND GERMANY

LUTHER AND THE REFORMATION IN GERMANY

---·•·---

Carl Truman

Of all of the historical figures associated with the Reformation, that of Martin Luther is the one who stands out most vividly in the popular imagination. The romanticized and unhistorical picture of the young monk defiantly nailing the Ninety-Five Theses against Indulgences to the church door at Wittenberg is one of the most dramatic and theatrical images of the Reformation. Of course, the European Reformation was not simply – or perhaps even primarily – about individuals and ideas, but about the larger social and economic changes which were transforming European society and politics. Nevertheless, the language used by the various parties involved to reflect upon their times and to make sense of what was going on around them was intimately linked to the theological battles in which Luther and his writings were such a key part. Thus, anyone who wishes to understand how the Reformation was understood by those who were actually involved must sooner or later come to terms with 'Dr Martin'.

LUTHER'S EARLY LIFE

Martin Luther was born, probably in 1482, in Eisleben in the county of Eisenach in Saxony. His father, Hans, was of farming stock, but because local law ensured that his younger brother, Heinz, inherited the farm, he turned to copper mining as a means of supporting his family. Luther, the giant of the German Reformation, thus had rather humble origins compared to his future significance.

There is very little documentary evidence to provide any insights into the relationship between the father and the son, despite the efforts made by some scholars to interpret Luther's later theological struggles as arising from the psychological impact of, among other things, uneasy family relationships.[1] Certainly, his later decision to abandon a career in the law for the life of an Augustinian friar was not to find favour with his parents, but regarding his early childhood one can assume only that it was full of the typical hardships and rigours of the day – to go any further than this is to indulge in speculation.

Luther spent the first fourteen years of his life in Mansfeld. His schooling was divided between three institutions, first at Mansfeld itself, then in Magdeburg and finally in Eisenach. From Eisenach, he proceeded to the University at Erfurt, where he matriculated in the summer of 1501. There he would have started his studies in the faculty of liberal arts where, upon successful completion of the course, he could move into one of the higher faculties for further study. It was at Erfurt that Luther would have been exposed for the first time to a number of intellectual influences that were to shape him, in both a negative and positive sense, for the rest of his life. The first was Aristotelian philosophy. Since the twelfth century not only Aristotelian logic but also Aristotelian metaphysics had been the staple of university education, particularly in terms of its philosophical underpinnings. The school of philosophy to which Luther was introduced at Erfurt was that known as 'nominalism', a fact not without significance for his later theology.[2]

The third influence was that of humanism, a term and movement notoriously difficult to define accurately.[3] Later, the major significance for Luther of this broad movement for cultural and educational reform was that it made available original texts of the early fathers, the reading of which was to be so crucial to Luther's own theological development. Also, through the philological endeavours of Erasmus of Rotterdam, the movement produced a Greek text of the New Testament, without which there would have been no Lutheranism of the kind that did develop. On another level, humanism also pitted itself against the scholasticism of the Middle Ages on the grounds of its crude Latin style and pedantic hair-splitting. At Erfurt, however, the humanism with which Luther came into contact was a fairly low-key affair which seems to have coexisted quite happily with the nominalism of the university. It seems unlikely that anything more than exposure to humanist rhetoric and some of their love for classical authors can be assigned to this period.

In 1505, having gained his master's degree, Luther turned his attention to law. Nevertheless, in the coming months a personal crisis ensured that his career as student of law was dramatically short-lived. What exactly led to this crisis is difficult to ascertain. Certainly, the older Luther talked about the sense of anxiety (*anfechtung*) which he felt as a young man. In addition, it would appear that after taking his master's degree he gave himself to deeper study of the Bible, which could well have raised existential questions about his eternal destiny. Whatever the reasons, the crisis itself erupted on 2 July 1505, while Luther was returning to Erfurt from Mansfeld. About four miles from Erfurt, near the village of Stotternheim, he was caught in an atrocious thunderstorm which culminated in a bolt of lightning striking the ground near him and throwing him down. In fear and despair, Luther is said to have cried out: 'Help me, St Anne. I will become a monk.' Whatever the long-term background to that cry, it was at that moment that Luther's future destiny was sealed.

Luther did not enter the monastery immediately. Some friends tried to dissuade him from fulfilling his vow and he himself regretted having made it. Nevertheless, he sold his books and, much to the disappointment of his father, entered the monastery of the Augustinian hermits in Erfurt. Once inside, Luther devoted himself body and soul to the life of a monk. The whole of life was regulated by the rules of the order and Luther committed himself to a passionate adherence to these rules as a means of ensuring his place in heaven.

Most important in his early years in the monastery was the celebration of the mass. The mass was the focal point of mediæval worship and theology – the sacrament which was superior to all others because it did not simply symbolize Christ or point to him, but actually contained him and conveyed him to the recipient. In preparation for his first mass, Luther had to study one of the standard texts on the theology of the mass: Gabriel Biel's *Exposition of the Sacred Canon of the Mass*, which had first been published in 1488.[4] The work was a classic piece of nominalist theology and thus philosophically of a piece with the logical tradition to which Luther was exposed at Erfurt. In addition, the work underlined the fact that, in the mass, the individual actually meets, both physically and spiritually, with Christ. On one level, this was bound to inspire a profound awe and devotion in Luther; but it also sowed the seeds of profound personal problems which were to bear fruit later, in his so-called Reformation theology. Primary among these was the question of worthiness: if Christ is actually encountered in the mass, on what grounds can the individual recipient be deemed at all worthy for this encounter? Within the kind of theology which Biel's work represented, that of the so-called *via moderna* or 'modern way', the answer was provided by the *pactum*, an arrangement freely made by God himself to enable sinners to come before him. The *pactum* was a kind of divine–human contract, the terms of which were as follows: to the one who does what is in them (i.e. does their best), God will not deny grace. The idea was that, although human beings could not possibly make themselves pure enough to come before God, provided they did their best, then God would treat them as if they had achieved the full level of righteousness needed. Thus the problem of human worthiness was solved: do your best and God will treat you as if you are worthy.

On one level, this seems a most satisfactory solution to the problem. The problem, however, is how one comes to know that one has done one's best. In the context of the mass, the question of personal purity became a pressing one: for example, no monk was meant to celebrate mass unless he had confessed all his sins, and even an involuntary nocturnal emission was enough to prevent such celebration. Doing one's best was therefore an extremely difficult, if not impossible, thing to do: however perfectly one confessed or guarded one's thoughts, could one be sure of having done these things to the best of one's ability? Such a theology, combined with the emphasis upon the worthiness of the mass celebrant, thus created a marvellous context for morbid introspection, particularly for a serious-minded monastic zealot such as Luther.

By the spring of 1507, Luther had received the various ordinations needed to make him a full priest and arrangements were made for the celebration of his first mass on 2 May. The celebration precipitated yet another crisis in Luther's life, though this time without the dramatic change of circumstances associated with the Stotternheim experience. Standing at the altar, Luther found himself having to face God by himself, with no one to mediate for him, and wondering how on earth he could be worthy enough to do this. The answer was, he felt deep inside, that he could not, and this created for him a profound personal problem. The question with which it confronted him, and which he was to face again and again over the coming years, was simply this: 'How can I, a sinner, find a gracious God?'

The crisis at Stotternheim, with the imminence of death and judgement which it symbolized, was a microcosm of Luther's time as a monk. His reputation in the monastery was as one who had an almost pathological obsession with his own sinfulness, with confession and with the need to prepare himself for meeting with God's judgement at any moment. Nevertheless, this did not stop his clear gifts as a scholar from being noticed by the authorities and this led in 1508 to his temporary transfer to the place where he was to spend much of the rest of his life: Wittenberg. There he started by lecturing on Aristotle's *Nicomachean Ethics*. While doing this, however, his principal interest appears to have been studying the Bible and continuing his theological studies under the famous Augustinian Johannes von Staupitz, who was also to be Luther's spiritual mentor for some years.[5] In 1509, Luther gained his bachelor's degree in theology and was about to embark on the typical rite of passage for one intending a career in theology – that is lecturing on the standard mediæval theological textbook, Peter Lombard's *Four Books of Sentences* – when he was recalled to Erfurt to undertake teaching duties there. The period immediately subsequent was not to be of major significance to his development, with one exception: his visit to Rome to negotiate with the papacy on behalf of those congregations of the Augustinian order who were concerned that recent disputes and agreements within the order had jeopardized the internal reforms to which it had been committed.

The politics of the trip were not ultimately as important as the impression which Rome made upon the young monk. While in later life Rome came to symbolize for Luther all that he considered wrong with Christendom, at this point he was overwhelmed with the opportunities for pious devotion. Although the visit was a failure in terms of its political intent, from a religious point of view it had a profound impact upon him. While there, he said mass at various holy sites, made pilgrimages to the various significant churches and to the catacombs, and even climbed the steps from Pilate's palace, saying the 'Our Father' on each step. The visit to Rome, then, was not just another part of his monastic routine – in many ways, it symbolized the apex of his devotion to monastic piety. Thus, despite the decadence and corruption which he witnessed, Luther came away from Rome with an overall positive image which was, perhaps surprisingly, to stay with him for some number of years.

On his return to Erfurt, a division occurred within the Augustinian order there over the authority of Staupitz as Vicar General of the order: Luther was part of the minority that supported Staupitz. The situation deteriorated and, probably by the autumn, Luther along with other members of the order, had been transferred back to Wittenberg. It was here that he was to carry out his most significant work.

THE EARLY YEARS AT WITTENBERG

While Wittenberg was physically a comparatively small settlement – with a population of approximately 2,500 – this size hid its political significance. Wittenberg was the capital of electoral Saxony and Saxony was one of the most powerful of the German political states. Thus Luther's move to Wittenberg, while superficially placing him in a narrower environment than had been the case at Erfurt, in fact moved him nearer to one of the centres of political power. This was something which was to invest his theological and ecclesiastical activities with a political significance which they might not otherwise have enjoyed.

The university in Wittenberg was of recent vintage, having been established by the elector, Frederick the Wise, in 1502 – although papal confirmation of its status was not obtained until 1507. When Luther arrived, there were around 200 students matriculating annually, a number which was to increase dramatically after Luther rose to prominence for his reforming activities.

Luther's early years at the university are marked by a slow but clear theological progression. Much has been written about the so-called 'Reformation break-through', but careful analysis of his lectures during his first years at Wittenberg has revealed that Luther's theology did not simply change overnight but was slowly transformed over a period of time. The key to understanding his develop-ment would appear to be the same inner volition that had motivated his move to the monastery and his utter devotion to monastic practices once inside: the need to find favour with God.

The first lectures which survive of Luther's teaching in Wittenberg are a series on the Book of Psalms known as the *Dictata super Psalterium* which were probably delivered in 1514–15, followed by lectures on St Paul's Letter to the Romans in 1515–16.[6] The theology of the early lectures has been characterized as a theology of humility. Put simply, this involved the individual acknowledging their hopeless sinfulness before God and accepting the justice of God's condemnation upon them. Then, seeking no longer to assert the self over against God or as a basis for approaching God, the individual should approach God in a spirit of humility and of self-condemnation: such a one will find that God is gracious. This theological position, while not the mature thought of the later reformer, did bring to the fore key elements of Luther's later position: the facts that humanity is so sinful, it cannot stand before God in its own strength; and that the only basis for approaching God is ultimately God's own mercy, not humanity's merit. This is crucial: ever since the incident in the thunderstorm, Luther had found himself confronted with the God of judgement and condemnation, something which his officiating at mass had continually underlined for him. Now (in the years between 1513–16) the God of mercy, not simply judgement, began to emerge: humans were still utterly sinful, but there was hope, not in themselves, but in the mercy of a gracious God.

THE CRISIS OVER INDULGENCES

The crisis which was to bring Luther to international prominence was, of course, that over the issue of indulgences, in which the theology of humility outlined above played a crucial role. Indulgences had, since the papal bull *Unigenitus* of Clement VI in 1343, been linked with the so-called 'treasury of merits', that accu-mulation of works of supererogation by saints which could be transferred to the account of those who were not so holy. This had been extended by a second bull, *Salvator noster*, by Sixtus IV in 1476 to cover souls in purgatory – the shadowy realm of purification between heaven and hell. Between them, these two bulls provided the official backing and theological justification for the sale of indul-gences to the public.

Luther was aware of the indulgence issue before the famous events of 1517. In 1516, he preached on the issue no less than three times. On the third occasion (Halloween), he made the cutting point that it was rather audacious of the pope to guarantee release of souls from purgatory and that, if he had the power so to do, he was rather cruel not to do it for all without any conditions. Luther was not completely opposed to the practice: what he disliked was the abuses and the false confidence they engendered. Nevertheless, to speak out against indulgences was a politically brave, or even foolhardy, thing to do: indulgences were a good source of revenue for the authorities and any attack upon them would also be seen as an attack upon the powers which they helped to fund. Indeed, it appears that the elector was not happy with Luther's Halloween sermon, but his annoyance in 1516 was to be nothing compared to the event triggered by the arrival of Tetzel the indulgence salesman in 1517. Nevertheless, in light of the ever-present temptation to interpret Luther's reformation campaign as a fundamentally nationalist phenomenon, it is important to bear in mind that Luther's first attacks on indulgences were not caused by an Italian papacy bleeding Germans dry, but by a revenue-raising operation that helped fund the Castle Church and the University of Wittenberg itself. Far from striking a blow against foreign imperialism, Luther was, it could be argued, biting the hand that fed him.

The crisis of 1517 was rather different in origin, arising from the political ambitions of one of the leading German houses – that of Hohenzollern – who wished to gain substantial control of ecclesiastical politics in Germany. A member of this house, Albrecht of Brandenburg, wished to add to the sees of which he was already in charge (Halberstadt and Magdeburg) the archbishopric of Mainz. This he could do for the princely sum of 10,000 ducats. In addition, he had to obtain papal permission to hold three sees simultaneously and this he determined to do by buying official approval for his move from the pope himself. Using the Fuggers – a major German banking house – as intermediaries, Albrecht negotiated a deal with the then pope, Leo X. Leo was himself in financial difficulties, left with the task of finishing (and paying for) the new St Peter's at Rome, which his predecessor, Julius II, had started. Thus it was agreed that Albrecht should pay Leo 10,000 ducats and in return Leo allowed Albrecht to take the archbishopric. More important, however, was Leo's agreement that Albrecht should be granted the privilege of raising indulgences in his territory for a period of eight years, with half of the receipts going towards the rebuilding of St Peter's and half going towards repaying the Fuggers.

The proclamation of the indulgence was entrusted to the experienced Dominican Johann Tetzel, who set about his task with zeal. The indulgences were never actually sold in Luther's parish – to have done so would have required the permission of Frederick the Wise and he would not give such permission lest a further indulgence should interfere with his own source of revenue from that quarter. Nevertheless, Tetzel did ply his trade near enough to Luther's parish for his parishioners to be able to make the journey to him and to return with the objects of their desire. It was this hawking, with its specious promises of salvation, that enraged Luther and led him, so tradition has it, to post his Ninety-Five Theses against Indulgences on the church door in Wittenberg.[7]

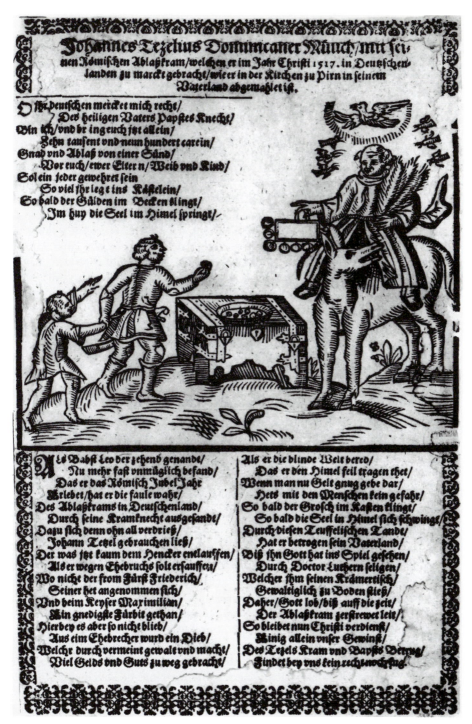

Figure 5.1 The indulgence trade. Johann Tetzel peddles indulgences to the credulous poor. (Wittenberg, Lutherhalle)

It is important at this point to realize that the posting of the theses was not quite as radical and revolutionary a step as later Protestant mythology has made it. What Luther was in essence doing was availing himself of the standard way of advertising a series of points for debate, with the choice of the church door possessing no real significance in and of itself. Luther made no attempt to disseminate them among his people – they were aimed at the scholars and intended as an invitation to debate. While the theses differed from many of the same genre in that they were written with angry passion, the point which they were making – that God's grace and favour could not be bought with money – was scarcely revolutionary. What catapulted Luther to prominence at this point was not the theological content of the theses but the fact that he had challenged Albrecht of Brandenburg's source of revenue. It was this that brought him to the attention of the church authorities.

Albrecht forwarded the theses to the pope who decided to take a fairly low-key approach to the whole affair and to have Luther dealt with by the Augustinian order itself at its triennial meeting at Heidelberg. It was here that Luther was truly to enter the wider stage of the Reformation and to give public voice to a theology which was breaking radically with its mediæval background.

The one great irony of the situation is that Luther had, in fact, dealt a much more radical blow against the church's theology earlier in 1517, when he had launched his *Disputation against Scholastic Theology*.[8] In this disputation, he had attacked the very Aristotelian foundations upon which the mediæval doctors had constructed their theology and it is this which could arguably be regarded as the start of the theological Reformation. The fact, then, that it was the later controversy over indulgences, with its profound implications for the revenue-raising powers of the political establishment, which really launched Luther's career as a reformer speaks eloquently about the importance of economic and political factors in the great chain of events that were to follow.

FROM THE HEIDELBERG DISPUTATION TO THE MISSION OF MILTITZ

The Heidelberg Disputation, which could have proved a flashpoint for opposition to Luther, in fact turned out to be something of a personal triumph for the young monk.[9] While he had expected opposition and some unpleasantness, Luther was actually fêted at Heidelberg as a guest of honour, dining with the Count Palatine and Staupitz, and being taken on guided tours of the chapel and other notable places. While letters of complaint against Luther were presented to the order, nothing was done, and in the public disputation Luther acquitted himself in a way that won the admiration of his audience and which was to inspire at least one young man, Martin Bucer, to attach himself to the reform movement. Indeed, such was Luther's success that, at the end of the meeting, he was invited to ride some of the way home with the Nuremberg delegation.

Church politics, however, were much wider than the internal affairs of the Augustinian order and the Dominicans, their great rivals, were spoiling for a fight. First, they gave Tetzel a doctorate which gave him a public and professional theological platform from which to defend the sale of indulgences. Luther responded by producing a series of sermons which both expounded and, indeed, expanded upon the original theses against indulgences.[10] This time, the attack was more far-reaching, questioning the superiority of the Roman church and, when hearing that he was under the ban of the church, querying the authority of bishops to ban in this way. What is important to remember, however, is that at this point Luther still regarded himself as pitted against those who corrupted the church, not against the church itself. With what seems in retrospect a touching naivety, Luther dedicated the *Resolutions* on the ninety-five theses to the pope, giving Staupitz a copy to send on to him.

Things could not, of course, be allowed to go on unchecked and, on 7 August, Luther received a summons from Rome which gave him sixty days to appear for trial there. This summons marked the real turning-point in the political situation and transformed what had first been a debate within the Augustinian order, and then a battle between Augustinians and Dominicans, into a major confrontation over national and church authority. Luther was now entirely at the mercy of the political powers and utterly dependent upon them for his personal survival. The first move on the part of Luther was a request to Frederick the Wise via his chaplain, George Spalatin, that he intervene in the matter. Frederick always kept Luther at a distance, being careful to use Luther's cause rather than to identify himself with it. Nevertheless, he managed to negotiate with the great scholar and churchman, Cardinal Cajetan, and arranged for Luther to be interviewed by Cajetan at Augsburg before his journey to Rome. The pope at the time was concerned about Emperor Maximilian's plans to have his nephew, Charles V of Spain, elected as king of the Romans. It would appear that the need for the elector's support on this issue helped in brokering the compromise deal over the location of Luther's trial.

Thus it was that on 7 October 1518 Luther arrived not in Rome but in Augsburg to be interviewed by Cajetan. Three interviews took place from 12–14 October. At the first, Cajetan told Luther he must recant, to which Luther replied that he wished first to be instructed about his errors. Over the next three days, the two men clashed over a whole variety of issues, from the treasury of merits to the final authority of the pope in scriptural interpretation. What became clear was that what had started as a complaint about the abuse of the practice of indulgences had developed into a wholesale clash of theologies. With no resolution in sight and with dark rumours of the cardinal having been empowered to arrest and detain Luther, the young monk fled with the help of friends back to Wittenberg. Cajetan, disappointed at the outcome, sent his report to Frederick the Wise. It was not favourable to Luther.

Luther's position, now dependent upon Frederick the Wise, was nonetheless a somewhat fortunate one. Frederick, as an elector, was central to European politics at the time. The pope relied to a large extent for his own political position on maintaining a careful balance between the interests of Spain and the interests of France. As most of the electors were German, they played a singularly important role in this balance – the pope could not afford to alienate them. It was for this reason that Luther was fortunate in having as his patron a man whom the pope had

Figure 5.2 Luther before Cajetan. From Rabus, *Historien*, 1557. (Wittenberg, Lutherhalle)

little desire to alienate in any dramatic way. If Frederick was to act against Luther, the pope realized that it would have to be because he felt it to be in his own best interest.

With this is mind, the pope appointed as assistant to Cajetan one Karl von Miltitz. Miltitz brought various papal privileges to Frederick and, in addition, the gift of a golden rose which was deposited with the Fuggers at Augsburg. Dark rumours circulated that the gift of the rose was to be conditional on Frederick handing Luther over to the authorities. When Miltitz himself met Luther, he asked him to subscribe to a new papal decree, an offer that Luther declined. Thus Miltitz's attempts to bring the crisis to an end failed.

THE LEIPZIG DISPUTATION

It was now that perhaps Luther's most famous – and certainly one of his most formidable – opponents stepped forward: Johann Eck of the University of Ingolstadt. Eck, who was in essence a professional debater and lived for the cut-and-thrust of argument, approached the patron of Leipzig, Duke George the Bearded, and obtained his agreement for a debate at Leipzig between Eck and Andreas Bodenstein von Karlstadt, despite the disapproval of the theologians there. Neither the choice of Leipzig, nor of Karlstadt, was without significance.

Politically, Leipzig represented a different part of Saxony to that of Wittenberg. It was not, however, the geography which was so significant – of more importance was the fact that this debate over the most theological of issues was to take place at a territorial university and not within the confines of an ecclesiastical institution. Duke George almost certainly had Frederick the Wise's permission to do this – and in so doing, the secular powers were again sending a clear signal to the church that the Luther problem was an issue which was to be resolved as much by the secular powers as by their religious counterparts.

The choice of Karlstadt as opponent was interesting in that it generated a certain amount of tension. Karlstadt, who was later to throw in his lot with the radicals and break with Luther, was at this point more conservative than Luther on the one issue which was to become the crux at Leipzig: the issue of papal authority. In his own counter-theses to Eck's theses for debate, Luther pointed out that the authority of the pope had only been fixed some 400 years earlier and was, therefore, a somewhat dubious matter. Karlstadt, when he read this, was nervous and went to great lengths to stress his loyalty to the Roman church. At this point in time, at least, he was still less radical than Luther.

The debate itself took place in July 1519 in the auditorium of the castle.[11] After the various procedural matters had been decided, the debate proper got underway. Eck and Karlstadt debated for a week over the depravity of humanity; then Luther entered the lists to debate the issue of papal authority, its antiquity and whether it was a divine or human institution. It was this that led to Eck's masterstroke: in denying the divine superiority of the Roman church, he claimed, Luther was doing no more than resurrecting the thought of the Englishman, John Wyclif, and the Czech, John Hus, which had been condemned 100 years previously at the Council of Constance.[12] Luther angrily repudiated the charge, but during an interlude in proceedings he took the opportunity to read up on Hus's condemnation. To his amazement, he discovered that Hus had been condemned for identifying the universal church with the number of the elect and as seeing the church's unity as based upon election. For him, this was simply Augustine's position and, at the next session, he took the opportunity of commending many of Hus's beliefs as sound and evangelical. He also suggested that some of the articles for which the records of the Council claimed Hus was condemned must have been interpolated at a later date. The damage was done, however. At Leipzig, Luther had effectively thrown in his lot with the heretics.

THE DECISIVE TURNING-POINT (1520–1)

In the following year, 1520, Luther produced three works which, taken as a whole, set out his basic reform programme. The first of these, *To the Christian Nobility of the German Nation*, was an overtly political treatise.[13] In it, he called upon the German nobility to take the reform of the church into its own hands, to throw off the burden of tributes to Rome, clerical celibacy, masses for the dead and other trappings of the mediæval church. In so doing, he was effectively inciting open political rebellion against Rome at the highest level. The second treatise, *On the Babylonian Captivity of the Church*, attacked the various abuses of the eucharist which were tolerated and even encouraged by the papacy, and argued instead for what Luther regarded as a more biblical approach, with a particular emphasis on communion in both kinds. Not insignificantly, this was also a distinctive belief of the followers of Hus in the previous century.[14] Finally, there was *The Freedom of the Christian*, a work which set out Luther's own understanding of justification, emphasizing the futility of human works as a means of finding favour with God and stressing instead the work of Christ as the basis and content of the Christian's righteousness.[15] This, of course, was Luther's famous doctrine of justification by faith, which stood at the very heart of his theological reformation. It was unlikely to appeal to the ecclesiastical authorities because it cut right across the elaborate penitential system, with its concomitant revenues and mechanisms of power, which the mediæval church had so carefully developed over the years.

Meanwhile, at Rome the papacy had decided that it could not put up with Luther's potentially damaging criticism for much longer. That Luther had been allowed to carry on his writing and preaching for three years with the apparent approval of the German princes and that his strikes against the church were becoming increasingly radical, could only be a source of great concern to the established ecclesiastical powers. Matters had moved a long way from the local dispute about indulgences of 1517. Thus, on 15 June 1520, the pope issued a bull, *Exsurge Domine*, which censured Luther's theology as heretical, ordered the burning of his books and, perhaps more in hope than expectation, gave him sixty days to recant.

The bull did not reach Luther until 10 October and immediately prompted from him a tract whose title is a good guide to its content: *Against the Execrable Bull of Antichrist*. Luther, never one to shrink from conflict or to indulge in understatement, repudiated the bull and declared at the end of the tract that ultimately God would judge the cause. Then, on 15 December, he publicly burned the bull and a few volumes of canon law in what had to be his most provocative public show of contempt for the papacy so far and which he justified in a typically vitriolic piece: *Why the Books of the Pope and his Disciples were Burned*.[16] His fate was now effectively sealed. Weeks later, on 3 January 1521, the pope invoked against Luther the ultimate spiritual sanction, that of excommunication, in the bull *Decet Romanum*.

The crucial development in 1520, however, was Frederick the Wise's decision to continue to support Luther and now to plead his cause with the emperor. While he claimed to have no particular vested interest in Luther's theology and to wish only for Luther to have a fair trial, it is obvious in retrospect that other issues were at play here. Luther's books were being burned in Germany, Luther at the end of the year himself burned a papal bull; the role that Frederick was in fact playing was only speciously that of neutral arbiter – in practice, it was that of opponent of Rome. In defending Luther, he was effectively declaring it legitimate for a German to defy the pope.

The appeal to the emperor was virtually the only course left open. At Rome the procedures against Luther were now inevitable and non-negotiable. The emperor himself subscribed at his coronation to a constitution which, among other things, declared that no German should be taken to be tried outside his own country and that no German should be condemned without a proper trial. The clauses were clearly both significant – and fortuitous – for Martin Luther. The result was, after various discussions and delays, that an imperial diet was convened in the city of Worms in April 1521 to try the case of Martin Luther before the emperor.

At the diet, Luther was once again confronted by a Catholic establishment which wished him to recant.[17] Arriving on 16 April, on the following day the examination began. Luther was shown by his examiner, Eck (not the Eck of Leipzig fame), a pile of his books and asked, first, if he acknowledged them as his own and, second, whether he wished to defend all or part of them. Luther replied affirmatively to the first question and then hesitated and asked for more time before answering the second. His reasons for this are not entirely plain, but it was not beyond the realm of possibility that Luther, faced with the overwhelming gravity of the situation, suffered a momentary crisis of confidence. Whatever the case, the delay was granted to him and the assembly adjourned until the next day, 18 April. Then, when confronted with the same two questions, Luther acknowledged the works as his own and then distinguished them into three kinds: those which set forth the faith so simply that even his enemies had to acknowledge their worth; those which lamented the ungodly state of Christendom, a state of affairs which everyone could see; and those which attacked individuals, where he acknowledged that his tone had not always been as moderate as perhaps it should have been. When pressed on these points by Eck, Luther is said to have replied with the famous, though possibly apocryphal, statement: 'Here I stand, I can do no other'.

Having had his chance to speak, Luther was now in the hands of the electors who were summoned by the emperor. The emperor had an edict drawn up which declared Luther a heretic and placed him under the imperial ban. While all six electors professed support for this move, only four actually signed. Those abstaining were Ludwig of the Palatinate and, to Luther's good fortune, Frederick of Saxony. While the emperor had sufficient backing to proceed with enforcing the edict, Luther almost immediately became the focus of nationalist and political insurgency. That very night placards depicting the *Bundschuh* – the clog worn by the peasants and a symbol of peasant revolution – appeared all over Worms. The obvious implication was that, if Luther perished, the peasants would rise against the authorities, bringing to a head many years of increasing social tension. Thus it was that, though the final edict was dated 6 May, it was not in fact issued until 26 May – by which time, most of those attending the diet had gone home and a true consensus was impossible.

THE WARTBURG AND THE PEASANTS' WAR

Having left Worms for Wittenberg, Luther and his companions were just entering the woods on the outskirts of Eisenach when they were intercepted and kidnapped. It was not, however, the act of the emperor – on the contrary, it was carried out on the orders of Frederick the Wise and with the full knowledge of Luther. The kidnapping was staged in order to remove Luther from the line of fire and to place him in safe keeping at the Wartburg Castle, where he was known as 'Junker Jörg'. While there – in between bouts of physical illness, constipation and insomnia – he translated the whole of the New Testament into German.

More significant than Luther's confinement, however, was the fact that the

Reformation in Wittenberg now moved ahead without him under the leadership of the academic wunderkind, Philip Melanchthon (1497–1560).[18] Even without Luther, reforms continued apace. Clerical celibacy was abolished – a position urged by Luther in his writings, yet not put into practice prior to Worms. Then, the mass was administered in both kinds. This was a particularly powerful symbol – not only did it realize what Luther had advocated in *The Babylonian Captivity* but it also pointed to a potent similarity between the German Reformation and the appeal of the Bohemian Hussites of the previous century for precisely the same reform.

With all of this Luther was well pleased, but there was one issue which concerned him and that was the non-publication of a number of tracts which he had despatched to Wittenberg from the Wartburg. To find out the reason for this, he left the castle incognito and entered Wittenberg on 4 December 1521. On the day before he arrived, however, there had been a riot when students and townsfolk had armed themselves and stormed the parish church in the name of reform. Events were now moving a little too fast both for Luther and, more significantly, Frederick the Wise. In an attempt to stem the tide, the latter issued an order on 19 December to the effect that discussion might continue on theological matters, but no changes to the mass were to be introduced until such time as a unanimous consensus on reform could be reached. Karlstadt, already emerging as a more radical force within the Wittenberg Reformation than many of his colleagues, defied the order on Christmas Day by officiating in a simple black gown at a mass with a highly abbreviated liturgy followed by a declaration that faith alone, not fasting or confession, was all that was needed for celebrating mass.

Over the coming weeks Karlstadt pushed on with the reforms, culminating in the banning of begging and a vigorous attack on the use of art and images in worship. Frederick finally lost patience and issued instructions on 13 February which, while not abolishing the reforms, called a halt to the present rapid progress and appealed for reflection on what had been done so far. Frederick was keen that any implementation of reform should not be done autonomously by town councils but should be based on a territorial consensus and kept under territorial control. In this way, he must have thought, he stood a greater chance of controlling the beast which he himself had been so instrumental in creating.

The town council, however, had other ideas. While Karlstadt had agreed not to preach, the matter of reform was not to be allowed to stagnate under the pretence of discussion and consultation. Thus an invitation was extended to Luther to return – an invitation which lacked the blessing of Frederick. As a result, when Luther accepted the invitation and returned to Wittenberg in 1522, it was in many ways the greatest gamble of his career: for the first time since he had embarked on his reforming crusade, he could not rely on the protection of powerful secular forces to keep him safe.

Back in Wittenberg, however, Luther found that he was not so much living in fear of his life as the uncrowned king of the reform movement. Indeed, he exerted something of a moderating influence on the radicals such as Karlstadt, managing to broker compromises on such things as celebration of the mass. In addition, by sending a letter to a diet at Nuremberg exculpating Frederick for any responsibility for his return from the Wartburg, Luther was able to placate his prince and go some way to rebuilding the relationship with his patron which was so crucial to his survival. With Frederick's implicit backing, Luther was able to proceed with his moderate reform programme – moderate, that is, in comparison with the iconoclastic crusade of Karlstadt and company.

Meanwhile, elsewhere in Germany Luther's reform programme was being adopted and adapted by other cities – something which cemented the importance of the Reformation as a social and political movement and which was thus crucial to its survival. Clearly the Reformation had struck something of a chord with urban communities. Cities were, of course, the centres of cultural endeavour and were thus where the printing presses, so vital to the propagation of Reformation ideology, were based. They were also centres for preaching which both intensified the impact of the pamphlets and communicated central Reformation ideas to the illiterate. Many such preachers emerged from the mediæval mendicant orders – the Dominicans, Franciscans and Augustinians – whose principle houses were within the cities.

Within these urban contexts, Lutheran ideas and especially Lutheran preaching served to focus the tension between the mass of people and the city magistrates. Increasingly, Lutheran ideology came to serve as a rallying cry for social and political change. Thus, in northern Germany, the introduction of Reformation ideas and principles came hot on the heels of social and political upheavals which displaced the old patrician rulers with committees run by the citizens. Then, through the intervention of Luther's close ally and friend, Johannes Bugenhagen, Reformation rites were peacefully introduced in the new social set-up.

Elsewhere in Germany not dissimilar patterns were followed. In this context, it was in central Germany that Lutheranism found its most secure urban bases in the mid-1520s, thus securing its own immediate survival. In Nuremberg we find reform of laws on poor relief in 1522 being followed, in 1525, by both the suppression of monasteries – a move with social *and* theological significance – and the establishment of a new German mass. Elsewhere in this area, a large number of towns were taking positive steps to establish the Lutheran Reformation by the mid-1520s.

In the west, the most significant centre was Strasbourg, a city well-endowed with preachers. While attempts were made early on to confine preachers solely to matters of immediate scriptural import, by 1524 the city was celebrating communion in both kinds and had instituted its first German mass and baptismal rites. It was here that Martin Bucer came to prominence and thus Strasbourg was, theologically and ecclesiastically, to hold something of a middle ground between the Lutherans and the Reformed in the years to come.

For Luther, by the time of his return to Wittenberg, the breach with Rome was irreparable and he set about building a Christian society free from the papacy. What was so devastating, however, was not so much the breach with the papacy but the rapid disintegration of the Protestant consensus. Luther, as a German reformer standing defiant against the rights of a foreign pope on German soil, had become a symbolic focus for a number of vested interests. At Worms, the presence of powerful nationalist knights such as Hutten and Sickingen had helped secure his

Figure 5.3 Hans Baldung Grien, *Luther as an Augustinian Monk*, 1521. The nimbus and dove give the reformer the attributes of a mediæval saint, a confusion of doctrine of which the evangelical theologians, who rejected the cult of saints, could scarcely approve.

safety, with these soldiers identifying his theological crusade with their own more narrowly political and nationalist interests. There had also been the dark intimations of peasant unrest, linked explicitly to the fate of Luther at the diet. In addition, groups within the theological party had begun to push in more radical directions – the obvious example being the impetuous reforms Karlstadt introduced at Wittenberg in Luther's absence. After Luther's return, Karlstadt's radicalism became more pronounced – he came to reject the real presence of Christ's body in the eucharist, he rejected infant baptism and he began to advocate things such as sabbatarianism and the compulsory marriage of clergy. To Luther, these things were a foul concoction of heresy and a new legalism. Added to this was Karlstadt's affected behaviour: he donned peasant garb and posed, one might now say, as a 'man of the people' – a posture which Luther found simply ridiculous.

In addition to Karlstadt, a more dangerous figure also emerged on the 'left' of the reform party, that of Thomas Müntzer.[19] Müntzer rejected the authority of the written word as too static, just a mass of paper, and emphasized instead the direct leading of God's Spirit. In addition, he combined this theological emphasis with a notion of church activity very similar to that of a Holy War: the children of God could recognize each other and should therefore covenant together; those who were outside of this covenant were worthy only of death and it was the church's responsibility to slaughter the ungodly as a means of inaugurating God's kingdom on earth. Müntzer became a real danger in 1523–4 when he was elected as a minister in the village of Allstedt. Luther wrote to the authorities, warning them of Karlstadt's radicalism and linking him with the threat which Müntzer posed, particularly if he gained anything like a popular following. As a result, Karlstadt – one-time ally of Luther – was expelled from Saxony. As for Müntzer, having heard him preach at Weimar, Frederick saw his crazy schemes for what they were and decided not to give him any support.

Things came to a head with Müntzer in 1525, when the Peasants' War which had been threatening for many years erupted and was put down with full severity by the powers that be with the full support and encouragement of Martin Luther.[20] Müntzer himself was captured and beheaded. For Luther, however, and for the German Reformation as a whole, the war was a turning point. The action of the authorities and the attitude of Luther shattered once and for all any link that had existed between Luther's Reformation and the social and political goals of certain radical elements. The papacy had not been overthrown in Germany to make way for radical reform but, in practice, to allow the German princes a greater control over their own affairs, and Luther was happy to work as part of that programme.

As a last tragic footnote to this episode, Karlstadt, fleeing from the débâcle of the Peasants' War, sought shelter with the man who, more than any other, had both shaped his life and ensured his ultimate destruction. On the very night of Luther's wedding to the nun, Katherina von Bora, Karlstadt arrived on Luther's doorstep in Wittenberg and was taken in temporarily by his erstwhile friend.

CONFLICTS WITH ERASMUS AND ZWINGLI

In addition to the Peasants' War, one other conflict of a more rarefied kind occupied Luther in the middle of the 1520s: that with the great humanist, Erasmus of Rotterdam. Erasmus was the pre-eminent northern European humanist of his day and his work on the Greek text of the New Testament was crucial to the Reformation. In addition, his attacks on church abuses placed him, superficially at least, close to reformers such as Luther. There was, however, a fundamental difference: while Erasmus attacked the outward corruption of papal religion, Luther saw himself as striking at its very heart in terms of its theological beliefs. For Luther, the problem could not be solved by attending to the reform of outward abuses; one first had to deal with the root cause of the problem, the apostate theology.

When it emerged that Luther was not a man with whom a moderate Catholic such as Erasmus could do business, pressure grew on the latter to do something to distinguish his reform programme from the more radical German alternative. This Erasmus did in the shape of a major treatise entitled *Diatribe on Free Will*. What Erasmus did in this work was to put his finger on the hinge upon which Luther's whole theology of justification by faith turned: the idea that human beings are ultimately impotent to effect their own salvation and utterly dependent upon God even for the first motions of their will towards Him. To Erasmus, this was unbiblical and in clear contradiction to the church's teaching.

Luther replied with his massive work *On the Bondage of the Will*, which is at times a line-by-line refutation of Erasmus's treatise.[21] While thanking Erasmus for focusing on an issue of importance, rather than upon side issues such as the papacy, Luther proceeded to ridicule almost every statement Erasmus made on the issue. In opposition, Luther defended a vigorous doctrine of double predestination whereby God decided, on the basis of his omnipotence and omniscience, who went to heaven and who went to hell, arguing that this position was both biblical and the historic position of the church.

The debate might seem to many today to be somewhat obscure. Its importance, however, lay not so much in its content but in the fact that it destroyed once and for all any hope of reconciliation between reform-minded Catholics and Luther's followers. A line in the sand had been drawn which was to separate the two groups. Strange to tell, Luther's second-in-command, Melanchthon, was to argue for a doctrine of human ability very similar to Erasmus in the very near future without suffering the hot coals heaped on the Dutchman; but Melanchthon, of course, was on the right side.

The other major conflict of the 1520s was that with the Zurich reformer, Huldrych Zwingli.[22] Zwingli had developed a reform programme in his own city in independence, so he claimed, from events in Germany. His reform was marked by a more radical tinge, particularly in its dislike of images and any pomp in church ceremonies. There were similarities between Zwinglian reform and that of radicals such as Karlstadt, particularly in their shared iconoclasm and sacramentarian views. These similarities were not lost on Martin Luther and did not endear the Swiss Reformation to him.

During the late 1520s, Luther and Zwingli exchanged a number of polemical pamphlets on the issue of the eucharist.[23] The theological issues involved are quite complex but came down to a fairly straightforward point: was the physical human body and blood of Christ really present in the bread and wine or was it there only in a symbolic sense? Luther affirmed the former, Zwingli the latter. Without going into details, Luther regarded Zwingli's view as theologically and pastorally disastrous: God could only be approached through the humanity of Jesus; to try to approach him in any other way brought one into contact not with God's grace and mercy but God's wrath and judgement.

Politically, however, an alliance between reform movements in Germany and Switzerland would have proved very useful. Philip of Hesse, a convert to the Lutheran cause, regarded the continuation of Catholic territories in Germany, along with their continued affirmation of the Edict of Worms, as a permanent threat to the Protestants. After the Peasants' War, these Catholic powers had used the war as an excuse for wholesale butchering of Lutheran ministers. Thus anything that strengthened the hand of the Lutherans at home and abroad was to be welcomed.

With this in mind, he convened a meeting between Luther and his colleagues and Zwingli and the Swiss Reformers at the Castle of Marburg in 1529.[24] The aim was to produce a joint confessional document to which both sides could agree and which would then form the basis of a political alliance for mutual support. In the event, the debates were long and tortuous and achieved agreement on fourteen-and-a-half points out of fifteen. The point of disagreement was, inevitably, that dealing with the presence of Christ in the eucharist. It was only half a point, but it was enough to shipwreck any joint confession and any political alliance which this might have facilitated. Luther left the colloquy, declaring that Zwingli and his cohorts were of a different spirit to the Lutherans. In the event, the failure of the alliance was of more significance to Zwingli than to Luther, as the former was killed at the Battle of Kappel in 1531. Luther's laconic response upon hearing the news was simply to declare that those who live by the sword should expect to die by the sword.

THE AUGSBURG CONFESSION

With the possibility of an alliance with the Swiss now gone, the Lutherans were left to fend for themselves. The opportunity to put their case to the empire once again came in 1530 when Emperor Charles arrived in Germany and convened a diet at Augsburg. Luther himself was not permitted to attend and, for the second time in his life, was confined to a castle, Feste Coburg, for six months. His place at the diet was taken by his young deputy, Philip Melanchthon. Melanchthon, for all his devotion to Luther, still hoped for a reconciliation with the Catholic moderates, led at the diet by Albrecht, Archbishop of Mainz, and seized the opportunity with both hands. At Marburg, he had genuinely sought a compromise with the Reformed and this left Luther with some misgivings about his ability to hold the line in the face of Catholic pressure, but he need not have worried. The Augsburg Confession was a firmly Protestant document and a key moment in defining Protestantism. Again the eucharist proved a stumbling block to the Swiss, but a broad consensus of Lutheran opinion was achieved. Indeed, when the confession was made public on 25 June 1530, the battle-lines between the Lutherans and the Catholics, and the Lutheran princes and the Holy Roman Empire had been formally established. Reconciliation was now impossible and the Reformation in Germany was truly established.

With the production of the Augsburg Confession, Lutheranism now had a confessional theological identity which defined it over and against the two major alternatives, Roman Catholicism and the Reformed theology of the Swiss. In addition, it had by now established the basic trajectory of its political development. Lutheranism, like Luther himself, committed itself to a radical separation of the heavenly and earthly realms, a separation which in practice allowed great freedom to the political powers to do as they wished. It thus had the ideology to prove a most conducive religion to those territorial princes interested in using the Reformation as a means of sloughing off the imperial yoke while still holding the line against more radical political and theological forces. To this extent, the really significant work of Luther and his colleagues came to the end of its most important phase in 1530.

THE LAST YEARS

The last sixteen years of Luther's life, from the Augsburg Confession to his death in 1546, were not marked by the same frantic activity that had marked his life from 1517. The Lutheran church was now properly established and no longer depended upon him personally for its future. Nevertheless, while the time of theological and ecclesiastical creativity may now have been behind him, these last years witnessed a number of disappointments of great significance in the life of the reformer.

First, and most famous, was the bigamy of Landgrave Philip of Hesse. Married for reasons of political expediency to the daughter of Duke George at the age of nineteen, he had satisfied his sexual appetite by living a life of carefree promiscuity. Upon his conversion to the Lutheran cause, however, he had become haunted by guilt and thus sought a monogamous relationship which would enable him to gain some level of sexual self-control. Luther would countenance neither annulment nor divorce, but (on the basis of Old Testament precedents) allowed Philip to marry a second wife, while keeping this secret from the people as it was a clear contravention of the law of the land. The bride's mother, however, would not keep silent and Luther then advised that George should simply lie to save face. By this time it was too late, for the bigamy was already well known and none of the parties, including Luther, emerged with any credit. Politically, the incident was disastrous as well, as it led to Philip receiving a pardon from the emperor at the price of abandoning a military alliance with the Protestants.

Second, Luther's disappointment at the pace and shape of reform led to his writings becoming increasingly bitter in tone. The imagery in the pamphlets became more and more obscene and scatological,[25] and his attitude towards certain groups – Anabaptists, papists and most notoriously the Jews – hardened in a dramatic manner. In part, this was the result of the failure of the Reformation to make a significant impact on these groups. The Münster débâcle fixed Anabaptism in the

Figure 5.4 Burial sermon for Luther. From Rabus, *Historien*, 1557. (Wittenberg, Lutherhalle)

popular mind as a movement of anarchy, violence and excess; the resistance of the papacy to the Reformation gave it an eschatological role in the struggle of good versus evil; and the failure of the Jews to recognize the Messiah called forth from Luther one of his most distasteful and – from a post-Holocaust perspective – deeply disturbing tracts, *On the Jews and Their Lies* (1543), which argued for enforced deportation of Jews to Palestine or, failing that, their subjection to a kind of slave labour. For good measure, Luther also advocated the burning down of synagogues.[26]

In these later tracts we see the culmination of a lifetime of polemical overstatement. Luther knew the power of the presses and he knew that the Reformation would be won or lost on the basis of printed material. In using earthy images, he appealed over the heads of the elite to the masses who would respond to such language. Thus we see in these tracts against Jews, papists and Anabaptists, the logical conclusion of a Reformation driven at one level by the populist instincts of its leading personality. They also form a rather tasteless, though perhaps not inappropriate, endnote to a rather colourful theological career.

CONCLUSION

The impact of the life and thought of Luther on the Reformation in Germany and beyond can scarcely be underestimated. Theologically, he set the agenda for ecclesiastical debate for the middle decades of the sixteenth century. His break with Zwingli and his radical emphasis upon justification by faith both served as basic points of contention with the Reformed and the Roman Catholic churches respectively and helped to shape and define all three confessional traditions. Politically, it was Luther's reforming activities that provided the context and the opportunity for the German princes to break with Rome while maintaining territorial control over church affairs. If the Holy Roman Empire and the church structure to which it was inextricably linked would inevitably have been transformed in any case by the forces of social, economic and political change, there can be no doubt that the specific shape of those changes, and the language through which those changes were understood, owed a profound debt to the monk of Wittenberg.

NOTES

1 Erik H. Erikson, *Young Man Luther: A Study in Psychoanalysis and History* (New York, 1958).
2 For a good discussion of nominalism, see Heiko A. Oberman, *The Harvest of Medieval Theology* (Durham, 1983).
3 See Chapter 4.
4 For more on Biel, see Oberman, *Harvest*.
5 On Staupitz, see David C. Steinmetz, *Misericordia Dei: The Theology of Johannes von Staupitz in Its Late Medieval Setting* (Leiden, 1968); on his relationship with Luther, see Steinmetz, *Luther and Staupitz: An Essay in the Intellectual Origins of the Reformation* (Durham, 1980).
6 W. Pauck (ed. and trans.), *Lectures on Romans* (Philadelphia, 1961). These lectures lay unpublished until 1908, when their 'discovery' revolutionized the scholarly understanding of Luther's intellectual development: see the introduction to the Pauck translation.
7 For the text, see J. Pelikan and H.T. Lehmann (ed.), *Luther's Works* (Philadelphia and St Louis, 1955–86), vol. 31; hereafter *LW*.

8   For the text, see *LW*, vol. 31.
9   For the text, see *LW*, vol. 31.
10 For the text, see *LW*, vol. 31.
11 For the text, see *LW*, vol. 31.
12 John Wyclif (*c*.1329–84) was an English scholastic philosopher and theologian most famous for his rejection of the doctrine of transubstantiation in the mass. John Hus (*c*.1372–1415) was a Czech preacher much influenced by Wyclif's writings, particularly on predestination and ecclesiology. Wyclif's teachings were condemned at the Council of Constance, as was Hus, who was burned at the stake for (among other things) agreeing with Wyclif on the mass – ironically a point on which he actually dissented from the Englishman and remained orthodox.
13 For the text, see *LW*, vol. 44.
14 For the text, see *LW*, vol. 36.
15 For the text, see *LW*, vol. 31.
16 For the text, see *LW*, vol. 31.
17 For the text, see *LW*, vol. 32.
18 A good introductory biography of Melanchthon is that by Robert Stupperich, *Melanchthon* (London, 1966).
19 On Müntzer, see Tom Scott, *Thomas Müntzer: Theology and Revolution in the German Reformation* (London, 1989). Müntzer's works have been translated and edited by Peter Matheson, *The Collected Works of Thomas Müntzer* (Edinburgh, 1988).
20 See Chapter 8.
21 For the text, see *LW*, vol. 33.
22 On Zwingli's life, see G.R. Potter, *Zwingli* (Cambridge, 1976); on his theology, see W.P. Stephens, *The Theology of Huldrych Zwingli* (Oxford, 1986).
23 For the relevant Luther texts, see *LW*, vols 36–8. Various translations of works by Zwingli are available: see the bibliography in W.P. Stephens, *Zwingli: An Introduction to His Thought* (Oxford, 1992), pp. 149–50.
24 For various accounts of the colloquy, written from both Lutheran and Zwinglian standpoints, see *LW*, vol. 38.
25 On this issue, see Peter Matheson, *The Rhetoric of the Reformation* (Edinburgh, 1998).
26 For the text, see *LW*, vol. 47.

FURTHER READING

The most complete English edition of Luther's works, replete with good introductions to each text, is the Philadelphia Edition, edited by J. Pelikan and H.T. Lehmann (Philadelphia and St Louis, 1955–86). A good popular biography is that by Roland Bainton, *Here I Stand* (Tring, 1983). The standard scholarly biography is, and is likely to remain for the indefinite future, that by Martin Brecht, *Martin Luther* (trans. James L. Schaaf; 3 vols; Minneapolis, 1993). Studies of Luther's theology are plentiful. Among the most helpful introductions is still that of E.G. Rupp, *The Righteousness of God: Luther Studies* (London, 1968). For a more recent collection of essays on Luther's life and theology, see David C. Steinmetz, *Luther in Context* (Grand Rapids, 1995). On Luther's conflict with the Catholic church, see Scott H. Hendrix, *Luther and the Papacy* (Philadelphia, 1981); for a more detailed study of particular Catholic opponents, see D.V.N. Bagchi, *Luther's Earliest Opponents: Catholic Controversialists, 1518–25* (Minneapolis, 1991). One of the most radically psychological interpretations of Luther is that of Erik H. Erikson, *Young Man Luther: A Study in Psychoanalysis and History* (New York, 1958). Erikson's views, while influential outside the academic world in the presentation of Luther in the work of individuals such as the playwright John Osborne, have not enjoyed much popularity among scholars, although echoes of his approach are to be found in the creative study of Luther by Heiko A. Oberman, *Luther: Man Between God and Devil* (New Haven, 1989). Luther's impact on the wider sphere of German life, politics and culture has received extensive attention from scholars. In this context, it is worth consulting Mark U. Edwards, *Printing, Propaganda and Martin Luther* (Los Angeles, 1994) and Peter Matheson, *The Rhetoric of the Reformation* (Edinburgh, 1998). On the relationship between Luther, lay piety and the broader German culture, see R.W. Scribner, *Popular Culture and Popular Movements in Reformation Germany* (London, 1987).

LUTHER'S CATHOLIC OPPONENTS

David Bagchi

Successful as the early Lutheran movement was in capturing German hearts and minds, it is important to remember that many – perhaps the majority – proved resistant or hostile to its message. This negative reaction can be attributed in some cases to an apathy towards matters seemingly remote from the concerns of day-to-day survival or in others to an unthinking conservatism, a desire to keep a hold of Mother Church for fear of finding something worse. But what might have been the considered grounds for opposing the gospel according to Luther? The official Catholic response gives few clues. The papal bull *Exsurge Domine* lists forty-one statements taken from Luther's writings that were to be regarded as 'variously heretical, scandalous, false, offensive to pious ears, misleading of simple minds, or contrary to Catholic truth'. But the bull does not indicate which statements were heretical and which merely offensive, nor does it explain in what way each statement departed from Catholic truth. It established the fact but not the degree of Luther's error.

The best evidence we have for identifying the limits of the appeal of evangelical teaching comes from a group of Catholic writers – usually referred to as the Catholic controversialists – who used the press to put forward the Catholic case in much the same way as the reformers did theirs. The most intense period of their activity was during the so-called 'pamphlet war' of 1520–5, when each side bombarded the other with cheap, mass-produced works of religious propaganda. About sixty Catholic writers were involved in this campaign and between them they produced over 200 books and pamphlets against the Reformation, mainly against Luther. The purpose of this chapter is to provide a brief introduction to the personalities involved, to some of the problems they faced in using the printing press to defend the Catholic cause and to the leading ideas that determined their opposition to Luther.

THE CATHOLIC CONTROVERSIALISTS

Neither Protestant nor Catholic historians have generally had much good to say about the controversialists. Protestants have criticized their favoured tactic of appealing to the tradition and customs of the church as begging the question. For

Catholics, the fact that the controversialists took it upon themselves to defend the faith and therefore spoke without the authority of Rome lessens the value of their achievements. This largely negative evaluation has resulted in the caricature of the typical controversialist one frequently encounters: a man much older than Luther, a monk and most probably a Dominican, a scholastic theologian and a knee-jerk reactionary prepared to condemn Luther without waiting to see what he had to say. As with all caricatures, this picture contains a germ of truth. Silvestro Mazzolini da Prierio, or Prierias, the curial theologian who was appointed to judge Luther's case but who nonetheless took the opportunity to 'descend into the arena in single combat' with him, seems to fit it exactly. But in all its main features the caricature is misleading. Take for instance the highly influential misconception illustrated by the following quotation:

> In 1517, Luther was thirty-four. Most of his followers were thirty years old or younger. ... Most of Luther's opponents were fifty years old or older. Erasmus was just under fifty, and Dr Johannes Eck, a major opponent, was a bit younger [than Luther]. But otherwise all of his opponents were much older men.[1]

If, however, we take just those opponents of Luther active before 1525, we find that (of the thirty or so whose dates of birth are known to us) less than a quarter were fifty or older in 1517, while about half were either younger than Luther or, like him, they were still in their thirties.[2] And after 1525, Luther would have found his opponents becoming, like policemen, younger by the year. In suggesting that Luther's opponents were much older than him and his supporters, historians have given the impression that the intellectual opposition to Luther came from ineffectual churchmen and academics left over from the last century. This view overlooks the strength and depth of the opposition he had to face from his own generation. But it also overlooks the important point that these older men often wielded considerable personal authority and so were more, not less, formidable opponents. It also does an injustice to someone like Cardinal Cajetan, who could easily be pigeonholed alongside Prierias as an older man, a Dominican, a Thomist and an Italian with a strong disdain for the barbaric Germans. Yet for all his peremptory treatment of Luther at the Diet of Augsburg, he shared many of Luther's own objections to indulgences. At the same time as Luther was writing the Ninety-Five Theses, Cajetan was in Rome preparing a private memorandum on the theology of indulgences along remarkably similar lines. A year later, in November 1518, Cajetan was responsible for drafting the famous bull *Cum postquam*. This bull goes so far towards answering Luther's original objections that, had it been published thirteen months earlier, Luther would not have posted his theses.

We should not assume either that Luther's opponents were all dyed-in-the-wool adherents of scholastic theology. It is true that, of the Catholic authors who wrote against Luther before 1526 for whom we have appropriate information, nineteen had received an exclusively scholastic training. But against them there were twelve pure humanists and a further five belonging to the hybrid category of 'scholastic humanists'. One was Johann Eck, who gave Luther a famous mauling at the Leipzig disputation. He could boast that his training had encompassed not only both the scholastic *viae* but also the New Learning: 'I should be thought of as a bat, for I am neither a mouse nor a bird.'[3] In short, Luther had ranged against him as many conservative opponents with some background in humanism as there were schoolmen. It meant that Luther could not rely on the automatic support of humanists for his cause and it may be the reason why, after 1519, he dropped the humanist affectation of græcizing his name as 'Eleutherius'. It meant also that his opponents could not be dismissed as time-servers and placemen totally uninterested in church reform, when such ruthless critics of ecclesiastical abuses as Thomas Murner — the imperial poet laureate — and of course Erasmus himself threw their weight so decisively against him.

Finally, we should not think of the conservative opposition to Luther as predominantly Dominican or even predominantly monastic. Of the fifty-seven controversialists who wrote against Luther during the pamphlet war, only twelve were members of the Dominican order. It is true that the Dominicans (who had a customary obligation to root out heresy) vastly outnumbered their fellow-religious: the Franciscans, in second place, had only five. But the Franciscans actually out-published the Dominicans, so that even here the Dominican contribution is easily exaggerated. Moreover, the strong Franciscan contribution guaranteed that at least some of Luther's opponents were supporters of a more or less muted conciliarism (notably Murner, Augustinus von Alveld and Kaspar Schatzgeyer) and that Luther encountered a defence of traditional religion based exclusively on scripture. Schatzgeyer in particular is well worth reading as one of the few Catholics who tried to develop a genuinely biblical theology, rather than simply mining scripture for proof-texts wrenched out of context. It should, however, be noted that by far the greatest contribution to the Catholic literary cause came not from monks or friars but from the ranks of the secular clergy: men like Eck, Johann Cochlaeus, Johann Dietenberger and Hieronymus Emser. The opposition which Luther faced was younger, more vigorous, in many ways more thoughtful and certainly more formidable than is generally conceded.

INTERNAL AND EXTERNAL CONSTRAINTS ON THE CATHOLIC RESPONSE

The existence of a large and capable body of Catholic theologians, ready to wield the pen in defence of their faith, was not enough to ensure victory. At the height of the pamphlet war in Germany, between 1520 and 1525, evangelical books and pamphlets consistently outnumbered the Catholic by five or six to one. Luther alone published twice as much as all his Catholic opponents put together during this period: in statistical terms, it was more of a rout than a war.

This imbalance is problematic, given that there were at least as many talented Catholic writers as there were Protestant, and no shortage of Catholic humanists with access to humanist presses and distribution networks. Part of the reason was that most of the Catholic controversialists, some thirty of the first fifty-seven, wrote just once and never re-entered the lists. Another was that the Catholics

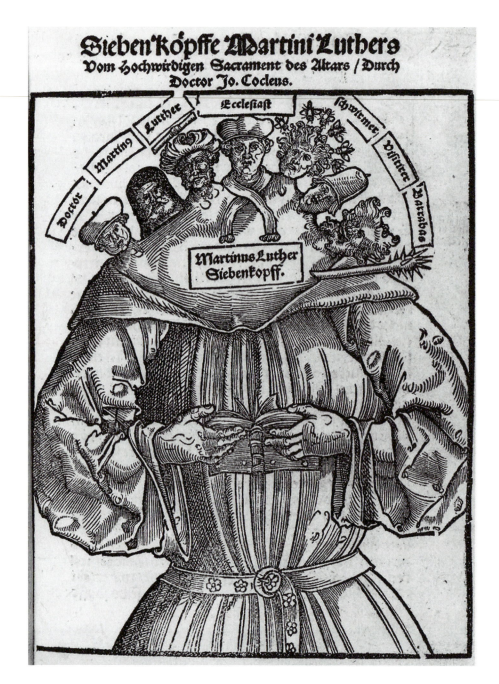

Figure 6.1 Cochlæus, *Luther as a Seven-Headed Monster*, 1552. The controversialists quarried Luther's voluminous writings for contradictions and inconsistencies. This woodcut illustrated Luther's readiness to speak differently according to the hat, or even the head, he happened to be wearing at the time. (London, British Library)

adopted a deliberately non-popular and inaccessible style, which had a predictable impact on sales. Their pamphlets tended to be longer than evangelical ones, were often written in a heavy, academic style, and were more often than not in Latin. Although the 'techno-fear' which had accompanied the spread of printing in the fifteenth century had by now largely died out, few Catholics were entirely happy with using the press for the purpose of religious controversy. First, they were acutely conscious of the danger of discussing theological matters in public. It implied that the public had the right to decide for itself between competing view-points, when the ultimate authority in such matters was the church's *magisterium*. On the other hand, if they addressed their works to Luther himself rather than the general public, there was the danger of appearing to be disputing with a heretic. It had been an important principle at least since the time of Tertullian that the church should never argue with those who have shown themselves to be heretics, because heretics are inspired by the Devil and deaf to reasoned argument. To dispute with them implies that the truth is open to negotiation and again the authority of the church is lessened. Second, the authoritative condemnations of Luther (namely, the judgements against him published by the universities of Louvain, Cologne and Paris in 1519, as well as *Exsurge Domine* itself in 1520) posed a problem already mentioned. Because these condemnations simply listed propositions taken out of Luther's writings and baldly declared them to be in error, there would be (as some controversialists pointed out) many intelligent readers who would find themselves unable to accept the condemnations as valid unless the reasons were also given and, once again, the church's authority would suffer. So Jacobus Latomus of Louvain and Jodocus Clichtoves of the Sorbonne, amongst others, saw their work as commentaries on these official condemnations. But this involved another danger, which Eck, for instance, appreciated: to provide an explanation of an authoritative judgement suggests that that judgement is inadequate by itself. The contentious are given something to argue about and again the church's *magisterium* is brought into doubt.

This minefield of potential dangers made the Catholic use of the press against Luther a hazardous enterprise and perhaps it is not surprising that most of his opponents wrote only one book against him. It also made the Catholic authors extremely suspect in the eyes of the Roman curia. The controversialists bombarded Rome with requests for financial help towards the cost of publishing, secretarial assistance, access to better libraries and postings to sinecures to enable them to refute Protestants at leisure. But these requests fell largely on deaf ears. One reason why the controversialists were so often disappointed was, ironically, the abuses inherent in the system they defended. Eck complains in his private letters of being cheated of lucrative canonries in the pope's gift by rivals worse qualified in all but birth. Even Lutheran lay noblemen, he claimed, were preferred to him! One sympathizes with his protest that the man who at Leipzig had done so much to defend the papacy was now rejected by it. Eck's fellow-labourer (and occasional rival for these posts) Johann Cochlaeus was moved by repeated disappointment to warn the German nuncio, Cardinal Aleander, that he would defect to Wittenberg unless he were paid immediately. But more significant was Aleander's response, which represents the official Roman view that the Reformation was a political, not a theological, problem: 'The cause of the revolution in Germany is something other than the sacraments', he replied. 'Disputations solve nothing'.[4] He even went so far as to say that if Eck had not disputed with Luther at Leipzig, the Luther affair would simply have fizzled out through lack of interest. This is revealing, because it shows that members of the curia actually held the controversialists partly to blame for the spread of the Reformation by supplying it with the oxygen of publicity.

The controversialists were not entirely without friends in high places. Pope Adrian VI took them seriously and consulted them extensively. But Adrian was a reforming pope and, like other reforming popes of more recent memory, he died an untimely death, after reigning only a matter of months. Much more forthcoming were secular rulers. Duke George of Saxony was an outstanding patron. He made sure that when benefices in his lands fell vacant they went to controversialists and he ensured that his printers handled only Catholic propaganda, even though (as they complained) it was bad for business. George turned his own hand to writing against the Reformation in prose and verse. But the most illustrious princely controversialist was of course King Henry VIII of England, who entered the lists against Luther with his own *Defence of the Seven Sacraments* (1521), for which he was awarded the papal title *fidei defensor*. In addition, Henry mobilized his own subjects such as Thomas More, John Fisher and Edward Powell to write as part of a vigorous anti-Lutheran campaign and entertained such polemicists from abroad as Thomas Murner and Johann Eck. But such princes were few, their support fitful and they hardly compensated for the lack of a centralized 'office of propaganda' such as the curia was uniquely able to provide. The isolation the Catholic controversialists experienced as a result is typified by the case of Georg Witzel. Witzel threw in his lot with Lutheranism at an early stage, but then converted back to Catholicism when he discovered that the morals of Protestants were no better that those of the church he had left. He spent the rest of his life despised and distrusted by both sides, harried from pillar to post together with the wife and family he had acquired as a Lutheran pastor, while writing discerning critiques of Lutheranism as one who knew it from the inside.

THE MESSAGE OF THE CONTROVERSIALISTS

Despite the internal and external constraints which exercised the controversialists, a literary response to Luther was nonetheless mounted by them, and what they each regarded as the Catholic case put forward. Since the response was a reactive one, the most effective way of summarizing their message is by reference to those aspects of Luther's teaching to which they most strongly objected. These can be considered in chronological order.

A feature of Luther's early writings (i.e. before the Peasants' War of 1525) was his concern for the laity, particularly where he thought pastoral care was deficient. This concern emerged as early as the Ninety-Five Theses of 1517, when he listed the sort of aspects of indulgences which might worry ordinary people who thought about their faith. It alarmed those Catholics who responded to the theses. To permit the doubts of ordinary Christians to govern the theological agenda was for

wie dem luther sein leib fal mit
einem katzen geschrei begangen würt.

Es luthers leren zögt mir an
Wie das die meß kein frucht sol han
In dem dot vnd in dem leben

Figure 6.2 Murner, *The Great Lutheran Fool*, 1522. In this brilliant verse satire Murner, ridiculed in print as the tonsured cat 'Murmaw', turned the tables on his Lutheran opponents. Here the Franciscan cat reads a requiem for Luther as he is interred in a privy. (London, British Library)

them a short step from anarchy and mob violence. When Luther demanded, in his ninetieth thesis, that the Church use reason with the laity rather than brute force, Eck replied: 'In that case, the clergy could scarcely be defended from the insults of the laity, let alone from their swords.'[5] Eck was not unusual in holding this view. It was common enough in the Middle Ages and the early modern period to regard civilization as only a veneer, beneath which violence and anarchy lay ever ready for an opportunity to erupt.

The most systematic refutation of Luther's ideas on the theological competence of the laity came from John Fisher, Bishop of Rochester and Chancellor of Cambridge University. In his defence of King Henry's book, he argued that the laity have a very limited role in respect of the church's teaching: they have the right to agree, but not the right to disagree or the right to judge. The controversialists were particularly dismissive of lay people, such as Melanchthon, who had pretensions to theological learning. Johann Dietenberger called them 'the striped laity' – neither laity nor clergy. But it is significant that a social distinction was made even here: lay people were allowed a theological competence, provided that they were monarchs. The literary interventions of King Henry of England and Duke George of Saxony were therefore regarded not as unwarranted lay intrusion, but as the continuation of a benign tradition in the church of royal defences of true doctrine, begun by Emperor Constantine at Nicaea and maintained by Emperor Sigismund at Constance.

Central to Luther's teaching was his belief that, through faith in God's promises, which are not vague intentions but concrete assurances *pro nobis*, believers could be certain of their salvation. This notion seemed highly presumptuous to his Catholic opponents, who held to the mediæval belief that the soul was a traveller on a journey, never sure of getting to its destination until it arrived. The uncertainty of salvation was important to them because it reinforced the necessity of using the church's sacramental machinery. When Luther appeared before Cardinal Cajetan in 1518, he was accused of trying to 'build a new Church' with his revolutionary ideas on assurance. Prierias defended indulgences as a necessary insurance policy precisely because one cannot be sure that divine forgiveness follows priestly absolution.

A third area of disagreement centred on Luther's belief that Christ's death on the cross atoned for all the sins of all people. Mediæval theology held that, at baptism the merits of the Cross dealt with original sin and with any actual sins committed up to the time of baptism. Post-baptismal sins had to be dealt with primarily by one's own acts of penance, though God in his mercy would release some of Christ's merit to compensate for sins genuinely overlooked in the confessional or in cases where the priest had imposed too light a penance. Luther, on the contrary, believed that the merits of Christ's death are continually available to the believer through faith, without need of the sacrament of penance (though that sacrament might be psychologically necessary to a bruised conscience). The grace of baptism is never lost or exhausted, because God's grace is inexhaustible. Luther's Catholic opponents were united in their opposition to Luther on this issue. They held to a belief in the 'treasury of merits', the mediæval idea that the Cross of Christ had generated an infinite amount of merit, of which only a little was needed to atone for people's original sin. An infinity of merit still remained, to which was added the great merits of the Blessed Virgin Mary and the other saints. The contents of this store of grace could be dispensed to the faithful, though only for good cause, through the pope's power of the keys (Matthew 16:19), which was delegated to individual priests.

It was apparent that Luther and his opponents operated with incompatible understandings of grace. Luther saw God's grace as the attitude by which God wills to save people. This had much in common with the doctrine of divine acceptation held by Duns Scotus, by which our works have value in God's sight not because of any intrinsic merit, but because God has decided to accept them. Luther took this Scotist belief a stage further with his belief that God can accept us as righteous without any merit on our part. This idea of grace-as-attitude contrasted strongly with the controversialists' Thomist view of grace as a sort of highly rarefied substance which could be stored away in the treasury of merits, added to or subtracted from, applied to people or withheld from them.

The most important implication of this understanding of grace as a physical entity was that God could not give it freely. Although the entire system of divine grace and human cooperation was itself the result of God's gratuitous love, within that system no grace could be dispensed from the treasury without some good cause, some earnest (however small and inadequate) of our intentions in the form of an act of love on our part. Luther's idea that God's grace is given freely (echoing Augustine's dictum that grace is not grace unless it is gratuitous) was foreign to this idea.

Luther's appeal to the normative role of scripture was one of the most important platforms of his – and of the other reformers' – programme. Luther's use of scripture differed, however, from that of his fellow reformers in that he made a qualitative distinction between different books of the Bible. This distinction was based on his division of the Word of God into 'law' and 'gospel': those parts of the Bible which spoke of gospel were more to be valued than those which spoke of law. So he rated John's gospel above the synoptics and the letters of St Paul (especially Romans, Galatians and Ephesians) above the letter of St James, which he once described as 'an epistle of straw' in comparison, 'for it has nothing of the nature of the Gospel about it'.

Luther's Catholic opponents were understandably astonished that he could take such a high-handed attitude to the canon, accepting and rejecting what pleased him. They were equally astonished that he could set scripture up as a norm, separate from and contrary to the other sources of authority accepted by the church – conciliar and papal decrees in canon law, the writings of the early fathers, the writings of the scholastics and custom. It was illogical, they argued, to accept the authority of the New Testament but not the authority of the church which had formed it, or to honour the apostolic fathers who wrote the New Testament but not the later fathers, or to honour the later fathers but not the schoolmen. All these authorities were members of the same church to which Christ had promised the Holy Spirit to lead it into all truth.

Luther's opponents therefore adopted two strategies in arguing against him. The first (followed by Schatzgeyer and Dietenberger) was to show that Luther could be refuted in his own terms, by scripture alone. The second, adopted by the majority of controversialists (including, interestingly enough, the English Catholic writers: King Henry, Thomas More, John Fisher, Edward Powell), was to argue that scripture represented only part of God's revelation and that one needed to listen to the tradition of the church as well. While Luther made a qualitative distinction between authorities based on proximity to the gospel, the Catholics were more interested in the quantity of authorities, on the principle of the more witnesses the better. Their attitude to custom is also interesting. Against the objection of Luther and his colleagues that many of the church's practices were of recent invention and not hallowed by antiquity, a Catholic like Henry could argue that the Spirit, as well as blowing where it wills, also blows when it wills, so a thing is no less true and good just because it is recent.[6] This belief in the providential guidance of the church by the Holy Spirit was so strong that many Catholic controversialists believed – or at least this is the implication of their anti-Lutheran arguments – that whatever the church does is therefore right and that even abuses of recent invention could be defended as customary. The most vehement assertions of this principle came from the pen of Thomas More, which perhaps conflicts with the received image of him as one of the more humane and self-critical of Roman loyalists.

The most famous aspect of Luther's teaching was of course his proclamation of justification by grace through faith alone. The astonishing thing about the early Catholic response to the Reformation was that this doctrine simply did not figure at all prominently in the controversy. The reason was (and this is a point that has been made many times by Roman Catholic historians, but which Protestant historians tend to ignore) that justification by grace through faith was a highly traditional teaching, which no one in the sixteenth century could actually deny. Yet if this doctrine were made central to Christianity, as it was by Luther, the external means of salvation (the church itself, the elaborate sacramental system and the priesthood) might become marginal to the Christian life. The tactic adopted by the controversialists was to concede the truth of the doctrine while warning of the consequences of disseminating it abroad. Thus Johann Eck claimed that he fully accepted justification by faith alone, but had to oppose it because he thought that the common people would take it as an excuse for immorality.[7] Erasmus went so far as to say that he would defend Catholic penitential teaching, even if he did not believe himself, because it helped to keep the people in order.[8] Even the controversialist who prompted Luther to pen his most scholarly exposition of justification by faith alone, Jacobus Latomus, argued only that this doctrine was heretical 'in the sense which Luther uses and expounds', that is, with apparent prejudice to morality.[9] Even King Henry joins in the chorus: 'I do not object to the fact that Luther attributes so much to faith, so long as he does not use it to defend evil lives.'[10]

The thread which connects these several objections is the conviction that Lutheranism was inherently subversive of authority, both ecclesiastical (in terms of the sacramental system, for instance) and social (in terms of private morality and public order). This tactic undoubtedly served a rhetorical purpose, for it would have encouraged secular authorities to believe it to be in their interests to suppress

Lutheran preaching. But there are good reasons for supposing that a belief in order, both as the means by which God communicates His saving will to the world and as the means by which He is in the process of saving it, was fundamental to the controversialists' world-view. The theme of the hierarchical ordering of heaven, of earth and of the church recurs throughout their writings. Whether the origin of this concern lay in the demands of rhetoric or whether it was implicit in their spirituality, it enabled the controversialists to equate evangelicalism and social disorder, and to predict that Luther's gospel would inevitably usher in the tumult of the Peasants' War.

NOTES

1 Lewis W. Spitz, 'Luther and Humanism', in Marilyn J. Harran (ed.), *Luther and Learning* (Selinsgrove, 1985), p. 70.
2 The following figures for controversialists active between 1517 and 1525 are based on research carried out for my study *Luther's Earliest Opponents*, but not presented there. The right-hand column shows that the younger writers were also more productive.

Date of birth	No. of writers in each age group	Total no. of titles attributable to writers in each age group
before 1467	7	11
1467–72	7	10
1473–77	4	24
1478–83	7	47
after 1483	6	19

3 Cited in E. Iserloh, *Johannes Eck, 1486–1543: Scholastiker, Humanist, Kontroverstheologe* (Katholisches Leben und Kirchenreform 41; Münster, 1981), p. 14.
4 W. Friedensburg, 'Beiträge zum Briefwechsel der katholischen Gelehrten Deutschlands im Reformationszeitalter (aus italienischen Archiven und Bibliotheken)', *Zeitschrift für Kirchengeschichte* 18 (1898), p. 120, n. 6. The correspondence edited by Friedensburg gives a lively picture of the problems faced by the German controversialists at home and abroad.
5 Johann Eck, *Obelisci Eckii* 29, in *WA*, vol. 1, pp. 312f.
6 King Henry VIII, *Assertio septem sacramentorum adversus Martinum Lutherum*, ed. P. Fraenkel (Corpus Catholicorum 43; Münster, 1992), p. 143.
7 Cited in E. Iserloh (ed.), *Katholische Theologen der Reformationszeit* (Münster, 1984), vol. 1, p. 70.
8 E.G. Rupp and P.S. Watson (eds), *Luther and Erasmus: Free Will and Salvation* (London, 1969), p. 40.
9 Latomus, *De ecclesia* (1525), in *Opera omnia* (Louvain, 1579), p. 87v.
10 Henry, *Assertio*, p. 169.

FURTHER READING

Most scholarship on this subject is in German. In English, the most comprehensive work is D.V.N. Bagchi, *Luther's Earliest Opponents: Catholic Controversialists, 1518–25* (Minneapolis, 1991), which contains extensive bibliographies. Further useful statistics and observations relating to Catholic pamphlets can be found in M.U. Edwards, Jr, *Printing, Propaganda and Martin Luther* (Berkeley, 1994), Chapters 1, 3 and 7. B. Gogan, *The Common Corps of Christendom: Ecclesiological Themes in the Writings of Sir Thomas More* (Leiden, 1982), and R.A.W. Rex, *The Theology of John Fisher* (Cambridge, 1991), are unrivalled in the insights they provide into the theology of the most famous English controversialists, while H.J. McSorley, *Luther: Right or Wrong?* (Minneapolis, 1969), and M. O'Rourke Boyle, *Rhetoric and Reform: Erasmus's Civil Dispute with Luther* (Harvard, 1983), are invaluable on Erasmus as theologian and as polemicist respectively. More recently, there has been a trend towards setting the polemical output of the controversialists in the context of their wider achievements. See especially M. Samuel-Scheyder, *Johannes Cochlaeus: Humaniste et adversaire de Luther* (Nancy, 1993), and M. Tavuzzi, *Prierias: The Life and Works of Silvestro Mazzolini da Prierio, 1456–1527* (Durham, NC, 1997). For an easily accessible example of Catholic controversial prose, see Sir Thomas More's *Responsio ad Lutherum*, translated into English and furnished with much helpful apparatus in J.M. Headley (ed.), *The Complete Works of St Thomas More* (New Haven, 1967), vol. 5.

BOOKS, PAMPHLETS AND POLEMIC

Andrew Pettegree

BOOKS AND PUBLIC DEBATE BEFORE THE REFORMATION

The Reformation did not create the book industry. Even before the invention of moveable type in the mid-fifteenth century, the later Middle Ages had witnessed the growth of a lively book trade. By the fifteenth century the hunger for texts was such that many works were being replicated in hundreds of manuscript copies: it is almost possible to speak of a fully developed market in manuscript books. Originally organized in the scriptoria of Europe's monastic houses, this copying trade had by the fifteenth century also moved into the cities, fuelled by the educational revolution of the later Middle Ages and the consequent demand for texts among Europe's increasingly numerous lay readers. The survival today of more than 800 manuscript copies of one such text, the devotional classic *The Imitation of Christ*, attests to the size and buoyancy of this market.[1] And it is worth pointing out that, even after the invention of printing, the manuscript continued to play an important role as a vehicle for religious debate, especially among more intimate circles. Indeed, there is some indication that participants in religious controversies regarded the manuscript in precisely this light, as an opportunity for franker exchanges than would be appropriate in the medium of print. It is no surprise that among the first group of texts censored by the conservative theology faculty of the University of Paris in the 1540s, half the texts named were manuscripts rather than books.[2]

Nevertheless, it is undeniable that the invention of moveable type opened up new possibilities for bringing texts to a wider public. The rapidity with which the new invention spread after its development in Mainz and Strasbourg around 1450 attests to the speed with which contemporaries grasped the potential of the new medium. The growth of printing fed off the huge demand for reliable editions of standard school texts and for those texts newly popularized by the growth of humanism. Its success was also intimately connected with the growth of universities and of lay literacy in precisely this period. Soon a printing press seemed as indispensable to a lively urban community as the local Latin school. Thus the new technology, almost ruinously expensive to the first generation of pioneers, spread with astonishing rapidity. By 1470, printing had been established in at least thirty cities. Twenty years later, there were presses in over 100 locations and certain

European cities, such as Venice, Paris, Rome and Antwerp, had already established a reputation as major centres of book production.

By this time the book, so recently the most experimental of technologies, was also attaining its mature form. Certain basic techniques and practices, such as the practice of marking up individual gatherings of leaves to aid correct ordering of the finished artifact and the publication of the printer's address on the title-page or at the end of the book (colophon), had become generalized through the industry. In the larger better-financed houses, printers had successfully experimented with the use of more sophisticated specialized types such as Hebrew and Greek fonts. The initial slavish imitation of the appearance of manuscript through a uniform body of text in one font size had given way to more ambitious compositions, using varying types, marginalia, decorative initial letters and, in the most sophisticated books, woodcut text illustrations. As the publishing industry became established in this way, there sprang up around it a range of associated specialist trades: the bookbinder, type-founder and merchants who specialized exclusively in the distribution and sale of books. The vastly increased demand for paper had spawned a huge increase in the number and quality of local paper mills. Most of all, printers had by now mastered the techniques for producing reliable texts at relatively modest prices and this in turn had begun to transform the market for books. Books now seemed less wholly elite objects. Though they remained outside the reach of more plebeian households, in the houses of the upper strata of urban society it was possible to consider a book as a casual purchase rather than merely a professional tool. With this the book entered a new age as a potential weapon in public controversies. Even before Luther, the book had demonstrated its capacity to spread local intellectual debates across international boundaries. It had also demonstrated that, in the hands of able publicists, fortunes were to be made in the new art, whether by authors, such as Erasmus, or the respectable scholar-publishers like Johann Froben of Basle, whose output fed the apparently insatiable demand for the new texts.

THE REFORMATION DEBATES

All of the above is not to deny that the controversies unleashed by Luther had a transforming effect on the European book trade and indeed on the book itself. From the time that Luther's Ninety-Five Theses against Indulgences were first published (in nearby Leipzig, but then swiftly reprinted in Augsburg and Basle), the debates surrounding Luther and his developing criticisms of the church unleashed a flood of printed books, which reached a crescendo in the period 1521–5. The bare statistics of this publishing explosion tell their own story. Between 1500 and 1530, over 10,000 pamphlets were published in Germany (in itself a remarkable volume of works). Three quarters of these were published in the seven years between 1520 and 1526.

In this explosion of book publishing it is impossible to deny the leading role of Martin Luther. In the first years of the Reformation Luther revealed himself to be a publicist of genius. Indeed, one can argue that his radical decision to publish his sermon on indulgences in German in 1518, and thus address a new audience beyond that naturally concerned in scholarly theological debate, was the event that really ignited the Reformation. In the next ten years Luther would totally domi-nate book production in Germany, with a flood of sermons, polemical defences and devotional works all issuing from his pen. Luther developed to an astonishing extent the ability to write in different voices to reach different audiences. In print at least, there was a Luther for every situation and taste. Between 1518 and 1544 he oversaw the publication of a massive 2,550 editions of his German works (not including his German Bible): this was more than the combined output of the seventeen next most important evangelical publicists and five times as many as all of his Catholic opponents. It is hardly any wonder that, in this first generation at least, the Reformation and the book seemed to be so intimately connected.

In the process, the Reformation transformed the book. During the period when it was in effect commandeered for the Reformation controversies, the book changed both its physical appearance and its audience. Books became shorter. Fifty per cent of the pamphlets published in this period were no longer than sixteen pages, that is two sheets in printing terms. The German *Flugschriften* were charac-teristically small quarto works of fewer than thirty pages of text. This period also witnessed a significant, perhaps decisive, shift from publication in Latin to the vernacular: a shift, in effect, from the book as the property of the scholarly elite to a wider educated public.

In recent scholarship there has been a tendency to play down the importance of the book in spreading the evangelical message. In an age when literacy seldom reached 20 per cent of the population, could a textual medium ultimately have played a decisive role in the promulgation of new doctrines? This scepticism can be attributed partly to a laudable desire to probe other methods of dissemination (for instance the sermon, and oral culture more generally) and partly to the shifts of historical fashion: the association of books and Reformation has become such a cliché that it almost demands re-examination. But if we allow ourselves to be guided by contemporary observers of the Reformation controversies, it is clear that they quickly came to discern the power of the book. The effectiveness of the printed medium as a vehicle both for theological controversies and wider social criticism was recognized on all sides, even by Luther's Catholic opponents as they struggled to find an effective response to the barrage of printed criticism. Finally, the sheer scale of the publishing achievement is itself eloquent testimony to the power of the new medium. It is estimated that by 1530 there were some six million *Flugscriften* in circulation in German: that is, twenty for each literate member of the population. Even the most elaborate and expensive product of evangelical publishing, the German Bible, sold in quite phenomenal amounts.

PUBLISHING IN WITTENBERG

Not the least significant aspect of this phenomenal growth in the book trade was that many people made a great deal of money. The printers of Wittenberg had particular reason to bless their most famous inhabitant; indeed, Wittenberg is a classic example of an economy transformed by a single trade, in this case books and the education industry.

Around 1500 Wittenberg was still a sleepy backwater of about 2,000 inhabitants. The foundation of a university (and with it a printing press) in 1502 was part of a conscious effort by the ambitious Frederick the Wise to give his electoral capital a higher profile, although until Luther made Wittenberg famous this could hardly be said to have succeeded. Before the Reformation the small local market for books was easily served by one printer and this early Wittenberg work was often of uncertain quality; this explains Luther's decision to have many of his first tracts printed in Leipzig. In 1519 the exasperated regents of the university, seconded by Luther, appealed to the elector to establish a more competent printer in the town. The problem was solved by the huge demand for Luther's book. Between 1521 and 1529, nine new printers established businesses in the town, including such well-known industry figures as Melchior Lotter, Hans Lufft and Georg Rhau.

These men knew that there were huge profits to be made in publishing Luther, though not without risk. Projects such as Luther's German Bible required a large investment which, even with the near certainty of a large return, was beyond the means of small printers. If one assumes an average edition size of 3,000 for such a work, the production of a folio Bible would completely occupy two printing presses for up to four months: a heavy prior investment in wages, plant and (particularly) paper before any return could be expected. Such consideration encouraged the formation of publishing syndicates, sometimes involving merchants and investors not otherwise concerned with the publishing industry. In 1533 rights to publish Luther's Bible in Wittenberg were passed to such a syndicate.

Evangelical publishing could be a cut-throat business. Melchior Lotter, who produced some of the finest early editions of Luther's works, was effectively ruined when Luther withdrew his patronage after Lotter had been convicted of assaulting a bookbinder. With none of Luther's works to publish, Lotter abandoned Wittenberg within a year. Nothing illustrates the nature of this competition better than the brief publishing career of Lucas Cranach, best known as the distinguished Reformation painter (see Chapter 25). Cranach in fact pursued a number of lucrative business ventures, so it was no surprise that the buoyant market for books should tempt him to try his hand at printing. Between 1523 and 1525 Cranach and a partner published a substantial number of Wittenberg Luther editions, including (to the irritation of their dispossessed competitors) a high proportion of first editions of new writings, inevitably the most profitable. But by 1525 the market was overheated and Cranach decided to cease printing – in any case he could continue to profit from the book trade through his near monopoly of the supply of woodcuts from his artist's workshop (see Figures 7.1 and 7.2).

For those without Cranach's connections the printing trade could be perilous and several of the most famous names in Wittenberg printing ran into financial difficulties later in life. Particularly resented were unauthorized reprints of Wittenberg works published outside the city. For while the frequent reprints of Wittenberg works published during these years at Leipzig, Erfurt, Augsburg, Nuremberg or Strasbourg undoubtedly assisted the spread of the new teachings, they also cut into profits. Luther himself was aware of this and did his best to protect his printers from the erosion of their market.

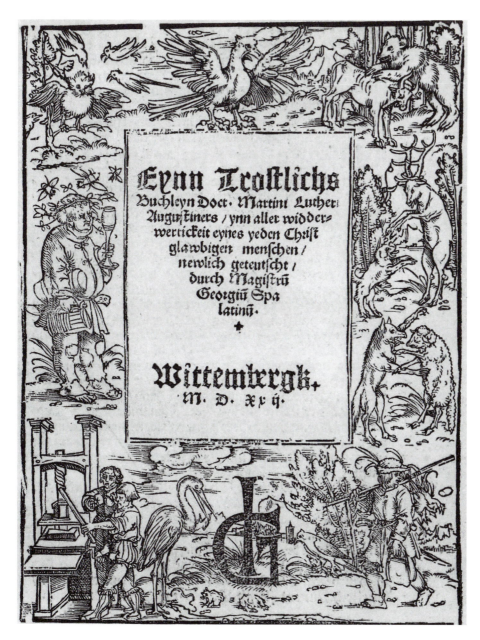

Figure 7.1 Title-page woodcut with Renaissance border from the Cranach workshop for Martin Luther, *Trostliche Buchleyn*, 1522. (Wittenberg, Lutherhalle)

Figure 7.2 Title-page woodcut with Conversion of St Paul for Martin Luther, *Auslegung der Episteln und Evangelien vom Advent an bis auff Ostern*, 1528. A fine example of the more explicitly evangelical work of the developing Cranach workshop. (Wittenberg, Lutherhalle)

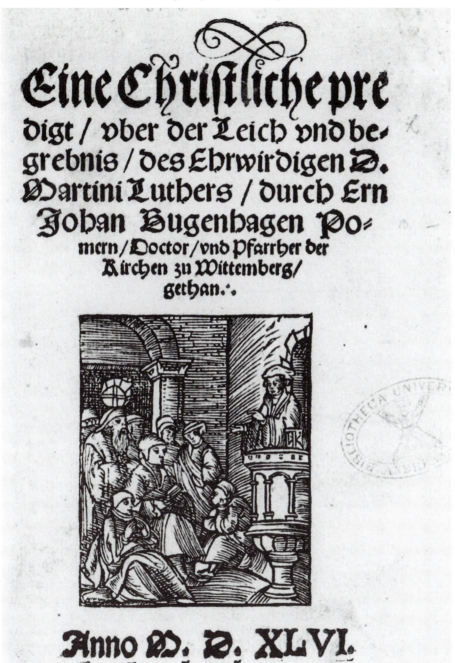

Figure 7.3 Johannes Bugenhagen, *Eine Christliche predigt uber der Leich Martini Luthers* (Wittenberg), 1546. Catholics expected that on his death Luther would be carried off by the devil. It was therefore important for Luther's lieutenants to demonstrate to the world that he had died well and peacefully; editions of Bugenhagen's sermon were hurried off the press. (St Andrews University Library)

Fortunately for the Reformation, Luther's representations had little impact. For the failure to regulate the market effectively was one of the major factors in the Reformation's rapid spread. In Saxony small printers outside Wittenberg when banned from reprinting Luther's works turned to other sources of work: not least manifestos of the Peasants' War. Further afield, printers in Augsburg and Strasbourg simply ignored the Wittenberg printers' rights. For small books it made infinitely more economic sense to reprint locally rather than pay for them to be shipped long distances. It also allowed for far greater immediacy: an edition of a two-sheet *Flugschrift* of sixteen pages could be turned off the press in a couple of days. The existence of these local reprints greatly assisted the swift spread of the Reformation message through Germany. It was a sign of diminished vitality for the Reformation when (as was the case after 1530) the printing of Luther's works was largely once more confined to Wittenberg. Where a market was successfully controlled, as we will see occurring in many places in Europe in the second half of the century, the free flow of innovative theological speculation was greatly inhibited.

TRANSLATIONS OF THE BIBLE

In any survey of the Reformation book, the Bible deserves a special chapter. Luther regarded the translation of the Bible into German as his greatest achievement – indeed, as the only one of his writings which deserved to outlive him. But it was also a publishing achievement of the highest order.

Luther completed his translation of the Bible in stages through the period 1520–34, building on the achievement of the year of enforced absence from Wittenberg after the Diet of Worms. The year of solitude in the Wartburg produced a translation of the New Testament which, suitably revised, was issued in Wittenberg in September 1522. The translation was an immediate success and inaugurated a publishing phenomenon. The New Testament went through forty-three editions in just over three years: a total of probably over 100,000 copies of what was bound to be an expensive book. The publication in 1523 of a Low German edition opened the text to inhabitants of northern Germany. The first complete Bible followed in 1534.

These Bible editions were often beautiful and elaborate books. Cranach, Holbein and other artists of note produced many of their finest woodcut designs for Bible text illustrations, a feature which both enriched the text and greatly increased the price of the Bible. These were elaborate books also in the increasing multiplication of glosses and marginal citations. Luther had determined from the outset that it was appropriate to present the text of scripture with suitable aids to interpretation and his lead was followed throughout the developing Protestant tradition. In later generations the scripture text was almost buried beneath a forest of explanatory materials, maps and diagrams: a somewhat ironic development for a movement which had initially trumpeted the virtues of the pure word of scripture (*rein Evangelium*) against mediæval scholasticism.

The thirst for vernacular scripture was by no means confined to Luther's home-land. Luther's Bible was soon published in the Swiss German lands, principally at Basle, by this point a major centre of fine evangelical printing. These early Basle

Bibles were notable not least for a fine series of illustrative woodcuts by the young Hans Holbein. The first Dutch vernacular Bible text followed in 1522; again heavily influenced by Luther, it inaugurated an extended series of New Testaments and Bible editions which attested to the lively demand for the scriptures in the Low Countries. In all, there were some sixty-five editions of the Dutch scriptures published between 1522 and 1545. The Netherlands was exceptional in providing a relatively free market in both Protestant and Catholic translations of the scripture text, an enviable licence which was scarcely replicated in any other major European publishing tradition. In France, for example, conservative forces in the University and Parlement of Paris achieved in 1525 a complete ban on the publication of vernacular scripture within the kingdom. This was a disaster for the printers of Paris, who had extensive experience in bringing out precisely this sort of large-format expensive book and could certainly see the potential of such a market. In France, after all, the tradition of critical Biblical translation was already well established through the distinguished work of Jacques Lefèvre d'Etaples. But the French authorities would not budge and the Parisian printers fell reluctantly into line; hereafter Bibles in French were published exclusively either abroad, first in Antwerp, later in multiple editions at Geneva, or far distant from the Paris censors at Lyons (see Figures 7.4 and 12.2, p. 220). In consequence the vernacular Bible became, more certainly than in the Netherlands, exclusively Protestant in character; the first French Bible published for Catholic users did not see the light of day until 1566.

The history of English Bibles closely mirrored the French experience. When William Tyndale failed to persuade the Bishop of London to sponsor an official English translation of scripture, he withdrew to pursue his project on the Continent, first in Worms and later in Antwerp. The successful publication of his translation of the New Testament in 1526 made Tyndale a marked man; thereafter the English authorities strove both to apprehend the translator and to intercept supplies of his books on their way back to England. Finally betrayed and arrested by the Netherlandish authorities, Tyndale was tried and put to death at Vilvoorde in 1536. Within a couple of years a new regime in England had embraced both reform and Tyndale's Bible project.

CENSORSHIP AND THE INTERNATIONAL BOOK TRADE

The tribulation of printers in parts of Europe that were turning away from Luther's Reformation bring us face to face with two other pertinent aspects of the Reformation book world: the international trade in books and the attempt to control the spread of the evangelical doctrines through censorship.

Luther's writings quickly commanded attention outside his homeland. In 1519 the Basle printer Johann Froben published a collected Latin edition of Luther's works, for which he found an immediate demand as far afield as Paris, the Low Countries, Spain and England. The circulation of Luther's works in Latin was soon followed by local reprints of both Latin works and translations into local vernaculars.[3] The Latin book trade was inevitably the more international of the two. It also functioned in a rather different way from the trade in vernacular books. On

Figure 7.4 *La Sainte Bible* (Lyons), 1561. Beginning of Exodus. Safe from the disapproval of both Paris and Geneva, Lyons printers specialized in a unique hybrid tradition of highly illustrated Protestant Bibles. (St Andrews University Library)

the whole, Latin books tended to be published in the larger formats and larger editions. Rather than meet the cost of a new edition locally, booksellers would normally find it more convenient with these more specialized works to purchase copies from the original publisher. Latin books tended therefore to be supplied over much longer distances.

This pattern of trade had been established before the Reformation; nevertheless the Reformation did bring about a significant reorientation of the international book trade. At the beginning of the century the key nodal points of the European book market would have been Antwerp and Paris in the north, Venice and Basle in the south, with Frankfurt at the pivotal point of exchange and Vienna and Prague as the eastern outposts. The Reformation initially reinforced the status of Basle as a centre of production and Frankfurt as a book fair, by this time a biannual event which for many publishers established the rhythms of their own production schedule. The particular circumstances of the Reformation in Germany created a new centre of production in Wittenberg and a new entrepôt in Strasbourg. Meanwhile Venice and Paris were virtually excluded from the market in evangelical books, while Antwerp printers struggled with the conflicting pressures of strong local demand and equally strong official hostility to the publication of evangelical texts.

Despite the obvious local interest in Luther's teachings, official attitudes to the Reformation in both France and the Netherlands remained bleakly hostile. The local universities at Paris and Louvain were among the first to condemn Luther and the local rulers, Francis I and Charles V, both remained strongly committed to religious orthodoxy. As part of his own personal crusade against Luther, Charles V focused much regulatory attention on the most visible signs of the new heresy in his dominions: evangelical preaching and the book trade. In both France and the Netherlands printers were soon subjected to a rigorous regime of inspection and regulation designed to stamp out the new heresies.

With these measures, reinforced by a series of highly publicized book-burnings of seized stock, the relationship between the book and the Reformation had taken an ugly turn. For the book was no longer merely word and text stimulating controversy and debate. It was also now the incriminating proof of heretical belief which could bring people to their deaths. Over the next several decades, numerous evangelicals apprehended in possession of forbidden books were among the several thousand executed for the beliefs in lands where the Reformation was proscribed. Among their number were several printers and many of the travelling booksellers (colporteurs) who now became the mainstay of the perilous trade in forbidden books.

Naturally those involved in the publication of Protestant books in this hostile environment took steps to avoid such a fate. Increasingly, the publication of Protestant texts for these lands moved abroad, beyond the reach of the secular and ecclesiastical authorities. But it was not only the publication of such works that was hazardous: in countries such as Spain, France and, at this stage, England and the Netherlands, mere possession of heretical literature became evidence of unorthodox belief.

Protestant printers therefore moved increasingly to protect their readers by disguising their books. Translated works by major reformers seldom acknowledge their authorship by name: what was a selling-point in Germany was dangerously incriminating in these other lands. And as the heresy hunters themselves became more experienced, publishers increasingly dissembled their own involvement by suppressing all mention of the place of publication on the title-page – particularly if this were a known centre of heretical publishing. Thus of the very small number of Luther's works translated into English during the reformer's own lifetime, none acknowledge his authorship and most (although printed secretly in Antwerp) have false addresses. Some of the French translations of Luther are so effectively disguised as harmless devotional tracts that one, a translation of Luther's major 1520 work, *On the Liberty of a Christian Man*, has only recently been rediscovered, four centuries after publication.[4]

The increase of religious persecution in the middle years of the sixteenth century thus spawned whole new centres of book production in Europe. When in 1553 the accession of Queen Mary ended the brief period of Protestant ascendancy in England under Edward VI, many of the printers who had published Protestant literature during the former reign joined the Protestant exodus to the Continent. There they re-established their presses, putting out a steady stream of exhortatory religious literature for those they had left behind. The new Catholic authorities struggled in vain to prevent large quantities of this literature entering England.

The most remarkable phenomenon of this era of persecution and religious emigration was the emergence of Geneva as a major centre of Protestant printing. Beginning in the 1540s, the presence of John Calvin transformed the fortunes of this recently reformed city. Strategically placed between France and the Swiss Confederation, the city proved an increasingly powerful magnet for refugees from Calvin's native France. This was the time when Calvin was beginning to establish his international reputation and his facility for words proved to rival that of Martin Luther. Soon publication of his writings and those of his collaborators Guillaume Farel and Pierre Viret was providing a profitable living for a number of printers. Among them were representatives of the Paris printing fraternity, driven to relocate in Geneva by the rigorously maintained prohibition on entering the lucrative market in evangelical books. Such men also injected into the Genevan industry new capital resources; by the 1550s this combination of circumstances meant that Geneva was able totally to dominate the trade in French Protestant books. The authorities within France, aware that such books were seeping back into the kingdom, promulgated special regulations to inhibit any contact with the heretical city.

However, the Genevan authorities had learned important lessons from the experience of Wittenberg. Aware that too many competing firms would risk swamping the market, in 1560 the city introduced strict limits on the number of presses that might operate within the city. The thirty-four presses were allocated on a quota system to the existing Genevan printing houses. The new regulations also established a committee charged with inspecting the texts of all new books within the city before the printers brought them to the press. In return for submitting to this regulation, printers would generally be given exclusive rights to print the text for a stated number of years: a passable replication of the system of privilege with which many of the printers would have been familiar from their former lives in Paris. The system was enforced, as was characteristic of Geneva, with extreme thoroughness. Over the years most printers fell foul of the regulations at one time or other: one musically minded printer was famously reproved for *correcting* a false note in the Genevan psalter without prior permission. But although indignant when they were the victims, Geneva's publishers generally welcomed close regulation of the industry and fought hard to protect their exclusive rights to lucrative works. And certainly, in the years when Calvinism was just putting down roots in France, the close control of the Genevan printing industry ensured that its printers published an unusually coherent and theologically focused body of works. This was undoubtedly a material factor in explaining Calvin's growing intellectual dominance of the evangelical movement in France.

POLEMICAL LITERATURE IN THE AGE OF RELIGIOUS WARS

The rise of Calvinism initiated a new age in the Reformation conflicts and with it a new age in the history of print culture. Both the French Wars of Religion and the outbreak of the Dutch Revolt were accompanied by a new barrage of religious propaganda. In France, the six years of intense religious and political strife surrounding the first conflict, 1560–5, saw the publication of more than a thousand vernacular religious works on the Protestant side alone, works that covered the complete spectrum from Bibles and serious works of theology to scabrous attacks on the Catholic priesthood. In the Netherlands the outbreak of the revolt against Spain was accompanied by a torrent of literature justifying the Protestant position. This was undoubtedly the most serious attempt to engage the loyalties of a mass public through the medium of print since the first evangelical assault in Germany in the 1520s.

Nevertheless the literature of the era of religious wars was different from the earlier campaign in several respects. First, and in obvious contrast to Luther's movement, this second Protestant polemical onslaught had been preceded by a long period of preparation. For France, as we have seen, the French Calvinist print campaign had been carefully nurtured in Geneva; for the Netherlands, the north German port city of Emden – home to a large colony of Dutch religious exiles – played a similar role. For England, the importance of exile literature during Mary's reign has already been touched upon. This age of exile certainly left its mark on the physical appearance of the book. The *Flugschriften* of Luther's day were remarkably uniform in size and character: almost all printed in a quarto format of approximately twenty centimetres. These were eye-catching and distinctive works, but less suitable for clandestine distribution for which the smaller octavo format was infinitely preferable. It was in this and even smaller sizes that most books smuggled back from exile to the secret congregations in France and the Netherlands were printed and, by the outbreak of the religious wars, this format was thoroughly established in the public mind as the medium of religious polemical writing (see Figure 7.5). By and large this typographical practice was simply retained when the Protestant printing moved back from exile to presses at home, as they inevitably did when printing restrictions were relaxed. The speed with

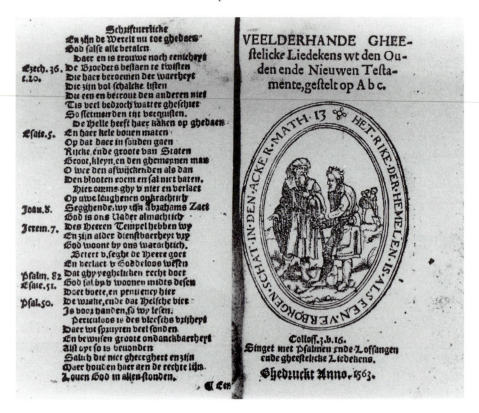

Figure 7.5 *Veelderhande Gheestelicke Liedekens wt den Ouden ende Nieuwen Testamente* (Emden), 1563. This collection of songs for congregational worship was typical of the small books published by the exile presses. The distinctive printer's mark was later counterfeited by unscrupulous printers in the Netherlands keen to pass off their work as that of the highly regarded Emden presses.

which the exile presses relinquished their grip on Protestant publishing is an important if little remarked aspect of the publishing history of this era. Geneva, for instance, from a position of near dominance until 1559, quickly surrendered a large part of its market share of French Protestant books in the succeeding decade.[5] This unsentimental abandonment of the exile towns made good commercial and practical sense. With demand for Protestant books so buoyant it made sense to establish presses nearer the market, whether that be in Lyons, Normandy or even, more tentatively, in Paris itself. This was particularly necessary with respect to the small political and religious tracts responding to particular events or replying to Catholic polemics, a form of writing particularly characteristic of the publishing of these years.

The second major difference from the German experience was that the medium of print was now far less exclusively the Protestants' alone. The response to Luther might have been sluggish and hesitant, but by now Catholic authors had found their voice. In the French conflicts, Catholic writers matched Protestants for the weight and effectiveness of their publications from the beginning of the wars. From the time that the Protestant offensive was losing momentum at the end of the 1560s, Catholic writers actually attained domination of the print medium, a domination they maintained until the end of the century and beyond. Significantly, most of the major French Catholic authors of the day made a contribution to this vernacular print campaign against heresy. Gone was the diffidence that had persuaded Luther's Catholic opponents to leave evangelical domination of the vernacular virtually unchallenged.

Reading these works one can see that Catholic writers had succeeded in finding a popular voice. The new confidence that came from the successful conclusion of the Council of Trent flowed through into the popular arena. Catholic preachers now developed some highly effective lines of attack against the heretics in their midst. The violence of the Catholic assault introduced a new defensiveness into much Protestant writing, forced to parry allegations that their meetings were the cover for all manner of devilish and perverted practices reminiscent of the heresies of the antique and mediæval period.

PRINT AND ORAL CULTURE

If the nature of popular religious debate had changed, so too had the medium. Surveying this mass of religious writings from the second half of the century, it is possible, for instance, to see a profound change in Protestant attitudes to visual media. One of the most interesting aspects of writings of the first Lutheran generation in Germany is the synergy of word and image in print. The German pamphlets drew on a rich visual tradition, a tradition which was itself developed and adapted by the Reformation, whether this be in the development of the tradition of Bible illustration, satirical print or, most famously, the illustrated single-page broadsheet.[6] But in the forty years that had elapsed since the first great age of evangelical pamphlets, Protestant attitudes to illustrations in books – and to the visual arts more generally – had undergone a profound change. In particular, Calvinist churches took an altogether more sceptical view of the place of art in the representation of Holy things: they called for a far more radical cleansing than had Luther of wicked 'idols' (see Chapter 25).

This has inevitable consequences for book culture, as is evident in changing attitudes to illustrations in the Bible (see Figure 7.6). Whereas the first generation of reform had seen a gradual move towards richly illustrated Protestant Bibles, constrained only by expense and the capacities of the local print industries, this was drastically cut back in the second generation. The Calvinist Bible tradition, by and large, permitted no illustration beyond maps and technical diagrams such as representations of the Ark of the Covenant. The influence on wider book culture was equally profound. The more than 300 Dutch Protestant books published in Emden contain not one single text illustration between them.

Instead, Calvinist communities sought other means to bridge the gap between the literate elite and the broader population. In particular they sought to engage the loyalties of the masses through the medium of song. It is well known that Calvin had a strong belief in the value of congregational singing in the worship

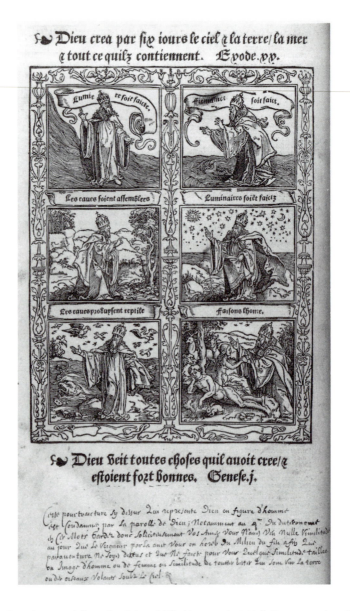

Figure 7.6 Creation panel from *La Sainte Bible* (Antwerp), 1534. Protestant hostility to images also affected book art. A sixteenth-century owner of this copy has annotated this fine Creation panel with a manuscript note condemning representation of the deity in human form. The text reads: 'Ceste pourtraicture sy dessus qui represente Dieu en figure d'homme est condamne par la parolle de Dieu, notamment au 4e du duteronome en ces mots. Gardez donc soliciteusement vos ames vous n'avez vue nulle similitude au jour que le seigneur par la avec bous en horeb du milieu du feu afin que paraventure ne soyez dessus et que ne faicte pour vous quelque similitude taillee ou image d'homme ou de femme ou similitude de touttes bestes qui sont sur la terre ou des oiseoux volants soubz le ciel.' (Grand Rapids, H. Henry Meeter Center for Calvin Research)

service, particularly of the psalms. One of the greatest achievements of his last years was to supervise the production of a complete version of the Psalms in metre for unison singing.

The metrical psalms became the cornerstone of a whole new genre of popular Protestant print. Publication of the metrical psalms was itself a publishing phenomenon, for the completion of the work in 1561 stimulated a unique and coordinated publishing operation to see that they were swiftly made available to the French congregations. An agent acting for the Genevan ministers licensed publication of the psalter to over twenty printers in Lyons, Paris and provincial France, in addition to those in Geneva itself, in an unparalleled suspension of the usual practices of competition and privilege. The goal was to bring 35,000 copies onto the market within two years, a remarkable achievement when one considers that almost all were published with the full musical notation, with all the practical and technical problems associated with music printing (see Figure 26.3, p. 500). As the tunes became popularized, the metrical psalms emerged as a uniquely effective means of expressing the essence of Calvinist cultural identity and spreading this beyond the realms of the literate. Psalm-singing became *the* defining activity of Calvinist activism. The psalms also spawned a whole host of associated verse works, which used the now familiar tunes for more scabrous polemical purposes: ridiculing the Catholic priesthood and the Catholic political leadership, and lauding Protestant heroes and Protestant victories. Large numbers of these songs also found their way into print.

CONCLUSION

With song Protestantism had found a truly popular medium, arguably one of far more genuine general application than visual propaganda. Certainly song seems to have replaced the broadsheet as the elusive bridge between literate and non-literate culture. This opened the possibility of a genuinely popular Reformation in areas where printing and book culture had made little previous impact, as for instance in the Highlands of Scotland.[7] Whatever the truth of this (and this debate has a long way to run), the Calvinist discovery of verse certainly demonstrated the adaptability of print as a medium of communication in the sixteenth century. The first generation of reformers had effectively reinvented the book, adopting and adapting a new technology only just finding its feet as the dominant medium of text. The *Flugschriften* of the first evangelical generation were a startlingly original cultural artifact, which boldly redefined the potentialities of the book and revolutionized its readership. This was a process of evolution that continued through the Reformation century. Conflicting pressures – such as censorship and persecution, Catholic competition and changing attitudes towards image – all caused changes to the physical appearance and the mediatory purpose of the book, as its role in successive generations of reform was constantly redefined and refined. Its striking success as a mode of communication owed a great deal to its flexibility as a medium in these changing circumstances.

NOTES

1   B.J.H. Biggs (ed.), *The Imitation of Christ* (Early English Text Society, Oxford, 1997), p. xxxv.
2   Francis Higman, *Censorship and the Sorbonne* (Geneva, 1979).
3   Bernd Moeller, 'Luther in Europe: His Works in Translation, 1517–46', in E.I. Kouri and Tom Scott (eds), *Politics and Society in Reformation Europe* (Houndmills, 1987), pp. 235–51.
4   Francis Higman, 'Les traductions françaises de Luther', in *Lire et découvrir: La circulation des idées au temps de la Réforme* (Geneva, 1998), pp. 212–18.
5   For the six years analysed fully for the purposes of this study, 1560–5, Genevan presses accounted overall for only 30 per cent of Protestant publications.
6   Robert Scribner, *For the Sake of Simple Folk: Popular Propaganda for the German Reformation* (Cambridge, 1981); W.L. Strauss, *The German Illustrated Broadsheet, 1500–1550* (4 vols; New York, 1975).
7   Jane Dawson, 'Calvinism and the Gaidhealtachd in Scotland', in Andrew Pettegree, Alastair Duke and Gillian Lewis (eds), *Calvinism in Europe, 1540–1620* (Cambridge, 1994), pp. 231–53.

FURTHER READING

A splendid introduction to the place of print in the early modern world is Lucien Febvre and Henri-Jean Martin, *The Coming of the Book: The Impact of Printing, 1450–1800* (1958; English translation, London, 1984). Elizabeth Eisenstein, *The Printing Press as an Agent of Change* (Cambridge, 1980), is a much admired classic, also available is a single volume condensed text, *The Printing Revolution in Early Modern Europe* (Cambridge, 1983). On the origins of printing, Albert Kapr, *Johann Gutenberg: The Man and His Invention* (Aldershot, 1996), is a recent and scholarly biography. On the scribal tradition and textual survival, see L.D. Reynolds and N.G. Wilson, *Scribes and Scholars: A Guide to the Transmission of Greek and Latin Literature* (Oxford, 1968). On literacy, R.A. Houston's *Literacy in Early Modern Europe: Culture and Education, 1500–1800* (London, 1988) is a broad-ranging survey of scholarship on the issue. On the technical aspects of book production, Philip Gaskell's *A New Introduction to Bibliography* (Oxford, 1972) is an authoritative guide. The literature on the Reformation and the book is fairly dispersed, although Jean-François Gilmont, *The Reformation and the Book* (English edn; Aldershot, 1998), provides a masterly series of introductory essays. Much of interest is to be found in the specialist essays collected each year in the *Gutenberg Jahrbuch*. For Germany, Mark E. Edwards' *Printing, Propaganda and Martin Luther* (Berkeley, 1994) is a useful survey; Miriam Usher Chrisman, *Lay Culture, Learned Culture: Books and Social Change in Strasbourg, 1480–1599* (New Haven, 1982), is a classic case study. Robert Scribner's *For the Sake of Simple Folk: Popular Propaganda for the German Reformation* (Cambridge, 1981) is the classic study of the dissemination of the Reformation message through visual media. The issues raised by Scribner are intelligently pursued in Helga Robinson-Hammerstein (ed.), *The Transmission of Ideas in the Lutheran Reformation* (Dublin, 1989). On France, Francis Higman's *Lire et découvrir: La circulation des idées au temps de la Réforme* (Geneva, 1998) is a collection of masterful essays, many of them in English. On England there is surprisingly little to replace the classic volumes of H.S. Bennett, *English Books and Readers* (2nd edn; Cambridge, 1970), though Tessa Watt's *Cheap Print and Popular Piety, 1550–1640* (Cambridge, 1991) is an impressive and innovative study of the reception of Protestantism in the later part of the sixteenth century.

THE GERMAN PEASANTS' WAR AND THE RURAL REFORMATION

James M. Stayer

The rural Reformation antedated the German Peasants' War and outlasted it. The Peasants' War was, among other things, the high point of the early radical revolutionary phase of the Reformation in German-speaking territories.

The conception of a 'rural Reformation' is the obverse of the older better-established idea of the 'Reformation in the towns'. It is necessary, however, to remind ourselves that the rural/urban divide was much less drastic in the sixteenth than the nineteenth or twentieth centuries. The rural aristocracy and the urban patriciate intermingled and intermarried and, as Thomas Brady has argued in the case of Strasbourg, were essentially one ruling class.[1] Vinegrowers, gardeners and lower guilds in the towns did agrarian work, while village cottagers often supplemented their income with manufacture or craftsmanship. The smaller territorial towns of a few hundred residents (which Tom Scott classes as 'peasant–burgher towns') were not qualitatively different from peasant villages, with which they shared many economic interests.[2]

THE IMPERIAL KNIGHTS

The keynote of the rural Reformation was Martin Luther's *Address to the Christian Nobility of the German Nation* (1520). It is a matter of some debate whether this tract was addressed chiefly to the higher princely nobility or to the lesser nobility. The tract's programme of church reform on an imperial level through the Reichstag could only have been carried out by the German princes. On the other hand, Luther seems to have been encouraged to articulate suggestions for reform by formal pledges of friendship and protection of his cause that he received from two lesser nobles, Sylvester von Schaumberg and Franz von Sickingen. Schaumberg claimed to speak on behalf of 100 Franconian knights and Sickingen offered Luther protection at his Rhenish estate, the Ebernburg.

The Ebernburg has been described as constituting, from 1521 to 1523, 'the third evangelical community to be formed in Germany',[3] after Wittenberg and Nuremberg. Sickingen was associated with humanist reform efforts, championing Johannes Reuchlin against the Dominican inquisitors at Cologne before he adopted Luther's cause. The knight had once had Reuchlin as a tutor and in July 1519 he issued a declaration of feud against the Dominicans, seeking justice on Reuchlin's behalf.

Although feuds were outlawed as part of an imperial reform mandate of 1495, to dismiss the ideas of private justice associated with the feud as the sole province of anachronistic 'robber barons' leads to a good deal of misunderstanding about the early stages of the rural Reformation and the Peasants' War as well. Towns and peasants, as well as noblemen, sought justice for themselves through the violent direct action of the feud, although there was more customary legitimacy granted to the aristocratic feud. The imperial courts were neither invariably capable of enforcing their decisions against powerful offenders, nor totally free of the suspicion of corruption. The nobles' claim that their estate sought justice for the oppressed seemed to be substantiated by Sickingen's championing of Reuchlin and Luther.

Contrary to the 'robber baron' stereotype, Sickingen's evangelical convictions appear to have been genuine. At the Ebernburg and neighbouring communities he provided shelter not only for Ulrich von Hutten, humanist and anti-papal polemicist, but also for future luminaries of the Reformation such as Martin Bucer and Johannes Oecolampadius. He orchestrated a publication campaign in the course of which more than thirty Reformation pamphlets issued from the Ebernburg. The most prolific devotional writer of the group was Sickingen's cousin, Hartmut von Cronberg. The messages of these pamphlets were simple: they supported Luther without a detailed grasp of his ideas, advocating use of German in worship and communion in both kinds for the laity, opposing prayers to the saints and contrasting the Word of God with papal customs. Monasteries should be closed and the lands they had extorted from the nobles' ancestors should be reclaimed. Once clerical properties were repossessed there would be enough for everyone, even the poor peasantry.

The knights who assembled around Sickingen connected their claims to be champions of justice for the helpless with an assertion of religious leadership. A pastor committed to the Reformation wrote at the height of the celebrity of the Ebernburg in 1522 that it was a centre of 'evangelical Christian discourse'.

> No man in orders, however spiritual … nor any theologian, however learned, could speak so discerningly … in praise of God and with regard to salvation as this group of noblemen. … The nobility now seek the honour and love of God instead of power and wealth.[4]

At a time when territorial princes and town councillors were more fearful of the imperial sanctions connected with the Edict of Worms, evangelically inclined noblemen were willing to take the risks that ensued from instituting reform in their rural villages and estates.

Next came the assault on territories of the clergy. Six hundred knights of the Upper Rhine formed a Christian confederation in August 1522 and pursued Sickingen's feud against Richard von Greiffenklau, Archbishop of Trier, a notorious opponent of Lutheranism. The movement spread as Franconian knights attacked the prince-bishops of their region: the Bishops of Bamberg and Würzburg. However, the Knights' Revolt of 1522–3 quickly turned into a fiasco. The order of the empire was defended by princes, regardless of whether they were sympathetic or hostile to Luther, and by the Swabian League, the Habsburg-sponsored peace-keeper in southern Germany. Sickingen was killed defending one of his castles, Cronberg lost his estates and dozens of imperial knights in the Rhineland and Franconia suffered the destruction of their castles. Luther adeptly disassociated himself from the failed undertaking, making it clear in *On Temporal Authority* (1523) that such authority in the empire belonged to the princes.

The knightly reforms were not necessarily violent. In Liegnitz in Silesia, Caspar von Schwenckfeld began reforming activities as early as Sickingen, yet peaceably accepted exile in 1529. Nor did the knights as an estate side with the Reformation. In the years before 1524 whether to side with Luther or the pope still seemed an individual matter, but the dependencies of evangelical lesser nobles were one of the first places to put the Reformation into practice.

The idea that clerical land – especially monastic land – had been obtained by fraud was first proclaimed in knightly propaganda, but it quickly took hold in the other rural estate – the peasantry. In 1523, the year of the suppression of the Knights' Revolt, widespread refusal to pay tithes began, especially those owed to cathedral chapters and monasteries. These actions occurred particularly at the Rhenish and Franconian scene of the Knights' Revolt and in the rural dependencies of urban centres of the Reformation. They touched Lutheran Nuremberg, Zwingli's Zurich, and Memmingen, where the major programmes of the Peasants' War were to be printed in 1525. Although the urban reformers had denounced the old church's practice of using excommunication to compel the payment of tithes, they were generally unsympathetic to direct action against tithes by rural villagers. In Zurich, for instance, tithe resistance started in Witikon and neigh-bouring villages at the instigation of the radical priest Wilhelm Reublin. It gained the support of the group impatient with the slow pace of the Zurich Reformation who started the Anabaptist movement in 1525.

Like the Knights' Revolt, the tithe resistance was accompanied by pamphlet propaganda. The major writer against tithes was an ex-monk, Otto Brunfels, who had enjoyed the protection of Ulrich von Hutten in 1521 and 1522. His *On Ecclesiastical Tithes* (1524) emphasized that the tithe was not commanded in the New Testament and thus was not a religious obligation for Christians. He considered it alms that could properly go to temporal authorities, the parish clergy or the poor, but that had been expropriated abusively in the papal order by monasteries and cathedral chapters. The knightly anti-monastic propaganda and the attacks on tithes in pamphlets and through refusal of payment in the villages led inexorably to the sacking of monasteries which marked the beginning of the Peasants' War.

THE PEASANTS' WAR

Erasmus in Basle observed the Peasants' War most closely in its Alsatian version. Alsace had been a territory of widespread tithe refusal in 1523 and 1524, followed by a series of attacks on monasteries in 1525. Erasmus viewed what occurred as a debasement of the church reform movement, but nevertheless as an expression of it. 'Although it seems terrible that the peasants destroyed certain monasteries,' he remarked, 'the wickedness of the latter provoked them to it, since they could not be controlled by law.'[5]

The action of rural commoners and unprivileged townspeople against clerical and lay lords in the misnamed Peasants' War of 1525 had the marks of a feud – an attempt to extort justice from mighty estates which 'could not be controlled by law.' The bands of resisters were part political assemblies, part boycott enforcers and only in the latter desperate stages of the movement did they become armies – usually ineffectual armies. From the standpoint of the victorious princes and the Swabian League the events of 1525 were a war to subdue and punish rebellious subjects; from the standpoint of the resisting commons they were an armed boycott or general strike which ended in disaster.

The fact that Martin Luther saw things through the eyes of the princes rather than the commons – and that Zwingli and Bucer shunned any connection with illegality and at best offered themselves as mediators – does not break the connection between the Peasants' War and the Reformation.

A number of outbreaks in the Black Forest area, starting in May and June 1524, foreshadowed the general upheaval of the first half of 1525. Both the wealthy abbey of St Blasien and the county of Lupfen and Stühlingen were the scene of a refusal of dues and services. The movement led by the former mercenary, Hans Müller from Bulgenbach, combined the traits of a strike and a public demonstration. Mixing in the turmoil was the small Black Forest town of Waldshut, whose radical pastor Balthasar Hubmaier had been initiating the Reformation since late 1523 in defiance of the town's Austrian ruler, Ferdinand of Habsburg. Hubmaier, who became an Anabaptist in 1525, sought protection against the Austrians both from Müller's Black Forest band and from a group of volunteers from Zurich. These volunteers, associated with the future Anabaptist movement in Zurich, were the tool of Zurich's expansionism, which sought covertly to extend both Zurich territory and the Reformation. In 1524, however, despite its economic anticlericalism and alliance with the forces of the Reformation, the Black Forest peasants' movement was not in itself of an evangelical character.

When the commoners' resistance moved to Upper Swabia in the first weeks of 1525 it took on explicitly religious coloration. The Baltringen area, near Ulm, began to be restive around Christmas 1524 and by the end of February a band of 30,000 peasants had assembled. Groups of armed peasants moved from village to village, certainly for purposes of extorting solidarity from the timid and the reluctant. When asked what they were doing, they said that they were exchanging Lenten cakes. This was after all the pre-Lenten season of carnival, when mockery of persons of high estate was given a certain licence. But the Baltringen leader Ulrich Schmid introduced the idea that a 'divine justice' derived from the gospel legitimated the peasant demands. He induced the Memmingen preacher, Christopher Schappler, who had won acclaim for denouncing ecclesiastical tithes, and the lay preacher and Reformation pamphleteer, Sebastian Lotzer, as experts in the Word of God to edit the 300 articles of grievance of the Baltringen villages. The result was the Twelve Articles of Memmingen,[6] published in early March, which served as a model for the uprising in all regions touched by the Peasants' War, except for northern Switzerland and the Alpine territories of Tyrol and Salzburg.

THE TWELVE ARTICLES

The Twelve Articles, which Peter Blickle has identified as the 'conceptual glue' of the Peasants' War, provide good insight into how religious language and objectives inspired by the Reformation mixed with social, economic and political grievances. They were a manifesto of the social gospel of the Reformation in the countryside. In the prologue it was stated that 'the basis of all the articles of the peasants' was 'to hear the gospel and live accordingly'. The opening statement was a refutation of the accusation of 'many antichrists' that the Reformation was subversive of spiritual and temporal power, as evidenced by the peasants' movement. This prologue argued that the gospel could not possibly cause rebellion because it tells of Christ and his peaceful message. The disorder and rebellion were the fault of the enemies of the commoners and the gospel.

The first two articles of the twelve gave communities the right to elect and depose pastors and reserved the control of the great tithe in grain to the villages, for the primary purpose of supporting pastors and helping the poor, with what was left over devoted to defence of the land. The small tithe, levied primarily on meat products, was to be abolished, 'for the Lord God created cattle for man's free use; and it is an unjust tithe invented by men alone'. The twelfth article offered to drop any peasant demand that was not in agreement with the Bible and – the most revolutionary notion of all – reserved the right to advance further demands against practices shown by scripture to be 'offensive to God and a burden to our neighbour'.

Although framed with Reformation principles in the prologue and Articles 1, 2 and 12, and accompanied in the marginalia to all articles by Bible citations, the Twelve Articles had definite social, economic and political objectives that contributed to their appeal throughout south and central Germany. Article 3, which denounced serfdom on the grounds that Christ had died for everyone, 'the lowliest shepherd as well as the greatest lord', and proclaimed that therefore it was unseemly for one human being to be the property of another, had great resonance in Upper Swabia. There the landowners, including the monasteries, were using serfdom to establish the foundation of small territorial states. Serfdom was less of an issue elsewhere, since it was virtually non-existent in Thuringia or the Tyrol.

Articles 4, 5 and 10, expressing peasant resentment at being excluded from use of the products of forests, waterways and meadows, including game and fish, touched the biggest and most general economic grievance throughout the rebellious territories. They reflected the manner in which aggressive lords were squeezing the peasantry out of their traditional sources of supplementary income, wood for building and fuel, grazing land, possibilities for irrigation as well as fish and game, not to mention the villagers' resentment of the way protected wild animals destroyed crops. Aside from the aristocrats' cultivation of hunting sport, the rationally administered monasteries were most prominent in their exploitation of waterways, meadows and forests, and particularly resented because they, unlike the nobles, seemed to make no contribution at all to the 'common good'.

Articles 6, 7, 8 and 9 referred to labour services owed both to landlords and rulers, rents that ate up an inordinate part of the product of the land and arbitrary penalties that departed from customary law. They expressed the country people's miscellaneous grievances against overlords both religious and lay. At their base the issues touched in these articles were economic because they squeezed the livelihood of the commons. The same point applies to Article 11, which attacked the death dues connected with serfdom.

But the economic grievances of the Twelve Articles were above all those of the village elite, the relatively well-to-do landholding peasants. The political programme inherent in the Twelve Articles was the reduction of the power of overlords so as to benefit the autonomous village communes. As a practical matter the village elite would appoint and dismiss pastors (Article 1), disburse the great tithe in grain (Article 2) and control the waterways, forests and common meadows and fields (Articles 4, 5 and 10). Recent research has made us aware of the social stratification of the countryside, in which the landholding class with either life tenure or hereditary tenure dominated the usually poor cottagers and landless labourers.[7] Generally, however, in 1525 the ideal of the 'common good' of the village was defined by the landholders and accepted by their peasant neighbours who were socially and economically weaker. At most, social tension among the various strata of villagers played its role when mercenaries recruited from the rural population eventually did the princes' bidding and suppressed the uprising. At first there was considerable worry about whether the mercenary soldiers could be depended upon to fight against their brothers and cousins.

THE FEDERAL ORDINANCE

The second major document published in Memmingen at the beginning of March 1525 was the Federal Ordinance.[8] It was the product of a conference from 5–7 March which established a union of the three major peasant organizations of Upper Swabia, the Baltringen, Allgau and Lake Constance bands. It aimed at a perpetual Swiss-type confederation of local communes ('towns, villages and rural regions'). The idea that the peasant movement might expand Switzerland, or at least the Swiss confederal system, was current both among its friends and enemies. The radical peasant pamphlet, *To the Assembly of Common Peasantry*, published in Nuremberg in May, carried on its cover page the provocative jingle: 'Wer meret Schwytz / Der herren gytz.' ('What makes Switzerland grow? The greed of the lords.') It referred to the proverb that a cow would bawl on the bridge at Ulm and be heard in the middle of Switzerland, altering the wording to 'when a cow stands on the Schwanberg and bawls, she'll be heard in the middle of Switzerland.' (The mythical Schwanberg was the Franconian mountain where Frederick Barbarossa was supposed to return and rescue the empire.) In the recent Swabian War of 1499–1500 Switzerland had expanded at the expense of the empire by absorbing the Swiss-type confederation of Graubünden and it seemed thinkable that the upheaval of 1525 might provide the occasion for Upper Swabia and perhaps the neighbouring regions of south Germany to 'turn Swiss'.[9] In any case the Federal Ordinance was disseminated beyond Upper Swabia to the neighbouring Upper Rhine area, where it re-emerged, modified to suit local conditions, both in the

Black Forest area and in Alsace. The 'Letter of Articles' of May 1525, which was formerly regarded as a distinct peasant programme, now seems to have been a covering letter for a Black Forest version of the Federal Ordinance. It contained the outlines of a 'temporal excommunication', a systematic boycott breaking off all personal and economic contact with those castles, monasteries and chapters whose possessors refused to subject themselves to the confederation.

The Federal Ordinance, probably drafted by the same Sebastian Lotzer who was the chief compiler of the Twelve Articles, clearly reflected his allegiance to the Reformation. It aimed to establish a 'Christian union and league', 'for the praise and honour of the almighty, eternal God, to call upon the holy Gospel and the Word of God, and to protect justice and the divine law'. It named fourteen pious and learned arbitrators to define the content of divine law. These persons turned out to be the leading Reformation theologians: among them Martin Luther, Huldrych Zwingli, Philip Melanchthon, Andreas Osiander, Johannes Brenz, Matthew Zell and Jakob Strauss. No supporters of the old faith were included and only Strauss could be construed as a Reformation radical.

The scholars who minimized the connection of the peasants' movement with the Reformation have argued that the language of the Reformation in the Twelve Articles and the Federal Ordinance represented only the views of Schappeler and Lotzer, not of the ordinary commoners in the uprising. It is very difficult to speculate about the convictions of anonymous masses, but the peasant documents we possess demonstrate the Reformation allegiance of the leaders and show that the movement was at least exposed to the anti-papalist rhetoric of the Reformation. For instance, the cover picture of 'To the Assembly of Common Peasantry' opposes 'peasants, good Christians' to 'Romanists and sophists'. The documents of the Klettgau revolt, just across from Zurich on the imperial side of the Swiss border, show a peasantry which began in 1524 by appealing to 'God and the saints', then went on in the following year to make the Old and New Testaments the basis of their demands, and resisted to the end of 1525 their overlord's insistence that they return to 'the old Christian order'. The Tauber Valley programme of April 1525 contained the explicitly Protestant formula: 'this common assembly will raise up the holy Word of God, the evangelical teaching, which henceforth will be preached purely and clearly without adulteration by human teaching or additions'. Michael Gaismair's draft of a Tyrolean Territorial Constitution (1526) proposed that the mass be forbidden, that books of canon law and scholastic theology be destroyed, and that they be replaced by the Bible as the sole basis of university instruction. Thomas Müntzer, the most prominent preacher in the Thuringian uprising, was second to none in his rejection of the old faith and allegiance to the Reformation, even if he opposed Martin Luther's version of the Reformation.

The Upper Swabian uprising was above all an assault on the power of monasteries, which held extensive lands in that region. It began with the subjects of the Abbot of Kempten, whose predecessors had been quarrelling with their peasantry and trying to enserf them for years previously. Only at a second stage did lay aristocratic lords come under attack. Economic anticlericalism, which had deep pre-Reformation roots, has been described as the hinge which connected the economic grievances of the peasantry with the Reformation.[10]

An die versamlung gemayner Pawer-
schafft/so in Hochteütscher Nation/vnd vil ande
rer ort/mit empörung vñ aufftrür entstandē. ⁊c.
oß ir empörung billicher oder vnpillicher ge
stalt geschehe/ vnd was sie der Oberkait
schuldig oder nicht schuldig seind. ⁊c.
gegründet auß der heyligen Göt-
lichen geschrifft/ von Oberlen-
dischen mitbrüdern gütter
maynung aufgangen
vnd beschriben. ⁊c.

Hie ist des Glückradts stund vnd zeyt
Gott wayst wer der oberist bleybt.

Hie Pawrßman güt Christen.   Hie Romanisten vnd Sophisten.

Wer meret Schwytz   Der herren gytz.

Figure 8.1 Peasant propaganda: *An die Versammlung gemanyer Pawerschafft*, 1525. A popular pamphlet from the height of the Peasants' War shows in the centre the wheel of fortune, on which is the Pope, clad in armour, accompanied by his supporters. Opposing them the 'Peasants and Good Christians'. Dame Fortune rotates the wheel. From Horst Buszello, *Der Deutsche Bauernkrieg von 1525 als Politische Bewegung*, Colloquium, 1969.

The slogan of enforcing the 'divine law', a standard of social, economic and political justice based on the newly recovered norm of God's Word, unadulterated by Romanist customs, was the common denominator of the programmes of the resisting commoners. Grievances like those against serfdom, or social pressures like rising population, varied from region to region affected by the uprising. The regions that rebelled had strong traditions of communal self-government at the local level – traditions that neighbouring Bavaria, untouched by the Peasants' War, lacked. But if communal institutions were necessary for the Peasants' War they were not sufficient to cause it. Grievances over forests, waterways and meadows were general among the rebellious regions but they were not new. What was new was the Reformation. The Peasants' War brought the Reformation to the ordinary people of the countryside of south and central Germany. Without the Reformation there would not have been a massive popular upheaval in 1525.

THE DEFEAT OF THE UPRISING

But the Reformation also handicapped the commoners in dealing realistically and resolutely with the privileged estates. This was particularly the case in the Upper Swabian heartland of the rebellion, where figures like Schappeler imagined that the divine law could win the day through its inherent righteousness without resort to violence.[11] None of the fourteen Reformation theologians appealed to in the Federal Ordinance, not even Jakob Strauss with his economic radicalism, rallied to the side of the commoners. Thomas Müntzer alone, temporarily exiled from Mühlhausen and travelling in southwest Germany shortly after the uprising began, seems to have been positively impressed. Martin Luther's response to the Twelve Articles was that he would always oppose rebels, no matter how just their cause. So the commoners appealed to the gospel and waited vainly for it to work by itself, while the princes and Habsburgs working through the Swabian League raised an army to suppress them.

The supply of trained mercenaries of south German origin (*Landsknechte*) was limited, many of them fighting for Emperor Charles V against the French in Italy. The major imperial victory at Pavia on 24 February 1525, released them for service with the Swabian League, which was organizing an army to suppress the peasants. The cause was not popular at first; contingents of mercenaries refused to serve against commoners from their own region, who were perceived in the early less-violent phase of the movement to have justice on their side. Eventually, at the very end of March, the League's army took the field, financed by a Fugger loan, under the command of George of Waldburg, an experienced professional soldier and one of the greatest territorial rulers in Upper Swabia. The League's original force was 1,500 cavalry and 7,000 footsoldiers.

Forced to fight, the Upper Swabian peasantry did poorly. The first major battle at Leipheim on 3–4 April was a massacre and soon afterwards the demoralized Baltringen band, the source of the Twelve Articles, dissolved itself. The advantage held by the League's army was that it had cavalry and was better equipped with cannon and handguns than the peasant bands it faced. The peasants included a good number of former mercenaries, and even hired professional soldiers, but they faced considerable disadvantages. There was no unified command. Even in Upper Swabia, supposedly united by the Federal Ordinance, the main bands would not leave their own territory to help one another. Hence they could be, and were, destroyed piecemeal. Unlike commoners' rebellions in previous centuries, this one developed no military innovations to counter the aristocratic cavalry. One thinks of the massed pike formations of the Swiss or the wagon fortresses of the Hussites, both of which went on from being the special tactics of rebelling commoners to be absorbed into general military practice.

When George of Waldburg's army faced the Lake Constance band at Weingarten on 15 April, one of the defining moments of the uprising had arrived. The peasant army was numerically superior, well equipped with fire power, peppered with experienced soldiers and in a tactical position that the League's horsemen could attack only with difficulty. Waldburg was not sure of victory and feared the consequences throughout south Germany should his army be defeated.[12] So instead of attacking he negotiated the disbanding of the opposing forces in return for the promise of hearing their grievances. By this time word of mouth and printed versions of the Twelve Articles had occasioned uprisings in Württemberg, Franconia, Thuringia and Alsace. Had the peasants fought and won at Weingarten the uprising could have taken on an aura of invincibility that would have made it much harder to suppress.

In the same days of late March that George of Waldburg was getting his army into commission, the uprising spread over Franconia, where it was to assume its most impressive character from a military standpoint. In the Tauber valley on 26 March the rebellion began with plundering of monastic property. The Franconian region was spotted with large prince-bishoprics, rich but militarily weak – important territories of the Archbishopric of Mainz, where the Primate of Germany ruled, as well as the Bishoprics of Bamberg and Würzburg. Powerful patrician Nuremberg managed with timely concessions to keep its rural subjects peaceful, but in Heilbronn the peasants seized control of the imperial city through the assistance of an urban dissident movement. The peasant armies of Franconia destroyed or dismantled hundreds of monasteries, castles and fortresses and forced the submission of the regent of the Archbishop of Mainz, who totally failed to raise a force to oppose them. They aimed their major attack against Würzburg, where they captured the town but failed to secure the formidable fortress, the Marienburg. At the beginning of June the Swabian League army, fresh from victory over the rebels in Württemberg, defeated the Franconian peasants and ended the siege of the Marienburg. Effectively George of Waldburg's victory at Königshofen on 2 June broke the back of the rebellion.

Although the Black Forest, Upper Swabia and Franconia were arguably at the heart of the Peasants' War of 1525, it also spread over Alsace, Thuringia, the Tyrol and the Archbishopric of Salzburg, as well as the northern borderlands of Switzerland. In Alsace it was suppressed in mid-May by the army of Duke Anthony of Lorraine at Saverne. At virtually the same time the united forces of the Lutheran Philip of Hesse, who had also been a major mover in suppressing Sickingen's knights in 1523, and the ultra-Catholic Duke George of Saxony slaughtered the Thuringian peasant army at Frankenhausen. Thomas Müntzer was the best-known pastor of the Frankenhausen band and arguably its spiritual leader. He saw the Peasants' War as a sign of the apocalypse and associated the Thuringian peasants with his covenant of the elect. However, his concrete objective in allying with the rebels was defence of his version of the Reformation. The Saxon princes and Philip of Hesse seemed to be planning to subdue the imperial city of Mühlhausen where Müntzer was a leading preacher. Marxist historians have been attracted to Müntzer because of his dramatic rivalry and polemical exchanges with Luther, but he seems to have been a peripheral figure in the Peasants' War.

A late, spectacular phase of the uprising began in May when Michael Gaismair managed to secure the treasure of the Archbishop of Brixen in the South Tyrol. He used it to hire mercenaries and mount a successful resistance against the Habsburg rulers.[13] A parallel revolt in the Archbishopric of Salzburg allied itself with Gaismair. At Schladming in Styria with the assistance of Salzburg miners the rebels won a renowned military victory on 3 July 1525. Despite a continuance of resistance into 1526, however, Ferdinand of Austria was able to overcome the Gaismair movement by a skilful combination of political and military measures. Clearly the church principalities, Brixen and Salzburg, embedded in Habsburg lands were particularly vulnerable to rebellion. Exiled in Switzerland in 1526, Gaismair composed a draft constitution for a liberated Tyrol, according to which all privileged orders would be levelled; in this same manifesto Gaismair repudiated the Roman church and all its practices.

The older historical viewpoint that the Peasants' War ran amok in utopianism needs to be substantially revised. It is true that its early preference for non-violent resistance and its appeal to the major theologians of the Reformation appear in hindsight to have been naive. But Switzerland stood as a demonstration that a commoners' confederation was a viable alternative to rule by aristocrats and princes. In territorial states like Württemberg or the Tyrol the rural commoners were prepared to work for reform together with nobles and townsmen in already instituted representative assemblies. Only the clergy was to be completely stripped of political power. The Peasants' War was limited to portions of south and central Germany; it left north Germany untouched. Its leaders had practical regional objectives; they were entirely innocent of German nationalism.[14]

CONSEQUENCES

In one respect the Peasants' War determined the course of the Reformation. Before 1525, even when they were personally and religiously on the side of the Reformation, the German princes avoided committing themselves institutionally. Frederick the Wise, Luther's protector, maintained the façade of religious neutrality to his death in 1525. Such reforms as took place occurred at the initiative of lesser nobles and town councils. The Peasants' War of 1525 changed all that. It taught the princes that the Reformation was so politically and socially explosive that it had to be managed and controlled. Peter Blickle writes:

> Now the princes had to take over the Reformation. Only if they could bring
> it under political control could revolt be eliminated root and branch. They

had to shear the Reformation of its revolutionary components, which they did by denying the communal principle as a mode of Christian life both in theory and practice.[15]

Blickle's standpoint is sympathetic to the commoners' resistance movement, which he calls the Revolution of 1525, and critical of Luther. But it receives surprising confirmation from Karl Holl, the father of the Luther Renaissance.[16] Holl presents Luther as approving of the piecemeal emergence of the early Reformation in Saxony through various kinds of local initiative. Such a decentralized, more or less spontaneous emergence of the Reformation suited the distinctions he made between church and temporal authority in *On Temporal Authority* (1523). In Holl's view, when the government of electoral Saxony began to occupy itself systematically with the spiritual as well as the physical welfare of its subjects through organizing the Visitation of 1528, Luther adopted an attitude of 'silent protest'. Eventually he grudgingly accepted princely authority in evangelical territorial churches, but only as a provisional necessity to deal with the moral and political chaos of the time.

At any rate, in the aftermath of 1525 the 'magisterial Reformation', controlled and directed by princes and ruling town councils, became the prevailing reality. There was no more general, spontaneous resistance to ecclesiastical tithes; such matters became objects of governmental regulation. Preaching of the Word of God was no longer something the commoner struggled for but a benefit he received from his ruler. Standing out from this magisterial Reformation and the object of its repression were the nonconformist supporters of the Reformation who refused to come to terms with the new official churches. These people carried the anticlerical impulse of the Reformation to the point of being radically distrustful of the evangelical clergy set up by the new established churches. If they set up voluntary church structures in defiance of the established churches and their governmental sponsors, they were called 'Anabaptists', since most of these nonconformist groups practised believers' baptism on mature persons. They rejected infant baptism, which seemed to them to automatically enrol everyone, believing or unbelieving, in the established church of a territory (see Chapter 14).

In areas that had experienced a more violent version of the Peasants' War – Franconia, Thuringia and the South Tyrol – former followers of Thomas Müntzer and Michael Gaismair became Anabaptists. The most prominent south and central German Anabaptist leaders emerged from the circle around Müntzer – Hans Denck, Hans Hut, Hans Römer and Melchior Rinck. These successors of Müntzer usually toned down his militancy. Only Hans Römer seems to have continued insurrectionary activity and hoped for a second round of the Peasants' War, starting with an assault on Erfurt at the beginning of 1528. Hans Hut played on Müntzer's apocalypticism, predicting the end of the world and punishment of the ungodly at Pentecost 1528, three-and-a-half years after the Peasants' War. Denck and Rinck turned away from violent resistance completely. Nevertheless, the news that many of Müntzer's followers had located a new covenant in Anabaptism was bound to evoke fright in the governments that had just experienced the Peasants' War.[17]

THE TAMING OF THE RURAL REFORMATION

In the years before 1525 the 'evangelical peasant Karsthans' (Hans of the Hoe) was a popular character in a dozen or more pro-Reformation pamphlets.[18] This fictitious peasant (or an equivalent peasant spokesman) invariably grasps the biblical message and shows himself the superior of courtiers, friars and learned doctors. He praises Luther and denounces Erasmus for his cowardice in deserting the Reformation cause. It cannot be shown that a single Reformation pamphlet was actually written by a peasant. Nevertheless, in the early 1520s the evangelical

Figure 8.2 Luther in 1526. This fine psychological study by Luther's friend and supporter Lucas Cranach shows the strain of years when the Reformation faced its first serious crisis. (Wolfenbüttel, Herzog August Bibliothek)

peasant was the symbolic embodiment of the Reformation ideal of the priesthood of all believers projected to the countryside.

A pamphlet entitled 'New Karsthans' that issued from the Ebernburg had gone so far as to suggest that the knights and the peasantry should become allies in the reform of the empire and the church. Obviously after 1525 the glorification of the peasantry in pro-Reformation literature ceased completely. After 1525 pamphleteers from the lesser nobility suggested that since both the first estate (the clergy) and the third estate (the commons) had betrayed the gospel, the gospel cause fell by right to their own, second estate. Noble writers like Jakob Schenck von Stauffenberg and Wilhelm von Isenburg could denounce the pretensions of 'scribes' (learned scholars) to control the interpretation of the Bible with some of the acerbity that Thomas Müntzer had directed against Egranus or Luther. The lesser nobility continued indeed as important executors of the rural Reformation, because through their rights of patronage they frequently nominated and sometimes even chose the evangelical pastors in the villages. Moreover, besides and under the surface of a bureaucratized princely Reformation in the territorial states, the reality of noble power persisted. In the religious peace of Augsburg in 1555, the imperial knights won the right to opt either for the old faith or the religion of the Augsburg Confession on their estates, just like the princes in their territories. More important, the character of the princely territories was not absolutist but dualist in the sixteenth century. In their projects and their finances the princes relied on the advice and consent of their estates; in Protestant lands that meant the nobles and the burghers, with the clergy removed.

Nevertheless, the Reformation of the princes did begin in 1526. In that year, at the first Diet of Speyer, the Catholic and Lutheran princes agreed to disagree, to maintain order in their territories and, pending a general council, each to direct his territorial church 'in such a way as he will be responsible for to God and the Emperor'. The attempt of the imperial government to rescind this licence for religious division at the second Diet of Speyer in 1529 provoked the Protestation that gave the Protestants their name. The emperor's effort to undo the damage by his personal presence at the Diet of Augsburg (1530) led to Philip Melanchthon's Augsburg Confession, the foundational document of the Lutheran churches. At first in the southwest of the empire, in Alsace and Swabia, the competing influence of the Swiss Reformers, Zwingli and Oecolampadius, challenged Luther's theology. But both these leaders died in 1531, the Swiss Reformed retired into isolation and the Wittenberg Concord of 1536 amounted to an acceptance of Luther's authority by Martin Bucer, the pre-eminent Reformer of southwestern Germany. For the time being (pending the encroachments of Calvinism in the second half of the sixteenth century) to be Protestant or evangelical in Germany meant to be Lutheran. Luther himself further defined the substance of confessional Lutheranism with the Schmalkaldic Articles (1537) which singled out the *Rechtfertigungslehre* (teaching of justification) as 'the article upon which the church stands or falls'. For evangelical rural Germany, the princely governments adopted these central confessions as their official creed, supposedly the basis of a good Christian life. Their challenge was to see that Lutheran theology was taught, inculcated, into the population.

The recent social history of the Reformation has speculated that there were great numbers of 'involuntary Protestants' in the rural parts of evangelical territories.[19] The basis for this idea that the majority were lukewarm, minimally observant in the new faith, was the system of visitations conducted regularly, particularly in the rural areas, by the Lutheran territorial governments. The first, in 1528 in electoral Saxony, was a commission of legally trained councillors and theologians sent out to inspect the material and spiritual state of the parishes under the prince's authority. The ignorance of Christian basics such as the Ten Commandments, Apostles' Creed and Lord's Prayer was so appalling to Luther that he immediately sat down to compose his Large and Small Catechisms in 1529. The Large Catechism, based on Luther's sermons of the previous year, was for the theological education of pastors; the Small Catechism, a series of carefully constructed questions and answers, was for the indoctrination of the young.[20]

To preach sermons and teach catechisms was the duty of the new evangelical clergy. This group was by the middle of the century competent in its way, but thoroughly resented by the rural congregations. Their excellent education in theology and languages set them apart from their flocks. They were seldom of local origin and they intermarried with each other's families rather than with their parishioners. The original anticlerical impulse of the Reformation was to be rid of the 'plague of priests', and indeed the numbers of clergy were now much smaller, the ceremonies less costly and elaborate. The Reformation 'downsized' religion, but it oversimplifies to call it 'cheap religion'. Villagers now were obliged to resume paying their tithes and to assume the upkeep of the church and the manse after an interval of freedom from such obligations in the first years of the collapse of the old order.[21] Moreover, they did not have the control over clerical appointments and disposal of church monies that, for instance, had been demanded in the Twelve Articles. The evangelical pastor was, far more than the former Romanist priest had been, an agent of the central government of the territory.

The visitation records strongly suggest that the villagers did not maintain the churches, support the pastors, attend sermons, learn their catechisms or regenerate their lives in the way that was required of them. In many respects they behaved in exactly the way that Lutheran theology with its extreme stress on human depravity would have expected them to behave. Unlike Catholics or even Anabaptists, Lutherans were taught that good works were not the way to salvation. Yet, once they had learned this insight and taken it to heart, the Lutheran laity were required spontaneously to come forth with good works. That this did not happen was at once anticipated and deplored by visitors and pastors. Luther himself would never identify the territorial evangelical church with the true church, which was 'visible only to faith' and consisted of the few among the many in the external congregations.

An electoral Saxon visitation of 1554 showed little or no improvement over the past two decades. Although village schools were now widespread, only a few children could recite the catechism and those who learned it as children tended to forget it as adults. A typical report reads: 'A crude folk, ignorant and untaught. Since they never go to church, most of them cannot even say their prayers.'[22] Visitations were the general practice not only in Saxony but throughout rural

Lutheran Germany. In the larger towns, councils and powerful pastors sometimes had the influence at court to refuse to receive the visitors, but in the countryside pastors and their flocks felt compelled to submit to humiliating interrogations. The results were almost never deemed satisfactory. In contrast to Catholic territories, the Lutheran visitors were never content with mere religious observance and, unlike later Calvinists, they did not think that compelling the recalcitrant redounded to God's greater glory. They wanted through teaching and preaching to win the hearts and minds of ordinary people in the villages, and they were almost always disappointed.

A recent study of the territorial Reformation of Brandenburg-Ansbach-Kulmbach (Lutheran territories around Nuremberg ruled by a branch of the Hohenzollern family) illustrates the great difficulties of the new pastorate in introducing the morality and religion of Lutheranism into the Franconian countryside.[23] Often the pastors were thwarted by their lay counterparts, by the village elite or even the local official of the ruling prince. One area of friction arose in social activities of mediæval origin like spinning bees and church fairs that the pastors denounced as licentious, while the lay powers often viewed them as desirable diversions from workaday drudgery. Nor in these Lutheran territories, in contrast to the Swiss and early southwest German Reformation which began on a wave of iconoclasm, did the religiosity of the laity depart from the old mediæval church in the way the pastors would have wished. Holy pictures, water from the baptismal font that seemed to have the potency of holy water and consecrated bells made the paraphernalia of Lutheran worship rather similar to Catholic sacramentals. And if the pastors knew that Lutheran sacraments were completely different from Roman sacraments, the parishioners' concern with absolution after confession and the reverence they showed the host indicated that they were not so aware of the difference.

The visitation reports about rural Lutherans contrasted strikingly with the reputation of the hunted sectarians. In Württemberg there are reports that people who lived irreproachable lives without cursing or carousing easily fell under suspicion of being Anabaptists. Alternatively, quarrelsome and violent behaviour helped one to defend one's reputation against suspicion of Anabaptism.[24] Of course the piety of the sectarians was written off as hypocrisy, but the territorial churches nevertheless wished that they could match the sects in holiness.

Against this picture of the failure of the Reformation in the countryside in the middle of the sixteenth century must be placed the equally striking failure of the attempt at a Catholic restoration in the years 1546–52. In 1547, the year following Luther's death, the Schmalkaldic War ended in total victory for the Spanish troops of Charles V. The leading princes of the magisterial Reformation, Elector John Frederick of Saxony and Philip of Hesse, were prisoners of the emperor. Charles V seems to have thought that at that moment he could abolish Lutheranism with the stroke of a pen. Instead, as an act of statesmanlike compromise, he promulgated the Augsburg Interim of 1548, which was to hold sway in Protestant lands pending a final settlement by a general council of the church. It substantially restored the mass and Catholic doctrine, conceding only clerical marriage and lay communion in both kinds. The Interim was enforced under the eyes of imperial soldiers in the cities of south Germany, but in the north it was universally resisted by the princes and, it is said, by the people. In 1552 a princes' revolt led by Maurice of Saxony, Charles' ally of 1546–7, took the emperor by surprise and drove him out of Germany. Thus was established the foundation for the Religious Peace of Augsburg (1555), which in substance restored and consolidated the arrangements of the first Diet of Speyer of 1526.

The Lutheran resistance in the years of the Interim was real enough and to contemporaries it was a remarkable testimonial to the vitality of the religion outlined in the Augsburg Confession. What does it say about the current interpretative dispute about 'involuntary Protestants'? Provisionally it may be suggested that Lutheranism was strongest among the lesser nobility and townspeople. In the illustrated pamphlet propaganda against the Interim, unlike that of the early 1520s, the Lutheran congregations appear not as evangelical peasants but as comfortable burghers.[25] The Peace of Augsburg gave distinct rights not only to Lutheran princes but to Lutheran lesser nobles, both imperial knights and nobles living in Catholic ecclesiastical territories. The north German princes in 1552 no doubt wanted to defend Lutheranism as a matter of personal religion, not only out of considerations of power politics. But they also had to consider the elites of town and countryside, burghers and nobles, who had habituated themselves to Lutheranism for a generation. Below these elites, the ordinary folk of the villages probably had no desire for the now foreign religion of the Interim or the pope, but they seem to have benefited from the Reformation chiefly in the sense that it let them off with less religion. They clung to social and religious attitudes that antedated Protestantism. The visitation reports probably picture them correctly as a recalcitrant flock for the new Lutheran clergy.

NOTES

1 Thomas A. Brady, Jr, *Ruling Class, Regime and Reformation at Strasbourg, 1520–1555* (Leiden, 1978).
2 Tom Scott, 'The Peasants' War: A Historiographical Review', *Historical Journal* 22 (1979), pp. 693–720, 953–74.
3 Miriam Usher Chrisman, *Conflicting Visions of Reform: German Lay Propaganda Pamphlets, 1519–1530* (Atlantic Highlands, NJ, 1996), pp. 65–6.
4 Ibid., p. 69.
5 Heiko A. Oberman, 'The Gospel of Social Unrest', in R.W. Scribner and Gerhard Benecke (eds), *The German Peasant War 1525: New Viewpoints* (London, 1979), p. 45.
6 English translation in Peter Blickle, *The Revolution of 1525: The German Peasants' War from a New Perspective* (Baltimore, 1981), pp. 195–201.
7 David Sabean, *Landbesitz und Gesellschaft am Vorabend des Bauernkriegs* (Stuttgart, 1972).
8 Gottfried Seebass, *Artikelbrief, Bundesordnung und Verfassungsentwurf* (Heidelberg, 1988).
9 Thomas A. Brady, Jr, *Turning Swiss: Cities and Empire, 1450–1550* (Cambridge, 1985).
10 Henry J. Cohn, 'Anticlericalism in the German Peasants' War 1525', *Past and Present* 83 (1979), pp. 3–31.
11 Oberman, 'Gospel of Social Unrest', pp. 47–8.
12 Tom Scott and R.W. Scribner (ed. and trans.), *The German Peasants' War: A History in Documents* (Atlantic Highlands, NJ, 1991), pp.156–8.
13 Jürgen Bücking, *Michael Gaismair: Reformer-Sozialrebell-Revolutionär. Seine Rolle im Tiroler 'Bauernkrieg' (1525/32)* (Stuttgart, 1978).

14 Horst Buszello, *Der Deutsche Bauernkrieg von 1525 als politische Bewegung* (Berlin, 1969). Cf. Buszello's recent nuanced assessment of Blickle's influential interpretation of the Peasants' War, in 'Deutungen und Wertungen aus fünf Jahrhunderten', in *Studien zum deutschen Bauernkrieg: Drei Essays*, Mühlhäuser Beiträge, special issue 10 (1997), pp. 18–22.

15 Blickle, *Revolution of 1525*, p. 185.

16 Karl Holl, *Gesammelte Aufsätze zur Kirchengeschichte, I: Luther* (Tübingen, 1921), pp. 279–325.

17 James M. Stayer, *The German Peasants' War and Anabaptist Community of Goods* (Montreal, 1991), pp. 61–92, 186–200.

18 Werner O. Packull, 'The Image of the Common Man in the Early Pamphlets of the Reformation (1520–1525)', *Historical Reflections* 12 (1985), pp. 253–77.

19 R.W. Scribner, *The German Reformation* (Atlantic Highlands, NJ, 1986), p. 34.

20 Gerald Strauss, *Luther's House of Learning: Indoctrination of the Young in the German Reformation* (Baltimore, 1978).

21 Gerald Strauss, 'Local Anticlericalism in Reformation Germany', in Peter A. Dykema and Heiko A. Oberman (eds), *Anticlericalism in Late Medieval and Early Modern Europe* (Leiden, 1993), pp. 625–37.

22 Strauss, *Luther's House of Learning*, p. 270.

23 C. Scott Dixon, *The Reformation and Rural Society: The Parishes of Brandenburg-Ansbach-Kulmbach, 1528–1603* (Cambridge, 1996), pp. 102–207.

24 Harold S. Bender, 'The Anabaptist Vision', in James M. Stayer and Werner O. Packull (eds), *The Anabaptists and Thomas Müntzer* (Dubuque, IO, 1980), p. 19.

25 R.W. Scribner, *For the Sake of Simple Folk: Popular Propaganda for the German Reformation* (Cambridge, 1981).

FURTHER READING

There is no satisfactory treatment of the Knights' Revolt. William R. Hitchcock, *The Background of the Knights Revolt* (Berkeley, 1958) presents the dated notion of the imperial knights as a declining class. The chapter 'The Knights as Propagandists' in Miriam Usher Chrisman, *Conflicting Visions of Reform: German Lay Propaganda Pamphlets, 1519–1530* (Atlantic Highlands, NJ, 1996), takes the adherence of the knights to the Reformation entirely seriously. For interpretations pertaining to the nobility I am particularly indebted to my Ph.D. student, Victor Thiessen, whose dissertation, 'Nobles' Reformation: the reception and adaption of Reformation ideas in the pamphlets of Noble writers from 1520 to 1530', was completed in 1998.

On the Peasants' War, Günther Franz, *Der deutsche Bauernkrieg* (Munich and Berlin, 1933) presented the Peasants' War as a regionally disparate and basically non-religious event. Peter Blickle, *The Revolution of 1525: The German Peasants' War from a New Perspective*, trans. Thomas A. Brady, Jr, and H.C. Erik Midelfort (Baltimore, 1981), attempts a multi-causal but unified presentation that connects the Peasants' War and the Reformation. Tom Scott, *Freiburg and the Breisgau: Town–Country Relations in the Age of Reformation and Peasants' War* (Oxford, 1986), views the structural hostilities between town and country as the Achilles' heel of the peasant rebellion. Tom Scott and R.W. Scribner (ed. and trans.), *The German Peasants' War: A History in Documents* (Atlantic Highlands, NJ, 1991), is not only a substantial collection of documents but also in the long introduction the best narrative account in English. It is probably the most useful book on the topic. A shorter collection of documents and interpretations is Janos Bak (ed.), *The German Peasant War* (London, 1976). R.W. Scribner and Gerhard Benecke (eds), *The German Peasant War: New Viewpoints* (London, 1979), is a more representative collection of interpretative essays.

Bridging the Peasants' War and Anabaptism and arguing for their connection is my *The German Peasants' War and Anabaptist Community of Goods* (Montreal, 1991). The best English work on Müntzer is Hans-Jürgen Goertz, *Thomas Müntzer: Apocalyptic Mystic and*

Revolutionary, trans. Jocelyn Jacquiery (Edinburgh, 1993). Also not superseded and a more conservative complement to Goertz's presentation of Müntzer as a revolutionary is the Müntzer biography in Part III of Gordon Rupp, *Patterns of Reformation* (London, 1969).

On the educational, moral and spiritual state of rural parishes in the Lutheran territorial churches, Gerald Strauss, *Luther's House of Learning: Indoctrination of the Young in the German Reformation* (Baltimore, 1978) presents an arresting sketch of the failure of the Reformers' original hopes. Strauss's findings are controversial. Cf. the rejoinder of James Kittelson, 'Successes and Failures in the German Reformation: The Report from Strasbourg', in *Archiv für Reformationsgeschichte* 73 (1982), pp. 153–75, which calls for thorough local studies. Such a study is the excellent monograph by C. Scott Dixon, *The Reformation in Rural Society: The Parishes of Brandenburg-Ansbach-Kulmbach, 1528–1603* (Cambridge, 1996), which substantiates and elaborates the interpretation originally presented by Strauss.

THE PRINCELY REFORMATION IN GERMANY

C. Scott Dixon

Even if the Reformation had done no other service, wrote the church historian Johann Matthias Schröckh in the eighteenth century, 'it could still lay claim to the gratitude of all princes and also of all subjects ... that royal authority regained possession of all that the tyrants of the Church for so long withheld from it.' For Schröckh, as for most thinkers of his day, personal liberty and freedom of conscience were corollaries of the Reformation. No longer subject to the coercion and oppression of the Catholic church, the Protestant faithful in the German lands could fashion a personal relationship with God without suffering the 'tyranny' of papal censure. Martin Luther's rereading of scripture's central message made this act of religious reinterpretation possible. But equally important, as Schröckh points out, was the shift in relations of power that made the long-term existence of the Protestant church possible. The Reformation did not just modify systems of belief. In sixteenth-century Germany the reform movement changed the relationship between church and state. It deprived the Catholic church of its sovereignty over subjects and souls, and it invested the state with the power and the right to govern the visible church. The Protestant church in the German lands was thus a state church; this was a collusion of power and rule that was in place at the very outset of the movement. And it has long been held a truth of German history. As late as 1919 Reinhold Moeller, addressing the evangelical church parliament in Dresden, spoke of how 'since the days of the Reformation there has been the closest relationship between the evangelical church ... and the public power of the state.'[1]

THE GERMAN STATES AND THE EMPIRE

The German Reformation originated in Saxony, a territory in the Holy Roman Empire. Saxony, like other German principalities such as Bavaria, Hesse or Württemberg, was a subject-power in the empire. The Holy Roman Emperor, an elected sovereign, was the titular head of the monarchy, and all of the states (from the Saxons to the Swiss) were his dependants. In the German lands, as a consequence, two notions (or types) of state were in evidence. On the one hand, there was the idea of a Holy Roman Empire of the German Nation (this latter appellation added in 1486), a single monarchy and a subject people. On the other hand, there was the myriad of territories and smaller dependencies that made up the empire. In practice and perception, these dependent territories were like independent states.

When Luther first posted his theses in Wittenberg (31 October 1517), the idea of empire was on the wane. Germans had long recognized the failure of the empire to provide the framework for a functional unified monarchy, and throughout the fifteenth and early sixteenth centuries a number of reform proposals emerged which did little more than expose the failures of the imperial system. An effective reform movement did not develop until the late fifteenth century, while Maximilian I was on the throne. At the Worms Reichstag of 1495, perpetual peace was declared, a Common Penny was introduced and the Imperial Chamber Court (*Reichskammergericht*) was re-established; in 1500 a ruling council (*Reichsregiment*) was created; and in 1512 the empire was divided up into a series of circles (*Reichskreise*) to facilitate more effective rule.[2] But these changes came too late to make an effective monarchy out of the vague configurations of empire and by the late fifteenth century the power of rule in the German lands was not in the hands of the emperors but rather in the hands of the German princes. Historians refer to this phenomenon as 'particularism', a term used to describe the powers of rule exercised by the periphery (the territories) at the expense of the centre (the empire). For this reason, the fusion of church and state which characterized the German Reformation would not take place at the level of empire, but at the level of the princely territory.

The princely territories of Germany did not together comprise a kingdom, as the historian Veit Ludwig von Seckendorff observed in *The German Princely State* (1660), but they were prone to the same problems of rule and invested with a similar range of power as any large monarchy. As such, Seckendorff continued, it is best to conceive of them as we would 'any great kingdom of the world'.[3] And indeed the powers of the German princes might be compared with those of a European monarch, save one major limitation: the German prince derived his powers from the emperor. Of course, there were different levels of noble status, passed on from one generation to the next, and these levels had some degree of fixed reality in the constitutional framework. But real power lay in the rights and responsibilities given to the princes by the emperor and as such the hierarchy of noble status in the German lands was largely determined by relations to the empire. In order to claim princely status, the candidate had to participate in imperial rule, and this meant sitting in councils and court, holding ceremonial offices and honouring the empire and its legal constitution. In return the candidate held an imperial fief – a principality – along with independent rights of rule, including powers of jurisdiction, defence, taxation and regalia. All of these rights and privileges comprised the princes' sovereignty (*Herrschaft*), the range of powers a prince might exercise. This, in addition to the size of the principality, was what distinguished a major prince such as the Elector of Saxony, the Margrave of Brandenburg or the Duke of Bavaria from the lesser nobility of the realm (counts, barons, knights). In the Holy Roman Empire, however, there were certain restrictions placed on the exercise of princely sovereignty. The prince was subject to the emperor and had to honour the constitution of the realm. Beyond this, the German prince also had to learn to negotiate the traditional laws of the principality, the territorial estates which upheld the laws, and the complex and fragile legal situation in a land where rights of rule and jurisdiction intermeshed. He could not, as Seckendorff observed, rule like a master over his journeymen.[4] Nevertheless, by the late mediæval period, the German princes had acquired extensive powers of governance, and a select few – the Elector of Saxony, perhaps, or the Duke of Bavaria – might consider themselves the equal of any monarch in Europe. They ruled, in effect, autonomous states within the Holy Roman Empire.

The princely territory in Germany, as Thomas Brady has remarked, was 'in many ways … the largest and strongest of all those local powers who developed more effective institutions of governance during the later Middle Ages'.[5] Throughout the mediæval period the princes had been able to alienate the power of the German emperors. In defence of 'German liberty' the princes blocked those reform initiatives which smacked of centralization. At the same time they set about consolidating rule in their own territories. More effective methods and organs of governance were introduced. This was the age which saw the emergence of public officials (chancellors, treasurers, councillors) and public offices (courts of justice and finance, the treasury, the prince's councils). The Bavarian ordinance of 1511–12 speaks of the chancellery, the treasury, the department of finance, and by 1520 the territory had a centralized judicial system based on Roman law. In Baden the first chancellery regulation was published in 1504, a central court established in 1509. This occurred throughout the German lands – from the duchies of Bavaria and Württemberg to the south, to the electorates of Saxony, Brandenburg and the Palatinate, to the centrally located lands of Hesse, Brunswick and Brandenburg-Ansbach. In all of the larger principalities, the late mediæval period witnessed an increase in the powers exercised by the territorial prince, new notions of sovereignty and a programme of centralization and institutional sophistication which helped consolidate territorial rule. Not all of the princes would welcome the evangelical movement as it took root in the cities, but it was clear from the very outset that the principality was the political and institutional setting where the fate of the Reformation would be decided. The relationship between the Protestant church and the princely state was thus not created by circumstance: it was inherent in the very nature of rule in the German lands.

THE MEDIÆVAL BEGINNINGS OF REFORM

In the late mediæval period, the German princes exercised considerable control over the church in their lands. It is worth remembering this, for it is often assumed that the Reformation created the territorial church out of nothing, when in fact the basic structural preconditions were already in place well before the sixteenth century. Granted, nothing in the mediæval world prepared the ground for the spiritual authority later claimed by the Protestant rulers, but the extension of secular rule to the ecclesiastical realm began centuries before the Reformation. Certain boundaries remained in place. The princes did not challenge the powers of the papacy, for instance, nor was the church's jurisdictional status ever seriously threatened. But as the principalities evolved in late mediæval Germany, the process of consolidation weakened and often eclipsed the powers of lesser sovereigns, and this included the Catholic bishops.

We can see this process at work in Luther's land of Saxony. Due to the need for military protection during the thirteenth and fourteenth centuries, the Bishops of Meissen, Merseburg and Naumburg signed treaties of mutual assistance with the ruling house of Saxony; but what began as a contract between equal partners soon evolved into a feudal protectorship. The bishops, in effect, became the vassals of the prince. The dioceses were forced to forfeit the right to mint their own coins, the princes extended their rights of advocacy in return for more ecclesiastical land, while the prelates became little more than ministers of the emerging Saxon state. Close ties with the papacy also worked to weaken the power of the bishoprics. In the fourteenth century, with the pope and the emperor at odds, support for the papacy earned the Saxon princes additional privileges, including the right to occupy important offices in Meissen, Naumburg and Merseburg. By 1485 the house of Saxony more or less had the Meissen bishopric at its disposal.[6]

The situation was similar in other principalities. In Jülich-Berg, as in Saxony, the territorial rulers used their relations with the pope to weaken the powers of the bishop. The dukes had long sought to exclude the jurisdiction of the Cologne archbishopric from their lands and in 1501 Duke William IV's plan to neutralize the judgement of the ecclesiastical courts in secular affairs received papal approval. In the electoral Palatinate, the two main bishoprics of Worms and Speyer had become little more than satellites of the state. In 1349 the cathedral chapter of Worms made an oath to the effect that it would never elect a primate who might bring harm on the land. And in the Palatinate, as in Saxony, the bishops often served as trusted court officials: from 1464 Matthias von Rammung was both Bishop of Speyer and the elector's court chancellor. As a final example among the great princes we might look at the Dukes of Württemberg, a line of secular rulers whose policy of aggrandizement was so successful that the duchy created its own special court to deal with church disputes. Indeed, the Württemberg dukes held the neighbouring bishops in such disregard that Eberhard the Bearded once appointed a clergyman to the church in Lauffen without first presenting him to Würzburg. Eberhard assured his subjects that this appointment was just as legal and binding 'as if he had been confirmed by a bishop of Würzburg. It needs no further confirmation.'[7] Even in the smaller territories the secular lords chipped away at the powers of the bishoprics. The duchy of Zweibrücken was subject to the dioceses of Mainz, Worms, Speyer, Strasbourg, Trier and Metz, but that did not stop the dukes from extending rights of protection and safeguard (*Schutz und Schirm*) over the new foundations, alienating the judgements of the ecclesiastical courts and publishing secular mandates (such as the 1442 Police Ordinance) that clearly touched on spiritual concerns.[8] In most of the secular territories in the empire, the late mediæval period witnessed a waning of diocesan power in the face of evolving princely rule.

With the bishops kept at arm's length, the late mediæval German princes were able to exercise considerable sovereignty over the church in their territories. But it was a purely instrumental increase in power, not a new conception of rule between church and state (as would emerge with the Reformation). In essence, the princes increased their hold over the church by exploiting the two traditional rights at their disposal: the right of protection over a foundation and rights of patronage. Ultimately, the rule of all princes was grounded in the right to exercise jurisdiction (*Hochgerichtsbarkeit*); but there were other rights and methods of rule as well, including those related to protection and safeguard. Protectorship or guardianship involved a complex set of rights and relations between the prince and his subjects. The right to act as military guardian did not confer territorial or jurisdictional power; but it necessarily placed the lord in a favourable position and this was a relationship the princes exploited at the expense of ecclesiastical foundations. While the legal code of the Middle Ages made no necessary connection between sovereignty and guardianship, the princes were able to transform their duties as protectors of churches and monasteries into real power. In general, such local forms of protection and advocacy helped create the large territorial powers of the sixteenth and seventeenth centuries, and it helped the princes secure total control over the church.[9] Patronage, on the other hand, was a fairly simple matter, not because most parish churches were in the gift of the prince, but rather because most were in the gift of the nobility. The bishop still had the right to ordain the parish clergymen, but most other powers had fallen to the noble patron. However, as the prince intensified his policy of ecclesiastical protection, and as more church foundations fell subject first to his protectorship and then to his claims as sovereign over the territorial church, the clergy became, in effect, his vassals, and the princes gradually usurped the rights of patronage claimed by the lesser nobles. The Reformation would provide the prince with a theoretical (or a theological) apology for this usurpation, but the process was already under way in the fifteenth century.[10]

These practices, common in the late mediæval German territories, provided the basis for the absolute religious authority the Protestant princes would later exercise. With the Reformation came the claim that the secular rulers had the right and indeed the obligation to reform the church (*ius reformandi*). It was no longer just a matter of protecting the church, but of ruling its inner workings and deciding its fate. Protestant scholars would later justify this transfer of power in massive and complex legal tomes. In the beginning, however, it was the right of protection and safeguard that allowed for the princes to stake a claim to the territorial church.[11] This made the princely territory a suitable framework for the introduction of religious reform and that is why Martin Luther turned to the secular princes of the German nation.

LUTHERAN CONCEPTS OF AUTHORITY

In February 1520 unrest broke out between citizens and students in the university town of Wittenberg. By July the citizens were arming themselves; fears spread that the students might set the town alight; shots were fired. On 15 July 1520 Luther spoke of the uprising in a sermon. In his eyes it was clearly the work of the Devil, for even if the unrest had been in the service of a good cause (such as God's Word), rebellion could never be justified. It was the duty – the God-given duty – of the secular authorities to put down unrest and maintain order. The following year, with Luther away at the Wartburg, a much more serious term of disorder gripped the town. Students were again at the forefront of the movement, but this time they could look for leadership in Gabriel Zwilling and Andreas Karlstadt. Historians sometimes refer to this as the Wittenberg movement (1521–2) and it was in essence the first attempt in the German lands to force through the Reformation. Unlike later attempts, however, it was not based on compromise and secular mandate, but threats and violence. Karlstadt and Zwilling succeeded to a degree, for the council was forced to concede to their demands and a new church ordinance was introduced (25 January 1522), but ultimately the movement came to nothing. Once back in Wittenberg, Luther referred to events in a series of sermons (March 1522) and again outlined his understanding of church and state. Reform, he advised, should not be forced on people; the Word should first be preached and weaker consciences won to the cause. However, if reforms must be pushed through, the power to make this decision does not lie with the common man or the city council, but rather with the sovereign appointed by God – the prince. Only when the Reformation was implemented by the territorial prince could the faithful be certain that it 'comes of God'.[12]

From the Wittenberg movement to the last days of his life, Luther never departed from his belief that the territorial prince had the authority to implement the Reformation. Luther had first turned to the princes in his *Address to the Christian Nobility of the German Nation* (1520), when he called on the secular authorities to assume the mantle of religious reform. But as the movement took shape, so too did the need for a sophisticated model (and a convincing defence) of the new relations between church and state. Luther's vision developed out of his evangelical theology. His notion of the priesthood of all believers did away with the distinction between the secular and spiritual realms. The earthly church, as a consequence, became an institution as any other, and it required governance and protection. To prevent the confusion of authority rife in the mediæval church, Luther developed his doctrine of the Two Kingdoms, an idea he presented in his work *On Secular Authority* (1523). Mankind is subject to two forms of rule: the rule of the church and the rule of the state. God's Word ruled the true church; and this was a matter left to the conscience of the believer. The rule of the state, however, was an external matter, put in place by God to impose order over Fallen Man. No less than the rule of the church, the rule of the state was a divine ordinance. It was created to make the world safe for Christians and allow for the preaching of the Word. As a consequence, to follow Luther's line of thinking, the secular arm had the right to impose order on the external form of the Christian church, for a church in a state of disorder was a threat to the public peace and a hazard to salvation. With this, the basic theoretical foundations of the territorial church were in place.

But it would be Luther's followers, more than Luther himself, who provided the final justification for the territorial church in Protestant principalities. Later Reformers did not look to the late mediæval tradition of protection and safeguard to justify secular intervention, nor did they view it as a temporary measure in a crisis situation (as Luther did). In Melanchthon's view, the prince had a God-given obligation to intervene and reform the church. The prince held a special place as 'chief member of the church' (*praecipuum membrum ecclesiae*), not because he enjoyed any favoured sacerdotal status, but rather because he had been invested with the power to rule over the Christian community. In the absence of action from the bishops, responsibility for the church thus fell to the prince and brotherly love made it obligatory. What gave this idea such power was the place the prince assumed in the divine order. He was God's agent on earth, put there to rule over the visible church just as he ruled over the state. The godly ruler, as Melanchthon wrote to the princes of Brunswick and Lüneburg, 'is God's image on earth, and the Eternal one himself protects and supports him.' Of all the Reformers who built on this theme, Johannes Brenz, the architect of the Württemberg church order, did the most to turn it into an ecclesiological programme. Citing Old Testament histories to support his case, Brenz argued that it was the duty of the prince to secure the welfare of his subjects, including their spiritual welfare. False worship, he concluded, would foster unrest and lead to damnation. By mid-century, Brenz believed that the central task of the secular authority was to secure the preaching of the Word, and this meant maintaining peace and order and watching over the church. 'Secular authority', he wrote, 'was established in order that man ... might be able to lead a tranquil life on earth, and thus be able to know and to serve God.' The prince had become the custodian of his subjects' salvation.[13]

The Protestant princes in the German lands were not slow to exploit the union between church and state. In 1533 Duke Ernst of Brunswick-Lüneburg published a tract in defence of his decision to introduce the Reformation. God's honour and his Christian obligation left him no other option, he wrote. There could be no greater good than the preaching of God's Word in a peaceful realm. Like Brenz, Ernst drew on the Old Testament histories to liken his situation to that of his biblical predecessors; and, like Brenz, he did not think of his intervention as a temporary expedient, but a permanent responsibility. Princes ruled, as the church ordinance of Calenberg explained, 'in place of God', and their duties did not end with the upkeep of secular order but also extended to the welfare of their subjects' souls. And as Julius of Wolfenbüttel made clear in the preface to his 1569 church ordinance, this responsibility also meant that the prince had to take decisions which touched on the service and worship of God. Duke Christopher of Württemberg did not hesitate to claim that his main role was that of protector of God's honour and the true faith – that was why he had been placed in office. The secular authorities in the Reformed (or Calvinist) principalities spoke in similar terms, even if the conditions of the Second Reformation made it necessary to provide a more detailed defence.[14]

German princes had made similar claims before. William of Thuringia thought of himself as God's agent on earth as he set about reforming the Saxon monasteries in the fifteenth century. Like any later Protestant prince, he did it for 'the honour of God' and the spiritual welfare of his subjects. And we have already seen above how the late mediæval princes could dominate and manipulate the church in their territories. But nothing in pre-Reformation Germany prepared the ground for the authority the Protestant prince would assume in church affairs. He was not just the steward of a church system, working within the bounds of an unchallenged religion. With the Reformation the prince became the legislator and the arbiter of a territorial church, and that included matters which touched on public religious confession and private belief. This type of power was not a continuation of a mediæval tradition, but a creation of the Reformation.

PRINCELY RESPONSES TO THE REFORMATION

The early evangelical movement did not have the support of the princes. Of course, Frederick the Wise (Luther's patron and prince) famously offered his Wittenberg professor safe conduct to his meetings with the Catholic authorities and the imperial diet in Worms (1521). Frederick also allowed for the preaching of the Word 'clear and pure' in his lands (which was seen by some as a mandate for reform) and let the Wittenberg reformers publish and preach. But he did not legitimate the movement or take steps to establish a new church. Instead, the movement developed independently of the prince; in fact it was only in response to the widespread support for the Reformation that the elector was forced to take a stand. Troubles in Wittenberg, Gotha and Weida, for instance, forced Frederick to intervene, but by 1524 most of the towns in Ernestine Saxony had become evangelical without any princely measures in support of the Reformation. This suggests two things: first, the evangelical movement had a broad spectrum of support which did not rely on princely fiat for its development; second, despite the movement's early momentum, the princes were slow to support it. This was certainly the state of affairs in Brandenburg-Ansbach-Kulmbach. As in Ernestine Saxony, the territorial towns became the first sites of reform activity and ultimately the setting for initial change. In Ansbach, Schwabach, Kulmbach, Wunsiedel, Crailsheim, Hof and a host of other towns, Lutheran supporters were active in the early 1520s. Even in the rural parishes the movement had taken hold. In the village of Wendelstein, to cite a famous example, the parishioners published a statement in 1524 calling for the reform of the parish and the introduction of an evangelical service. Casimir, the resident margrave, reacted no differently than Frederick of Saxony: he allowed for the preaching of the Word 'clear and pure' and let the reformers teach and publish, but he did not encourage or support the movement. But here, as elsewhere, the Reformation took root despite the lack of encouragement from the prince. There is no greater testimony to the depth of popular support than events in the lands of Albertine Saxony. Even in this principality, where duke George made every effort to put down the movement, Luther gathered followers. There seemed to be little a prince could do to stop the spread of the movement in the early 1520s, just as there was little the German princes seemed to offer in support of it.[15]

Luther's excommunication in 1520 and the Edict of Worms (1521) bound the princes to take a public stand, but few reacted with any conviction. The ban was only reluctantly enforced, for the princes feared it would spark unrest among the common people. But as the princes dissimulated, the movement continued to spread and the imperial council could do little to control the situation. A series of imperial diets was held in Nuremberg (1522–4) at which the Luther Affair was discussed and some decisions taken. The second recess of Nuremberg (February 1523) would only tolerate 'the holy gospel according to Scripture' to be preached.

Figure 9.1 Albrecht Dürer, *Frederick the Wise*, 1524. The artistry of Albrecht Dürer presents a fine image of a prince whose fierce pride in his local university – and its turbulent preacher – enabled him to combine a devout Catholicism with a refusal to turn over Luther to his enemies.

It also promised a general council which would deal with reform. The third recess (April 1524) reissued the Edict of Worms, exhorting the princes to impose it 'as far as it was possible' and again spoke of the forthcoming council (set for Speyer). But this was also rather vague non-committal politics, made even less effective after Charles V forbade the proposed council in Speyer. The princes were thus forced to think on their feet and it gave rise to a range of different reactions.

Some princes viewed Luther as a heretic and the movement as a threat to the public peace. These rulers did not just remain true to the traditional church, but were quite active opponents of the early Reformation. By 1523 most of the German prince-bishops had recognized the threat Luther presented and combed their dioceses for his followers. Of the secular princes, William of Bavaria and George of Saxony were the most dogged and inflexible, while others (such as Joachim of Brandenburg, Christopher of Bremen-Verden and Henry of Wolfenbüttel) were satisfied imposing measures which ensured the public peace. George of Saxony did not just resist the movement: he took active measures to stamp it out. In 1522 Lutheran sympathizers in Albertine Saxony were to be placed under arrest and the same year George published a mandate which put an end to all religious change. Only the Dukes of Bavaria, led by the formidable Leonard von Eck, could come close to George's anti-Lutheran zeal. As in Saxony, the Bavarian initiative was a campaign designed to root the Lutherans out through arrest and expulsion. Far more common in the early years was the reaction of princes like Casimir of Brandenburg-Kulmbach or Philip of Baden. Rather than take a firm decision on the early Reformation, these princes let the evangelical movement gather momentum. Loyalty to the emperor and distrust of all popular movements meant that some restrictions were imposed, but few, if any, effective steps were taken to stamp out the movement. Henry of Mecklenburg, Ludwig of the Palatinate, the Dukes of Jülich-Cleve-Berg, Philip of Baden – all of these princes granted the preaching of the Word 'clear and pure' and allowed for some degree of religious innovation, but they did not throw full support behind the Wittenberg version of Reformation. Even the two princely icons of early Lutheranism, Frederick the Wise and Philip of Hesse, did nothing positive to develop the Reformation in their lands in the early years. There was no need to – political circumstances did not necessitate it. But this would soon change.[16]

In the 1520s a series of events occurred which placed the Reformation at the centre of the imperial agenda. The Peasants' War of 1525, inspired in large part by evangelical demands, forced the princes to take action against the more threatening aspects of the reform movement. For Casimir of Brandenburg-Ansbach-Kulmbach, the preaching of the Word had given rise to the unrest and it was the duty of the secular lord to intervene and restore order. Casimir interpreted this to mean a turn back to traditional worship. For others, such as John the Steadfast (who succeeded Frederick the Wise as Elector of Saxony), the aftermath of the Peasants' War was the occasion for reform initiatives. The following year the imperial diet at Speyer (1526) issued a temporary resolution which gave reform-friendly princes the opportunity to let the Reformation develop. With the empire in a state of stalemate, the recess of Speyer (27 August 1526) commanded the estates to conduct their affairs 'as [they] hope and trust to answer to God and his

Imperial Majesty' until a council could resolve the religious issue. This was a political, not a legal, solution, but in practice it granted the same freedom of movement that the Peace of Augsburg (1555) would later confirm in its famous formula *cuius regio eius religio* ('whose the rule, his the religion'), a law which secured the right of Reformation for the Protestant princes. Archduke Ferdinand rescinded the concessions of 1526 at the diet which met in Speyer in 1529, but by this stage a fairly powerful evangelical party had already emerged. Indeed, in response to the threats of Speyer (1529) a group of evangelical cities and princes submitted a common protest to the empire (and were henceforth termed Protestants). The Protestant party (which included the princes of electoral Saxony, Hesse, Brandenburg-Ansbach, Brunswick-Lüneburg and Anhalt-Bernberg) acquired a common religious identity when the Augsburg Confession (1530) was submitted to the imperial diet and a common political destiny when a group of Protestant powers joined together in the Schmalkaldic League (1531). Thus, by the mid-1530s the German princes could no longer sit on the fence. Two confessional parties were at odds and the princes had to make a choice for or against the Reformation. It was a difficult decision, one tempered by personal conviction, selfish interest and political expediency, but every secular ruler in the German lands had to face it. And it first became a possibility with the 1526 recess of Speyer, when the princes were afforded the latitude to introduce reform.

Up to the outbreak of the Peasants' War in 1525, the reform movement had taken root in the cities and the rural parishes as a form of Communal Reformation. Thus for the princes who introduced the Reformation in the 1520s, the challenge was not just to create a new church *ex nihilo*, but rather to take the initiative away from the subject population. Philip of Hesse was the first prince to take positive action. Soon after the 1526 recess of Speyer he called his clergy together in Homburg (October 1526) and, with the help of the clergyman Franz Lambert of Avignon, drew up a model of reform in the *Reformatio Ecclesiarum Hassiae*. Luther spoke out against this proposal, however, and it came to nothing. As a consequence, evangelical princes like Philip of Hesse turned to Luther's Saxony for guidance.

In Saxony, measures to establish an evangelical church were introduced after the accession of John the Steadfast (1525–32). The Wittenberg vision of reform was imposed throughout the principality: evangelical clergymen were appointed, troublesome Catholics were dismissed; church services were standardized (definitively with Luther's *German Mass* in 1526); the church and monasteries were placed under the supervision of the secular authorities. But the most effective measure was the visitation process, for this enabled the prince to take the Reformation into the parishes. The visitation commission met for the first time in late 1526; a draft of visitation instructions was completed the following year. Melanchthon then provided the prince with a doctrinal statement in his *Instructions for the Visitors of Parish Pastors in Electoral Saxony* (1528). A more detailed system of church rule would develop later in the century, but the central pillars of the Lutheran church had been put in place – Saxony had a statement of the faith, princely mandate controlled the church and the visitation took the Reformation into the parishes. Other princes followed the Saxon lead. Philip of Hesse borrowed from the Saxon model for his own Reformation, as did Ernst of

Brunswick-Lüneburg. But of all the princes who followed the Saxon initiative in the early years, the most important was Margrave George of Brandenburg-Ansbach. George assumed rule of his Franconian inheritance after the death of Casimir in 1527 and from the moment of his accession he set about introducing the Reformation in his principality. On 3 March 1528 he issued a resolution which made it law to preach the Word 'clearly and purely'; any clergyman under his patronage who did not honour the margrave's religious directives would be dismissed from office. Using the Saxon visitation as a model, the higher clergy of Brandenburg-Ansbach, together with officials from the imperial city of Nuremberg, saw through their own visitation in 1528. And over the next few years the two powers worked together again to draw up the Brandenburg–Nuremberg Church Order (1533), one of the most sophisticated and influential statements of Lutheranism in the empire.[17]

The early reform initiatives taken by Saxony, Hesse and Brandenburg-Ansbach were crucial for the development and ultimate survival of Lutheranism in Germany and yet, even in 1529 when the signatories submitted their protest, the Reformation was still on weak ground. In the 1530s, however, two important conversions helped to secure the faith. In 1534 Landgrave Philip of Hesse helped restore Duke Ulrich to his patrimony of Württemberg. The land had been confiscated by the Habsburgs in 1519, but with French and Bavarian backing, under Philip's fortuitous leadership, Ulrich resumed powers of rule in Stuttgart. Initially, the reform of the principality was subject to a strong Zwinglian influence, but eventually the duke opted for Lutheranism and immediately introduced the Reformation into his lands. Johannes Brenz was summoned from Schwäbisch Hall to serve as a theological adviser and, together Brenz and the Dukes of Württemberg, fashioned one of the most influential territorial church structures in Europe. Moreover, with the emergence of the church in Württemberg, the Lutheran faith had been established in a powerful territory in the German southwest. Lutheranism eclipsed Zwinglianism as a confessional force among the German princes once and for all: the southern cities waned in the shadow of this Lutheran principality, and when Ulrich joined the Schmalkaldic League in 1536 an important strategic position was won for German Protestantism. The other important conversion occurred in the lands of Albertine Saxony. Duke George, German Catholicism's most forceful prince, died on 17 April 1539, leaving the reins of rule in the hands of his brother Henry. Lutheranism was introduced immediately. Both Melanchthon and Luther offered advice on the reform process and indeed many of the steps that were taken (such as the visitations, the church order) were modelled directly on the Ernestine equivalents. When Duke Maurice took over rule from Henry in 1541, he was able to force through the Reformation by insisting that the *Heinrichsagenda*, a statement of the faith for the principality, was honoured by the resident clergy.[18] Albertine Saxony was an important conquest for the Protestant powers, not only for its intrinsic worth as a territory in the empire, but for its symbolic value. One of Germany's most prominent Catholic territories turned Lutheran on the death of its prince and there was no reason to doubt that others might follow in train.

Despite the hopes that were raised in mid-century with the signing of the Peace of Augsburg (1555), the Reformation did not carry all before it. This was due in large part to the strength of the Catholic response. The Council of Trent (1545–63) gave the Catholic church a sense of mission – and a clarity of dogma and purpose – that had been lacking for centuries. But just as fateful for the progress of Lutheranism in the German principalities was the emergence of an alternative model of Protestant reform, what historians sometimes refer to as the Second Reformation. It occurred later in the century, experiencing most of its progress in the years from 1580 to 1620, and it was a movement which took its inspiration from the Swiss (or Reformed) tradition of evangelical thought. The works of Huldrych Zwingli and John Calvin, rather than those of Martin Luther, provided the theological framework for the movement. As a process or a campaign of religious reform, however, the Second Reformation relied on the same basic methods as the early Lutheran programmes. The prince assumed control of the church, statements of the faith were published, visitations were carried out, clergymen were put in office or replaced, and a new service and liturgy (usually Calvinist in inspiration) was introduced. A revised theology gave rise to changes in worship – the most important (at least symbolically) being the breaking of bread and the cleansing of churches. But perhaps the most significant difference between the Lutheran Reformation of the early sixteenth century and the Second Reformation was the stress the princes placed on the organization of church and society. In the eyes of the rulers who adopted the Reformed confession, they were not implementing a new reform movement so much as completing what Martin Luther had begun. It was necessary to reform life, just as it had been necessary to reform doctrine, and once again it was the responsibility of the pious prince to see this vision through. In view of this, the Second Reformation should be thought of as a continuation of the first, one which brought an even closer union of church and state.[19]

THE PROCESS OF REFORMATION

The decision to introduce the Reformation was one of the most important a sovereign would ever make and there was a complex of factors and considerations that had to be taken into account. Political determinants often played a role, as did the promise of increased income, the threat of violence, the benefits of extended rule, the power of territorial identities and the liability of dynastic relations. Nor should we forget the deep piety behind decisions of this kind. When Princess Elisabeth of Calenberg drafted a testimony for her son and spoke of him as God's servant on earth and protector of the Lutheran church, her words were not meant to disguise a darker purpose. She believed it.[20] For these reasons – and many more besides – the German princes ventured to introduce the Reformation into the German lands. It was a decision which brought with it certain risks, as well as certain consequences.

The process of Reformation helped to transform the mediæval German principality into the early modern state. Historians think of the sixteenth century as an age which saw a turn towards more modern forms of statecraft. Independent councils, written constitutions, complex bureaucracies, standardized legal codes and university-educated ministers of government replaced the highly personalized household rule of the Middle Ages. In Protestant Germany, the fusion of church and state encouraged this process.[21] To start with, the prince now had more land under his control. Soon after the introduction of the Reformation in Albertine Saxony, for instance, the Bishop of Meissen was forced to cede the administrative district of Stolpen to the prince. Equally, the monastic territories of Altzella, Chemnitz, Grünhain, Zschillen-Wechselburg and Remse were turned into secular units.

But the simple expansion of area was not enough. In order to see through the Reformation and then to maintain the faith once it had been introduced, the prince had first to construct, then to control, a fairly sophisticated system of church rule. In the early years of the reform movement, the system of church government was usually the result of adaptation and compromise between the territorial sovereigns and the leading reformers. Luther worked with the princes of Saxony; George of Brandenburg-Ansbach with Andreas Althamer and Johannes Brenz; the dukes of Pomerania with Johannes Bugenhagen. In these early Lutheran principalities the Reformation began with a visitation, the existing chapters were divided up into new church districts (superintendencies), the diocese officials were replaced by Lutheran clergy (each district acquiring its own superintendent) and the clergy gathered together in yearly synods. But perhaps the most important union was that between Johannes Brenz and the dukes of Württemberg, for the system of church government that was developed in Württemberg served as a model for many of the Lutheran churches in Germany. Here too the Reformation began with a visitation in 1536 and the emergence of superintendents (or visitors), all of which was managed by the court. But by mid-century a separate form of church government emerged. In 1547 an administrative body was set up to deal with church matters: in 1553 a church consistory was established, a new superintendents' ordinance was issued and a church treasury was created. All of this was given final definition in the Great Church Ordinance (1559), which specified the membership and functions of the consistory, the responsibilities of the church officials (secular and spiritual alike) and supervised the visitations and the church treasury. At the very apex of this system of church rule was the Duke of Württemberg. The prince was the final authority in all matters relating to church government: this was just another aspect of his expanding powers of rule in the sixteenth century. The fact that it was the rule of the church, however, meant that it was an assumption of power and a quality of power without precedence in European history.[22]

In many ways, the broader process of Protestant reform was played out at the local level with the sequestration of the monasteries. As we have seen above, German princes had interfered in monastic life before. William III of Thuringia introduced a reform programme in the mid-fifteenth century which relied on secular officials for its implementation. But William never challenged the right or the utility of the church foundations – indeed, his reform initiative of 1450 received the pope's approbation. The Protestant princes, on the other hand, did not want to reform the monasteries, but disband and abolish them, and this required a different approach. Philip of Hesse was one of the first princes to deal directly with this problem. Using the Peasants' War as initial justification, Philip ordered an inventory (February 1525) of the foundation wealth in the landgravate.

The valuables of the church, including important documents, were confiscated. Following Luther's advice, the prince did not use force to empty the foundations: the clergy were free to go or stay, they were compensated (as were the patrons) and the monasteries and nunneries were left standing until the clergy died out. Once a recess (15 October 1527) had made this into law, Philip appointed secular officials to supervise the foundations, while the populated monasteries and nunneries were forced to take on an evangelical preacher. The Hessian prince now had complete control of the former Catholic foundations: they were integrated into the secular system of rule, and the wealth and income was combined with the court treasury. Other sovereigns reacted similarly. The Reformation granted all German princes the right to lay claim to the ecclesiastical foundations and this resulted in both a considerable extension of sovereignty and an influx of wealth. For the rulers of Baden-Durlach, this meant placing a secular overseer into each of the monasteries and channelling the money into the new church. For the rulers of the Palatinate, it meant transforming former abbots into princely officials and turning former monasteries into new schools. For the dukes of Württemberg, it meant they could finally claim complete control of the fourteen big foundations and it also meant the University of Tübingen could at last have a suitable anatomy theatre.[23]

But for most of the Protestant princes of the sixteenth century, the Reformation's ultimate purpose was not the conversion of doubtful clergy or the liquidation of moribund Catholic institutions. The Reformation had been introduced in an effort to realize the potential of God's Word on earth and this meant a *complete* reform of society and its members. Religion thus became central to the development of the Protestant state in Germany, not only because the public confession created the intellectual framework for the state's evolving sense of identity, but also because it was religion more than any other theme in this age which provided the dynamic for social and political relations. Historians refer to this state of affairs as confessionalization, a concept which is meant to convey how important the change of religion was for the development of the modern state.[24] Opinions still vary about its degree of applicability, but the concept makes two claims that seem beyond doubt: first, the introduction of the Reformation led to increased control of the belief and behaviour of the subject population; second, religious division gave rise to a new context of foreign relations. Both had profound consequences for the German princes.

The sovereign, as the Hohenlohe Church Order (1553) made clear, had been placed in office 'not only to preserve the common peace, and with it all honour and discipline', but also to preserve the true Christian religion, and this meant he had to enforce all requirements of the Decalogue. Not just the preservation of the peace, but the preservation of the faith fell within his purview. In the words of the Hohenlohe Order, it was the prince's duty 'to protect God's name and his Word' and to ensure that the faithful 'were protected from error in pure, sound teaching and proper belief'. Throughout the German lands in the sixteenth century the princes defined the nature of acceptable belief in church orders, secular mandates and educational programmes. George of Brandenburg-Ansbach, for instance, empowered Johannes Brenz to work alongside Nuremberg's Andreas Osiander in drafting the Brandenburg–Nuremberg Church Order (1533). Once it was published, all clergy and all parishioners were obliged to honour this Lutheran statement of the faith. It was introduced into the churches, taught in the schools and Osiander's catechism (appended to the order) was used to indoctrinate the young. The margrave had thus mandated what his subjects might believe; all other religions (Catholicism, Anabaptism, Calvinism) were anathema. In essence, as the example of Ansbach illustrates, the Protestant prince was acting like a bishop, legislating what people might believe and how they should come to believe it. Such was the nature of church rule in all of the Protestant territories in Germany, from Württemberg to Pomerania, Albertine Saxony to the Rhine Palatinate. The Reformation had invested the sovereigns with the right to police their subjects' thoughts as they previously policed their actions.[25]

Philip of Hesse made similar claims in his Church Order of 1526, though he placed even more stress on the other aspect of his duty as the guardian of God's laws. For Philip, the safekeeping of 'honourable, disciplined life, Christian unity, upstanding morals, and the preservation of the common good' was the sovereign's first obligation. Just as the prince had to ensure that the true faith was preached, so too was he commissioned by God to preserve peace, the common weal and Christian conduct on earth. The secular authorities had always been responsible for disciplining the subject population, but now that the prince had become the custodian of God's church on earth the range and reach of responsibilities had been amplified. Indeed, the idea of the prince as the ultimate arbiter of all earthly conduct was built into the very fabric of the Protestant church. The Reformation in Zweibrücken, for instance, gave rise to an entirely new system of moral control. The implementation of the Reformation began with visitations from 1539 to 1544 and this immediately exposed the conduct of the parishioners to the duchy's higher officials (the chancellor, a councillor and the superintendent). The visitation commission had the writ to investigate all aspects of parish life (from marriages to the condition of the schools to the nature of popular culture) and report all suspect cases to the district officials. Practice was then turned into law when the chancellor Ulrich Sitzinger worked together with the clergyman Cunmann Flinsbach in 1557 to draft a church ordinance designed to police secular affairs in a manner 'which would not prove detrimental to the godly laws'. A year later a marriage court was created, followed by a consistory, both of which were staffed by clergy and laity, and both of which then helped the territorial courts preserve the dictates of the secular and spiritual ordinances.[26] Church governance and temporal governance had merged, united in their mission to discipline the thought and conduct of the parishioners. This happened throughout Protestant Germany to such an extent that historians now speak of the increase of social disciplining in the sixteenth century. The Reformation had made it possible for the territorial princes to exercise even more control over the subject population.

Finally, we should not forget how confessional division influenced the broader framework of power politics in the empire. In 1523, as the evangelical movement was taking root in Hesse, a group of peasants in Balhorn wrote to the landgrave Philip and vowed that 'your princely Grace shall be our Pope and Emperor'. By the end of the century, this was not too far from the truth. The Protestant princes of the Holy Roman Empire could act as bishops (if not popes) in their lands. The church was a construct of the state; it was just another apparatus of princely rule. The prince determined the faith of his subjects and he had the divine obligation, as the bishops once had the divine obligation, to make sure the true Christian faith was preserved. Moreover, the prince had been put into office to uphold God's honour and this meant punishing the wicked and safeguarding the good (Romans 13:1–4). In all but name, the prince was bishop in his land. The Balhorn peasants were also not so far from the truth when they compared the prince to an emperor. Granted, he had nothing near the range of powers once reserved for the German emperors, but he did have a new quality of sovereignty that made him much more powerful than his mediæval predecessors. Moreover, a changed context of international relations did in a sense make it possible for him to think in terms of empire. The Protestant prince was now caught up in a new political dynamic, a constellation of European power politics created by the religious divisions of the sixteenth century. The German rulers were no longer just members of a ghostly federation of enfeoffed territories and imperial cities, but a European state system which was allied, divided and transformed on the basis of religious belief.[27] A new political dynamic had emerged in the sixteenth century, one which made it possible for the territorial sovereigns of the Holy Roman Empire to assume a prominent place in western Europe's international affairs. Like many of the profound changes experienced by the German princes in the sixteenth century, this too was a transformation brought about by the Reformation.

ACKNOWLEDGEMENTS

I would like to thank Anita Traninger and Hillay Zmora for their comments and corrections.

NOTES

1   Schröckh cited in Ernst Walter Zeeden, *The Legacy of Luther* (London, 1954), p. 202; Moeller cited in Manfred Schulze, *Fürsten und Reformation: Geistliche Reformpolitik weltlicher Fürsten vor der Reformation* (Tübingen, 1991), p. 2.

2   Karl-Friedrich Krieger, *König, Reich und Reichsreform im Spätmittelalter* (Munich, 1992), pp. 36–53.

3   Veit Ludwig von Seckendorff, *Teutscher Fürsten-Stat* (Frankfurt, 1660), p. 85.

4   Seckendorff, *Teutscher Fürsten-Stat*, pp. 21–39, 31; Ernst Schubert, *Fürstliche Herrschaft und Territorium im späten Mittelalter* (Munich, 1996), pp. 5–41.

5   Thomas A. Brady, Jr, *The Politics of the Reformation in Germany: Jacob Sturm (1489–1553) of Strasbourg* (New Jersey, 1997), pp. 20, 14–25.

6   Irmgard Höss, 'Die Problematik des spätmittelalterlichen Landeskirchentums am Beispiel Sachsens', *Geschichte in Wissenschaft und Unterricht* 10 (1959), pp. 352–62; Schulze, *Fürsten und Reformation*, pp. 41–3.

7   Schulze, *Fürsten und Reformation*, pp. 25, 17–45; Isnard W. Frank, 'Kirchengewalt und Kirchenregiment in Spätmittelalter und Früher Neuzeit', *Innsbrucker Historische Studien* 1 (1978), pp. 33–60; Justus Hashagen, 'Die vorreformatorische Bedeutung des spätmittelalterlichen landesherrlichen Kirchenregiments', *Zeitschrift für Kirchengeschichte* 41 (1922), pp. 63–93.

8 Frank Konersmann, *Kirchenregiment und Kirchenzucht im frühneuzeitlichen Kleinstaat: Studien zu den herrschaftlichen und gesellschaftlichen Grundlagen des Kirchenregiments der Herzöge von Pfalz-Zweibrücken 1410–1793* (Cologne, 1996), pp. 73–95.

9 Dietmar Willoweit, *Rechtsgrundlagen der Territorialgewalt: Landesobrigkeit, Herrschaftsrechte und Territorium in der Rechtswissenschaft der Neuzeit* (Cologne and Vienna, 1975), pp. 87, 34–110; Schubert, *Fürstliche Herrschaft und Territorium*, pp. 38, 38–41. Historians have been able to trace this process in detail in the duchy of Württemberg, where the dukes of the fifteenth century used these methods to create a territorial church well before the Reformation. Dieter Stievermann, *Landesherrschaft und Klosterwesen im spätmittelalterlichen Württemberg* (Sigmaringen, 1989), passim; Peter Dykema, 'The Reforms of Count Eberhard of Württemberg: "Confessionalization" in the Fifteenth Century', in Beat Kümin (ed.), *Reformations Old and New: Essays on the Socio-Economic Impact of Religious Change c. 1470–1630* (Aldershot, 1996), pp. 39–56.

10 Jörn Sieglerschmidt, *Territorialstaat und Kirchenregiment: Studien zur Rechtsdogmatik des Kirchenpatronatsrechts im 15. und 16. Jahrhundert* (Cologne and Vienna, 1987), pp. 8–23.

11 Burkhard von Bonin, *Die praktische Bedeutung des Ius Reformandi* (Stuttgart, 1902), pp. 1–15; Martin Heckel, *Staat und Kirche nach den Lehren der evangelischen Juristen Deutschlands in der ersten Hälfte des 17. Jahrhunderts* (Munich, 1968), pp. 1–163.

12 Ulrich Bubenheimer, 'Luthers Stellung zum Aufruhr in Wittenberg 1520–1522 und die frühreformatorischen Wurzeln des landesherrlichen Kirchenregiments', *Zeitschrift der Savigny-Stiftung für Rechtsgeschichte* 102 (1985), pp. 208, 147–214; Berndt Hamm, 'Reformation "von unten" und Reformation "von oben". Zur Problematik reformationshistorischer Klassifizierung', in Hans R. Guggisberg and Gottfried G. Krodel (eds), *Die Reformation in Deutschland und Europa: Interpretationen und Debatten* (Gütersloh, 1993), pp. 274–9.

13 Jürgen Ricklefs, 'Das Bemühen der Reformatoren um die jungen Fürsten in der Lutherzeit: Melanchthons Brief an den Fürsten Franz Otto und seine Brüder, Herzöge von Braunschweig und Lüneburg, um 1542', *Jahrbuch des Gesellschaft für Niedersächsische Kirchengeschichte* 81 (1983), pp. 89, 75–93; James Martin Estes, *Christian Magistrate and State Church: The Reforming Career of Johannes Brenz* (Toronto, 1982), pp. 54, 35–58.

14 Heinrich Schmidt, 'Kirchenregiment und Landesherrschaft im Selbstverständnis niedersächsischer Fürsten des 16. Jahrhunderts', *Niedersächsisches Jahrbuch für Landesgeschichte* 56 (1984), pp. 31–58; Hans-Walter Krumwiede, 'Reformation und Kirchenregiment in Württemberg', *Blätter für Württembergische Kirchengeschichte*, 68–9 (1968–9), pp. 81–111; Paul Münch, *Zucht und Ordnung: Reformierte Kirchenverfassungen im 16. und 17. Jahrhundert (Nassau-Dillenberg, Kurpfalz, Hessen-Kassel)* (Stuttgart, 1978), pp. 30–3, 162.

15 Thomas Klein, 'Ernestinisches Sachsen, kleinere thüringische Gebiete', in Anton Schindling and Walter Ziegler (eds), *Die Territorien des Reichs im Zeitalter der Reformation und Konfessionalisierung* (Münster, 1992), vol. 4, pp. 8–24; C. Scott Dixon, *The Reformation and Rural Society: The Parishes of Brandenburg-Ansbach-Kulmbach, 1528–1603* (Cambridge, 1996), pp.14–26; Günther Wartenberg, *Landesherrschaft und Reformation: Moritz von Sachsen und die albertinische Kirchenpolitik bis 1546* (Weimar, 1988), pp. 27–61.

16 Eike Wolgast, 'Die deutschen Territorialfürsten und die frühe Reformation', in Stephen E. Buckwalter and Bernd Moeller (eds), *Die frühe Reformation in Deutschland als Umbruch* (Gütersloh, 1998), pp. 407–34.

17 Eike Wolgast, 'Formen landesfürstlicher Reformation in Deutschland: Kursachsen-Württemberg/Brandenburg-Kurpfalz', in Leif Grane and Kai Hørby (eds), *Die dänische Reformation vor ihrem internationalen Hintergrund* (Göttingen, 1990), pp. 68–72; Klein, 'Ernestinisches Sachsen, kleinere thüringische Gebiete', in Schindling and Ziegler (eds), *Die Territorien des Reichs im Zeitalter der Reformation und Konfessionalisierung*, vol. 4, pp. 14–19; Dixon, *The Reformation and Rural Society*, pp. 26–32.

18 Estes, *Christian Magistrate and State Church*, pp. 59–80; Wartenberg, *Landesherrschaft und Reformation*, pp. 61–176.

19 See Chapter 22. Heinz Schilling, 'The Second Reformation: Problems and Issues', *Religion, Political Culture and the Emergence of Early Modern Society* (Leiden, 1992), pp. 247–301; Bodo Nischan, *Prince, People, and Confession: The Second Reformation in Brandenburg* (Philadelphia, 1994).

20 Eike Wolgast, 'Einführung der Reformation als politische Entscheidung', in Guggisberg and Krodel (eds), *Die Reformation in Deutschland und Europa*, pp. 465–86; Schmidt, 'Kirchenregiment und Landesherrschaft', pp. 43–4.

21 Karlheinz Blaschke, 'Wechselwirkungen zwischen der Reformation und dem Aufbau des Territorialstaates', *Der Staat* 9 (1970), pp. 347–64; Karlheinz Blaschke, 'Reformation und Modernisierung', in Guggisberg and Krodel (eds), *Die Reformation in Deutschland und Europa*, pp. 511–20.

22 Joachim Wächter, 'Das Verhältnis von Territorialgewalt und Kirche in Pommern nach Einführung der Reformation (1534/35)', *Jahrbuch der Gesellschaft für Niedersächsische Kirchengeschichte* 86 (1988), pp. 93–107; Estes, *Christian Magistrate and State Church*, pp. 59–80; Martin Brecht, *Kirchenordnung und Kirchenzucht in Württemberg vom 16. bis zum 18. Jahrhundert* (Stuttgart, 1967), pp. 23–39.

23 Eckhart G. Franz, 'Die hessischen Klöster und ihre Konvente in der Reformation', *Hessisches Jahrbuch für Landesgeschichte* 19 (1969), pp. 147–73; Richard Cahill, 'The Sequestration of the Hessian Monasteries', in Kümin (ed.), *Reformations Old and New*, pp. 39–56; Meinrad Schaab, 'Territorialstaat und Kirchengut bis zum Dreißigjährigen Krieg: Die Sonderentwicklung in der Kurpfalz im Vergleich mit Baden und Württemberg', *Zeitschrift für die Geschichte des Oberrheins* 138 (1990), pp. 241–58.

24 Wolfgang Reinhard, 'Pressures Towards Confessionalization? Prolegomena to a Theory of the Confessional Age', in C. Scott Dixon (ed.), *The German Reformation: The Essential Readings* (Oxford, 1999), pp. 172–92; Heinrich Richard Schmidt, *Konfessionalisierung im 16. Jahrhundert* (Munich, 1992).

25 Emil Sehling (ed.), *Die evangelischen Kirchenordnungen des XVI. Jahrhunderts* (Tübingen, 1977), 15 (Württemberg I), pp. 55–6; Dixon, *The Reformation and Rural Society*, pp. 47–54, 143–62.

26 Sehling (ed.), *Die evangelischen Kirchenordnungen des XVI. Jahrhunderts* (Tübingen, 1965), 8 (Hessen I), pp. 55–6; Konersmann, *Kirchenregiment und Kirchenzucht im frühneuzeitlichen Kleinstaat*, pp. 154–212.

27 Heinz Schilling, 'Konfessionalisierung und Formierung eines internationalen Systems während der frühen Neuzeit', in Guggisberg and Krodel (eds), *Die Reformation in Deutschland und Europa*, pp. 591–613; Heinz Schilling, 'Nationale Identität und Konfession in der europäischen Neuzeit', in Bernhard Giesen (ed.), *Nationale und kulturelle Indentität* (Frankfurt, 1996), pp. 192–252.

FURTHER READING

The princely Reformation in Germany has not yet been the subject of a general survey in English. Hans J. Hillerbrand (ed.), *The Oxford Encyclopedia of the Reformation* (4 vols; Oxford, 1996), and Mark Greengrass, *The European Reformation, c. 1500–1618* (London, 1998), are recent reference works with essential information, but there is no extended narrative on the theme.

General surveys of late mediæval Germany include Michael Hughes, *Early Modern Germany, 1477–1806* (London, 1992), and F.R.H. Du Boulay, *Germany in the Later Middle Ages* (London, 1983). Princely sovereignty is addressed in J.A.F. Thomson, *Popes and Princes, 1417–1517: Politics and Piety in the Late Medieval Church* (London, 1980), with analytical rigour in Otto Brunner, *Land and Lordship: Structures of Governance in Medieval Austria* (Philadelphia, 1992). Brunner's interpretation has been re-examined in Hillay Zmora, *State and Nobility in Early Modern Germany: The Knightly Feud in Franconia, 1440–1567* (Cambridge, 1997). More detailed investigations of late mediæval princely rule in Germany can be found in H.J. Cohn, *The Government of the Rhine Palatinate in the*

Fifteenth Century (Oxford, 1965), and F.L. Carsten, *Princes and Parliaments in Germany from the Fifteenth to the Eighteenth Century* (Oxford, 1963). See also the articles by Stievermann, Moraw and Press in Ronald D. Asch and Adolf M. Birke (eds), *Princes, Patronage and the Nobility: The Court at the Beginning of the Modern Age, c. 1350–1650* (London, 1991).

For the relationship between the Lutheran reform movement and the German princely state, see the selection of articles in James D. Tracy (ed.), *Luther and the Modern State in Germany* (Kirksville, 1986); James Martin Estes, *Christian Magistrate and State Church: The Reforming Career of Johannes Brenz* (London, 1982); Hans J. Hillerbrand, *Landgrave Philip of Hesse, 1504–1567* (London, 1967); and G.G. Krodel, 'State and Church in Brandenburg-Ansbach-Kulmbach, 1524–1526', *Studies in Medieval and Renaissance History* 5 (1968), pp. 141–213. A good introduction to the basic development of the Lutheran church in Germany is Irmgard Höss, 'The Lutheran Church of the Reformation: Problems of its Organization and Formation', in L.P. Buck and J.W. Zophy (eds), *The Social History of the Reformation* (Columbus, 1972), pp. 317–39. The Reformed church of the Second Reformation is discussed by Henry J. Cohn, 'The Territorial Princes in Germany's Second Reformation, 1559–1622', in Menna Prestwich (ed.), *International Calvinism 1541–1715* (Oxford, 1985), pp. 135–65, and Bodo Nischan, *Prince, People and Confession: The Second Reformation in Brandenburg* (Philadelphia, 1994).

Different approaches to the effect of the Reformation on the nature of princely rule can be found in Thomas Robisheaux, *Rural Society and the Search for Order in Early Modern Germany* (Cambridge, 1989); C. Scott Dixon, *The Reformation and Rural Society: The Parishes of Brandenburg-Ansbach-Kulmbach, 1528–1603* (Cambridge, 1996); and P.S. Fichtner, *Protestantism and Primogeniture in Early Modern Germany* (London, 1989). Longer-term consequences, including the effect of religious change on the development of the German state, can be found in Mary Fulbrook, *Piety and Politics: Religion and the Rise of Absolutism in England, Württemberg and Prussia* (Cambridge, 1983); R. Po-Chia Hsia, *Social Discipline in the Reformation: Central Europe 1550–1750* (London, 1989); Heinz Schilling, *Religion, Political Culture and the Emergence of Early Modern Society* (Leiden, 1992); G. Oestreich, *Neostoicism and the Early Modern State* (Cambridge, 1982); and the articles by van Dülmen and Reinhard in C. Scott Dixon, *The German Reformation: The Essential Readings* (Oxford, 1999).

PART III

THE REFORMATION OUTSIDE GERMANY

CHAPTER TEN

SWITZERLAND

————◆•◆————

Mark Taplin

Sixteenth-century Europe presents a bewildering patchwork of competing and overlapping jurisdictions: monarchical, aristocratic, ecclesiastical and civic. Despite this, modern study of the Reformation continues to be dominated by an essentially 'national' approach which reflects twentieth-century political and social circumstances more than it does those of the early modern period. We still speak of an English Reformation, a German Reformation and so forth. However, most scholars would also now accept that such terms can distort our understanding of the Reformation. Usually it was local concerns and circumstances which determined how the reformers' ideas were received and how the new religious dispensation was implemented. Nowhere is this more apparent than in the area comprising modern Switzerland. The sixteenth-century Swiss Confederation or *Eidgenossenschaft* was not a state, but a loose and constantly evolving alliance of sovereign territories. The determining say in religious matters, the *ius reformandi*, lay not with the Confederation's federal body – the Diet – but with its member states, or even lower down, with local communities and parishes (*Gemeinden*). There was no single Swiss model of reform: the Protestant churches that emerged in Switzerland from 1525 shared some common features, but in organization and even theology they often ploughed their own furrow.

The diversity of Swiss Protestantism has, until relatively recently, tended to be obscured in the historiography by a concentration on the charismatic figure of Huldrych Zwingli and the religious revolution which he helped bring about in Zurich. Zwingli's contribution, both as a theologian and a statesman, was without doubt immense, but his centralizing vision of a Reformed Swiss Confederation – a vision which was only ever espoused in Zurich – met its end with him on the battlefield of Kappel in October 1531. One of the tasks of those now working on the Swiss Reformation is to broaden our perspective, both geographically and chronologically. It becomes necessary, first, to place the Zurich Reformation in the context of different patterns of religious change *throughout* Switzerland and, second, to look beyond the fevered confessional politics of the 1520s to the decades after 1531: Switzerland's 'long Reformation'.

THE SWISS CONFEDERATION

The original Swiss Confederation, consisting only of Uri, Schwyz and Unterwalden, took shape around the end of the thirteenth century in response to attempts by the Habsburgs to consolidate their hold over inner Switzerland. It did not, however, assume real significance until the 1350s, when the city-states of Berne, Zurich, Lucerne and Zug, along with rural Glarus, formed a series of alliances with the original confederates. The development of the Confederation received a further boost during the early decades of the fifteenth century, when combined military action by the Swiss states brought them control over areas such as Eschental and Aargau. The joint administration of these 'common lordships' (*Gemeine Herrschaften*) required regular consultation between the allies, which gradually became formalized as meetings of the Swiss Diet (*Tagsatzungen*). During the remainder of the fifteenth century the area under the Confederation's control expanded rapidly as the Swiss gained for themselves a fearsome military reputation, notably in the Burgundian Wars against Charles the Bold in the 1470s and the Swabian War two decades later.

The success of the Confederation encouraged neighbouring states to seek admission to its ranks. In 1481 Solothurn and Fribourg were received as full members. They were followed by Basle and Schaffhausen (1501) and Appenzell (1513). A sense of Swiss identity was also emerging. From the early fifteenth century the designation 'Schweizer', which originally referred only to inhabitants of Schwyz, began to be applied by foreigners to the Swiss as a whole. Although the Confederation's members included both rural leagues, like Uri, and city-states, like Berne, all shared, according to one scholar, a common 'peasant ideology', which found expression in the founding myths of Wilhelm Tell and the Rütli oath. Patriotic humanists like Heinrich Brennwald argued for the lineal descent of the Swiss from the ancient Helvetians, distinguishing them in the process from both the Germans proper and the Romance-speaking 'Welschen'.[1] This new self-awareness reflected the changing status of the Confederation within the empire. The Swabian War of the 1490s had gone some way towards undoing the traditional ties between the Swiss and southwest Germany. Significantly, the treaty of Basle, which brought the conflict to an end in September 1499, placed the Confederation beyond the reach of the imperial chamber (*Reichskammergericht*) and exempted it from Maximilian I's proposals for the reform of imperial government.

However, the centralizing impulses within the Confederation continued to be held in check by the particularism of its members. The eight *alte Orte* (original states), for example, were determined to maintain a legal distinction between themselves and those states which had joined during the fifteenth and early sixteenth centuries. Basle was only admitted to the Confederation in 1501 on condition that it agreed in future to seek the consent of its new allies before going to war with an outside power. Increasingly, the *alte Orte* were reluctant to accept new members even on such inferior terms. This led to the emergence of a group of so-called associated states (*zugewandte Orte*), which were restricted to a non-voting presence at the Diet. The most important of these were the Rhaetian Freestate (Graubünden), the Valais, the city and abbot of St Gallen, and the Swabian imperial cities of Rottweil

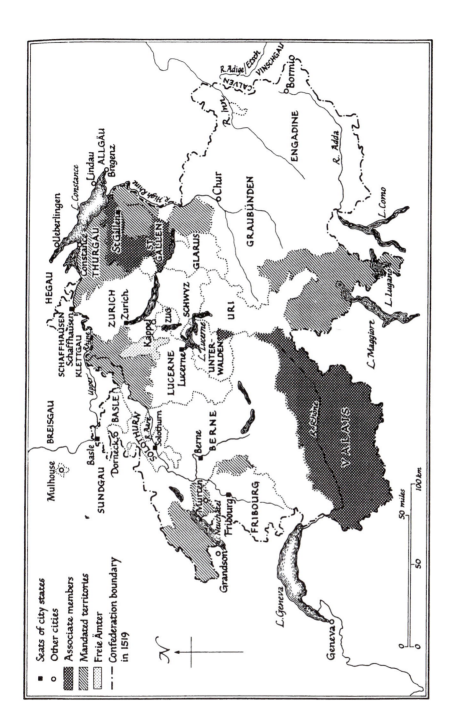

Figure 10.1 The Swiss Confederation in 1519. (Cambridge University Press)

and Mühlhausen. Relations between the *alte Orte* themselves were often tense. The more populous city-states of Zurich, Berne and Lucerne were keen to strengthen their position within the Confederation, but faced fierce resistance from its founder members in inner Switzerland. A war between the rural and urban states was only narrowly averted in 1481 by the so-called Stanser Verkommnis. Competition, as much as co-operation, characterized the relationships between individual states, whose strategic interests frequently clashed. Schwyz and Glarus, for instance, were suspicious of Zurich's ambitions in northeastern Switzerland and combined in the 1430s to prevent their rival annexing the estates of the extinct house of Toggenburg. Throughout the late mediæval period, the interests of individual states took precedence over their commitment to the Confederation as a whole, which was understood principally as an instrument for the advancement of those interests. Above all, the Confederation provided a secure framework from within which individual states could pursue expansionist and centralizing policies of their own: Berne and Zurich are the best examples of this.

THE SWISS CHURCH

The Swiss Confederation may have established itself as a distinct political entity by the beginning of the sixteenth century, but one can hardly speak of the emergence of a Swiss church in parallel with this development. Most of German-speaking Switzerland formed part of the sprawling diocese of Constance, which also embraced large swathes of southwestern Germany. Graubünden came under the jurisdiction of the Bishop of Chur, while to the west lay the sees of Sion, Lausanne and Basle. Except in Graubünden (to some extent) and the Valais, political and ecclesiastical boundaries rarely corresponded, making effective episcopal government difficult. The educational standards and moral conduct of the clergy in many areas fell far short of the canonical requirements. Most parish priests lived in permanent quasi-marital arrangements. Following the Council of Basle (1431–43) successive Bishops of Constance did attempt to improve matters within their diocese, by holding occasional synods of the clergy, by issuing mandates for the correction of abuses and by reinforcing the disciplinary powers of local deans.[2] In Lausanne, Bishop Aimon de Montfaucon issued a constitution for a diocesan synod and authorized a new missal in 1493.

Such initiatives had little long-term impact, however, because the bishops lacked the financial resources to carry them through and because the secular authorities in many parts of Switzerland were intent on pursuing a very different brand of reform, which had the effect of weakening the bishops' position still further. Like their counterparts in the cities of southwestern Germany, the magistrates of Zurich, Berne and other Swiss urban centres had long been campaigning to bring the religious life of their citizens, including the local clergy, under their direct control. This involved an attack on clerical judicial and financial immunities, as well as attempts to sideline the bishops' courts. In Zurich, a *Pfaffengericht* (priests' court) was created to deal with criminal cases involving clerics and lay people as early as 1304. By the late fifteenth century control over ecclesiastical appointments was largely in the hands of the civic authorities; even marital disputes were no longer automatically referred to the bishop. Episcopal authority was also steadily rolled back in rural inner Switzerland during the course of the fourteenth and fifteenth centuries. In response to perceived abuses of the church's power of excommunication and interdict, the confederates sought to reduce the areas subject to the jurisdiction of the bishop's court in Constance. The Convent of Our Lady in Schwyz, for example, was made to agree that all disputes between itself and the local inhabitants should be settled not by the bishop's court, but by the senior magistrate (*Ammann*) and a secular tribunal.[3]

Such actions did not amount to a form of 'proto-Reformation'. Rather, they were a lay response to what was seen as the failure of the bishops to deliver acceptable standards of pastoral care. By making the clergy answerable to the secular courts or by obtaining the right of presentation to their parish (as happened throughout central Switzerland during the course of the fifteenth century), local magistrates and communities hoped to ensure that this situation was put right. Their expectations of the church remained entirely conventional, with most emphasis on the availability and correct administration of the sacraments, along with the provision of masses for the dead. There are no signs that traditional Catholic devotion was in decline, rather the reverse. Late fifteenth-century Switzerland saw a state-sponsored boom in church-building together with improvements to existing structures, often funded through lay bequests. On the eve of the Reformation, Berne, with a population of only 4,500, could boast no less than seventy altars.[4] Pilgrimage centres like the Marian shrine at Einsiedeln in Schwyz and the tomb of St Beatus near Berne continued to thrive. On 12 June 1439, for example, 1,000 inhabitants of Basle made a mass pilgrimage to Einsiedeln to pray for relief from an outbreak of plague afflicting their city.[5]

However, alongside the traditional piety of the masses was emerging a literate culture deeply influenced by Christian humanist ideals. The pre-eminent centre of that culture in Switzerland was Basle, which by the end of the fifteenth century had developed into a centre of the publishing industry boasting more than seventy printers.[6] Editions of the Bible and the church fathers formed an important part of their output. Basle's international profile was later raised by the association of one of its printers, Johannes Froben, with Erasmus. Erasmus quickly attracted an enthusiastic Swiss following, which included some who later opposed the Reformation, such as the imperial poet laureate Heinrich Loriti (known as Glarean), but also many of Switzerland's most prominent reformers: Joachim Vadian of St Gallen, Oswald Myconius of Lucerne and, of course, Huldrych Zwingli.

ZWINGLI AND ZURICH

Zwingli was born at Wildhaus, in the Toggenburg, on 1 January 1484. The political status of his native territory was peculiar even by Swiss standards. Although subject to the lordship of the Abbot of St Gallen, the Toggenburg's inhabitants were also formally allied to Schwyz and Glarus, and therefore regarded themselves as belonging, however indirectly, to the Swiss Confederation. The fact that Zwingli originated from an area that lacked a clear separate identity but was committed to the confederal ideal may explain why he was later so reluctant to countenance a Reformation which failed to encompass all of Switzerland.[7]

After receiving elementary education from his uncle, the parish priest in Weesen, Zwingli attended Latin schools in Basle and Berne, before matriculating at the University of Vienna. He returned to Basle in 1502 to complete his studies and was appointed parish priest in Glarus four years later. The University of Basle was a conservative stronghold, but two of Zwingli's professors, Thomas Wittenbach and the liturgist Ulrich Surgant, were influenced by humanist currents and may have passed on this interest to their pupil. During his time in Glarus, certainly, Zwingli emerged as one of the leading lights of Swiss humanism. He began learning Greek in 1513 and devoted himself to the study of the fathers, particularly Origen and Jerome. Around 1516 Glarean introduced him to the works of Erasmus, a moment which Zwingli later came to see as marking his conversion to the cause of ecclesiastical reform. However, Zwingli's Erasmianism did not at first undermine his loyalty to the Roman church. His election as stipendiary priest (*Leutpriester*) at the Zurich Grossmünster in late 1518 was attributable in large measure to his status as a client of Cardinal Matthias Schiner, the Bishop of Sion, and hence as an adherent of the papalist party which currently held sway in Zurich.[8] During his early years in Zurich, Zwingli appears to have preached in a typically Erasmian vein, concentrating his fire on the 'superstitious' aspects of popular Catholicism. He also, famously, dispensed with the traditional pericopes in favour of the continuous exegesis of scripture. Like other humanists, Zwingli initially regarded the 'Luther affair' as simply another episode in the ongoing struggle between scholastic conservatives and supporters of the new learning. At some time during the period 1520–2, however, he accepted the key evangelical principles of justification by faith alone and *sola Scriptura*. Zwingli scholars have long debated whether he came to these insights through his reading of Luther or independently, as he later claimed. This question is unlikely ever to be resolved fully and I do not intend to dwell on it here.[9] What one can say with certainty is that Luther's protest, and the papacy's reaction to it, reinforced Zwingli's belief in the need for fundamental church reform.

The catalyst for Zwingli's public emergence as a reformer was an incidence of fast breaking which took place in the house of his friend, the printer Christoph Froschauer, during Lent 1522. Zwingli had been present at, but had not participated in, this 'Wurstessen'. However, when outraged citizens, along with the Bishop of Constance, called on the city council to punish the offenders, Zwingli came out in open support of their actions with his sermon *On Choice and Liberty in Food*. Shortly afterwards he organized a petition to the bishop demanding an end to compulsory clerical celibacy. Zwingli himself defied the ban by marrying secretly towards the end of 1522.

Zwingli's activities encountered considerable resistance within Zurich, both from among the conservative canons of the Grossmünster and in the city council. At this stage the primary concern of the civic authorities was the restoration of order and religious unity. It was with this in mind that they called a disputation for 29 January 1523, at which Zwingli was required to defend his preaching. The significance of the council's decision was not immediately apparent; it could be regarded as simply a further extension of the magistrate's power over the church in Zurich, in line with the late mediæval trend throughout Switzerland. Certainly a break with the Roman hierarchy was not intended: the Bishop of Constance was represented at this, the 'first Zurich disputation', by a substantial delegation. In hindsight, however, it would seem that the Zurich magistracy had taken a crucial step towards creating the conditions for a successful Reformation, effectively setting itself up as an arbiter in matters of doctrine and worship. Whether consciously or not, it had transformed the disputation from a forum for scholarly debate into a mechanism for the implementation of religious change.

Following the disputation, the Zurich council gave its official sanction to the principle of scriptural preaching advocated by Zwingli. This did not yet commit Zurich to the latter's programme of reform. What it did do, however, was give him the scope to press on with his evangelical campaign. During the course of 1523, Zurich's population became increasingly polarized between supporters and opponents of reform. The debate had by now moved on from the scripture principle to the potentially explosive questions of the mass and the cultic use of images. Once again, the council sought to restore consensus by means of a disputation (26–8 October 1523). This failed to deliver the fundamental reform of worship which Zwingli and other evangelicals were now demanding: for the time being, the mass continued to be said in its traditional form and images remained in place. The inconclusive outcome of the second Zurich disputation could not conceal the fact that the tide was running in Zwingli's favour, however. From the beginning of 1524 popular Catholic devotion in the city began to show signs of collapse, while acts of iconoclasm were reported from Höngg and Zollikon in the Zurich countryside. Under mounting pressure from below, the council ordered the removal of all images from city churches on 15 June. This move was followed by the secularization of the city's religious houses in December, although the abolition of the mass had to wait until June the following year.

It is easy, in retrospect, to see the triumph of the Reformation in Zurich as somehow inevitable, given the relative swiftness with which it was accomplished. In fact, Zwingli was obliged to proceed cautiously throughout in order to neutralize opposition to his proposed reforms. Initially, for example, he suggested only limited changes to the liturgy, rather than the replacement of the mass by a fully reformed Lord's Supper. The reformer was aware that he had many powerful adversaries, especially in the aristocratic guild known as the *Konstaffel* and in the Zurich Small Council, the committee which handled most day-to-day administration. Besides this, Zwingli's role in persuading Zurich to reject the mercenary alliance concluded between the Swiss and France in 1521 had not endeared him to the francophile party within the city. On the other hand, the reformer's preaching had made him a favourite of the Zurich populace and of the craft guilds, whose representatives dominated the full Zurich council (*Grosser Rat*). The key civic positions of *Burgermeister* and *Obristmeister* were also held by evangelical sympathizers during the first half of the 1520s. They were able to ensure that traditionalists were excluded from the commissions appointed to advise the council on religious questions. Even so, according to the (Catholic) chronicler Gerold Edlibach, the crucial vote for the abolition of the mass was passed by only a narrow majority, at a poorly attended night-time session of the council.[10] Zwingli himself long remained fearful that the reforms he had initiated might be reversed by his Zurich opponents in collaboration with foreign Catholic powers. It was at his urging that the council launched an investigation into the activities of several citizens accused of receiving pensions from France and the pope in September 1526, which led to the execution of one prominent conservative, Jakob Grebel.

The stability of the Reformation in Zurich was threatened not only by religious traditionalists, but by radicals among Zwingli's own followers. Differences of approach within the evangelical party had become apparent towards the end of 1523. The failure of the second Zurich disputation to deliver the immediate abolition of the mass led some evangelicals to question Zwingli's policy of 'tarrying for the magistrate' and to call for the establishment of a separate church of believers only. The radicals' rejection of the state church model to which Zwingli had committed himself was soon translated into an attack on infant baptism, the rite which determined membership of that church. From the second half of 1524 they began to put their alternative programme into effect, a process which culminated in the establishment of the first Anabaptist conventicle in Zollikon in January the following year. This congregation was quickly suppressed by the Zurich authorities, but the Swiss Brethren (as they are usually termed) long remained a thorn in the side of the Reformed establishment, clinging on in the Zurich countryside well into the seventeenth century despite occasional savage repression. Much of the polemical energy of Zwingli and his successor Heinrich Bullinger was poured into refuting the 'errors' of the Anabaptists, who also established a presence in Berne, Basle, St Gallen and Graubünden.

THE REFORMATION EXPANDS

In the Confederation as a whole, opposition to the reforms embarked on by Zurich quickly manifested itself. At a meeting in Beckenried on 8 April 1524 five states (Uri, Schwyz, Unterwalden, Zug and Lucerne) reaffirmed their commitment to the Catholic faith, condemning Zwingli along with Luther and Jan Hus. Various explanations have been offered for the failure of the Reformation to make an impact in central Switzerland. A major factor, certainly, was Zwingli's opposition to mercenary service, on which the inner Swiss states depended for their economic survival. Nor should one underestimate the attachment of rural populations to traditional forms of devotion, which took decades to overcome, even in nominally Reformed areas. Recently, Peter Blickle has suggested that the very success of many Swiss communities in emancipating themselves from the spiritual jurisdiction of the clergy and in taking control of their religious life in the decades prior to the Reformation diluted the appeal of the evangelical message. Many of the demands put forward by the German peasants in 1525, such as the right to elect their own parish priests, had already been realized by their counterparts in rural inner Switzerland.[11]

Outside the Catholic heartland of inner Switzerland the response to events in Zurich was less uniformly hostile. In Berne the council gave tentative backing to the scripture principle in December 1522, but fought shy of any reform of worship. Like its Zurich counterpart, it sought initially to steer a middle course between opponents and supporters of reform, both of which could be found in its own ranks. Thus, at the same time as steps were being taken to enforce the traditional ban on clerical marriage, citizens sympathetic to the Reformation were being permitted to read evangelical works in private. Basle, whose printing industry and geographical position on the Confederation's northern extremity made for easy access to the ideas of the German reformers as well as those of Zwingli, also gave out conflicting signals. Zwingli's theological ally Johannes Oecolampadius was allowed to preach and publish unmolested, but a powerful aristocratic elite within the city council resisted any attempt to cut ties with Rome or the Bishop of Basle.

At this early stage, the Reformation was making most progress in eastern Switzerland. In St Gallen and in Chur (the main urban centre of Graubünden), political factors worked in favour of the evangelicals. Both cities were engaged in an ongoing battle to free themselves from the domination of resident clerics, the Abbot of St Gallen and the Bishop of Chur respectively. It was easy for evangelicals to establish a connection between this struggle for political emancipation and religious reform. In April 1527 Johannes Comander was able to inform his St Gallen colleague Joachim Vadian that the mass and images had been abolished in Chur; around the same time the first Reformed eucharist was celebrated in St Gallen. The Reformation also registered gains in rural eastern Switzerland, where the 'communalization' of religion noted by Blickle for the inner states was far less pronounced. The Thurgau, Toggenburg and parts of Graubünden all saw significant peasant uprisings in 1525, fuelled by anticlericalism and calls for both economic and religious change. In Graubünden, where political and spiritual supremacy had hitherto been combined in the person of the Bishop of Chur, the peasantry succeeded, almost uniquely in central Europe, in having its demands incorporated by and large into the constitution of the state. The Second Ilanz Articles placed the right of presentation to benefices in the hands of the Rhaetian Freestate's member communes and empowered each to decide for itself whether or not to embrace the Reformation. A similar measure had already been agreed by the inhabitants of Appenzell (in April 1525).

The five Catholic states responded to these developments by attempting to isolate Zurich. In May 1526 they organized their own disputation in Baden, with the intention of resolving the religious question for the Confederation as a whole. As the Zurich council refused to allow Zwingli to attend because of fears for his safety, it was left to Johannes Oecolampadius of Basle to put the evangelical case. Oecolampadius proved no match as a disputant for the heavyweight team which had been assembled on the Catholic side. This was led by the Ingolstadt theologian Johann Eck, who mercilessly exposed inconsistencies in his opponent's arguments against the Catholic teaching on the eucharist. The result was a resounding endorsement of the status quo by the representatives of the Swiss states present. However, in the medium term the Baden disputation proved to be less of a blow to the Reformation in Switzerland than it first appeared. It actually drove a wedge between the five hard-line Catholic states and others, such as Berne, Basle and Solothurn, which were more inclined to adopt a mediating role. Berne in particular was incensed by the refusal of the inner Swiss states to allow it to scruti-nize the acts of the disputation prior to their publication. The Berne council elections of Easter 1527 brought decisive gains for the evangelical party in the city and saw the exclusion of two leading Catholics, Sebastian von Stein and Kaspar von Mülinen. By the end of July, the Bernese authorities had taken over the administration of all religious houses and over the coming months the mass was abandoned in some rural parishes. In Basle, too, the balance of power had shifted in favour of the evangelicals. In September 1527 the obligation on citizens to attend mass was lifted and three city churches were set aside for Reformed worship.

The following year saw even more spectacular successes, in the wake of Berne's decision to hold a disputation as a prelude to the introduction of full-scale reform. The disputation, which was attended by Zwingli and a large Zurich delegation, along with Vadian and Oecolampadius, finally ended Zurich's formal isolation within the Confederation. Berne was by far the largest and most powerful state in Switzerland and its defection to the Reformed camp encouraged others to follow suit. Later that year, an assembly of the Thurgau's inhabitants voted in favour of reform. With Zurich's encouragement, the authorities in St Gallen seized control of the city's cathedral church from the abbot in February 1529. In Basle, mean-while, the conservative city council fought hard to broker a compromise between the competing religious parties in the face of increasing pressure from the evangel-ical guilds. A disputation was arranged for 30 May 1529, but this was pre-empted by an outbreak of iconoclastic violence on 9 February which persuaded the council to throw in its lot with the Reformation. For many on the council, the Reformation represented the 'least worst' option: the guilds were also pressing for fundamental reform of the city's oligarchical constitution and the Basle ruling elite probably hoped to neutralize this aspect of their programme by conceding their religious demands.

THE KAPPEL WARS

These evangelical gains dramatically increased the stakes in the conflict between the Reformed and Catholic states, which responded by seeking an alliance with the Habsburgs (eventually concluded on 22 April 1529). By late 1528 it was clear that the two camps were drifting towards open conflict. In November, Catholic Unterwaldners offered military assistance to rebels in the Bernese Oberland who were resisting the magistracy's attempts to establish Reformed worship in the area. Berne responded by lodging a formal complaint against Unterwalden with the Diet. The affair rumbled on through the early months of 1529, with Zurich arguing that, as punishment for its actions, Unterwalden should be temporarily excluded from the administration of the common lordships. From this point onwards, the future confessional status of the common lordships was the main point at issue between the two sides. In May 1529 Schwyz executed Jakob Kaiser, a Zurich minister who had been attempting to evangelize the common lordship of Gaster. Shortly afterwards, Zurich and Berne mobilized their forces for an attack on the inner states.

The so-called first Kappel War proved to be a bloodless affair, swiftly brought to an end by the mediation of Basle and the remaining neutral states. In the resulting peace treaty, the Catholic states tacitly acknowledged that their Reformed rivals now held the upper hand within the Confederation. In the common lordships, the *Gemeindeprinzip* (communal principle) was established in matters of religion, paving the way for further defections to Protestantism. The Catholic states' pact with Austria was dissolved and the reforming measures already carried out within the evangelical states received legal recognition.

However, the treaty failed to meet a number of Zwingli's key demands. Above all, it did not commit the Catholic states to allowing evangelical preaching to take place on their territory: Protestantism would continue to be excluded from a high proportion of the Swiss lands for the foreseeable future. The first Kappel peace reflected the approach to Swiss politics not of Zurich, but of Berne, where the dominant voice was that of the artist, dramatist and councillor Niklaus Manuel. Manuel's Protestant credentials are not in doubt. As early as 1523, he had written a number of fiercely anti-papal plays. However, Manuel was also concerned to avoid conflict within the Confederation, even if that meant accepting a less than ideal settlement of the religious question.[12] Berne as a whole was not prepared to concede the principle of outside interference in the internal affairs of any particular state, which the demand for free preaching throughout the Confederation entailed.

For his part, Zwingli believed that the Reformation of inner Switzerland was being thwarted only by the stubborn resistance of a corrupt elite within the Catholic states. He argued that the principle of non-interference had to take second place to the divine imperative of ensuring that all had access to God's Word. Lack of support for this position from Berne forced him to look further afield for allies in pursuit of his ultimate goal of a Reformed Confederation. Zwingli had expressed a vague interest in a pan-Protestant alliance as far back as 1525, and in December 1527 Zurich concluded a defensive pact (*Burgrecht*) with Constance, which was subsequently extended to Berne, Biel, Basle, Mühlhausen and Schaffhausen (where the Reformation had been introduced under pressure from the existing Reformed states following the first Kappel War). Now Zwingli intensified contacts with Philip of Hesse, whose aim had long been to mediate an agreement between the Reformed Swiss states and Lutheran Saxony.

In the way of any such alliance stood Zwingli's differences with Luther over the eucharist, which led to acrimonious exchanges between the two men from early 1527. The celebrated colloquy of Marburg organized by Philip in early October 1529 brought Zwingli and Luther face to face for the first time, but failed to produce a formula on the mode of Christ's presence in the sacrament acceptable to both sides. Luther's habit of placing Zwingli in the same category as those he termed 'Schwärmer', radical reformers like Thomas Müntzer and the Anabaptists, undermined subsequent attempts to bring about a rapprochement between Swiss and German Protestantism. In January 1531 Zurich rejected Saxony's terms for admission to the Schmalkaldic League (which included subscription to the Augsburg Confession) and hopes of establishing a common anti-Catholic front evaporated. The imperial cities of southwest Germany, where Zwingli's brand of reform was popular, reluctantly chose to throw in their lot with the Lutherans rather than cut themselves off from the main body of the empire. During the first half of 1531, Zwingli was forced to fall back on unrealistic plans for alliances with France, Venice and other opponents of the Habsburgs.

Within the Confederation the common lordships remained, as before, the most likely flashpoint. Zwingli did not dictate Zurich's foreign policy, but there was a convergence of interests between his desire to promote reform beyond the boundaries of Zurich and the authorities' wish to bring more of northeastern Switzerland into their sphere of influence. During the period between the first and second Kappel Wars, Zurich helped to consolidate the ascendancy of the Reformed in the Thurgau and Toggenburg, and encouraged the subjects of the Abbot of St Gallen to repudiate his overlordship. The Reformation also began to make inroads into Bremgarten and the Freie Ämter, which formed a strategically crucial corridor between inner Switzerland and the Habsburg Breisgau. In the west, pressure from Berne led to the introduction of Reformed worship in Neuchâtel and Biel. By early April 1531 Zwingli was pressing for a further strike against the Catholic states, whom he accused of planning a massive attack on the Reformed in coalition with the Habsburgs and the Italian condottiere Giangiacomo de Medici, Castellan of Musso. Once again the differences in approach between Berne and Zurich came to the surface. Instead of military action, Berne proposed merely an economic blockade of inner Switzerland. Subsequently it expressed itself willing to rescind even this measure. The divisions within Reformed ranks left them ill-equipped to face the inevitable Catholic response to the blockade. On 11 October Zurich's forces were routed at Kappel; Zwingli was among those who fell. A further defeat at the Gubel two weeks later forced the Reformed to sue for peace.

The terms imposed by the victorious Catholic states were surprisingly moderate. No attempt was made to force Zurich and its allies to return to the old faith: like Berne, the inner Swiss respected the principle of non-interference in the internal affairs of each state. It is unlikely that they had the resources to force through a draconian settlement in any case. The real significance of the second Kappel peace lay in the articles dealing with the common lordships. Here Catholicism, described in the treaty as 'the true, undoubted Christian faith', was established in a clearly privileged position. Communities which had accepted the Reformation were permitted to return to the old religion, but not vice versa. Provision was also made for Catholic minorities to worship in predominantly Reformed areas, and to have a share in church buildings and revenue. In the common lordships of Bremgarten, Mellingen and the Freie Ämter, the Catholic states were given the authority to restore the mass by force.

RETRENCHMENT AND CONSOLIDATION

The months following Kappel saw a rolling back of Protestantism from many areas where Zwingli had helped establish it. A new Abbot of St Gallen, Diethelm Blarer, was installed and set about energetically re-catholicizing his subjects. In the common lordships of Sargans and Rheintal, the Catholic states exploited the so-called *Schmähverbot* in the second Kappel peace (which stipulated punishment for those who defamed the opposing faith) to make life for the Protestant minority, especially the Reformed clergy, well nigh impossible. All Protestant preaching could, after all, be interpreted as an attack on the good name of the Catholic church. In Solothurn, where the Reformed had been allowed the use of two city churches, conformity to Catholicism was swiftly re-imposed. The Reformation also suffered reverses in Appenzell and Glarus, which had been well on the way to becoming fully Reformed prior to the Protestant defeat.

The impact of the settlement was not felt equally throughout Switzerland. The main casualty of the war was Zurich and it was largely Zurich which paid by forfeiting much of its influence in the common lordships of the northeast. Even here, the Catholic states succeeded in bringing about only a partial restoration of Catholicism. The Thurgau remained overwhelmingly Protestant and in some places, like Altstätten and Berneck in Rheintal, new Reformed congregations were established in contravention of the terms of Kappel.[13] Significantly, the *zugewandte Orte* were unaffected by the anti-Reformed provisions contained in the second Kappel peace. In Graubünden, the Reformation's most impressive advances came during the decades after Kappel. From the end of the 1530s, Protestant communities appeared first in the Romantsch-speaking Engadine and then in the Italian-speaking communes of southern Rhaetia and the subject territories of the Valtellina and Chiavenna. This new wave of Reformed expansion was assisted by an influx of evangelical exiles from Italy, for whom Rhaetia represented a surrogate mission field. The exiles provided a pool of talent from which ministers to preside over the newly formed congregations could be drawn. They included Pier Paolo Vergerio (formerly Bishop of Capodistria), the Piedmontese Agostino Mainardi and the Neapolitan Scipione Lentolo.

In the same way, Kappel did not close off the possibility of further Protestant gains in western Switzerland. Berne, unlike Zurich, had emerged from the defeat of 1531 with its power largely intact. The importance of this was demonstrated in early 1536, when Berne responded to an appeal from newly Reformed Geneva for assistance against a possible attack from Savoy by occupying the Pays de Vaud. Within months of the conquest the Berne authorities had begun to implement a reform of worship. This followed the by now familiar pattern: after the 'truth' of the evangelical faith had been demonstrated at a disputation held in the former episcopal city of Lausanne, Reformation mandates were promulgated for the area. Over the coming decades the Pays de Vaud, along with Geneva, emerged as a centre of Protestant printing and education not only for the *Suisse romande*, but for France itself.

The formative years of the Swiss Reformation, the 1520s, had been dominated by Zwingli and by the conflict between the Catholic and Reformed states. With the Zurich reformer's removal from the scene and the establishment of an uneasy *modus vivendi* between the rival confessional camps, the differences and tensions within and between the individual Swiss Reformed churches were brought into sharper focus.

In Zurich, the defeat at Kappel had produced a backlash, centred on the rural areas, against the 'foreign' pastors who were seen as having led the state to disaster. Zwingli's successor, Heinrich Bullinger, was forced as a result to accept a diminished role for the clergy in political decision-making, although he continued to exercise considerable influence behind the scenes. The emphasis of Zurich policy, in both church and state, shifted away from the promotion of reform abroad to the internal consolidation of the Zwinglian settlement. The second half of the 1520s had seen the establishment of several core Reformed institutions: the *Prophezei*, a daily exercise in the reading and interpretation of scripture; the *Ehegericht*, a marriage and morals tribunal which assumed the powers formerly exercised by the bishop's court in Constance; and the synod, a twice-yearly meeting of the clergy. It was left to Bullinger and his colleagues to place these bodies on a permanent footing, however. The *Prophezei* developed into a fully fledged Reformed academy, the *Carolinum*, which served as a model for later institutions of this type in Berne, Lausanne, Geneva and the Empire. The presence there of such luminaries as Konrad Pellikan, Konrad Gesner and Peter Martyr Vermigli kept Zurich at the forefront of intellectual and theological developments within European Protestantism. The synod, meanwhile, became a key instrument for raising the educational, moral and pastoral standards of the Zurich clergy to the level demanded by the Reformed leadership.

Zurich retained an interest in the fate of Protestants in the Confederation as a whole, particularly in eastern Switzerland, but support was now delivered in more indirect ways. The *Carolinum*, for example, attracted a significant number of foreigners: of 529 students who matriculated there between 1559 and 1620, 156 were from other parts of Switzerland, with no less than 64 from Graubünden.[14] Zurich was also the principal source of candidates for the ministry in many of these areas, such as Reformed Appenzell, where over half of the pastors recorded for the period 1531–97 were Zurichers.[15] But Zwingli's strategy of promoting the Reformation by military means was now out of the question. In March 1555, Zurich had no choice but to stand by while the Catholic states expelled the evangelical minority from the common lordship of Locarno.

The institutions of the other Swiss Reformed churches were modelled in the first instance on those of Zurich. After Kappel, however, many of them began to develop along different lines. Zwingli, in the course of his disputes with the Anabaptists, had decisively rejected any notion of separation between the ecclesiastical and civil powers. Church and state were to work together in order to sanctify society and ensure that true worship was upheld. In practice, that meant the integration of the church into the apparatus of early modern government. Ministers became agents of social control, monitoring births and marriages; preaching against drunkenness, dancing and other 'vices'; ensuring that their flocks were kept informed of the council's decisions. However, in Zurich the church retained a degree of institutional independence: within the synod, the clergy were able to comment on and occasionally criticize council policy. This was not the case in Berne. Although the original Reformation mandates envisaged that synods be held every three years, such gatherings became increasingly infrequent, before ceasing altogether in the seventeenth century. Graubünden also saw a move away from the Zurich model of church–state relations, but in the opposite direction. There the weakness of central magisterial authority eventually forced the synod to sanction the independent exercise of ecclesiastical discipline, including the ban (excommunication, or exclusion from the sacraments), by congregations and regional colloquies of the sort which operated in the French Reformed churches. The Zwinglian vision of the clergy acting as supports to the godly magistrate simply proved unworkable in the context of a bi-confessional state.[16]

Theologically, too, some of the Swiss churches began to distance themselves from Zurich after Kappel. Even during the 1520s, Zwingli did not enjoy universal support from Swiss evangelicals. At the Berne disputation, for instance, Benedikt Burgauer of Schaffhausen contested the Zurich reformer's interpretation of the eucharist. Zwingli's death gave Switzerland's 'Lutherans' an opportunity to assert themselves. In 1532 a new constitution, known as the *Synodus*, was drawn up for the church of Berne by the Strasbourg reformer Wolfgang Capito. The document included formulations that were Lutheran and even Schwenckfeldian in tone. Under Peter Kunz and Sebastian Meyer, this Lutheranizing tendency became dominant within the leadership of the Bernese church, although large sections of the pastorate, led by Erasmus Ritter and Kaspar Megander, remained loyal to Zwingli's teachings. In 1537, however, Megander was dismissed for opposing changes to the Berne catechism proposed by Martin Bucer, to be replaced by another Lutheran sympathizer, Simon Sulzer. Not until Kunz's death in February 1544 did the balance of power begin to swing back in favour of the Zwinglians. In November 1547 Thomas Grynaeus was removed from the Berne academy for introducing Lutheran opinions and Bernese students enrolled at Wittenberg and other German universities were recalled. Sulzer and his Lutheran colleagues Beat Gering and Konrad Schmid were dismissed the following year, paving the way for the appointment of Bullinger's close friend Johannes Haller as *Antistes* (senior minister).

In Basle the church's confessional identity remained in dispute for even longer. Basle placed far more emphasis on its imperial links than either Berne or Zurich; this was understandable given its marginal position, both geographically and politically, within the Swiss Confederation. The death of Oecolampadius shortly after Kappel gave the green light to those Baslers keen to improve relations with the Lutherans. The Basle church, headed by Oswald Myconius, became an active participant in attempts to broker such a compromise during the mid-1530s. In 1536 it adhered to the ill-fated Wittenberg Concord negotiated with Luther by Bucer, only to be rejected by the Zurichers. Myconius was later succeeded as *Antistes* by Simon Sulzer, who simultaneously held the superintendency in the (Lutheran) margravate of Baden. During Sulzer's term of office Basle became increasingly estranged from the other Swiss Reformed states. Sulzer introduced Lutheran liturgical practices like the use of organs and polyphonic singing, and enraged the Zurichers by apparently endorsing the Augsburg Confession in September 1563.[17] At the time of his death in 1585 he was campaigning to have the Lutheran Formula of Concord approved by the Basle clergy.

In general, the religious culture of Basle was also more pluralist than that of its Reformed neighbours. The city tended to attract thinkers who held views at variance with both Lutheran and Reformed orthodoxy. These included the Dutch Anabaptist David Joris, the Savoyard Sebastian Castellio, who coordinated the protest against Calvin's role in the execution of Michael Servetus, and a whole host of Italian dissidents: Celio Secundo Curione, the Lucchese printer Pietro Perna and the anti-Trinitarian Fausto Sozzini. Basle was not, as is sometimes claimed, a centre of religious toleration. The remains of David Joris, who had lived in the city under the pseudonym Johann of Bruges, were exhumed and publicly burnt on the order of the magistrate after his true identity was revealed, while the activities of Castellio, Curione and Perna all came under investigation at different times. Nevertheless, it would seem that on the whole the Basle authorities were inclined to treat heterodoxy more leniently than their counterparts elsewhere. Hans Guggisberg suggests that Sulzer was held back from pursuing the radicals for tactical reasons: so long as their criticisms were directed principally against his own adversaries in Geneva and the other Swiss churches, he was happy to leave them undisturbed.[18]

For early modern Europeans it was axiomatic that religious and political unity went hand in hand. Consequently, few believed that the Swiss Confederation could survive in the long term as a bi-confessional entity. As Heinrich Bullinger observed in September 1532: 'We [the Swiss] no longer have a single faith, as in the past, which leads to such a division in all our dealings that no alliance is strong enough to hold us together.' Bullinger proposed that the Confederation be dissolved, with the common lordships partitioned between the former member states.[19] In fact, such predictions of the Confederation's demise proved ill-founded. The further strengthening of central institutions like the Diet was now out of the question, but Catholic and Reformed states continued to cooperate in the existing areas of pooled jurisdiction, notably the administration of the common lordships. The Swiss identity, which had emerged during the fifteenth century, was not wholly displaced by new confessional allegiances. Relations between Swiss Catholics and Protestants were often cordial: a shooting match held in Zurich in 1547, for instance, attracted participants from Catholic Lucerne, Schwyz, Zug and Solothurn as well as from the other Reformed states.[20] The relationship between the Protestant city of Basle and the Catholic bishopric of the same name offers a good example of political cooperation across the religious divide. In a recent study, Hans Berner notes that Basle repeatedly turned down requests from the bishop's Protestant subjects to bring them within the structures of the Basle church and ignored opportunities to promote the spread of the Reformation in the bishopric. When the city did intervene to strengthen its position within episcopal territory, the aim was usually to head off rival states like Berne and Solothurn which might also have designs on the area.

In many places the boundary between Catholic and Protestant remained relatively fluid throughout the first half of the sixteenth century. Church-sharing between the rival denominations was a feature of religious life in Glarus, parts of Graubünden and the Thurgau, which had around thirty such 'paritätische Gemeiden' in 1627.[21] In Diesse and Nods, where jurisdiction was shared between Berne and the Bishop of Basle, the pastor celebrated the mass and the Reformed liturgy on alternate Sundays until 1556.[22] A decade later, one finds Bullinger complaining about the fact that Catholic and Reformed clergy were holding joint synods in Rheintal; in Appenzell, altars were still standing in three Reformed churches as late as 1603.[23] Protestants continued to attend Catholic institutions of learning, as the travels of the future Basle physician Felix Platter in France during the 1550s demonstrate.[24] The proximity of Reformed and Catholic areas – for example, the Bernese Oberland and the Valais – meant that Protestants who were so minded could also continue to attend mass or visit pilgrimage sites on nearby Catholic territory. Traditional forms of devotion, such as the cult of the dead, persisted for decades among nominally Reformed populations, especially in the countryside. In 1567, for instance, the Zurich synod received reports from Freiamt that human remains were being dug up from cemeteries and re-interred in 'Beinhäuser' ('bone houses') where they could be used for magical rites.[25] From the disciplinary records of both the Zurich and the Rhaetian synods it would appear that catholicizing was a recurrent problem even among the Reformed clergy, many of whom were of course former priests.

From around 1550, however, there was a marked increase in religious tension at both a confederal and a local level. The so-called *Glarnerhandel* or *Tschudikrieg* of 1555–64 provides evidence of this trend. In Glarus, where Protestants outnumbered adherents of the old faith by around four to one, the Catholic minority accused their Reformed neighbours of failing to observe the terms of the *Landesvertrag* of November 1532, which regulated relations between the two confessions. During the ensuing controversy the five inner Swiss states intervened on behalf of their co-religionists, even contemplating the forcible re-catholicization of Glarus at one point. Although the dispute was eventually resolved peacefully, it exposed the growing divisions between Catholics and Protestants in Glarus. In the interests of self-preservation, the Catholic minority set up its own structures of authority, such as the Secret Council (*Geheimer Rat*), which has been described as a 'government within the government'.[26] In Appenzell, conflict between the two religious groups produced an even more drastic outcome: the effective partition of the state, in 1595, between the Catholic *Innerrhoden* and the Reformed *Ausserrhoden*.

These developments were accompanied by a strengthening of confessional identity on both the Catholic and the Protestant sides. The impact of Tridentine reform was beginning to be felt in Catholic Switzerland. Carlo Borromeo, the driving force of the Counter-Reformation in northern Italy, visited Switzerland four times, in 1567, 1570, 1581 and 1583. The same period saw the establishment of a Jesuit college in Lucerne (1574), and the introduction of the Capuchins in Altdorf, Stans, Lucerne and Schwyz. Swiss Catholicism was also showing signs of a new militancy: during the 1580s Protestant worship was suppressed in the bishopric of Basle, for instance. In 1586, the Catholic states of the Confederation concluded a confessional pact, the *Goldener Bund*, and shortly afterwards most of them entered into a formal alliance with Spain, for whom the Gotthard route across the Alps had taken on crucial strategic importance.

In the same way, Swiss Protestantism was acquiring a more settled look. Although Switzerland did not see anything equivalent to the 'Second Reformation' which has been posited for some parts of Protestant Germany, there is evidence of a certain harmonization in theology and general outlook among the various Swiss Reformed churches. A key factor in that process was the developing relationship of the Swiss churches with Geneva. Initially the prospects for agreement between the two sides seemed relatively bleak. Calvin and the Swiss differed fundamentally in their approach to the sacraments, predestination and church government. During the 1550s, the Pays de Vaud was the scene of a bitter struggle between the Berne council, supported by a number of local 'Zwinglian' pastors, and Pierre Viret, senior minister of Lausanne and a close ally of Calvin. Viret's repeated demands for the establishment in the Pays de Vaud of an autonomous system of ecclesiastical discipline on Calvinist lines eventually led to his dismissal in 1558. At one point Berne actually forbade its subjects from taking communion in Geneva. Despite these difficulties, however, Geneva and the Swiss churches did move slowly towards a common doctrinal position. Following intensive written exchanges, Bullinger and Calvin put their names to an agreed statement on the sacraments, the *Consensus Tigurinus*, in July 1549. In January 1560, the most vocal Zurich critic of Calvin's teaching on predestination, Theodor Bibliander, was removed from his post at the *Carolinum*, paving the way for agreement between Zurich and Geneva in this matter also. Eventually even Berne overcame its reservations about the Calvinist doctrine of double predestination.

Bullinger's Second Helvetic Confession of 1566 set the seal on this process of confession building. Moderate and relatively undogmatic in tone, it became the basis for lasting doctrinal unity between the Swiss churches. Zurich, Berne, Schaffhausen, St Gallen and the Reformed church of Graubünden, along with Geneva, were among the initial signatories. Only Basle, where Sulzer's Lutheranism continued to hold sway, remained aloof. However, Sulzer's successor as *Antistes*, Johann Jakob Grynaeus, brought the city back into the Reformed fold during the 1580s. In terms of its leadership, Swiss Protestantism was becoming both more homogeneous and more closely integrated into the pan-European 'Calvinist' movement. The reception of the Second Helvetic Confession by Reformed churches from France to Hungary highlighted the importance of these international connections, which Bullinger and his colleagues in Zurich did a good deal to foster through their voluminous correspondence.

By 1600, the Swiss Reformed churches had placed themselves on a sound doctrinal and institutional footing. Some of the objectives of the second generation of reformers, such as the creation of an educated ministry, had been more or less achieved. In Reformed areas, the most obvious manifestations of residual Catholic belief and piety were less in evidence. Establishing a genuine commitment to Reformed teaching and standards of behaviour among overwhelmingly rural populations was a task for the longer term, however. If the testimony of Daniel Müslin – minister of Vechigen near Berne in the early eighteenth century – is to be believed, it eventually proved beyond the capacities of the Reformed church authorities. Around 1727 Müslin wrote that his congregation remained, despite his best efforts, 'ignorant of even the most fundamental truths of the Christian religion, without love and without fear of God'.[27]

NOTES

1   U. Im Hof, *Mythos Schweiz: Identität-Nation-Geschichte 1291–1991* (Zurich, 1991), p. 42.
2   K. Maier, 'Die Konstanzer Diözesansynoden im Mittelalter und in der Neuzeit', *Rottenburger Jahrbuch für Kirchengeschichte* 5 (1986), pp. 53–70.

3   P. Blickle, 'Rechtsautonomie durch Kirchenkritik: Die Eidgenossen wehren sich gegen Bann und Interdikt', in B. Bietenhard (ed.), *Ansichten der Rechten Ordnung: Bilder über Normen und Normenverletzungen in der Geschichte* (Berne, 1991), pp. 99–112 (105).

4   K. Guggisberg, *Bernische Kirchengeschichte* (Berne, 1958), p. 18.

5   A. Hauser, *Was für ein Leben: Schweizer Alltag vom 15. bis 18. Jahrhundert* (Zurich, 1988), p. 122.

6   H. Guggisberg, *Basel in the Sixteenth Century: Aspects of the City Republic before, during and after the Reformation* (St Louis, 1982), p. 10.

7   E. Kobelt, *Die Bedeutung der Eidgenossenschaft für Huldrych Zwingli* (Zurich, 1970), p. 7.

8   J. Stayer, 'Zwingli before Zurich: Humanist Reformer and Papal Partisan', *Archiv für Reformationsgeschichte* 72 (1981), pp. 55–68.

9   The debate is summarized in U. Gäbler, *Huldrych Zwingli: His Life and Work* (Edinburgh, 1987), pp. 45–9.

10 W. Jacob, *Politische Führungsschicht und Reformation: Untersuchungen zur Reformation in Zürich 1519–1528* (Zurich, 1970), p. 36.

11 P. Blickle, 'Warum blieb die Innerschweiz katholisch?', *Mitteilungen des Historischen Vereins des Kantons Schwyz* 86 (1994), pp. 29–38.

12 B. Gordon, 'Toleration in the Early Swiss Reformation: The Art and Politics of Niklaus Manuel of Bern', in O. Grell and R. Scribner (eds), *Tolerance and Intolerance in the European Reformation* (Cambridge, 1996), pp. 128–44.

13 H. Meyer, *Der zweite Kappeler Krieg: Die Krise der Schweizerischen Reformation* (Zurich, 1976), p. 241.

14 K. Maag, *Seminary or University? The Genevan Academy and Reformed Higher Education, 1540–1620* (Aldershot, 1995), p. 136.

15 H. Büchler, *Die Politik des Landes Appenzell zwischen dem zweiten Kappeler Landfrieden und dem Goldenen Bund 1531–1584* (Bamberg, 1969), p. 112.

16 U. Pfister, 'Reformierte Sittenzucht zwischen kommunaler und territorialer Organisation: Graubünden, 16.–18. Jahrhundert', *Archiv für Reformationsgeschichte* 87 (1996), pp. 287–333.

17 A. Nelson Burnett, 'Simon Sulzer and the Consequences of the 1563 Strasbourg Consensus in Switzerland', *Archiv für Reformationsgeschichte* 83 (1992), pp. 154–79.

18 H. Guggisberg, 'Reformierter Stadtstaat und Zentrum der Spätrenaissance: Basel in der zweiten Hälfte des 16. Jahrhunderts', in A. Buck (ed.), *Renaissance-Reformation: Gegensätze und Gemeinsamkeiten* (Wiesbaden, 1984), pp. 197–216 (210).

19 H.U. Bächtold, 'Bullinger und die Krise der Zürcher Reformation im Jahre 1532', in U. Gäbler and E. Herkenrath (eds), *Heinrich Bullinger, 1502–1575: Gesammelte Aufsätze zum 400. Todestag* (2 vols; Zurich, 1975), vol. 1, pp. 269–89 (284–8).

20 K. Maeder, *Die Via Media in der Schweizerischen Reformation: Studien zum Problem der Kontinuität im Zeitalter der Glaubensspaltung* (Zurich, 1970), p. 187.

21 Meyer, *Der zweite Kappeler Krieg*, p. 241.

22 K. Guggisberg, *Bernische Kirchengeschichte*, p. 185.

23 Büchler, *Politik des Landes Appenzell*, pp. 89, 116.

24 E. Le Roy Ladurie, *The Beggar and the Professor: A Sixteenth-Century Family Saga* (Chicago, 1997).

25 H.U. Bächtold, *Heinrich Bullinger vor dem Rat: Zur Gestaltung und Verwaltung des Zürcher Staatswesens in den Jahren 1531 bis 1575* (Berne, 1982), p. 76; B. Gordon, *Clerical Discipline and the Rural Reformation: The Synod in Zürich, 1532–1580* (Berne, 1991), p. 175.

26 M. Wick, '"Der Glarnerhandel": Strukturgeschichtliche und konfliktsoziologische Hypothesen zum Glarner Konfessionsgegensatz', *Jahrbuch des Historischen Vereins des Kantons Glarus* 69 (1982), pp. 47–240 (128).

27 Cited in H.R. Schmidt, *Dorf und Religion: Reformierte Sittenzucht in Berner Landgemeinden der Frühen Neuzeit* (Stuttgart, 1995), p. 157.

FURTHER READING

There are several good general surveys of the Swiss Reformation. Rudolf Pfister, *Kirchengeschichte der Schweiz Bd. 2: Von der Reformation bis zum Zweiten Villmerger Krieg* (Zurich, 1974), provides more balanced coverage of Switzerland as a whole than Gottfried Locher, *Die Zwinglische Reformation im Rahmen der europaïschen Kirchengeschichte* (Göttingen, 1979), where the emphasis is on events in Zurich. The best short account in English is Bruce Gordon, 'Switzerland', in Andrew Pettegree (ed.), *The Early Reformation in Europe* (Cambridge, 1992), pp. 70–93.

On late mediæval religion in Switzerland, especially the relationship between the church and local communities, see Carl Pfaff, 'Pfarrei und Pfarreileben: Ein Beitrag zur spätmittelalterlichen Kirchengeschichte', in *Innerschweiz und frühe Eidgenossenschaft: Jubiläumsschrift 700 Jahre Eidgenossenschaft* (2 vols; Olten, 1990), vol. 1, pp. 203–82. Oskar Vasella, *Reform und Reformation in der Schweiz: Zur Würdigung der Anfänge der Glaubenskrise* (Münster, 1958) focuses on the shortcomings of the pre-Reformation clergy. On the 'secularization' of ecclesiastical authority, see Hans Morf, 'Obrigkeit und Kirche in Zürich bis zu Beginn der Reformation', *Zwingliana* 13 (1969–73), pp. 164–205.

The standard biography of Zwingli in English is G.R. Potter, *Zwingli* (Cambridge, 1976). Also useful are Martin Haas, *Huldrych Zwingli und seine Zeit: Leben und Werk des Zürcher Reformators* (Zurich, 1969), and Ulrich Gäbler, *Huldrych Zwingli: His Life and Work* (Edinburgh, 1987). On Zwingli's thought, see W.P. Stephens, *The Theology of Huldrych Zwingli* (Oxford, 1986). The ongoing publication of Bullinger's correspondence has yet to be matched by a modern biography of Zwingli's successor. However, see Ulrich Gäbler and Erland Herkenrath, *Heinrich Bullinger 1504–1575: Gesammelte Aufsätze zum 400. Todestag* (2 vols; Zurich, 1975). The principal study of Bullinger's theology in English is J. Wayne Baker, *Heinrich Bullinger and the Covenant: The Other Reformed Tradition* (Athens, OH, 1980). On Oecolampadius, see Ernst Staehelin, *Das theologische Lebenswerk Johannes Oekolampads* (Leipzig, 1939). On Vadian, see Werner Näf, *Vadian und seine Stadt St Gallen* (2 vols; St Gallen, 1944, 1957).

On Zwingli's supporters within the Zurich council, see Walter Jacob, *Politische Führungsschicht und Reformation: Untersuchungen zur Reformation in Zürich 1519–1528* (Zurich, 1970). The social and institutional aspects of the early Zurich Reformation receive attention in Lee Palmer Wandel, *Always Among Us: Images of the Poor in Zwingli's Zurich* (Cambridge, 1990), and Bruce Gordon, 'Die Entwicklung der Kirchenzucht in Zürich am Beginn der Reformation', in Heinz Schilling (ed.), *Kirchenzucht und Sozialdisziplinierung im frühneuzeitlichen Europa* (Berlin, 1994), pp. 65–90. Helmut Meyer, *Der zweite Kappeler Krieg: Die Krise der Schweizerischen Reformation* (Zurich, 1976), is the best guide to the second Kappel War and its aftermath. The Zurich church under Bullinger is scrutinized in Hans-Ulrich Bächtold, *Heinrich Bullinger vor dem Rat: Zur Gestaltung und Verwaltung des Zürcher Staatswesens in den Jahren 1531 bis 1575* (Berne, 1982); Pamela Biel, *Doorkeepers at the House of Righteousness: Heinrich Bullinger and the Zurich Clergy 1535–1575* (Berne, 1991); and Bruce Gordon, *Clerical Discipline and the Rural Reformation: The Synod in Zürich, 1532–1580* (Berne, 1991).

For an overview of the Reformation in Berne, see Kurt Guggisberg, *Bernische Kirchengeschichte* (Berne, 1958). On developments after 1531, see André Holenstein, 'Reformierte Konfessionalisierung und bernischer Territorialstaat', in Meinrad Schaab (ed.), *Territorialstaat und Calvinismus* (Stuttgart, 1993), pp. 5–33. Heinrich Richard Schmidt, *Dorf und Religion: Reformierte Sittenzucht in Berner Landgemeinden der Frühen Neuzeit* (Stuttgart, 1995), assesses the long-term impact of the Reformation on patterns of belief and behaviour. For the Pays de Vaud, the first volume of Henri Vuilleumier's *Histoire de l'église réformée du Pays de Vaud sous le régime bernois* (Lausanne, 1927–33) remains an essential point of reference. See also Eric Junod (ed.), *La dispute de Lausanne (1536): La théologie réformée après Zwingli et avant Calvin* (Lausanne, 1986).

On the background to the implementation of reform in Basle, see Paul Roth, *Durchbruch und Festsetzung der Reformation in Basel* (Basle, 1942). The iconoclasm of February 1529 is explored in Lee Palmer Wandel, *Voracious Idols and Violent Hands: Iconoclasm in Reformation Zurich, Strasbourg and Basel* (Cambridge, 1995). On Basle's ambiguous status after 1531, see Julia Gauss, 'Basels politisches Dilemma in der Reformationszeit', *Zwingliana* 15 (1982), pp. 509–48. Uwe Plath, *Calvin und Basel 1552–1556* (Zurich, 1974), and Hans Guggisberg, *Sebastian Castellio 1515–1563: Humanist und Verteidiger der religiösen Toleranz im konfessionellen Zeitalter* (Göttingen, 1996), provide an insight into the world of Basle's religious radicals.

On the economic and constitutional ramifications of the Reformation in Graubünden, see Oskar Vasella, *Geistliche und Bauern: Ausgewählte Aufsätze zu Spätmittelalter und Reformation in Graubünden und seinen Nachbargebieten* (Chur, 1996). For the Italian-speaking areas, see E. Camenisch, *Geschichte der Reformation und Gegenreformation in den italienischen Südtälern Graubündens* (Chur, 1950), and the forthcoming study by Conradin Bonorand.

On Catholic–Protestant relations, see Kurt Maeder, *Die Via Media in der Schweizerischen Reformation: Studien zum Problem der Kontinuität im Zeitalter der Glaubensspaltung* (Zurich, 1970), and Hans Berner, *'Die gute correspondenz': Die Politik der Stadt Basel gegenüber dem Fürstbistum Basel in den Jahren 1525–1585* (Basle, 1989). On contacts between the Swiss and Geneva, see Bruce Gordon, 'Calvin and the Swiss Reformed Churches', in Andrew Pettegree, Alistair Duke and Gillian Lewis (eds), *Calvinism in Europe 1540–1620* (Cambridge, 1994), pp. 64–81.

EASTERN EUROPE

Graeme Murdock

Eastern Europe was profoundly affected by the Protestant reformation. The impact of reform quickly spread across the region, and the vast majority of eastern European societies remained committed to Protestantism at the end of the sixteenth century. This Protestant achievement was at first slowly, and then in the 1620s dramatically and violently, undermined by the force of Catholic Counter Reformation. Catholic recovery proved to be so widespread and enduring as almost completely to obscure the previous significance of Protestantism in the region. The elaborate Baroque ostentation added to so many church buildings proclaimed the Roman church's apparent triumph, but this affectation of confidence could not conceal Catholic anxiety about the legacy of generations who had felt more at ease with simpler surroundings in which to worship.

Protestantism made swift progress across eastern Europe because of the perceived attractions of ideas about religious renewal, and also because of the political circumstances of the early and middle decades of the sixteenth century. Fundamental to this process were the threats posed to Hungary, Austria and Bohemia by the expansion of Ottoman power. In addition, rivalry between the ruling Habsburg dynasty and native nobilities significantly influenced the growth of support for Protestant religious reform. German-speaking areas were the first to be affected by Protestantism, but support for reformers had also spread by the mid-sixteenth century to Bohemian and Hungarian nobles. A variety of Protestant churches emerged from localized reform initiatives across the region and no single Protestant group proved to be strong enough to eclipse completely the Catholic church. Each of the Protestant churches instead battled to gain legal recognition from their Catholic monarchs. On the whole different confessional groups managed to coexist without major eruptions of communal violence, resulting in a remarkable degree of practical religious toleration during this period in eastern Europe. By the end of the sixteenth century Protestant churches were, however, increasingly placed on the defensive by programmes of Catholic counter-reform. In the end, with the notable exception of Hungary, Protestantism was everywhere put to flight by the 1620s.

Figure 11.1 Eastern Europe in the mid-sixteenth century. (Ian Johnston)

THE POLITICAL LANDSCAPE

The politics of sixteenth-century eastern Europe were primarily shaped by the triumphant progress of the armies of Suleiman the Magnificent into the northern Balkans. Suleiman's janissaries and sipahi cavalry were able to inflict successive defeats on Christian armies from the capture of Belgrade in 1521 until the 1568 peace of Adrianople finally brought war to an end. In the 1520s the burden of blocking Ottoman progress fell upon the shoulders of the Jagiellonian king of Bohemia and Hungary, Louis II. Louis led the Hungarian army against the Ottomans in southern Hungary at Mohács at the end of August 1526. However the Hungarians suffered a catastrophic defeat and by the end of the battle Hungary and Bohemia had lost their monarch and many leading Hungarian nobles, both Hungarian archbishops and five bishops lay dead alongside more than three-quarters of the army. In the wake of this calamity, the estates of Bohemia and Hungary had to elect new kings and Ferdinand, Habsburg archduke of the Austrian provinces, claimed succession to the thrones of both kingdoms through his marriage to Louis's sister and his sister's marriage to Louis. Ferdinand was elected king by the Bohemian diet in October 1526, but the Hungarian diet first elected János Zápolyai, from 1510 governor of Transylvania, before Ferdinand was able to garner enough support by promising to reverse Hungary's fortunes for his own rival election as king.

Both Zápolyai and Ferdinand then attempted to establish control over all of Hungary, but Ottoman armies encroached even further north in 1541, capturing Buda and Esztergom, and the rest of the Hungarian kingdom remained divided between a western kingdom under Habsburg control and an eastern kingdom under Zápolyai. Agreement between the two kingdoms was only finally reached in 1570, when Emperor Maximilian II accepted the authority of János Zsigmond Zápolyai as prince of Transylvania and in return János Zsigmond recognized Maximilian as king of Hungary with suzerainty over his principality. However when János Zsigmond died in 1571 the Transylvanian diet ignored Habsburg claims of succession, accepted Ottoman suzerainty over the principality and elected István Báthori as their new prince. The division between Royal Hungary and the Transylvanian principality solidified after 1570 and despite being precariously lodged between directly subjugated Ottoman territories in southern Hungary, Moldavia and Wallachia, the Transylvanian principality retained its semi-autonomous status under loose Ottoman overlordship throughout this period.

The disruption caused to government and the church in Hungary by the Ottoman invasion left the nobility to maintain order and direct local affairs. Even in areas of eastern Europe not immediately affected by war, royal authority was balanced against the power of the estates and this divided sovereignty was to prove crucial to the progress of Protestant reform. In Transylvania, princes ruled over the Hungarian, German and Romanian-speaking peoples of Transylvania proper (*partes trans-ilvanicae regni Hungariae*) and over Hungarian counties to the east of the Tisza river known as the Partium. Princes were elected by a single-chamber diet of delegates from the three Transylvanian nations, the Hungarian nobility, Saxon towns and Szeklers, who had been joined in a political union since 1437. Elected princes were able to invite princely officials and unlimited numbers of selected 'regalist' nobles to attend the diet, and usually got agreement to their requests for taxation. Princes were also able to exercise effective authority over central and local government in Transylvania, developing the powers of their chancery and treasury, able to dismiss members of the council and to select sheriffs for most of Transylvania's counties. The economic power and social significance of the urban centres was relatively weak in Transylvania, with neither the largest German town of Kronstadt (Brașov) nor Hungarian town of Kolozsvár (Cluj) containing more than 10,000 people.

Habsburg monarchs retained control over Royal Hungary and ruled over an arc of territory running from the Croatian coast to the German towns and Slovak, Ruthene and Magyar villages of Upper Hungary. Hungarian nobles maintained that their monarchy was determined by election in the diet, a principle only finally relinquished in 1687. In the absence of the king, government was supposed to operate through a palatine selected by the diet to act as Hungary's chief justice and as president of the council. However, after 1562 Habsburg kings governed through a carefully controlled regency council at the capital Pozsony (Bratislava). Noble indignation at this pattern of government was expressed within the diet, where leading magnates had rights of individual representation in the Upper Chamber, alongside a bench of archbishops and bishops. Gentry representatives from the counties sat in the Lower Chamber, overwhelming delegates from royal free towns and mining towns. The main function of the diet was to grant royal requests for taxation and after the two chambers heard royal proposals the estates were also permitted to respond with their own petitions. There were large numbers of legally privileged landowners in Hungary, forming over 5 per cent of the population, and they dominated Hungarian county society. A small number of major magnate families held vast estates across the countryside and nobles controlled powerful county courts and assemblies, with responsibilities to collect taxes and organize military defence. Only the small number of royal free towns were entirely exempt from the jurisdiction of county courts, with the councils of other market and mining towns exercising varying degrees of judicial and administrative competence.

The Habsburg family were also hereditary rulers of the Austrian provinces, but even here the court and chancery could only exert relatively weak central control over the estates. Habsburg authority was itself divided, with branches of the ruling house sustained at Graz in Inner Austria and at Innsbruck in the Tyrol. Lower Austria was governed from Vienna and tended to dominate both Upper Austria beyond the river Enns and the Inner Austrian provinces of Carniola, Carinthia and Styria. Provincial administration was led by a high sheriff, but independent-minded diets of clergy, magnates, knights and towns defended the corporate rights and local privileges of each province, and were able to levy taxation and organize military defence. These provincial diets were mostly directed by powerful magnate families, many of whom held lands across the Austrian provinces and sometimes also in neighbouring kingdoms.

To the north lay the lands of the Bohemian crown, stretching from the historical margravate of Moravia to the German duchies of Silesia and Lusatia. The king appointed a chancellor over all of the Bohemian lands, a governor for Moravia, while the supreme burgrave of Prague operated for the sovereign when absent from the kingdom of Bohemia proper. A Czech majority lived across the Bohemian countryside while the German-speaking minority was concentrated in towns and in northern and western districts. Although the ranks of privileged nobles were smaller in Bohemia than in Hungary, Habsburg kings still had to contend with powerful diets in each province and noble dominance of local administration. After the Hussite revolution, the clergy lost their place as the first estate of the kingdom and so by the sixteenth century the diet comprised only magnates who received individual invitations to attend diets, knights who were invited collectively and representatives from towns. The Bohemian diet held extensive powers, including rights to levy taxation, to sanction new legislation and confirm appointments of royal officials and members of the council. The diet in Moravia stoutly defended its territorial independence and was again commanded by major magnates, although knights, delegates from towns and Catholic prelates were also represented in the assembly.

Among the corporate rights which the Habsburgs as Bohemian kings were obliged to defend, were freedoms offered to non-Catholics after eastern Europe's first wave of religious reform. Jan Hus' execution in 1415 had failed to prevent the spread of a Hussite revolution and civil war in Bohemia during the 1420s and 1430s. Hus had proclaimed the need for spiritual renewal, the importance of the Bible in religious life and the primacy of Christ in effecting salvation. The central practical issue of Hussite reform was to open access to the chalice in the mass, intended to create a brotherhood of believers living in anticipation of Christ's imminent return and strengthened to defend God's laws. The Hussites split into two wings, with the vast majority held within an Utraquist church that offered communion in both kinds to the laity (*sub utraque specie*) and a small minority of more radical Taborites who rejected the priesthood and held a sharper eschatological vision of the social consequences of religious reform.

In 1436 the emperor reached an accommodation with Prague Utraquists by the Compacts of Basle, which apparently acknowledged that the laity could be offered the chalice. The Basle agreement was however left open to different interpretations by the two sides, was never confirmed by the papacy and was rejected by the Taborites. The Basle Compacts were however incorporated into Bohemian law in 1485 and Bohemian kings were obliged to promise on their election to uphold the freedom of both Catholic and Utraquist churches. By the early sixteenth century, Utraquists dominated Bohemian religion, with an administrator and consistory elected by the estates directing church affairs from Prague. Clergy were trained at Prague university and Utraquists controlled most urban schools. Catholic structures were, on the other hand, very badly disrupted in Bohemia, with the archbishopric of Prague vacant from 1471 until 1561 and Catholic benefices left in poverty after the transfer of much church land to noble control. The Taborites meanwhile remained without legal safeguards and their numbers dwindled, but from the 1450s the Unity of Bohemian Brethren (*Jednota Bratrská*) grew to represent the more radical tendency of Hussite reform. Brethren congregations under elected seniors rejected transubstantiation and the mass, but could only survive where they gained the patronage of sympathetic nobles.[1]

THE TRIUMPH OF REFORM

In the early 1520s the cause of religious reform in eastern Europe received fresh impetus. From Saxony, Luther appealed for a return to religion based solely upon the Bible, preaching that faith in Christ alone effected salvation and criticizing the papacy, clergy and monastic orders. Luther's message revealed strong humanist influences, but also carried clear similarities with Hussite reforms. It is hardly surprising therefore that many Utraquist clergy in Bohemia, in contact with humanist learning through universities at Prague and in Germany, also supported Lutheran ideas. Lutheran preaching spread first though to Germans in Silesia and Lusatia, bordering on Saxony, and to German-speaking Catholics in northern and western districts of Bohemia. Evangelical preaching then quickly extended across Bohemia under the protection of urban magistrates and nobles. Reform-minded Utraquist clergy became increasingly alienated from more conservative colleagues, who still sought unity with Rome if they could retain communion in both kinds. In 1526 Ferdinand had attempted to take advantage of this division and force a union between conservative Utraquists and Catholics. Despite the king's best efforts the position of reformers steadily strengthened during the 1530s and 1540s in Bohemia, with many clergy moving towards evangelical neo-Utraquism and Lutheranism.

Bohemian commitment to the evangelical cause was soon tested when, without consulting the diet, Ferdinand ordered the nobility to raise an army to support him in the Schmalkaldic War against German Protestant princes. This prodded some nobles to revolt in 1547, as much to defend political liberties in Bohemia as religious freedoms. When this revolt failed, Ferdinand ordered the expulsion of Lutheran preachers from within the Utraquist church and forced the Bohemian Brethren into exile in Poland and Moravia. However, once the Augsburg peace had been agreed in the empire in 1555, Lutheran preaching flowered again in Bohemia. Nobles questioned whether the Augsburg peace implied that their monarch could reform religion in Bohemia according to his will, arguing instead that noble privileges included the right to reform religion within their own lands. In any case, many noble patrons and urban magistrates simply selected Lutheran clergy for service in parishes during the 1550s and 1560s. The organization of Protestant churches in Bohemia nevertheless remained uncertain and dislocated, with Lutheran ministers no longer accepting the authority of the Prague consistory and looking instead to Saxony for leadership.

In Moravia the majority of nobles and parishes had also become Utraquist in the fifteenth century and the Utraquist church was legally recognized by the diet. The Catholic church, though, held on to more support in Moravia than in Bohemia, particularly in towns and in German-speaking areas. Evangelical Protestant ideas quickly gained support among Catholics and Utraquists alike in Moravia, as clergy spread the Lutheran message in towns and among magnates and knights. Some Moravian towns also provided refuge for German Anabaptists in the 1520s after the Peasants' War. Balthasar Hubmaier arrived in Nikolsburg (Mikulov) in 1526 and was joined by the millenarian Hans Hut and by many Anabaptist refugees from southern Germany. Jakob Hutter then tried to unite Anabaptist communities in southeastern Moravia around principles of communal economic activity and collective ownership of property. Although Anabaptists faced increased persecution in 1535 from urban authorities they found refuge on the lands of supportive nobles, as did Bohemian Brethren when exiled to Moravia in 1526 and again in 1547. In 1550 an overwhelming majority of the Moravian diet meeting at Brünn (Brno) asserted the principle that the estates held rights to reform religion. This left Ferdinand with little option but to concede religious freedom to the Moravian nobility in return for promises of political loyalty. Lutherans, Anabaptists and Bohemian Brethren were then shielded from persecution in pockets of the Moravian countryside where they could find noble protection. While the estates had secured the free practice of Protestant religion in Moravia, little was then done to unify Protestant groups or to develop effective church structures.

Austrian clergy were influenced by a mixture of humanist teaching at Vienna university and Protestant ideas from Wittenberg. Preachers in Lower and Upper Austria got an enthusiastic response for evangelical slogans from a majority of urban elites and nobles from the 1520s. The practice of Catholicism simply drained away, with the collapse of monastic houses and rising numbers of vernacular Bibles in circulation marking the sudden shift in patterns of religiosity. The pace and direction of Protestant reform in Austria was again determined by the nobility. Noble patrons of reform first prevented the Bishop of Passau from enforcing his jurisdiction over dissident clergy, and then from the 1540s supported the development of more identifiably Lutheran congregations with married clergy conducting communion services instead of the mass. In 1556 the Vienna diet then declared its support for the Lutheran Augsburg Confession and Ferdinand's ability to counteract this spread of Protestantism was hampered by his need for provincial diets to agree taxation to continue financing the Ottoman Wars. The organization of Lutheran congregations in the Austrian provinces, however, remained localized and inadequate, with weak administrative structures and some variety of beliefs and practices among Protestant parish clergy.[2]

In Hungary, support for religious reform from the 1520s was driven by a desire to purify the Catholic church, whose spiritual power was badly discredited by the Ottoman invasion. Catholic church structures were decimated in war-affected areas of Hungary, where there was little effective institutional resistance to clergy reformers, often influenced by study at Cracow and Wittenberg. The Hungarian diet was sufficiently concerned about clergy connections with German academic centres to pass measures to punish heretics as early as 1523. German-speaking towns were indeed the first to be infected with Protestantism, as itinerant preachers and merchants moved between the towns of Upper Hungary and Transylvania during the 1530s and 1540s. Local ministers who became disaffected with Catholic theology and traditional ritual received a sympathetic hearing almost everywhere from urban magistrates. The German towns of Upper Hungary had already adopted a variant of the Augsburg Confession by 1544, which they then anxiously defended against the Hungarian diet's clear denunciation in 1548 of Calvinist views of the sacraments. In Transylvania, Johannes Honter – who had studied and worked at Cracow, Vienna and Basle – introduced Lutheran liturgical changes at Kronstadt which were quickly copied in Transylvania's other Saxon towns. Transylvania's Catholic princes took advantage of growing support for reform among German and Hungarian clergy to bolster their own power and in 1556 the diet agreed that all church property be brought under the control of the prince. János Zsigmond then accepted the diet's demands for the legal recognition of Protestant religion and in 1557 the Saxon towns received approval for the free practice of Lutheranism.[3]

COMPETING CONFESSIONS

From the mid-sixteenth century the influence of Calvinist theologians began to be felt across eastern Europe. In the 1560s contacts expanded between the Bohemian Brethren and Reformed Protestants in western Europe, and the Brethren's 1567 confession mediated many aspects of Calvinist theology. Magyars in Hungary and Transylvania were mostly exposed to Protestant preaching from the 1550s, by which time southern German and Swiss cities had become the most dynamic continental centres of Protestant reform. Thus while Lutheran and Melanchthonian influences had been strong among early Hungarian reformers, parish clergy were increasingly drawn towards Reformed Protestant religion. Hungarian reformers were not as reliant as their German colleagues upon the support of urban magistrates, looking instead to great noble families for patronage, such as the Török, Nádasdy, Thurzó, Perényi and Drágfi families. While individual nobles were undoubtedly convinced about the need for religious renewal, broad support from many Hungarian nobles for Protestant doctrinal opinions also reflected continued insecurity about Ottoman power in the region and discontent with Habsburg rule. Hungarian nobles were anxious to defend their corporate privileges against the growing claims of crown sovereignty and this concern found a new focus from the middle decades of the century on the need to defend rights of religious liberty.

Reformed religion also won strong support in the small market towns of the Partium, particularly at Debrecen in the 1550s under the leadership of Márton Kálmáncsehi. The mass desertion from the Catholic church of ordinary clergy and parishioners in this area was marked by fervour for a religion purified of idolatry, as a response to apocalyptic signs of divine judgement which the Turkish invasion and ongoing occupation of Hungary was seen to entail. Apocalyptic interest in Hungary reached a peak in the late 1560s with predictions from one leading preacher that 1570 would bring the destruction of the Antichrist. Expectations in eastern Hungary reached fever pitch in 1569 with heavenly signs detected by local enthusiasts and the discovery of a 'black man' to lead a holy army against the Turks. This prophet, called György Karácsony, encamped with his supporters around Debrecen in 1569 and 1570. The captain of the Hungarian frontier fortress at Eger, Simon Forgách, wrote that his garrison had to be dissuaded from joining Karácsony, since 'religion had gripped them as if thunder-struck'. In expectation of a miraculous victory, Karácsony led a band of 600 men to the nearby frontier garrison at Törökszentmiklós only to be overwhelmed by Ottoman forces and scattered in confusion.

A Reformed church gradually emerged in Hungary and Transylvania from the late 1550s. Contact between Hungary and Geneva however remained minimal and when synods of Hungarian ministers agreed on confessional statements in the 1560s they proved to be rather eclectic mixtures of Calvinist, Bezan, Zwinglian and Melanchthonian ideas. In 1559 Hungarian ministers from Transylvania, the Partium and northeastern Hungary met in joint synod at Marosvásárhely (Tîrgu Mureş) and agreed upon a statement that communion services should be held as memorials of Christ's death. In 1567 the Reformed credentials of these ministers were more firmly established when a synod at Debrecen accepted Bullinger's Second Helvetic confession and agreed to a *Confessio Catholica* published in 1562 by Péter Méliusz Juhász and Gergely Szegedi. By 1570 the vast majority of Hungarian nobles adhered to one of the Protestant churches and while the royal towns and nobles of western Hungarian counties mostly remained Lutheran, Calvinism gained widespread support among the nobles, gentry and market towns of the eastern counties. Protestant churches to the west of the Danube were in fact slow to split into distinct Evangelical and Reformed branches and separate Reformed church structures only emerged there in the 1590s. This was partly because the Hungarian estates proved unable to win agreement from their Habsburg kings to the extension of legal rights to Lutherans and Calvinists. Indeed royal decrees continued to be promulgated against Calvinists in the 1560s and 1570s. Protestant ministers were left entirely dependent upon noble support and while most could easily find local patrons this delayed the development of the Protestant churches' organization. Meanwhile in Ottoman-occupied Hungary, strict controls were imposed on all Christian churches, with letters of approval required from the authorities to guarantee the undisturbed practice of religion. Even here, though, the cause of Protestant reform made progress, and Reformed clergy mostly came to hold sway over southern Hungarian congregations.[4]

In Transylvania the 1558 diet had condemned Calvinist views on communion, however support for Reformed ideas about the sacraments was expressed by Hungarian clergy in a series of doctrinal debates against local Lutherans. In 1564 the Transylvanian diet demanded that Saxon and Hungarian clergy try to resolve contested points of theology. When the two sides completely failed to agree, the diet recognized the existence of two distinct Protestant churches in Transylvania, one for Saxons and another for Hungarians, and proclaimed that parish ministers should preach according to the wishes of their local congregations. Three churches were then legally established within Transylvanian society, with the Reformed church receiving the support of most Hungarian nobles. Both Protestant churches had their own superintendent elected by a clergy synod and confirmed in office by the prince. The prince granted superintendents the right to hold synods, conduct ordinations and parish visitations, and over time the authority of these superintendents to discipline their clergy steadily increased. In the 1560s a fourth religion began to gain ground in Transylvania when a faction of Hungarian ministers questioned the doctrine of the Trinity. These anti-Trinitarians were influenced by Polish and Italian humanist intellectuals, and led by Ferenc Dávid, then superintendent of the Hungarian church. In June 1568 the Transylvanian diet met at Torda (Turda) and responded to this further confessional division by recognizing the constitutional validity of four 'received religions' within Transylvania's three nations. Legal status was extended to the Roman Catholic, Lutheran, Reformed and anti-Trinitarian churches, and freedom of worship granted to supporters of all four religions, with the diet instructing ministers to teach Christian religion according to their understanding of it.

This 1568 Torda agreement reflected the relative weakness of central political authority in Transylvania and was intended to balance the interests of the three nations represented in the diet. Given Transylvania's precarious international position, it was hoped that acceptance of religious division would prevent the implosion of the fledgling state under confessional conflict. Although political calculations were probably decisive in establishing religious toleration in Transylvania, there was also long experience within the principality of managing peaceful coexistence between different ethnic and religious groups. Therefore while clergy involved in theological debates entered into heated arguments about doctrinal and liturgical issues, the remarkable plurality of confessions in Transylvania fostered local traditions of successfully accommodating religious differences within regional communities, towns, neighbourhoods and even among families. The 1568 Torda diet described faith as a gift from God which could not be compelled and religious persecution proved to be minimal in Transylvania. Forced conversions were in any case prohibited by law and denominational disputes were only very rarely characterized by violence. In 1564 the diet tried to avoid future conflicts over the contentious issue of ownership of church buildings, by deciding that churches belonged to the confessional group with majority support in each parish. New occupants of churches were also supposed to provide an alternative place of worship for any displaced minority. Even landowners with rights to select local ministers were forbidden from introducing clergy of a different religion to that of the parish community. In practice, nonetheless, patterns of religious loyalty in Transylvania still tended largely to be determined by the rights of patronage and social power of the privileged elite, whether Hungarian nobles, Saxon burghers or Szekler lords.[5]

Anti-Trinitarian preachers had gained some endorsement from János Zsigmond before his death in 1571, and support for anti-Trinitarianism was particularly strong among the Szeklers in eastern Transylvania and also in Hungarian-speaking towns. However, under the new Catholic prince István Báthori support for anti-Trinitarianism began to contract. The church was weakened when the 1576 diet limited their superintendent's powers of visitation to the areas around Kolozsvár and Torda, leaving anti-Trinitarians elsewhere under the aegis of the Reformed superintendent. In 1572 Báthori had also encouraged the diet to outlaw any further theological innovation among ministers of the four received religions, in an effort to prevent the development of any more religious groups in the principality. This law was primarily aimed at the anti-Trinitarian church because of the emergence of a radical wing of anti-Trinitarian clergy, known as Sabbatarians, who denied the divinity of Christ. Ferenc Dávid was himself arrested under the 1572 law on suspicion of Sabbatarianism and died in prison in 1579. While the anti-Trinitarian church was gravely weakened by internal disputes over Sabbatarianism, Lutherans in Transylvania became largely isolated within the Saxon community. Transylvania's Romanians meanwhile mostly remained loyal to Eastern Orthodoxy, although some Romanian gentry were attracted to a Calvinist church sponsored by Hungarians from the 1560s. Since Romanians were not represented as a nation in the diet, their religion was not included within the 1568 settlement, but the free practice of Orthodox religion was granted as a privilege by the princes. Transylvanian Orthodox clergy received support to resist Protestant conversion efforts from their sister churches in the Romanian principalities. Only one rogue Moldavian prince, Jacob Basilicos Heraclides, took some steps to reform the Orthodox church in the sixteenth century. Heraclides however only succeeded in alienating both clergy and Moldavian nobles, and was assassinated in 1563.[6]

THE PROTESTANT ASCENDANCY

By the latter decades of the sixteenth century Protestantism dominated eastern European society. Around 1600 more than 80 per cent of over 5,000 parishes in Hungary were Protestant, with a majority of Protestant parishes held by the Reformed church. Of around 1,600 parishes in Bohemia, 1,400 were Protestant with 200 under the jurisdiction of the old Utraquist administrator, and the Archbishop of Prague was left controlling only around 200 parishes. This pattern of religious adherence had been decided by a mixture of geography and communication networks, pre-Reformation patterns of religiosity and ecclesiastical organization, as well as feudal, regional, local and family loyalties. Except among Anabaptists and Brethren there were no colonies of religious refugees in the region and in the rest of society only the privileged elite could consider making a personal choice about their religious affiliation. The role ethnic allegiance played in determining the outcome of the Reformation in eastern Europe has been much debated. Certainly Lutheranism received wide support from German-speakers, but Slovaks in Upper Hungary, Czechs and some Hungarians also became Lutheran. Calvinism, though, was almost exclusively the preserve of Hungarian communities and the Calvinist church in Transylvania proved to be almost entirely a Magyar affair. Ethnic cohesiveness cannot therefore be wholly discounted either in establishing or, perhaps more significantly, in reinforcing attachment to a particular religion. Many anomalies remain, however, with leading Hungarian reformers Gáspár Heltai and Ferenc Dávid in fact Saxon by origin, and in Transylvania not all Hungarian-speakers became Calvinists, with others Lutheran, remaining Catholic or turning to anti-Trinitarianism.

Protestant religiosity slowly spread into the towns and parishes of eastern Europe. Although Protestant systems of belief highly valued access to the scriptures it took until 1590 for Reformed minister Gáspár Károlyi to publish the first complete translation of the Bible in Hungarian, while Bohemian Brethren only produced a vernacular Bible at Kralice in Moravia in 1593. While there was a sharp rise in the production of vernacular books by Protestants in the latter decades of the sixteenth century, low rates of literacy ensured that preaching and oral instruction rather than books and popular pamphlets remained the prime means of transmitting ideas to local communities. Eastern European Lutherans and Calvinists could not in any case boast of outstanding native theologians, with the main sources of theological novelty in the region coming from radical anti-Trinitarians and Anabaptists. Standards of Protestant clergy education certainly rose, however, through extensive contacts with German universities, and local Protestant grammar schools become important centres of religious life. A new clergy elite slowly emerged to lead Protestant church organizations, although central control over parish clergy remained uncertain with secular patrons jealous of conceding rights to superintendents and clergy synods.

The clergy and church buildings of eastern Europe had been visibly altered by Reformation. Protestant ministers could marry and synods were anxious to regulate the appearance of both ministers and their wives according to strict codes of sober clothing. Churches had also clearly undergone reform, particularly at the hands of Calvinists, although even in Hungary there were only very isolated outbreaks of iconoclasm. Instead Reformed ministers and church patrons instigated the orderly removal of images, statues, ornamental windows, organs, candles and altars from church buildings. Protestant church services were also steadily established, with emphasis placed upon vernacular readings from the Bible and preaching. Sacramental liturgy was drastically simplified with Calvinist congregations most obviously abandoning traditional practices, by using ordinary water for infant baptism and bread in communion services held only seven times a year. Everywhere Protestant religious life was shorn of elaborate celebrations and ceremonies deemed to be superstitious, and church music was altered with Hungarian Calvinists particularly suspicious of using musical instruments in their services. There is limited evidence on the varying speed and enthusiasm with which local communities across the region adapted to these changes in church practices and religious life. While some ministers complained bitterly about the persistent survival of Catholic abuses, elsewhere there were clear signs of popular enthusiasm for the different forms of Protestant religion.

THE CATHOLIC COUNTER-ATTACK

The extent of this Protestant achievement in eastern Europe was soon tested by counter-reform pressure from the Catholic hierarchy and Habsburg dynasty, and by the disruption of renewed war against the Ottomans in the 1590s. The Catholic church's recovery came from a very low starting point in many areas. In Transylvania the Catholic church had almost ceased to exist after the loss of episcopal lands, of church buildings and of so many of its clergy. The secularization of church land gave the princes and many nobles a direct interest in limiting any Catholic revival, with even the palace of the former Bishop of Gyulafehérvár (Alba Iulia) converted for use as the main princely residence. While all the Protestant churches in Transylvania were led by superintendents the Catholic church alone had no bishop from 1542, with disagreement between the papacy and Habsburgs preventing any new appointment. Any remaining Catholic clergy in Transylvania had retired to the lands of a few sympathetic Hungarian nobles and Szekler lords. Even when István Báthori invited Jesuits to set up teaching stations at Gyulafehérvár, Kolozsvár and Nagyvárad (Oradea) in 1579, the diet ensured that they could not become involved in missionary work. Pressure from the diet forced the Jesuits' exclusion from the principality in 1588 and the order was readmitted only to be expelled twice more before 1606, further disrupting the halting progress of the

Counter Reformation within Transylvania. The Catholic church remained a much more significant institutional force in Royal Hungary than in Transylvania through episcopal representation in the Upper Chamber of the diet and with the chancellor always drawn from the ranks of bishops and archbishops. Significant efforts were also made to train a new generation of Catholic priests to replace those lost to the Protestant churches and a new seminary opened near the capital at Nagyszombat (Trnava) in 1590.

In the latter decades of the sixteenth century some momentum of Catholic recovery was generated in the Austrian provinces and Bohemia, with Jesuit colleges set up from the 1560s across Austria and at Prague, Brünn and Olmütz (Olomouc) in Moravia. This all focused the attention of the estates on the need to secure legal protection for Protestant liberties. In 1568 Lower Austrian nobles pushed Maximilian into accepting the free practice of Lutheranism on noble lands. Although these rights were not extended to towns in Lower Austria, from 1574 Lutheran nobles could also worship freely in Vienna. In 1572 Inner Austrian nobles gained verbal guarantees that Lutheran church services would not be disturbed, a promise confirmed at the 1576 diet in return for a subsidy. However, in the late 1570s a Catholic commission curtailed Protestant freedoms in Inner Austria and these attacks resumed when Ferdinand of Styria took over as governor of Inner Austria in 1596. Protestant clergy were banished from towns, Protestant schools were closed and by 1600 Graz was wholly Catholic once again. While Protestantism in Austrian towns was under severe threat by the turn of the century, the agreements reached between the Habsburgs and the nobility ensured that Protestantism in the Austrian countryside still remained largely unaffected by counter-reform measures.

The progress of Catholic recovery in Bohemia was also very slow before the 1590s, although the Catholic church could claim some important noble converts including Vilém Slavata and Karel Liechtenstein. The estates' reaction to royal attempts to coordinate the progress of counter-reform measures was to encourage clergy to reconcile their theological differences and draw up a unified Protestant confession. Most Bohemian Protestant clergy adhered to German Lutheran confessional statements, which had led to divisive arguments over Melanchthonian ideas. In 1575 Protestant nobles managed to broker agreement between Lutherans of all shades, reformist Utraquists and Bohemian Brethren to the *Confessio Bohemica*, which mostly followed the Melanchthonian version of the 1530 Augsburg Confession. The diet then succeeded in forcing Maximilian to give his assent for nobles to practise Protestant religion under this Bohemian confession. Ecclesiastical ordinances organized Bohemian Protestants under the protection of fifteen defenders appointed by the estates and in return for these concessions the diet voted new taxes and elected Rudolf II to succeed Maximilian.[7]

The cost of defending their lands against the Ottomans had long constrained the Habsburgs' ability to act more vigorously against Protestants living under their authority. Skirmishes along the borders of Ottoman-occupied Hungary flared up again in the early 1590s, with hostilities culminating in the first major attempt to push the Ottomans out of Hungary since the early 1540s. A joint Habsburg and Transylvanian army took the field, only to be defeated at the Battle of Mezökeresztes in 1596, with only minor and indecisive encounters continuing until 1606. Zsigmond Báthori, the chronically unstable Transylvanian prince, had first renounced Ottoman suzerainty to join these campaigns and then abandoned the Transylvanian estates to cope with invasions of the principality first by the Wallachian Prince Mihai Viteazul and then in 1603 by a Habsburg army under General Giorgio Basta. After five years of turmoil in Transylvania, a leading Calvinist noble, István Bocskai, had concluded that Habsburg control of Transylvania posed a greater threat to domestic stability, noble privileges and religious freedom than Ottoman suzerainty had done. Bocskai therefore joined with other dissident nobles who had already declared themselves opponents of Habsburg rule. Among nobles in Royal Hungary there was also growing anti-Habsburg sentiment fuelled by resentment at the inconclusive results of the Ottoman War and by indignation at Rudolf's heavy-handed attempts to reassert Habsburg sovereignty over all non-Ottoman Hungary, for both his dynasty and the Catholic church. Basta's vicious wartime governance of Transylvania was ably complemented by General Jacob Belgiojoso in Upper Hungary, with Protestants expelled from towns and the leading Protestant magnate István Illésházy was put on trial for sedition. The town of Kassa (Košice) became a particular flashpoint, when in January 1604 the Catholic bishop used imperial troops to occupy St Elizabeth's church and evicted Lutheran ministers from the town. When complaints were raised about events in Kassa at the Hungarian diet in February 1604, Archduke Matthias, acting for Rudolf, responded by asserting that anyone who raised religious issues at the diet was guilty of treason.

The response of the Hungarian estates to this potent cocktail of military, political and religious grievances amounted to a crisis of confidence in Habsburg authority to rule Hungary and resulted in a rebellious assertion of local corporate rights. István Bocskai led the revolt, supported first by bands of Hajduck mercenaries and then by the magnates, gentry and towns of eastern Hungary. Despite stiff resistance from Belgiojoso, Bocskai was able to enter Kassa in triumph in November 1604. By February 1605 Bocskai had been elected as the first Calvinist Prince of Transylvania and his rebel army advanced by April 1605 to Pozsony, while Hajduck bands backed by Ottoman forces reached as far as Lower Austria and Moravia. In April 1605 the Hungarian diet met at Szerencs and elected Bocskai as Prince Protector of Hungary, or 'Moses of the Hungarians'.[8]

The diet's use of Old Testament imagery to portray Bocskai reflected how Reformed preachers had consistently idealized the new prince as a defender of true religion and as a divinely appointed liberator of Hungary from tyrannical Habsburg government. Bocskai himself declared in an *Apology* that his aims in the revolt were 'the maintenance of ourselves, our nation's life and, further, of our religion, liberty and property'. This may seem only to amount to a rather muted echo of Huguenot monarchomach writings, but such claims do suggest that Bocskai's revolt was justified to some extent by Calvinistic theories of rights of resistance against sinning higher authorities. Bocskai though was careful to limit his use of religious rhetoric, anxious to appeal not only to Hungarian Calvinists but also to Lutheran nobles and towns. Bocskai instead mostly justified his actions by citing the thirty-first article of the 1222 Golden Bull of András II, which gave

Hungarian nobles the right to resist any ruler who ignored noble privileges. While Bocskai's rebellion was not therefore an immediate consequence of Calvinist influence over Hungarian politics, Reformed clergy were only too pleased to chime in with their spiritual blessing for noble aspirations to prevent the centralization of power in Hungary in the hands of the Habsburgs and the Catholic hierarchy.[9]

Bocskai was content to relinquish his claim to the Hungarian crown, once Rudolf was prepared to negotiate and accept Bocskai's rule as Prince of Transylvania. The terms of the Vienna peace agreed between Bocskai and Rudolf in June 1606 also dealt with the grievances of the Hungarian nobility and finally acknowledged the reality of confessional division in Royal Hungary. The treaty extended the free exercise of religion to the nobility, royal towns and military garrisons, and established the rights of both Lutheran and Reformed churches to regulate freely their own affairs. The gains made by Hungarian Protestants through the peace of Vienna, however, still had to be ratified by the Hungarian diet. In 1608 Protestant nobles took advantage of the struggle between the Habsburg brothers Rudolf and Matthias for control of Bohemia and Hungary, and in return for supporting Matthias won endorsement of the Vienna peace. This agreement at the 1608 diet effectively devolved absolute rights of religious patronage over local churches to the Hungarian nobility. The diet's articles also, however, contained an implicit suggestion that peasants across Hungary would gain religious liberties. Many Protestant nobles indeed supported the extension of freedom of worship to peasants, in so far as it permitted peasants who lived on the lands of Catholic nobles to become Protestant, an advantage calculated as outweighing the risk of losing peasants on Protestants' lands to the Catholic church.

With a stream of noble reconversions to the Catholic church from the 1610s, it soon became obvious, however, that Hungarian Protestants' confidence about the future had been misplaced. The increasing numbers of Catholic landowners, especially in western and northwestern counties of Royal Hungary, reclaimed control over church buildings and expelled Protestant ministers and teachers from their lands. Faced with this vulnerable position, Protestant nobles began to argue that the freedom of religion established by the 1608 diet could only have practical meaning if it was understood to include access to a place of worship. This argument was placed before the 1619 diet at Pozsony, by which time Catholics formed a majority in the Upper Chamber, with fifteen Catholic prelates sitting alongside sixty-six Catholic magnates and only sixty-one Protestant magnates. The complaints of Protestants in both chambers about Catholic interference with Protestant freedoms and especially over restricted access to church buildings, also received support from the Calvinist Transylvanian prince, Gábor Bethlen. The diet acknowledged that there was disagreement on whether freedom of religion in Hungary was *una cum templis*, that is entailing free use of churches, church bells and graveyards. This statement also recognized that there were differences of opinion in the diet as to whether the rights of landowners as church patrons or the rights of a majority within local communities took precedence in determining parishes' confessional allegiance.

THE DEFEAT OF PROTESTANTISM

The example of the Hungarian estates' resistance against monarchical centralization and Counter Reformation was not lost upon Protestant nobles in Bohemia, Moravia and Austria. Here too the estates were able to take advantage of the battle for power between Rudolf and Matthias. In 1608 the estates of Moravia, Upper and Lower Austria exacted a restatement of previous declarations on religious freedom from Matthias in return for their support. The Bohemian estates remained loyal to Rudolf, who agreed to a Letter of Majesty in July 1609 which offered religious liberty both to nobles and for the first time also to towns. In August 1609 the Silesian estates were also rewarded for their loyalty to Rudolf when he acknowledged the rights of Lutheran churches across the Silesian duchies. Once the crisis within the ruling dynasty was resolved in favour of Matthias, pressure was soon renewed upon Protestants across the Habsburg monarchy. Although Matthias confirmed the Letter of Majesty on his election as king of Bohemia in 1611, the estates' defenders of Protestant churches made repeated claims that their legal freedoms were being violated. A crisis between the Habsburgs and the Bohemian estates was set off in 1618 by the destruction of Protestant churches on crown lands at Braunau (Broumov) and Klostergrab (Hrob). The Bohemian estates deposed the staunchly Catholic Ferdinand of Styria and rebelled in defence of corporate privileges and Protestant freedoms. The Upper Austrian estates offered strong support to Bohemia and in turn nobles in Lower Austria, Silesia, Lusatia and Moravia joined the Protestant estates' confederation and refused to accept Ferdinand II's rule. There is some evidence of Calvinist coordination behind this resistance with contacts established between Bohemian nobles, the Upper Austrian Calvinist Georg Tschernembl and German Reformed courts, particularly at Heidelberg in the Palatinate.[10]

In August 1619 this new defiance of Habsburg authority spread to Hungary when Gábor Bethlen advanced the Transylvanian army to Pozsony in alliance with Frederick of the Palatinate and the Bohemian rebels. Bocskai's revolt had supplied the Transylvanian state with a clear sense of Protestant mission to oppose Habsburg claims of sovereignty over Hungary and efforts to impose counter-reform, and Bethlen's 1619 attack on Royal Hungary revived and strengthened this perception of the principality's role. By 1620 Bethlen, supported by his Ottoman overlords and by many Hungarian nobles, had apparently conquered Royal Hungary and the diet offered Bethlen the Hungarian crown in August 1620. Bethlen, however, refused to be crowned, unwilling to become the figurehead of the diet's vision of limited monarchy and concerned about the potentially hostile reaction at the Porte to his spectacular success. Bethlen's caution indeed proved astute, since the triumph of the confederation of Protestant estates in eastern Europe was short-lived. The Bohemian rebels' defeat at the White Mountain in November 1620, despite the presence of 8,000 troops sent by Bethlen, struck a severe blow against the pretensions of Protestant estates in the region. Left largely bereft of allies, Bethlen agreed to the Nikolsburg peace treaty with Ferdinand in December 1621, by which Ferdinand ceded territory in northeastern Hungary to Bethlen's control.

The collapse of Bohemian resistance in 1620 and peace with Bethlen in 1621 enabled Ferdinand to concentrate on crushing Protestantism and the power of estates within his monarchy. Ferdinand directly equated Protestantism with political disloyalty, and quickly moved to overturn previous guarantees of Protestant liberty. By 1625 Protestant worship had virtually ceased in Bohemia and the renewed constitution of 1627 summarily abrogated the Letter of Majesty, abolished elections for the Bohemian crown and only recognized the legality of the Catholic church. Protestants were left to conform to the new regime or leave Bohemia and with the execution or exile of leading rebels and Protestant nobles vast tracts of land were confiscated and transferred to Catholic ownership. The renewed constitution was extended to Moravia in 1628, again forcing nobles and clergy into exile, and Lutheran freedoms only remained intact in Silesia. In Upper Austria Protestant nobles who had made common cause with the Bohemian rebels were forced into exile and Protestant clergy were banished from the province in 1626. By 1630, 800 Inner Austrian Protestant nobles were also in exile and even in Lower Austria, where many nobles had remained loyal to the Habsburgs, Protestant preachers were expelled and pressure placed on nobles to convert. Denied noble protection and clergy leadership, Protestant congregations across the Austrian provinces offered little resistance to the imposition of Catholic clergy and worship.[11]

The Protestant challenge to Habsburg attempts to enforce Counter Reformation in the first two decades of the seventeenth century had certainly not been a popular movement. The acquisition and defence of Protestant freedoms instead relied almost exclusively upon noble estates, with the Hungarian diet alone able to preserve the concessions wrung out of Rudolf at Vienna in 1606. Hungarian Protestants certainly had several advantages which ensured that they were not persecuted to the same extent as their co-religionists elsewhere in the Habsburg monarchy. First, the combative strength provided by distinct Lutheran and Reformed confessional identities in Hungary may have stiffened resistance to counter-reform measures. Second, Hungarian Protestants did not have to rely solely upon the diet to defend their liberties, with the military strength of Transylvania's Calvinist princes able to place limits upon Habsburg power in Hungary. However, with both Bocskai and Bethlen directly backed by the Ottomans, Catholics in Hungary could make claims with some justification that Protestants had entered into a pact with the Turks.

Although the Protestant churches' legal freedoms remained intact in Hungary many of the most prominent magnate families converted back to the Catholic church after 1620. While some may sincerely have experienced a change in their private beliefs, many others hoped that showing loyalty to the Habsburgs' religion would lead to office and advancement. While Protestant gentry continued to be strongly represented in the Lower Chamber of the diet, they faced the combined force of the crown, magnates and Catholic hierarchy, and from the 1630s Protestants fought a long and ultimately unsuccessful battle to maintain their hard-won privileges. Protestants gained some concessions at the 1647 diet after military intervention by the Transylvanian Prince György I Rákóczi. However this settlement was steadily overturned in many localities as Catholic nobles re-imposed restrictions on the free practice of Protestantism and after 1648 Protestants turned to the diet for redress of their grievances entirely in vain. Ministers were expelled from their parishes, churches closed to Protestants, books confiscated, burials disturbed, Protestants forced to recognize Catholic holidays, blocks placed against Protestant guild membership and forced payments demanded for Catholic priests. Along with the outright destruction of Protestant churches and schools, these measures rendered the terms of the 1606 Vienna peace entirely meaningless. By the 1650s Protestant ministers in Ottoman Hungary were in many respects far more secure than their colleagues in Royal Hungary.

Hungarian Protestantism thus became increasingly reliant upon the political support of Transylvania's princes during the early seventeenth century. In earlier decades Protestant clergy in Hungary had relied heavily upon noble support and at the turn of the century Reformed ministers had enthusiastically backed the cause of noble rebellion against monarchical authority. Now the Reformed church in Transylvania became closely allied with the growing authority and power of Calvinist princes. The Reformed church in Transylvania indeed acquired the status of the public and orthodox religion of the principality. While maintaining the legal rights of the other confessions, Transylvania's princes resolutely promoted the interests of the Reformed church and its clergy, who received collective ennoblement from Bethlen in 1629. Bethlen and the Rákóczi princes were also generous in offering financial support for the education of Reformed student ministers. Bursaries were given for students to travel to western universities, mostly to Germany and the Dutch Republic, and princes paid for the development of local Reformed academies, schools and printing presses. Princes also responded to Reformed demands for action against Sabbatarianism and in 1638 even placed somewhat crude controls over mainstream anti-Trinitarians in the Unitarian church.

Contact with western co-religionists in the early seventeenth century led some Hungarian Calvinist ministers to support an agenda of yet further reformation of church practices and religious life. By the 1640s many clergy who had studied in the Dutch Republic and England advocated the imposition of tighter controls over the behaviour and morality of congregations. So-called puritan ministers encouraged greater personal piety among ordinary believers, the extension of educational opportunities, further reform of liturgical and sacramental practices to rid them of any semblance of surviving Catholic influences and greater lay involvement in running parishes to facilitate the implementation of these reforms. There was in fact broad acceptance within the church and among Reformed patrons of the need to impose higher standards of moral and social discipline. The suggestion, however, that this required the introduction of congregational presbyteries and wholesale changes to the pattern of hierarchical church government led to reforming ministers being stigmatized as puritan troublemakers and separatists. The advantages and disadvantages of reform plans were repeatedly debated from the late 1630s until the 1650s. However, after György II Rákóczi's disastrous campaign in Poland in 1657 left the principality gravely weakened, the Reformed church could no longer afford the luxury of internal debates. Transylvania's decline left the Reformed and other Protestant churches grimly defending their remaining privileges, freedoms, churches and schools in the face of increasing Catholic persecution and further losses of noble support.[12]

The eastern European Reformation proved to be largely a noble affair. Above all it had been the political circumstances of the sixteenth century which explain the dramatic rise in support for Protestantism, with noble elites adopting Reformed or Lutheran religion both from sincerely held convictions and also to bolster their political ambitions for autonomy from monarchical power. Nobles dominated Protestant church affairs from the Lobkovic family in Bohemia, the Budovec and Zerotín families in Moravia, to the Thurzós in northwestern Hungary and the Rákóczis in the Partium and Transylvania. Protestant strength was therefore intimately linked to the political fortunes of eastern European diets and the depth of loyalty among noble converts would prove crucial to Protestant churches' fortunes. Leading Protestant aristocrats tried to reinforce their position by developing links across the Habsburg monarchy and made some connections with German courts. Protestants in Bohemia also tried to reconcile their theological differences and present their Catholic monarchs with a united front, but could not mask internal divisions or break down robust local loyalties. When the storm of the Counter Reformation came, the foundations of Protestantism in eastern Europe simply proved too shallow to resist the onslaught of Habsburg confessional absolutism. Protestantism retained significant support only in Hungary, where both the Lutheran and Reformed churches had developed strong confessional identities and built up church structures which proved resilient to Catholic pressure. Hungarian nobles also held the strongest bargaining position in disputes with the Habsburgs, since in return for religious freedoms they could offer not only royal solvency and political loyalty in local administration, but also military cooperation against the Ottomans. Most importantly though, Hungarian Protestantism was bolstered and defended by Transylvania's princes and while support from the Transylvanian state guaranteed Protestant survival, elsewhere in eastern Europe Protestants were marginalized and persecuted by the growing power of Catholic states.

NOTES

1 Frantisek Kavka, 'Bohemia', in Robert Scribner, Roy Porter and Mikuláš Teich (eds), *The Reformation in National Context* (Cambridge, 1994), pp. 131–54. Frederick Heymann, 'The Hussite-Utraquist Church in the Fifteenth and Sixteenth Centuries', *Archiv für Reformationsgeschichte* 52 (1961), pp. 1–26.

2 Winfried Eberhard, 'Bohemia, Moravia and Austria', in Andrew Pettegree (ed.), *The Early Reformation in Europe* (Cambridge, 1992), pp. 23–48.

3 Jenö Zoványi, *A reformáczió magyarországon 1565-ig* (Budapest, 1921). Katalin Péter, 'Hungary', in Scribner *et al.*, *The Reformation in National Context*, pp. 155–68. David Daniel, 'Hungary', in Pettegree, *The Early Reformation*, pp. 49–69. William Toth, 'Highlights of the Hungarian Reformation', *Church History* 9 (1940), pp. 141–56. Kálmán Benda, 'La réforme en Hongrie', *Bulletin de la Société de l'histoire du Protestantisme Français* 122 (1976), pp. 30–53. László Makkai, 'The Crown and the Diets of Hungary and Transylvania in the Sixteenth Century', in Robert Evans and Trevor Thomas (eds), *Crown, Church and Estates: Central European Politics in the Sixteenth and Seventeenth Centuries* (London, 1991), pp. 80–91.

4 David Daniel, 'Calvinism in Hungary: The Theological and Ecclesiastical Transition to the Reformed Faith', in Andrew Pettegree, Alistair Duke and Gillian Lewis (eds), *Calvinism in Europe, 1540–1620* (Cambridge, 1994), pp. 205–30.

5   Katalin Péter, 'Tolerance and Intolerance in Sixteenth-Century Hungary', in Ole Grell and Robert Scribner (eds), *Tolerance and Intolerance in the European Reformation* (Cambridge, 1996), pp. 249–61.

6   Róbert Dán and Antal Pirnát (eds), *Antitrinitarianism in the Second Half of the Sixteenth Century* (Budapest, 1982). Earl Wilbur, *A History of Unitarianism in Transylvania, England and America* (Cambridge, MA, 1952), pp. 99–126.

7   David Daniel, 'Ecumenicity or Orthodoxy: The Dilemma of the Protestants in the Lands of the Austrian Habsburgs', *Church History* 49 (1980), pp. 387–400. Okatar Odlozilík, 'Bohemian Protestants and the Calvinist Churches', *Church History* 8 (1939), 342. Ivana Cornejová, 'The Religious Situation in Rudolfine Prague', in Eliska Fucíková *et al.* (eds), *Rudolf II and Prague* (London, 1997), pp. 310–22.

8   David Daniel, 'The Fifteen Years' War and the Protestant Response to Habsburg Absolutism in Hungary', *East Central Europe* 8 (1981), pp. 38–51.

9   Kálmán Benda, 'Le calvinisme et le droit de résistance des ordres hongrois au commencement du XVIIe siècle', *Études Européennes: Mélanges offerts à Victor-Lucien Tapié* (Publications de le Sorbonne 6; Paris, 1973), pp. 235–43.

10 Karin MacHardy, 'The Rise of Absolutism and Noble Rebellion in Early Modern Habsburg Austria, 1570–1620', *Comparative Studies in Society and History* 34 (1992), pp. 407–38. Jaroslav Pánek, 'The Religious Question and the Political System of Bohemia before and after the Battle of the White Mountain', in Evans and Thomas, *Crown, Church and Estates* (London, 1991), pp. 129–48. Joachim Bahlcke, 'Calvinism and Estate Liberation Movements in Bohemia and Hungary (1570–1620)', in Karin Maag (ed.), *The Reformation in Eastern and Central Europe* (Aldershot, 1997), pp. 72–91.

11 Gottfried Schramm, 'Armed Conflict in East-Central Europe: Protestant Noble Opposition and Catholic Royalist Factions, 1604–1620', in Evans and Thomas, *Crown, Church and Estates*, pp. 176–95.

12 László Makkai, 'The Hungarian Puritans and the English Revolution', *Acta Historica* 5 (1958), pp. 13–45.

FURTHER READING

Of a number of studies on the Habsburg monarchy and the political and social context for reformation in eastern Europe, Robert Evans' *The Making of the Habsburg Monarchy, 1550–1700* (Oxford, 1979) still leads the field. Also very helpful is his introduction and many of the articles in Robert Evans and Trevor Thomas (eds), *Crown, Church and Estates: Central European Politics in the Sixteenth and Seventeenth Centuries* (London, 1991). Further background can be gleaned from Robert Kann and Zdenek David, *The Peoples of the Eastern Habsburg Lands, 1526–1918: A History of East Central Europe* (London, 1984), vol. 6; Peter Sugar, *Southeastern Europe under Ottoman Rule, 1354–1804: A History of East Central Europe* (London, 1977), vol. 5, and Orest Subtelny, *Domination of Eastern Europe: Native Nobilities and Foreign Absolutism* (Gloucester, 1986). There is still a chronic shortage of effective treatments of many aspects of the eastern European Reformation. The collection of essays in Karin Maag (ed.), *The Reformation in Eastern and Central Europe* (Aldershot, 1997), offers some starting points. Winfried Eberhard has written a good overview of 'Reformation and Counter-Reformation in East Central Europe', in James Tracey, Thomas Brady and Heike Oberman (eds), *Handbook of European History, 1400–1600: Late Middle Ages, Renaissance and Reformation*, vol. 2, *Visions, Programs and Outcomes* (2 vols; Leiden, 1995). On Calvinism in the region, see Robert Evans, 'Calvinism in East Central Europe: Hungary and Her Neighbours', in Menna Prestwich (ed.), *International Calvinism, 1541–1715* (Oxford, 1985), and hopefully soon forthcoming is Graeme Murdock, *International Calvinism and the Reformed Church in Hungary and Transylvania*. Also on Hungarian Protestantism, Mihály Bucsay's *Der Protestantismus in Ungarn, 1521–1978: Ungarns Reformationskirchen in Geschichte und Gegenwart*, vol. 1, *Im Zeitalter der Reformation, Gegenreformation und katholischen Reform* (Vienna, 1977), remains the most important treatment in a western language. George

Williams, *The Radical Reformation* (Philadelphia, 1962), includes coverage of eastern Europe. Also on radical religion, Earl Wilbur's *A History of Unitarianism: Socinianism and Its Antecedents* (Cambridge, MA, 1946) has much on Transylvanian anti-Trinitarians, while also useful is Jarold Zeman, *The Anabaptists and the Czech Brethren in Moravia, 1526–1628* (The Hague, 1969). A Catholic perspective is provided by Robert Bireley, *Religion and Politics in the Age of the Counter-Reformation: Emperor Ferdinand II, Williama Lamormaini, S.J., and the Formation of Imperial Policy* (Chapel Hill, 1981).

FRANCE

---◆---

Jonathan A. Reid

No Protestant churches were established in France before 1555. Yet a minority Reformed church sprang up during the next seven years that was strong enough to secure a place within Catholic France after forty years of religious civil war. This striking fact colours interpretation of the earlier period. Many scholars portray the Reformation as a religious revolt against the church animated by the core doctrines of justification by faith alone and scripture as the sole authority for belief and practice. Others emphasize that Protestant communities, with their new church structures, clergy, disciplining institutions, rituals and ideas, changed the rhythm of social life and even modified people's world-view. Since French Huguenots fulfilled this double historical mission, the early French Reformation has often been approached as a prelude to their dynamic challenge. The story revolves around explaining how Reformation doctrines penetrated France despite official repression, but failed to produce a new religious order.

However, the earliest French reformers, 'Evangelicals', upset this plot-line. Although they held similar doctrines to German and Swiss Protestants, most contemplated no schism. Rather, while enduring persecution, they attempted to renew the church from within. Only gradually after 1540 did a classic Protestant movement come together under the influence of French reformers in exile, chiefly John Calvin, who offered a clear system of Reformed doctrine, a model church and a decided call to reject Catholicism.

EVANGELICAL GROWTH

Like many areas in Europe, religious devotion was on the rise in France at the end of the fifteenth century. After the devastation of the Hundred Years War, confraternities multiplied, some 900 churches were rebuilt, many more were sumptuously decorated, the ranks of the secular clergy and mendicant orders swelled, and people embraced new devotional practices such as the rosary. Fiery mendicant preachers spurred their listeners to greater piety by denouncing moral corruption. Some scholars have interpreted the laity's intensifying zeal for buying indulgences and founding obit masses as betraying deep fears about the pains of purgatory, even the surety of their salvation, that were excited by the church's teachings, but not assuaged by its economy of grace.

Rising lay piety, in any case, exacerbated the perception that the church was not functioning as it should. Institutionally, the failure to reform the church in 'head and members' – from the pope through the clerical ranks – following the four-teenth-century Great Schism, permitted anticlerical feelings to grow. While some 'lax' Benedictine, Dominican and Franciscan houses had been restored to strict observance of their rules by 1510, the movement foundered for lack of consistent royal support. Among the secular clergy, bishops provided little spiritual direction and parish priests remained woefully ill-trained since few had access to improved training programmes at the University of Paris.

After 1500, Christian humanists – with Erasmus of Rotterdam in the vanguard – offered an inspiring way forward. Reviling clerical failings and superstitious devotions, they proclaimed that teaching the simple gospel message, purified of scholastic obscurantism, would renew the faith. The leading French biblical humanist, Jacques Lefèvre d'Etaples, gave this goal material support by editing and writing commentaries on the Latin Vulgate Bible, starting with the Psalms in 1509, in which he expounded the scriptures' plain, 'vivifying' meaning. Scholastic theologians in turn attacked humanists like Lefèvre for questioning the authority of the Vulgate, as well as received doctrines of the church, in their biblical studies. Meanwhile, the Faculty of Theology (known as the Sorbonne) and the Parlement in Paris fought desperately against the Concordat of Bologna (1516) between Francis I (1515–47) and Leo X (1513–21), which abrogated the French church's fiscal and administrative liberty. As the Reformation era opened, religious expecta-tions were high but not fully met and rival groups were laying blame for lack of progress on each other.

When the strife over Martin Luther's ideas reached France in 1518, it electrified these doctrinal and ecclesiological tensions. Contemporary witnesses report that humanists, clerics, even Sorbonne theologians read Luther's books with enthu-siasm. Lefèvre sent warm greetings to Luther in 1519. Boniface Amerbach, a German student in the papal enclave of Avignon, imported Luther's works, which inspired the Franciscan François Lambert to journey to Wittenberg in 1522. In short order, Luther's admirers encountered opposition. In 1521, following the pope, the Faculty of Theology at Paris condemned the schismatic friars' doctrines as heretical and the Parlement of Paris outlawed books containing them. Thereafter, those sympathetic to doctrines dissenting from the church – for a long time libelled as 'Lutheran', whatever their nature or origin – had to explore such ideas under the threat of persecution. The telling questions for the spread of the Reformation in France would be how secular authorities, chiefly the king, would define true doctrine and to what degree they would enforce orthodoxy.

In 1518 Bishop Guillaume Briçonnet had inaugurated a novel reform in the diocese of Meaux near Paris and this now became a testing ground for these ques-tions. Appalled at the clergy's unwillingness to improve religious instruction, in 1521 he called Lefèvre and his disciples from Paris to lead an intensive preaching campaign. The group included Michel d'Arande, Gérard Roussel, Guillaume Farel, Pierre Caroli and Martial Masurier.

Lefèvre summarized their programme in his 1522 *Introductory Commentary on the Four Gospels* as 'to know the Gospel, to follow the Gospel and to proclaim the Gospel everywhere'. While ministers proclaimed this message in the diocese's thirty-two preaching circuits, Lefèvre and his closest disciples pursued their biblical scholarship. This included reading Protestant reformers' works, for which they had a growing but not uncritical admiration. Based on these studies, they commenced translating the Bible into French and produced a vernacular preaching handbook. Briçonnet distributed Lefèvre's Bible translations to the laity, who were then well-equipped to attend Roussel's daily lessons on Paul's letter to the Romans and on the Psalms for the more advanced.

At the same time, individuals associated with the Meaux group promoted evangelical renewal elsewhere in the realm. At court, the king's sister, Marguerite of Angoulême (of Navarre after 1527) summoned d'Arande to teach and circulated Briçonnet's letters of spiritual instruction as well as Lefèvre's translation of Paul's Epistles. During 1523–4 she had d'Arande preach in her territories at Alençon and Bourges, while promoting similar efforts by Aimé Meigret and Pierre de Sébiville in Rouen, Lyons and Grenoble.

Catholic conservatives throughout France detected 'Lutheran' heresy at every turn. Leading the way, the Faculty of Theology and Parlement of Paris indicted these preachers as Lutheran heretics for criticizing the cult of the saints, devotion to Mary, purgatory, indulgences and fees for masses. Their fears were confirmed by reports that d'Arande at court and Masurier in Meaux had argued: 'What Luther has said well, no man has said better, what he has said wrongly, no man has said worse, as St Jerome said of Origen.'[1] In 1524, a magistrate in Le Puy (Auvergne) blamed poor turnout during the jubilee pilgrimage to his town's miracle-working Black Virgin on d'Arande and Meigret's attacks in Bourges and Lyons. That winter, people coined the term 'Lutherans of Meaux' after commoners ripped down prayers to the Virgin and placards announcing a papal indulgence. When the German Peasants' War spread to Lorraine in the spring of 1525, anxious Parisians panicked at the rumour of a 'Lutheran' invasion.

Francis I's capture at the Battle of Pavia (February 1525) brought matters to a head. The Parlement of Paris warned the regent, Louise of Savoy, that this disaster was God's judgement for, among other faults, the court's protection of heretics. Royal intervention had indeed saved members of the Meaux group from successive heresy indictments. In 1523, the court had even liberated the courtier, Louis de Berquin, who had been caught red-handed with works by Luther, which he had translated. During the king's captivity, the conservatives were finally free to act. Lefèvre, Roussel, d'Arande and Caroli fled to Strasbourg, while Briçonnet, Berquin, several other preachers, as well as ten commoners from Meaux, stood trial. Returning in 1526, Francis I quashed these proceedings. Marguerite, recalling the exiles, appointed Lefèvre as tutor to the royal children, obtained a bishopric for d'Arande, installed Caroli as curate of Alençon and took Roussel as her personal minister.

By 1526, the Lutheran threat had become a national issue, but Reformation doctrines were understood by few. Persecution had forced native reformers to clarify their positions. Three camps emerged that would endure until the establishment

M. De Val.

Figure 12.1 Marguerite of Navarre and Jacques Lefèvre d'Etaples. Neither of these two leading figures in French evangelism would ultimately sever their connections with the

Roman church and embrace the Reformation. Despite this, both earned a place in Beza's portrait gallery of heroes of the Reformation, the *Icones*. (St Andrews University Library)

of the Reformed church. Reformist prelates attracted to the pedagogical promise of biblical humanism emulated Briçonnet, who backed away from evangelical reform when it incited the people to radical acts and provoked judicial inquiry. After one round of heresy accusations in 1523, he formally condemned Lutheran errors, revoked the licences of the most outspoken preachers, like Farel, and affirmed the doctrine of purgatory and the cult of the saints. After 1526, though a competent bishop, he did little more than repeat injunctions against clerical abuses. Those who, following the German and Swiss reformers, became convinced that obeying the gospel required rejecting the traditional church could either take Farel's route to exile or stay and risk the consequences. The remaining group, 'Evangelicals' like those succoured by Marguerite, sought strategic positions from which they might promote reform from within. While attracted to Protestant doctrines, they aimed chiefly at fostering 'living faith' among the laity, but balked at casting off the church, however deformed it may have appeared in the 'pure light of the gospel'.

As contemporaries recognized, the king's decision would matter most in determining France's religious orientation. Catholic conservatives remained frustrated after 1526 as Francis adopted no strident response to the new doctrines. He had certainly sworn at his coronation, 'to annihilate and drive out from the land subject to my jurisdiction, all heretics pointed out and denounced by the Church.'[2] Yet only after 1539 did he fully back the pursuit of heretics. Until then a *modus vivendi* reigned: so long as dissenters did not openly attack the faith, the king ignored conservatives' pleas for their eradication.

Often interpreted as hesitancy, Francis' stance balanced his interests. He could not accept the theologians' definition of heresy since they lumped together without distinction followers of Erasmus, Lefèvre and Luther as enemies of the faith. Francis, an avid patron of Renaissance letters, had previously invited Erasmus to enter his service and respected the internationally renowned Lefèvre. Moreover, the Faculty of Theology and the Parlement of Paris had used heresy charges against his *protégés* as a vehicle to attack royal policies. Secure in his control over the church under the Concordat, Francis had little reason to heed conservatives' denunciations, lest in acting he give occasion to undermine his regime.

THE CRISIS OF EVANGELISM

Francis I's position left the impression that he might support a magisterial Reformation. Hopes for a royal reform were never higher than during the early 1530s. In 1533, Marguerite had Roussel preach Lenten sermons in Paris, which attracted 5,000 eager listeners. From rival pulpits, preachers sent out by the Sorbonne urged the people to rise up against Roussel since the king was not acting. When Francis I banished the chief instigators for fomenting rebellion and forced the Faculty of Theology to retract its censure of Marguerite's recently published *Mirror of the Sinful Soul*, partisans of reform predicted imminent victory.

Seizing the moment, Nicolas Cop used his All Saints' Day address to the assembled University of Paris (1533) as a platform to condemn religious persecution and to advocate public preaching of the gospel. Possibly co-authored by his young friend, John Calvin, the sermon expounded theological themes from Luther and Erasmus and concluded with a rousing call to action whatever the consequences, which in Cop's case required immediate flight:

> The world and the wicked are wont to label as heretics, impostors, seducers and evil-speakers those who strive purely and sincerely to penetrate the minds of believers with the Gospel. ... But happy and blessed are they who endure all this with composure, giving thanks to God in the midst of affliction. ... Onward then, O Christians. With our every muscle let us strive to attain this great bliss.[3]

Cop's outspoken words raised a storm of criticism and a number of his circle were forced temporarily to withdraw from Paris. This might soon have been forgotten but for a far more serious outrage the following year, which in effect doomed the evangelical cause. On the night of 17–18 October 1534, the posting of violently worded placards against 'the horrible, great and insufferable papal mass devised in direct opposition to the Last Supper' in Paris, several regional cities and even, it was said, on the royal bedchamber at Amboise, played straight into the conservatives' hands. Attacking the mass as a 'blaspheme', priests as 'charlatans, pests and false antichrists' and the doctrine of transubstantiation as 'the doctrine of devils', the tract enraged the authorities. Faced with religious sedition, the king backed a brutal repression. Twenty-four were executed, others imprisoned, and over seventy suspected heretics fled, including the famed court poet Clément Marot, Pierre Caroli and Calvin.

Francis I ended the persecution on 16 July 1535 with the Edict of Coucy, which opened the gaols and offered amnesty to all exiles, excepting 'Sacramentarians' (those who held the Zwinglian doctrine of the eucharist articulated in the placards), if they would abjure their errors within six months. Francis intended most immediately to allay the anger of German Protestant princes, with whom he was trying to cement a political alliance based on a proposed religious colloquy with Philip Melanchthon. Yet, even after these negotiations failed, he extended the pardon to Sacramentarians in 1536, re-establishing his regime's *modus vivendi*.

Roussel's sermons, Cop's address and the placards were explosive exceptions to the largely clandestine spread of Evangelical and Protestant ideas during the early French Reformation. Persecution prevented any visible public leadership from forming, but policing was porous enough for the new doctrines to diffuse covertly. Occasionally from the parish pulpit, but more often in school rooms, nobles' courts, homes and workshops, people encountered such ideas by word of mouth and increasingly by consulting a spate of new religious books. Although the full scope of this dissemination is far from clear, research on heresy trial records and religious books has revealed much about its developing pace and content.

Among the centres of propagation to the elites, France's fifteen universities played a prominent role. The early enthusiasm for Luther at Paris was matched in Caen (1530) and Toulouse (1532), where authorities uncovered circles of professors discussing Protestant authors' works with town notables. At the same time in Bourges and Orleans, Calvin, Theodore Beza (Calvin's successor at Geneva) and fellow students heard the new doctrines expounded by their masters. As university students took up posts in society, they carried the new ideas across France. Some became regents of France's multiplying municipal schools – at least thirty new *collèges* were established from 1530–60. By one count, schoolmasters are known to have taught suspect doctrines in twenty-five cities by 1550.

Communication lines to uneducated commoners were less structured. Remarkably, one third of accused heretics whose occupations were noted at Toulouse (1510–60) and Paris (1547–9) were clerics. Nevertheless, the first estate remained massively loyal to the church. That contemporaries frequently complained about itinerant preachers propagating heresy, highlights the extraordinary difficulty that curates who converted must have had proselytizing in their home parishes. Telling evidence from Meaux shows that commoners taught one another. Inspired by the more radical preachers there, Jean Le Clerc, a wool-comber, was condemned for preaching at Metz in 1525. His last words spoke for all those commoners inspired to proclaim the gospel. 'Ah, my lords, do not be amazed if you see me here [i.e. a mere artisan], me, one who is going to die for the faith and for upholding the truth. ... God gave me a mouth so that I might speak and I pray Him to give me true faith.'[4] In the following decades authorities arrested other artisans from Meaux for instructing their confrères in Champagne and neighbouring regions. A similar phenomenon occurred in Normandy, which gained a reputation by 1530 as a 'little Germany'.

In the absence of widespread preaching, religious books enabled Reformation ideas to spread on all levels. The Latin works of Luther, Melanchthon, Bucer, Zwingli and other reformers circulated among the learned since censorship prevented only their domestic publication, not their distribution. Books in French reached a far broader audience, for although literacy rates were low, people habitually read aloud in groups.

Far fewer vernacular religious books circulated in France than did in the empire, where the twin engines of popular preaching and some three million pamphlets by 1525 powered the Reformation forward. The production of French heterodox books only began after that date. Yet such works made up a high proportion of the 1,300 editions of French religious books, totalling near one million copies that appeared from 1511–51; and this is a conservative estimate. Certainly this was enough to reach an extensive, largely urban audience. Towns, where literacy was highest and the Reformation eventually penetrated deepest, held 15 per cent of France's estimated fifteen to twenty million people.

People bought Bible translations more than any other text, despite a 1525 edict banning them. The Psalms, used as a prayer- and hymnbook, appeared in seventy-five editions, fifty-two in Marot's censured verse rendering. Bibles and New Testaments were reprinted from the Lefèvre translation (thirty-eight editions) and after 1535 from Olivétan's popular Protestant rendering (thirty-nine editions), which together supplanted two traditional versions (fourteen editions after 1521).

Until the mid-1530s, in addition to Bibles, evangelical authors and printers published short manuals of religious instruction. Simon Du Bois, an associate of the Meaux group, and other printers at Basle, Strasbourg and Antwerp presented Erasmus, Luther and other reformers' devotional and catechetical texts, which were designed to foster lay piety. Avoiding outright attacks on the church or its doctrine, these tracts nevertheless highlighted the need for reform. Translations of Luther's works figured prominently. Yet the reader encountered not the strident opponent of the papacy, but an always anonymous teacher, scriptural expositor and spiritual counsellor. *The Book of True and Perfect Prayer* (1528), the most popular devotional text in French with thirteen reprints, offered portions of Luther's exposition of the Lord's Prayer and Creed together with texts by Farel and more traditional Catholic writers. The *Brief Summation of the Substance and Foundation of Evangelical Doctrine* (Du Bois, 1525), epitomized the intent of such works. The unnamed author tells his 'faithful readers' thirsting for 'the Word of God' that since it was no longer possible to preach publicly, 'so that we do not completely abandon you, it remains possible, at least, for us never to stop aiding your faith in writings.' He warns them not to take vengeance against 'persecutors of the truth', but to pray for God to convert them as well as the king.[5]

After 1533 overtly Protestant literature appeared when Farel succeeded in establishing the Reformation in French-speaking territories east of France. From Neuchâtel, he, Antoine Marcourt and the printer Pierre de Vingle, exiles all, published polemics against Catholic doctrine and practice, of which the 1534 placard was a particularly inflammatory example. This activity centred on Geneva after 1536, whence Calvin would became the dominant voice of French Protestantism, having established his reputation with the *Institutes of the Christian Religion* (the first, Latin edition was published in 1536).

THE REFORMED ASCENDANCY

Reformed Protestantism coalesced in France after 1540 largely due to the efforts of Calvin, Farel and their Swiss colleague, Pierre Viret. They succeeded in broadcasting a galvanizing 'Reformed' Protestant doctrine from abroad just as the French crown was developing systematic means to extirpate heresy.

Calvin's influence in France emerged clearly with the publication of the French *Institutes* (1541). Its sensational impact prompted a royal edict banning it in the same year (1542) that a heretic at Rouen went to the stake quoting from it. As evidence of 'heresy' mounted, Francis I and Henry II adopted successive measures against what was now seen as a clear threat to social order. Francis I requested the Faculty of Theology to draw up Articles of Faith, which he published as the law of the realm (1543), along with a list of condemned books (1544), on which Calvin's works figured prominently. Initially magistrates – some sympathetic to the new doctrines, others indifferent – failed to enforce heresy laws effectively. Persecution grew real teeth when Henry II required magistrates to prove their orthodoxy and ordered regular searches in bookstalls and houses (27 June 1551, Edict of Châteaubriand). Genevan records of arriving refugees from 1549–60 reveal the effectiveness of these measures. French Protestants fled in a growing stream, including in the early 1550s scholars, printers and nobles such as Beza, Robert Estienne and Laurent de Normandie, who contributed to the vast increase in Genevan religious propaganda after 1550. Thus, persecution, while oppressing French Protestants, augmented the ability of Geneva to lead them from abroad.

Figure 12.2 Title-page of the Lefèvre Bible of 1530. Despite its enormous popularity, orthodox condemnation of vernacular translations of the Bible ensured that from 1525 editions of Lefèvre's translation were published abroad, to the frustration of Parisian printers thus excluded from a lucrative market. (St Andrews University Library)

As persecution grew, many factors contributed to Calvin's ascendancy over the French Protestant movement: his forceful prose, his extensive network of friends and admirers, a lack of domestic leadership, Geneva's proximity to Lyons – a hub of communications in France – and the spectacular output of the little city's many presses. Above all it was Calvin's teaching that persuaded. His *Institutes* offered the first clear doctrinal system in French containing a new vision of the Christian life and church. In the wake of the placards, his dedicatory epistle to Francis I served as an apology for committed Protestants. He affirmed their obedience to secular authority, but warned that on religious matters they owed a higher allegiance to God. His polemical writings – *Reply to Sadolet, Treatise on Relics, Little Treatise on the Lord's Supper, Little Treatise Showing What a Faithful Man Should Do Among the Papists, Apology to the Nicodemites* – attacked Catholics' 'false' beliefs and practices as well as 'faint-hearted' Evangelicals who acquiesced in them. Calvin exhorted true believers to adhere to God's truth without waiting for a royal reformation or dissembling in the face of persecution.

Some Evangelicals found his demands too severe. In 1544, the parliamentarian Antoine Fumée made a tortured appeal on behalf of French evangelicals. He complained that Calvin required the ultimate sacrifice in telling believers to abstain from the mass. Though recognizing it as an abuse, they would have to emigrate or face death to comply. Calvin maintained his position affirming that to truly 'honour God body and soul', flight or abstaining – whatever the consequences – were the only alternatives to 'polluting' oneself.

Calvin's signal contribution to the rise of Protestantism was to give direction to the evangelical conventicles that had sprung up since the early 1520s. At such gatherings people read scripture or discussed religious tracts, prayed and exhorted each other to a better life. The books of Calvin and his colleagues provided materials to enrich their meetings. Moreover, Calvin encouraged them to remain steadfast, sending consoling messages to prisoners and letters of advice to these embryonic Protestant communities. The precocious commoners at Meaux formed a church in 1545 on the model of a refugee church founded by Calvin in Strasbourg, but the authorities crushed it savagely. Fourteen leaders were burned and their experiment was not repeated for another ten years.

In the face of harsh repression, Calvin drew such communities into a network centred on Geneva through correspondence and direct contacts with leaders who visited him. By 1550, Calvin had ties with believers in Paris, Orleans, Bourges, Poitiers, Angoulême, Rouen, Lyons, Agen, as well as the regions of Brie, Provence, Dauphiné and Languedoc. That year Claude Baduel, regent at Nîmes, proclaimed Calvin's guiding role in a report to Philip Melanchthon. He announced that after Marguerite of Navarre's death (December 1549), French believers' only solace came from 'the teaching of God's Word', 'the Genevan church' and 'John Calvin, who through that piety, sound teaching and strength of soul that you know so well, consoles us in our deepest misfortune frequently and powerfully with his letters.'[6]

Just as Baduel's letter signals Calvin's ascendancy, so too it marks the decline of evangelical leadership in France. After the mid-1530s, Marguerite's influence on her brother diminished. Few figures of the first generation remained like Gérard

Roussel, Bishop of Oloron since 1536, who continued efforts at reform. Though embattled, he attempted to transform the mass and other rites in accordance with Evangelicals' emphasis upon faith in Christ alone as the root of salvation, even borrowing from Calvin's writings to do so. Nor did French Evangelicals produce many new devotional works. Rather evangelism took a literary turn. Marguerite, François Rabelais, Clément Marot, Victor Brodeau, Nicholas de Bourbon, Etienne Dolet and Charles de St-Marthe, among the most popular French writers, expressed their profound faith in poems, plays, satires and novellas. While heaping abuse on 'Sorbonagres', corrupt clerics and monks, and sometimes the intransigence of the Genevan reformers, they gave sophisticated cultural expression to the call for 'living faith', but offered no clear programme for renewal.

Who, then, were the clandestine Protestants turning to Calvin? To answer this question fully the evidential base remains frustratingly weak. The best statistics on the geographical distribution and social origins of French Protestants come from studies on the established Reformed churches. By then, the Protestant movement had undergone a profound transformation during its rapid growth from 1555–62. Genevan refugee records and trial records for the earlier period, however, reveal similar patterns. Geographically, Protestant doctrines had adherents throughout France, Brittany excepted, though their subsequent heavy concentration south of the Loire and in Normandy is harder to establish. Numerically, committed Protestants were probably far fewer than the 10 per cent of the population they would reach at their peak in the 1560s. Yet those yearning for a reform based on the gospel were certainly more numerous than those who would later join the minority Reformed church. Which social groups were attracted? Trial records show a disproportionate number of members of the clerical and urban elites indicted for heresy. But this figure may be inflated by the fact that accusers stood to gain a portion of the defendant's goods if convicted. The social origins of those fleeing to Geneva, on the other hand, were roughly equivalent to their proportions in the urban population, including numerous artisans. What attracted these people to the new religion? On this thorny, perhaps insoluble, problem most scholars reject an older thesis that posited a correlation between a broadening socio-economic crisis among urban artisans and their attraction in large numbers to the reform. Even the leading proponent of this thesis, Henry Heller, stresses Calvin's multifaceted ability to appeal to artisans as well as the elites.[7] Denis Crouzet has recently argued that apocalypticism and interest in astrologers' predictions of calamity fuelled religious passions as France moved towards the savage Wars of Religion.[8] Scholars have yet to assess the implications of this thesis for the growth of Protestantism, but such insights reinforce the need to consider further all the political, economic, social and mental coordinates by which contemporaries made their religious choices. Everyone saw the hands of God and Satan working in the world, but deciding whose was behind the religious alternatives depended upon the complex interplay of reading the book of life and the scriptures together.

CONCLUSION

Before 1555, it could hardly have been predicted that an independent Reformed church would eventually survive without royal support. Evangelicals' hope for a magisterial Reformation was thwarted by events: the defeat at Pavia, the placards and unfavourable international affairs. So their simple desire for another future, in which establishing the gospel did not engender violence, died away. Calvin and the example of Geneva convinced French believers not to accept the alternative. Transforming an underground movement into a visible church, however, would require a radical change in circumstances. In 1555, just as Lutherans secured their future at Augsburg, Calvin's party gained political ascendancy in Geneva, which allowed over 200 missionary pastors to be sent to France in the next years. And that same year, the first enduring French Protestant church formed in Paris under a nobleman's protection, a presage of the key ingredient for the rise of the Reformed church and the coming civil war: the armed support of the nobility for the new faith.

NOTES

1   Michel Veissière, *L'Évêque Guillaume Briçonnet, 1470–1534* (Provins, 1986), pp. 332–3.
2   J.H. Shennan, *Government and Society in France, 1461–1661* (London, 1969), p. 79.
3   Appendix III, in John Calvin, *Institutes of the Christian Religion*, 1536 edn, trans. Ford Lewis Battles (Grand Rapids, 1989), p. 371.
4   Nathaniel Weiss, 'Notes et documents sur la Réforme en Brie', *Bulletin de la Société de l'Histoire du Protestantisme Français* 46 (1897), pp. 642–3.
5   *Brief recueil de la substance et principal fondement de la doctrine Evangelique* (Paris, Simon Du Bois [1525]), sig. A ii r–v.
6   M.J. Ganfrès, 'Lettre de Claude Baduel à Phil. Mélanchthon (1550)', *Bulletin de la Société de l'Histoire du Protestantisme Français* 23 (1874), p. 547.
7   Henry Heller, *The Conquest of Poverty. The Calvinist Revolt in Sixteenth-Century France* (Leiden, 1986), esp. ch. 4.
8   Denis Crouzet, *Les guerriers de Dieu. La violence au temps des troubles de Religion vers 1525 – vers 1610* (2 vols, Seyssel, 1990).

FURTHER READING

Mark Greengrass, *The Reformation in France* (Oxford, 1987), is the best introduction in English. For comprehensive coverage, Denis Crouzet's *La genèse de la réforme française, 1520–1562* (Paris, 1996) provides an up-to-date synthesis framed around his innovative views. Pierre Imbart de la Tour, *Les Origines de la Réforme* (4 vols; reprint edn, Geneva, 1978), offers a classic interpretation and evidence to which all modern studies refer.

Important topical studies include: for field-defining views about religious sensibilities, Lucien Febvre, *Au coeur religieux du XVIe siècle* (Paris, 1983); for political context, R.J. Knecht, *Renaissance Warrior and Patron: The Reign of Francis I* (Cambridge, 1994); for social history, Natalie Zemon Davis, *Society and Culture in Early Modern France* (Stanford, 1975), and David J. Nicholls, 'Social Change and Early Protestantism in France: Normandy, 1520–62', *European Studies Review*, 10 (1980), pp. 279–308; for a socio-economic interpretation, often dismissed but rich in detail, Henry Heller, *The Conquest of Poverty: The Calvinist Revolt in Sixteenth-Century France* (Leiden, 1986); for conservative Catholics' reaction, James K. Farge, *Orthodoxy and Reform in Early Reformation France: The Faculty of Theology of Paris, 1500–1543* (Leiden, 1985). For Calvin's mission to France, Heiko A. Oberman, 'Europa afflicta: The Reformation of the Refugees', *Archiv für Reformationsgeschichte*, 83 (1992), pp. 91–111.

Studies on religious books have steadily driven the field forward. For access to the extensive literature in this field, see Francis M. Higman's collected articles (many in English), *Lire et découvrir: La circulation des idées au temps de la Réforme* (Droz, 1998), and his *Piety and the People: Religious Printing in French, 1511–1551* (Aldershot, 1996) for a comprehensive bibliography of French religious books. Reformed theologians have been studied extensively, French Evangelicals more unevenly. Consult the bibliographies in the works cited above for studies on Calvin, Farel, Viret Briçonnet, Lefèvre, Roussel, Marguerite of Navarre, Marot and Rabelais.

ENGLAND

Helen Parish

Fyrst the Kyngs maiestie vz. Henrie the 8 in the 24 yeare of his reign was wrongusly devorcide from his lawfull wyffe gratius Qweane Katheryn and mariede Ladye An Bullan, wich was crownyde Queyne of Englande on Whitsonday. Butt in the yeare followynge (anno domini 1533) the Pope of Rome withall his authoritie & powre was abolischide qwytte owtt of this realme, & then the Kyngs Majestie was proclamyde Supreme Heade nextt & immediatly under God of the Churche of Englande & Irelande.[1]

A STATE REFORMATION

In the Reformation narrative of the conservative Yorkshire cleric Robert Parkyn, these two events – the king's divorce and the abolition of the pope's authority – were the opening acts in a drama which was to engulf the English church for the next three decades. The second marriage of the king and the assertion of the royal supremacy over church and state were the first in a series of deeds and declarations which were to dismantle the physical and mental world of Parkyn and his parishioners, and reshape the structure of the church in England. In Parkyn's account, the Reformation in England was a series of acts of state, effected by the few but affecting the many, governed by the vicissitudes of high politics, but governing the life of the people, in this world and the next. Henry VIII's quest to secure the succession was the catalyst for the chain of events which followed. Politics, not Protestantism, brought about the Reformation in England.

The image of the royal supremacy certainly had a powerful resonance in the early English Reformation. The title page of the 1539 Great Bible depicted Henry VIII as the new David, bringing the Word of God to the people and wielding authority over church and state. The jurisdiction of David over the priests of the temple was invoked to justify Henry's claim to supreme headship over the English church and his authority over the clergy. Cuthbert Tunstall claimed that in exercising the office of the supreme headship, Henry 'acted as the chief and the best of the kings of Israel did'.[2] By this understanding, the Henrician Reformation was renovation rather than innovation, the restoration to the monarch of the authority usurped by the church. This promotion of the royal image was clearly of value in a country that lacked an effective police force or a standing army, but England was still a highly centralized state. Unlike the sprawling empire of Charles V, the size and structure of England made regulation of religion by statute a possibility, and a possibility which king and councillors were willing to explore. The ideology of the royal supremacy could be realized by bringing the authority of the king to bear upon religious practice in the parishes. Henry himself was certainly convinced that the theoretical authority of the king over the church should also be made a practical reality. His attempt to alter the wording of the Lord's Prayer in the Bishops' Book of 1537 was swiftly cut short by his archbishop, but the king still exercised a powerful influence over the reform of the church enacted in his name. The royal reservation of the right to determine the doctrine of the church was graphically demonstrated at the execution of John Lambert in November 1538. 'If you do commit yourself unto my judgement you must die', Henry told the accused, 'for I will not be a patron unto heretics.'[3]

The necessity of conformity to the mind of the king, albeit a mind of a capricious character, was demonstrated again in July 1540. Two days after the death of Cromwell, three evangelicals were executed in London alongside three conservative priests. The three executed evangelicals – Barnes, Garrett and Jerome – suffered because their vision of godly Reformation extended further and faster than that of the king. The Catholics – Abell, Featherstone and Powell – were hanged as traitors, after a long imprisonment for upholding the primacy of the pope and the validity of the Aragonese marriage. The royal supremacy had forged a link between political and religious dissent and allowed the king to play the role of arbiter in both.

Henry VIII's actions in the 1530s were enough to alarm those who had not previously appreciated that the supreme headship might be used to legitimate heretical belief. By a combination of statute and proclamation founded upon the authority of the king in matters spiritual, the power of the pope over the English church was abrogated, the monasteries were suppressed and the Bible was made available in the vernacular. Ecclesiastical patronage secured the appointment of bishops sympathetic to the break with Rome and the reform of the church: Cranmer himself, Latimer at Worcester and Shaxton at Salisbury. The martyred defender of papal supremacy, John Fisher, was succeeded at Rochester by John Hilsey, who led the campaign against images and relics in 1538. Two years previously, a set of royal injunctions had attacked the superstitious use of images and their exploitation for financial gain. The proliferation of festivals as part of the cult of the saints, it was argued, encouraged idleness; thus lesser feasts were to be abolished, especially those which fell at harvest time. Images were admitted to be of didactic value, but the clergy were admonished to instruct their congregations to remember the role of saints as intercessors and to direct their devotions to God, not to the saint or indeed the image of the saint. Thus the danger of idolatry and superstition could be avoided, while the immediate effect on popular piety and practice was mitigated. In 1538 a second set of Injunctions moved beyond these measured criticisms and initiated an attack which reached the heart of traditional cults. It was no longer just abuses which were to be rooted out, but the cults and relics themselves which were now deemed to incur 'great threats and maledictions of God'. The Holy Blood of Hailes, already considered suspect before the Reformation, was denounced as a fraud and the Rood of Boxley was brought to London and destroyed. The injunctions outlawed pilgrimage and prohibited the burning of candles before images, an act of doctrinal iconoclasm which broke apart the visual framework of popular devotion. In the hands of the more vehement evangelicals, such as Shaxton, the Injunctions were a manifesto for the purification of the church, but the Injunctions did not kindle iconoclastic fires in the hearts of the faithful. Despite pre-Reformation antagonism towards relics and images, the English Reformation was not marked by mob violence and vandalism. Few were enthusiastic enough to take matters into their own hands and the accidental conflagrations which followed the destruction of roods at St Margaret Pattens in 1538 and St Pauls in 1548 were widely interpreted as acts of divine vengeance.

When the king's mind took a conservative turn after 1538, the new, more hostile climate caused both physical and philosophical problems for Protestant writers who had been vigorous in their support of the royal supremacy. A royal proclamation condemned 'contentious and sinister' ideas which were circulating in printed treatises, forbade the import of English books without licence and prohibited further debate on the theology of the eucharist. Ceremonies such as creeping to the cross on Good Friday were upheld and those clergy who had presumed to marry were expelled from their benefices. Worse was to come, in the form of the Act of Six Articles (1539) with its rather optimistic aim of abolishing diversity in opinions. In its insistence upon clerical celibacy and its defence of private masses and auricular confession, the act was hardly the work of a godly Protestant monarch. Recent work has presented a persuasive case for the king himself, rather than the conservative bishops, as the major force behind the legislation. The prohibitions had been prefigured in Henry's statements in the preceding years and embodied the unresolved questions which had prevented an agreement with the German Lutherans in the autumn of 1538. Outside observers were quick to see the hand of the king in the act: Philip Melanchthon praised Henry for his attack on papal authority, but demanded that the king explain why, 'in the mean time, you defend and maintain the laws of that Romish Antichrist'.[4] English evangelical writers took refuge on the Continent, churning out tracts which denounced the continued presence of Catholic doctrine and practice in the new national English church. Henry VIII, the godly king who had given the Bible to the English people, was to take it away from a substantial proportion of them less than a decade later. The 1543 Act for the Advancement of True Religion condemned unorthodox translations of the Bible and listed those groups in society who would no longer be free to read or expound the scriptures – 'women, artificers, apprentices, husbandmen, labourers' among them. In the eyes of evangelical writers and propagandists, the last years of Henry's reign raised two questions: how far had the Reformation won the hearts and minds of the English people by 1547 and, more significantly, how far could the Henrician church itself claim to be truly reformed?

EDWARD VI

In the years before Henry's death, conservative and evangelical factions struggled to gain the upper hand at court. The king's marriage to Katherine Parr offered some hope to the reformers, but as late as 1546 their position was still far from secure. The London preacher Edward Crome was forced to recant and in July four London evangelicals, including John Lascells and Anne Askew, were burned for their beliefs. Events in the final months of the reign were to have profound implications for the future of the Reformation. Military success abroad put Edward Seymour, Earl of Hertford, in the ascendant and as Seymour gathered the support of Dudley and Parr, the conservative grouping under Bishop Gardiner and the Duke of Norfolk was catastrophically weakened by allegations of treason against Norfolk's son. Surrey was executed on the last day of the reign and the control of the regency council for the young King Edward fell into the hands of Seymour and his allies. The accession of the Edward raised the hopes of the reformers and, in his coronation sermon, Thomas Cranmer reminded the new king of his duty and calling.

> Your majesty is God's vicegerent, and Christ's vicar within your own dominions, to see, with your predecessor Josiah, God truly worshipped, and idolatry destroyed, the tyranny of the bishops of Rome banished from your subjects, and images removed. These acts be the sign of a second Josiah, who reformed the church of God in his days.[6]

In a sermon preached before the court in April 1549, Hugh Latimer returned to this theme, reminding the audience of how 'Josiah reformed his father's ways, who walked in idolatry'.[6]

The promotion of Edward VI as the new Josiah both delineated and validated an iconoclastic path for the Edwardian Reformation. In the Old Testament, Josiah's rule had been marked by religious reform and the destruction of idols was a key part of that reform. This image of Edward was promoted throughout the reign in court sermons and in the works of Protestant writers such as John Bale and William Turner, both of whom enjoyed the patronage of Protector Somerset. Iconoclasm reached to the heart of Catholic devotion, where theology was acted out in ritual and embodied in ceremony and statue. The Articles of 1547 recognized this relationship, demanding that shrines, images and 'all other monuments of feigned miracles' should be removed, 'so that there remain no memory of the same'. The 1549 Book of Common Prayer omitted the elevation of the consecrated elements, which was the physical representation of the theology of sacrifice and the centrepiece of late mediæval eucharistic devotion and adoration. The new Ordinal of 1550 removed all references to a sacrificing priesthood in the ordination rite, and in the same year altars were removed from churches. Physical change had its origins in doctrinal developments. Just as the presence of a statue in a church was the outward manifestation of the theology of the cult of the saints, so the material changes of Somerset's years – the destruction of images, the removal of roods and the appearance of legally married clergy – were the external results of a determined Protestantism which came to fruition after 1550.

ENGLAND AND THE CONTINENT

The English Reformation, particularly in the reign of Edward, was not simply an English event. Despite Henry VIII's personal hatred of Luther, discussions with German theologians were held in 1538 and Thomas Cranmer made repeated attempts to bring Philip Melanchthon to England. Evangelical writers who had taken refuge on the Continent in the aftermath of the Six Articles returned to England after 1547 with clear ambitions for the nascent national church. Thomas Cranmer's outlook was far from parochial: his own marriage provided a link with Osiander and the German Reformation, and by the end of 1548 several distinguished Continental divines had arrived in England, including Peter Martyr Vermigli, Bernardino Ochino, John à Lasco and Martin Bucer. The rapidly changing fortunes of Continental Protestantism made England a place of refuge after the military advance of Catholic forces in the empire in 1547. The arrival of French and Dutch refugees, and the subsequent foundation of the 'Stranger Churches' in London brought this already volatile community into contact with new theologies, new liturgies and new ideas of church government. However, the reforming zeal of à Lasco and his congregation, combined with John Hooper's determination to purge the English church of the remnants of Rome, threatened the order and unity of Ridley's diocese and indeed of the Edwardian church. When he was offered the see of Gloucester in 1550, Hooper refused to be consecrated in accordance with the Ordinal of the same year and launched a stinging attack upon the use of vestments in the supposedly reformed English church. His actions were roundly condemned by both Ridley and Cranmer, but condemned because of the challenge which they posed to uniformity and the supremacy of secular powers in determining the nature of reform in the church. The battles fought in 1550 and 1551 were certainly no attempt to salvage the mediæval heritage and compromise with the Catholic past.

The centrality of the royal supremacy to the English Reformation ensured that doctrinal deliberations were never far removed from practical politics. Thus the full implications of the institutional changes of the 1530s and 1540s were not always borne out by the theology of the Henrician church. In the early years of the Edwardian Reformation, conservative opposition to the radicalization of reform focused upon the question of the validity of doctrinal change conducted in the name of a minor. As the health of the young king failed in the winter of 1553, the fear that control of the national church would pass into the hands of a Catholic queen became a reality.

MARY: REACTION AND PERSECUTION

Northumberland's 'grand design' to alter the succession and secure the throne for Jane Grey ended in failure and served to encourage the notion that Protestantism and perfidy were one and the same. The capitulation of Northumberland and his last minute recantation suggested that the work of the godly Josiah could be easily reversed, and the level of popular and elite support for the accession of the rightful heir inspired the belief that there would be the same level of support for a return to Rome. This was certainly Robert Parkyn's assessment of the celebrations of July 1553: a Te Deum was sung in St Paul's and 'tholle comonalltie in all places in the northe partes grettlie reiocide makynge grett fyers, dryknynge wyne and aylle, prayssing God'.[7]

Although there was clearly a widespread expectation that the accession of Mary would bring an end to the religious changes of the last decades, it was less clear what form the restoration of Catholicism would take. Initial assessments suggested that once the vociferous evangelical minority who had led the people astray had been silenced, Catholic practice would be easily restored. A royal proclamation of August 1553 suggested that for the time being there would be no attempt to enforce conformity, but the same document also outlined the targets of the new regime: 'evil disposed persons' who took it upon themselves to expound the Word of God and the printers of 'false fond books and ballads ... touching the high points and mysteries of the Christian religion'. Foreign Protestants were encouraged to leave the realm, leading English evangelicals (including Cranmer, Hooper and Rogers) were imprisoned and parliament met in October 1553 to begin the work of dismantling the legal foundations of the Reformation. The path to restoration was neither straight nor smooth, complicated by the vexed question of the fate of church lands and the late arrival of the papal legate Pole on English soil. Efforts were made to improve preaching and pastoral care, and to strengthen the finances of the church, but in the early stages the implementation of Marian Catholicism was still dependent upon the queen's position as supreme head of the church, a title which she detested. Married priests, one of the most visible manifestations of Edwardian Protestantism, were among the first targets of the reaction. In the first parliament of the reign, all Edwardian religious legislation was repealed, including the act of 1549 which had lifted the prohibition on clerical marriage. Injunctions of March 1553–4 ordered that married clergy were to be deprived of their livings, a decision which affected and ran the risk of alienating some 2,000 parish clergy.

With the arrival of Pole and the revival of mediæval treason legislation in 1555, the campaign against heresy became more determined and wide-ranging. In February 1555 the Bible translator John Rogers was burned at Smithfield, the first of some 300 men and women who were to die for their beliefs before the end of the reign. Persecution for the sake of religion was no novelty in the sixteenth century; indeed the burnings in England claimed far fewer lives than many Continental campaigns against heresy. But as the campaign continued, its physical and mental effect upon the lives of the wider population increased: fewer people turned up to watch the executions and the government was forced to issue a proclamation in an effort to silence displays of sympathy with the martyrs. The spectre of martyrdom did not in itself effect widespread conversion or enthusiasm for Catholicism, but rather by their death those who suffered emerged as heroes and models of endurance for the sake of true religion. The Marian persecution was also to have a profound influence upon the future of English Protestantism. Those Edwardian Protestants who remained in England formed part of an underground evangelical congregation whose leaders, men such as Edmund Scambler, were to emerge as key figures in the Elizabethan church. The promotion of Parker and

Alleyn, who had spent the reign of Mary in internal exile, gave the impression of continuity between Edwardian Protestantism and the 1559 settlement. Some 800 men and women sought exile on the Continent, and the debates and divisions between exiles in Frankfurt and Geneva prefigured some of the later challenges to the integrity of the Elizabethan church. Equally important was the barrage of literature with which writers in exile bombarded the church and government at home. This included vernacular works which justified resistance to the monarch, attacked idolatry and false religion, and Latin treatises and martyrologies which brought the plight of English Protestantism to the attention of an international audience.

Writing in exile in 1554, John Foxe compiled a Latin account of the persecution of heresy in the fifteenth and sixteenth centuries. Five years later, the project was extended to include the martyrs of Mary's reign and in 1563 a much larger edition was dedicated to the new queen, Elizabeth. Foxe's history presented an image of the history of the church, and particularly the church in England, which was to influence the historiography of the Reformation for centuries to come. From the very beginning of the *Acts and Monuments*, Foxe makes clear the structure of his history: the division of humanity since the time of Cain and Abel into the true church and the false, and more particularly the persecution of the true church by the false. This theme was given visual expression on the title page of the work, where contrasting scenes from the two churches are arranged side by side (see Figure 13.1). At the bottom left a sermon is preached, while a reformed congregation listens attentively, books in hand and faces turned toward God. On the right, Catholic practice is caricatured: a monk preaches while men and women sit with their rosary beads and, in the background, a Corpus Christi procession leads others away. Above this, a priest celebrates mass with his back to the congregation, while the martyrs for the true church perish for their beliefs. At the top of the picture, the martyrs receive their crowns in heaven, while the erroneous and persecuting papists tumble into the jaws of hell.

The same division of the two churches is repeated in the woodcut allegory of Edward VI's reign in the ninth book of the *Acts and Monuments* (see Figure 13.2). On this occasion, the image is divided in half horizontally, with the representation of Catholic practice in the upper half, and the newly reformed English church at the bottom. In the top half of the picture, and an image is pulled down while the fleeing papists salvage what they can from the purging of the temple: the Mass Books, a pastoral staff, a censer and a papal tiara. The bottom left panel shows Edward delivering the Bible to the prelates, and in a church purged of all images and furnishings, a congregation of men, women and children are gathered to hear the Word of God expounded by a preacher. The woodcut illustrates the centrality of iconoclasm, and indeed of the Josiah propaganda, to the Edwardian Reformation. Two-church ideology and the polemical literature which surrounded it were fundamentally divisive. The physical and behavioural divide between the two halves of these illustrations suggests that there was no room for half-heartedness: an individual was either a member of the true church or the false and there could be no compromise between good and evil, between Christ and Antichrist.

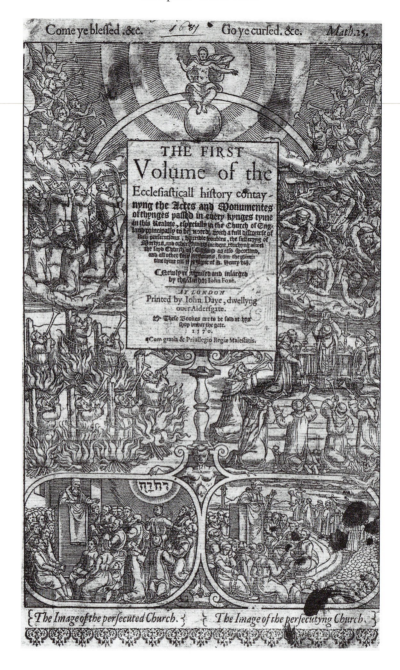

Figure 13.1 Foxe's *Actes and Monumentes*. The title-page of Foxe's *Book of Martyrs* sets Protestant against Catholic, true church against false, in a classic Protestant antithesis. Its lavish illustration helped introduce a religion of the word to a largely illiterate society. (Oxford, Bodleian Library)

Figure 13.2 The Reformation of the churches under Edward VI. Below, the young king gives the Bible to his people and the godly congregation partake of the Protestant sacraments. Above, the churches are 'cleansed' and the papists take flight. (Oxford, Bodleian Library)

THE IMPACT OF RELIGIOUS CHANGE

But is this stark division of humanity into the true church and the false reflected in the responses of individuals to the questions raised by the Reformation? What was the impact of propaganda in the parish? In recent decades, the historiography of the English Reformation has tended to focus around two key questions: was the Reformation imposed from above or demanded from below, and was conformity with Protestantism the result of conversion or coercion? Wills, bequests and churchwarden's accounts, where such materials survive, have been used to paint a picture of flourishing and popular mediæval parish religion. The years before the Reformation had witnessed a spate of lay bequests for the renovation of churches: St Mary Redcliffe at Bristol, parish churches in Bodmin and Cirencester, and the so-called 'wool churches' of East Anglia. Images of saints were erected or restored

233

in Ashburton and Morebath, and guilds and fraternities flourished in Lincoln, Northampton and Sussex. Such manifestations of popular piety would lend support to the theory that the Reformation was imposed from above, yet this is not to doubt its effectiveness. Indeed, in the light of such evidence, the dislocation caused by Reformation destruction appears all the more substantial and threatening. Even in the conservative southwest, the provision of masses for the dead all but ceased, roods were destroyed and images mutilated. Edwardian iconoclasm and the apparent lack of divine or even saintly intervention in defence of relics, rites and ceremonies shook confidence in the old church. Iconoclasm did not simply destroy the edifice of Catholicism, but also undermined the fundamentals of traditional belief.

The destruction of the visual and material aspects of Catholicism could be achieved with a hammer, but it took much more than this to build a Protestant community founded upon the word rather than the image. Thomas Hancock's sermons against the mass provoked violence in Poole in 1548 and the outbreak of rebellion in the West Country in 1549 suggests that religious passions ran high, at least among parts of the population. Recent work on the impact of the Reformation in London reveals a society deeply divided over religion by 1553 and Roger Edgeworth reported of the situation in Bristol at the start of Mary's reign that 'some will hear mass, some will hear none ... some will be shriven, some will not ... some will pray for the dead, some will not'.[8] The number of people who preferred exile or martyrdom over accommodation with Catholicism after 1553 suggests that Edwardian Protestantism had begun to make inroads in the parishes, but these groups make up only a small proportion of the population of the country. For others, the accession of Mary marked yet another change in the formulae of faith and one which offered no guarantee of permanence. The conduct of the clergy was likely to exercise a strong influence over responses to reform, and in this area the impact of the Reformation was particularly damaging. Those clergy who had married after 1549 had voluntarily embraced one aspect of Edwardian Protestantism, but many had also fulfilled the requirements of pre-Reformation Catholicism and the Henrician Reformation, and by far the majority were to acquiesce in the restoration of Catholicism under Mary. Few were prepared to stand in defence of the religious changes which had allowed them to marry – nearly all conformed with the disciplinary procedures, left their wives and sought reappointment as Catholic priests. The conduct of George Fairbank, a married priest in Tarring Neville in the diocese of Chichester was strongly criticized by an ironmaker, Richard Woodman. Fairbank, he claimed, 'often persuaded the people not to credit any other doctrine but that which he preached, taught and set forth in King Edward's days. And afterwards, in the beginning of queen Mary's reign, the said Fairbank, turning head to tail, preached the clean contrary to that which he had before taught'. It was not Fairbank's marriage to which Woodman objected, but the fact that he had been 'a fervent preacher against the Mass and all the idolatry thereof seven years before, then came and held with it again'.[9] His example illustrates well the situation of many of the English clergy and the confusion that three decades of religious change and controversy had caused. The conduct of Fairbank, and indeed most of the Edwardian married clergy, reveals some of the problems faced by the Marian church and indeed the sixteenth-century English church as a whole. Creating a committed ministry equipped for the Reformation of the English parishes would not be an easy task, given the propensity of the clergy to accommodate rather than agitate in defence of their beliefs. The Protestant message, even if it was preached by a minister with reformist sympathies, was likely to be treated with scepticism by those who had seen the same minister married in 1549, but separated from his wife and celebrating mass in 1554.

However even if the polemical image of the two churches does not provide a model for the conduct of the masses, the message of obedience to the king as the supreme head of the church had some impact even from the earliest days of the Reformation. In the aftermath of the Six Articles of 1539, one priest, John Foster, admitted to Cromwell that he had married a nun, claiming that he believed such marriages to be legal by the law of God. 'My disfortune has been to have conceived untruly God's Word', Foster confessed, 'and not only with my intellect to have thought it, but externally and really I have fulfilled the same'. Foster assured Cromwell that when he had become aware of Henry VIII's hostility to clerical marriage, he had sent his wife sixty miles away, presumably well out of the way of temptation. When confronted with the law of the king, Foster was prepared to admit that the law of God was open to misinterpretation. The apparent contradictions and ambiguities that made up the history of the English Reformation may well have been the result of many others acting on the same pragmatic principle.

NOTES

1 A.G. Dickens (ed.), 'Robert Parkyn's Narrative of the Reformation', *Reformation Studies* (London, 1982), p. 293.
2 Richard Rex, *Henry VIII and the English Reformation* (Basingstoke, 1993), p. 174.
3 Christopher Haish, *English Reformations* (Oxford, 1993), p. 137.
4 Quoted in John Foxe, *The Actes and Monumentes of these Latter and Perillous Dayes* (London , 1570), p. 1343.
5 J.E. Cox (ed.), *The Works of Archbishop Crammer* (2 vols, Cambridge, 1844), vol. 2, p. 127)
6 G.E. Corrie (ed.), *Sermons by Hugh Latimer* (Cambridge, 1844), p. 175.
7 Dickens, *Parkyn's Narrative*, p. 307.
8 David Palliser, 'Popular Reactions to the Reformation During the Years of Uncertainty 1530–1570', in Christopher Haigh (ed.), *The English Reformation Revised* (Cambridge, 1987), p. 105.
9 West Sussex Record Office, Ep 1/1/96. John Foxe, *Actes and Monumentes*, pp. 2171–95.

FURTHER READING

Recent debates in the history of the English Reformation are exemplified in A.G. Dickens, *The English Reformation* (London, 1989); Christopher Haigh, *English Reformations: Politics, Religion and Society under the Tudors* (Oxford, 1993); and Peter Marshall (ed.), *The Impact of the English Reformation* (London, 1997).

Studies of the reign of Henry VIII and the Reformation of the 1530s and 1540s include G.R. Elton, *Policy and Police: The Enforcement of the Henrician Reformation* (Cambridge, 1972); A. Fox and J. Guy, *Reassessing the Henrician Age* (Oxford, 1988); and D. MacCulloch (ed.), *The Reign of Henry VIII* (London, 1995).

There are no recent works devoted specifically to the Edwardian Reformation, although politics and religion are treated in M.L. Bush, *The Government Policy of Protector Somerset* (London, 1975), and in W.K. Jordan's older two-volume biography, *Edward VI: The Young King* (London, 1968) and *Edward VI: The Threshold of Power* (London, 1970). The best new treatment of the Edwardian Reformation is that embedded in D. MacCulloch, *Thomas Cranmer* (New Haven, 1996). The Marian restoration of Catholicism is discussed in David Loades, *The Reign of Mary Tudor* (London, 1979), while Andrew Pettegree's *Marian Protestantism: Six Studies* (Aldershot, 1996) gives much needed attention to the Protestant congregations and their problems in England in the same period.

More detailed studies of the impact of the Reformation in the parishes include Eamon Duffy, *The Stripping of the Altars* (New Haven, 1992); Margaret Bowker, *The Henrician Reformation: The Diocese of Lincoln under John Longland, 1521–1547* (Cambridge, 1981); Susan Brigden, *London and the Reformation* (Oxford, 1989); J.F. Davis, *Heresy and Reformation in the South-West of England, 1520–1559* (London, 1983); and Robert Whiting, *The Blind Devotion of the People: Popular Religion and the English Reformation* (Cambridge, 1989).

Recent work on Reformation imagery and iconography includes John King, *English Reformation Literature* (Princeton, 1982) and *Tudor Royal Iconography* (Princeton, 1989); Margaret Aston, *The King's Bedpost* (Cambridge, 1993); and Richard Rex, *Henry VIII and the English Reformation* (Basingstoke, 1993).

ANABAPTISM

Sigrun Haude

Anna Jansz. of Rotterdam joined the Dutch Anabaptists in 1535. Persecution drove her and her husband to England. She returned to the Netherlands upon her spouse's death. Again on the run, she was arrested for her religious convictions in 1538. Since Anna held firm to her beliefs, she was drowned in January 1539, twenty-eight years of age, leaving a fifteen-month-old child behind. On her way to the execution, she turned to the crowd seeking a caretaker for her son. A baker stepped forward and took the child together with the offered purse. Parts of the testament she left behind for her son read:

> Listen, my son, to the instruction of your mother. Today I go the path of the prophets, apostles and martyrs; I drink the cup that all of them drank before me; I go the path of Jesus Christ who had to drink this cup as well. I urge you, my son, submit to the yoke of Christ; endure it willingly, for it is a great honour and joy. Do not follow the majority of people; but when you hear about a poor, simple, repudiated handful of men and women cast out of the world, join them. Do not be ashamed to confess your faith. Do not fear the majority of people. It is better to let go of your life than to deviate from the truth.[1]

Anna Jansz.'s testament is a statement about an Anabaptist's willingness to sacrifice her life for her beliefs. It is the voice not of a leader but of one of the many witnesses to a faith that was persecuted by Protestants and Catholics alike.

What drove people like Anna to leave their churches and opt for persecution and death? Anna, a prosperous woman, only had to convert to Catholicism to save her own life and thus ensure care for her child. Or she could have pretended to have converted. Instead she chose death for herself and the protection of a stranger in the crowd for her child. Clearly, people like Anna found something wanting in the Catholic and Protestant churches.

Figure 14.1 Anna Jansz. of Rotterdam, on her way to execution, entrusts her son to a man in the crowd. Etching by Jan Luyken in Tielman Jansz van Bracht, *Het bloedig tooneel of martelaers spiegel* (*Martyrs' Mirror*) (2nd edn; Amsterdam, 1685). (North Newton, KS, Martyrs' Mirror Trust: Kaufman Museum; Goshen College, Mennonite Historical Library)

WHAT ARE ANABAPTISTS?

In the Reformation world of the sixteenth century, Anabaptists were the outlaws of society. They belonged to what is nowadays called the 'radical Reformation', a term coined by George Hunston Williams. The new terminology replaced Roland Bainton's older designation 'left wing of the Reformation', which had relegated Anabaptism to the religious and political fringes of society. Anabaptism, rather than being a marginal phenomenon, arose from the centres of the Reformation and must be understood in this dialectic relationship. Although some unease among scholars remains, 'radical Reformation' has been accepted as a convenient umbrella-label for a host of movements and individuals that cannot be fitted under Lutheran, Zwinglian, Calvinist, Anglican or Catholic headings. What was 'radical' about these people, however, has been defined differently by various historians. Williams understood 'radical' to connote the reformers' break with the 'magisterial Reformation'.

'Anabaptists' means 're-baptizers'. The term was used by their opponents and, since Anabaptists did not acknowledge infant baptism as a proper, legitimate baptism, 'Anabaptist' is an out-group designation which does not reflect the beliefs of the group: believer's baptism constituted the one and only, not a second, baptism. Anabaptists frequently referred to themselves as 'Brethren'. For the last few decades, German scholars have taken this fact into account and used the word 'Täufer' (Baptists) rather than 'Wiedertäufer' (Anabaptists), a solution not viable in the United States or the rest of the English-speaking world because of its easy confusion with modern-day Baptists.

There is some disagreement regarding how one ought to define Anabaptism. The majority of historians argues that an Anabaptist is someone who rejects the baptizing of infants and practises a visible form of believer's baptism. According to this definition, Thomas Müntzer (d.1525), who opposed infant baptism but did not perform believer's baptism, was not an Anabaptist although he exerted a great influence on some of the Brethren. Anabaptists repudiate infant baptism because they hold that in baptism a Christian makes a conscious decision for Christ, which an infant is unable to do. Beyond a commitment to faith in Christ, the believer pledges to lead a disciplined, Christian, 'reformed' life.

RELIGIOUS AND SOCIAL CRITICISM

Hans-Jürgen Goertz has underlined the significance of anticlericalism as a force during the Reformation era in general and for Anabaptism in particular. Anabaptists shared with the evangelical reformers their criticism of the papacy. Yet, in the eyes of the Anabaptists, the evangelical reformers had not improved the state of the church. Luther and Zwingli had laid bare the treachery and tricks of 'papal holiness', but they had failed to build something better in its place. People continued in their old sinful ways instead of doing penance and striving toward a holy life. The Anabaptists believed that the reformers' failure to make a complete break with the mediæval Catholic church was responsible for the lack of improvement. Their retention particularly of infant baptism and the eucharist precluded a Christian lifestyle. Unless one made certainty of faith and commitment to Christian living the conditions for baptism – something an infant was incapable of – people would not become sincere Christians. The Anabaptists, therefore, were convinced that Luther and Zwingli had started on the right road, but had abandoned their mission halfway. Instead, so the Anabaptists charged, they had made compromises with the secular authorities.

Among the motives for the Anabaptists' break with the evangelical reformers, frustration about the lack of morals, the retention of infant baptism as well as the eucharist, and the new alliances with the secular powers rank highest. Still, such frustration was hardly enough to make them endure persecution and execution. Anna Jansz's testament gives a glimpse of the spiritual resources on which Anabaptists drew. They believed that they stood in a long line that began with Jesus Christ and his apostles, continued with the martyrs of the early church and extended to Christians persecuted since. Anabaptists took their strength from the knowledge of being heirs to a long, noble tradition, of carrying on what Jesus

Christ and many others before them had endured. Discipleship meant suffering. To them, a comfortable Christian life was a contradiction in terms. In fact, martyrdom was considered evidence for being on the right path to the heavenly kingdom.

The Anabaptist critique did not focus solely on theology and religious practices. In many instances, religious criticism merged with social and economic grievances. The complex nexus between Anabaptism and the Peasants' War, as demonstrated by James Stayer, provides clear evidence of the social and economic concerns, particularly among the South German and Austrian Anabaptists. Similarly, the widespread practice of a community of goods (in imitation of Acts 2 and 4) was, according to Stayer, the Anabaptist response to social exploitation. Furthermore, during the reign of Münster (1534–5) Anabaptists erected not only a religious but also a social and political counter-culture to the existing order. These examples underline that religious criticism was seldom independent of social, economic and political protest. Such blending has led several historians to conclude that Anabaptism constituted in effect a socio-economic movement which expressed its material concerns in religious language. However, this scholarly position owes more to a twentieth-century perspective than to a close reading of sixteenth-century realities. In a society where religious, political, economic and social concerns were tightly interwoven, often inseparable, it seems natural that Anabaptist criticism would reflect a similarly integrated spectrum of concerns.

IDEOLOGICAL CONTEXTS OF ANABAPTISM

Anabaptism emerged from a complex background. The Reformation provided one significant context. Since several Anabaptist leaders had originated from the circles of Luther and Zwingli, these connections are as undeniable as are the Anabaptists' frustration with and eventual split from their early companions. Many historians have emphasized the Anabaptists' (unconscious) indebtedness to the mediæval church and to pre-Reformation developments. While the mystical character of some Anabaptist groups, elements of apocalypticism and influences of the Modern Devotion and humanism on a sizeable number of their leaders all offer evidence to this effect, such traits may not necessarily distinguish Anabaptists from Evangelical or Catholic reformers. More telling is the Anabaptists' focus on sanctification, on leading a pure, morally exemplary life, which they share with reformers of the mediæval Catholic church, as well as with humanists such as Erasmus.

While Anabaptists conceded a certain debt to the Evangelical reformers, they did not acknowledge any link to the Catholic church. In fact, the Anabaptists' criticism of the Evangelicals had been that these had failed to make a complete, a *radical*, break from it. Instead, the Anabaptists saw themselves most closely connected to a much more distant context: the people and teachings of the early Christian church. They understood themselves to be the true heirs of Christ's church. Catholic and Evangelical critics agreed that the Anabaptists' pedigree went back as far as the early church. However, in their eyes the Anabaptists' true predecessors were the first heretics (such as Donatists and Manicheans), not the apostles. Similarly, Anabaptist connections to the Middle Ages, according to their opponents, existed in such heretical groups as the Cathars and Waldensians, not in the legitimate mediæval reform movements. For Catholics, the Anabaptists' most recent and immediate ancestors were the Evangelicals themselves; while for Luther the Anabaptists were the new papists because they had turned human works and human initiative into preconditions for baptism and divine acceptance. Once again, salvation depended on moral conduct. Luther, Zwingli and other Evangelical reformers tried hard to distance themselves from their erstwhile colleagues and considered Anabaptists as usurpers of their reformation efforts.

Finally, a group of radical reformers – Thomas Müntzer, Andreas Karlstadt (d.1541), Caspar Schwenckfeld (d.1561) and Sebastian Franck (d.1542) – provided the most influential context for early Anabaptist leaders. While none of these reformers practised believer's baptism, they did criticize the practice of infant baptism and formulated many of the later Anabaptist positions.

GEOGRAPHICAL AND IDEOLOGICAL ORIGINS

Over the past few decades, our understanding of Anabaptism's origins has undergone substantial revisions. Following Harold Bender, historians had long assumed that Anabaptism originated from a single source in Switzerland. In the early 1970s, Klaus Deppermann, Werner Packull and James Stayer argued convincingly in a groundbreaking article that polygenesis (several origins) rather than monogenesis (one origin) most accurately describes the beginnings of Anabaptism. Furthermore, while Bender and his followers had searched for a normative Anabaptism, studies from the 1970s on emphasized the diversity within Anabaptism. An important issue in the search for 'Anabaptism proper' had been to portray the true Brethren as a peaceful group of believers and to ostracize those who had resorted to violence. James Stayer's study *Anabaptism and the Sword* put an end to this endeavour by demonstrating that at 'no time in the sixteenth century was there a truly united non-resistant Anabaptist movement'.[2] According to Stayer, what 'was typically Anabaptist was not violence or non-violence but rejection of the wickedness of the world, as represented by the established church and government'.[3]

Lately, Anabaptist scholarship has shifted its focus once again. Granting Anabaptism's heterogeneity, historians have begun to steer us back towards the unifying themes among the various movements. James Stayer found that visions of a community of goods cut across the dividing lines between religious groups; Werner Packull's work on the Hutterites has led him to similar conclusions. Walter Klaassen showed that apocalypticism was an important issue not only for the South German and Dutch Anabaptists, but in an altered form also for the Swiss Brethren. And against Hans-Jürgen Goertz's emphasis on theological plurality among the believers, Arnold Snyder contends: 'we see in early Anabaptism a movement with significant internal theological agreement and coherence'.[4] Even Goertz, who maintains that one will find little religious unity among the Anabaptist leadership, has recently turned his attention toward areas of greater homogeneity, namely the Anabaptists' great mass. Discrepancies disappear, Goertz argues, when one looks at the 'simple' Anabaptists who were much closer in their religious convictions.[5]

Anabaptism consisted of several groups which embraced both similar and differing ideas. Whatever divided various Anabaptist groups, most of them shared a quest for authenticity and simplicity. They desired to leave behind all the additions and the developments that ensued when Christianity changed from a persecuted sect to a state church during the fourth century. Church hierarchy, the onerous administration, ceremonies and elaborate liturgies, fancy vestments, the establishment of the seven sacraments, ostentatious church buildings – all this had nothing to do with Christ's message to his disciples. The Anabaptists perceived that, with its institutionalization and its subsequent meddling in politics, the church had abandoned Christ's original mission. Among the common characteristics of Anabaptists, therefore, was a return to early Christianity, to an unadorned faith and to a sincere commitment to Christ. Their rejection of infant baptism (a second common trait) expresses this sense of sincerity, as does the third unifying aspect: the practice of believer's baptism.

Despite these similarities, the Anabaptist movement was divided over a number of issues. Some of the differences stem from the diverse origins of the various Anabaptist groups. Most scholars today agree that there existed at least three distinct movements: the Swiss Brethren, the South/Central German and Austrian Anabaptists, and the North German and Dutch Anabaptists. Arnold Snyder has drawn attention to the fact that in the beginning there was much fluidity between what, over time, emerged as distinct features of these movements. For example, although the Swiss Brethren would become known for their strong adherence to scripture and the South German Anabaptists for their embracing of the Spirit, those dividing lines were initially far from stark and frequently crossed. Furthermore, these movements were complex enough to encompass a variety of persons (such as Pilgram Marpeck, d.1556) situated on the periphery, where diverse groups touched and sometimes overlapped.

The earliest among these movements were the Swiss Brethren. Several of its leaders, including Conrad Grebel (d.1526) and Felix Mantz (d.1527), had initially been colleagues of Huldrych Zwingli in Zurich. Their alliance broke over the issues of the tithe and, more importantly, infant baptism. Pushed out of the Reformation movement, Grebel and Mantz were soon joined by people from city and countryside. On 21 January 1525, probably at the home of Mantz's mother in Zurich, the Swiss Brethren performed the first recorded believer's baptism of the Anabaptist movements. Those committed to the community of the faithful accepted the ban as the form of disciplining if they went astray. After repeated admonition, unrepentant members could be expelled since they endangered the congregation's purity and unity. However, as Michael Sattler (d.1527) would urge, the ban should be applied with love, not with zealousness. The Supper meant a commemoration of Christ and a celebration of their unity and fellowship.

Although over time separatism, pacifism and biblicism would emerge as the trademarks of 'Swiss' Anabaptism ('Swiss' increasingly came to denote a type of Anabaptism, not its geographic location), in the beginning Swiss Anabaptists were neither separatist nor united in their pacifism nor strictly biblicist. Their early visions of reform involved the entire society, yet persecutions left them no alternative but to live a sectarian existence. Similarly, not every member of the Brethren embraced pacifism. While Grebel and Mantz advocated non-violence, Balthasar Hubmaier (d.1528), for example, the reformer of Waldshut, participated in the Peasants' War (1524–5). And although the Swiss always put great emphasis on the letter of the Bible, in the beginning they left room for a spiritual interpretation as well.

After the failure of the Peasants' War and the persecutions of 1527, which virtually wiped out the Anabaptist leadership, much of the early fluidity in positions disappeared. By 1526 Michael Sattler emerged as the leader of the Swiss Anabaptists and in February 1527 a meeting took place at Schleitheim, where those present defined the future course of Swiss Anabaptism. The Schleitheim Articles underscored biblicism, separation from the unbelievers and non-violence. The separatist nature of the Swiss Brethren meant that they remained apolitical and thus refused to serve in civic offices, swear oaths and take up arms to defend the country. In this climate of persecution, many Swiss Brethren fled to more tolerant territories.

The South German (more precisely, the South and Central German and Austrian) Anabaptists constituted the second major movement. This segment, with its centre in Augsburg, was heavily influenced by Thomas Müntzer and the Peasants' War. Here, too, we find a broad array of groups with varying ideas. Its most prominent leaders during the early phase were Hans Hut (d.1527), Melchior Rinck (d. between 1553–60) and Hans Denck (d.1527). Hut was a book peddler throughout South Germany, Austria and as far north as Wittenberg. He and the former Lutheran preacher Rinck and possibly even Denck (a former schoolmaster in Nuremberg) had fought at Müntzer's side during the Peasants' War but escaped being killed. On the day of Pentecost, 1526, Denck baptized Hut in Augsburg. Hut's brand of Anabaptism differed in several aspects from that of the Swiss Brethren. While he too rejected infant baptism and advocated believer's baptism, his theology and practice were marked by a greater militancy and a much more prominent emphasis on the Spirit. Promoting a fervent mysticism and apocalypticism, he believed that the end of the world was at hand. Herein lies the explanation for his vigorous missionary activity. Stayer has shown that Hut and other South German Anabaptist leaders directed their message particularly towards the disillusioned survivors of the Peasants' War, where they found ready followers. The content of their message, Stayer suggests, emphasized 'apocalyptic vengeance for the Peasants' War'.[6] Different from the Swiss understanding, baptism here meant a sealing of the elect. Those who were baptized belonged to the chosen few of the Last Days. In addition, Hut believed he could predict the time when the end of the world would come.

In August 1527, South German Anabaptist leaders (and some Swiss Brethren) met in Augsburg over three days to discuss, in particular, Hut's end-time predictions. The meeting earned the label 'Martyrs' Synod' since soon thereafter many of its participants gave their life for their faith. Because of its emphasis on the Spirit and its expectation of the imminent end, the movement had little organization and uniformity. After 1527, with the loss of leadership and the failure of Hut's prophecies to come true, the South German Anabaptists split into further groups.

The third movement, the North German and Dutch Anabaptists (or Melchiorites, named after their founder) formed in 1530. This group was largely untouched by the experiences of the Peasants' War. Instead, in the Netherlands it absorbed much of Sacramentarianism, the country's own brand of the early Reformation movement. Scholars generally divide the history of North German and Dutch Anabaptism into three phases: the first lasting from 1530 to 1533. Its most important leader, the Swabian furrier Melchior Hoffman (d.1543), had been a lay preacher of the Reformation in northern Europe before he turned Anabaptist. But even his early teachings in the Baltic area reflected more closely the ideas of Luther's colleague, Karlstadt, than those of Luther himself. Subsequently Hoffman went to Strasbourg, where he encountered a pot pourri of heterodox people and received much food for Anabaptist thought. Immersed in prophesies, he founded his own Anabaptist movement, the Melchiorites. Fleeing imprisonment in 1531, he took his teaching to the Netherlands, where it spread rapidly to Holland's cities, as well as to Friesland and Overijssel. Hoffman's followers brought his ideas to Antwerp and northern Germany: Münster, Cologne, Aachen and Wesel were among their destinations. Klaus Deppermann and Albert Mellink have pointed to the deteriorating economic conditions in the Netherlands during the early 1530s as a major reason why people joined the Melchiorites. Samme Zijlstra, however, rejects this argument. His research has shown that, during this time, food prices did not rise astronomically nor did wages fall. Therefore the economic motive could not have been very strong.

Relentless anticlericalism, a heightened apocalypticism and a conviction that Christ did not really become flesh (the early Christian heresy, Docetism) marked Hoffman's teachings. He preached that, before the Second Coming of Christ, the world would be cleansed of the godless, but Hoffman did not permit the elect to take up the sword to this end. Instead he believed that pious rulers might become God's instruments in bringing about the new heaven and the new earth. However, not all northern Anabaptists followed Hoffman in his rejection of violence. Melchior Hoffman saw himself as the messenger of the apocalypse, which he had predicted for 1533, and proclaimed Strasbourg as the New Jerusalem where the 144,000 elect would gather to await the end of the world. When he returned to Strasbourg in 1533, he let himself be arrested hoping that this event would usher in the Last Days. Instead he died in prison ten years later.

Hoffman's apocalyptic preaching, as well as his missionary activity in northern Germany and the Netherlands, provided the backdrop for the establishment of an Anabaptist reign in Münster (1534–5), the second phase of this movement. Münster in Westphalia, having just turned Protestant, began to turn towards Anabaptism during the summer of 1533. Crucial for the transition from Protestantism to Anabaptism was Münster's most influential theologian, Bernhard Rothmann (d.1535?), as well as the arrival of Anabaptists from the lower Rhineland and the Netherlands, both regions the stamping ground of Melchior Hoffman. The success of Anabaptism in the Westphalian city brought throngs of Dutch emigrants to Münster, among them the tailor Jan van Leiden (d.1536), who would become King of the Münsterites. The Anabaptists were legally voted into power and, as historian Karl-Heinz Kirchhoff has shown, there existed a peaceful

Anabaptist congregation in Münster until the bishop's aggression outside the city walls provoked an equivalent response from the Anabaptists within. The Münsterites thus eventually transformed Hoffman's theology from a passive into an active apocalypticism, as did some of the Anabaptist groups in the Netherlands.

The Münsterites managed to defend the city for sixteen months against the ever-growing military forces from throughout the empire. In the beginning, they forced those who were unwilling to accept believer's baptism to leave the city. They abolished private property and destroyed all documents that gave evidence of the former political and spiritual jurisdiction, including court records, title deeds, account books and civic privileges. Twice during 1534, Münster's bishop, Franz of Waldeck, attempted to overthrow the Anabaptists and both times his disorderly troops suffered an embarrassing defeat at the hands of the determined and highly disciplined Münsterites. Since his concerted assaults proved unsuccessful, Franz focused on building a circle of blockhouses around the city to cut off supplies and starve the population to death. On Easter 1534, the Anabaptists lost their first leader, Jan Matthijs, who tried to bring about the Kingdom of God by charging into the besieging troops. He died instead, and Jan van Leiden took over. The new leader, who was soon proclaimed king, established a royal household and made it known that his goal was world dominion. In addition to community of goods, in July 1534 the Anabaptist leadership introduced polygyny. Jan van Leiden's enemies alleged that he did so because the already married leader lusted after Jan Matthijs' beautiful widow. Be that as it may, Münster's population now counted three times as many women as men and polygyny was a way to provide security for the women. There are also indications that the Anabaptist leadership was concerned about keeping women under male control.

The introduction of polygyny not only horrified observers but also led to unrest within the city. Women twelve years and older were forced to take a husband and many resisted these regulations. Jan himself took sixteen wives and exercised a harsh rule during the last months of the siege. By then, food had become scarce and morale low. The city finally fell through treason on 25 June 1535. The troops entering the city killed most men and some women. The leaders of the Münsterites were arrested, interrogated and tried. Tortured with glowing tongs, then stabbed and beheaded, their bodies were placed in iron cages and hung from the tower of the Lamberti Church in Münster – a showcase of the horrible punishment that awaited heretics. Replicas of the empty cages still hang there today.

After the fall of Münster, during the third phase, the North German and Dutch Anabaptists split into several factions. Except for the followers of Jan van Batenburg (d.1538), Melchiorites overwhelmingly adopted pacifism. Among their various leaders, the most influential would be Menno Simons (d.1561), founder of the Mennonites.

THE SOCIAL MATRIX

Historians and theologians have often argued that Anabaptism was a revolutionary movement, driven by the poor and underprivileged in a desire to improve their social conditions. Given the disparate nature of the Anabaptist movements, it is difficult to make a general statement about their social composition. Local studies have yielded different results for various regions. It is nevertheless clear that the concept of a lower-class movement for Anabaptism as a whole is distorted and faulty: Konrad Grebel, leader of the Swiss Brethren, was the son of a patrician; Felix Mantz had a humanist training; many of the Anabaptists had been former monks or priests, others were learned artisans. In several instances, members of the nobility sympathized with Anabaptists and cooperated with them by providing shelter. Recent research corroborates the view that the Anabaptist movement did not represent exclusively any one societal segment. With regard to the Netherlands, Albert Mellink and Samme Zijlstra argue that, although artisans made up the largest section, Dutch Anabaptism still reflected a typical cross-section of sixteenth-century society. Then again, in other regions (e.g. the Grisons), the lower classes outnumbered the rest more than usual. In Italy, too, as Antonio Rotondó has pointed out, Anabaptism found followers particularly among the poor.

Another revision in scholarship focuses on the question of whether the social matrix of Anabaptism can be found primarily in the city or in the countryside. Having ascertained that during the 1520s almost two out of three Swiss and South German Anabaptists came from urban areas, Claus-Peter Clasen argued that Anabaptism's social origins lay in the city. It was only in its later phase, when persecution destroyed the urban base, that Anabaptism became overwhelmingly rural. Indeed, Clasen noted, by the second half of the sixteenth century, the number of burghers had dropped drastically to 16 per cent.[7] Because of the initially predominantly urban character of Anabaptism, Clasen furthermore asserted that 'the evidence … does not show a link between the peasant uprising and the Anabaptist movement'.[8] Scholars of the Reformation in general, and the Peasants' War in particular, have since pointed out that in the sixteenth century 'urban' and 'rural' could not neatly be separated. The worlds of the countryside and the city did not constitute two distinct entities, but were in numerous ways connected with each other. Moreover, the 'Peasants' War' is a misleading label since, during the uprisings, peasants and underprivileged people from cities and towns fought side by side for improved conditions.

Therefore, in contrast to Clasen, Stayer argues that even in its beginnings Swiss and South German Anabaptism was much more rural than urban, with only 30–40 per cent coming from commercial cities and craft towns. Perhaps even more important are Stayer's findings regarding Anabaptism and the Peasants' War. Most scholars today believe that there is a significant connection between these two phenomena. James Stayer investigated the links closely and discovered that the circuit of influence went from the Peasants' War to Anabaptism, not vice versa. Although several early Anabaptist leaders participated in the uprisings, Anabaptism was much more shaped by the negative outcome of the rebellion. Not every region was equally tied to the Peasants' War, but according to Stayer there can be no doubt that the Peasants' War does much to explain early Anabaptism in South Germany and Switzerland.[9]

It is difficult to assess how many of the Anabaptists were women. In his social study of the movement in the south, Clasen found low numbers for females, which led him to believe that women made up only a third of the group; Stayer, however, pointed out that in some areas women numbered up to 70 per cent of the community. Reliable estimates are hard to come by since authorities often recorded only the number of Anabaptists that had been apprehended or reported. Moreover, there is much evidence that officers tended to overlook the role of female Anabaptists. Women were considered simple-minded and easily led astray by their husbands. It is likely that this disregard of female initiative is also reflected in the recorded numbers for women.

ANABAPTIST WOMEN

During the last two decades, Anabaptist scholarship has turned increasingly towards women and their role within the Anabaptist movements. Historians differ in their assessment of opportunities for females. Claus-Peter Clasen and Joyce Irwin argue that Anabaptist women enjoyed no greater role than other sixteenth-century women, while George Williams and Jennifer Reed claim that there existed virtual equality between Anabaptist men and women. Without a doubt, female Anabaptists preached, taught, interpreted scripture, evangelized, engaged in theological debates and led Anabaptist circles, but these cases were likely to have been exceptions among Anabaptist women. There is no conclusive evidence, as Linda Huebert Hecht has pointed out, that women performed baptism. Most women were involved in performing scores of small but critical tasks that sustained the movements, such as functioning as messengers for meetings, writing and carrying letters, and hosting gatherings in their homes. Since secular authorities took women less seriously than men, they could move around more easily without being apprehended. Women indeed often took advantage of male perceptions regarding female simple-mindedness.

It is evident that women's roles differed according to the nature of the Anabaptist group. Females experienced the greatest equality with men in congregations that emphasized visions, prophecies and the Spirit above scripture. In Strasbourg, Saxony and Franconia, Anabaptist prophetesses held exceptional places in their congregations. These women based their activities on their direct call from God and thus rejected any other authority. Furthermore, females dissolved and re-entered marriage freely with whomever the Spirit allegedly suggested. Unlike polygynous Münster, where many women were forced to enter into marriage with one husband (a practice engineered by their male leaders) women elsewhere could choose their own spouses. Thus, communities led by the Spirit provided the greatest opportunity for women to expand their roles.

Scholars tend to distinguish between an early, unstructured phase, in which Anabaptist women had a greater degree of freedom, and a later, more institutionalized period during which women were forced back into their traditional societal roles. Nevertheless, this two-phase model, so successfully applied to women's situation during other times of upheaval, may provide too easy an answer for a much more complex reality. Not only did continued persecutions make women's extensive support crucial; females also had their own way of dealing with the boundaries set before them by their male contemporaries.

THE DEMOGRAPHIC EXTENT OF ANABAPTISM

The demographic extent of Anabaptism is a further contested topic among historians. Claus-Peter Clasen made a stir in 1972 when his social study led him to conclude that Anabaptism was numerically insignificant. Clasen's moderate statistics challenged earlier estimates of tens of thousands of Anabaptist martyrs. Indeed, today scholars have significantly scaled down their figures and assume that 2,000 represents a more accurate approximation. It is nevertheless hardly surprising that Clasen's verdict of the Anabaptist movement as 'a minor episode in the history of sixteenth-century German society' both in terms of its quantity and quality did not go uncontested among Anabaptist historians.[10] Scholars have pointed out that Clasen studied precisely the areas, South Germany and Switzerland, where Anabaptism was severely persecuted and suppressed. Quite a different picture emerges when one looks at regions to which Anabaptists fled, such as northern Europe and Moravia. Werner Packull estimates that the Anabaptists made up about 10 per cent of the population of South Eastern Moravia. Samme Zijlstra argues that in the northern Netherlands Anabaptists counted for 20–30 per cent of the population. Other studies for northern Europe offer similar results. In more tolerant areas, therefore, Anabaptism was much in evidence. It is most likely that the Brethren, where they encountered greater persecution, were much lower in number. However, one also has to keep in mind the difficulty of assessing the extent of an underground movement.

REACTIONS TO ANABAPTISM

Anabaptism was not tolerated in the Holy Roman Empire. The imperial Recess of 1529 stipulated that all re-baptized persons were to be punished with the death penalty. Those who recanted had a chance to be pardoned, but Anabaptist leaders, obstinate believers and those who had been pardoned before but had relapsed could expect no leniency. The edict was based on the *Codex Justinianus* (533), a code of law formulated during the late Roman Empire, which in this particular case addressed early Christian heresies (Donatism, Manicheanism, re-baptism). To Hans-Jürgen Goertz, the 1529 edict 'sounded the death knell of Anabaptism', but Clasen's point is well taken that prosecution lay with the territories and cities, not with the empire. Consequently, while no authority accepted Anabaptism as a viable form of religion, the enactment of the imperial order could differ widely. It was not easy to ferret out Anabaptists. Common people rarely betrayed their Anabaptist neighbours. Shortly after the first adult baptism in 1525, pastors began to introduce baptismal registers as a means to detect those who rejected infant baptism. Eventually parish visitations, during which the officials would interrogate those who did not attend church or the eucharist, emerged as the most effective method for discovering Anabaptists.

Traditional punishment of Anabaptists included death, imprisonment and expulsion, but territories and cities varied in their application of such treatments. Burning at the stake (the mediæval punishment for heretics), beheading and drowning were the most widespread forms of execution during the first half of the

1500s. Still, many cities and territories simply banished the culprits from the area, even though (in the case of Strasbourg) the ministers advised against such a strategy and instead recommended that convicted Anabaptists should be put to work for the community. Indeed, expulsion never solved the problem of heresy. In the best of cases, it exported the problem to another area; in the worst, it merely bought a little time before the expelled returned to their communities.

For a long time, the fact that Catholics and Protestants concurred regarding their opposition to Anabaptism and would even cooperate in combating these alleged heretics (as in the case of Münster), led scholars to presume that their treatment of Anabaptists was the same. But Clasen's studies proved these assumptions wrong. Catholics pursued a much more relentless course against Anabaptists. Protestant territories rarely resorted to torture. Furthermore, for Germany and Switzerland Clasen's evidence showed 81 executions of Anabaptists by Protestant authorities, as opposed to 709 by Catholic governments; 'indeed, all the larger Catholic territories resorted to executions to stamp out Anabaptism.'[11] And, finally, as the sixteenth century wore on, Protestant authorities adopted a much more lenient policy toward Anabaptists than did Catholics. Nevertheless, one ought not confuse greater moderation among Protestants with toleration. Protestant Strasbourg, with the reformer Martin Bucer and the broad-minded politician Jacob Sturm, provided (at least until the late 1530s) a haven for dissenters; Landgrave Philip of Hesse, leader of the Protestant defensive league, went far in listening to Anabaptist concerns – but these cases were exceptions in sixteenth-century Europe.

Political and religious authorities considered Anabaptists to be heretics, which implied, on one hand, that they held a dangerous religious creed. Judged as liars who twisted scripture and made common cause with the Devil, Anabaptists could potentially infect whole areas with their 'poisonous' teachings. On the other hand, the label 'heretic' denoted a political and social threat. Governments were convinced that heretics would invariably stir unrest, and thus disturb the order and peace so vital in an unstable world. Moreover, official proclamations highlight the social and moral depravity of Anabaptists by discussing them in one breath with criminals, prostitutes and other people on the margins of society.

One of the reasons for the political leaders' fierce response, therefore, was the fear of social and political chaos. Anything out of the ordinary was perceived as a threat to the fragile political system, held together by a weak police force. In fact, Anabaptist practices did tend to undermine the established social system. Their habit of leaving their spouses and children to find a new husband or wife among the faithful upset one of the most important stabilizing factors in society – marriage. Once this crucial institution started to crumble, it would shake up society at large. Anabaptists also refused to serve in civic offices, to bear arms and to swear oaths. Because of the persecutions, Anabaptists had fallen back on secret gatherings. But it was exactly this secrecy which made the magistrates suspicious. Moreover, not all Anabaptists were pacifists. Authorities linked the Anabaptists to the Peasants' War of 1524–5, which in their eyes provided clear proof that these heretics were rebels. Their conviction was dramatically reinforced ten years later, in 1534–5, when Anabaptists seized the city of Münster and established a kingdom there. The world around them looked on in shock as they introduced community of goods and polygyny. Their apostles travelled throughout the Netherlands and northern Germany to win converts. Soldiers in front of Münster's gates, hired to fight the Anabaptists, instead joined their cause. And the Münsterites' king, Jan van Leiden, aspired to no less than world dominion. Indeed, if the empire's political leaders had wanted any confirmation of their view that Anabaptists were devilish architects of rebellion, the Peasants' War and the Anabaptist take-over of Münster abundantly provided it.

Still, the attitudes of neighbours toward Anabaptists in city and countryside may have been quite different from those in power. Evidently the comportment of (peaceful) Anabaptists made a strong impression on their neighbours, who admired the Anabaptists' proper lifestyle as well as their care for the poor and suffering. People were even more intrigued by the Anabaptists' willingness to suffer death for their beliefs. In the face of these experiences, people started wondering about the official portraits of Anabaptists as seditious, immoral and Satanic. One story tells about an evangelical pastor, Nick, who lived an exemplary life. During a visitation from his superiors, Nick broke down in tears and told them that his salary was too small and his housing situation abominable, especially during the winter. It had come to the point that the Anabaptists had offered him support. Asked about these supposed heretics, Nick said that many of them had kind hearts, but some of them were quarrelsome, especially one woman. We hear the tone of admiration, leniency and caution in the words of this Protestant minister.

Both Catholic and Protestant religious leaders were aware of the dangerous attraction these Anabaptists held for many people. Philip Melanchthon, Luther's colleague in Wittenberg, warned his readers:

> Do not let yourself be deceived by the comportment of the Anabaptists, by their lifestyle, and by their willingness to become martyrs for their faith. All their revelations are lies, their humility is pretence, so is their great broth-erly love, their patient endurance of suffering, and the audacity and stubbornness with which they approach their death. All these are tricks of the devil.[12]

Amandus, a Franciscan in Saalfelden, warned his listeners from his pulpit in a similar fashion: 'The persistence and reckless audacity of the Anabaptists should not make anybody doubt about our Christian faith. Their martyrdom does not prove that they are right.'[13] The recurring and insistent warnings against being taken in by Anabaptists makes it unlikely that religious leaders were simply fighting against a phantom of their imagination. Rather, it indicates that the Anabaptists must have scored some frightening successes among the members of Catholic and Protestant congregations.

DEVELOPMENT OF ANABAPTISM TO 1600

Arnold Snyder has criticized Anabaptist scholarship for being overwhelmingly concerned with the origins of Anabaptism at the expense of its subsequent devel-opment, which had its own intriguing dynamic. Having argued for a common theological 'grammar' among diverse Anabaptist groups during their early phase, he finds even greater unity when looking at the further evolution of Anabaptism throughout the sixteenth century.

The beginnings of the first Anabaptist movements lay in Switzerland, Germany and the Netherlands. It was largely through persecution that Anabaptism spread to other parts of Europe. Persecution of German and Swiss Anabaptists had been particularly vicious in 1527 and 1528. In central Germany, Anabaptism ceased to exist as a movement by about 1540. Its members either fled or, prompted by the unique Philip of Hesse and Martin Bucer, joined Protestantism. For the Swiss Brethren, the countryside of Switzerland provided some means to hide and survive. Thus, from the late 1520s on, Anabaptism became a much more rural movement.

Persecutions furthermore led to significant internal migrations within Germany and Switzerland, as well as between these countries. Anabaptists left more oppressive territories and settled in areas of greater moderation. Some moved to the more tolerant south German cities Strasbourg, Augsburg and Esslingen, which provided sanctuary until the 1530s. Others departed for the Tyrol and spread along the Danube in Austria, but fierce Habsburg suppression forced them to seek new lands. They joined the general Anabaptist exodus to Moravia in eastern Europe.

Parts of Italy served as a temporary sanctuary for Anabaptists from the Tyrol. The first evidence of Anabaptists in Italy comes from 1526, when persecuted peasants around Michael Gaismair found refuge in the republic of Venice. According to Manfred Welti, Anabaptism became the most popular Reformation movement in the Venetian republic.[14] By the early 1530s, anti-Trinitarians emerged alongside the Anabaptists. Both groups were linked by spiritualism, but only the latter group – those who practised believer's baptism – can properly be termed Anabaptist. Aldo Stella distinguishes between an early, revolutionary phase (until about 1535) and a second, quiet period during which the persecuted followers tried to defend themselves against accusations of rebelliousness. While the anti-Trinitarians attracted followers particularly in Padua, the intellectual centre of the Veneto, the Anabaptists drew their supporters mostly from towns in the countryside. Even though the Veneto, unlike other parts of Italy, offered a certain degree of tolerance during these years, it is amazing that in 1550 the nonconformists were able to hold a synod in Venice on major issues dividing the two groups. Just prior to this meeting, in 1546, about forty Anabaptists and anti-Trinitarians, some of eminent renown, had come together to discuss their differences regarding the divinity of Christ, but were unable to resolve them. The meeting in 1550 probably did not muster the same illustrious list of participants as that of four years earlier, but it marked a high point before disaster struck the Venetian congregations a year later. Except for one group of delegates, the assembled agreed that Jesus Christ was not God. Shortly thereafter, a fierce persecution set in after lists of the conference's participants had fallen into the hands of the Inquisition. Those who stayed returned to the Roman Catholic faith or became Nicodemites. Yet once more persecution fuelled the spread of Anabaptism into other countries as men and women fled to places as far away as Salonici in the Ottoman Empire and Austerlitz in Moravia.

Formally a part of the Holy Roman Empire, Moravia was nearly an independent kingdom and tolerated a plurality of confessions. This country in the east therefore emerged as the most sought-after destination, despite the fact that it experienced occasional waves of persecution too – as after the Anabaptist reign of Münster. At these places of refuge, members of diverse Anabaptist movements met. In Nikolsburg, Moravia, three distinct groups came in close contact: the non-separatist Anabaptists (Hubmaier), the separatist Swiss Brethren (Sattler/Schleitheim) and the apocalyptic South German Anabaptists. For a while they coexisted peacefully and discussed their theological differences, but eventually the disagreements between the 'staff bearers' (*Stäbler*) and the 'sword bearers' (*Schwertler*) led to schism. The *Stäbler*, following the precepts of Schleitheim, carried 'neither pikes nor picks' and refused to perform military service, while the *Schwertler*, like Hubmaier, believed that the Anabaptist government and its subjects had the right to bear arms. The *Stäbler* were forced to leave Nikolsburg and moved on to other parts of Moravia to form communal settlements. Not surprisingly, however, the climate of cross-fertilization by various Anabaptist groups in Nikolsburg had an influence on the original Schleitheim Brethren. In addition to their separation and absolute non-resistance, they embraced notions of Hans Hut's apocalypticism and soon added a strict communitarianism.

James Stayer has pointed out that communitarian ideas were one of the common characteristics of early Anabaptism. Under pressure of persecution, the Swiss Brethren had abandoned their ideas about community of goods and had adopted the concept of mutual aid. The south German and Austrian Anabaptists, influenced by Thomas Müntzer's 'anti-materialist spiritualism', held on to a much more rigorous understanding of community of goods and Moravia offered the opportunity to realize these ideas.

The early communitarian experiments in Moravia's Austerlitz and Auspitz were plagued by conflict and a crisis of leadership. Eventually, in the early 1530s, Jakob Hutter (d.1536), who had arrived from Tyrol, and his supporters split from the rest of the congregation and established their own Hutterite communes. In these so-called *Bruderhöfe*, Anabaptists lived, worked and worshipped together. Their community of goods, the distinct mark of the Hutterites, symbolized that they had reached a state of *Gelassenheit* (the ability to let go which leads to tranquillity) in which material benefits did not matter; all that counted was their love of God and neighbour. The Hutterite *Bruderhöfe* were so tightly structured and highly committed that they survived Hutter's death – he was executed in 1536 during a trip to his native Tyrol where he had gone to recruit members for his congregation – and several waves of persecution. By the second half of the sixteenth century, for them a time of religious and economic prosperity, they counted 120 *Bruderhöfe* with 200–400 Hutterites each. While there existed other pacifist and communitarian groups in Moravia, the Hutterite *Bruderhöfe* emerged as the most representative of Moravian Anabaptism. Nothing, however, remained of the Nikolsburg 'sword bearers'.

With the defeat of the Münsterites (1535) came severe persecutions of the Melchiorites in the Netherlands and northern Germany. In addition, a meeting at Bocholt in the summer of 1536 exposed the friction within the movement. Militant Anabaptist groups like the followers of Jan van Batenburg envisioned a much more active role in bringing about God's Kingdom on earth than those whose apocalypticism remained pacifist. Still, the diverse parties worked towards union. David Joris (d.1556), with the brothers Dirk and Obbe Philips (both d.1568) the most important leader of northern Anabaptism at this time, proved a shrewd negotiator and able to create a temporary compromise between the groups. Batenburg, whose circle had increasingly resorted to church robberies and killings, was executed in 1538.

The first half of the 1540s was marked by an intense rivalry between the old central figure in Northern Anabaptism, David Joris (he left for Basle in 1546), and the emerging new leader, Menno Simons, a former priest from Friesland. Simons aimed to gather the various Anabaptist groups into a peaceful movement, but dissension among the leaders over beliefs and practices kept the Dutch and North German Anabaptists disunited. Disagreements regarding how strictly separation from the world ought to be practised led to the Wismar Agreements in 1554. While Leenhaert Bouwens and Dirk Philips advocated a rigid course of separation, Menno Simons maintained that love and moderation should be used in following the guidelines laid down in Wismar. The expectation of God's Kingdom was transformed into the belief that the baptized members were already living in the time of grace. The congregation of God's elect constituted the New Jerusalem in the midst of a condemned world. The Mennonites accepted Melchior Hoffman's teachings that Christ did not take on the flesh of Mary and thus had nothing in common with man. This understanding in turn led to an emphasis in Mennonite congregations on purity and rejection of everything carnal and worldly in order to become a community 'without spot and wrinkle'.

Anabaptism remained the most important expression of the Reformation in the Netherlands until the waves of persecution under Alva and the emergence of Calvinism around 1560. Calvinism in the Netherlands aimed to liberate the country from political and religious oppression. Thus the combination of militancy, nationalism and religion offered an attractive alternative to Anabaptism. The Mennonites were nearly the only group of Melchiorites that survived into the seventeenth century. Gradually the Anabaptists had made the transition from active to passive dissenters and had become the 'quiet in the land'.

Persecutions in the Netherlands during the years 1532 to 1535 brought Anabaptism to England. Fleeing across the Channel, Anabaptist refugees adopted England for a home and thereby spread Melchiorite ideas throughout the island. By 1535 Anabaptists were so numerous that English authorities reacted with edicts against them. Although the initial impetus had come from abroad, Anabaptism in England soon acquired characteristics typical of native nonconformity. It is likely that the Anabaptists in England merged with the last of the Lollard movement, but we lack conclusive evidence for such a claim. According to Irvin Horst, the English Anabaptists were neither separatists nor re-baptizers. If indeed the English movement did not practise believer's baptism, then it would not meet what most scholars define as essential Anabaptist characteristics. George Williams, on the other hand, in his monumental work *The Radical Reformation*, showed how multifaceted was English Anabaptism. Over the decades, Dutch Anabaptists continued to seek refuge and to influence Anabaptism in England. Furthermore, distinct indigenous groups of Anabaptists emerged, some of which practised re-baptism. Even though they were confronted with a certain degree of persecution, particularly after news of the events in Münster reached the island, England proved to be one of the more tolerant countries in Europe.

Despite persecution Anabaptists persevered. However, it was the pacifist branches that survived. The Anabaptists remained an irksome companion of other Evangelical and Catholic churches throughout the sixteenth century. Scores of them fled to safer havens in Europe and eventually many left the Old World for the New. It was particularly in America that these Anabaptists – as Mennonites, Hutterites, Amish and several groups of Brethren – had a chance to develop in freedom. At the same time they demonstrated that their convictions did not corrode public order, as their opponents had feared and predicted. Rather they became part of the fabric and pillars of a new and vigorous society.

NOTES

1 For the original of this abbreviated and modernized version, see Thielmann J. Van Bracht (ed.), *The Bloody Theater or Martyrs' Mirror* (Scottsdale, 1950), pp. 453–4. For a critical assessment of Anna's role within Dutch Anabaptism, see C. Arnold Snyder and Linda A. Huebert Hecht (eds), *Profiles of Anabaptist Women: Sixteenth-Century Reforming Pioneers* (Waterloo, Ont., 1998), pp. 336–43.
2 James M. Stayer, *Anabaptists and the Sword* (Lawrence, 1976), p. 334.
3 James M. Stayer, *The German Peasants' War and Anabaptist Community of Goods* (Montreal, 1991), p. 123.
4 C. Arnold Snyder, *Anabaptist History and Theology: An Introduction* (Kitchener, Ont., 1995), p. 97.
5 Hans-Jürgen Goertz, *The Anabaptists* (London, 1996), p. 112.
6 Stayer, *German Peasants' War*, p. 86.
7 Claus-Peter Clasen, *Anabaptism: A Social History, 1525–1618. Switzerland, Austria, Moravia, South and Central Germany* (Ithaca, 1972), p. 305. See also Paul Peachey, *Die soziale Herkunft der Schweizer Täufer in der Reformationszeit: Eine religionssoziologische Untersuchung* (Karlsruhe, 1954).
8 Clasen, *Anabaptism*, p. 157.
9 Stayer, *German Peasants' War*, p. 4.
10 Clasen, *Anabaptism*, p. 428.
11 Ibid., p. 373.
12 Philip Melanchthon, 'Verlegung etlicher unchristlicher Artickel Welche die Widerteuffer furgeben' (1536), on microfiche in *Gustav Freytag Flugschriftensammlung*, no. 3439, sig. eiijv.
13 Sermon preached by Amandus (1535), *Gustav Freytag Flugschriftensammlung*, no. 3431, sig. aijr–aijv.
14 Manfred E. Welti, *Kleine Geschichte der italienischen Reformation* (Gütersloh, 1985), p. 77.

FURTHER READING

James M. Stayer has been one of the most influential scholars in the recovery and redefinition of Anabaptist history. His *Anabaptists and the Sword* (Lawrence, 1976) put an end to the search for 'normative' Anabaptism as exemplified by Harold S. Bender, 'The Anabaptist Vision', *Mennonite Quarterly Review* 31 (1944), pp. 67–88. He co-authored an article with Klaus Deppermann and Werner O. Packull, 'From Monogenesis to Polygenesis: The Historical Discussion of Anabaptist Origins', *Mennonite Quarterly Review* 49 (1975), pp. 83–122, which moved scholarship's search for Anabaptist origins from monogenesis – see Bender as well as Fritz Blanke, *Brüder in Christo: Die Geschichte der ältesten Täufergemeinde, Zolikon 1525* (Zurich, 1955) – to polygenesis. And in *The German Peasants' War and Anabaptist Community of Goods* (Montreal, 1991), Stayer showed the importance of the Peasants' War for Anabaptism as well as the pervasiveness of community of goods among diverse Anabaptist groups. The most monumental work on Anabaptism and the broader radical Reformation is still George Hunston Williams' *The Radical Reformation* (3rd revised edn; Kirksville, MO, 1992), which introduced a new terminology, replacing Roland Bainton's 'The Left Wing of the Reformation', *Journal of Religion* 21 (1941), pp. 124–34. See also Heinold Fast (ed.), *Der linke Flügel der Reformation: Glaubenszeugnisse der Täufer, Spiritualisten, Schwärmer und Antitrinitarier* (Bremen, 1962). A number of important collections of articles have appeared since, among them Hans-Jürgen Goertz (ed.), *Umstrittenes Täufertum 1525–1975: Neue Forschungen* (Göttingen, 1977); Marc Lienhard (ed.), *The Origins and Characteristics of Anabaptism* (The Hague, 1977), and Hans J. Hillerbrand (ed.), *Radical Tendencies in the Reformation: Divergent Perspectives* (Kirksville, MO, 1986). Richard van Dülmen, *Reformation als Revolution: Soziale Bewegung und religiöser Radikalismus in der deutschen Reformation* (Munich, 1977), focused his discussion of radicalism on Thomas Müntzer and the Anabaptist reign of Münster. Important recent studies on Anabaptism are Hans-Jürgen Goertz, *The Anabaptists* (London, 1996), and C. Arnold Snyder, *Anabaptist History and Theology: An Introduction* (Kitchener, Ont., 1995). See also Snyder's abbreviated and more graphic *Anabaptist History and Theology: Revised Student Edition* (Kitchener, Ont., 1995).

For important studies on major figures in Anabaptism, see Harold S. Bender, *Conrad Grebel, 1498–1526: The Founder of the Swiss Brethren, Sometimes Called Anabaptists* (Goshen, 1950); Torsten Bergsten, *Balthasar Hubmaier: Anabaptist Theologian and Martyr* (Valley Forge, PA, 1978); Steven B. Boyd, *Pilgram Marpeck: His Life and Social Theology* (Durham, NC, 1992); Klaus Deppermann, *Melchior Hoffman: Soziale Unruhen und apokalyptische Visionen im Zeitalter der Reformation* (Göttingen, 1979); Gottfried Seebass, *Müntzers Erbe: Werk, Leben und Theologie des Hans Hut* (Erlangen, 1972); C. Arnold Snyder, *The Life and Thought of Michael Sattler* (Kitchener, Ont., 1984); and Gary K. Waite, *David Joris and Dutch Anabaptism, 1524–1543* (Waterloo, Ont., 1990). Goertz's *Profiles of Radical Reformers* (Scottdale, PA, 1982) provides brief summaries of radical reformers.

Claus-Peter Clasen, *Anabaptism: A Social History, 1525–1618. Switzerland, Austria, Moravia, South and Central Germany* (Ithaca, 1972), stands as the most important social study on Anabaptism. Karl-Heinz Kirchhoff's *Die Täufer in Münster 1534/35: Untersuchungen zum Umfang der Sozialstruktur der Bewegung* (Münster, 1973) investigates the social composition of the Münsterites. Important articles on the social dimension of Anabaptism are Albert F. Mellink, 'Das niederländisch-westfälische Täufertum im 16. Jahrhundert', in *Umstrittenes Täufertum*, pp. 206–22; Jochen Oltmer and Anton Schindling, 'Der soziale Charakter des Täuferreichs zu Münster 1534/35: Anmerkungen zur Forschungslage', *Historisches Jahrbuch* 110 (1990), pp. 476–91; Heinz Schilling, 'Aufstandsbewegungen in der Stadtbürgerlichen Gesellschaft des Alten Reiches: Die Vorgeschichte des Münsteraner Täuferreiches, 1525–1534', in Hans-Ulrich Wehler (ed.), *Der Deutsche Bauernkrieg 1524–26* (Göttingen, 1975), pp. 193–238; and Gary K. Waite, 'The Anabaptist Movement in Amsterdam and the Netherlands, 1531–1535: An Initial Investigation into its Genesis and Social Dynamics', *Sixteenth Century Journal* 18 (1987), pp. 249–65. C. Arnold Snyder and Linda A. Huebert Hecht (eds), *Profiles of Anabaptist Women: Sixteenth-Century Reforming Pioneers* (Waterloo, Ont., 1998), furnish valuable short biographies of Anabaptist women as well as excerpts of their writings. See further Joyce Irwin, *Womanhood in Radical Protestantism 1525–1675* (New York, 1975); Jennifer H. Reed, 'Dutch Anabaptist Female Martyrs and their response to the Reformation (M.A. thesis, University of South Florida, 1991). Sigrun Haude, 'Anabaptist Women – Radical Women?', in Max Reinhart (ed.), *Infinite Boundaries: Order, Disorder and Reorder in Early Modern German Culture* (Kirksville, MO, 1998), pp. 313–27, discusses general themes in scholarship and provides references for further literature on Anabaptist women, including unpublished master theses.

For Anabaptism in England, consult Irvin B. Horst, *The Radical Brethren: Anabaptism and the English Reformation to 1558* (Nieuwkoop, 1972); for the Netherlands, Cornelius Krahn, *Dutch Anabaptism: Origin, Spread, Life and Thought (1450–1600)* (The Hague, 1968), and Albert F. Mellink, *De Wederdopers in de Noordelijke Nederlanden, 1531–1544* (Groningen, 1954); for Moravia and the Hutterites, Werner O. Packull, *Hutterite Beginnings: Communitarian Experiments during the Reformation* (Baltimore, 1995); for Italy, Aldo Stella's *Anabattismo e Antitrinitarismo in Italia nel XVI Secolo* (Padua, 1969) and his *Dall'Anabattismo al Socinianesimo nel Cinquecento Veneto* (Padua, 1967), as well as Antonio Rotondó, 'I movimenti ereticali nell'Europa del'Cinquecento', *Studi e Ricerche di storia ereticale Italiana del Cinquecento* (Torino, 1974), pp. 5–56.

The Anabaptist reign of Münster has stimulated much scholarship. Carl A. Cornelius, *Geschichte des Münsterischen Aufruhrs* (2 vols; Leipzig, 1855, 1860), is particularly known for his edition of documents. Karl-Heinz Kirchhoff's work on Anabaptist Münster has been invaluable. Several of his articles are compiled in Franz Petri, Peter Schöller, Heinz Stoob and Peter Johanek (eds), *Forschungen zur Geschichte von Stadt und Stift Münster* (Warendorf, 1988). Ralf Klötzer, *Die Täuferherrschaft von Münster: Stadtreformation und Welterneuerung* (Münster, 1992), brings a fresh look to the events of Münster. Albert F. Mellink investigated 'The Mutual Relations between the Münster Anabaptists and the Netherlands', *Archiv für Reformationsgeschichte* 50 (1959), pp. 16–39. Walter Klaassen, *Living at the End of the Ages: Apocalyptic Expectation in the Radical Reformation* (New York, 1992), pursues the theme of apocalypticism within Anabaptism. Günter Vogler, 'The Anabaptist Kingdom of Münster in the Tension between Anabaptism and Imperial Policy', in *Radical Tendencies*, pp. 99–116, places the problem of Anabaptism in the larger context of imperial politics.

SCANDINAVIA

Ole Peter Grell

Evangelical ideas made an early impact in Scandinavia, reaching the region around 1520. By the mid-1520s the inhabitants of most of the major towns had encountered the new religious ideas either on their visits to the main Baltic ports of Danzig and Lübeck or through visiting German merchants and itinerant German preachers, or from the German evangelical pamphlets they brought with them. It was also at this point that the first native evangelical preachers began their preaching. The larger towns, Copenhagen, Malmø and Stockholm, all possessed a significant resident German merchant population, who more often than not were intermarried with the emerging Scandinavian civic families; together these families formed the driving force behind the movement for religious reform.

Thus, as in the Holy Roman Empire, support for the Reformation came primarily from the urban centres. Bearing this in mind we should not be surprised to find that popular support for the evangelical movement was stronger in Denmark than any of the other Scandinavian countries. Here alone anticlericalism was a significant factor, while the Catholic church appears to have been unable to generate much grass-root support by the beginning of the sixteenth century.

These differences are probably best explained by the fact that Denmark was the most urbanized of the Nordic countries. More than 10 per cent of the population lived in towns, several of which (such as Copenhagen, Malmø, Elsinore, Odense, Aalborg, Aarhus and Ribe) ranged in size from 2,000 to 8,000 inhabitants. In Sweden less than 5 per cent of the population lived in towns and only Stockholm, which had between 4,000 and 6,000 inhabitants, could lay any real claim to urban status. Most other Swedish towns were little more than large villages. Norway and Finland were even more rural in character. Thus Denmark, with its closer contacts to the major urban evangelical centres in Germany, not least due to its geographical position, provided social conditions particularly conducive to the introduction of the Reformation.

Proof that popular support for the new evangelical ideas was much stronger in Denmark than in Sweden can also be found in the differences in the evangelical literature and the way it was produced in the two countries. The Danish literature, including translations, was initially produced on local initiative and outside princely control in the towns of Viborg, Malmø and later Copenhagen. It was doctrinally diverse, in contrast to the Swedish evangelical literature which was printed in Stockholm under royal control. The uniformity of the Swedish publications are indicative of an evangelical movement which, apart from a brief intermezzo in Stockholm, depended nearly exclusively on princely initiatives and support, whereas the diversity of evangelical ideas in the Danish evangelical works demonstrates the strength of popular support for the Reformation among the urban population of this country.

THE POLITICAL CONTEXT

In Scandinavia, as in Germany, the evangelical programme for religious change and renewal became intertwined with the political and social upheavals which had begun in the late Middle Ages. By the sixteenth century the defeudalization process had led to a growing confrontation between lay and ecclesiastical aristocracy, peasants, burghers and the crown in the Nordic countries. From 1524 to 1542 a succession of peasant rebellions and a major civil war came to dominate events in these countries. The revolts were all primarily social and economic in origin, but more often than not they were inflamed and aggravated by the growing conflict between new and old in the religious domain.

As in Germany, the political centre came under increasing pressure from the periphery. By 1520 Luther had already, willingly or unwillingly, become a pawn in the political struggle between the territorial princes in Germany and their Habsburg emperor. Similarly the Reformation in Scandinavia became intrinsically linked to the weakening of the political centre and undoubtedly helped to accelerate the dissolution of the Scandinavian Union, created in 1397, into territorial national states. By the beginning of the sixteenth century the Union was on the verge of collapse. The Union, which comprised the kingdoms of Denmark (which then included Scania, Halland and Belkinge, now in southern Sweden), the duchies of Schleswig and Holstein, Norway, and Sweden and Finland, had always been an unwieldy entity. But the often arbitrary attempts of King Christian II to secure further power for the crown which, among other things, manifested itself in the execution of more than eighty leading members of the Swedish lay and ecclesiastical aristocracy in Stockholm in November 1520, brought about a rebellion in Sweden. It was led by the Swedish nobleman Gustav Vasa whose father had been among those executed in Stockholm. A year later he was in total control of Sweden while Christian II was facing mounting difficulties in Denmark. By early 1523 the king's attempts to weaken the political influence of the Danish nobility led to his deposition by the Danish Council (Rigsrådet). Rather than confronting the rebels, Christian fled Denmark for the Netherlands, seeking protection and support from his Habsburg relations (he had married Emperor Charles V's sister, Elisabeth, in 1515). In his place the Danish Council elected his uncle, Duke Frederik of Schleswig and Holstein, who had supported the rebels. Thus by the summer of 1523 two usurpers, Gustav Vasa and Frederik I, had succeeded to the thrones of Sweden/Finland and Denmark/Norway respectively and the Union of the Scandinavian Kingdoms had collapsed. Both monarchs proved positively inclined towards the new evangelical ideas and sought to establish some form of national church under royal control. However, in terms of religious commitment they appear to have differed significantly. Where Gustav Vasa's interest in evangelical reform was predominantly determined by political and economic considerations, Frederik I's (and later, to an even greater extent, his son, Christian III's) views were dictated as much by faith as by political priorities.

Until the 1530s the deposed King Christian II and his Habsburg family continued to present some hazard to the new Scandinavian rulers, and this encouraged some hesitant political collaboration between Gustav Vasa and Frederik I. The Swedish king, however, always doubted the political sincerity of Frederik I and later, even more so, that of his son Christian III whom he was convinced nurtured secret ambitions of re-establishing the Scandinavian Union, thus once more bringing Sweden under Danish hegemony. In addition Gustav Vasa's kingship was far from secure, at least until the 1540s, facing, as he did, constant internal revolts, as well as a lack of external recognition of the legitimacy of his rule. Frederik I and later his son, Christian III, never encountered similar domestic problems and, while their legitimacy might also be questioned, they at least belonged to the royal family and had been next in the line of succession to Christian II. These circumstances undoubtedly helped to make their rule internationally more acceptable.

As was the case with the Catholic church in the Holy Roman Empire, the three Scandinavian church provinces had witnessed increased papal and royal interference in church affairs during the fifteenth century. By the 1520s, however, the Catholic church in the Nordic countries was in considerably worse shape than was the case in Germany. Monasticism was on the retreat across Scandinavia. Even in Denmark where its position had been the strongest, with larger and richer monasteries, and where the traditional orders as well as the mendicants were well represented, recruitment had proved difficult for most orders in the decades leading up to the Reformation. Well before the emergence of the evangelical movement several monasteries were close to dissolution. Their overall weakness in terms of personnel and standing had caused many of them to accept the control and management of lay noblemen.

However, it was the lack of leadership within the Scandinavian Catholic church which more than anything else proved detrimental to the church in its attempt to counter the new evangelical ideas. Not only were those bishops who were in place of a questionable quality, but the number of vacant dioceses was unusually large. In December 1522 the rebellious members of the Danish Council had signified in their open letter that among their main reasons for rebelling against Christian II was the king's disregard for the Catholic church and his promotion of 'Lutheranism'. In addition, they added, 'unfortunately, we are daily faced with the fact that there are no archbishops in these three kingdoms, Denmark, Sweden and Norway, who should preside over the holy Christian faith next to our holy father, the pope'.[1] Indeed on the eve of the Reformation the three archbishoprics of Lund, Uppsala and Trondheim were all unoccupied. While in Denmark all eight bishoprics, including Schleswig, had an incumbent, half the dioceses in Norway and Sweden were vacant.[2]

Their uncertain hold over the political loyalties of their kingdom apart, Gustav

Vasa and Frederik I shared one other problem: they were both deeply in debt. Gustav Vasa's financial problems were the greater because of the protracted military campaign necessary to oust the supporters of Christian II in Sweden and Finland, but even Frederik I's largely unopposed military advance through Denmark to Copenhagen had proved costly. In Sweden, as well as in Denmark, this caused serious fiscal problems for years to come. These difficulties were further aggravated by the need for constant extra defence expenditure during the 1520s because of the threat of an invasion by Christian II. Furthermore, the many rebellions in Sweden by a dissatisfied, predominantly conservative and Catholic rural population, not to mention the civil war in Denmark (*Grevens Fejde*) between 1534 and 1536, added to the economic woes of these countries. Economic necessity alone would have dictated some form of action to appropriate the wealth of church, given that in the Nordic countries the church establishment possessed around 40 per cent of the land and at least an interest in a third of plots and houses in the major towns, and yet was traditionally exempt from taxation. Thus the Swedish and Danish governments both had sound economic reasons for supporting the evangelical movement. Consequently, the depleted leadership of the Catholic church in Scandinavia already found itself on the defensive for economic and political reasons, before the evangelical movement added to their woes.

SCHLESWIG-HOLSTEIN

Initially the Reformation was most successful in the duchies of Schleswig-Holstein. Here its progress owed much to the support of the young Duke Christian (later King Christian III of Denmark and Norway), who had begun playing an active part in the government of Schleswig-Holstein from 1525. In 1528 the duke was able to introduce the first evangelical Church Order in Scandinavia, in his personal fief, Haderslev-Tønning, in Schleswig. Together with the orders of Brunswick and Saxony from the same year, it was one of the first Lutheran Church Orders.[3] By then most of the towns in Schleswig-Holstein had been won over to the Reformation, primarily through princely initiatives rather than by popular support. For political and geographical reasons, however, the duchies did not sustain the pace of reform. In this, their mixed nationality and allegiance (Holstein was part of the Holy Roman Empire while Schleswig was a fief of the kingdom of Denmark) played a role. They thus fell behind the evangelical developments which took place in Denmark during the 1530s: Denmark received a Lutheran Church Order in 1537, five years before the duchies as a whole.

Evangelical preaching had already begun in Schleswig-Holstein in the town of Husum in 1522, where the Wittenberg-trained minister Hermann Tast had started to spread the evangelical message in Low German. Husum appears to have provided fertile ground and Tast was soon joined by other former Catholic clergy in the town. The Wittenberg connection was to characterize the Reformation in the duchies from the outset. Duke Christian, who had been present at the Diet of Worms in 1521, was an early convert to Lutheranism. This may owe less to Luther's impressive performance at the diet than the influence of his Lutheran and

Wittenberg-educated councillors. The young duke's evangelical commitment appears to have hampered his early career, as later in 1533 it was to delay his succession to the Danish throne. Opposition among the lay and ecclesiastical aristocracy in the duchies prevented his father, King Frederik I, from making him stadtholder of Schleswig-Holstein before 1526. In the meantime, in 1525, Christian was given the fief of Haderslev-Tønning to sharpen his political and administrative teeth. By then, however, the tide had already begun to turn against the Catholic church in the duchies. The Diet of Rendsburg in 1525 demonstrated that the traditional solidarity between lay and ecclesiastical leaders was disintegrating. In a situation where increased taxes were needed in order to pay for the armaments and troops to counter the threat of an invasion from the deposed king, Christian II, the lay aristocracy abandoned their colleagues within the church. They demanded that the clergy pay the greatest share of the increased tax-burden as a condition of their continued support against the reformers. Despite agreeing, the Catholic leaders found that the diet also took the opportunity to circumscribe and weaken their ecclesiastical jurisdiction, ordering that in future the gospel should be preached purely and in the vernacular in the duchies.

These events encouraged Duke Christian to proceed to reform his fief. He commenced his campaign by dismissing the dean of the collegiate chapter in Haderslev, simultaneously clashing with the Bishops of Schleswig and Ribe over everything from tithes to ecclesiastical jurisdiction. Despite losing some of these early clashes, the duke was able to continue to promote the evangelical cause in Haderslev-Tønning. In 1526 he recruited two German evangelical theologians, Eberhardt Weidensee and Johann Wenth, to assist him in the reformation of his fief. Both came to play influential parts in the Reformation of Schleswig-Holstein, Weidensee in the capacity of superintendent, while the Wittenberg graduate, Wenth, became one of the authors of the Danish Lutheran Church Order of 1537–9 and the Schleswig-Holstein Order of 1542. Both were produced under the supervision of Luther's friend and collaborator, Johannes Bugenhagen.

When the Catholic church was further weakened politically at the Diet of Kiel in 1526, Christian took the opportunity to call a synod of the clergy in and around Haderslev. They were presented with new evangelical articles of faith, drawn up by Weidensee and Wenth, most likely identical with the later Haderslev Church Order of 1528. The duke had seen his political power significantly strengthened when he was appointed stadtholder of Schleswig-Holstein on 25 May 1526. By the end of 1527 most parish churches in urban areas had received evangelical preachers, often Wittenberg-educated, most personally introduced by either King Frederik I or Duke Christian. In Haderslev, Johann Wenth had turned the collegiate chapter-school into the first training academy for new evangelical ministers in Scandinavia. It became a model for similar schools in Denmark which were established in the towns of Malmø and Viborg within a few years. The Reformation of the towns of Schleswig-Holstein proved a quiet affair with minimal disruption, controlled and promoted by the prince.

The example of Husum illustrates the considerable degree of continuity between the old and new in terms of personnel. Fifteen of the original nineteen priests in the town remained in place after the Reformation. In an agreement between the magistracy and the Catholic church, the clergy were guaranteed their salaries for life as long as they abstained from celebrating mass. One can only conclude that self-interest easily outweighed religious commitment to Catholicism among the clergy in the town. Henceforth only evangelical services were allowed in Husum, but a strong sense of continuity must have existed among its citizens attending 'Protestant' services conducted by ministers who only recently, as priests, had been saying mass. Simultaneously the magistracy not only surveyed all property belonging to the church, but took over its administration, deciding that part of it should be used to pay for a schoolmaster and parish clerks.

In 1528, when Duke Christian called another synod, this time of all the clergy in Haderslev-Tønning, only the Reformation of the countryside needed further attention. The village clergy were presented with the Haderslev Church Order, which in its first paragraph denounced the lack of uniformity in ceremonies and teaching which had necessitated its formulation. The shortage of evangelical ministers evidently argued for a tolerant and positive attitude towards rural Catholic priests whose commitment to Protestantism was at best vague, but who were willing to continue their work exchanging the pope for the duke as their master. Often the priests would have been tempted to stay on for purely social and practical reasons. The chance of legitimating their domestic set-up – where many, if not most, lived intimately with their 'housekeeper' (with whom they often had children) – through marriage would have appealed to them. All the evidence from Schleswig-Holstein indicates that most of the Catholic incumbents stayed on in the countryside, where only a handful of village priests refused to accept the Haderslev Church Order and had to be expelled. The old Catholic priests were, in other words, preferable to no ministers, even if this meant that the gospel was not necessarily purely preached. This, however, was expected to be remedied through teaching and instruction, as laid down in the Church Order.

The dependence of the Haderslev Order on Wittenberg is evident. All ministers were advised to follow Luther's *Kirchenpostille* in their sermons and warned only to preach the gospel: a reminder not to revert to the old Catholic ways. Parishes less than a mile from the towns of Haderslev and Ribe were obliged to recruit their parish clerks from the Latin schools there, thereby making sure that they at least might benefit from the recent evangelical instruction given to pupils. The ministers were told to catechize their congregations after each Sunday sermon. Similarly they were expected to explain the catechism in half-yearly series of sermons. A number of rural deans should carry out yearly visitations on the duke's behalf similar to those Philip Melanchthon had prescribed for Saxony, to secure uniformity and good administration.

Christian's reasons for introducing an oath of allegiance for new ministers in 1528, repudiating the teachings of sacramentarians and Anabaptists, may not solely have been inspired by developments in Germany, but also by the arrival of the radical reformer Melchior Hoffmann in Kiel in February 1527. If Christian was not already intent on ridding his duchies of this volatile preacher by 1528, a letter from Martin Luther prompted him to action, and Hoffmann was expelled from the duchies the following year. This correspondence initiated what proved to be lifelong close contacts between Christian and the leading Wittenberg theologians. But further progress for the evangelical cause proved much slower during the next decade. When Christian was declared Duke of Schleswig-Holstein upon his father's death in 1533, the Diet of Kiel decided to await developments in Germany and Denmark before final decisions were made about religious and ecclesiastical matters. Despite this official setback, which allowed Catholic services to continue, Christian continued to press for further concessions for the evangelicals, forcing the Bishop of Schleswig to allow Protestant services to take place in his cathedral. Legally, however, the duchies had to wait another decade before receiving a Protestant Church Order covering the whole territory.

Christian's victory in the civil war (*Grevens Fejde*) in Denmark, and his succession to the Danish throne depended in no small measure on the loyal support of both lay and ecclesiastical aristocracy in Schleswig-Holstein. Thus, when he tried to introduce the recently issued Danish Church Order in the duchies and encountered significant opposition to such a step from a considerable number of local nobles and Catholic churchmen, he immediately abandoned his plans, accepting their mainly constitutional objections. This 'conservative' and Catholic faction of the nobility in the duchies wanted to maintain the independence of the duchies, while family loyalty and general respect for Schleswig's elderly bishop, Gottschalk Ahlefeldt, may well have affected their views too. Instead, Christian continued the piecemeal and localized approach to religious change that he had used for years. Avoiding the diets, the duke called a synod in the duchies, consisting of ministers and local lay officials (such as town councillors) to deliberate a new Church Order. A practical result of the synod was the appointment of four inspectors for the towns and countryside around Haderslev, Husum, Schleswig and Flensburg.

By 1540 Christian must have felt that the time was ripe for another attempt to have a Protestant Church Order for Schleswig-Holstein accepted. By then he had commissioned a translation of the Danish Church Order into Low German. Still, he failed to convince a substantial Catholic minority at the Diet of Flensburg and once more the plans were dropped. As previously, Christian opted instead for further practical reforms. The four inspectors were given additional authority. They were upgraded to superintendents and a reformation of the remaining Catholic monasteries and convents was organized, halting their Catholic activities while forcing them to appoint and pay for evangelical lecturers who should catechize them in the new evangelical teachings. When the Bishop of Schleswig died in January 1541, the already shrinking Catholic minority within the aristocracy of the duchies lost its standard-bearer and fourteen months later a Lutheran Church Order was issued for the whole of Schleswig-Holstein. It was essentially a translation of the Danish Church Order of 1537, which itself had been inspired by the Haderslev Church Order of 1528, and like its Danish counterpart it had been drawn up under the supervision of Johannes Bugenhagen.

Thus, within two decades of Hermann Tast beginning to disseminate the evangelical message in Husum, the duchies had witnessed a full Reformation. The popular element in the Reformation of Schleswig-Holstein was, however, insignificant. The success of the Reformation in this region depended on the initiative of Duke Christian. It was his personal commitment to Protestantism which saw most of the ecclesiastical changes through, well before the Diet finally accepted the new

Church Order of 1542. In his reforms, however, Christian depended not solely on the advice of Bugenhagen and the other leading Wittenberg theologians, but also on the more direct input from a considerable number of Wittenberg-educated ministers. The Reformation of Schleswig-Holstein appears to have had a distinct Lutheran–Melanchthonian flavour from beginning to end, with the brief incursion of Melchior Hoffman the only exception to this pattern. That, of course, does not tell us how fast and to what extent the Reformation succeeded in winning over the population of the duchies. Catholic traditions and practices undoubtedly survived for generations, especially in rural parishes, but the Protestant emphasis on education and catechism may well have borne fruit within a couple of generations. Thus the School Order of May 1544 provided the foundation for an expansion and improvement of the educational facilities in the duchies, not least with regard to religious instruction.[4]

The fact that the Counter Reformation made little impact and that the Jesuits never undertook any major missionary activity in the duchies is the best proof that little if any Catholicism survived towards the end of the sixteenth century. Only within the town of Flensburg do the Jesuits appear to have had reasonable connections.

DENMARK

Even if the Reformation in Denmark also benefited from increasing princely support over time it differed substantially from the Reformation of the duchies. In Denmark the evangelical movement was far more heterodox than in the duchies and during the first ten to fifteen years it relied heavily on popular and local magisterial support. Initially it had been promoted by Christian II, who appreciated its potential use in connection with his absolutist plans for the kingdom. For a while the king had surrounded himself with Wittenberg-trained humanists and theologians who were allowed to preach in Copenhagen. Here they appear to have found a receptive audience, especially within the university, where humanist and Erasmian interests had already been reinforced by the creation of a Carmelite college in 1519. It was from this college that several of the leading lights of the Danish Reformation, such as Frants Vormordsen and Peder Laurentsen were to emerge in the late 1520s.

When Frederik I succeeded his deposed nephew, Christian II, as king in 1523, his power was severely circumscribed by the conservative and Catholic majority within the Rigsrådet. Initially, therefore, the king offered only passive support for the evangelical movement, supplemented by a policy of issuing royal letters of protection for individual evangelical preachers. Among the first to benefit were Hans Tausen and Jørgen Jensen Sadolin, both Wittenberg-educated, who had generated considerable support for the evangelical cause in the Jutland town of Viborg. By 1526 most of the market towns in Jutland appear to have been won over to the Reformation, often (as in the case of Viborg) with strong support from their magistracies.

The parliaments of 1526 and 1527 broke the traditional links to Rome and created a national (if still Catholic) church. Until then the contacts between the

Danish church and Rome had been excellent. More than 800 documents and letters were exchanged in the thirteen years leading up to 1526. Thereafter, for the nine years from 1527 leading up to the official Reformation in 1536, only 60 documents and letters exist, and most of these were directed to the exiled Christian II and his associates.[5] Yet the Danish bishops and church leaders had proved unable to force the king to intervene against the growing number of evangelical preachers in the country, despite his promise in his coronation charter to fight Lutheranism. A consequence of this national stalemate in religious affairs led the bishops to try to combat the evangelical movement locally within their individual dioceses, while the king continued his piecemeal policy of issuing royal letters of protection to individual evangelical preachers.

By 1528, however, the evangelical movement in Denmark had moved on from the towns in Jutland in general and Viborg to the much larger and commercially far more important cities at the Sound – Malmø and Copenhagen. Compared with their Hanseatic and German counterparts, these cities were not only smaller (with between 6,000 and 8,000 inhabitants), but they were also relatively new as urban centres, having experienced dramatic growth during the second half of the fifteenth century. This recent rapid expansion had allowed no time for the development of urban oligarchies. Consequently the division often seen in German cities between a small conservative and Catholic group of old merchant families, who controlled the city councils, and a larger opposition party of new merchants and craftsmen supporting the evangelical movement was not evident.[6] In Malmø especially, encouraged and assisted by the city's strong and united magistracy, Protestantism blossomed. The commitment to the new teachings by Malmø's leading mayor, Jørgen Kock, proved particularly important. It was he who secured the royal privileges for the city which by 1530 had led Malmø to become a fully reformed city. From 1529 he had been aided by the presence in Malmø of two of the leading evangelical theologians of the Danish Reformation, Frants Vormordsen and Peder Laurentsen. Both were present in Copenhagen in July 1530 when the parliament met and Frederik I intimated plans to reform his kingdom. However, these plans had to be abandoned owing to the threat of an impending invasion by his deposed nephew, Christian II, and consequently only the market towns received a general charter, allowing them to introduce evangelical services.

This was how matters stood when Frederik I died in April 1533. In this power-vacuum the Catholic bishops and their lay supporters within the council, who constituted a majority, dominated the parliament which gathered in Copenhagen that summer. The bishops realized that this was their last chance to prevent the country from becoming fully reformed. Even if no obvious alternative candidate was on offer, they at all costs wanted to avoid electing Frederik's oldest son, the Lutheran Duke Christian. Instead, an interim government of the council was established until another parliament could meet the following year. This attempt to turn the clock back, religiously as well as politically, resulted in a civil war (*Grevens Fejde*). Malmø commenced the rebellion in May 1534 and the city's alliance with Copenhagen and Lübeck quickly forced a split within the council. Two months later the aristocracy in Jutland and Funen felt their political and military position untenable and elected Duke Christian king.

Figure 15.1 Communion in both kinds. Contemporary Danish altar-painting in the style of the School of Cranach. (Copenhagen, National Gallery)

When Copenhagen surrendered two years later, Christian III was the victor of the civil war. The country was now ready for a royal Reformation, having already experienced the popular, as well as the magisterial phases. Most of the ecclesiastical and lay aristocracy, especially the bishops, had been deeply compromised by the events following the parliament of 1533. The bishops were held responsible for the civil war and imprisoned on 12 August 1536. The parliament which followed decided to remove the bishops and replace them with other 'Christian bishops and superintendents' and to introduce an evangelical Church Order. This was achieved in 1537 when the Danish Church Order received royal confirmation.

Cathedral chapters, monasteries and rural convents were, however, allowed to continue for the time being. In contrast to the dismissed Catholic bishops, who appear to have settled down quite happily as feudal landowners and even in some cases to have converted to Lutheranism, these institutions were to constitute the last visible bastions of the old faith. During the 1540s and 1550s the canons in the two most prestigious chapters, those of Lund and Roskilde, fought a rearguard action against the Reformation. The government realized the potential for obstruction and subversive action within these chapters and accordingly attached two of the leading reformers, Hans Tausen and Peder Laurentsen, as lecturers to them, thus turning them – together with the rest of the chapters – into one-man evangelical divinity schools. However, the government still found it necessary to intervene directly during the 1540s by forcing recalcitrant canons to sign the new Lutheran confession. Apart from the obstinacy of a handful of canons, most of the Catholic clergy appear to have been absorbed into the new Lutheran church without any complaints or attempts at obstruction. Thus only a few examples can be found of rural ministers who continued to use Catholic rites and who were defrocked for false teaching.

Dealing with a small clerical Catholic residue, however, was not the most crucial problem for the Lutheran church in Denmark. The new evangelical teachings had to be disseminated among the laity and the Reformation had yet to make an impact in the countryside. A major educational effort was needed to promote the Lutheran faith among an at least passively Catholic peasantry – a necessity which had already been acknowledged by the evangelical preachers from as early as 1530.

As in the case of the German territorial churches, the new Lutheran church in Denmark concentrated most of its efforts on education and social provision, such as hospitals and poor relief. The University of Copenhagen, which had been closed in 1531 because it had been considered a major centre for the dissemination of evangelical ideas, was reopened in 1537, remodelled on the University of Wittenberg which had recently been reformed by Melanchthon. Lack of money and the university's inability to attract students, however, guaranteed that it remained a backwater until Christian III's son and successor, Frederik II, provided it with adequate funds in 1570.

The government fared considerably better with regard to secondary education. Before Christian III's death in 1559, nearly all towns in the kingdom had been provided with Latin schools. The administration, however, appears to have concentrated its efforts within secondary education and demonstrated only limited interest in providing elementary schooling for the majority of the population. However, the religious instruction given in elementary schools and supplemented by the teaching provided by ministers and parish clerks in the rural areas was considered essential in bringing the Reformation to the people. The first Protestant Bishop of Zealand, Peder Palladius, hoped that the children who benefited from this instruction would teach the evangelical message to their elders. The king and his chancellor, Johan Friis, took considerable personal interest in education, supporting Danish students in Wittenberg and providing capital for the establishment of Latin schools. However, many of the plans for improvement within the educational sector had to await the improved economic conditions of the reign of Frederik II.

The new ecclesiastical administration monitored the clergy and laity's adherence to the Protestant faith. The superintendents constantly inspected their dioceses and examined candidates for the ministry. Their visitations were supplemented on the local level by rural deans. A constant synodal activity, from national via provincial down to local synods, helped secure a measure of uniformity. As can be seen from the detailed provisions laid down for the visitations by

Peder Palladius, the evolutionary implementation of the Reformation through education and catechizing was paramount to the new Lutheran church.

The acts of the diocesan synods of Zealand from 1554 to 1569 show the constant preoccupation with the need to ensure that local churches and ministers had the necessary books. These included the Bible, books of sermons by Luther, Melanchthon and Brenz, Melanchthon's *Loci communes*, Brenz's and Palladius's catechisms – not to mention the new Danish Church Order. Much was lacking in the first decades after the official Reformation. Unqualified and unauthorized ministers were seen as a constant threat by the authorities, while incumbents repeatedly had to be admonished to preach and not read their sermons from books, and to fulfil their obligation to catechize their congregations every Sunday. If the clergy was in need of constant censure, so was the rural population. Peasants were reminded that they were obliged to send their children to school and that continued refusal to comply would be punished by lay authority. That failure to take heed of the ecclesiastical authorities could have dire consequences can be seen from the example of the tenant-farmer who in 1574 lost his farm because he had been excommunicated by his vicar for lack of church attendance for more than six years, during which time he had never received communion.[7]

If the activities of Hans Mikkelsen, Bishop of Odense between 1626 and 1641, are anything to go by, the concern for annual visitations did not abate among the next generations of Lutheran bishops in Denmark. From late spring through summer, Hans Mikkelsen was on the road visiting the local parishes in his diocese, paying particular attention to the instruction of the local children, conscientiously noting whether or not they were well taught. His diary indicates that by then the Reformation had proved a success, even if constant supervision and admonition were still needed. The occasional minister who was unable to read could still be found, and now and again a parish clerk had to be disciplined or even dismissed. However, the most remarkable aspect of Hans Mikkelsen's visitations is the extent to which the local lay population were able to have their views considered and their complaints acted upon. Thus, when carrying out his visitation of Hørup church and parish in 1629, Hans Mikkelsen was presented by the parishioners with three complaints about their minister. Apparently he scolded them in his sermons, while not finishing his preaching within reasonable time. Furthermore, he demanded a thaler from those who were to be engaged. That the bishop should have prevented the local minister from charging young couples about to get married is hardly surprising, but that he accepted the parishioners' complaints about the style and length of his sermons is startling. Evidently, the local lay input in the newly established Lutheran church was considerable and much greater than recognized by church historians.[8]

The discipline of the new church was still not universally accepted even by this late date. Thus, when the bishop was visiting Årslev church in 1627, only three children bothered to turn up to face him, while the rest of the parish's children were 'behaving in an uproarious manner' just outside the church. Two years later Hans Mikkelsen reported that a peasant who had been given public absolution in St Knud's church in Odense had shown his disdain by roaring with laughter. He had subsequently been chained in the street and exposed to public ridicule.[9]

Furthermore, many Catholic traditions refused to die within a Lutheran Church which permitted most high altars, side altars, images of saints and frescoes to remain in place. Many rural ministers, who might well have started their careers as Catholic priests, continued to elevate the communion wine and bread while the congregation knelt according to Catholic custom. Similarly, the same ministers would more often than not follow the Catholic tradition and consume all the remaining communion wine and bread, showing the empty chalice and dish to their congregations. If some of the clergy found it difficult to adjust fully to the new order, many of their parishioners struggled too. As was the case prior to the Reformation, popular demand in the countryside for benedictions of food and seed-corn around Easter remained strong, while pilgrimages to popular shrines often continued unabated. Thus, in Zealand the shrines in Egede dedicated to the Trinity and also the shrine in Bistrup continued to attract crowds during the 1560s. Large sums were donated to these shrines and the strong local opposition to their closure was as much economically as religiously motivated, since the money was divided between the local church, their ministers and their poor.[10] In Denmark pilgrimages to holy springs became particularly important after the Reformation. They were tolerated by the Lutheran clergy, not least because of the prominent place allocated to the Creation in Reformation theology, but possibly also because they recognized the need for some outlet for popular beliefs. As such, these springs served as a compensation for the loss of other previously acceptable avenues of miraculous healing, now considered as expressions of Catholic superstition.[11]

The extended period of peace and tranquillity which reigned in Denmark from 1536 after Christian III's victory in the civil war, served the new Protestant church well and offered it conditions which most territorial Lutheran churches in Germany would have envied. Despite a lack of local, detailed studies of how the Lutheran church functioned in Denmark in the second half of the sixteenth and early seventeenth centuries, we can safely assume that the Danish Reformation proved a success within a couple of generations of its formal introduction, even if the religious commitment of the population at large may well have been less fervent and spontaneous than the new church leaders might have hoped.

NORWAY

The overwhelmingly rural character of early modern Norway, even when compared with Denmark, may well explain why the evangelical movement seems to have made little or no impact at the popular level before the Reformation was introduced as a *fait accompli* by Christian III in 1537. The only place where evangelical preachers appear to have been active before this date was Bergen. It is no coincidence that the German Hansa had its staple here, and the first people to bring the evangelical message to Norway were undoubtedly German itinerant preachers who appealed to the resident Germans.

The Danish Church Order included a separate chapter outlining what was necessary for a Reformation of Norway. The king was to appoint new superintendents for the Norwegian dioceses as quickly as possible. They in turn were to ensure that good evangelical ministers – those who were willing to obey the new Church Order – were available in all parishes. More importantly it publicly stated that Christian III should personally visit Norway and together with the new superintendents supervise the introduction of a Lutheran Church Order, specifically geared to Norwegian conditions. Considering the active opposition to his rule and to the Reformation (which had found its greatest exponent in Norway's last Catholic archbishop, Olav Engelbriktsson), Christian III's concerns for Norway seem well placed.

In terms of practical policy, however, little if anything was done. Norway did not receive its own Church Order until 1607 and until this date was left to follow the Danish Order. Neither did Christian III find the time to visit the country, while it proved generally difficult to find suitable and willing candidates for the Norwegian superintendencies or bishoprics. Apart from Geble Pederssøn, who was appointed superintendent in Bergen, most of the other posts remained vacant for years. In the case of the united sees of Oslo and Hamar, the government took the unusual step of re-appointing the former Catholic Bishop of Oslo, Hans Reff, in 1541, only four years after his removal.

The government in Copenhagen clearly recognized the strength of Catholicism in Norway and the limitations of the fledgling Lutheran church it had created. Its instructions to the royal administrator in Bergen, Esge Bille, suggested he quietly permitted Catholic priests to remain in place rather than seek to appoint new evangelical preachers in their stead, in order to avoid generating unease and disturbances among the population. Considering the government's difficulties in finding suitable evangelical superintendents, the chances of the Norwegian administration being able to appoint evangelical ministers must have been remote indeed. When one considers the strength of Catholicism in Norway throughout the sixteenth century, it can hardly be surprising that the Jesuit who masterminded the attempts to introduce the Counter Reformation in Scandinavia was a Norwegian, Laurentius Nicolai. Indeed, Norwegians constituted the majority of Scandinavians who attended the Jesuit college in Braunsberg.

It was not until the second generation of superintendents/bishops were appointed in Norway that some form of Lutheranism was successfully promoted. As opposed to their predecessors they were all of Danish origin. Clearly by then the government in Copenhagen must have felt confident enough to disregard the question of nationality and opt for a more forceful Lutheran reform. Frants Berg, who served as Bishop of Oslo and Hamar from 1548 to 1580, led the way by improving the financial foundation of new Lutheran church in Norway, while also assisting in raising the educational standards of the clergy. Jens Skjelderup, who succeeded Geble Pederssøn in Bergen in 1577, also made a significant contribution to the improvement of clerical training, while spending considerable energy in ridding the country of traditional Catholic rites. Thus he clashed with the magistracy in Bergen when he attempted to have images of saints removed from the town's churches.

By far the most influential among this second generation of Lutheran bishops was Skjelderup's son-in-law, Jørgen Eriksson, who became Bishop of Stavanger in 1571. Through tireless visitations and synods of his diocese, Erickssøn did much to raise the educational profile of his clergy and the evangelical awareness of the laity. His significance is probably best illustrated by the fact that contemporaries labelled him 'the Norwegian Luther'. The lack of a Norwegian Church Order undoubtedly hampered the new Lutheran bishops and ministers in their work. That they had to wait seventy years might well be seen as indicative of how much the Norwegian Reformation lagged behind its Danish counterpart. Evidently it took a couple of generations to make up for the near total lack of popular support for the evangelical cause in 1537.

SWEDEN

The Reformation in Sweden (and Finland, which was part of the kingdom) was a protracted affair. Outside Stockholm, with its many influential German residents, it lacked significant popular support until the mid-sixteenth century. The spiritual crisis that had engulfed the Catholic church in Germany and Denmark appears to have left Sweden unaffected. As on the Continent, a growing hostility towards the monastic orders in general and towards the mendicant orders in particular was in evidence, but lay support for the Catholic church remained strong at parish level. The reason for this was undoubtedly closely related to the decentralized nature of the Catholic church in Sweden and Finland, where local churches exercised considerable independence and lay involvement at parish level (especially concerning financial affairs) was significant.

The Reformation therefore depended on princely initiative. The fact that Gustav Vasa, who had usurped the Swedish throne in 1523, never became a committed Protestant only served to muddy the waters. On one hand, the king was encouraged to promote a reformation of the Swedish church because of the obvious political and economic advantages to be gained by the crown. On the other hand, the king's lack of a genuine Protestant faith, coupled with his lack of dynastic legitimacy, meant that the confessional foundation for the Reformation in Sweden were not put in place until well after his death. Thus Sweden did not receive a Protestant Church Order until 1571, while confessionally it did not opt for Lutheranism until the Uppsala Assembly of 1593. Gustav Vasa's cause was not helped by the many social, economic and religious rebellions he encountered between 1527 and 1543.

The cost of the war of liberation from Denmark meant that Gustav Vasa took a considerable interest in ecclesiastical affairs from the start. Pragmatically, the church represented the most likely source for the funds necessary to pay his financiers within the German Hansa. Furthermore, the Catholic church in Sweden was short of leaders since most bishoprics were vacant. Most of the bishops, including the Archbishop of Uppsala, had owed their promotion to Christian II and had fled the country. Gustav made sure that their successors were loyal to him rather than to the Catholic church. Only one among all the bishops elected in the wake of Gustav Vasa's accession to the throne, Peder Månsson, managed to obtain papal confirmation.

Initially, Gustav Vasa appears to have hoped for some accommodation with the curia in his ambition to create a semi-detached Swedish church, but by 1524 he abandoned these plans and openly encouraged the nascent evangelical movement in the country. Two leading evangelicals, the Archdeacon of Strängnäs, Laurentius Andreae, and another Strängnäs theologian, Olaus Petri, were promoted to leading positions, respectively royal chancellor and the important post of clerk and minister to the town of Stockholm. They were to spearhead the evangelical movement under the king's protection until the early 1530s, at which time Gustav appears to have been uncertain of whether to proceed to further reform. Initially, he had offered the reformers all the support they wanted, providing them with access to printing presses while closing down the press set up and financed by Hans Brask, the Bishop of Linköping and leader of the Catholic faction. The expulsion of Melchior Hoffmann from Stockholm in January 1527 had until then been the only setback for the evangelical movement in Sweden; but, by the summer of 1529, the king had decided to suspend further moves towards Reformation.

In spite of the success of the parliament (Riksdag) of Västerås in 1527 in dismantling the economic and political power of the Catholic church, Gustav Vasa also had to face the first serious peasant rebellion – the so-called Daljunkeren's Revolt – in that year. This had served as a reminder to the king of the volatile social and economic situation in the realm, caused to a considerable extent by the increased royal taxation needed to pay for the recent war of independence against Christian II. Significantly, however, the revolt had been fanned by religious disaffection with the new Protestant teachings.

The inability of the national synod of Örebro in 1529 to reach an ecclesiastical compromise which satisfied the predominantly Catholic peasantry, as well as the evangelical burghers of Stockholm, not only led to disturbances in Stockholm, but caused a far more dangerous peasant uprising in southwest Sweden in April. This time the anti-evangelical overtones were much stronger than before, with local nobles providing leadership for the revolt. Only by promising to retain the status quo in religion and distancing himself from the reforms already introduced did Gustav Vasa manage to contain the danger. Consequently, Laurentius Andreae and Olaus Petri found themselves out of royal favour. Andreae lost his position as chancellor in 1531, while Petri (who had initially replaced him) was removed only two years later.

Gustav Vasa's actions may not have been motivated solely by the social and religious unrest generated by the evangelical movement within his realm. He may well have been alarmed by the social-radical tendencies demonstrated by parts of the evangelical movement in Germany, while the Catholic reaction which had followed the death of Frederik I in Denmark may have added to his doubts. Whatever the reasons, the Reformation was put on ice in Sweden until 1536, when a victorious Christian III had turned the Danish church into a territorial Lutheran church. Significantly, in that year another national synod introduced major changes to the order and ceremonies of the Swedish church. However, it did not manage to resolve the growing controversy between church and state. The Swedish reformers led by Olaus Petri and Laurentius Andreae wanted a Lutheran territorial church as independent of civil authority as possible, while Gustav Vasa wanted it firmly under royal supremacy. This dispute was to preoccupy Swedish church policy well into the seventeenth century.

Continuing protests among the peasantry combined with what the king considered to be the reformers' unwillingness to preach obedience to secular authority, convinced Gustav Vasa that further action was necessary. During the parliament of Örebro in December 1539, Gustav Vasa finally secured full control over the Swedish church. He had been encouraged to this initiative by his growing number of German advisers, especially his councillor, Conrad von Pyhy, and the Wittenberg-educated theologian, Georg Norman. A new church organization was introduced in parallel with the episcopal system. Thus by 1540 the Swedish church had finally experienced what amounted to a princely Reformation, though only in church government. Most of the changes, however, proved short-lived. Yet another peasant revolt in 1542, caused as much by economic grievances as dissatisfaction with the ecclesiastical changes (though Georg Norman's visitations were especially singled out for complaint), guaranteed that most of the innovations had gone by 1545. Gustav Vasa remained firmly in control of the Swedish church until his death in 1560. But the lack of any firm doctrinal foundation for the new semi-evangelical church was to cause serious and protracted difficulties for decades to come.

Gustav Vasa had provided two of his three sons, Erik and Karl, with Calvinist tutors, Dionysius Beurreus and Jan van Herboville. Together with a number of Calvinist refugees from East Friesland they attempted to promote Calvinism in Sweden during the first years of the reign of Erik XIV. This all came to an end in 1565 when the Calvinist position had come under fierce attack by the archbishop, Laurentius Petri, forcing Erik to reverse his father's policy of inviting persecuted Calvinists to settle in Sweden, while at the same time forbidding Calvinist agitation in his kingdom.[12]

When Johan III succeeded his deposed brother in 1568, the potential dangers of the Swedish church's lack of doctrinal foundation came to the fore once more. This time the principal threat came from the Catholic Counter Reformation. Despite having finally been given a Protestant Church Order in 1571, Sweden proved fertile ground for Jesuit missionary efforts in the late 1570s.

Johan III, who had married a Catholic Polish princess, Katarina, was personally attracted to the splendour of the Counter-Reformation church. Theologically, he was heavily influenced by the writings of Georg Cassander, an irenically minded Catholic churchman, as can be seen from the king's amendments to the Church Order – the *Nova Ordinantia* of 1575. The prospects of the Swedish church's imminent return to the Catholic fold were positively interpreted by the leading Polish Jesuit, Warzewicki, who had provided Queen Katarina with spiritual guidance since 1574. His reports encouraged Pope Gregory XIII to send the Norwegian Jesuit, Laurentius Nicolai ('Klosterlasse'), to Sweden in 1576. The Norwegian served as an undercover agent for the curia and proved an immediate success with Johan III, who allowed him to open a theological college in the former Franciscan monastery in Stockholm. Education had been in a deplorable state in Sweden since 1516 when the University of Uppsala had been closed and, in spite of attempts by Erik XIV and Johan III to reinvigorate it, no place existed in the country where ministers could be properly trained.

Meanwhile, an official embassy from Johan to Pope Gregory XIII encouraged the pope to send a former secretary-general of the Jesuit Order, Antonio Possevino, to Sweden. With his arrival in 1577 and Johan's introduction that year of a new, more Catholic liturgy – known as the Red Book because of its cover – the Catholic missionary efforts began to bear fruit, especially within the Swedish aristocracy. However, the new liturgy was fiercely opposed by a majority of churchmen in Sweden. Their fear of a papist conspiracy to re-Catholicize the country was confirmed when in 1578 Laurentius Nicolai revealed himself as a Jesuit. The following year fear turned into panic among Swedish Protestants, when Possevino – who had returned from Rome, this time in full clerical garb – ordered all Catholic priests to throw aside their disguises. The violent anti-Catholic reactions which followed (including riots in Stockholm), lost Possevino and Laurentius Nicolai the royal support they had enjoyed and they were forced to leave Sweden. A few Catholic priests were allowed to stay with the Queen, but by the time of Katarina's death in 1583 the Counter-Reformation threat to the Swedish church had receded.[13]

If anything, the Jesuit attempt to infiltrate Sweden ultimately served only to undermine the reign of Johan's son, the Catholic King Sigismund, who was deposed in 1598 after only six years on the throne. During these years the Protestant opponents of the high-church, crypto-Catholic policies of Johan and Sigismund had benefited from the protection and encouragement of Duke Karl, Johan's brother. It was from the safe haven of his duchy that some of the leading Lutheran theologians of the Swedish church materialized during the 1590s. Karl, who retained strong Calvinist sympathies, succeeded his nephew Sigismund, but failed in his attempt to resolve the ongoing struggle between church and state for control of ecclesiastical affairs. Ironically, the predominantly Lutheran churchmen he had protected during their years of persecution now turned against him, defending the independence of the church while accusing him of heterodox beliefs. He, on the other hand, did his utmost to impose royal supremacy on the church, but his Lutheran bishops kept him at bay until he died in 1611.

Thus the Swedish Reformation turned out to be the slowest and doctrinally most insecure of the Scandinavian Reformations. Initially it not only lacked popular support, but also faced the greatest opposition of any of the Nordic countries, especially from its peasant population. From the outset it was subject to the predominantly political and economic calculations of Gustav Vasa. The fact that the country had to wait more than forty years before an evangelical Church Order was finally issued in 1571, and then in a remarkably vague form, did little to cement the evangelical achievements of the preceding decades. Furthermore, the religious heterodoxy of Gustav Vasa's sons meant that doctrinal stability had to wait until the Uppsala Assembly in 1593. This ensured that the Swedish church remained on the defensive throughout the sixteenth century, keenly defending some sort of Lutheran orthodoxy, while simultaneously seeking to protect the church against royal encroachments.

NOTES

1   This document is cited in C. Paludan-Müller, *De første Konger af den Oldenborgske Slægt* (Copenhagen, 1874), pp. 442–3. A translation of the relevant section is cited in O.P. Grell, 'The Catholic church and Its Leadership', in O.P. Grell (ed.), *The Scandinavian Reformation: From Evangelical Movement to Institutionalisation of Reform* (Cambridge, 1995), p. 72.

2   The eight Danish bishoprics were, besides the archbishopric of Lund, those of Roskilde, Odense, Børglum, Aarhus, Viborg, Ribe and Schleswig. The Swedish church consisted of the archbishopric of Uppsala and the bishoprics of Linköping, Skara, Strängnäs, Västerås, Växjö and Åbo in Finland. Apart from the archbishopric of Trondheim, the four Norwegian bishoprics were Bergen, Oslo, Stavanger and Hamar.

3   See H.V. Gregersen, *Reformationen i Sønderjylland* (Aabenraa, 1986), pp. 244–9.

4   See H.F. Rørdam, 'En mærkelig Forordning for Hertugdømmerne om Kristendomsundervisningen', *Kirkehistoriske Samlinger* 3, 5 (1884–6), pp. 153–9.

5   See A. Krarup and J. Lindbæk (eds), *Acta Pontificium Danica, 1316–1536* (Copenhagen, 1913), vol. 6.

6   Within recent Danish Reformation historiography a couple of purely speculative and unconvincing attempts to interpret the Danish Reformation within the traditional Marxist framework of class hostility have appeared. See H. Lundbak, *... Såfremt som vi skulle være deres lydige borgere* (Odense, 1985), and A. Wittendorf, 'Popular Mentalities and the Danish Reformation', in L. Grane and K. Hørby (eds), *The Danish Reformation against Its International Background* (Göttingen, 1990), pp. 211–22.

7   For the diocesan acts, see H.F. Rørdam, 'Forhandlinger paa Roskilde Landemode 1554–1569', *Kirkehistoriske Samlinger*, new series, 2 (1860–2), pp. 441–511.

8   A. Riising and M. Seidelin, *Biskop Hans Mikkelsens dagbøger 1626–1641* (Odense, 1991), p. 42.

9   Ibid., pp. 20, 48.

10 See Troels-Lund, *Dagligt Liv i Norden i det sekstende Århundrede* (Copenhagen, 1969).

11 J.C.V. Johansen, 'Holy Springs and Protestantism in Early Modern Denmark: A Medical Rationale for a Religious Practice', *Medical History* 41 (1997), pp. 59–69.

12 See S. Kjöllerström, *Striden kring kalvinismen i Sverige under Erik XIV* (Lund, 1935), and O.P. Grell, 'Exile and Tolerance', in O.P. Grell and Bob Scribner (eds), *Tolerance and Intolerance in the European Reformation* (Cambridge, 1996), pp. 164–81.

13 See O. Garstein, *Rome and the Counter Reformation in Scandinavia* (vol. 1, Oslo 1963; vol. 2, Copenhagen 1980; vols 3 and 4, Leiden 1992).

FURTHER READING

The best study of the Scandinavian Reformation is O.P. Grell (ed.), *The Scandinavian Reformation: From Evangelical Movement to Institutionalisation of Reform* (Cambridge, 1995), which covers events in the Nordic countries until the mid-seventeenth century. For the Reformation of Iceland, which is not included in this work, see my article in the second volume of the forthcoming *Cambridge History of Scandinavia* (Cambridge, 1999). However, a definitive and detailed study of the Scandinavian Reformation has still to be published.

My two recent articles on Scandinavia, in A. Pettegree (ed.), *The Early Reformation in Europe* (Cambridge, 1992), and Bob Scribner, Roy Porter and Mikuláš Teich (eds), *The Reformation in National Context* (Cambridge, 1994), add supplementary perspectives and detail to the present survey. The detailed studies published in German and English in L.Grane and K. Hørby (eds), *The Danish Reformation against Its International Background* (Forschungen zur Kirchen- und Dogmengeschichte 46; Göttingen, 1990), provide interesting perspectives on the significance of humanism, princes, learning and education, popular reception, ecclesiastical discipline and cities for the Danish Reformation. To this can be added my article 'The City of Malmø and the Danish Reformation', *Archiv für Reformationsgeschichte* 79 (1988), pp. 311–39.

The effect of the Reformation on health care and poor relief in Scandinavia is discussed by E.I. Kouri, E. Ladewig Petersen and T. Riis, in O.P. Grell and A. Cunningham (eds), *Health Care and Poor Relief in Protestant Europe, 1500–1700* (London, 1997). A couple of articles on the fashionable subject of gender and the role of women in the Scandinavian Reformation have been published by G. Jacobsen: 'Nordic Women and the Reformation', in S. Marshall (ed.), *Women in Reformation and Counter-Reformation Europe: Private and Public Worlds* (Bloomington, IN, 1989), and 'The Reformation of the Women II: A Response from a Northern Perspective', in H.R. Guggisberg and G.G. Krodel (eds), *Die Reformation in Deutschland und Europa: Interpretationen und Debatten* (Sonderband Archiv für Reformationsgeschichte; Gütersloh 1993). Despite their titles, these articles are nearly exclusively concerned with Denmark.

ITALY

————◆◆◆————

Bruce Gordon

If we think of Reformation along the lines of events in northern Europe during the sixteenth century, then we search in vain for something comparable in Italy. One leading historian has recently declared the Italian Reformation to have been a 'non-event'. Indeed, not a single city, town or state adopted the Reformation. Yet the peninsula was by no means isolated from the religious tumults of the sixteenth century; Protestant thought made its way south of the Alps and found a receptive audience. The central ideas of the northern reformers, however, formed only one strand of an intricate fabric in which various forms of religious belief and traditions were woven together.

For Luther, Zwingli and (later) Calvin, the True Church was invisible and eternal, but Reformation concerned the external manifestation of the Body of Christ – the parochial church. This not only required the connivance of temporal authorities, whether they were electors of the empire or magistrates of imperial cities, but led to the formulation of enduring concepts of the godly prince and magistrate. In the north, Protestantism made its peace with worldly authority with haste and this had profound consequences for the whole movement. By declaring that good Christians were also good citizens, Protestantism not only sanctified external works but also placed in doubt its central tenets of *sola fide* and *sola scriptura*, as its critics never ceased to declare. Both of these principles were works of the Spirit, but ultimately they were domesticated by the restrictions imposed by a vast array of church ordinances written by Protestant churchmen in the service of their political masters. The issue went deeper: by resisting the attacks of 'spiritualists', those who espoused an unfettered form of religion free from the profane concerns of the state, Protestant reformers revealed the profundity of their indebtedness to older Catholic ideas about questions of doctrine and tradition. Zwingli was not alone among the Protestant reformers in willingly citing mediæval scholastic authors (in his case Duns Scotus) when the occasion demanded it. Those who resisted the accommodation of religion and worldly authority, men like Caspar Schwenkfeld or Melchior Hoffman, were quickly marginalized, labelled radicals or spiritualists.

This tension between spirit and world, which was both the strength of the Protestant message and its greatest stumbling block, was also profoundly felt in Italy. The breathtaking grandeur of the papal courts of the late fifteenth century did not even pretend to mask a world of simony and nepotism. The nervous splendour of Medicean Florence was displayed against the storm clouds of Girolamo Savonarola's thunderous preaching in the Duomo. Famously, Michelangelo in old age commented that when he closed his eyes he could still hear the words of Savonarola. The contrasts of Italian religious life through the early decades of the sixteenth century were wrought by the destructive wars that had plagued the peninsula following the French invasion of 1494. Italy was a corpse torn apart by rival vultures, whose stripping of the bones culminated in the Sack of Rome of 1527. In the nearly forty years of chaos which reigned in Italy between 1494 and 1530 (when Emperor Charles V made peace with Pope Clement VII), popular religious life was dominated by prophetic visions of the Antichrist and the Day of Judgement. Itinerant preachers, holy men and women, ballad singers, as well as regular clergy, interpreted natural phenomena as signs of catastrophe and castigation. Above all, monstrous births were understood to bespeak divine displeasure.[1] Among the educated elite there were also many voices crying out for reform, as the words of Savonarola continued to inspire. Humanist culture gave rise to a generation of men committed to restoring the church to its ancient roots and to using the pedagogical and intellectual advances of the Renaissance to battle ignorance and superstition. While the illnesses of the church in Italy mirrored those in other parts of Europe, the circumstances created by the collapse of Italian Renaissance culture were distinctive.

Although Protestant thought arrived in Italy during the earliest years of the Reformation, it would be wrong to speak of Italian 'Protestantism' before the 1540s. During the 1530s and 1540s the principal exponents of evangelical thought were well rooted within the Catholic church. Bernardino Ochino was General of the Capuchins, Juan de Valdés held a benefice in the diocese of Cuenca and Peter Martyr Vermigli was a member of the Lateran canons. The patrons of these men were senior members of the Roman hierarchy. Although the term 'evangelical' has been much disputed in the scholarship of sixteenth-century Italian religious history, we shall use it here to describe the non-dogmatic, fluid thought which flowered in the period before the Council of Trent.

The traditional historiography of the Reformation in Italy has emphasized the year 1542 as marking the end of the evangelical movement. Without doubt, a year which saw the departure from Italy of Bernardino Ochino (the most sensational event of the period), the departure of Peter Martyr Vermigli (who had been regarded as a possible candidate for a bishopric), the founding of the Roman Inquisition and the death of Cardinal Contarini, has to be regarded as remarkable. As we shall see, however, it was in the period after 1542 that the Reformation in Italy became a public event. Silvana Seidel Menchi has recently proposed a chronology of events that demonstrates not only the enduring character of the Reformation, but its protean nature. She divides the Reformation into four phases: 1518–42, 'The theological call to arms'; 1542–55, 'Spontaneous diffusion'; 1555–71, 'Repression'; and 1571–88, 'Extinction'.[2] By 1559 the Inquisition was putting serious pressure on evangelicals; it was a crime to possess 'heretical' books and the Inquisition was increasingly infiltrating groups thought to hold heterodox beliefs.

PRINTING AND THE REFORMATION IN ITALY

At an early stage the ideas of the northern Reformation had begun to make their way into Italy. In 1525 Huldrych Zwingli, reformer of Zurich, wrote in the preface to his work *Concerning True and False Religion* that he had been petitioned to write a summary of Christian doctrine by brethren in Italy and France. Evidence is sketchy, but men such as Peter Martyr in Naples are said to have read works by Zwingli in Italy before their flight north. In the Swiss city of Chur, the reformer Johannes Commander spoke of how he had been asked by evangelical sympathizers in Italy to supply works of the northern reformers. Similarly, the first works of Luther were published in Venice in 1518. At first these works were generally read by aristocrats. Venice's unique place in Italy enabled an unusual religious environment to develop; there was a swirl of ideas into which northern Protestant texts were added. There was a tradition of religious doubt expressed towards traditional doctrine and Luther's works, replete with criticism of the papacy and the ecclesiastical hierarchy, found a welcome. The evidence of the Venetian Inquisition suggests that during the 1520s and 1530s not one person was charged with making Lutheran statements. It was not until the early 1540s that the Inquisition, which was in the hands of the Franciscans, began to take aim at lay religious attitudes. Before this point the Inquisition was active, but primarily against indolent clerics.

The availability of Protestant books from the north enabled evangelical ideas to take hold across Italy during the 1530s. After Luther was excommunicated in 1518, no openly Protestant book was printed in Italy and therefore, as Rozzo and Seidel Menchi have shown, the publication of evangelical religious literature in Italy took on a clandestine nature.[3] What makes this literature so difficult to identify was that alongside the works of Protestant reformers there was a continuous flow of reform literature that embraced certain, but by no means all, ideas from the north. Most Protestant literature circulating in Italy was brought in from outside the country, though there were sporadic periods of native printing activity. The first sign of covert Protestant printing activity was in Venice, where a collection of dialogues (including two by Luther) was printed in 1525. During the period 1530 to 1560 the printing of Protestant literature was sporadic, with the most active period being between 1540 and 1550, the time of the Regensburg Colloquy and the rise of public support for the evangelical cause. Production was ended in 1560 with the appearance of the first Roman Index of 1559, together with the zeal of the Inquisition.

Silvana Seidel Menchi has shown that ground for Protestant literature was prepared by the work of Erasmus, who was widely read in Italy between 1520 and 1530.[4] It was not only the intellectual elite who were reading the Dutch humanist, but literate artisans and merchants. The closeness of humanism and reform in Italy meant that when Luther's works began to appear they were read in the spirit of Erasmus's books. Luther's thought in the 1530s in Italy was mediated through the work of Erasmus and the two figures were closely identified. This conjunction resulted in the vilification of Erasmus in the eyes of Italian Catholics, who saw him as a heretic, and his works quickly appeared on the Index.

After 1542, when many of the leading Italian evangelicals (men such as Peter Martyr Vermigli, Bernardino Ochino, Celio Secundo Curione, Camillo Renato, Francesco Negri, Giulio della Rovere and Pier Paolo Vergerio) had fled, the bulk of Italian evangelical literature began to flow from the presses of Basle and Geneva. After his flight in 1549, Vergerio became involved with the printer Dolfino Landolfi, who had been at work in Poschiavo in the Grisons since 1547, to produce a flood of polemical works which were widely circulated in the northeast of Italy. The most widely circulated books by Italian authors printed outside Italy were Negri's *Tragedy of Free Will*, Ochino's *Prediche* and *Beneficio di Cristo* (the Benefice of Christ). As befitting their intended use among clandestine groups, the books were often small and hastily printed. Their size allowed them to be easily carried or concealed.

The penetration of Protestant ideas from outside Italy reached its zenith around 1540. The circulation of 'heretical' texts was largely carried out by students, merchants and clergy. Books printed north of the Alps could be in Italy within a month. Until 1535 Luther's works were predominant among Protestant literature available in Italy, but after this date other authors emerged. During the late 1530s and 1540s the Swiss Protestant theologians (including Calvin) overtook the Wittenberg reformer in popularity. An important figure was that of Pietro Perna, a bookseller from Lucca who had emigrated to Basle. Acting as an agent for the Basle printer Oporinus, Perna zealously circulated the writings of the Swiss reformers among the cities of central and northern Italy (Venice, Bologna, Bergamo, Padua, Milan and Lucca). By the middle of the 1540s it was clearly the work of John Calvin which was most significant and from 1541 there was great demand for his *Institutes of the Christian Religion*. Rozzo and Seidel Menchi have written that 'it seems possible to conclude that from around 1540, Italian pressure for religious change was centred around Calvin, especially since as well as his *Institutes*, Bibles with Calvin-inspired commentaries were circulating in vast numbers in Italy, and since influential nobles collaborated with rich merchants in organising trips to Geneva "to bring back barrel-loads of sermons".'[5]

Although there was a continuous supply of Protestant works into Italy, supplementing the small amount of home production, historians have cautioned us not to over-emphasize the role played by books: most of the writings were in Latin, and therefore not very accessible, so the principal means by which these ideas were disseminated was preaching and word of mouth.

We shall return to the popular elements of evangelical religion in Italy, but it is right to attend to those influential circles of churchmen and laity that were primarily responsible for the propagation of evangelical ideas. The men who occupied these circles were known as the *spirituali*, a term used by contemporaries and subsequently adopted by modern scholars. It can be defined as those 'distinguished ladies, humanists and cardinals' drawn, by and large, from the highest levels of Italian society, ecclesiastical and lay, who formed groups to discuss matters relating to theology and the reform of the church. The most important circles were those formed around Gasparo Contarini in Venice, Juan de Valdés in Naples and (later) Reginald Pole in Viterbo. Although these groups retained their separate identities, their members were able to maintain considerable links with each other, through correspondence and also through itinerant preachers like Bernardino Ochino.

As a group, the *spirituali* did not last long, yet their influence was enduring. The Farnese pope, Paul III, elected in 1534, immediately announced his desire for reform and in the following year he promoted a number of the leading *spirituali* (Contarini, Pole and Jacopo Sadoleto) to the cardinalate. In 1536 Paul appointed a distinguished group of prelates and cardinals to draft a report on ecclesiastical reform and again the *spirituali* were well represented, though balanced by hardliners as such Gianpietro Carafa and Girolamo Aleandro. The report of the commission, completed in 1537, was entitled the *Consilium de emendanda ecclesia* and although its recommendations were sound, it was quickly shelved.

CONTARINI AND THE *SPIRITUALI*

Scholars have long recognized that the most important figure of Italian religious reform during the 1530s and early 1540s was the Venetian Gasparo Contarini, a humanist patrician born in 1483. Contarini was closely associated with two other prominent Venetians, Tommaso Giustiniani and Vincenzo Quirini – all of them were searching for spiritual renewal. Whereas Quirini and Giustiniani would find solace in the retreat to the monastic life, Contarini was a man of the world. Following the great humanists of his time, Contarini was profoundly influenced by his reading of Paul, especially Romans. This stirred a critical attitude towards works as the means to salvation. Contarini adhered to the primacy of grace and when Luther's writings began to appear in Italy in the 1520s, he read them with approval. Yet Contarini's beliefs were ultimately more akin to Erasmus than to the Wittenberg reformer; he never denied free will and remained unswervingly loyal to Rome.

Contarini might have spent his life in the diplomatic service of his native Venice had he not been drawn to Rome by the papal curia's desire to respond to the crisis begun by Luther.[6] Contarini was made a cardinal in May 1535 by Paul III, who was concerned to reconcile the institutional church with the spiritual currents swirling around Europe. Contarini travelled to Rome to take up residence in the Vatican and became one of the pope's closest advisers. It was Contarini who proposed the reform commission of 1536, in anticipation of a council to take place in Mantua in 1537. The commission met during the first three months of 1537 and then presented its report to Paul III in early March.

Contarini himself brought the report before the pope and its contents must have raised a few ecclesiastical eyebrows. The commission spared no one in its findings and although the text contained a clear declaration of papal authority, it also declared the incumbents of Peter's See to have been the cause of much of the ruination of the church:

> And your Holiness, taught by the Spirit of God who (as Augustine says) speaks in hearts without the din of words, had rightly acknowledged that

the origin of these evils was due to the fact that some popes, your predecessors, in the words of the Apostle Paul 'having itching ears heaped up to themselves teachers according to their own lusts' (II Timothy 4:3), not that they might learn from them what they should do, but that they might find through the application and cleverness of these teachers a justification for what it pleased them to do. Then it came about, besides the fact that flattery follows all dominion as the shadow does the body and that truth's access to the ears of princes has always been most difficult, that teachers at once appeared who taught that the pope is the lord of all benefices and that therefore, since a lord may sell by right what is his own, it necessarily follows that the pope cannot be guilty of simony. Thus the will of the pope, of whatever kind it may be, is the rule governing his activities and deeds; whence it may be shown without doubt that whatever is pleasing is also permitted.[7]

In contrast to those earlier popes who had allowed error and abuse to destroy the fabric of the church, Paul III was praised in the text for his reforming zeal. Nevertheless, the commission proceeded to enumerate a long list of disfiguring practices within the church: clerical behaviour, abuse of church offices (in particular benefices), pluralism, the decline of the religious orders, pagan tendencies in education and the purchase of absolution by those who commit simony, to give a few examples. About the city of Rome itself, the commission recorded:

Also in this city harlots walk about like matrons or ride on mules, attended in broad daylight by noble members of the cardinals' households and by clerics. In no city do we see this corruption except in this model for all cities. Indeed they even dwell in fine houses. This foul abuse must also be corrected.[8]

In each case the report set forth proposals for the remedying of these ills; for instance, the religious orders:

Another abuse which must be corrected with regard to the religious orders, for many have become so deformed that they are a great scandal to the laity and do grave harm by their example. We think that all conventual orders ought to be done away with, not however that injury be done to anyone, but by prohibiting the admission of novices. Thus they might be quickly abolished without wronging anyone, and good religious could be substituted for them. In fact, we now think that it would be best if all boys who have not been professed were removed from their monasteries.[9]

What distinguished this text from the vast corpus of reform literature produced in the late fifteenth and early sixteenth centuries was its attention to the pastoral context in which the improvements were to be made. The proposals are redolent of the authors' concerns for the renewal of spirituality within the church. The institutions of the church are not merely the external mechanics; they form the Body of

Christ, with offices commissioned by Christ himself, radiating the spirituality that comes from the indwelling of the Holy Spirit. The Body must be cleansed and made 'as beautiful as a dove, at peace with itself'. The reform of the church lay in the reform of its hierarchy. Law, office and spirituality were envisaged as a seamless robe. It was this understanding of the church and its nature that rendered impossible any acceptance of Protestant views.

The commission had proposed a radical reform plan for the church and Contarini had emerged as the leading spokesman for change. Vittoria Colonna, patroness of Juan de Valdés, wrote to Contarini that he had sustained the bark of Peter by his labours and that '[the Church] is secure from shipwreck, and Your Excellency holds the tiller'.[10]

The reception accorded the *Consilium* brought into relief the forces within the Catholic church arrayed against reform. The college of cardinals was riven by the report, with a conservative majority concerned to maintain the status quo. Most cardinals did not want radical change; they understood all too well that they had a great deal to lose if the reforms were implemented. It was evident to all that the pope could not bring about reform, even if he had wanted to, simply by decree. Powerful cardinals within the Vatican used their connections to frustrate the work of the commission. Their opposition, however, was not entirely venal; some had predicted that the *Consilium* would be grist for the Protestant mill and they were correct. Martin Luther produced a German translation of the *Consilium* and added a hostile gloss; the title page has a woodcut of three cardinals trying to sweep the church with foxtails. Luther portrayed Contarini and his colleagues as charlatans attempting to dupe the Christian people with their sham reforms.

The *Consilium* may not have been implemented in the manner hoped for by its authors, but we should see it as one of the most important pieces of Catholic reform literature to appear after the outbreak of the Reformation. The institutional reforms outlined in the *Consilium* anticipated the work of the Council of Trent. The crucial difference, however, was that ten years after the *Consilium*, the Tridentine fathers would not discuss papal authority or the power of the cardinals, but would begin their reforms with detailed doctrinal debates.

Under Paul III the *spirituali* became prominent in the papal curia, but, as the *Consilium* of 1537 demonstrated, their influence was constrained. As John Martin has written, 'in the increasingly courtly climate of sixteenth-century Italy, connections and patronage still counted for more than commitment and piety in the elevation of a man to the office of cardinal.'[11]

Contarini represented a line of reform thought which sought to align the best of Protestant thought with a zeal for restoring the Catholic hierarchy through cleansing its offices. Without doubt there was a considerable degree of overlap with Protestant writers on certain ideas; the shared influence of Paul and St Augustine was evident in discussions on many points. Contarini, like Erasmus, believed passionately in maintaining the unity of the church and he eschewed questions of doctrinal exactitude that could divide. Protestants, he was in no doubt, were heretics, but they were not beyond the pale; they could be reconciled. Such a view was not shared by his contemporary Gianpietro Carafa, who made it clear that whilst he agreed with the other authors of the *Consilium* that abuses and failings within the church were a major stumbling block, the purgation of which the commission wrote would only take place once heretics had been extirpated.

The conflict between the *spirituali* and the more hardline members of the papal curia was softened by the fact that there was no doctrinal orthodoxy in the Catholic church before the Council of Trent. There was a great deal of latitude in how concepts such as grace, works and faith were interpreted. With the dissolution of the scholastic synthesis of Thomas Aquinas, rival schools of theology had existed within the Catholic church and much of the language of theology was fairly elastic, permitting a spectrum of interpretations. Luther's error for many within the Catholic church lay in his rejection of papal authority, rather than the direction of his theology. As long as one upheld the authority of the hierarchy, there was room to differ on theological points.

The ambiguous nature of religious language in the sixteenth century encouraged the *spirituali* to pursue their goal of revitalizing the church through fostering inward spirituality and by seeking accord with Protestants. Their major contribution to the first was through their patronage of important religious thinkers in the second half of the 1530s. These included men like Juan de Valdés, Bernardino Ochino and Peter Martyr Vermigli. These circles and the writings that emerged from them will be discussed later.

The hopes of the *spirituali* for healing the breach between Rome and the Lutherans lay with the Imperial Diet of Regensburg in 1541. Emperor Charles V had placed considerable pressure on the papacy to make peace with German Protestants and Paul III gave his official support to the negotiations held in the city. Cardinal Contarini was appointed papal legate to the colloquy and many hoped that his theological position on justification would help bring the two sides together. On the issue of justification a formula was agreed, though it was not to the liking of many on both sides. The stumbling block proved to be the issue of transubstantiation and the talks broke down.

It was in 1541 that Contarini wrote his *Epistola de iustificatione*, a lucid articulation of his own beliefs. Essentially Contarini wanted to demonstrate that the theory of double justification worked out at Regensburg was consonant with Catholic theology.[12] Contarini believed that faith was essential to salvation and in his explanation he drew near to Luther's conception of faith as trust and hope in God's mercy. Good works are not essential to salvation, but rather proof that one is saved. As Elizabeth Gleason has written: 'Contarini undoubtedly had goodwill and sympathy for Lutheran theology, but ... he was too unsystematic, thus unable to give his opinions cogency and clarity or to organize them into a coherent theological argument.'[13] Contarini was not a trained theologian and although his humanism led him to reject the intellectual structures of scholastic theology, what replaced it was a deeply felt, non-dogmatic spirituality which was ultimately drawn from a hybrid of sources.

The *spirituali* had staked their hopes on Regensburg as the means to heal the divide within the church and they had failed. The tide had turned. In the wake of Regensburg, the Roman Congregation of the Holy Office was founded (the Roman Inquisition) on 21 July 1541. The Roman Inquisition, which theoretically had jurisdiction over all of Christendom though in practice was limited to Italian lands, signalled that a new initiative against doctrinal heresy was underway. The vision of reconciliation was abandoned. Just over a month later, Contarini died, bringing to an end hopes of bringing Protestants back into the fold. This was not, however, the end of the *spirituali*; they would suffer another serious reverse in 1547 with the Tridentine decree on justification, but scholars suggest that men imbued with the views of the *spirituali* remained until around 1565.

The supporters of the *spirituali* found themselves under great pressure; the evangelical cause appeared to have been defeated by those who believed that doctrinal clarification was the only path to restoring the true Catholic church. Nevertheless, there were still important figures in influential positions who laboured to retain the reforming spirit. Gian Matteo Giberti (1495–1543) belonged to the same circle of reformers as Contarini and Carafa, and as Bishop of Verona he sought to implement many of the pastoral and spiritual qualities contained in the *Consilium*. He was passionately devoted to being a worthy bishop and he served the diocese of Verona (not least by actually residing in it) from 1524 until his death. He was a humanist with an impressive library replete with Greek texts; he installed a printing press and was a patron of scholars and poets. He established a society for the care of the poor and he was rigorous in visiting his parishes in a root-and-branch effort to reinvigorate his diocese. His work was directed towards practical reforms and his efforts demonstrated that the reforming spirit that animated the *spirituali* did make its way down to the ground level. Giberti wrote a series of ordinances and guidelines concerning the religious life and discipline in his diocese, and these were collectively printed as his *Constitutions* in 1542. The work received the approval of Paul III. The flavour of Giberti's work is found in the following admonition concerning preaching:

> We ask all religious, after they have received permission from us to preach in the city and our diocese, by the compassion of our Lord Jesus Christ to preach and proclaim His Gospel sincerely to the people and to follow in His footsteps when he taught the Apostles 'Preach the Gospel to every creature' and again 'Teach all nations to observe whatever I have commanded you'. Let them put their reliance in the interpretations of the holy doctors of the Church of old, as has also been decreed in the Lateran Council under pain of excommunication. Let them avoid in those holy sermons citations of profane laws not at all necessary, the superfluous appeal to the authority of poets, the advancing of subtle themes very often worthless. Let them be ever mindful that he who teaches and instructs uneducated minds ought to be able to adapt himself to the intelligence of those of his audience. Let them instruct the people to observe the precepts of God so that they may firmly keep the faith and obey the commands of God and the Church. Nor let them deviate from the decrees and ordinances of the same Church.[14]

For men such as Giberti, Contarini and Reginald Pole the question was how to prevent a spontaneous Reformation from breaking out; a fissure which they knew would prove disastrous. Pole and Contarini, through their patronage of men like Ochino and Vermigli, were largely responsible for the widespread evangelical preaching and now, in 1541, they sought to control it. Against the background of the ferment stirring in Modena, Pole and Contarini sought a formula which made room for their central belief – that faith was central to salvation – whilst preserving order (see the discussion of Modena below). The difficulty seemed to rest on two contradictory principles: a notion of salvation clearly articulated by Paul in his letter to the Romans, and loyalty to a church whose theology had a different foundation. Through 1541 and the summer of 1542, before Contarini's untimely death, he and Cardinal Pole sought to balance these deeply held convictions.

The *spirituali* found themselves not only between the Catholic doctrine of atonement and the evangelical position of justification by faith alone, but between two warring parties: Protestants and the Papal curia. On the one hand, Protestants had broken with the Roman church precisely because, in their eyes, *sola fide* precluded the Catholic sacramental system; on the other hand, the members of the curia rejected *sola fide* out of court as a pernicious attack on the authority of the church. For both Pole and Contarini, embracing the central concept of Lutheranism (a term which was used loosely in Italy) was tempered by obedience to the church. As Dermot Fenlon has written:

> What kept [Contarini] secure in the faith to which he adhered was his confidence that, beyond theology and the resources of human ingenuity, there lay the indefectibly established authority of the Church. Some might assert the doctrine of salvation by works alone, others presumptuously abandon the Church: Pole and he must submit to the Church's doctrine. Let them steer securely through Scylla and Charybdis, 'not abandoning the doctrine of the Church, but believing in it more than in our wits'.[15]

Cardinal Pole proposed to his preachers in the summer of 1542 that they declare justification by faith alone, eliminate scholastic language from their sermons and preach the simple gospel whilst affirming all that the church believed. The cardinal could see the storm clouds gathering and there was a great deal of suspicion of the religious circles that had sprung up across Italy.

JUAN DE VALDÉS

Crucial to the understanding of what Italian evangelical thought entailed is the shadowy figure of Juan de Valdés (*c*.1510–41). Having fled his native Spain, he settled first in Rome and then, from 1535, in Naples. Valdés enjoyed much patronage in Naples, being made inspector of fortifications by Pedro de Toledo. More importantly, he established a circle containing prominent noblewomen such as Giulia Gonzaga and Vittoria Colonna, as well as some leading religious figures, Bernardino Ochino and Peter Martyr Vermigli. It is extremely difficult to put together a coherent picture of the sources of Valdés' thought; with the exception of one Erasmian dialogue printed in 1529, all of his writings were published posthumously. The time in Naples was fecund and Valdés wrote a series of works: *Christian Alphabet* (1537), *Commentary on First Book of Psalms* (1519–21), *Commentary on Romans* (1538), *Commentary on First Corinthians* (1539), *CX Divine Considerations* (1540) and a *Commentary on St Matthew* (1541). Despite the volume of extant work, the nature of Valdés' thought has continued to perplex historians. Valdés supported the idea of justification by faith, but not the Reformation cause. He attacked the reformers for breaking the unity of the church, yet he denounced the external ceremonies of the Roman Catholic church. The ambiguity of his faith is represented in the diverging careers of his supporters. Marcantonio Flaminio (who had been a member of the Divine Oratory) was later offered the secretaryship of the Council of Trent, while Peter Martyr and Bernardino Ochino chose exile and went to dwell among the northern Protestant churches.

Recent scholarship has argued for the importance of Luther's influence on Valdés. Carlos Gilly has shown that as early as 1529 Valdés made extensive use of two of Luther's catechetical works written in 1518 and 1520. The traditional argument that Valdés was influenced by Erasmus has been weakened by evidence which demonstrates that Valdés' work written whilst still in Spain has only a superficial Erasmian quality, intended to deflect the eye of the Inquisition. Gilly has further argued that Valdés continued to be influenced by Luther's work after his arrival in Italy. Important themes from Luther which scholars have found in Valdés include the use of the terms *beneficium Christi* and *beneficium Dei*, and the link between Christ's crucifixion and the believer's incorporation in Christ. It has also been shown that Valdés was aware of Luther's important work on the Psalms, *Dicta super Psalterium* and *Operationes in Psalmos*. Massimo Firpo, who is currently engaged in a study of the Valdesian circle, has recently stated that the real significance of Valdés' work was his 'creative synthesis of Erasmianism, *alumbradismo* and Lutheranism.'

The essence of Valdés' thought lay in his emphasis on direct revelation and the role of the Spirit. The individual is illuminated by the Spirit and requires, therefore, no material aid; even scripture is seen as auxiliary to the Spirit. His placing of the Spirit over all else and indifference to the outward forms of the church meant that Valdés' writings were hardly more digestible for Protestants than they were for Catholics. Many believed that Bernardino Ochino was the public face of Valdés, though this was not entirely fair to Ochino, and Theodore Beza in Geneva blamed Valdés for Ochino's heretical views. The northern reformers saw in Valdés the same dangerous spiritualism they had been battling among their own. There can be no doubt, however, that the influence of Valdés can be seen in those Italian evangelicals who fled north to Switzerland but found they could not stomach the ecclesiology or doctrinal formulations of the established Protestant churches there.

At the conclusion of his *Christian Alphabet*, a dialogue with the patrician Giulia Gonzaga concerning her scruples about her faith, Valdés speaks of Christian perfection:

Now, turning to the subject, I wish, signora, that you set before the view of your soul the idea of Christian perfection, according to what we have discussed, and that you set yourself to be enamoured of it, and when enamoured of it, you will not satisfy yourself until you have reached very near to it; and consider that you will then be near it when you shall know in truth that your heart is not inclined to love anything out of God, nor your tongue taste sweetness in naming any other name than that of God, and this only when naming it for his glory. And when you shall feel that you are not inclined to perform anything that may not be conformable to the will of God; and when you shall find your mind most obedient and submissive to your superiors, and far removed from all ire and all revenge and rancour, filled with peace and humility; and as far removed from all sensual vice that you will not find in it a thought that is not chaste; and so poor in spirit, that you would incline your desire to nothing more than to preserve what it has; and so fervent in love toward your neighbour that you would not only never speak to his prejudice, but if you hear others speak so, you excuse and exculpate him as much as possible; by all this I wish to say, that when you shall feel yourself as dead to the outward affections and appetites as to the interior, that neither the estimation of the world exalts you nor its dishonour abases you, that neither anger overrules you nor envy molests, not less the flesh disturbs you – then well and truly may you believe that you are indeed near to Christian perfection.[16]

The papal pronotary Pietro Carnesecchi, who was deeply influenced by Valdés, left this account of the man:

At Naples, however, the friendship grew to be a spiritual one, for I found him entirely given up to the Spirit, and wholly intent on the study of Scripture. [Carnesecchi added that his view of Valdés would not have been so exalted] had I not observed what a high place he occupied in the eyes of Fra Bernardino Ochino, who then was preaching, to the admiration of everybody, at Naples, and who professed to receive the themes of many of his sermons from Valdés, from whom he used to get a note on the evening preceding the morning on which he was to ascend the pulpit.[17]

Carnesecchi, the noblewoman Giulia Gonzaga and the head of the Capuchins, Ochino, were but a few of the prominent people who came within Valdés' circle: others included Peter Martyr Vermigli, Pier Paulo Vergerio (Bishop of Capo d'Istria and papal nuncio), the poet Marcantonio Flaminio, the Duchess of Amalfi Constanza d'Avalos and Vittoria Colonna, Marquise of Pescara. When Valdés died in 1541 the group was left rudderless. Like Contarini and Pole, they could sense the winds of change. Flaminio and Carnesecchi took up residence in the house of Cardinal Pole in September 1541. This became the Viterbo circle, consisting of Flaminio, Vittoria Colonna (who placed herself under Pole's spiritual guidance), Carnesecchi, the Venetian merchant Donato Rullo, Vittore Soranzo and Vergerio. Pole, along with Contarini and Morone, commissioned Martyr and Ochino as their preachers, and their relationship with these men remained close until Ochino's sensational flight from Italy in August 1542, following the death of Contarini.

BENEFICIO DI CRISTO (THE BENEFICE OF CHRIST)

The encroachments of the Roman Inquisition upon those who favoured reform were very real, and both Peter Martyr and Bernardino Ochino could have expected to end their days in flames had they not chosen exile. Nevertheless, evangelical ideas continued to exercise a hold on the minds and hearts of laity and clergy alike in Italy. The clearest evidence for this was the publication in Venice in 1543 of an anonymous book *Beneficio di Cristo*. When the work appeared it was an immediate success; Vergerio, probably with exaggeration, wrote that 40,000 copies had been sold. Nevertheless, the work was well received by many leading churchmen: Giovanni Morone, Bishop of Modena, found the *Beneficio* 'very spiritual' and promoted its sale in his diocese. Cardinal Cortese, who had been sent to report on heretical activities in Modena, wrote colourfully that 'when I dress in the morning, I cannot cloak myself in anything better than this *Beneficio di Cristo*'. Cardinal Pole and the Viterbo circle promoted the circulation of the book, while Marcello Cervini (the future Pope Marcellus II) wrote in 1544 after he had examined the text that he had found 'many good things and many bad things'. What displeased Cervini was the insufficient treatment, from a Catholic viewpoint, of the vexatious issue of justification. Cervini, who worked for the Roman Inquisition, did not, however, believe that the book should simply be banned, but that those found in possession of the text should be admonished and the 'dubious, subtle and overly confusing things' in the text should be carefully explained in order to prevent others from falling into error.[18] The book was eventually banned, placed on the first Venetian Index of 1549 and publicly burnt in Naples. The Inquisition was thought to have been so effective in eradicating the text that, until a copy was found in 1843 in Cambridge, the book was thought to have vanished.

There has been a good deal of ink spilt considering the authorship of this important text, but there is now a scholarly consensus that it was initially the work of a Benedictine, Don Benedetto, and then revised by Flaminio. Equally contentious have been the debates over the *Beneficio*'s theological nature. Clearly the text was intended as a spiritual guide, to lay out the road to salvation. Its central theme is the remission of sins as a gift, or benefit, received on account of Christ's passion. There is no place for works in obtaining salvation and each person is enjoined to the imitation of Christ.

In many ways the *Beneficio di Cristo* was the mirror of the evangelical movement in Italy. The work is discursive and rather unstructured, a patchwork of Italian and foreign (mostly northern Protestant) thought. Scholars have detected the influence of the Greek fathers, Benedictine spirituality, Juan de Valdés, as well as Luther, Melanchthon and Calvin, portions of whose *Institutes of the Christian Religion* appear verbatim in the *Beneficio*. The manner in which these sources have been employed was idiosyncratic, the authors have woven together the thought of various writers and traditions in a manner which suited their purposes, and by modern standards this resulted in a less than absolute fidelity to the original text. We may never know exactly how the text came to acquire its present form, but it was certainly a product of the friendship between Don Benedetto and Marcantonio Flaminio. As Kenneth Austin has written,

Italian evangelism was a movement characterized more by personal bonds of friendship between individuals who shared similar religious outlooks. Of course, some figures achieved greater prominence, or could command greater respect, than others, but it would be incorrect to view these Italian circles of reform as composed of leaders and followers.[19]

The first four chapters of the *Beneficio* are concerned with justification by faith alone and the rejection of the place of good works. Such works have their place in the lives of those who have been justified by the grace of God. Works are the fruit of faith. The fifth chapter is a meditation on the need for Christians to rejoice in suffering humiliation and persecution at the hands of false Christians. Against this the faithful are exhorted to follow the example of Christ, and the weapons at their disposal are prayer, frequent communion, the recollection of baptism and an awareness of predestination. The eucharist gives the soul of each Christian the assurance of salvation, it is the seal of redemption. It was the passages on the eucharist which had so moved Morone.

The *Beneficio di Cristo* was an important development in the Italian Reformation; it was the first coherent articulation of the evangelical ideas circulating on the peninsula and it reflected the hybrid nature of those beliefs. Its central concern was with justification, the very issue which animated supporters and foes of the evangelical movement. The reaction of Marcello Cervini, a staunch supporter of the Roman hierarchy, suggests that the *Beneficio di Cristo* captured something of the attitudes prevalent among Christians of all stripes in Italy, a passionate desire to fire the inner spirituality of the church and to restore pastoral care. While there was fundamental division on crucial theological matters, we can, more broadly speaking, identify a shared sense of the urgency of reform and a yearning to embrace the message of the Bible. This consensus had its roots in the apocalyptic spirituality of the fifteenth century and in the intellectual and spiritual developments of the Renaissance.

EVANGELICAL ACTION

After the collapse of Regensburg in 1541 the situation in the Italian cities was extremely volatile and evangelical proponents were becoming increasingly vocal. Bishop Giovanni Morone faced especially strong opposition in his diocese of Modena, where there emerged a group of reformers known as the *accademia*, a circle of humanist scholars fluent in Greek and Latin who were deeply impressed by evangelical teachings. This circle demanded that better interpretations of scripture, less dependent upon scholastic thought, be made available. Although the group remained in the shadows, it was widely believed that it harboured Lutheran sympathies. In the light of day, however, preachers expounded evangelical doctrines and were 'pitted against one another in an attempt to gain followers'.[20] The situation was spiralling out of control and the Governor of Modena, Batistino Strozzi, had to supplicate the duke to restore order. Morone, who had been an absentee bishop, returned in May 1542 and wrote:

Here I have found things infinitely afflicting me, giving me no rest, knowing the dangers and being uncertain, yet not knowing how to solve this problem for the salvation of this flock, which I wish with my blood that I could hand over to Christ. ... I am inflamed by shame, hearing in every place I've been and being advised from every place, that this city is Lutheran.[21]

Paul III was so concerned that he sent Gregorio Cortese to Modena on 10 December 1541 to report on the situation. The pope wrote:

Having the confidence in your uprightness, piety and learning, We enjoin upon you, with your ability, as much as possible to investigate whether in your native city of Modena, there are Lutheran or other heresies. If you find that something of this nature is cropping up in that place, write to us concerning both the matter and your own advice in regard to it, so that we ourselves may be able to make provisions from on high.[22]

Cortese's mission proved extremely difficult, as the members of the Academy were suspicious that they were being lured into an admission of heresy. Through emollient diplomacy Cortese arrived at a resolution whereby the whole city (the Academy, leading clergy and Bishop Morone himself) signed a confession of faith, which was a catechism written by Contarini in June 1542. By the first few days of September all those who had resisted Morone had signed the catechism, but this by no means brought the troubles to an end. The *accademici* became Nicodemites, disguising their real views, and later they assisted in the spread of popular evangelical activity by drawing in artisans. The group survived until finally broken up in the 1560s.

Throughout central and northern Italy evangelical ideas spread through towns and cities, cutting across social classes. In Modena, Siena, Lucca and (later) in Venice, popular movements took shape, inspired by the preaching and writings of men such as Bernadino Ochino and Peter Martyr Vermigli. In Siena, famine and social tension fanned the flames of religious dissent as rival groups of preachers stirred the people with sermons calling for repentance and criticizing ecclesiastical and bourgeois wealth. The turbulent situation was exacerbated by the evangelizing efforts of Lelio Sozzini and Basilio Guerrieri in the mid- to late 1540s. Lucca was the city of Peter Martyr Vermigli and under his influence significant acts of defiance took place: a Zwinglian eucharist was celebrated in the monastery of St Agostino; another Lateran canon openly declared his doubts about papal authority and there were rumours of lay eucharistic services.[23]

A series of local studies has revealed the breadth and depth of Italian evangelical culture in the first half of the sixteenth century. John Martin, in his book on Venice, has shown that there was an active evangelical culture in the city centred on the workplace, the tavern and urban festivities – all sites and occasions which made possible the dissemination of religious ideas by word of mouth. Inquisition records from 1542–55 provide evidence of the existence of over forty groups in northern and central Italy working openly for the propagation of Protestant views. These groups were almost exclusively urban and artisans predominated. It was also during this period that more radical trends became evident.

In Venice, Anabaptist and anti-Trinitarian groups sprang up. Unlike the *spirituali* of the 1530s and 1540s, who had envisaged moderate reform of the church, these people appropriated aspects of evangelical thought which, combined with their own studies of scripture, they endeavoured to make their own. Radical groups spread across northern Italy as northern Anabaptist ideas were brought south from the Grisons by a shadowy missionary named Tiziano, who arrived in 1549. The ideas brought by Tiziano became mixed with views propagated by the Anabaptist leader Girolamo Busale. Busale's story is fascinating. A member of the Valdés circle, he too drifted after the Spaniard's death in 1541. He was of Jewish extraction and he joined up with another Spaniard, Juan de Villafranca, who may also have had a Jewish background. The two men were talented humanist textual scholars and they employed the techniques of Valla and Erasmus. The ends to which they employed them, however, were very radical. The conclusions at which they arrived resulted in the dismissal of almost all Christian doctrine, including the idea that Christ is the Son of God. Under the leadership of these men, Venetian Anabaptism drew upon humanist culture and evangelical ideas, patching together different teachings to formulate its own view of Christianity. John Martin has written:

> what mattered to them to them fundamentally were the ethical dimensions of their religious convictions. In Jesus, who was the son of Joseph, they saw not a mediator (as both Catholic and the Protestant churches portrayed him) but a teacher; like other Anabaptists, they placed special emphasis on Jesus' Sermon on the Mount as the basis for a Christian life. Ultimately, it seems, this popular anti-Trinitarianism was a way of making Jesus their own. It was a popular Christology, moreover, that could lead the Anabaptists to an extreme identification with Jesus himself.[24]

In the decade following the death of Contarini in 1542 there were a variety of religious currents flowing through Venice, of which the evangelical, with its connections with northern Protestant thought, was the strongest. Anabaptist and millenarian groups, however, were also in evidence and there was considerable public discussion of theological ideas. These debates were not only about justification by faith, the issue that would dominate the early phase of the Reformation in Italy, but about the figure of Jesus and the nature of redemption.[25]

Through the 1540s and later there is ample evidence for crypto-Protestant activity in Italy. The conventicles in Venice continued to thrive, led by jewellers, tailors and barbers in discussions of theological questions. In Padua, Siena, Lucca, Vicenza and Modena, scholars have found evidence of evangelical groups. They met in private, holding study sessions, prayer meetings and conversations hidden from the authorities. This form of behaviour became known as Nicodemism – the dissimulation of Protestant beliefs alongside outward conformity with Catholic rites. While an able defence against the growing power of the Inquisition in Italy, Nicodemism meant that the conventicles which were spread across Italy never developed into churches.

By 1560 Italian evangelicals had withdrawn from the streets and churches (where in the 1540s and 1550s they had professed their beliefs) to conventicles which were increasingly oriented towards Calvin's Geneva in their theology. It has also been shown that the movement became more political as Italian Protestants followed with eager anticipation the fate of the Huguenots in the French Wars of Religion.[26] By the 1570s the movement was exhausted. The Inquisition and the vigour of the post-Tridentine Catholic church had choked the life out of the Protestants in Italy. The culture in which they were living was now hostile on all social levels. Many of the Protestants had already left for Geneva, where at its height the exile community numbered about 1,000 souls. Italians would continue to play an important role in the development of European Protestantism, but no longer in their homeland.

ACKNOWLEDGEMENT

My thanks to Mark Taplin for his helpful comments on a draft of this article.

NOTES

1 See the important book, Ottavia Niccoli, *Prophecy and People in Renaissance Italy*, trans. Lydia G. Cochrane (Princeton, 1990).
2 Silvana Seidel Menchi, 'Italy', in Bob Scribner, Roy Porter and Mikuláš Teich (eds), *The Reformation in National Context* (Cambridge, 1994), pp. 181–201.
3 Ugo Rozzo and Silvana Seidel Menchi, 'The Book and the Reformation in Italy', in Jean-François Gilmont (ed.), *The Reformation and the Book*, trans. Karin Maag (St Andrews Studies in Reformation History; Aldershot, 1998), p. 321.
4 Silvana Seidel Menchi, *Erasmus als Ketzer: Reformation und Inquisition im Italien des 16. Jahrhunderts* (Leiden, 1992), pp. 79–83.
5 Rozzo and Seidel Menchi, 'The Book and the Reformation in Italy', pp. 342–3.
6 John Martin, *Venice's Hidden Enemies: Italian Heretics in a Renaissance City* (Berkeley and Los Angeles, 1993), p. 37.
7 Quoted from John C. Olin, *The Catholic Reformation: Savonarola to Ignatius Loyola* (New York, 1992), p. 186–7.
8 Ibid., p. 196.
9 Ibid., p. 193.
10 Quoted from Elizabeth Gleason, *Gasparo Contarini: Venice, Rome and Reform* (Berkeley and Los Angeles, 1993), p. 149.
11 Martin, *Venice's Hidden Enemies*, p. 39.
12 See Gleason, *Gasparo Contarini*, pp. 228–35.
13 Ibid., p. 232.
14 Olin, *Catholic Reformation*, p. 146.
15 Dermot Fenlon, *Heresy and Obedience in Tridentine Italy: Cardinal Pole and the Counter Reformation* (Cambridge, 1972), p. 65.
16 Quoted from George Hunston Williams and Angel M. Mergal (eds), *Spiritual and Anabaptist Writers* (Philadelphia, 1957), p. 388.
17 Ibid., p. 304.
18 William V. Hudon, *Marcello Cervini and Ecclesiastical Government in Tridentine Italy* (Dekalb, 1992), p. 119.
19 Kenneth Austin, 'The *Beneficio di Cristo* and the Italian *Spirituali*: The Life of a Text in Evangelical Circles' (unpublished honours dissertation; St Andrews, 1997), p. 55.

20 Francesco C. Cesareo, *Humanism and Catholic Reform: The Life and Work of Gregorio Cortese (1483–1548)* (New York, 1990), p. 126.
21 Ibid., p. 127.
22 Op. cit.
23 Euan Cameron, 'Italy', in Andrew Pettegree (ed.), *The Early Reformation in Europe* (Cambridge, 1992), pp. 202–3.
24 Martin, *Venice's Hidden Enemies*, p. 111.
25 Ibid., p. 121.
26 Seidel Menchi, 'Italy', pp. 193–4.

FURTHER READING

The literature in English has greatly expanded in the last decade. Two excellent survey essays are Euan Cameron, 'Italy', in Andrew Pettegree (ed.), *The Early Reformation in Europe* (Cambridge, 1992), pp. 188–214, and Silvana Seidel Menchi, 'Italy', in Bob Scribner, Roy Porter and Mikuláš Teich (eds), *The Reformation in National Context* (Cambridge, 1994), pp. 181–201. The historiography of the period is well covered in Anne Jacobson Schutte, 'Periodization of Sixteenth-Century Italian Religious History', *Journal of Modern History* 61 (1989), pp. 269–82. As background it would be useful to read the excellent Denys Hay, *The Church in Italy in the Fifteenth Century* (Cambridge, 1977). On popular religious culture in Italy at the beginning of the sixteenth century, Ottavia Niccoli, *Prophecy and People in Renaissance Italy*, trans. Lydia G. Cochrane (Princeton, 1990). On books and printing, see Paul F. Grendler's *The Roman Inquisition and the Venetian Press, 1540–1605* (Princeton, 1977) and his 'The Circulation of Protestant Books in Italy', in Joseph C. McLelland (ed.), *Peter Martyr Vermigli and Italian Reform* (Waterloo, Ont., 1980), pp. 5–16; Ugo Rozzo and Silvana Seidel Menchi, 'The Book and the Reformation in Italy', in Jean-François Gilmont (ed.), *The Reformation and the Book*, trans. Karin Maag (St Andrews Studies in Reformation History; Aldershot, 1998), pp. 319–67; Anne Jacobson Schutte, *Printed Italian Vernacular Books, 1450–1550: A Finding List* (Geneva, 1983). On the reception of Reformation ideas, see Elizabeth Gleason, 'Sixteenth-Century Italian Interpretations of Luther', *Archiv für Reformationsgeschichte* 60 (1969), pp. 160–73. On the *spirituali* there is a rich literature: Elizabeth Gleason, *Gasparo Contarini: Venice, Rome and Reform* (Berkeley and Los Angeles, 1993); Dermot Fenlon, *Heresy and Obedience in Tridentine Italy: Cardinal Pole and the Counter Reformation* (Cambridge, 1972); Peter Matheson, *Cardinal Contarini at Regensburg* (Oxford, 1972); William V. Hudon, *Marcello Cervini and Ecclesiastical Government in Tridentine Italy* (Dekalb, 1992); Francesco C. Cesareo, *Humanism and Catholic Reform: The Life and Work of Gregorio Cortese*, and Anne Jacobson Schutte, *Pier Paolo Vergerio: The Making of an Italian Reformer* (Geneva, 1977); also Carol Maddison, *Marcantonio Flaminio: Poet, Humanist and Reformer* (London, 1965). There is also a growing literature on the principal evangelical figures: Massimo Firpo, 'The Italian Reformation and Juan de Valdés', *Sixteenth Century Journal* 27 (1996), pp. 353–64, and Jose C. Nieto, *Juan de Valdés and the Origins of the Spanish and Italian Reformation* (Geneva, 1970). On Ochino, the only work in English remains Karl Benrath, *Bernardino Ochino of Siena: A Contribution towards the History of the Reformation*, trans. Helen Zimmern (London, 1876). Some of Ochino's work has been made available in Rita Belladona, *Bernardino Ochino: Seven Dialogues* (Toronto, 1988). On Peter Martyr Vermigli there has been much recent interest: Philip McNair, *Peter Martyr in Italy: An Anatomy of Apostasy* (Oxford, 1967); Joseph C. McLelland and G.E. Duffield, *The Life, Early Letters and Eucharistic Writings of Peter Martyr* (Oxford, 1988). There is an ongoing project dedicated to the translation of Martyr's works into English. On *Beneficio di Cristo* (the Benefice of Christ), see Barry Collett, *Italian Benedictine Scholars and the Reformation: The Congregation of Santa Giustina of Padua* (Oxford, 1985). Important work on the social context of religious movements has been published by John Martin. See John J. Martin's *Venice's Hidden Enemies: Italian Heretics in a Renaissance City* (Berkeley and Los Angeles, 1993), his 'Salvation and Society in Sixteenth-Century Venice: Popular Evangelism in a

Renaissance City', *Journal of Modern History* 60 (1988), pp. 593–610, and his 'Popular Culture and the Shaping of Popular Heresy in Renaissance Venice', in Stephen Haliczer (ed.) *Inquisition and Society in Early Modern Europe*, pp. 115–28.

SPAIN

———◆◆◆———

David Coleman

From the time of the conquest of the Philippine archipelago in 1564–5, Spanish King Philip II (reigned 1556–98) ruled the world's first 'empire upon which the sun never set'. With domains stretching from the western Pacific to the tip of South America to the Netherlands and Italy, Philip was (in the words of one contemporary English observer) 'the most potent monarch in Christendome'[1] and the linchpin of European power politics. During the reigns of Philip and his predecessor and father, Holy Roman Emperor Charles V (also King of Spain as Charles I, 1516–56), Spain became Europe's great military superpower.

Although at the centre of European political and military history during this period, Spain remained on the periphery of one of sixteenth-century Europe's most consequential cultural and religious developments: the Protestant Reformation. Unlike most of its western and central European neighbours, Spain in the sixteenth century experienced no sustained and lasting Protestant movement.

This does not mean, however, that Reformation-era religious controversy by-passed Spain entirely. In 1557–8, for instance, officials of the Spanish Inquisition discovered and arrested dozens of members of what they unequivocally called conventicles of 'Lutherans' centred in the cities of Seville and Valladolid. Whether or not these groups constituted a genuine Spanish expression of Protestantism has long been a matter of great debate among historians. Protestant or not, the presence of dissenting groups in this bastion of Catholic orthodoxy aroused great public turmoil and controversy. Following a series of dramatic public spectacles called *autos-da-fé* held in Valladolid and Seville between 1559 and 1562, the inquisitors handed many of the leaders of these evangelical conventicles over to secular authorities to be put to death. In the wake of the Inquisition's crackdown in the late 1550s and 1560s, open religious heterodoxy largely vanished from the Spanish landscape.

Historians have offered a variety of explanations for Protestantism's failure to make significant inroads in Spain. One common line of argument asserts that Protestant reform was wholly unnecessary in sixteenth-century Spain. Proponents of this thesis argue that fervent popular spirituality combined with institutional reforms initiated by exemplary Spanish clergymen combined to create in Spain a vibrant and dynamic Catholicism that was impervious to the growth of Protestant heresy.

Scholars of this opinion typically contend that the Seville and Valladolid heretics were in fact not Protestants at all, but rather simply energetic Erasmians who sought spiritual renewal within the context of the established Catholic church.

A second school of thought, however, generally rejects such glowing evaluations of the religious state of affairs in sixteenth-century Spain, emphasizing instead the essentially oppressive character of the Spanish Catholic establishment. According to supporters of this point of view, the relative scarcity of Protestants in Spain reflected not the internal strength of Spanish Catholicism, but rather the stern resolution of church and state authorities, particularly the much feared Spanish Inquisition, to eradicate all forms of domestic religious dissent. To scholars of this camp, the Seville and Valladolid heretics represent much more than misunderstood Erasmianism. Recent research by historians Robert Spach and the late A. Gordon Kinder, among others, has demonstrated convincingly that the Seville and Valladolid groups were in fact Protestant, both in doctrine and practice. These historians grant that Protestantism did not achieve the level of quantitative significance in Spain that it achieved in northern Europe. Nonetheless, they contend that the oppressive policies of crown and Inquisition in the 1550s and 1560s effectively destroyed a genuinely Protestant movement; a movement that had grown gradually from the early sixteenth century in response to many of the same conditions that shaped the development of Protestantism elsewhere.

SPAIN BEFORE THE REFORMATION, 1500–20

In Spain, as in much of the rest of Europe, the early sixteenth century was a time of dramatic religious change and spiritual ferment. The absence of a strong and lasting Protestant movement in Spain is in fact somewhat surprising given the degree to which Spain shared many of the preconditions that contributed to the growth of Protestantism in northern and central Europe.

First, the late mediæval revival in individualistic lay spirituality represented in the north by movements such as the *devotio moderna* and the Brethren of the Common Life also affected Spain in particularly powerful ways. As in the rest of Europe, the growth of printing with moveable type made available to an increasingly literate Spanish populace a wide variety of books, and devotional works were always among the sixteenth century's best-sellers. Many books from the northern European spiritual tradition enjoyed immense popularity in Spain, including Ludolf of Saxony's *Life of Christ* and Thomas à Kempis's *Imitation of Christ*. Spain also housed in the early decades of the sixteenth century a native individualistic spiritual movement based largely on the concept of *recogimiento* or 'recollection' as a means of contemplative prayerful contact with God. Growing largely from the work of the early sixteenth-century spiritual writer García de Cisneros, this movement found its strongest expression in the 1527 *Spiritual Alphabet* of Franciscan author Francisco de Osuna. Osuna's stress on a disciplined and methodical approach to private mental prayer in turn exerted immense influence on almost all subsequent sixteenth-century Spanish devotional thought, from the heretical illuminist movement discussed below to the writings of well-known future saints such as Teresa of Avila and Ignatius Loyola.[2]

Second, Spain was also a centre of the sort of meticulous biblical scholarship and philology characteristic of the Christian humanist academic tradition, a tradition which directly influenced the scriptural focus of the northern Protestant reformers. Of particular significance in this regard was the work of the Archbishop of Toledo, Francisco Jiménez de Cisneros, who founded the University of Alcalá in 1508 as a centre of Spanish humanist study. Under Cisneros's direction, scholars at Alcalá in 1517–20 published the landmark Complutensian Polyglot Bible, a three-columned book in which the text of the Latin Vulgate (the official Bible of the Roman Catholic church) was flanked by the original Hebrew and Greek scriptures from which it had been translated. The Complutensian Polyglot represented one of the great achievements of sixteenth-century biblical scholarship, allowing scholars at a glance to check the accuracy of specific passages from St Jerome's fifth-century Latin Vulgate translation. In addition, both the popular and academic writings of Erasmus of Rotterdam, the most celebrated contemporary northern Christian humanist scholar, enjoyed immense popularity in Spain, especially in the late 1510s and 1520s.

Although sixteenth-century Spain shared much with its western and central European neighbours, it was in many ways unique. An understanding of some of these differences provides critical clues to an explanation of why the Protestant Reformation failed to attract a large Spanish following.

First, Spain in the late fifteenth and early sixteenth centuries was home to much larger communities of ethnic and religious minorities than could be found in other regions of Europe. Specifically, Spain's sixteenth-century population included large numbers of formerly Jewish converts to Catholicism (or recent descendants of such converts), called *conversos*, and formerly Muslim converts, called *moriscos*. Christians in many cases only by reason of coercion or force of circumstance, the *conversos* and *moriscos* alike were continually suspected by state and Church authorities of secretly maintaining the faith of their Jewish or Muslim ancestors while feigning allegiance to the Roman Catholic church.

Second, in an explicit response to the perceived problem of insincere conversion among their formerly Jewish subjects, Spain's Catholic monarchs Isabella and Ferdinand established the Spanish Inquisition as a formal institutional means of combating religious heterodoxy within their kingdoms. Approved by a papal letter of 1478, the Inquisition had tribunals operating in nearly all of Spain's major cities by the end of the 1480s. The Inquisition directed its attention in these early years first to rooting out crypto-Judaic practices among the *conversos* and later also to eradicating the vestiges of Islamic observances among the *moriscos*. The Spanish Inquisition, then, was already nearly four decades old by the time Martin Luther posted his Ninety-Five Theses on the door of the Castle Church in Wittenberg in 1517. The foundation and early history of the Inquisition thus had nothing to do with combating Protestantism. At the dawn of the Reformation era, however, Spain was the only nation in Europe that had an extensive and experienced bureaucratic institution whose explicit mission was the eradication of religious heterodoxy.

THE SPANISH INQUISITION AND THE SPECTRE OF MARTIN LUTHER, 1521–33

For Spain's inquisitors, the birth of Protestant heresies elsewhere in Europe occurred at a very opportune moment. By 1520, the Inquisition faced a severe crisis, a victim largely of its own success. Sustained campaigns against backsliding *conversos* had by that point already rooted out most crypto-Judaism and the excessive zeal of some inquisitors in their search for new business aroused great dissatisfaction among many sectors of Spain's population, *converso* and Old Christian alike. To many, the Inquisition appeared to be a corrupt, disruptive and obsolete institution. As early as 1508, an ecclesiastical congregation had been held in the city of Toledo to investigate alleged abuses among Inquisition officials. The Inquisition again came under attack during the 1520–1 *Comuneros* uprising, when rebellious municipal councils included among their complaints to the crown numerous accusations of corruption and abuse among the inquisitors.

Faced by these challenges, the Inquisition found in the growth of Protestant heresies in northern Europe a new justification for its own existence: specifically, keeping Spain free from Protestant contagion. From the 1520s onward, inquisitors and religious conservatives began to create in Spain an atmosphere of increasing suspicion through their attempts to root out what they considered to be dissident thought. In the fairly open intellectual and religious climate that continued to characterize Spain through the first decade of Charles V's reign, the inquisitors and their allies found a variety of targets, ranging from Erasmian humanist intellectuals to popular spiritual visionaries and mystics.

As King of Spain, Charles typically lent cautious support to the Inquisition. Having already seen his German lands torn asunder by the rise of Lutheranism, Emperor Charles hoped to avoid similar religious discord in his Spanish possessions. Nonetheless, although Charles was no scholar, he was a reasonably well-educated man and an advocate of a large degree of intellectual liberty. Having grown up in the Low Countries and having spent most of his adult life travelling throughout his vast and scattered European dominions, Charles was highly cosmopolitan in his interests. He was particularly fond of the Christian humanist intellectual tradition represented by the works of Erasmus of Rotterdam and, when the ideas of Erasmus came under attack in Spain in the late 1520s, Charles proved to be one of the Dutch humanist's strongest defenders.

The controversy over Erasmus that developed in Spain in the 1520s and culminated in a 1527 ecclesiastical conference in Valladolid serves to illustrate the difficulty historians face in unravelling the complex threads of Spanish religious thought in the early years of Charles's reign. It is true that these years saw increasing attempts among some Spanish conservatives to label Erasmus's works heretical and to condemn his Spanish supporters. Yet, ironically, the man who headed the Inquisition in these years, Archbishop of Seville and Inquisitor General Alonso Manrique, was an avowed supporter of Erasmus. In 1520, Manrique called many of Spain's leading theologians to the Valladolid conference in order, he hoped, to put an end to the controversy by issuing a definitive decree confirming Erasmus's orthodoxy. The range of opinions expressed by the scholars who attended the conference was vast, with most choosing simultaneously to support certain propositions of Erasmus while condemning others.[3] The conference ended inconclusively and issued no blanket statement one way or the other concerning Erasmus's Catholic orthodoxy. At this stage, there was certainly no official prohibition of Erasmus's works and Spanish scholars continued to read and cite the Dutch humanist frequently for decades. Following the Valladolid conference, Charles V wrote a letter to Erasmus confirming his personal support: '(A)s though, so long as we are here, one could make a decision contrary to Erasmus, whose Christian piety is well known to us. ... Take courage and be assured that we shall always hold your honour and repute in the greatest esteem.'[4]

Although the anti-Erasmian cause certainly did not, as is sometimes claimed, triumph at the Valladolid conference, it is true that many prominent Spanish intellectuals in the late 1520s and 1530s began to feel growing pressure from an increasingly hostile, suspicious and aggressive Spanish Inquisition. The year 1529 marked a critical turning point in this regard. That year Charles V left Spain, bound for his Italian possessions, taking with him many of the prominent humanist scholars of the royal court. Also in 1529, the disgraced Erasmian Archbishop Manrique was demoted from his position as Inquisitor General and sent back to his see of Seville. These developments allowed conservatives among the Inquisition hierarchy greater liberty to pursue thinkers whom they considered dangerous. In order to avoid persecution, many Spanish intellectuals, including the prominent humanist and *converso* Juan de Valdés, chose to flee from their native land and continue their studies abroad.

Besides intellectuals such as Valdés, the Inquisition's targets in the 1520s and 1530s included adherents to a uniquely Spanish tradition of mystical spirituality called illuminism. Drawing from similar sources to the more orthodox *recogimiento* school – exemplified by the work of Osuna – the illuminists (or *alumbrados*) went beyond other contemporary Spanish spiritual groups in their emphasis on purely passive spiritual union with God through giving oneself up entirely to the empowering action of the Holy Spirit in the individual human soul. Led by visionary women such as Isabel de la Cruz and Francisca Hernández, and numbering among its followers many *conversos* (perhaps searching for a meaningful spiritual life outside of the formal observances of traditional Catholicism), the illuminist movement proved particularly vulnerable to inquisitorial persecution. A systematic Inquisition campaign to eradicate illuminism began in 1525 with a formal edict condemning a wide variety of common illuminist tenets. Although only five people were actually executed as a result of this wave of persecution, many more were arrested and given punishments ranging from fines to imprisonment. By the early 1530s, illuminism had all but disappeared.

In what ways, if at all, did these various strands of Spanish spirituality and religious thought reflect the direct influence of Luther or other northern Protestant reformers? From the point of view of some inquisitors and religious conservatives, the ranks of the illuminists and humanists were filled with Lutheran heretics. As the century progressed, the inquisitors' taxonomy of offences increasingly conflated all sorts of suspicious thought, from illuminism and Erasmianism to Calvinism and other forms of Protantism practised by foreigners within Spain's borders, under the single heading Lutheranism. As one historian has put it, Martin Luther became a 'bogeyman' in the eyes of the Inquisition and the inquisitors effectively used the perceived threat of a possible Spanish repeat of Luther's religious revolt as a pretext for their campaigns to enforce a strict definition of religious orthodoxy.[5]

At least before the mid-1530s, however, the direct influence of Protestantism in Spain appears to have been extremely slight. This is not to say that the humanists and illuminists were completely unfamiliar with Protestant thought. Valdés and other Spanish humanists had certainly read some Protestant writings and certain passages from Valdés' 1529 *Dialogue on Christian Doctrine* in particular clearly reflect the influence of Luther and other Protestants whose works he had consulted and admired.[6] With regard to the illuminists, there is one reference in Inquisition documentation to the discovery of some Protestant writings among the possessions of members of an *alumbrado* group in Toledo.[7] Nonetheless, the early growth of both humanism and illuminism in Spain predated by decades the posting of Luther's Ninety-Five Theses in 1517 and the general development of each movement can certainly be understood without reference to extensive Protestant influence. That is to say, while such movements may have shared with northern Protestantism common historical roots in the general European spiritual ferment of the late fifteenth and early sixteenth centuries, they were by no means caused by the Protestant Reformation, nor may they be accurately understood as expressions of Protestantism in Spain. By the middle decades of the sixteenth century, however, the situation had changed dramatically. Beginning in 1557, the inquisitors found themselves faced with a small but genuine Protestant challenge within the borders of Spain itself.

THE LIFE AND DEATH OF SPANISH PROTESTANTISM, 1534–70

As early as 1521, the same year that Luther appeared before the emperor at the Diet of Worms, Pope Leo X issued to the Spanish crown a warning to take great care to prevent the spread of heretical writings and ideas from the north among the people of Spain. The government of Charles V in Spain entrusted to the Inquisition the oversight and policing of the domestic printing industry and the import of books from outside Spain's borders. From the 1520s through the 1550s, there are occasional notices of caches of heretical books seized by various Inquisition tribunals throughout Spain, particularly in port cities. The Inquisition's censorship efforts became more formalized in 1551 with the publication of Spain's first Index of Prohibited Books. This lengthy list of banned books included not only works by Protestant leaders such as Luther and Calvin, but also many works of the Christian humanist tradition (including some, but not all, of Erasmus's writings), as well as some native Spanish devotional literature.

It proved impossible, however, to build an absolutely impenetrable wall against the spread of heretical ideas in Spain. Supposedly banned books continued to circulate clandestinely in many areas. In 1557 in the city of Seville, for instance, the local Inquisition tribunal followed an informant's tip to discover in the possession of a man named Julián Hernández Protestant writings and propaganda that he had brought back with him from a recent trip to France. Beginning with Hernández and his friends and associates, the inquisitors' investigations over the next five years gradually unravelled an entire network of native Spanish evangelical Protestants, numbering perhaps 1,000 adherents. It stretched from the wealthy port city of Seville and surrounding regions to the long-time administrative capital of Castile, Valladolid.

As noted earlier, some scholars deny that these groups might legitimately be called Protestant. However, historians who hold that these evangelical conventicles in Seville and Valladolid did in fact constitute a genuine expression of Protestantism in Spain are able to marshal in support of their thesis a wide array of compelling evidence. First, at the level of doctrine, the testimony of those members of these groups who were brought up for trial bears the clear stamp of Protestant theology. One of the accused in Seville, for example, made a fairly clear statement of the common Protestant doctrine of faith alone when she testified that she had learned from the leaders of the movement that Christ had already done for us everything that was necessary for our salvation, and that 'giving oneself up to works and afflicting oneself was excessive.'[8] Others in both the Seville and Valladolid groups explained that their leaders had further taught them that devotional images were mere idols, that the doctrine of purgatory was a human invention with no scriptural basis and that genuine Christians need only to confess their sins to Christ, not to a priest. All these were common tenets among various Protestant denominations outside Spain.

Second, the testimony of the accused in these cases also included various indications of conscious affinity with northern European Protestantism. Some of the defendants, for instance, noted that it was commonly felt among the members of their conventicles that the Lutherans of Germany in particular were good, caring people. Others stated clearly that many members of their groups hoped to leave Spain and move north in order to live and worship freely among the Protestants.

Third, even if we consider suspect the testimony given by these defendants under threat of inquisitorial torture or punishment, the fate of those members of the Seville and Valladolid conventicles who managed to escape the Inquisition's grasp presents further evidence of the consciously Protestant nature of these groups. Dozens of them, particularly from the Seville circle, managed both before and during the frenzied persecution of 1557–62 to flee from Spain entirely. Nearly all of the escapees later surfaced in England or in Protestant regions of Germany or the Low Countries, where they formed Spanish Protestant communities in exile or merged into local Protestant congregations.

The Inquisition's investigations revealed a great deal about the origins and growth of these heretical conventicles, and one of the things that most shocked Inquisition and crown officials alike was the social prominence of much of the movement's leadership. The Seville and Valladolid groups alike had been led, they discovered, not by disenchanted social outcasts, but rather by prominent clergymen and political officials.

The Seville group, for instance, had grown from the mid-1530s largely under the guidance of a highly respected clergyman named Juan Gil or 'Dr Egidio'. Educated at the University of Alcalá, Gil received appointment in 1534 to a position as canon in Seville's cathedral chapter from the Erasmian archbishop and former Inquisitor General Alonso Manrique. By 1548, Gil's reputation as a teacher and preacher had grown to the point that he received the crown's nomination to fill the vacant bishopric of Tortosa. Local conservatives in Seville who doubted Gil's orthodoxy, however, denounced him to the Inquisition in order to block the appointment, and Gil was arrested and imprisoned in 1549. After enduring the humiliation of appearing in an *auto-da-fé* in Seville in 1552, Gil was banned for ten years from preaching and teaching and ordered not to travel beyond the borders of Spain. After his release from inquisitorial incarceration in 1553, however, Gil was allowed to return to his position as canon. The strength of his reputation among his colleagues was such that he was even sent as the Seville cathedral chapter's representative to a 1555 ecclesiastical conference in Valladolid. Gil's death in Seville later that same year, however, spared him from the fires of persecution that consumed so many of his followers after 1557.

While in Valladolid in 1555, the inquisitors later discovered, Gil had secretly met and discussed theology with the similarly prominent leaders of that city's smaller but growing Protestant conventicle. Dr Agustín Cazalla, the most eminent of the Valladolid Protestants, had even served as royal chaplain in the courts of both Charles V and Philip II. Also present at the meetings with Gil was the founder of the Valladolid Protestant circle, the Italian-born Carlos de Seso, who held the prestigious political post of royal civil governor (*corregidor*) of the nearby city of Toro.

The fact that heresy had grown within Spain's borders under the guidance of such prominent subjects aroused a state of near panic on the part of the monarchy. Having already abdicated the Spanish throne in favour of his son Philip in 1556, the former king and Holy Roman Emperor Charles V wrote from his retirement in the monastery of Yuste in southwestern Spain in 1558 a particularly poignant letter to his daughter Juana (Juana was at the time serving as regent during Philip's absence in the Netherlands):

> This business has caused and still causes me more anxiety and pain than I can express, for while the king and I were abroad these realms remained in perfect peace, free from calamity, but now that I have returned here to rest and recuperate and serve our Lord, this great outrage and treachery, implicating such notable persons, occurs in my presence and yours. You know that because of this I suffered and went through great trials and expenses in Germany, and lost so much of my good health. ... Believe me, my daughter, if so great an evil is not suppressed and remedied without distinction of persons from the very beginning, I cannot promise that the king or anyone else will be in a position to do it afterwards.[9]

Just as his father Charles had seen firsthand the effects of religious discord in Germany, so too had Philip witnessed the bloodshed associated with Reformation-era religious division in England during his brief marriage to Queen Mary I. From his own experiences and the lessons of his father's life, the young King Philip emerged staunchly determined to destroy in its infancy any expression of Protestant heresy in Spain.

Philip thus lent his full support to the Inquisition's campaign of persecution and, in a series of seven *autos-da-fé* held in Seville and Valladolid between 1559 and 1562, the inquisitors issued punishments ranging from service in the galleys to burning at the stake to nearly 200 of the leading figures of the Protestant conventicles. Philip himself underscored the significance of these events by personally attending the 8 October 1559 *auto* in Valladolid at which his former royal governor Carlos de Seso was handed over to the secular authorities for execution. According to some accounts, when Seso was marched off to die, he cried out to the king: 'How can you let me burn?' Philip reportedly responded flatly: 'If my own son were as wicked as you, I would carry the wood to burn him myself!'[10]

Two more *autos-da-fé* in Saragossa in 1560 and 1562 sufficed to root out a smaller circle of Protestants in Aragon and, by the end of 1562, the efforts of the inquisitors had resulted in the effective eradication of organized domestic Protestantism in Spain. The Inquisition's active campaign against Protestantism in Spain continued through the end of the century, periodically classifying as Lutheran the occasional indiscreet Spanish subject who let slip from their lips some careless statement against the Catholic clergy or in praise of the Protestants. Such penitents usually received only instructive correction and mild punishment. After 1562, in fact, the Inquisition limited its serious efforts at persecution of Protestantism almost exclusively to foreigners living within Spain's borders. As one historian puts it, 'the great Protestant hunt of the 1560s involved little more than tracking down Frenchmen.'[11]

In the Spain of Philip II, heresy had no place. After the 1557–62 crackdown, organized Spanish Protestantism survived only among the communities of refugees who had fled north in order to avoid inquisitorial persecution. Embittered by their experiences, some of these Spanish expatriates voiced biting criticism of their homeland, contributing in the process to the growth of what twentieth-century historians have retrospectively labelled the 'Black Legend' of Spanish cruelty and depravity. In 1567, for instance, an anonymous refugee from the Seville conventicle writing under the pen-name Reginaldus Gonsalvius Montanus published in Heidelberg a stinging exposé of the inhumane practices of the Spanish Inquisition. The work was quickly translated into all major European languages and in 1568 an English edition appeared under the title *A Discovery and Plaine Declaration of the Sundry Subtill Practices of the Holy Inquisition in Spain*. Another escapee from the Seville conventicle, the former monk Cipriano de Valera, rose to prominence in London in the Armada year of 1588 as a polemicist in the ideological war against Spain. In one of his works, Valera explicitly asserted that Protestantism would have grown in Spain had it not been for the Inquisition's cruel persecution of those who preached and taught the 'true gospel'.[12]

Such counter-factual speculation is, of course, inherently ahistorical and there is certainly no way to know what might have happened to the Seville and Valladolid conventicles had there been no Inquisition in Spain. Valera's musings, however, do provide an interesting perspective. The blanket condemnations of sixteenth-century Spanish society and culture typical of attitudes informed by the Black Legend are no doubt unjustified. As other chapters in this volume illustrate, Spain among the states of sixteenth-century Europe certainly held no monopoly on religious perse-cution and intolerance. Nonetheless, the presence and strength of the Inquisition made Spain's experience with Protestantism unique. Emerging from the very same devotional and intellectual currents that fed the growth of Lutheranism, Calvinism and other heretical denominations in the north, Spain did in fact house in the middle decades of the sixteenth century a small but genuinely Protestant move-ment. This legitimate expression of Protestantism was, however, destroyed in the fires of the 1559–1562 *autos-da-fé* in Seville and Vallodolid.

NOTES

1   Geoffrey Parker, *Philip II* (3rd edn; Chicago, 1995), p. 159.
2   Melquíades Andrés Martín, *Los recogidos: Nueva visión de la mística española (1500–1700)* (Madrid, 1976).
3   Lu Ann Homza, 'Erasmus as Hero, or Heretic? Spanish Humanism and the Valladolid Assembly of 1527', *Renaissance Quarterly* 50 (1997), pp. 78–118.
4   Henry Kamen, *Inquisition and Society in Spain in the Sixteenth and Seventeenth Centuries* (Bloomington, 1985), p. 65.
5   Jaime Contreras, 'The Impact of Protestantism in Spain 1520–1600', in Stephen Haliczer (ed.), *Inquisition and Society in Early Modern Europe* (Totowa, 1987), pp. 47–63.
6   A. Gordon Kinder, 'Spain', in Andrew Pettegree (ed.), *The Early Reformation in Europe* (Cambridge, 1992), p. 223.
7   Ibid., p. 220.
8   Robert Spach, 'Juan Gil and Sixteenth-Century Spanish Protestantism', *Sixteenth Century Journal* 26 (1995), p. 865.
9   Kamen, *Inquisition and Society*, p. 75.
10 Parker, *Philip II*, p. 100.
11 William Monter, *Frontiers of Heresy: The Spanish Inquisition from the Basque Lands to Sicily* (Cambridge, 1990), p. 234.
12 A. Gordon Kinder, 'Protestantism in Sixteenth-Century Spain: Doctrines and Practices as confessed to Inquisitors', *Mediterranean Studies* 4 (1994), p. 77.

FURTHER READING

There is no book-length study in English of Spain's sixteenth-century Protestant move-ment. The most detailed research was done by the late A. Gordon Kinder, who unfortunately never published a monograph on the subject. Besides the works mentioned in the notes, see also his article 'Spain's Little-Known "Noble Army of Martyrs" and the Black Legend', in Lesley K. Twomey (ed.), *Faith and Fanaticism: Religious Fervour in Early Modern Spain* (Aldershot, 1997). See also Robert Spach's recent article on Juan Gil, also mentioned in the notes. For the opinion of one historian who does not believe that the Seville and Valladolid conventicles merit the label Protestant, see Jaime Contreras' 'The Impact of Protestantism in Spain 1520–1600', in Stephen Haliczer (ed.), *Inquisition and Society in Early Modern Europe* (Totowa, 1987), pp. 47–63. The history of the Spanish Inqui-sition as a whole also lacks a good recent study. Henry Kamen's *Inquisition and Society in Spain in the Sixteenth and Seventeenth Centuries* (Bloomington, 1985), although still useful as a general introduction, is becoming somewhat dated. This is largely because of the recent appearance of many good local and regional studies. See Sara Nalle, *God in La Mancha: Religious Reform and the People of Cuenca, 1500–1650* (Baltimore, 1992); Stephen Haliczer, *Inquisition and Society in the Kingdom of Valencia, 1478–1834* (Berkeley and Los Angeles, 1990); Henry Kamen, *The Phoenix and the Flame: Catalonia and the Counter Reformation* (New Haven, 1993), and William Monter, *Frontiers of Heresy: The Spanish Inquisition from the Basque Lands to Sicily* (Cambridge, 1990).

PART IV

CALVINISM AND THE SECOND REFORMATION

CHAPTER EIGHTEEN

CALVIN AND GENEVA

·•·

William G. Naphy

It would be hard to overestimate the importance of the relationship between Calvin, the internationally famous theologian, and Geneva, the birthplace and forge of the Calvinist 'model'. During nearly three decades in Geneva, Calvin struggled (with varying degrees of success) to mould the city into his ideal Christian commonwealth. However, it is often forgotten that Geneva also managed consciously and unconsciously to stamp that model with the peculiarities of its polity, society, culture and even geography. This interplay of Calvin, the theoretician, and Geneva, the home of the movement, gave Calvinism many of its distinctive and idiosyncratic characteristics. If Calvin was the weaver then Geneva was the loom on which he had to work. To understand how this model for other Calvinist polities came to be, one must chart the course of Calvin's often tortured relationship with the city.

GENEVA

In the first thirty years of the sixteenth century, Geneva had been involved in a complex and rather laconic revolution. Geneva's politics and geography conspired to place the city in a difficult, confusing and potentially dangerous situation. Geneva was the premier city of the Duchy of Savoy. With 10,000 inhabitants it was also one of the largest cities in the region. With easy access to Lac Leman and the Rhône, the city should also have been an economic powerhouse. The fact that it was not draws attention to one of Geneva's greatest problems. France, its powerful neighbour to the west, was flexing its political and economic muscles to secure dynastic claims to northern Italy. The kingdom had granted extensive privileges to Lyon, which had greatly weakened Geneva's economic pre-eminence. France also coveted the strategically important lands of the Duchy of Savoy.

As if the French 'rock' to the west were not enough, on the east, Geneva faced the threat of a Swiss 'hard place'. Berne and Fribourg had long desired to expand at the expense of Savoy's northern marches. In this westward push, Berne was by far the senior military partner. Events added a dash of colour and complexity with Berne's conversion to Protestantism in 1528. Thus, on the west, Geneva faced

France, who saw the city and Savoy as the strategic thoroughfare into Italy and, on the east, the dynamic but religiously divided duo, Berne and Fribourg.

Even this complex state of affairs is comparatively simple when compared with the city's domestic situation. There were three ways of viewing Geneva's situation. First, many citizens would have stressed that Geneva was an imperial city. Second, the clergy saw the city as a prince-bishopric in which most of the rural holdings and much of the political power were in the hands of clerics. Third, the Duke of Savoy held Geneva to be the duchy's chief city, the key to holding his northern possessions and, increasingly in the early decades of the century, a possible capital and residence. As is readily apparent, these political presuppositions are (and were) mutually incompatible. In effect, Geneva was governed by a triangular political arrangement in which any astute individual or group could play two sides against the third. Alternatively, any single section could try to ally itself with the duchy's external enemies in an attempt to secure its own position.

In 1519, an element in the merchant-dominated citizenry made an attempt to recruit Swiss support to break from Savoy. However, Savoy was able to marshal diplomatic support from neighbouring states, which forced Berne and Fribourg to accept a negotiated settlement. All sides backed away from a military clash and some of the Genevans who had sought to challenge the agreement were executed. The result was twofold. On one hand, Savoy's opponents were hardened in their resolve and ever more distrustful of the duke. On the other hand, the voices raised against the duke in Geneva had been temporarily stilled. To stamp his authority more firmly on Geneva, the duke took up residence in the city in 1523–4. Again, in the short term, this was politically astute. However, not only did it infuriate those citizens who already resented the duke's power, but it also worried the clerics and the duchy's neighbours. If the duke were to make Geneva his permanent residence, this could undermine clerical power and potentially thwart Franco-Swiss ambitions.

When the next political and military crisis arose, in the late 1520s, Savoy, faced by all these potential adversaries, was not able to defuse the situation. Genevan society fractured (not for the last time) into political factions. The smallest was the ducal party (called *Seigneuristes* or *Mamelus*). A slightly larger faction supported the bishop (*Peneysans*). The final and largest group (*Enfants de Genève* or *Eidguenots*)[1] sought independence, preferably within the Swiss Confederation. Since the latter needed Swiss (that is, Bernese) military support it increasingly allied itself with Berne's Protestant religious preferences. This sharpened the clash with the bishop and his ecclesiastical bureaucracy: not only could patriots reject his political pretensions, they could also refute his religious claims. The duke's supporters withdrew quickly while the bishop attempted to serve as a bridge between Savoy and the *Enfants*. This complicated situation was resolved when a Bernese army swept into northern Savoy. This secured the city's freedom from Savoy and adherence to Protestantism. Henceforth, Catholicism would be inextricably linked to Savoyard (or French) domination and Protestantism to Genevan patriotism (and liberty).

Another crisis immediately broke. Much to the horror of the *Enfants*, the Bernese 'army of liberation' stayed. Moreover, Geneva beheld the image of the bishopric of nearby Lausanne disappearing into the maw of 'greater' Berne. Geneva feared that it would be next on the menu. Fortunately for the city, so did France. The possibility of French intervention convinced Berne to depart.

At this moment, Calvin wandered on to the Genevan stage. Around him, he beheld a city gripped by patriotic passions and inflamed with revolutionary fervour. Large numbers of prominent citizens had fled into exile, the political structure was in chaos, the government was *ad hoc*, the society in turmoil. More importantly, beneath the carnage and debris littering the Genevan tableau was the unresolved question of the relationship between the newly freed but defenceless city and its military protector, Berne.

CALVIN'S INTRODUCTION TO GENEVA (1536–8)

In 1536, Calvin became an employee of this revolutionary republican state. Thus began the first phase of his relationship with Geneva. For those who follow Calvin's own interpretation of events, these years have been seen as a losing battle against various forces within Geneva opposed to Calvin's views of a truly reformed community. His opponents have been characterized as libertines, Catholics and even Anabaptists. In reality, Calvin (along with his senior co-minister, Farel) was simply a casualty of domestic political discord.

In these circumstances it is worth asking what had brought Calvin to Geneva and why Farel was so keen to have as a colleague someone so little known that the city records simply refer to him as *ille gallus* ('that Frenchman'). Calvin had been born in Noyon (France) in 1509 and was therefore twenty-seven years old when he arrived in Geneva. He had had solid training as a lawyer and, as a part of any good university education, a good grounding in theology. More importantly, Calvin was known by this time as a humanist and supporter of religious reform. His involvement in the events in Paris in 1534–5 which led to his flight from France, most particularly his association with Nicholas Cop, the disgraced rector of the University of Paris, may have brought him to the attention of Farel. For all that, Calvin's 'fame' in 1536 was undoubtedly limited to a select band of educated men. It was based on a limited œuvre: a commentary on Seneca's *De Clementia* and two prefaces to Olivétan's French Bible. His attack on the Anabaptist belief in 'soul-sleep' (*Psychopannychia*) was at this point unpublished. More importantly for his future renown, in March 1536 Calvin published (in Basle) the first (Latin) edition of his *magnum opus*, *Institutes of the Christian Religion*.

Prior to his arrival in Geneva, Calvin had visited the court of Marguerite of Navarre as well as Basle. In other words, Calvin, a young religious enthusiast with a recognizably good mind, had been making the rounds of reforming communities and was gaining a reputation and contacts. Farel recognized in Calvin the stable, learned colleague that he needed to consolidate the Genevan Reformation. Given time and peace, there was every reason to believe that they might have succeeded.

It was not to be. In 1536 the city's magistrates were faced with a dangerous and delicate foreign policy situation. Geneva was wholly dependent on Berne's military protection. However, Berne had overt desires on many of the lands seized from the prince-bishop and a covert desire to absorb the republic. Thus the Genevan politicians had to find some way to maintain Bernese support while avoiding the slippery slide from protectorate into province. In 1538 the municipal elections gave power to the faction bent on appeasing Berne at any cost short of outright occupation.

The political realities of Genevan society merit a brief description at this point. A Genevan was a *citoyen* (the native-born child of a *citoyen* or *bourgeois*), a *bourgeois* (a person naturalized gratis or upon payment of a fee) or an *habitant* (a legal resident alien). Every adult *citoyen* and *bourgeois* could attend and vote in the annual meeting of the Conseil Générale. In February, this body validated rulings made by the higher councils the previous year and elected magistrates for the coming year. From this body was chosen the Conseil des Deux Cents which set wine and grain prices and elected the city's investigative and prosecutorial team in November. This large council supplied the membership of the smaller Conseil des Soixante which met to consider extremely important or contentious issues (primarily in foreign affairs). A segment of this council was the Petit Conseil (Senate) comprising the four ruling syndics, a treasurer, secretary, factor (*saultier*) and other senators for a total of (around) twenty-five. Any *bourgeois* or *citoyen* could vote in the elections for these offices but only *citoyens* could serve in the Senate.

Thus the Genevan political system was unusually active and inclusive. Slightly more than 10 per cent of adult males had some magisterial duties. Geneva was not a democracy; elections were between candidates nominated in a co-optive manner. Nevertheless, Geneva was very responsive to public opinion and, with annual elections, the government could change radically and swiftly. In addition since a *bourgeois* could exercise civic rights from the moment of naturalization, he had immediate political power. Thus the admission of large numbers of new *bourgeois* could have an immediate effect on the political balance within the city. Moreover, *bourgeois* status was bought. In other words, although new *bourgeois* could be politically destabilizing, they could also be a very lucrative source of revenue for the republic. Since the revolution and Bernese liberation had left the city heavily indebted to the Swiss, this was no mean concern.

In 1538, Calvin became a victim of Geneva's volatile politics. The party of appeasement conformed Geneva's ecclesiastical system to that of Berne. In practice, as Calvin admitted, this was unimportant. Calvin and Farel opposed not the end, but the means. They refused to accept that the Senate (the secular magistracy) could, without reference to the church (the ministers), take religious decisions. Calvin and Farel refused to accept the changes and were expelled. New ministers were hired, among them Antoine Marcourt, the man credited with writing the famous placard which so incensed Francis I of France. Thus ended Calvin's first stay in Geneva. He left and, after journeying through Switzerland, settled in Strasbourg. Although Calvin eventually returned, Farel never regained his post.

EXILE (1538–41)

The next phase of Calvin's career lasted almost four years. There are a number of key questions which must be answered in examining this period. What was the character of Geneva's religious life in Calvin's absence? What lessons might Calvin have learned from his expulsion and exile? Why was Calvin able to return? As one might expect though, the immediate aftermath of the expulsion was turmoil in the church. In the short term, the speedy arrival of Marcourt and Morand restored equilibrium. On two very different levels, though, there were dramatic shifts in the city's religious life. First, the entire ministerial cadre acknowledged the primacy of the state in all aspects of Geneva's life, including the sacred. That is, their approach to church–state relations was that which prevailed throughout Protestant Switzerland. In this (Zwinglian) model, the magistrates were competent, indeed obliged by their God-given offices, to undertake decisions on religious matters with or without ministerial approval or consultation.

More importantly, the ecclesiastical situation became a focus for political protest. Those opposed to the appeasement of Berne had little opportunity for open political protest. Outright action could have been interpreted as treasonable or, at best, endangering the Bernese alliance. However, in Calvin and Farel, these politicians had martyrs who could serve a political end. By siding with the exiled ministers, this group was able to criticize the government with some degree of safety. Calvin saw this from his exile in Strasbourg and explicitly condemned it. He advised local Genevans to accept the new ecclesiastical situation.

Clearly, however, Calvin would have drawn some vital lessons from the events surrounding his expulsion and exile. First, the ministers had to be united if they were to resist magisterial interference in ecclesiastical matters. Second, Calvin had been given a dramatic lesson in Genevan factionalism and the crucial need to have local political support. To weather the violent sea-changes in Geneva, one needed a strong, stable and secure power base.

In the end, and much against his will, Calvin was enticed back to Geneva. In 1540, yet another political upheaval resulted in the disgrace of Calvin's political opponents. In this year the city's rulers negotiated a new settlement with Berne in which they surrendered all disputed territory. When these Articles were finally published, the anti-appeasement party (which became known as *Guillermins* or *Farets* after Guillaume Farel) was able to capitalize on the popular fury. The makers of the treaty (*Articulants* or *Artichaux*) were swept from power and the treaty repudiated. New elections had brought to power the very men who had been harassing Calvin and Farel's replacements. In the frenzied atmosphere following the election, Marcourt and Morand judged their positions untenable and left. Bereft of its finest ministers and in the midst of turmoil, suspicion and animosity, the magistrates recalled Calvin.

BUILDING A CHURCH (1541–6)

Upon his arrival, Calvin was given two crucial tasks. He was placed on two committees: one to draft regulations for Geneva's church, and the other to draft a secular constitution for the republic. At this stage the city was as keen to exploit Calvin's expertise as a lawyer as his leadership of the church. The new constitution was necessary to reflect the changed governmental structure since the expulsion of the bishop: it replaced ducal, episcopal and cathedral powers and personnel with magistrates and thus validated and confirmed the city's transformation from a prince-bishopric under ducal suzerainty into an independent republic.

Likewise, the Ecclesiastical Ordinances were radical yet conservative. The initial draft, which explicitly made the church free in its own sphere, was watered down to a formula that implied magisterial overlordship. The establishment of a consistory was radical but not novel. Berne had consistories and Geneva had discussed setting one up during Calvin's exile. On at least one point, Calvin was less successful than Marcourt and Morand. They had managed to get the Senate to discuss establishing a diaconate under ministerial control for regulating social welfare. Yet under the new settlement this sphere always remained strictly under magisterial control and the city never established an office of deacon.

Once the ecclesiastical structure was in place, Calvin set about giving it sinews and muscles. In this period (1541–6), he was occupied with two major tasks. First, he had to collect a strong and unified ministerial cohort (the Company of Pastors). Second, he wanted a stable body of councillors to work with the Company to form an effective and efficient Consistory. By 1546, Calvin had gathered round himself a group of extremely gifted, well educated, socially prominent and financially secure French religious refugee ministers. Also, after a few shifts in personnel, Calvin managed to gather a group of elders who would serve with him and the rest of the ministers on the Consistory for nearly a decade. Thus, by 1546, Calvin was in a very secure position supported by the entirety of the Company and buttressed by the elders.

More importantly, by 1546, Calvin was well on his way to putting sinews and flesh on the skeleton of a 'Calvinist' system of ecclesiology. The basic facets are imbedded in the Ordinances and were quickly put into practice. The Company of Pastors, a meeting of the state's ministers for discussion, improvement, admonition and support was, in effect, a Genevan synod (alternatively called General Assembly or *coitus* depending on the nation). The Consistory (ministers and elders) was an ecclesiastical court which, deprived of overt and determined magisterial support, could become the local governing body (presbytery, kirk session) of the church. The local school system remained under state control but Calvin and the ministers involved themselves in the provision of teachers (doctors) and strove for years to convince the city to establish and fund a higher facility for training ministers; they succeeded in 1559 with the foundation of the Academy. Calvin never gained clear control of the provision of poor relief (under the oversight of deacons) though the system operated by the private fund to support poor French refugees (*Bourse française*) as well as the state-controlled *Hôpital* provided a model for other Calvinist communities and governments.

This summary leaves one major question unanswered. How original or unique was the system developed in Geneva under Calvin? In its constituent parts it is not at all unique. Geneva's magistrates and ministers (in Calvin's absence) had already held discussions on the establishment of consistories and deacons, clearly taking their lead from the Protestant churches in the Swiss Confederacy. The local school system pre-dated the Reformation and was a vital part of Geneva's civic structure. Just as importantly, the provision of social welfare was one of the first things centralized and rationalized by the newly reformed republic.

However, the integration of these ecclesiastical and social elements and their relationship to one another as well as to the Genevan state made the system in its totality unique. Regardless of the verbal obfuscation of the Ordinances it is clear that Calvin had placed the ministers on a level footing with the magistrates. In their own fields of expertise they claimed full competence and responsibility. For example, the Consistory claimed it had absolute power to excommunicate, though the magistrates long resisted this assertion (see below). In the long run, Calvin was successful in freeing the ministers from the oversight of the magistracy in many 'religious' areas.

This rather optimistic interpretation can only be held in conjunction with some serious reservations. The truth of the matter is that the system most commonly called 'Calvinistic' does not really ever become fully apparent in Geneva. For example, there was never a city diaconate under ministerial control. Indeed, the 'Calvinist' system, in which the elders and the local minister control the church (especially the provision of poor relief) and then provide representatives (almost always ministers) for higher bodies (synods, coitus, presbyteries, assemblies) only develops in larger states. One must never forget that the Genevan system assumed that all the nation's ministers would – and could – meet together every week. The Genevan system also created a Consistory in which ministers and elders were represented, broadly speaking, in equal numbers. When one stood before the Genevan Consistory one faced not only twelve elders, but quite often nearly a dozen ministers. This Genevan 'Calvinistic' system was devised entirely for a small city-state republic.

That this system was successfully moulded, stretched and altered to fit larger geographical areas and differing socio-political systems is a testimony both to its inherent resilience (one factor which made it unique) and to Calvin's fame. In addition, its popularity was in no small measure due to Geneva's receptiveness and hospitality to religious refugees. Hundreds of future ministers and political leaders, as well as thousands of lay people, received asylum in Geneva, were nurtured in its church and went forth determined to reproduce in their homelands the apparently successful model they had come to know so intimately both through word (Calvin's writings) and deed (Geneva's example).

A HARBINGER OF TROUBLE (1546–50)

Unfortunately for Calvin, the new-found security of his position was shaken by a series of clashes just as the ecclesiastical structure was taking shape. First, a significant number of senators and their wives were accused of dancing at the wedding of a certain Antoine Lect. They all denied the charge. Eventually one senator, Amblard Corne, broke the conspiracy of silence and confessed.

At the same time, the Consistory (led by the ministers) clashed with the Senate over excommunication. The final version of the Ordinances was intentionally vague on this point. Originally Calvin had proposed that the power be left wholly in the hands of the Consistory. The magistrates baulked at this. The result was a wording that could support the ministers' right to excommunicate or only allow them to recommend people deserving of excommunication to the Senate. The Senate, until 1555, consistently ruled that the proper role of the Consistory (and hence the ministers) was to admonish sinners and, should that prove ineffective, to recommend their excommunication to the magistrates. With similar consistency and obstinacy, Calvin (a foreign employee of the state) refused to accept this ruling.

The most serious clash involved a seemingly obscure issue: baptismal names. Calvin and the ministers wanted names untainted by Catholic, non-biblical practices and beliefs. Hence, they outlawed the traditional names for the Magi (Balthasar, Gaspard and Melchior) and names associated with the Deity (e.g. Emmanuel). However, they also wanted to ban Claude, the most popular name for boys in Geneva and the third most popular for girls. The rationale was understandable. The shrine of St Claude was nearby and the ministers thought the name implied a lingering attachment to the saint. The name was in any case considerably less common in France, whence the ministers came. Most native Genevans took the view that the name was a traditional local name. The ministers' methods of implementing their decision did not help. The first occasion can serve as an example for the rest. A man presented his son for baptism. The minister asked for the name and was told 'Claude'. He promptly baptized the child 'Abraham'. A near riot ensued; later manifestations of this dispute were, in fact, accompanied by actual rioting. The magistrates asked the ministers to provide a list of proscribed names. The ministers complied but seemed to reserve the power to make *ad hoc* decisions at the font when necessary.

With provocations of this nature, Calvin's cadre of foreign ministers and loyal elders seemed headed for a complete rupture with leading magistrates by the end of 1546. However, the threat of religious war in Germany and large Catholic armies passing near Geneva *en route*, forced peace on the city. This period of enforced calm lasted until 1551 when the consensus began to break down.

THE STORM BREAKS (1551–4)

As the threat from Germany receded, Geneva confronted another external problem: waves of French Protestants fleeing persecution at home. While Germany concentrated Genevan minds on unity and stability, the refugees threatened the very social fabric of the city. The numbers alone demonstrate the danger: Geneva was forced to accommodate 3,000–5,000 refugees.

In the wake of this flood of refugees came a rising tide of xenophobia amongst native Genevans. The refugees were mostly men with skills who represented a real threat to the economic position of locals. Their presence pushed up prices, rents and property values. Some refugees were able to transfer to Geneva considerable economic resources. Also, not a few were of noble birth. The introduction of nobles, with all their prejudices and social expectations further complicated the situation. Geneva was a merchant society without nobility and prominent citizens resented the pretensions of refugee nobles – including some of the ministers. The city grappled with the problem of how to integrate so many new *bourgeois* while limiting their impact on Geneva's finely balanced politics.

During these years too, two celebrated individual cases troubled the city: the controversies raised by Jerome Bolsec and Michael Servetus. In 1551, Bolsec challenged Calvin's teachings on predestination. Since the Zwinglian Swiss cities were also troubled by Calvin's views, it is not surprising that Geneva was unsure of the best course to pursue. Geneva, and the ministers, sought the opinion of the Swiss Protestants. Their responses showed a lack of enthusiasm for Calvin's theology but a clear support for institutional stability and the status quo. Geneva responded to this cautious and conservative advice by expelling Bolsec. But an important precedent had been set: when making critical domestic decisions both magistrates and ministers recognized the need for support from the other Swiss cantons.

The procedure followed with regard to Bolsec established the pattern of events that would unfold when Geneva faced the challenge posed by the Servetus case. In 1553, Servetus appeared in Geneva fleeing a sentence of death for heresy in Catholic Vienne. There is little doubt that the ministers then instigated his arrest. From this point onwards the case (as with Bolsec) was prosecuted before the criminal courts. Calvin was asked to evaluate Servetus' views as a theological specialist. He denounced Servetus as an anti-Trinitarian. This placed the city's leaders in a quandary. Normally Geneva had dealt with religious heterodoxy (e.g. Anabaptism) by banishing the heretic. This leniency (by normative sixteenth-century standards) had already raised eyebrows and had resulted in a rumour amongst Catholics that Geneva tolerated, if not secretly favoured, Anabaptism. The consensus between church and state was that Servetus would have to be dealt with harshly.

However, the magistrates were clearly loath to act. They offered Servetus the chance to return to Vienne; he refused. Then, unwilling to act alone, the magistrates turned to the Swiss for advice and, perhaps, mutual culpability. Although some have read these events as a sign either of support for Servetus or a desire to use him against Calvin, the truth is that the city lacked any enthusiasm for executing heretics. Since many (Protestant) Genevans regularly did business in Catholic cities (e.g. Lyons, Chambéry) and some had been arrested and executed there for their faith, one can understand the hesitation. Diplomatically, Geneva's complaints against executions for heresy would be greatly weakened once the city indulged in the same. Nevertheless, once the Swiss opinions arrived (counselling death), the city moved quickly. Servetus was convicted and sentenced to death immediately.

These two high-profile cases prompt some comment on Calvin's theology. In particular they highlight the extent to which the 'high theology' of Trinitarianism and predestination was just as capable of becoming a matter of popular debate, argument and conflict as the 'practical theology' of baptismal names and excommunication. For later commentators, the two most important (one might fairly say, unique) aspects of Calvin's theology were the stress he laid on predestination and the 'spiritual' presence in the eucharist. These two doctrines were major stumbling blocks for Geneva's Protestant allies in Switzerland. The predominately Zwinglian ministers favoured a purely symbolic understanding of the Lord's Supper. For them, the bread and wine were representational only. They had held this view, to the great detriment of pan-Protestant cooperation, against Luther and his consubstantial eucharist. Although Calvin also rejected the physicality of Luther's views, it is clear that his understanding of what happened at communion was more in line with Luther (and, one might argue, Catholics) than the radical reinterpretation offered by Zwingli. However, since Calvin also stressed that only believers benefited from a spiritual presence, this refinement – together with the enthusiasm of Swiss magistrates and ministers (especially, Bullinger) for conciliation – meant the issue was not insuperable. In 1549 Calvin took a vital initiative to promote consensus between Geneva and Zurich, by steering an initially reluctant Bullinger towards a joint statement of eucharistic theology – the *Consensus Tigurinus*. This would prove the basis of the later and vital unity between the Swiss churches on this crucial question.[2]

In some ways, the issue of predestination posed a greater problem. There is no reason to think that Calvin's views were radically out of step with other reformers. After all, one need only read Luther's *De servo arbitrio* (or indeed much of Augustine) to realize how widespread this 'Calvinist' understanding of predestination was. The problem for Calvin's Swiss colleagues (both ministerial and magisterial) was the prominence Calvin gave to this point of 'high' theology in his 'practical' theology. Not without cause, Luther expressed his radical views on predestination in Latin, not the vernacular. Many were troubled, if not incensed, that Calvin preached on predestination, election and reprobation on a regular basis. They did not sympathize with his insistence that these beliefs were a great source of consolation and strength to believers.

The difference, of course, was the situation of the particular believer. In settled reformed societies, these beliefs were troublesome and disturbing to the laity. However, to Protestants being persecuted, exiled and executed for their faith, these doctrines were a source of great reassurance. Calvin, whose eyes never strayed from the suffering of Protestants in his native France, understood the strength these beliefs could give both to his compatriots in France but also to his fellow refugees (and, perhaps, himself) in Geneva. Sufferings, persecution, exile, deprivation and even death were not meaningless and, ultimately, were part of God's eternal plan for the elect. If one saw in all things the hand of one's God, then all things were bearable, all things endurable. One could see in these punishments the refining work of God. However, in a settled Protestant society it was much more difficult individually to discern God's will, plan or election and this doctrine therefore left many lay people concerned and troubled. In this dichotomy one can understand the unease the strenuous preaching of these doctrines could engender in magistrates and ministers in securely Protestant states.

TRIUMPH AND CONSOLIDATION (1555–9)

The crisis which finally settled Calvin's position in Geneva came to a head in late 1554 and early 1555. The increasing anti-French sentiment manifested itself in attacks on refugees and rioting. Calvin and the other French in the city found support amongst local Genevans who saw the refugees as religious martyrs deserving of help. In addition, Calvin's supporters recognized in the French a tool with which they could lever out of power Geneva's dominant political faction (centred on his old adversary, Ami Perrin). The Perrinists, part of the *Guillermin* faction of 1538–42, were the largest single grouping in Genevan politics, though not an outright majority. Although elections throughout the early 1550s had returned Perrinist or pro-Perrinist governments, these proved unable to bring stability or unity to Geneva. They faced two insuperable problems. First, the unified front presented by the Company and the Consistory meant the Senate was unable to bring the ecclesiastical structure to heel. Also, the flood of refugees increasingly embroiled Geneva in French affairs and detracted from the effort to join the Swiss Confederation, a policy the Perrinists favoured.

In 1555, the electorate swayed slightly against the pro-Swiss, anti-French Perrinists, and their opponents gained a one-vote majority. Acting with a speed and ruthlessness never contemplated by the Perrinists, the new government moved to secure its narrow electoral base. Despite legal and extra-legal protests by the Perrinists, French immigrants were admitted as *bourgeois* in large numbers.[3] By May, the Perrinists realized they were unlikely ever to regain political power. A drunken riot on the night of 16 May was described as an attempted coup and deemed treasonable. Perrinists were arrested or fled. Within six months, a third of Geneva's ruling elite had gone into exile. Perrinists' estates were confiscated. The Swiss responded with fury and horror. However, after twenty years Geneva gained domestic unity, a secure ecclesiastical settlement (with the church given a free hand in its own affairs) and had irrevocably turned its face away from membership in the Confederacy. In protest, Berne allowed their defensive alliance to lapse.

Henceforth, Geneva would be an independent city, under Swiss protection, with a substantial French population, guided by Calvin. The city abandoned its previous attempts to 'turn Swiss' and threw itself into supporting the Reformation in France.

There was no single explanation for Calvin's ultimate triumph. However, if one were to stress one aspect of Calvin's Genevan ministry that contributed to his success then the vital importance of his pulpit ministry becomes clear. By 1549 sermons were being held in the city every day and thrice on Sunday. In addition, each week saw catechism classes, theological debates and Bible studies (*congréga-tions*), meetings of the ministers and a Consistory session. In other words, Calvin (and the other ministers) was the visible face – and audible voice – of authority in the city. Calvin interpreted the Scriptures, declared God's Word, admonished, cajoled and threatened the people of Geneva, day in and day out. Against his control (and use) of the pulpit ministry, Calvin's opponents had no comparable forum in which they could propound and defend their position.

These reflections highlight the importance, against a tendency in Calvinist studies to focus on Calvin the theologian and writer, of Calvin's role as a minister. This emphasis on theology is perhaps understandable, since Calvin has left an enormous body of printed literature. Moreover, the bulk of his literary production was not, in fact, directed at Geneva. Calvin devoted much of his literary activity to nurturing, promoting and stabilizing French Protestantism. However, this bifur-cation of Calvin is artificial and unfair. Calvin was, first and foremost, a pastor. He devoted endless time and energy to his flock in Geneva as well as the flock he felt responsible for in France. In addition, this historiographical approach (and confes-sional fixation) overlooks the importance of the local Genevan context in shaping much of what one now calls Calvinism. Not only was the ecclesiastical model a local creation but also the practical working out of the place of ministerial freedom and the role of excommunication were thrashed out in the republic. Of course,

Figure 18.1 Anon., *John Calvin*. Sometimes (very doubtfully) attributed to Hans Holbein, though it is hard to see how the paths of the painter and the Genevan reformer could ever have crossed. (Grand Rapids, H. Henry Meeter Center for Calvin Research)

some of Calvin's views emerged as the result of interactions with and reactions to issues, persons and ideas beyond Geneva's gates. Nevertheless, there is a very real sense in which one should never cease to view Calvin, his work, his writing and his beliefs as the product of his local ministry. Much of the advice and counsel he gave to his distant and persecuted flock in France arose from the experiences he had working with his local Genevan congregation.

After the convulsions of 1555, Calvin continued in his Genevan ministry another nine years. The final component of Calvin's ecclesiastical model did not appear immediately after his victory. It was not until 1559 that the city agreed to use the Perrinists' property to fund the new Genevan Academy. This was the high-water mark of Calvin's ministry. The city had a functioning (and mostly independent)

Consistory, a high quality Company of Pastors, a ministerially dominated public school system and a seminary for training (foreign) ministers. However, Calvin was not wholly supreme. His attempt to introduce draconian morals' legislation in 1557 had been rejected by the Conseil Générale as 'too severe'. Also, the city never relinquished control of poor relief to the church. Geneva had elected magistrates who served as *procureurs*, never deacons.[4] Despite these few failures, the system that one identifies as 'Calvinism' was in place and functioning by 1559.

THE FINAL YEARS (1560–4)

After 1559, Calvin's health began to fail. The arrival of Beza in 1559 provided Calvin with a key supporter and obvious successor. Although ill, Calvin was still asked to head the committee (which included the refugee lawyer, Colladon) selected to redraft the 1542 Constitution. Calvin did not live to see the project finished, but there is little reason to doubt that he had a major input into the subsequent 1568 Constitution.

Calvin's relationship with Geneva had been tumultuous. And yet, by 1555–9, Geneva was serving as a model for Calvinists across Europe. Why would others want to visit the same traumas upon their homeland? The key point to remember is that many of the non-French refugees (especially the English and Scots) arrived after the worst of the 1555 crisis. Thus they saw a Geneva purged of opposition, full of zealous refugees. Truly, it must have been a place of enthusiasm, learning, devotion and determination.

The post-1555 magistrates were largely drawn from the Consistory and had a close working relationship with Calvin. In them and their relationship with the Company of Pastors, these temporary residents of Geneva beheld a city full of and led by zealots united by religious fervour. The price paid to reach this happy pass was unknown: the crises, the riots, the rupture with the Swiss Protestants, the exiles. Men like Knox went away striving to emulate an artificial creation. Calvin had not overseen the conversion of the Genevans into a Calvinist community but the transformation of Geneva into a Calvinist camp; in effect, a gathered community.

NOTES

1   *Eidguenots* from *Eidgenossen* (Swiss for 'confederates'), a reference to the *Enfants'* desire to join the Confederacy. Some suggest this may be the source for the word Huguenot.
2   Paul Rorem, *Calvin and Bullinger on the Lord's Supper* (Nottingham, 1989).
3   In 1555, 127 were admitted and another 144 the following year. This total of 271 compares with 269 for the entire period 1543–54.
4   Though the administrators of the privately funded *bourses* that aided refugees were styled deacons.

FURTHER READING

In a general sense, for those interested in pursuing aspects of the above discussion in greater detail, one can divide the secondary literature into three broad categories: Genevan history, biographies of Calvin and Calvin's theology. In the area of Genevan history, one might usefully consult the works of Robert M. Kingdon, William Monter and William Naphy. Robert Kingdon, *Geneva and the Coming of the Wars of Religion in France, 1555–1563* (Geneva, 1956) and *Adultery and Divorce in Calvin's Geneva* (Cambridge, MA, 1995). See also now the ongoing project to publish the *Registres du Consistoire de Genève au temps de Calvin*, ed. Thomas A. Lambert and Isabella Watt (vol. 1, Geneva, 1996), progressing under the direction of Kingdon. E. William Monter, *Studies in Genevan Government* (Geneva, 1964) and *Calvin's Geneva* (London, 1967). William G. Naphy, *Calvin and the Consolidation of the Genevan Reformation* (Manchester, 1994). J.A. Gautier, *Histoire de Genève* (9 vols; Geneva, 1898), although historiographically dated, remains the best starting point. One might also consider Henri Naef's *Les Origines de la Réforme à Genève* (2 vols; Geneva, 1936), which gives the best detailed analysis of the early phases of the Genevan Reformation. In addition one might usefully consult William C. Innes, *Social Concerns in Calvin's Geneva* (Allison Park, 1983); Jeannine Olsen, *Calvin and Social Welfare: Deacons and the Bourse Française* (Sellingsgrove, 1989), and T.H.L. Parker, *Calvin's Preaching* (Edinburgh, 1992).

In the realm of biographies, the list is almost endless. The most detailed work (and one which has stood the test of time very well indeed) is Emile Doumergue's magisterial *Jean Calvin: Les hommes et les choses de son temps* (7 vols; Lausanne, 1899–1917). More recent biographies include William J. Bouwsma's somewhat idiosyncratic *John Calvin: A Sixteenth-Century Portrait* (Oxford, 1988). Also of interest is Quirinus Breen's *John Calvin: A Study in French Humanism* (Hamden, 1968). See also Alexandre Ganoczy, *The Young Calvin* (Philadelphia, 1987); Alistair McGrath, *A Life of John Calvin* (Oxford, 1990); T.H.L. Parker, *John Calvin: A Biography* (London, 1975), and François Wendel, *John Calvin* (London, 1963).

While Genevan history has attracted only a few non-Genevan historians and Calvin has inspired so many biographers, his theology has been an even greater source of fascination and debate to scholars. See especially Willem Balke, *Calvin and the Anabaptist Radicals* (Grand Rapids, 1981); André Bieler, *Pensée economique et sociale de Calvin* (Geneva, 1961); Robert Kingdon and Robert Linder (eds), *Calvin and Calvinism* (Lexington, 1970); Harro Höpfl, *The Christian Polity of John Calvin* (Cambridge, 1982); Francis Higman, *The Style of John Calvin in his French Polemical Treatises* (Oxford, 1957); Brian Gerrish, *Grace and Gratitude: The Eucharistic Theology of John Calvin* (Minneapolis, 1993); Donald K. McKim (ed.), *Readings in Calvin's Theology* (Grand Rapids, 1984), and Richard Gamble (ed.), *Articles on Calvin and Calvinism* (London, 1992).

CHAPTER NINETEEN

THE FRENCH WARS OF RELIGION

Raymond A. Mentzer

The confessional tensions arising from the Reformation led to prolonged and intense conflict in France, as elsewhere throughout Europe. Highly organized and reasonably well-financed warfare, as well as less premeditated, more spontaneous outbreaks of popular violence – tumultuous local revolts, murderous riots and brutal massacres – underscored the deep fissures and explosive pressures which surrounded competing notions of the sacred. Catholics and Protestants bitterly opposed one another over what they perceived to be fundamental questions regarding the nature of the godly and, accordingly, how the community ought best to be organized. The religious transformations and consequent attempts to reorder society proved a difficult and uncertain process, one indelibly marked by discord and strife. Altogether, the Reformation was deeply divisive for the people who lived within the French realm, from the lowest to the highest orders.

The wars, which shattered France internally for decades and led to external conflict, principally with Spain, began with the massacre at Vassy in 1562, subsided after the Edict of Nantes in 1598 and erupted again briefly in the 1620s. The conflict was first and foremost an encounter between communities of believers, people who worshipped and prayed together. It was rooted in collective practices of piety and went well beyond quarrelling over a body of beliefs. Antagonisms between rival religious cultures focused on everyday conduct and ideas regarding appropriate devotion. Protestants vehemently rejected, for instance, the 'idolatries' of the mass and the veneration of saints and their relics, while Catholics took offence at Reformed sermon services and the singing of the Psalms in the vernacular. Each side viewed the other as having profaned the Lord and polluted the community. The ensuing cleansing and purifying process was at best contentious and frequently lethal.

While the wars sprang primarily from the fierce confessional competition between Protestant and Catholic, political, social and economic elements soon became entangled in the struggle. The eruption of religious friction coincided with a grave political crisis in France. The unexpected death of King Henry II in 1559 led to a power struggle at the highest levels and stirred the nobility to assert claims for a greater role in the governance of the realm. The monarchical crisis and aristocratic unrest triggered dangerous institutional instability. In addition, the fighting reverberated profoundly through the economy. Military activity on and off the battlefield, as well as various popular disturbances, severely disrupted agricultural and artisan production. Famine and epidemic were, as ever, the close accompaniment of war. The disorder spilled into the social realm too, unleashing latent tensions. During the late 1570s, harsh wartime conditions and the breakdown of authority in Vivarais prompted peasants' revolts and artisan risings, while in neighbouring Dauphiné the disruptive conflict contributed to the emergence of hostilities between the nobility and the urban bourgeoisie.[1] Later, in the 1590s, the social upheaval became more widespread and more serious. The activities of the Catholic League at Paris and provincial towns exacerbated existing strains in the social fabric. In the end, the faultlines of discord were multiple: economic, social, political and, above all, religious. Indeed, the conjunction of the religious and political aspects during the late 1550s and early 1560s led directly to the firestorm that engulfed France for the next forty years and beyond.

THE DRIFT TO WAR

Notions of religious reform had circulated in France since the beginning of the century (see Chapter 12). Widespread conflict and the resort to arms, however, began only in the early 1560s. Throughout the previous decade, the Reformed movement instituted by John Calvin at Geneva had attracted increasing numbers of converts in his native France. Among other things, Calvin's followers had undertaken an intense and successful evangelization effort. The growth continued into the initial decade of warfare. Janine Garrisson estimates that some 1,400 Reformed churches were established in the kingdom between 1560 and 1570, which was undoubtedly the high-point of French Protestant fortunes. In terms of the total number of faithful, Mack Holt suggests that there were some 1.8 million French Protestants, about 10 per cent of the entire population, during the same period.[2] In addition, the Huguenots (as French Protestants came to be called) were heavily concentrated in the western and southern portions of the kingdom. They lived along the Atlantic coast at La Rochelle and throughout the provinces of Normandy and Poitou. The French Reformed churches also had deep roots in southern France, a region known as the Midi. Towns such as Castres, Montauban and Nîmes and the many Protestant villages of the Cévennes mountains became legendary in the history of the French Reformation. Roughly four-fifths of all Huguenots lived in these areas. The solid Reformed presence in these locales afforded a measure of protection as Protestants set about constructing the churches and consistories, colloquies and synods which in turn formed the basis for an extensive and uniform national system.

The rapid expansion of Protestantism coincided with the marked deterioration of political stability. The key event was death of Henry II in July 1559 following a jousting accident. The king's passing initiated a political crisis, which in combination with the mounting religious tension led to open warfare. Henry's fifteen-year-old son, Francis II, succeeded him on the throne. Not surprisingly, the new king lacked experience and judgement. As a result, noble factions vied for dominance during his seventeen-month reign. In the short term, the Queen Mother

Catherine de Medici and members of the ultra-Catholic Guise family controlled the government.

Competition among aristocratic affiliations only worsened an already tense situation. As the Reformed movement gathered strength in France, especially in the larger cities and among urban professionals and artisans, the conversion of ever more aristocrats meant that confessional divisions had serious political consequences. The interests of great families figured prominently in the wars and the noble elite divided into several competing factions. The royal house of Valois remained Catholic, although it repeatedly sought a middle course amid the religious turmoil. The Guise family emerged as the great defender of the Catholic faith, while the Bourbons led the Protestant cause. Another important household was the Montmorency, whose members included both moderate Catholics and resolute Protestants. These powerful families, along with their many allies and clients, provided political, diplomatic and military leadership throughout the wars.

Catherine de Medici oversaw the fortunes of the Valois house following the death of her husband Henry II. While Catholic, she was also a pragmatic woman who sought to advance the political interests of the royal children. Three of her sons wore the crown of France during this turbulent era: Francis II (reigned 1559–60), Charles IX (reigned 1560–74) and Henry III (reigned 1574–89). One daughter, Elizabeth, married King Philip II of Spain and another, Marguerite, was for a time married to Henry of Navarre, the future King Henry IV (reigned 1589–1610).

The Guise, whose lands lay to the east in and around Lorraine, were ardently Catholic and virulently anti-Protestant. They were a powerful clan whose members held important feudal titles, royal offices and ecclesiastical appointments. Their ties to King Francis II were especially strong. He had married Mary Stuart, Queen of Scots, whose mother was Mary of Guise. Thus the elder Guise spokesmen – Francis, Duke of Guise, and Charles, Cardinal of Lorraine – wielded enormous influence during the young king's brief rule. The duke had a distinguished military career and the cardinal was among the richest and most powerful prelates in France.

Opposed to the Guise were the largely Protestant Bourbons, princes of the blood who stood to succeed to the throne in event of the extinction of the ruling Valois house. In fact, this occurred with the succession of Henry of Navarre following the murder of King Henry III in 1589. On the eve of the religious wars, Antoine de Bourbon (who was King of Navarre by virtue of his marriage to Jeanne d'Albret) was titular head of the family. He proved a weak and vacillating figure whose ultimate religious loyalties remained uncertain. Far more steadfast in her dedication to the Reformed faith was his wife Jeanne d'Albret, Queen of Navarre. She exercised considerable moral and political influence within the Huguenot camp until her death in June 1572. Their son, born in 1553, was Henry of Navarre, future King of Navarre and of France. Louis de Bourbon, Prince of Condé and Antoine's younger brother, was also deeply committed to the Huguenot cause. Condé directed the Protestant efforts during the first three wars.

Anne de Montmorency, Constable of France, headed a fourth family with extensive influence. The constable had been a close adviser to Henry II and was a staunch and sincere Catholic. Others within his family, however, were Protestants or moderate Catholics. His sister, Louise de Châtillon, favoured the Reform and her three sons became leaders of the Huguenot movement. The best known was Gaspard de Coligny, Admiral of France, whose assassination in August 1572 was the opening event in the St Bartholomew's Day massacres. Given their religious affinities, the Châtillons were close allies of the Bourbons. Finally, two of Montmorency's sons — Francis, Marshal of France, and Henri de Damville, Governor of Languedoc — were moderate Catholics who were willing when necessary to work with the Huguenots.

The first outward sign of the drift towards civil war occurred in March 1560 when a group of Protestant nobles, mostly youthful lesser figures who resented Guise influence over Francis II, engaged in the impulsive conspiracy of Amboise. Their plan was to capture Francis II while the royal court wintered at the château of Amboise and thereby remove him from Guise tutelage. The plot failed miserably and many of the conspirators were quickly executed as traitors. Nonetheless, the incident alarmed conservative Catholics throughout the kingdom. It seemed ample evidence of the disruptive and seditious character of the Protestant heresy. Yet the king and his Guise advisers were unable to stem the spreading religious unrest or calm the volatile political situation.

Francis II died suddenly from a severe ear infection in December 1560 and with the accession of his nine-year-old brother, Charles IX, Guise influence over the crown diminished. The queen mother became regent in her son's minority and replaced the Guise with her supporters on the royal council. She appointed Antoine de Bourbon, King of Navarre, as lieutenant-general of the realm and even appointed the Protestant Gaspard de Coligny to the council. For the first time, Protestants had a direct voice in the governance of France. The queen mother then embarked upon a policy of compromise and increased religious tolerance in the hope of avoiding armed strife. Many officials, such as the chancellor Michel de l'Hôpital, fully supported her moderate course and urged that the religious issues be settled peacefully. The critical need for public order and tranquillity engendered, according to this view, a call for practical toleration.

Catherine de Medici began by summoning a national council or colloquy of the French church to meet at Poissy near Paris in September 1561 (see Figure 19.1). The expectation was that Catholic and Protestant ecclesiastical officials and theologians would find some common religious ground within the larger framework of a Gallican church. The notion of a church administratively dominated by the monarchy and relatively independent of the Roman papacy had long found favour in France. Yet the queen mother's attempt collapsed because neither side was in a mood to compromise. Again, the principal effect appears to have been the mobilization of Catholics, who began to organize their opposition with even greater diligence. Duke Francis of Guise, Constable Montmorency and Marshal Saint-André formed a military triumvirate in late 1561 to put pressure on the crown. Their open call for the elimination of the Protestants measurably increased the prospect of war.

Figure 19.1 The Colloquy of Poissy. The bishops and magistrates of the Parlement of Paris are drawn up to left and right while the reformers, led by Theodore Beza, plead their case at the bar. The young king and Catherine de Medici preside. From Perressin and Tortorell, *Quarante tableaux touchant les troubles en France*, 1570. (St Andrews University Library)

The queen mother remained undeterred in her views. She issued an edict of toleration in January 1562. This so-called Edict of January granted the Huguenots formal recognition and allowed them to practise their religion under limited circumstances. They could assemble for worship outside town walls during the daytime, but were expressly forbidden to arm themselves. The government's chief concern was the maintenance of public order. From the Protestants' perspective, although the concessions were minimal, they could now hold their sermon services openly and peacefully. Predictably, the edict aroused immediate strong opposition from the triumvirs, as well as from the French Catholic hierarchy and the powerful judges who sat on the sovereign high court of the Parlement of Paris. The Parlement baulked at registering the edict as required by law and did so on 6 March 1562 only at the express command of the monarch. By then the incendiary event had already occurred. Less than a week earlier on 1 March, the Duke of Guise and a group of armed followers, while travelling in Champagne, had come upon a Huguenot congregation worshipping within the town of Vassy, in violation of the edict. Guise and his men promptly slew many of the Protestants. The duke then marched on Paris and with the other triumvirs began to raise a Catholic army. They even managed to convince Antoine de Bourbon to enter their camp. Eventually, the queen mother and royalist forces joined them in the attempt to suppress the Protestants.

The Huguenots, for their part, had been no less active. The national synod of the Reformed churches of France, meeting at Orleans in April, asked Louis de Bourbon, Prince of Condé, to gather soldiers for the protection of the faithful. Condé, in turn, issued the call to oppose the Guise. The French Reformed churches possessed a highly developed hierarchy of ecclesiastical institutions, local churches, regional colloquies, provincial and national synods, which in conjunction with Condé's endeavours, were utilized to raise money and arms throughout France during the spring of 1562. The southern French church of Nîmes, for example, responded with the dispatch of money in March 1562. At Le Mans, southwest of Paris, the Huguenot nobility sought to raise money and muster men, while the elders of the local Reformed church identified those men in the congregation who were fit for service and thereby able to contribute to the town's defence.[3]

THE SEARCH FOR PEACE

A series of eight wars, interspersed on an official level by peace treaties and truces, ensued. At the local level, however, the tensions rarely subsided: the violence was widespread and ongoing. Hostilities plagued the towns of southern France, for example, throughout the late winter and spring of 1562. In February, Protestants at Nîmes killed several Catholics who refused to repudiate the 'false' worship of the mass. The next month at Castelnaudary, participants in a passing Catholic procession slew dozens of Protestants who had gathered for a preaching service.[4] Similar incidents occurred in nearly every corner of the kingdom.

The first of the religious wars was a stalemate. While the Catholics won the only major engagement, at Dreux in December 1562, the death of Marshal Saint-

André tempered their victory. In addition, the rival commanders, the Constable Montmorency and the Prince of Condé, were captured. Antoine de Bourbon had already perished from wounds received in the Siege of Rouen. Losses among the leadership culminated with the assassination of Duke Francis of Guise while besieging Orleans in February 1563. Catherine de Medici then acted swiftly to end the fighting. She secured the release of Montmorency and Condé; together, they arranged the Edict of Amboise in March. It was a compromise settlement that, much as the earlier Edict of January 1562, permitted the Protestants limited freedom of worship.

This initial war, its conduct and conclusion were a model that would, in many ways, be replayed time and again until the end of the century. Neither side was capable of gaining significant advantage on the battlefield. Upon expending their limited energies and resources, they agreed upon a compromise arrangement that was wholly unenforceable. The peace was at best temporary, a truce or interim that allowed each camp to regroup and renew the fight at a later date. The other aspect of the first war which reoccurred with regularity, was the involvement of outside powers. Both Catholics and Protestants sought and received aid in the form of money and troops from their respective foreign supporters: Philip II of Spain on the Catholic side; for the Huguenots Elizabeth of England, various German princes and other lesser powers. Although fought on French soil, the wars became the focus of a European clash.

After the Peace of Amboise, the royal court embarked on a two-year tour of the provinces, beginning in March 1565. It was an attempt to maintain the peace and strengthen the position of the monarch. The campaign yielded meagre results. Furthermore, the Catholic faction, led by the deceased Duke of Guise's two brothers – Claude, Duke of Aumale, and Charles, Cardinal of Lorraine – continued to dominate the court. A second war, which lasted about half a year, broke out by September 1567. It began over Huguenot apprehensions that a Spanish army marching along the eastern frontier of France would be diverted from its announced goal of suppressing the Revolt of the Netherlands. Fearful of a combined Spanish-French campaign against their co-religionists, Coligny and Condé attempted unsuccessfully to kidnap the royal court at Meaux and, once more, free the king from Guise control. The war that followed was another military stalemate. The most notable event was the death of Constable Montmorency from wounds received at the Battle of Saint-Denis in November 1567. The original triumvirs were now dead. The Edict of Longjumeau, which was signed in March 1568, mostly reiterated the earlier Edict of Amboise; again, the fighting ended but once more temporarily.

Another war began almost immediately, as the Cardinal of Lorraine persuaded the royal council to seek the arrest of Condé and Admiral Coligny. The two Huguenot leaders, who managed to elude capture, took refuge at La Rochelle and by September 1568 the third civil war was under way. After Condé was killed at the Battle of Jarnac in March 1569, Coligny regrouped the Huguenot forces and prevented the royal army from capitalizing on its victory. The Edict of Saint-Germain, negotiated in August 1570 and only slightly more favourable to the Huguenots than previous peace arrangements, concluded this third round of hostilities with yet another compromise settlement. Neither Catholic nor Protestant had been able to achieve convincing victory. Instead, they were left with little more than heightened mistrust and apprehensions. Indeed, by the late 1560s, the growth among Catholics of fiery popular piety and crusading zeal, evidenced especially in the activities of confraternities, emphasized an additional deadly element in the confessional tension. Hereafter, a savage collective rage, more intense than previous local disturbances, accompanied the various military campaigns.

ST BARTHOLOMEW'S DAY AND ITS CONSEQUENCES

With the death of the major factional leaders in the first three wars, Catherine de Medici returned to her policy of restraint and reconciliation. The cornerstone of the attempt to turn the fragile truce into a permanent peace became the negotiated union between her daughter Marguerite of Valois and Henry of Navarre, Jeanne d'Albret's son who was now King of Navarre and nominal head of the Huguenot forces. The marriage took place in Paris on 18 August 1572. A week later, the celebration of the wedding alliance between the Bourbon and Valois families gave way to the most famous bloodbath of the sixteenth century. The St Bartholomew's Day massacres began with the assassination of Admiral Coligny and the slaughter of the Huguenot wedding guests housed in and near the Louvre Palace. The killing quickly spread through Paris and eventually involved several provincial cities. The result was the frightful murder of thousands of French Protestants.

The St Bartholomew's Day killing was one of the most horrifying and tragic episodes associated with the Reformation. At the same time, the events of August 1572 cannot be viewed in isolation. They were the culmination of a larger pattern of confessional animosity and rising collective violence. Popular religious tensions had been building for some time in Paris and a number of other cities. Grisly riots had occurred in the months immediately preceding the royal marriage and provided an ominous setting for August's homicidal frenzy.

The series of murders known collectively as the St Bartholomew's Day massacres began on 22 August 1572 with the attempted assassination of Admiral Gaspard de Coligny, who was the principal political and military commander of the Protestant forces. He and many other Huguenot leaders had remained in Paris to discuss violations of the latest peace settlement with the king. While returning to his residence following a meeting with Charles IX, Coligny was shot in the hand and arm from the upper window of a house. Although this initial attack seems to have been directed solely at Coligny and was not part of a larger, more nefarious offensive against Protestants, the violence would soon escalate to widespread killing. The admiral and most of the Huguenot nobles made a fateful decision to remain in Paris after assurances from the king that the attackers would be apprehended. The next day, Saturday 23 August, the royal council met to discuss the growing strain and fears of Huguenot reprisals for the attempt on Coligny's life. In fact, some 4,000 Huguenot soldiers under the command of Coligny's brother-in-law stood outside the capital. Council members appear to have agreed that the best course of action to prevent the Huguenots from taking revenge was to strike first. The king and queen mother supported the plan and ordered the royal guards to slay the several dozen Huguenot leaders still in Paris. The political assassinations of Coligny and other Protestant aristocrats took place in the early hours of Sunday 24 August. Again the violence, however reprehensible, appears not to have been premeditated and focused on a limited number of key persons. The king, queen mother and their advisers did not intend it to be a wholesale slaughter of the Huguenot population.

As word of events in and around the Louvre Palace spread through Paris, the popular religious anxieties that had been mounting for some time exploded with deadly fury. The general massacre began on Sunday morning, St Bartholomew's Day, and continued for three days. Fanatical Catholics, outraged by Protestant contamination and driven to a collective zeal, committed most of the carnage. They shot, stabbed and impaled their victims. Women, particularly pregnant women, received especially harsh treatment. The rioters often took particular care to kill the foetus. They also mutilated Protestant corpses, cutting off heads, limbs and genitalia.

In seeking to explain this bloodthirsty behaviour, Natalie Davis has emphasized the ritual structure of the crowd's cruel performance.[5] These 'rites of violence' constituted neither exceptional nor abnormal behaviour. The fierce collective conduct followed discernible patterns and was far from random and senseless. The actions were closely tied to the life of worship and time-honoured purificatory traditions. Catholics saw the Protestants as an acute danger to the political and social order. Accordingly, they had to be annihilated. The Huguenots, including the unborn and those already dead, deserved utter humiliation and dehumanization for, after all, they had trespassed upon all that was sacred within the community as Catholics interpreted it. Indeed, throwing corpses into the Seine and burning victims' houses, common acts in the massacres, suggest long-established rituals of cleansing with water or purifying by fire.

Participants in the massacres undoubtedly believed that they were acting with royal authorization, as well as carrying out the divine will. Henry, the youthful Duke of Guise following the assassination of his father Francis in 1563, led the assault on Coligny and the other Huguenot leaders. He was overheard to have said that the murders took place at the 'king's command'. Parisian Catholics apparently read the remark as conferring a sense of public purpose upon their savagery; they believed that Charles IX endorsed the killing. Catholic preachers and pamphleteers had, in addition, been labouring since the conclusion of the third religious war two years earlier to convince people that God could and did use common folk as instruments of divine justice. If, furthermore, God was angry with Parisians for tolerating heretics in their midst, St Bartholomew's Day offered an opportunity to right the horrible wrong and fulfil the divine will.

In the weeks that followed, as news of the events at Paris reverberated through the provinces, a string of additional massacres took place in a dozen different urban centres, including Bordeaux, Lyon, Orleans, Rouen and Toulouse. Although Catholics controlled these towns and constituted a strong majority, each had a significant Huguenot presence. All had experienced considerable religious strife and internal division during the early years of warfare. In several cases, the Huguenot minority had actually seized power for a brief time. Again, Protestants had contaminated Catholic religious culture and posed a grave danger to the body social.

Holt puts the number of Parisian victims at roughly 2,000 and estimates that another 3,000 Protestants died in the provincial aftermath.[6] Much of the political and military elite, in particular, was dead. Many other Huguenots went into hiding or fled the kingdom. In addition, a substantial number of the faithful, deeply discouraged if not thoroughly terrified, defected to Catholicism. Altogether, the St Bartholomew's Day massacres had a profound and enduring impact upon the French Protestant movement. The initial confidence, dramatic growth and euphoric expectation of converting France to the true religion vanished. Exhilaration gave way to despair. Numbers declined, energies dissipated and enthusiasm waned. The events of August 1572 marked a decisive point in the French Reformation.

The sheer magnitude of St Bartholomew's Day has overshadowed the confessional violence at other moments and especially for towns outside Paris. Protestants, furthermore, could be as bloodthirsty as Catholics. Earlier Huguenot rage at Nîmes led to the *Michelade*, named after the day on which it occurred, St Michael's Feast (29 September) 1567. It was the massacre of a hundred or so Catholics, mostly priests and prominent laymen at the hands of their Protestant neighbours. Few towns escaped the episodic violence and some suffered repeatedly from both sides. At Gaillac in Languedoc, for example, Catholics massacred Protestants in 1562 and 1572; Protestants attacked the Catholics in 1568.[7] Neither faith had a monopoly on cruelty and misguided fervour. The assassination of individual leaders, beginning with the murder of Duke Francis of Guise in 1563, was equally common. Catholics killed the Huguenot leader Coligny in 1572. Royal guards cut down Henry of Guise in 1588. Extremist Catholic assassins murdered Henry III in 1589 and Henry IV in 1610. Numerous lesser figures perished in similar fashion. Accordingly, St Bartholomew's Day must be understood as the most extensive and dramatic in a succession of collective and individual acts of murder stemming from powerful and passionate confessional hatreds.

An immediate consequence of the 1572 massacres was the resumption of warfare. Most of the fighting centred on Charles IX's inconclusive siege of La Rochelle. After substantial loss of life and depletion of financial resources, the Peace of La Rochelle negotiated in July 1573 ended the fourth religious war. The new settlement resembled the 1570 Peace of Saint-Germain with the notable exception of the toleration clauses. The revisions theoretically granted the Huguenots freedom of conscience but severely restricted their right to worship. The arrangements also did little to stabilize France. Despite the enormity of the massacres, the kingdom had not been purged of Huguenots. They retained political and military strength, particularly in the south, where they refused to lay down their arms. There Protestants openly defied the terms of the Peace of La Rochelle. At the same time, Catholic suspicions and apprehensions hardly lessened. The death of Charles IX in May 1574 and the coronation of his younger brother, Henry III, formerly Duke of Anjou and briefly King of Poland, only worsened the troubled situation.

If St Bartholomew's Day and its repercussions weakened French Protestants, it also moved them to rethink their political position. Thoroughly disgusted by a monarchical government that had permitted atrocities on an unimaginable scale, Protestants in southern France formed a federal or republican government complete with local assemblies. Some historians have labelled the enterprise a 'United Provinces of the Midi' in an obvious comparison to developments in the Netherlands.[8] Huguenot leaders from the region also allied themselves to the Governor of Languedoc, Henri de Damville. The son of Constable Montmorency, Damville was part of an emerging group of moderate Catholics who opposed royal policy. Given the prominence of Damville's position and family, his willingness to support the Huguenots suggests the depth of division within the kingdom.

Other Protestants were even more forceful in their anti-monarchical sentiment and began to propose a variety of resistance theories. They reasoned that a government which was deeply implicated in detestable acts such as those experienced in 1572 had degenerated into tyranny. It had utterly failed its subjects and therefore forfeited all right to obedience. A number of tracts, published in the mid-1570s, expressed these views forcefully. Among the most influential were the anonymous *Reveille-Matin* (1574), François Hotman's *Francogallia* (1573), Theodore Beza's *Du droit des magistrates* (1574) and the pseudonymous *Vindiciae contra tyrannos* (1579), probably written by Philippe Duplessis-Mornay.

The *Reveille-Matin*, which contained a detailed account of the events of St Bartholomew's Day, was an open attack on the crown. Wide-ranging in its approach, the treatise offered a number of anti-monarchical arguments and included a republican constitution, which had been drafted by an unknown group of Protestants in late 1572. This blueprint for a new order called for a decentralized federal government and emphasized the concept of popular sovereignty. The *Francogallia*, for its part, was essentially an historical work. In it, Hotman argued that the principal elements of the ancient Frankish constitution were an elective monarchy and a national assembly. According to his interpretation, this framework had been largely dismantled, especially by Louis XI in the fifteenth century, and sorely needed repair. Hotman also noted the inability of women to govern and recounted the offences of past queen mothers. Few readers would have misread the allusion.

Beza's *Du droit des magistrates* made the case for government on the basis of a contract between king and people. Violation of the compact by a tyrant voided the arrangement and permitted his overthrow by the people in a corporate sense. Sovereignty, after all, resided ultimately with the governed. Despite this assertion of the rights of the sovereign community, Beza did not grant private persons the authority to resist. Rather, it was the duly constituted inferior magistrates, the natural leaders of society, who had the right – if not the duty – to oppose tyranny. Both Hotman and Beza looked to the French Estates-General, a representative body that incorporated the notion of a national assembly or inferior magistrate, to resist the tyranny of the Valois monarchy. The *Vindiciae contra tyrannos*, on the other hand, attributed the right of resistance to an even broader group of magistrates. It undercut the role of the Estates-General by extending the power of resistance to a wide range of aristocrats, judges and other officials, including foreign princes.

THE COLLAPSE OF MONARCHICAL AUTHORITY

The circumstances could hardly have been more difficult for the new French monarch. Henry, Duke of Anjou and younger sibling of Charles IX, had been elected King of Poland in 1573. Upon receiving news of his brother's death in May 1574, he immediately abandoned his Polish crown to become Henry III of France. The realm was on the verge of splintering and the king, while intelligent and cultured, lacked the requisite strength and experience. Simply put, he was unable to provide the leadership to restore harmony and unity. Instead, over the next decade another three wars would perpetuate the deadly rhythm of hostilities with which French men and women had become all too familiar.

The immediate challenge to Henry III came from his ambitious younger brother Francis, Duke of Alençon. In September 1575, the duke fled the court, where he had been under close watch, and quickly announced, in tones mirroring the Huguenot resistance pamphlets, armed opposition to his brother's tyranny. Alençon led a group of malcontent Catholic nobles who joined forces with the coalition that had earlier been forged between Henri de Damville, the moderate Catholic Governor of Languedoc, and the insurgent Huguenots of the Midi. Alençon's position as direct successor to the French throne in the event of Henry III's death only compounded the gravity of the rebellion. In February 1576, Henry of Navarre, who had survived the St Bartholomew's Day massacres by converting to Catholicism, escaped the royal court where he had been forcibly detained. He immediately returned to the Reformed faith and together with Alençon, Damville and Henry, Prince of Condé (son of Louis de Bourbon, the previous Prince of Condé), led a group of Huguenots and *politiques* (moderates who were willing to accept confessional coexistence for the greater well-being of the state). The members of this alliance further strengthened their position with military support from the Calvinist Elector of the Palatinate in the German Rhineland. Faced with mounting opposition, Henry III and Catherine de Medici yielded and agreed to the Edict of Beaulieu in May 1576.

The edict was also called the Peace of Monsieur (the eldest brother of the king was customarily designated 'Monsieur') in recognition of the fact that Alençon appeared to force it upon the king. It concluded the fifth war of religion by granting the Huguenots generous concessions. Protestants received the right to worship openly and to build temples everywhere in France except Paris. The edict also called for the creation of special law courts for Protestant litigants so that they might avoid prejudiced Catholic judges and it awarded the Huguenots eight surety towns, chiefly in southern France. Francis, Duke of Alençon, received the important Duchy of Anjou and was thereby reconciled with the king who, for his part, agreed to summon a meeting of the Estates-General.

The overwhelmingly Catholic deputies to the Estates-General that met at Blois in November 1576 bitterly disagreed with the peace arrangements. They believed that the settlement had largely ignored their demands and much preferred renewed warfare. Only a minority of the delegates urged a negotiated peace and at least temporary tolerance of the Protestants. Among the moderates was Jean Bodin whose *Six livres de la République* had just appeared. The work stressed the sacred character of the monarchy and stood in marked contrast to the Huguenot promotion of a political ideology based on popular sovereignty. The author was a *politique* who sought a return to tranquillity – even though he would later join the Catholic League, most likely in a cautious effort to protect himself. Apprehensive, along with many others, over the destructive anarchy in France, Bodin's stabilizing solution was to concentrate sovereign power in the person and office of the monarch. Political authority was not, in his view, shared between the crown and institutions such as the Estates-General. It belonged indivisibly and absolutely to the king. While the monarch was subject to divine and natural law as well as the fundamental law of the kingdom, he depended on no one. The king was both executive and legislator; he had complete power to command his subjects. Bodin's skilful and dynamic argument would ultimately have persuasive effect in France.

The militants at Blois soon organized a Catholic association or League under the direction of Henry, Duke of Guise. They especially resented Henry III's closest advisers and companions, whom they derisively dubbed the *mignons* or pretty ones. The king's friendship with the *mignons* and his failure to father children eventually gave rise to rumours that he was homosexual. His more belligerent Catholic opponents certainly used the issue against him. More to the point, extremists accused the king of betraying the Catholic church and weakening royal authority. He came under intense pressure to act and had little choice but to return to the battlefield. A sixth war, brief and inconclusive, began in December 1576. The Peace of Bergerac, issued in September 1577, halted the sporadic fighting. The compromise settlement restricted the liberal terms accorded Huguenots in the previous Peace of Monsieur but failed to satisfy the stern demands of dedicated Catholics. It offered no more than a short respite in the incessant conflict.

Another war, the seventh, was fought in 1580. The immediate circumstances were Henry of Navarre's attempt to capture several Catholic bastions in the southwest. Neither side possessed sufficient resources to maintain a sustained offensive and a truce was arranged by November 1580. The Peace of Fleix, negotiated between Navarre and the king's younger brother Francis, now Duke of Anjou, did little more than confirm existing Protestant political and religious privileges.

THE RISE OF THE CATHOLIC LEAGUE

The tangled and tense situation worsened considerably in June 1584 with the death of King Henry III's brother and heir, Francis, Duke of Anjou. The duke's passing had momentous consequences. As the king had no children, his nearest male relative, the Protestant Henry of Navarre was now heir presumptive under the provisions of Salic law. The possibility of a relapsed heretic wearing the crown of France provoked swift and intense opposition from the Catholic majority. The religious and political struggle entered into its most complicated and chaotic phase.

Henry of Navarre's proximity to the throne pushed Huguenots to reconsider their carefully crafted resistance theories. Notions of a strong dynastic monarchy held fresh appeal. Catholics, on the other hand, began to advance a constitutional argument in which the Catholicity of the 'Most Christian King' (as the French monarch traditionally styled himself) took precedence over secular arrangements, such as the ancient Salic law of succession. In the political arena, they revived the Catholic League. Yet the new organization was far more fanatical than its 1576 predecessor. The most extreme expression was at Paris. There and in numerous other towns, Catholic notables established league councils and allied themselves to aristocratic clients of the Guise family. King Henry III attempted unsuccessfully to steer a course between the Huguenots under Navarre's command and the Catholic League dominated by the Duke of Guise. The catastrophic result has been tagged the War of the Three Henries, aptly summarizing the three-sided conflict between royalists under Henry III, Protestants led by Henry of Navarre and Catholics dominated by Henry of Guise.

The League was a complex institution that drew upon a wide range of supporters: nobles, judicial magistrates, the clergy, bourgeois merchants, legal professionals, artisans and workers. Moreover, it was only loosely under command of the Guise. The bond that held the unwieldy confederation together was a shared perspective on the crown. Leaguers regarded the Catholicity of the sovereign monarch as implicit in France's unwritten constitution. The sacral monarchy and Catholicism were inextricably joined. Consequently, the succession of the Protestant Henry of Navarre was unthinkable; it threatened the basic fabric of France's religious-political culture. Even Henry III was held suspect for his failure to fight vigorously for the extirpation of heresy throughout the kingdom.

The Catholic League, led by Duke Henry of Guise, signed a treaty with Spanish emissaries at Joinville in December 1584. King Philip II was alarmed at the prospect of a heretic on the French throne and, in addition, saw an opportunity to increase Spanish leverage in French affairs. From the viewpoint of the League and Guise family, the alliance secured backing from the wealthiest and most powerful state in Europe. The signatories agreed to join in the effort to eradicate Protestantism in France and in the Netherlands, over which Philip II ruled. The treaty marked the beginning of some ten years of direct Spanish intervention in the French civil wars.

The League was in reality a multi-layered union that arose in response to a perceived threat to Catholicism. At the highest political and social levels, the Guise brothers – Duke Henry and his brother Charles, Duke of Mayenne – directed an aristocratic group that provided vital military, political and diplomatic leadership. An urban league composed of bourgeois notables commanded broad popular support and was more radical in its policies. Strong leagues existed at other provincial centres such as Nantes and Toulouse. The association was especially energetic in Paris, where a revolutionary group called the Sixteen (after the sixteen municipal wards in which it had organized cells) won backing from the critical middle groups within urban society. Its membership included clergymen, judges, lawyers and royal officials. The association proved highly adept at mobilizing Catholic sentiment among the petty bourgeois and lower orders. Eventually, the Sixteen became independent of the crown, the Guises and even the Paris municipal authorities.

The popular figure of Henry, Duke of Guise, led the Holy Union of aristocrats and urban notables in their insistence upon the restoration of the one true Catholic faith. In a public statement of March 1585, the league outlined its main objectives:

armed opposition to the heretic Henry of Navarre and recognition of Navarre's Catholic uncle, Cardinal Charles of Bourbon, as rightful successor to the throne. Leaguers were also harshly critical of Henry III for excessive taxation and the tolerance he extended to the Protestants. The king, much as he had when the first League appeared in late 1576, sought to gain control over the movement. Still, he was in a weak financial and military position. Recognizing the circumstances, he negotiated the Treaty of Nemours with the Duke of Guise in July 1585. It revoked the edicts of pacification and forbade the practice of Protestantism. Two months later, the pope excommunicated Henry of Navarre and the other principal Huguenot commander, the Prince of Condé. In Catholic eyes, Navarre was unequivocally barred from the French succession.

All sides once again took up arms. The Duke of Joyeuse, one of the king's favourites, commanded an army that marched south to confront Henry of Navarre. But the Huguenots defeated the royal troops at Coutras and killed Joyeuse in the process. The victory was offset, however, when the Duke of Guise crushed an army of German mercenaries that was seeking to link with Navarre's soldiers. The Huguenot cause was further weakened by the death of Condé in early 1588. Though the Catholic forces appeared on the verge of triumph, divisions within their ranks precluded any quick conclusion to the fighting. Instead, a fundamental split developed between royalist Catholics who supported Henry III and the Leaguers who bitterly opposed him. Even the League itself was beginning to show signs of strain as the Parisian Sixteen acted with increasing independence of the aristocratic group controlled by Guise. The crisis of royal authority and the growing zeal of the extreme Catholics, especially those associated with the Sixteen, were unmistakable in the frenetic developments surrounding the Day of the Barricades in May 1588.

The Sixteen had apparently planned an uprising against the royal government for some time. When the militant organization mobilized its followers in the spring of 1588, the Duke of Guise decided to seize the opportunity. On 9 May he entered Paris, despite the express prohibition of Henry III. The king, hoping to defend royal authority with a show of armed force, dispatched some 4,000 Swiss guards to occupy strategic positions within the city. The plan quickly turned against the monarch. The soldiers' presence merely incited the populace to erect barricades on 12 May and effectively block the guards' movement. With the League militants threatening to trap him in the Louvre, Henry III lost his nerve and fled the city in disgrace. Guise and the Sixteen sealed their triumph by purging the municipal government and placing their supporters in charge of the capital. Two months later, Guise and the League forced Henry III to sign the Edict of Union and accept the humiliating defeat. The monarch recognized the revolutionary Parisian commune, pledged renewed energy in the war against the Huguenots, acknowledged the Cardinal of Bourbon as his heir and agreed to convene the Estates-General. The role of the Estates-General, in particular, assumed crucial importance as Leaguer political theorists proposed notions of popular sovereignty akin to those put forth earlier by the Huguenots. If the king endangered the spiritual welfare of his subjects, representative assemblies could apply corrective action. But events moved in an entirely different direction.

When the League-dominated Estates-General assembled at Blois in October

1588, the king saw an opportunity to avenge his recent disgrace. Hoping as well to strike a decisive blow against the Catholic opposition, Henry III decided to eliminate the Guise brothers and imprison their closest companions. On 23 December, he summoned the Duke and Cardinal of Guise to his apartments in the château at Blois. The royal guards immediately murdered the duke and arrested his brother the cardinal. The latter was killed in his cell the following day. Henry III had his revenge but, in the process, infuriated the League. Resistance at Paris and among the Catholic nobility only intensified. A Guise cousin, the Duke of Aumale, became Governor of Paris and the League's Council of Forty named the youngest Guise brother – Charles, Duke of Mayenne – lieutenant-general of the realm. By early January 1589, the Sorbonne theologians declared the king deposed and called upon all French people to rise against him in defence of the Catholic faith. Catholic propagandists and pamphleteers portrayed Henry III as a tyrant and declared it proper and legitimate for the people to depose and even kill the despot. In his 1589 tract *De justa Henrici tertii abdicatione* (Just Deposition of Henry III), the Sorbonne theologian Jean Boucher went so far as to grant private persons the right to resist and rid the community of the tyrant.

Catherine de Medici, who might have been able to negotiate with the Catholic militants, died in January 1589. Henry III, now more isolated than ever, turned to the Protestant Henry of Navarre and in April they struck an alliance. The king recognized Navarre as his legitimate successor and together they marched their armies toward Paris to seize the capital from a mutual enemy. Their approach and impending clash with the Catholic forces commanded by Mayenne and Aumale spawned an intense propaganda effort within Paris. Preachers and publicists justified the killing of the tyrant and pushed religious passions to a fever pitch. Jacques Clément, a young Dominican lay brother, became caught up in the frenzy and on 1 August 1589 made his way into the royal camp at St Cloud near Paris. He fatally stabbed the king, who died the following day. The Valois dynasty ended. Henry of Navarre was, according to Salic law, King of France; according to those who held for the Catholicity of the crown, he was not.

THE TRIUMPH OF HENRY IV

Catholics in Paris and other League cities rejoiced in Henry III's assassination, regarding it as divine retribution. Protestants, though certainly less exuberant, took comfort in Navarre's succession; they could ask for no more powerful temporal protector. The new king, however, faced a daunting task. The realm was bitterly divided, foreign enemies threatened and the king's own Reformed faith was an enormous barrier to his assumption of full power. Henry IV had to retain the loyalty of the Huguenots and simultaneously secure the backing of the moderate Catholics. Another religious conversion was not immediately possible. The king first needed to strengthen his military and political position. Still, he committed himself to the Catholic character of the crown and kingdom. Henry IV's stance won over many Catholic ecclesiastical official and royal officers who disliked the League's ultramontane ties to Rome and Spain. They much preferred an independent Gallican church.

Henry IV achieved a measure of success on the battlefield, defeating League armies in two successive engagements and laying siege to Paris by the spring of 1590. Only a Spanish army dispatched from the Netherlands saved the city after six months of suffering and starvation. Within the capital, the Sixteen had embarked upon a campaign of terror directed against anyone suspected of moderate or *politique* views. The zealotry soon caused a rift within Leaguer ranks. The Parlement of Paris protested vehemently and several persons withdrew from the Sixteen. The Catholic League in other towns experienced similar internal divisions. To make matters worse, the League pretender to the throne, Cardinal Charles of Bourbon, died in 1590, leaving extreme Catholics with no other reasonable claimant to the throne.

The friction between the noble League led by Duke of Mayenne and the revolutionary Sixteen culminated in November 1591 when the latter purged the Parlement of Paris and executed three judges. The deaths convinced Mayenne to march into Paris, put an end to the dreadful developments and hang four members of the Sixteen. Mayenne, acting in his capacity as lieutenant-general of the realm, next called the Estates-General to elect a Catholic king. The meeting had been an integral part of the League's political agenda since Henry III's assassination.

When the delegates to the League Estates assembled at Paris in January 1593, the Spanish ambassador proposed the candidacy of Philip II's daughter – the Infanta, Isabella Clara Eugenia. Though she possessed Valois blood through her mother Elizabeth of Valois, Salic law precluded succession by a female or even through the female line. A foreigner on the throne was also unpalatable. The Spaniards countered with the suggestion that she marry a suitable French prince, perhaps a Guise. While the controversy continued, moderate Leaguers began meeting with Catholic supporters of Henry IV. By mid-May 1593, the king dramatically broke the deadlock by promising to seek instruction in the Catholic faith. The climactic ceremony of abjuration and absolution took place at the abbey church of Saint-Denis on 25 July 1593. By March 1594, even the city of Paris, long the centre of ardent Catholicism and extreme League activity, opened its gates to the king, who went directly to Notre Dame and piously heard mass. The conservative theologians of the Sorbonne declared Henry IV a sincere Catholic and recognized him as king in late April. Finally, in September 1595, Pope Clement VIII lifted the papal excommunication that had been imposed a decade earlier.

A few militants were, certainly, sceptical of Henry's Catholicism. Attempts on his life were commonplace and, indeed, the assassin François Ravaillac finally succeeded in May 1610. Still, most Catholics became convinced of the value of the king's conversion rather than his permanent exclusion from the throne. The settlement implicit in Henry's confessional transformation and entry into Paris allowed the gradual but deliberate process of healing a kingdom painfully rent by civil and religious war. No one wished to continue the chaos of the past and the monarch alone stood as the guarantor of public order. At issue was the sacred character of monarchy and the stability of French society. The conversion unified and stabilized the kingdom.

THE PROCESS OF PACIFICATION

The Edict of Nantes, which Henry IV proclaimed in April 1598, marked the beginning of a pacification process, which after forty years of war was neither rapid nor facile. The edict provided a legal and political structure for ending the conflict, fostering confessional coexistence and reconstructing the ravaged kingdom. As such, its provisions and procedures were many and complex. The edict had four parts: ninety-two published articles, fifty-six secret articles and two royal brevets. It recognized the legal existence of the French Reformed churches and granted Protestants the same civil rights as Catholics. The edict delineated the circumstances of Huguenot worship and, in particular, established surety towns where Protestants could practise their religion freely and under the protection of their own garrisons. The edict also created special courts, the *chambres de l'Edit*, which were attached to the Parlements of Bordeaux, Grenoble, Toulouse and, in more limited fashion, to the high courts at Paris and Rouen. The Protestant and Catholic judges who sat on these tribunals were empowered to settle any dispute, civil or criminal, in which one of the litigant parties was Protestant. The chambers assured Protestants access to equitable justice or, at least, justice as fair and impartial as possible in the religiously divided world of sixteenth- and seventeenth-century France. The edict also provided Huguenot access to royal offices, professional occupations, schools and universities. While the edict did not give Protestantism complete parity with Catholicism, it did provide a coherent framework for adherents of the two faiths to live together in a semblance of peace.

To ensure its proper application, the king appointed commissioners, one Catholic and the other Protestant, to verify and execute the Edict of Nantes in each province. On a practical level, the commissioners sought to guarantee Protestant worship in those towns where it was permitted under the terms of the edict, re-establish the celebration of the mass throughout the kingdom, and ensure individual and collective security for both Catholics and Protestants.

The provisions of the Edict of Nantes also contained the seeds for conflict in the seventeenth century, a deadly postscript to the violence of the previous age. Although the crown confirmed the edict at the moment of Louis XIII's succession in 1610, the provisions allowing Huguenots a strong measure of political and military autonomy (the notion of a 'state within the state') were soon viewed as detrimental to the best interests of the monarchy. Tensions between crown and Huguenot multiplied in the early 1610s. Matters came to a head in 1617 when Louis XIII restored Catholic worship and all church property in the territory of Béarn, the rump kingdom of Navarre which technically was not covered by the Edict of Nantes. Opposition from Protestants in Béarn persuaded Louis XIII to lead an army southward in the summer of 1620. Béarn quickly submitted, much to the shock of Huguenots elsewhere. Would the crown next compel them to surrender their fortified towns and cease holding political assemblies? When Protestant militants gathered at La Rochelle in defiance of the king's command, a second royal military campaign took place in 1621. This time the Protestants, under the command of Henry, Duke of Rohan, offered greater resistance. Louis XIII's forces captured Saint-Jean d'Angély, which guarded La Rochelle, but did not capitalize on the gain. They also failed in their siege of Montauban. Yet a third campaign in 1622 led to a near total Huguenot capitulation. Under the terms of the Peace of Montpellier (October 1622), the Protestants relinquished nearly half of their garrisoned towns and were forbidden to hold further political assemblies.

The last of the seventeenth-century wars of religion centred on the Protestant fortress of La Rochelle. The city, supported by Protestant England, refused to submit to the royal will and by 1627 Cardinal Richelieu persuaded the king that it threatened the royal capacity to be 'absolute' within the realm. The ensuing siege lasted a brutal fourteen months and led to the death of nearly half the 25,000 inhabitants. Surrender came on 28 October 1628 and was followed by the Peace of Alais in June 1629. The peace reaffirmed the articles of the Edict of Nantes but pointedly excluded the royal brevets, which had accorded the Huguenots military and political autonomy. The religious wars were over, even if confessional antagonism and friction continued in other less bellicose ways.

The long and destructive struggle for religious supremacy and control of the state ended with the sheer physical and psychological exhaustion of the combatants. The wars, particularly in the later stages, exacerbated existing structural difficulties in the economy. People's distress was considerable, pressed as they were by famine, plague and the fiscal demands of the crown.[9] Psychological uncertainty, including the recurrent threat of death, compounded physical hardships. Political and religious authorities, for their part, feared the anarchy implicit in the ongoing warfare. Social tensions mounted and popular revolts increased as the years wore on. Both the members of the lower orders and the governing notables came eventually to view the monarchy as the sole institution capable of providing order and safeguarding the realm.

The wars unquestionably contributed to an increase in the power of the monarchical state. The foundations of the absolute monarchy lay in the turmoil of the sixteenth century. Following the disorder of the wars and chaotic rule of the last Valois kings, Henry IV and his advisers made an energetic, pragmatic effort to bolster royal authority. Notions of popular sovereignty, resistance theories and calls for the Estates-General as a permanent functioning part of the government gave way to the king's absolute will, a society of orders and reason of state. Finally, the conflict fostered a sense of the practical value of confessional coexistence. Catholics and Protestants still regarded one another with deep suspicion. Counter-Reformation Catholics repeatedly contested the status and privilege accorded Protestants. Yet few within either religious culture continued to regard war, massacre and assassination as appropriate recourse for settling religious differences.

NOTES

1   Emmanuel Le Roy Ladurie, *Carnival in Romans* (New York, 1979). J.H.M. Salmon, *Renaissance and Revolt: Essays in the Intellectual and Social History of Early Modern France* (Cambridge, 1987), pp. 211–34.

2   Janine Garrisson-Estèbe, *Protestants du Midi, 1559–1598* (Toulouse, 1980), p. 64. Mack P. Holt, *The French Wars of Religion, 1562–1629* (Cambridge, 1995), p. 30.

3   H. Anjubault and H. Chardon, *Papier et registre du Consistoire de l'Eglise du Mans, réformée selon l'evangile, 1560–1561 (1561–1562 nouveau style)* (Le Mans, 1867), pp. liv,

lviii. Anne H. Guggenheim, 'Beza, Viret and the Church of Nîmes: National Leadership and Local Initiative in the Outbreak of the Religious Wars', *Bibliothèque d'Humanisme et Renaissance* 37 (1975), pp. 33–47.

4   Dom Claude de Vic and Dom J. Vaissète, *Histoire générale de Languedoc* (16 vols; Toulouse, 1872–1904), vol. 12, pp. 88–91.

5   Natalie Zemon Davis, 'The Rites of Violence: Religious Riot in Sixteenth-Century France', in *Society and Culture in Early Modern France* (Stanford, 1975), pp. 152–87.

6   Holt, *The French Wars of Religion*, p. 94.

7   Mathieu Blouin, *Les troubles à Gaillac*, ed. Ernest Nègre (Toulouse, 1976).

8   Garrison-Estèbe, *Protestants du Midi*, pp. 177–224.

9   Philip Benedict, 'Civil War and Natural Disaster in Northern France', and Mark Greengrass, 'The Later Wars of Religion in the French Midi', in Peter Clark (ed.), *The European Crisis of the 1590s: Essays in Comparative History* (London, 1985), pp. 84–105, 106–34.

FURTHER READING

Mack P. Holt, *The French Wars of Religion, 1562–1629* (Cambridge, 1995), and J.H.M. Salmon, *Society in Crisis: France in the Sixteenth Century* (London and New York, 1975), are excellent, succinct introductions to the principal issues. Denis Crouzet, *Les guerriers de Dieu: La violence au temps des troubles de religion (vers 1525–vers 1610)* (2 vols; Seyssel, 1990), is a much longer yet valuable account. Arlette Jouanna is currently preparing a major study of the Wars of Religion. Meanwhile, her *La France du XVIe, 1483–1598* (Paris, 1996) offers a superb synthesis. Another, highly readable survey is Frederic J. Baumgartner, *France in the Sixteenth Century* (New York, 1995). More traditional in their approach to the wars are Michel Pernot, *Les guerres de religion en France, 1559–1598* (Paris, 1987), and Georges Livet, *Les guerres de religion* (8th edn; Paris, 1996).

Several good local studies have appeared in recent years. For developments in the south of France, the best account is Janine Garrisson-Estèbe, *Protestants du Midi, 1559–1598* (Toulouse, 1980). Inquiries into the clash at the municipal level include Philip Benedict, *Rouen during the Wars of Religion* (Cambridge, 1981); Wolfgang Kaiser, *Marseille au temps des troubles, 1559–1596: Morphologie sociale et luttes de factions* (Paris, 1992); Michel Cassan, *Le temps des guerres de religion: Le cas du Limousin (vers 1530–vers 1630)* (Paris, 1996), and Penny Roberts, *A City in Conflict: Troyes during the French Wars of Religion* (Manchester, 1996).

Studies of the St Bartholomew's Day massacres by Barbara Deifendorf, *Beneath the Cross: Catholics and Huguenots in Sixteenth-Century Paris* (Oxford, 1991); Denis Crouzet, *La nuit de la Saint-Barthélemy: Un rêve perdu de la Renaissance* (Paris, 1994), and Philip Benedict, 'The Saint Bartholomew's Massacres in the Provinces', *Historical Journal* 21 (1978), pp. 205–25, have added enormously to our understanding of the subject. The collection of articles by Natalie Zemon Davis, *Society and Culture in Early Modern France* (Stanford, 1975), remains the most imaginative overall exploration of iconoclastic riots, massacres and popular culture.

For military aspects of the conflict, James B. Wood, *The King's Army: Warfare, Soldiers and Society during the Wars of Religion in France, 1562–1576* (Cambridge, 1996), is invaluable. J.H. Burns and Mark Goldie (eds), *The Cambridge History of Political Thought, 1450–1700* (Cambridge, 1991), and Quentin Skinner, *The Foundations of Modern Political Thought: The Reformation* (Cambridge, 1978), are good introductions to the development of political thought. Perhaps the best general discussion of the Catholic League is Jean-Marie Constant, *La Ligue* (Paris, 1996). Nancy L. Roelker, *One King, One Faith: The Parlement of Paris and the Religious Reformations of the Sixteenth Century* (Berkeley and Los Angeles, 1996), presents a synthetic account of the Parlement's place in the turbulent events. Michael Wolfe, *The Conversion of Henri IV: Politics, Power and Religious Belief in Early Modern France* (Cambridge, MA, 1993), meticulously examines Henry IV's conversion to Catholicism and assumption of full monarchical power. Finally, the 400th anniversary of the Edict of

Nantes saw the publication of several fine studies, including Bernard Cottret, *1598: L'Edit de Nantes. Pour en finir avec les guerres de religion* (Paris, 1997); Janine Garrisson, *L'édit de Nantes* (Paris, 1998), and Michel Grandjean and Bernard Roussel (eds), *Coexister dans l'intolérance: L'édit de Nantes (1598)* (Geneva, 1998).

THE NETHERLANDS

Guido Marnef

The Netherlandish Reformation got off to a promising start soon after Luther's call for reform in Germany. Especially in Antwerp, the commercial hub of northwestern Europe, the evangelical message found a quick and powerful response. As early as 1518, Luther's works were on sale and the Antwerp Augustinians were staunchly supportive of their brother in Wittenberg. Nevertheless, the fortunes of the Reformation in the Netherlands and Germany soon diverged. In the Low Countries Charles V and his central government enacted a series of edicts which forced religious dissent underground.[1] From the 1560s onwards, the course of the Reformation movement became closely interwoven with an open revolt against Spanish Habsburg policy in the Netherlands, with unpredictable results. Protestantism would eventually prevail precisely where it had initially been the weakest, notably in the northern Netherlands, and Calvinism became the dominant religion in a new nation – the Dutch Republic.

THE EARLY REFORMATION MOVEMENT

It was not by accident that the evangelical movement found fertile soil in the Netherlands. In the middle of the sixteenth century, the Low Countries were economically and culturally one of the most advanced areas in Europe. The period from the end of the fifteenth century until around 1565 witnessed rapid economic and demographic growth. Flanders, Brabant, Holland and Zeeland constituted the economic heartland, bringing in more than 80 per cent of the taxes levied by the central government in the 1540s. In these highly urbanized provinces, cities of 10,000 and more inhabitants were common. Most of them could boast a rich and self-conscious civic culture embodied in architecture, literature and public festivals. Big cities and many smaller towns boasted a well-organized educational system and a busy printing industry. These cultural media, together with economic mobility, stimulated the intellectual emancipation of the citizens, especially that of the prosperous and numerous middle classes.

At first sight, the old Roman Catholic church was still flourishing at the end of the fifteenth century. The clergy was omnipresent within the city walls. An abundance of institutionalized channels of mediation, such as indulgences, relics, fraternities and chantries was available to sinful men and women looking for salvation. Yet there are strong indications that the early 1520s constituted a watershed. Laymen increasingly distanced themselves from the late mediæval economy of salvation. The causes of this shift in religious attitude are many and difficult to pinpoint. The influence of Erasmus and church reformers such as Martin Luther certainly played an important role. In 1523, for instance, the churchwardens of St George in Antwerp complained that the devotional gifts of the faithful had fallen off sharply 'since the disturbances and opinions of Lutherus have reigned'.[2] The theatrical plays performed by the Chambers of Rhetoric voiced the religious ideas that thrived in the urban middle classes, and many of them took a pronounced anticlerical line while emphasizing faith in Christ and the authority of the Bible.

Martin Luther's teachings were clearly popular, if printed books can be taken as an accurate indication. Between 1520–2, no less than twelve Latin and ten Dutch editions of Luther's writings were printed in Antwerp, while additional works were produced by presses in minor printing centres such as Amsterdam, Leiden and Zwolle. Yet the ecclesiastical and lay authorities were determined to halt the new heresy. In November 1519, the theologians of the University of Louvain vigorously condemned Luther and, in May 1521, Charles V issued a version of the Edict of Worms. Public book-burnings in a number of Brabant and Flanders cities accompanied the offensive against Lutheranism. Around the same time, the Augustinian monastery in Antwerp was dissolved. Most of the friars recanted but two, Hendrik Voes and Johannes van Esschen, were burned at the stake in Brussels on 1 July 1523. They were the first of a long series of Netherlands martyrs. With the dissolution of the Antwerp monastery, Lutheranism lost its firmest base and the impact of Martin Luther faded in the Low Countries.[3] During the next decades his influence was mainly limited to the Antwerp German merchant colony which had permanent contacts with the Lutheran homeland.

The first wave of repression did not, however, succeed in eradicating heresy. For the next twenty years the evangelical movement continued to exist, although in a fragmented, eclectic and non-institutionalized way. Secret assemblies – the conventicles – played an important role in the articulation of dissident religious ideas. At these small gatherings, usually attended by between ten and twenty people, Bible passages were read and discussed and dissident religious ideas were voiced. Among the participants were evangelically minded clerics, skilled craftsmen and artists. Often family ties led to occupational homogeneity. Most of the participants possessed at least a modest level of learning, though it should be remarked that prominent humanists remained aloof. Obviously, they followed more careful paths after the open rupture between Erasmus and Luther and the start of harsh repression.

The secret conventicles did not replace but rather supplemented the traditional parish services. Those present at the secret meetings usually still belonged to the old Catholic church. At the gatherings a variety of 'new ideas' could be heard, which is hardly surprising given the absence of a formal and supra-local degree of organization. At meetings held in Brussels in the mid-1520s, the evangelical priest Claes van der Elst refuted the mediating role of the saints and the value of indulgences while others spoke about the priesthood of all believers and rejected the real presence of Christ in the eucharist. This last claim took such a prominent place in the eyes of the persecuting authorities that they labelled the dissenters as 'sacramentarians', though it should be emphasized that the evangelicals were far from unanimous on this issue. The embryonic secret organization of dissent led to a creeping institutionalization, while at the same time the repressive policy of the authorities reinforced the sectarian tendencies. Nevertheless, the evangelicals did not yet form real counter-churches with a clear-cut confessional identity. This situation changed in the early 1530s when the Anabaptist movement came to the fore.

Anabaptism was introduced in the Netherlands by Melchior Hoffmann. His apocalyptic vision attracted many simple people, especially in Friesland and Holland. His followers were obliged to separate themselves from the sinful world and joined the covenant through adult baptism. Already in 1531 the Melchiorites at Amsterdam were celebrating the Lord's Supper. Hoffmann's separatist and apocalyptic teachings were radicalized by Jan Matthijs and Bernhard Rothmann, who identified the Westphalian city of Münster as the New Jerusalem where the Lord would preserve his people. When they succeeded in gaining control of Münster in February 1534, their prophesies had an extraordinarily strong appeal in the northern Netherlands. New congregations sprang up, and many adherents travelled to Münster. The fall of the Anabaptist Kingdom at Münster in June 1535 provoked a bloody repression in the Netherlands and cast a revolutionary stain on Anabaptism even when it followed a pacific line in the next decades. As a consequence, the Anabaptist movement was decimated and internally divided. Eventually, it was the Friesian ex-priest Menno Simons who emerged as a new leader in the 1540s and brought a new period of expansion to the Anabaptist brotherhood.

THE RISE OF CALVINISM

Apart from the Anabaptists, the evangelicals in the Low Countries did not form real counter-churches until the middle of the sixteenth century. The transition from non-confessional dissent within or at the margins of the Catholic church to open schism entered a new phase in the 1540s. This development started in the cities of the southern Netherlands and did not reach the northern provinces until the 1560s. The most important characteristic in the formation of Reformed Protestantism in this region was the varying influences felt not only from Calvin's Geneva but also from other Protestant centres and from the refugee churches such as London and Emden.

Calvin's first involvement in the Netherlands goes back to 1544 when Pierre Brully was sent from Strasbourg to the French-speaking cities of Tournai and Valenciennes in order to organize their small evangelical communities into an established church with a proper organization. Soon after his arrival in Tournai he was arrested by the city authorities, and in February 1545 he was executed together with four co-religionists. A considerable part of the Tournai community fled to Wesel in the German Rhineland. The harsh repression launched by Charles V and his central government after Brully's mission struck a heavy blow to the Reformed movement. The organization of the nascent Reformed communities in the Netherlands was retarded but at the same time contacts with Geneva and foreign refugee centres intensified.

It was not until 1554 that an organized Reformed church was established in the Low Countries. This occurred first in Antwerp. This commercial metropolis had active economic links with the rest of Europe and was, in consequence, well adapted to the rapid circulation of ideas and people. Furthermore, the city government tried to follow a cautious policy towards Protestants in order to safeguard the commercial interests of the city. In 1554, a French or 'Walloon' Reformed church was established in Antwerp, followed the next year by a Dutch-speaking congregation. The minister, Gaspar van der Heyden, was the architect of the Dutch church 'under the cross'. He had served the Antwerp community for almost four years when he set up an organizational structure in 1555. He compiled a Church Order and required from each member a confession of faith. He followed a very strict line and wanted to exclude all those 'who yet sometimes partake of the Roman abominations and superstitions'.[4] Both Antwerp congregations had preachers, elders and deacons and greatly benefited from contacts with the refugee churches. It is even possible that they received decisive stimuli from returning exiles who left England after the accession of the Catholic Mary Tudor in 1553.

Reformed Protestantism experienced an obvious expansion from the mid-1550s onwards, at least in the southern Netherlands, Zeeland included. In the northern provinces, organized congregations with a distinct Reformed confession did not exist before 1566. It was often Antwerp that acted as a bridgehead from which Reformed life was carried into the surrounding towns and districts. This applies in the first place to the Duchy of Brabant where Reformed communities in Brussels, Mechelen and Breda were highly dependent upon the support of the Antwerp brethren. Even in the county of Flanders, the young congregations of Bruges and Ghent received invaluable help from Antwerp. The industrialized area of west Flanders, the so-called *Westkwartier*, was another important focus of growth for the Reformed church. Here, significant stimuli came from both London and Antwerp, and after 1561 to an even greater extent from the militant exile community at Sandwich. In the French-speaking region Tournai took a prominent place, with Antwerp's influence also felt. At Tournai the transition towards an organized church was not accomplished until Guy de Brès returned as a permanent minister in 1559. From there he gave guidance to the churches of Lille, Valenciennes and other smaller places.

From the beginning, the Netherlands Reformed church was integrated into an international network. Influence was exerted by major Reformed centres such as Geneva and Zurich, and by refugee centres at London and Emden in East Friesland. As a consequence, early Reformed Protestantism developed a pluriform character. A statement made by Jacob Dieusart from Nieuwkerke in the *Westkwartier* during his imprisonment in 1560 is illuminating in this respect. His statement identified as the guiding influences of the new movement not only Zwingli and Calvin, but also the leaders of the refugee churches, Marten Micron and John à Lasco. It was only from the 1560s that the Netherlands Reformed movement increasingly took a Calvinist stance. This evolution went quicker and more vigorously in the French-speaking churches, which generally had more direct contacts with Geneva.

At the same time, the dispersed Reformed churches under the cross were brought towards more unity. The mobility of the Reformed leaders, the common experience in foreign refugee centres and the prominence of a few churches, such as Antwerp and Tournai, contributed to this process. A synodical structure which strengthened the bonds between the local churches functioned from at least 1562. These synods were as 'national' as the difficult circumstances permitted and were attended by representatives of the two language groups. Antwerp was the site for all but one of the synodical assemblies organized in the Netherlands before 1571. Equally important were the acceptance and use of the same writings, such as the psalms by Jan Utenhove and Pieter Datheen. It was, however, the *Confession de Foy*, composed in 1561 by Guy de Brès, that contributed most to confessional unity. A synod held in Antwerp in 1566 adopted it as the confession of all the Calvinist churches in the Netherlands.

The process of religious confessionalization was even strengthened by competition within the broad Protestant movement. The first generation Calvinists had not only to face the dominant Catholic church but they were also obliged to struggle with the Anabaptists for supremacy. The latter had an obvious chronological advantage. Well-organized communities had been at their disposal for more than twenty years before the Reformed established their first churches. Furthermore, the peaceful Anabaptism moulded by Menno Simons not only attracted many adherents in the northern provinces but also in the Dutch-speaking south. The prolonged exchange of controversial pamphlets bears witness to the increasing conflict between Reformed and Anabaptists. A substantial number of these pamphlets were printed at Emden, which emerged as a major Reformed printing centre after the dissolution of the London refugee churches in 1553. The Confession of Faith compiled by Guy de Brès explicitly condemned the teachings of the Anabaptists on the incarnation, baptism and the civil powers.

The Anabaptists not only forced the Reformed to adopt a stricter confessional profile, they also had an impact at the organizational level. Menno Simons and his followers tried to achieve a pure community, a brotherhood 'without spot or stain'. This pure brotherhood of adult believers could not be preserved without strict discipline. Therefore the Calvinists too were obliged to pay sufficient attention to discipline, since co-religionists disappointed with lax discipline in their ranks could decide to join the Anabaptist congregation. This constant preoccupation with Anabaptism gave the Reformed movement in the Netherlands a peculiar character and reinforced its sectarian tendencies.

On the other hand, competition from the Lutherans was limited to Antwerp. There the Lutherans increasingly worried about the rise of the *secta sacramentariorum*, by which they meant the Reformed. They solicited the help of leading orthodox Lutheran theologians such as Joachim Westphal and Matthias Flacius in order to build a dam against the rising tide of Calvinism.

The Calvinist churches under the cross did not enjoy an easy existence. The risk of persecution and the competition of other confessions imposed hard burdens upon their members who had to accept strict rules. Gaspar van der Heyden and the Antwerp consistory clearly distinguished between the Children of God – those who made the confession of faith and submitted to ecclesiastical discipline – and the Children of the World. Thus it is hardly surprising that membership of such exclusive and demanding churches remained low. In Antwerp, the Dutch-speaking congregation was divided at the beginning of 1558 into sixteen or eighteen sections, each of which comprised eight to twelve people. Until the early 1560s membership never surpassed a few hundred and the situation was no different in Flemish cities such as Ghent and Bruges. The industrialized Flemish *Westkwartier* presents another picture. There Calvinism was already a mass movement around 1560. Even the helpless judges of the Court of Flanders realized that strict enforcement of the heresy edicts would entail a terrible and bloody slaughter. It is, however, impossible to derive quantitative data from such impressionistic evidence. The same applies to the situation in some Walloon towns, especially Tournai and Valenciennes, where Calvinism expanded rapidly after the Peace of Cateau-Cambrésis (1559). This treaty brought peace between France and the Netherlands and at the same time facilitated contacts with the French Huguenots.

Yet it would be wrong to judge the impact of Calvinism only on the strength of its real membership. Besides the core members there was a wider circle of interested sympathizers who did not yet want to make a far-reaching commitment. Some of them probably acted out of principle while others hesitated to risk their lives and property. The 'salon' preachings held by Adriaan van Haemstede for the well-to-do were condemned by the Antwerp church elders and caused considerable tension within the Reformed community. This tension between members and sympathizers (in Dutch, *liefhebbers* or 'lovers') would remain an important factor in the history of the Netherlands Calvinist church, even after it had gained its liberty in the Dutch Republic.

The half-heartedness of the prudent sympathizers did not escape the attention of John Calvin. He violently condemned such 'Nicodemites', so-named after the Pharisee who visited Jesus at night – like him they dared not confess their faith purely and openly. It was certainly not by chance that Calvin's *Institutes* was not translated into Dutch before 1560, while his *Excuse à messieurs les Nicodemites* appeared in Dutch in 1554. The printing presses of Emden produced a significant number of anti-Nicodemite works, among them translations of Calvin's tracts. In any case, the Reformed following was substantially increased by Van Haemstede's preachings outside the congregation. A public sermon held outside the city walls at the end of 1558 even attracted 2,000 listeners.

The attractiveness of the Calvinist movement also appears from an analysis of the occupations of those prosecuted by the Inquisition and the lay courts. In the cities of Brabant, Flanders and the Walloon provinces, Calvinism recruited from the whole spectrum of urban society, though occupations that required some geographical mobility and a 'certain nobility of the spirit' were remarkably well represented.[5] At this point, there was a sharp contrast with the Anabaptists who overwhelmingly worked in crafts that required specific but fairly simple manual labour. Furthermore, most of them owned no property. A partial explanation for this contrast certainly lies in the different attitude of both confessions towards the secular world. The refusal of Anabaptists to bear arms or hold office and the rejection of taking oaths before secular authorities confined their appeal to the lower classes. The Calvinists, on the contrary, respected the burghers' ethos and even harboured the desire to take over power in the towns.

In passing, it should be emphasized that the religious situation in the Low Countries displays strong geographical contrasts. The development of the Reformed movement was thus far mostly confined to the economically advanced southern provinces. In Holland and even more in the peripheral provinces Groningen, Friesland and Overijssel, religious relations were less polarized. These northern provinces were only added to Charles V's territories in the 1520s and 1530s (see Figure 20.1) and had retained a measure of independence towards the central government in Brussels. The town authorities in the north offered surprisingly ample room for 'protestantizing' priests within the Catholic church. In 1559, Steven Silvius was appointed curate of the St Martin's Church at Groningen. While serving at Leeuwarden, he had declared twice from the pulpit that he doubted Christ's real presence in the eucharist but this was no obstacle for the Groningen city fathers. Silvius even took a doctor's degree at the Lutheran University of Heidelberg before accepting his new position at Groningen. Similar protestantizing priests served in a number of other northern towns. They were very close to the evangelical teachings and made, in a certain way, the need for a real Reformed counter-church less compelling. Before 1566, only the Anabaptists succeeded in establishing organized congregations in these northern provinces, Holland included.

The different policy towards the repression of Protestantism accentuates even more the differing situations in north and south. In theory, the heresy placards issued by the central government in Brussels applied to all the seventeen Netherlandish provinces. The Perpetual Edict (better known as the 'bloody edict') which Charles V proclaimed for his Netherlandish territories on 29 April 1550, remained the guideline for the central government's policy during the next decades. It consolidated all the previous ordinances and added a number of stricter provisions. In practice, however, the enforcement of the Perpetual Edict depended greatly upon the collaboration of the provincial and local authorities. Resistance or passive opposition was, apparently, easier in the northern provinces. In Amsterdam, the sheriff Willem Bardes adopted a tolerant attitude from 1554 onwards. As a result, nobody was executed until the arrival of the Duke of Alva in 1567. Some councillors of the provincial Court of Friesland openly declared in the mid-1550s that it was impossible to put the heresy placards into practice. They refused to punish poor Anabaptists who did no harm and were thought merely misguided in their beliefs. Statistically, the contrast between north and south is striking. In the period 1550–66, 200 people were executed for heresy in Flanders, 131 in Antwerp and 97 in the Walloon towns of Lille, Mons, Tournai and Valenciennes, but only 52 in Holland.[6] Furthermore, in the northern provinces executions had effectively ceased by 1560. In the Dutch-speaking areas, the overwhelming majority of death sentences were passed on Anabaptists while the Reformed were usually punished with banishment. The repression reinforced the sectarian tendencies of the Netherlandish Reformation, especially in the south where the persecution was most effective.

In the 1560s more and more political leaders, even in the central government circles, became convinced that the harsh repression of heresy was not appropriate. These moderates acted for humane or political reasons. In the latter case, they

Figure 20.1 The Netherlands under Charles V, showing when territories were acquired. (Oxford University Press)

wanted to protect local privileges or maintain civic order since public executions could stir up riots. As a result, from 1564 the number of executions dropped substantially in the southern provinces. Philip II was not, however, prepared to change his policy. His notorious letters from the Segovia Woods (October 1565) ordered a relentless application of the heresy edicts.

In the meantime, the self-confident Reformed movement increasingly adopted a militant stance. Within the Reformed church a debate developed about the attitude to be taken towards hostile authorities. A synod of Reformed churches held at Antwerp in 1562 decided that it was permissible to use force to free one's fellow believers from prison. In the Flemish *Westkwartier*, radical Calvinist leaders put theory into practice and committed armed prison-breaking and other violent actions. Public manifestations of Calvinist strength also took place in 1562–4 in Antwerp, Tournai and Valenciennes. At the same time, the printing presses in the refugee centres produced a steady flow of polemical literature that encouraged co-religionists in the Low Countries. The year 1565 represented a high-point for the output of the busy Emden presses. The Calvinist potential for power nevertheless only became clear during the Wonderyear of 1566–7.

CALVINIST ASCENDANCY DURING THE WONDERYEAR

The Wonderyear, or *annus mirabilis*, spanning the period from spring 1566 until spring 1567, profoundly altered the political and religious situation in the Netherlands. The pressure for a moderate religious policy and the subsequent concessions made by the central government had created a vacuum from which the Calvinist movement benefited tremendously. Already in 1565 the grandee nobles and the lesser nobility were articulating increasing dismay at the king's policy towards heresy, especially after the publication of the letters from the Segovia Woods. In December, a group among the lesser nobility formed a league, the so-called 'Compromise of the Nobility'. In a petition presented to the regent, Margaret of Parma, on 5 April 1566, they demanded that the Inquisition be abolished and the edicts against heresy suspended. This presentation had an enormous impact and boosted the self-confidence of the Protestants. The news immediately reached the refugee churches and over the next months many exiles returned to their homeland, attracted by the promising outlook. In June 1566, a synod of the Calvinist churches held in Antwerp decided it was time to come into the open. Mass gatherings were organized in Flanders, Brabant, Zeeland, Tournai and Valenciennes and later, from July onwards, also in Holland. These so-called 'hedge-preachings', held outside the city walls, attracted crowds numbering hundreds and even thousands. On 14 July, 25,000 listeners gathered outside Antwerp. Meetings of similar proportions were reported somewhat later at Ghent and Ypres.

That the Calvinists were able to attract thousands of new listeners within a short timespan indicates that there was ample room for expansion once the movement could come into the open. Yet it is evident that the thousands who attended the preachings did not instantly become convinced Calvinists. Many of them belonged to the undecided religious middle groups and leaned towards Protestantism once the political context changed. Some probably acted out of curiosity, while others, sympathetic towards new doctrines, were still unwilling to commit themselves to an organized church with a strict ecclesiastical discipline. Thus even during the Wonderyear the distinction between full members and the large group of sympathizers continued to exist.

While the large-scale hedge-preachings were certainly impressive, worship within the city walls remained an unrealized ambition. In this regard the icono-clastic fury which began on 10 August 1566 near Steenvoorde in west Flanders and which swept through the Netherlands over the next months was path-breaking. The iconoclasm was certainly ideologically motivated, but it also constituted a deliberate *acte de présence* by which the Reformed claimed their rights within the city. In some places, the image breaking happened at the instigation of Calvinist preachers, while elsewhere the consistories were the driving force. In the north, across the great rivers, the iconoclasts could not fall back upon a similar degree of Reformed church organization. In several towns of Holland and in Utrecht there were violent attacks on the churches, while elsewhere, especially in the more peripheral northern provinces, images were removed in an orderly way.

In any case, the iconoclastic fury did not miss its target. An intimidated Margaret of Parma surrendered to the demands for toleration and reluctantly conceded freedom of Protestant worship in all areas where it was already taking place. She asked the grandee nobles to enforce this 23 August Accord in the places under their command. The agreement of 2 September 1566, negotiated by William of Orange in Antwerp, granted basic rights to the Protestants, permitting Calvinists and Lutherans to build churches within the city walls. Similar accords were reached in Amsterdam and Utrecht. In practice these accords applied only to the Reformed. The Lutherans only constituted a force in Antwerp and the Anabaptists

Figure 20.2 *Christ and the Pope.* This well-known anti-papal image clearly takes its inspiration from Cranach's *Passional Christi und Antichristi.* Although relatively well known as a printed broadsheet, few examples survive as fine as this Dutch painted panel. (Glasgow, The Stirling Maxwell Collection, Pollock House)

were still perceived as a sect. Thus, in the short run, the iconoclastic fury was very fruitful for the Reformed movement. In several towns a consistory was set up in the days and weeks following the image breaking. Another remarkable fact after the outbreak of the iconoclasm was the extremely weak response of the Catholic community. In many places, Catholic religious life was paralyzed for some time after the iconoclastic riots.

Another aspect that underscores the impact of Calvinism is its dynamic social recruitment. In Antwerp, Bruges and Ghent, the social and occupational profile of the congregations underwent a remarkable change during the Wonderyear. This is especially clear when one concentrates on the leading circles of the movement. Wealthy merchants and well-to-do people belonging to the crafts, applied arts and professions came to the fore. In Valenciennes and Middelburg, the consistories were drawn from merchants and well-to-do citizens, whereas previously 'the meaner sort of folk' had served as elders or deacons. This change in social recruitment must be attributed to the changed legal and political context. The dangers associated with belonging to a secret church under the cross, forbidden by the authorities, fell away during the Wonderyear. As a consequence, wealthy and respectable people could convert without fear. Among these 'converts' were a number of previous Nicodemites who sympathized with the underground Reformed movement but had maintained a discreet distance. These Nicodemites, repudiated by Calvin, were now invaluable. The merchants and prosperous citizens who went over to Calvinism in 1566 not only gave financial support, they also lent their power and prestige at a time when the church was struggling for official recognition.

Yet the iconoclastic fury did not only bring advantages to the Calvinist church. Many moderates were shocked by the sudden outburst of violence and henceforth perceived the Calvinist church as a seditious, aggressive sect. Among the confederate nobles, distrust towards the Calvinists also increased and many rallied behind the regent. As Margaret of Parma re-established her authority in the autumn and winter of 1566, she decided to retract the rights reluctantly granted to the Calvinists, if necessary by the use of armed force.

In this changed context, the Calvinist church opted for overt opposition and armed resistance. It was especially the Antwerp committee of deputies that served as a kind of headquarters for the resistance movement. This committee of eight deputies, all rich merchants, was a political body that represented the interests of the Reformed community before local, central and even international authorities. The sophisticated political organization of the Calvinists could not, however, prevent the regent from triumphing. The Calvinists lacked sufficient financial resources and military experience. Furthermore, the resistance movement lacked unity. Calvinists and nobles did not succeed in creating a united front and the Lutherans did not want to join an unlawful revolt. The defeat of the rebels at Oosterweel near Antwerp and the capture of Valenciennes by central government troops, both in March 1567, showed clearly that the rebellion had failed.

AFTER THE WONDERYEAR: BETWEEN REPRESSION AND EXILE

By the middle of 1567, Margaret of Parma was master of the situation. Protestant churches were closed or demolished. William of Orange and thousands of Protestants – among them Reformed ministers and the ringleaders of the troubles – fled into exile. The refugees scattered in all directions. They reinforced already established exile centres and stimulated the foundation of a number of new congregations in England and Germany. The size of this large-scale emigration is difficult to establish, although the influx in a few centres might give a concrete idea. No less than 4,000 Netherlanders moved to East Friesland, especially to Emden. In Norwich the refugee community numbered 1,471 people in 1568, 2,825 in 1569 and 3,900 in 1571.

The arrival of the Duke of Alva, heading 10,000 Spanish soldiers, in August 1567 was the prelude to severe repression in the Low Countries. In the following month an extraordinary tribunal, the Council of Troubles, was set up to punish the culprits of the Wonderyear, such as Reformed ministers, members of consistories, iconoclasts and other rebels. Over the next six years, the Council of Troubles pronounced 1,100 death sentences and more than 10,000 banishments *in absentia*. The majority of the condemned originated from southern cities such as Tournai, Valenciennes and Antwerp, and a number of smaller places in the *Westkwartier*. Meanwhile, the traditional legal institutions, such as the town magistracies, continued to deal with 'ordinary' cases of heresy. Yet the period in which provincial and local judges could pursue their own policy belonged to the past. Alva and his council kept a critical watch and did not hesitate to interfere if necessary.

Alva's determined policy had a serious impact on the religious situation. Many Protestants decided to return to the fold of the Roman Catholic church. After the proclamation of a royal and papal pardon in 1570, 17,852 persons reconciled themselves in the diocese of Antwerp, 14,128 in the city of Antwerp alone. For the archbishopric of Mechelen and the bishopric of 's-Hertogenbosch, the numbers were respectively 10,906 and around 6,000. Such figures once again indicate that many who converted to Protestantism during the Wonderyear were certainly not hardliners. They also underscore the impact of political circumstances upon religious mentality. Massive repression could lead to large-scale defections among Protestants, just as happened in France after the St Bartholomew's Day massacre.

Many among the steadfast Protestants went into exile, but others chose to remain. They had to face a hard life, bereft of leadership and constantly exposed to the danger of persecution. It is difficult to determine the extent and nature of Reformed life during Alva's regency, given the scanty sources. In 1568–9 there were still Reformed cells in Friesland, Haarlem and Delft which received support from the Emden refugee church. Apparently, there was a loose organization but real churches did not exist. The situation was even more difficult in the southern provinces where Alva's repression was most intense. Yet there are strong indications that the Reformed communities were still better developed there. Just as before the Wonderyear, Antwerp played a leading and pivotal role. An organized underground church with elders and deacons continued to exist in the city. In

1571 an arrested minister, Jan Cornelissen, revealed that the city was divided into four quarters, each of which had four elders, deacons and messengers. Contacts between Calvinists in the exile centres and co-religionists in the Low Countries were often maintained through the commercial channels of the Antwerp metropolis. Besides Antwerp, there were organized Calvinist communities in Brussels, Ghent and the *Westkwartier*, and in a number of Walloon towns. It is, however, very unlikely that these places harboured uninterruptedly organized churches, as was the case in Antwerp.

The problems that the underground churches had to face were manifold. There were, for instance, the repression, the constant lack of money, the competition from the Anabaptists and Nicodemism. In this regard, the support of the many refugee centres in England and the German empire proved to be invaluable. They offered a safe haven to the persecuted, collected money for the needy churches under the cross, trained and sent preachers, and gave advice. Furthermore, the refugee churches contributed significantly to the formation of an international Calvinism. The many merchants and enterpreneurs from Antwerp, Amsterdam, Tournai and some other places who left the country after the Wonderyear, created a commercial network that linked Calvinists in different countries. A similar role was played by the Reformed universities and academies. In Heidelberg, Geneva, Basle and elsewhere, students from the Netherlands and other countries met one another and formed contacts which might bear fruit when they later participated in the creation of a Calvinist church in the Netherlands.

The Reformed leaders in the refugee centres also took measures for the building of a future free Calvinist church in the Netherlands. Particularly important in this regard was the general synod of Netherlandish churches held at Emden in October 1571. The representatives from the churches under the cross and the refugee churches made clear arrangements about church doctrine, affirming the French and Netherlands confessions of faith as the common doctrinal statements and the Geneva and Heidelberg catechisms as the recommended congregational texts. At the organizational level, they adopted a presbyterian church order, affirming that 'no church shall exercise dominion over another church'.[7] The consistory was the first level of a hierarchy of assemblies, ascending through the *classis* and provincial synods to the general or national synod. The blueprint of *classis* and provincial synods betrays a great deal of optimism. For the northern provinces, the Calvinist leaders gathered at Emden decided that 'the congregations of Amsterdam, Delft and other churches in Holland, Overijssel and West Friesland will constitute one *classis*'. It was clear to everyone that the realization of such a structure depended to a large extent upon the evolving political and military situation in the Netherlands.

REVOLUTIONARY REFORMATIONS IN THE 1570s AND 1580s

Half a year after the synod of Emden, the situation in Holland changed completely. William of Orange, who since 1568 had been the undisputed leader of the resistance movement in the Netherlands, eventually achieved a major success in 1572. On 1 April 1572 the Sea-Beggars captured Den Briel, a small port in the south of Holland. During the next months, many towns in Holland and Zeeland joined the revolt, although often reluctantly. The refugee centres in England and Germany collected money and raised troops, and thus contributed significantly to the military victory. At the first free assembly of the States of Holland, held in July 1572 at Dordrecht, Philip Marnix de St Aldegonde declared that it was Orange's intention 'that there will be freedom of religion for both Reformed and Catholics and that everyone will have public and free exercise of his religion in some church or chapel'.[8]

Yet Orange's ideals were difficult to realize in a climate of civil war. The agreements reached between the town magistracy and the commanders of the Beggars were often violated soon after the Beggar troops entered the towns. From then onwards, a 'revolutionary Reformation' was implemented.[9] The religious status quo or religious peace, stipulated in the terms of agreement, was always short-lived. In most places, the Calvinist ascendancy followed a familiar pattern. Beggar troops or small groups of Calvinists harassed the Catholic clergy, attacked the parish churches and committed acts of iconoclasm. Subsequently, churches were taken over by the Calvinists and the clergy were evicted. By the spring of 1573 the parish churches were either closed or already in use by the Calvinists in the chief towns of Holland, such as Dordrecht, Gouda, Leiden, Haarlem, Rotterdam and Delft. Only Amsterdam remained a safe-haven for Catholics, and did not join the revolt until 1578.

The building up and the consolidation of the Calvinist church was a difficult and protracted task. First of all, there was a pressing need for competent ministers, although the refugee churches sent their most experienced men. Equally important was the formation of consistories. By 1573, the Reformed congregations at Delft, Leiden, Dordrecht, Rotterdam, Gorcum and Alkmaar had consistories. The first Lord's Supper was probably administered at Enkhuizen on 1 November 1572. From mid-1573 this also happened in the chief towns of south Holland, which by then still had relatively small congregations. At Enkhuizen's first Lord's Supper 156 adults sat at the table and at Dordrecht there were 368 in July 1573. At Delft, 180 communicant members were counted in 1572. These are very small numbers if one realizes that Dordrecht and Delft had total populations of respectively 10,500 and 14,000 around 1560.[10]

As a result of the revolt, the Calvinist church obtained a dominant position in Holland and Zeeland, the small size of its congregations notwithstanding. The Calvinist church enjoyed a privileged situation and was recognized by the state as the only public church. The Calvinist leaders hoped to create a godly society in which Calvinism permeated all areas of social life. Yet the secular authorities were more and more unwilling to give free reign to the Calvinists. The relationship between state and church was especially strained in Holland where many town magistrates were of a moderate and non-dogmatic religious stamp. From the beginning, they tried to temper the power of the Calvinist church. In 1575, the States of Holland even suggested putting the consistories under the control of the town magistrates and abolishing the ecclesiastical structure of *classis* and synod. One year later, they argued that the church of Holland had ceased to be a secret church of exiles, but was now 'a public community which is free under the magistrates of her own land'.[11] It belonged to the competence of the civil authorities to draw up laws for the realm of religion. As a result, the success of the Reformed church in Holland was largely dependent upon the relationship with the local authorities. In Gouda and Leiden, the magistrates deeply resented an institutionalized religion of the Calvinist type and rejected the supremacy of the Calvinist church. They supported moderate ministers who were usually repudiated by orthodox Calvinists. In Dordrecht and Delft there was, on the contrary, a close collaboration between the Calvinist church and the magistrates.

From 1577 onwards, the course of the Revolt created new opportunities for the Calvinists in the southern Netherlands. The Pacification of Ghent, proclaimed on 8 November 1576, asked for the suspension of the heresy edicts and the withdrawal of the Spanish soldiers. William of Orange gained influence in a number of cities in Flanders and Brabant, while Calvinist exiles started to return to their homeland. The subsequent process of Calvinist ascendancy resembled the pattern of Holland. In general, things developed more rapidly and more radically in Flanders than in Brabant.

In the county of Flanders it was Ghent that took the lead.[12] On 1 November 1577, a Committee of Eighteen in charge of the city's military defence was established. It was headed by Jan van Hembyze, a Calvinist radical, and consisted of partisans of William of Orange who soon manifested themselves as Calvinists. A few months later, the city council was purged in a similar way. The new regime was based on two pillars: the restoration of the city's autonomy and privileges, and the advancement of the Calvinist religion. The situation of the Calvinist church changed completely soon after the installation of the new regime. Already, before the political turnover, the Calvinist church was well organized. A consistory and at least three ministers were active in Ghent. In February 1578 public preaching started and at the beginning of July Catholic churches and convents were despoiled. By the end of August 1578, Catholic worship had ceased. All churches were closed, except those used by the Calvinists. Over the next months the city of Ghent subjugated the surrounding countryside and introduced the Reformed religion, often by force, in most Flemish towns and villages. The religious policy followed by the new city rulers was so radical that it even thwarted William of Orange's pleas for a religious peace.

In the duchy of Brabant, the Calvinists likewise benefited from the new political situation.[13] In Antwerp and Brussels the Calvinists could rely on an already existing church structure. From the end of 1577 onwards, the magistracies of both cities took the side of William of Orange, but unlike Ghent, the Calvinists did not dominate the city government until 1579. In 1578–9 religious peace settlements granted church buildings to Calvinists and Lutherans in Antwerp and Brussels. In practice, these peace settlements were soon rendered out of date as a consequence of the polarization of the revolt. The Catholic clergy was gradually expelled and, in 1581, the city governments of Antwerp and Brussels prohibited the exercise of the Catholic religion. Calvinists and Lutherans took possession of the main parish churches. A similar process was accomplished in Mechelen (1580–5) and in Tournai (1579–81).

The 'revolutionary Reformation' carried through in Flanders and Brabant was possible because the Calvinists were fully backed by the purged city governments. In these provinces the civil authorities were much more devoted to the advancement of the Reformed church than they usually were in Holland. When the consistory of Ghent wrote about the growth of the Reformed church, it explicitly referred to the role of the new city government, declaring that 'God created a godly Authority which aims to reform the church of God in such a way that our city will become an example for all the Netherlands. In realizing this, the city fathers are prepared to help us with all their power given them by God.'[14] The significant overlap that existed between city government and consistory in the so-called Calvinist Republics of Brabant and Flanders is another indication of the close collaboration between civil authorities and Calvinist church.

It is beyond doubt that Protestantism experienced a massive growth after the political revolution in the south. The correspondence exchanged between the ministers and their former refugee churches contain compelling evidence on this point. Thomas van Thielt, a minister active in Antwerp, wrote on 19 December 1578: 'As far as this congregation goes, by God's grace the hearers and members increase daily. 560 new members have been registered, of which many are rich people and the like. Yesterday the Lord's Supper was celebrated at Saint Andrew's and the Dominican's Church. The total number of communicants was 1,240.' Five months later, his colleague Johannes Cubus reported that 'the church is increasing not only among the common people, but also among the prominent ... so that we already have 12,000 hearers and more than 3,000 incorporated members.'[15] These testimonies point once again to a pattern that was already present during the Wonderyear: the well-to-do people only took the decisive step once the position of the Calvinist church was more or less consolidated. Furthermore, the two Antwerp ministers systematically distinguished between the officially registered members who were admitted to the Lord's Supper and the wider circle of 'hearers' (*toehoerers*) or sympathizers who merely attended the sermons. Ministers active in Kortrijk and Mechelen made similar observations.[16] Data about the numerical strength of the different confessions is only available for Antwerp. Immediately after the capitulation of the city in August 1585, the citizens' guard was purged. The new rulers compiled a list containing the names of 10,688 adult men who had served in the citizens' guard and systematically indicated their religious persuasions. Of them, 45 per cent were classified as Catholic, 26 per cent as Calvinist, 15 per cent as Lutheran and 2 per cent as Anabaptist. For around 12 per cent no religion could be traced. An extrapolation based on a total population of 82,000 inhabitants would give 37,000 Catholics, 21,000 Calvinists, 12,000 Lutherans and 1,600 Anabaptists.

Eventually, the fate of the Protestants in the southern Netherlands was determined by the course of the Revolt. In 1583–5, the Spanish governor Alexander Farnese succeeded in recapturing the cities of the south one after the other. A massive emigration, now overwhelmingly directed towards the Dutch Republic, started. The population of Antwerp dwindled to 42,000 within four years, and Ghent and Bruges also lost about half of their inhabitants. It is beyond doubt that the thousands of emigrants from Brabant, Flanders and the Walloon towns significantly reinforced the Protestant congregations in the republic, especially in

Holland and Zeeland. The Calvinist Walloon churches and the Lutheran churches were almost all established after the large-scale emigration from the south.

THE REFORMATION IN THE EARLY DUTCH REPUBLIC

From the late 1570s onwards, the Calvinist religion gradually gained influence outside Holland and Zeeland, in parallel with the process of political radicalization. The geographical spread of Calvinism is clearly reflected in the churches represented at the national synod held at Middelburg in June 1581. There were not only representatives from the churches in Holland, Zeeland, Brabant and Flanders, but also from those in Friesland, Overijssel, Gelderland and Utrecht. The same year a general proclamation prohibited the exercise of Catholic worship in the Dutch Republic. Yet the size of the Calvinist congregations remained relatively modest. In 1587, the president of the Court of Holland declared that not even 10 per cent of the people in Holland belonged to the Calvinist church.

The reasons for this sluggish response to the Calvinist religion are many. Especially in the countryside, where well-trained ministers were scarce, ignorance and adhesion to old, often superstitious, practices remained remarkably strong. Furthermore, there was the competition from other Protestant confessions. The Anabaptist congregations were particularly strong in Friesland and Groningen, and in the major towns and some rural areas of Holland. In 1574 the representatives of the *classis* of Voorne and Putten asked at the provincial synod of Holland

> how they could best resist the sect of the Anabaptists. As you know, they do not come to hear the Word of God and we cannot get them to a disputation. In the meanwhile, their false teaching creeps as a cancer. In the village of Swartewael most of the heap adheres to this sect, creeping from there through the complete land of Voorne, ... yes, in some villages not a single child is baptized.[17]

From 1585 onwards, the Lutherans, too, tried to recruit new followers among the still non-confessionalized masses. The recently established Lutheran communities were perceived as a threat by the Calvinist leaders and provoked hostile reactions in a number of Dutch towns, such as in Amsterdam during the 1590s. Thus it may be true that Lutheranism loomed larger in the Dutch consciousness of the late sixteenth century than is often realized, as Jonathan Israel suggests.

Another important element for the limited participation, emphasized in recent scholarship, is that the obstacles to the swift growth of Calvinism were self-imposed. The members of the Calvinist congregations had to meet high standards. Only those who professed the confession of faith and accepted consistorial discipline were worthy to sit at the table of the Lord and were, by consequence, full members of the congregation. The Lord's Supper and discipline were inseparable. Yet submission to discipline was voluntary, a situation that did not exist in Geneva, Scotland and many other places. The numerous sympathizers or *liefhebbers* did not want to make such a radical engagement and merely went to the sermons. Two factors account for this peculiar Dutch situation. First, in the time of persecution and exile membership was by definition voluntary. The memory of the exclusive communities still loomed in the Calvinist mentality. Second, there was the constant presence of the Anabaptists who maintained rigorous moral standards and consequently put pressure on the Calvinist congregations.

Furthermore, Benjamin Kaplan emphasized the existence of a broad group of 'Libertines' within Dutch society.[18] These Libertines rejected any form of discipline and perceived the consistorial discipline as a new introduction of the Spanish Inquisition. Their anti-confessional piety was formed by spiritualism, late mediæval mysticism and anticlericalism. Calvinist critics stigmatized the Libertines as people without religion and morals. The Calvinist minister at Delft, Reginald Donteclock, undoubtedly had these Libertines in mind when he wrote about 'the greatest sect in the country, ... notably those who stay on their own without going to any visible church or religion'.[19] Such statements underscore the impact of the Libertines. Many who attended the Reformed sermons undoubtedly sympathized with this Libertine mentality. Furthermore, the Libertines had considerable influence in the town governments of, for instance, Gouda, Leiden and Utrecht.

In the first place it was the civil authorities that determined the parameters within which the Calvinist church would operate. Especially in Holland and Utrecht, many liberal erastian town magistrates wanted to curb the influence of the Calvinist church in a pluralist society. As a result, magistrates and ministers frequently disputed about the control of poor relief, the regulation of education and the place of other confessions in civic society. In many cases, the magistrates found a solution by distinguishing public and private spheres. The Calvinist church, as the public church, enjoyed a monopoly on public worship. Thus church buildings were reserved for the Calvinists. People belonging to other religions were only allowed to practise their faith within the confines of private homes. The practical application of this principle of freedom of conscience could, of course, vary from time to time and from place to place.

It is difficult to measure the size and impact of the public Calvinist church. Fragmentary quantitative evidence seems to indicate that the members of the Calvinist church accounted for between 10 and 20 per cent in the first two decades of the seventeenth century. In the countryside, the percentages were much lower. By 1620, about half of the population had made its religious choice at Haarlem: 20 per cent were Calvinist, 12 per cent Catholic, 14 per cent Anabaptist, 1 per cent Lutheran and 1 per cent belonged to the Walloon church. The proportion of those who did not belong to a church is difficult to trace but everything seems to indicate that they outnumbered the Calvinist members.

The situation of the Dutch Republic was quite unique in a Europe character-ized by an increasing hardening of confessional boundaries. In the republic there were no collaborative efforts by state and church to rally their subjects behind one creed. The religious landscape always remained pluriform. The public church was the church of a minority. The contrast with the Spanish Netherlands, where the archdukes Albert and Isabella successfully promoted Tridentine Catholicism is striking. Nevertheless, the position of the Calvinist church was stronger than the low membership suggests. The Calvinists were an exceptionally determined minority and had at their disposal a very good organization, built up in times of persecution and exile. Furthermore, they had significantly contributed to the war against Spain, a fact that the secular authorities could not ignore. In the second decade of the seventeenth century, a dispute about predestination between the moderate Jacobus Arminius and the orthodox Franciscus Gommarus caused a deep conflict in the Calvinist church and even led to the schism of the moderate Remonstrants. The national synod of Dordrecht (1618–19) sealed the victory of orthodox ministers. In the years that followed, confessional Calvinism gained an ever more dominant influence in Dutch society and culture; but it still remained the religion of a minority.

NOTES

1 For the heresy legislation, see Aline Goosens, *Les Inquisitions modernes dans les Pays-Bas méridionaux*, vol. 1, *La legislation* (Brussels, 1997).

2 W.H. Vroom, *De Onze-Lieve-Vrouwekerk te Antwerpen. De financiering van de bouw tot de Beeldenstorm* (Antwerp, 1983), p. 59.

3 Emphasized by G. Hammer, 'Der Streit um Bucer in Antwerpen: Ein rätselvoller Textfund und ein unbekannter Lutherbrief', in G. Hammer and K.-H. zur Mühlen (eds), *Lutheriana: Zum 500. Geburtstag Martin Luthers* (Cologne and Vienna, 1984), pp. 393–454.

4 G. van der Heyden to the consistory of Emden, 17 December 1555, quoted in Alastair Duke, Gillian Lewis and Andrew Pettegree (eds), *Calvinism in Europe, 1540–1610* (Manchester, 1992), p. 134.

5 An observation of the contemporary Catholic author Florimond de Raemond quoted in Philip Benedict, *Rouen during the Wars of Religion* (Cambridge, 1981), p. 80.

6 Data based on the tables in Alastair Duke, *Reformation and Revolt in the Low Countries* (London, 1990), p. 99, and Guido Marnef, *Antwerp in the Age of Reformation: Underground Protestantism in a Commercial Metropolis, 1550–1577* (Baltimore and London, 1996), p. 84.

7 *Acta van de Nederlandse synoden der zestiende eeuw*, ed. F.L. Rutgers (2nd edn, Dordrecht, 1980), pp.55–6.

8 Quoted in R.C. Bakhuizen van den Brink, *Cartons voor de geschiedenis van den Nederlandschen vrijheidsoorlog* (2 vols, The Hague, 1891–8), vol. II, p. 205.

9 The expression was introduced by H.A. Enno van Gelder, *Revolutionaire Reformatie: De vestiging van de Gereformeerde Kerk in de Nederlandse gewesten, gedurende de eerste jaren van de Opstand tegen Filips II, 1572–1585* (Amsterdam, 1943).

10 Figures based on Duke, *Reformation and Revolt*, p. 211, and Jonathan Israel, *The Dutch Republic: Its Rise, Greatness and Fall, 1477–1806* (Oxford, 1995), p. 114.

11 D. Nauta and J.P. van Dooren (eds), *De nationale synode van Dordrecht 1578* (Amsterdam, 1978), p. 133.

12 There is no survey in English on the developments in Ghent and Flanders. See therefore Johan Decavele, 'Gent, Calvinistisch en republikeins strijdcentrum in de Nederlandse Opstand (1577–1584)', in *Willem van Oranje 1584–1984* (Brussels, 1984), pp. 65–86, and Johan Decavele (ed.), *Het eind van een rebelse droom: Opstellen over het calvinistisch bewind te Gent (1577–1584)* (Ghent, 1984).

13 Guido Marnef, 'Brabants calvinisme in opmars: de weg naar de calvinistische republieken in Antwerpen, Brussel en Mechelen, 1577–1580', *Bijdragen tot de Geschiedenis* 70 (1987), pp. 7–21.

14 Quoted in J.H. Hessels (ed.), *Ecclesiae Londino-Batavae Archivum* (3 vols in 4; Cambridge, 1889–97), III-1, p. 526.

15 Both passages are quoted in Guido Marnef, 'The Changing Face of Calvinism in Antwerp, 1550–1585', in Andrew Pettegree, Alastair Duke and Gillian Lewis (eds), *Calvinism in Europe, 1540–1620* (Cambridge, 1994), p. 156.

16 Guido Marnef, *Het Calvinistisch Bewind te Mechelen, 1580–1585* (Kortrijk, 1987), pp. 245–6; *Ecclesiae Londino-Batavae*, III-1, pp. 568–9.

17 F.L. Rutgers (ed.), *Acta van de Nederlandsche synoden der zestiende eeuw* (2nd edn; Dordrecht, 1980), p. 196.

18 See the select bibliography below and Benjamin J. Kaplan, 'Remnants of the Papal Yoke: Apathy and Opposition in the Dutch Reformation', *Sixteenth Century Journal* 25 (1994), pp. 653–69.

19 Quoted in A. Ph. F. Wouters and P.H.A.M. Abels, *Nieuw en ongezien. Kerk en samenleving in de classis Delft en Delfland, 1572–1621* (2 vols, Delft, 1994), vol. I, p. 243.

FURTHER READING

Jonathan Israel, *The Dutch Republic: Its Rise, Greatness and Fall, 1477–1806* (Oxford, 1995), offers an excellent and comprehensive survey of the period. He also covers the history of the southern Netherlands until the late sixteenth century. A survey of the political context is indispensable for the second half of the sixteenth century. See the classic work of Geoffrey Parker, *The Dutch Revolt* (2nd edn; London, 1985), which integrates the struggle in the Low Countries into the international political setting. J.J. Woltjer, *Tussen vrijheidsoorlog en burgeroorlog: Over de Nederlandse Opstand 1555–1580* (Amsterdam, 1994), is indispensable for political and religious relations within the Netherlands. Philip Benedict, Guido Marnef, Henk van Nierop and Marc Venard (eds), *Reformation, Revolt and Civil War in France and the Netherlands, 1555–1585* (Amsterdam, 1999), is an important collection of articles that places the developments in the Netherlands in a comparative perspective. Equally interesting from a comparative perspective is Heinz Schilling, *Religion, Political Culture and the Emergence of Early Modern Society: Essays in German and Dutch History* (Leiden, 1992).

There is no recent general survey of the Reformation in the Netherlands. Wiebe Bergsma, 'The Low Countries', in Bob Scribner, Roy Porter and Mikuláš Teich (eds), *The Reformation in National Context* (Cambridge, 1994), presents a brief outline. Alastair Duke, *Reformation and Revolt in the Low Countries* (London, 1990), is a superb collection of articles that runs from the early Reformation until the religious situation in the early Dutch Republic. To this collection should be added Alastair Duke, 'The Netherlands', in Andrew Pettegree (ed.), *The Early Reformation in Europe* (Cambridge, 1992), pp. 142–65. A number of important studies chart the progress of Protestantism in the era of persecution at the local and regional level: Gérard Moreau, *Histoire du Protestantisme à Tournai jusqu'à la veille de la Révolution des Pays-Bas* (Paris, 1962); J.J. Woltjer, *Friesland in Hervormingstijd* (Leiden, 1962); Johan Decavele, *De dageraad van de Reformatie in Vlaanderen, 1520–1565* (2 vols; Brussels, 1975), and Guido Marnef, *Antwerp in the Age of Reformation: Underground Protestantism in a Commercial Metropolis, 1550–1577* (Baltimore and London, 1996). Robert S. DuPlessis, *Lille and the Dutch Revolt: Urban Stability in an Era of Revolution, 1500–1582* (Cambridge, 1991), is a long-term study that incorporates religious developments. The history of the Reformation in the Netherlands cannot be separated from the refugee centres in Germany and England. See especially Andrew Pettegree's *Foreign Protestant Communities in Sixteenth-Century London* (Oxford, 1986) and *Emden and the Dutch Revolt: Exile and the Development of Reformed Protestantism* (Oxford, 1992).

The development of the Reformed movement during the Wonderyear is analyzed by Guido Marnef, 'The Dynamics of Reformed Militancy in the Low Countries: The Wonderyear', in N. Scott Amos, Andrew Pettegree and Henk van Nierop (eds), *The Education of a Christian Society: Humanism and Reformation in Britain and the Netherlands* (Aldershot, 1999). Studies on the Reformation in the northern Netherlands since 1572 mainly focus on Holland. See Andrew Pettegree, 'Coming to Terms with Victory: The Upbuilding of a Calvinist Church in Holland, 1572–1590', in Andrew Pettegree, Alastair Duke and Gillian Lewis (eds), *Calvinism in Europe, 1540–1620* (Cambridge, 1994), pp. 160–80; C.C. Hibben, *Gouda in Revolt: Particularism and Pacifism in the Revolt of the Netherlands,*

1572–1588 (Utrecht, 1983), and Benjamin J. Kaplan, *Calvinists and Libertines: Confession and Community in Utrecht, 1578–1620* (Oxford, 1995). A.Th. van Deursen, *Bavianen en Slijkgeuzen: Kerk en kerkvolk ten tijde van Maurits en Oldebarnevelt* (Assen, 1974), presents a fascinating survey of the Reformed church during the first quarter of the seventeenth century, paying special attention to the conflict between Remonstrants and Contra-Remonstrants. The precarious relationship between state and Calvinist church and the question of tolerance have received ample attention. See J.D. Tracy, 'Public Church, *Gemeente Christi*, or Volkskerk: Holland's Reformed Church in Civil and Ecclesiastical Perspective', in H.R. Guggisberg and G.G. Krodel (eds), *Die Reformation in Deutschland und Europa: Interpretationen und Debatten* (Gütersloh, 1993), pp. 487–510; C. Berkvens-Stevelinck, J. Israel and G. Posthumus Meyjes (eds), *The Emergence of Tolerance in the Dutch Republic* (Leiden, 1997); Andrew Pettegree, 'The Politics of Toleration in the Free Netherlands, 1572–1620', in Ole Peter Grell and Bob Scribner (eds), *Tolerance and Intolerance in the European Reformation* (Cambridge, 1996), pp. 182–98.

ENGLAND AFTER 1558

Margo Todd

It was once the case that histories of the English Reformation dealt almost exclusively with the two decades between the Henrician legislation separating the Church of England from Rome and the Edwardian Prayer Books and Articles of Religion. Those that looked beyond the death of Edward VI saw the Marian martyrs as clear evidence of England's thoroughgoing Protestantism by the 1550s, and with the accession of Elizabeth the story simply petered out. What made such truncated accounts possible was a top-down view of the Reformation: Protestantism was achieved, in this view, by parliamentary statute and royal proclamation, reinforced by the preaching of clerical converts and administered by reforming bishops. The government ordered Reformation; the realm was thenceforth Protestant.

What the received version did not take into account is the matter of what was actually going on at the parochial level and it is this question that increasingly occupies historians. We are no longer content to define the Reformation so narrowly as to be satisfied by a study of edicts and sermons. Recognizing with the earliest Protestants that at the heart of the reformers' message was individual belief, conversion and the adoption of a new kind of piety and disciplined living, we have delved anew into the archives and, indeed, into the physical remains of sixteenth-century parishes to seek evidence for the kind of transformation that really constituted Reformation. As Helen Parish's earlier chapter suggests, that new research has uncovered considerably more resistance to Protestant ideas than was earlier acknowledged and has made it increasingly difficult to date the Protestantization of England. As it turns out, for every Marian martyr there was a parishioner bringing carefully hidden mass-books and icons back into use; for every exile there was a craftsman busily restoring rood screens and altars. The precise degree of resistance remains unclear, but certainly traditions and beliefs condemned by the reformers survived Edward's reign. In fact, reluctant acquiescence rather than willing embrace of Protestantism continued to be the order of the day for much of the population well into the Elizabethan period. And if the Reformation was constituted by the sort of cultural transformation we see in sixteenth-century Geneva or Zurich, we must look to the mid-seventeenth century to find a vigorously Protestant government attempting to effect a reformed English society.

Protestant clerical complaint in the 1580s of popular 'superstition' and igno-rance of Reformed doctrine seems after all an accurate reflection of the limited nature of the Elizabethan Protestant achievement. George Gifford found in his Essex parish in 1582 a 'hatred ... exceeding great against the gospel' and no more than 'five among five score which are able to understand the necessary grounds and principles of religion'. In the following year, Philip Stubbes complained that people continued their traditional sabbath observance, not by attending Protestant sermons, but 'in frequenting of bawdy stage plays, ... May games, church ales, feasts and wakes; in piping, dancing, dicing, carding, bowling, tennis-playing; in bear-baiting, cock-fighting, hawking, hunting, and such ... other devilish pastimes'.[1] This was not entirely exaggeration: Elizabethan church courts had ample cause to prosecute both Sabbath breach and the persistence of 'popish' doctrines and festive practices, as well as retention in many parish churches of Catholic furnishings and images. Episcopal and archidiaconal visitations in York, Chester and Hereford in the 1580s were still investigating the survival of altars, images and Catholic vestments.[2] If contemporaries were thus unconvinced that the Reformation had been accomplished meaningfully by this date, surely we must reassess our own judgement.

What this will require is a clear set of criteria for measuring the success of the Reformation. If we accept the minimalist criterion of outward conformity to mandated observances, the Elizabethan Settlement and the subsequent campaigns against those who disavowed it might suffice to complete our story of the Reformation. But Catholicism persisted in later sixteenth-century England against increasing popular opposition, suggesting that the story of rising anti-popery as a defining element of Protestantism also deserves attention. The negative definition of Protestantism as anti-Catholicism is one that would have satisfied many contemporaries, especially after the 1570 papal excommunication of the queen, the Armada of 1588 and later the Gunpowder Plot made popery synonymous with military threat and treason and reinforced the Protestantism of Englishness. Contemporary clergy, however, especially Puritans, would demand more than this negative definition; they sought a minimal level of theological understanding in Protestant converts. If we define 'Reformation' in doctrinal terms, our story will have to include the remarkable Elizabethan campaigns for systematic Reformed catechizing and for an educated preaching clergy.

Yet even these increasingly demanding definitions stop short of the one that the most zealous of Protestants would require. With its emphasis on faith and conver-sion, on the experience of repentance and amendment of life in gratitude for grace, on personal piety and evangelical zeal, Protestantism was a religion of the heart. The reformers demanded of believers a transforming experience of saving faith, not mere outward profession. Their expectation, moreover, was that this experience would transform not only the individual believer, but the entire community. When hearts were converted, scripture would truly rule the behaviour of Christians and a disciplined, godly community would attest to the providential design for England. This transformation would entail both a rejection of tradi-tional Catholic culture, with its seasonal festivities, cult of saints, painted and sculpted images, and religious ritual and drama, and an acceptance of the more austere, word-centred Protestant culture of sermon attendance, catechism, Bible-reading and prayer. In the eyes of the most vigorous Protestants, anything short of this bore witness to the fact that England's Reformation had been stillborn, or at best had progressed only part of the way. For many of the Marian exiles, Calvin's Geneva provided the pattern for full reformation of church and community, and on their return they proceeded to try to reproduce it. But achievement of that ideal was difficult enough for a small city-state; its implementation in a sizeable national church with a not particularly religious ruler was quite another matter.

What the Reformation finally established in Elizabeth's England was a state church united both negatively in its opposition to popery and positively in its formal identity with Protestant doctrine, but at the same time fundamentally divided by the demands of Calvinist doctrine and piety. For all its theoretical inclusiveness, the Elizabethan church was riven by an unrelenting tension between those most fully committed to continuing the movement that had come so far in Edward's reign and those who were either satisfied that the movement had come far enough or who had merely submitted outwardly to required change in each reign. The first group, the self-professed 'godly', known in modern parlance as Puritans, identified themselves with the biblical remnant of elect saints surrounded by the unregenerate masses. Their predestinarianism was 'experimental': founded in the individual experience of repentance and conversion, reinforced by the personal struggle to achieve assurance of election. To these, the 'hotter sort of Protestants', those mere outward professors of the faith who lacked the inward change so central to Protestant conversion were, like the most active sinners, an affront to God and true believers, and the direct cause of providential judgements on all England. The 'mere' conformists' simply credal faith, their satisfaction with a 'half-way Reformation' and their intermittent harassment of the godly, were constant sources of worry and complaint by their more zealously Protestant brethren.

The story of the later English Reformation is the story of how this tension at the centre of the reformed church worked itself out; initially in the achievement of a measure of uneasy consensus and compromise, but eventually in the steadily heightening conflict that culminated in what one historian has called the last of the European Wars of Religion. The Civil War of the 1640s, sometimes labelled the Puritan Revolution, was the final effort of the godly fully to realize the English Reformation for the nation. If they failed, it was surely because their agenda, their criteria for true Protestant faith, was more demanding of individual spiritual experience than most ordinary people could manage. For their spiritual heirs, the Dissenters of the post-Restoration era, the campaign would continue on the more limited scale of the gathered congregation and later the revivalism of the Methodists. The most recent larger treatment of England's later Reformation accordingly resigns itself to a 'Long Reformation' with a terminal date of 1800. The present chapter stops short of that too-expansive view and examines the efforts of a century of Protestants following the official Henrician/Edwardian legislation to achieve the full Reformation of the national church. It concludes with a glance at the ultimate failure of the seventeenth-century godly – military victors in the 1640s – to win the Reformation that was supposed to ensue. The forced retreat of the most zealous from the pinnacle of Protestant achievement after the 1660 Restoration inaugurates a Protestant history of mere dissent from established religious formalism and ends the story of the more ambitious English Reformation.

THE ELIZABETHAN SETTLEMENT

Elizabeth found at her accession in 1558 that her own agenda was best served by adopting the religious reforms of her brother's government, but no more. Those reforms were, of course, thoroughly Protestant. Given her principal aim of securing the stability of her realm and the loyalty of her subjects, the queen's choice suggests that she gauged popular support for the reformed faith to be substantial – an important testimony to the achievements of the Edwardian Reformation. Elizabeth was no fool and her judgement surely gives the lie to revisionist views of the earlier English Reformation as forced from above on an unwilling populace. She took seriously the distinctly Protestant pageantry that greeted her entry into London and straightaway distanced herself from her Catholic sister's grim reputation by returning to a Protestant stance. The parliament that promulgated the religious settlement was likewise sensible of the utility of public approbation of their programme; at least the members of the Commons perceived sufficient support for the Reformation from their propertied constituents. Their concern was not exclusively spiritual, of course: they and their constituents were anxious to retain ownership of the monastic lands seized by Henry. But they were also politicians and recognized that a new set of beliefs and behaviours was more easily secured from a populace already in some measure committed to it. And a substantial minority clearly held strong Protestant convictions themselves: it is worth noting that even in Mary's reign, a quarter of M.P.s had had the courage to vote against the restoration of Catholicism.[3]

Accordingly the new government proceeded to issue injunctions that replaced stone altars with portable communion tables and ordered the destruction of images, rood lofts and popish vestments like chasubles and copes. In place of images, the words of the Creed and the Ten Commandments now decorated church walls, along with the royal arms to underpin visually the ruler's headship of the Protestant church. Parliament retained an orderly liturgical service by reissuing the Book of Common Prayer. Its communion formula was modified from the 1552 version with an awkward combination of the formulae of the two Edwardian Prayer Books in order to allow for a wide breadth of interpretation of the sacrament, ranging from Zwinglian commemoration to a real presence; however, little else changed. The earlier linguistic shift from 'priest' to 'minister', 'altar' to 'table' underpinned the Protestantism of a liturgical order that in general structure continued to follow the order of the mass, but in the vernacular and with congregational participation. The queen retained episcopal polity as most supportive of monarchical authority, rejecting the Presbyterian alternative advocated by the Genevan exiles. Between 1559 and 1561 she filled sees vacated by Catholic opponents of the Settlement (and by victims of the 1558 influenza epidemic) with staunchly but not radically Protestant bishops, including some former exiles. In 1563 parliament adopted the Thirty-Nine Articles (a slight adaptation of

Edward's Forty-Two), including the clearly predestinarian Article 17, and a Calvinist catechism was promulgated. With a reauthorized English Bible and an expanded Book of Homilies, the latter a handy tool for ministers unaccustomed to preaching, the official English Reformation was concluded. This Elizabethan Settlement would continue virtually unamended to govern the religious life of the people of early modern England.

Were the English people hereby rendered Protestant? Certainly most conformed outwardly to the demands of the Settlement, though there was regional variation. Generally London and the more densely populated southeast welcomed the return of Protestantism, as did ports and areas involved in cloth manufacture and trade; more remote and isolated areas, having less contact with new and especially Continental ideas, were slower to comply. Enforcement was not particularly draconian during the decade of the 1560s and many traditionalists found it possible to retain their Catholic beliefs but still attend the new communion service the required three times a year. These 'church papists' generally escaped the attention of the authorities and outright recusancy (refusal to attend Church of England services) was at first rare. The church courts, which continued to operate as they had before the Reformation, continued to deal mostly with cases of sexual and other misbehaviour, although they did examine parishes to determine that they had purchased Bibles and Prayer Books and eliminated their altars, icons, rood lofts and vestments (other than the surplice). Royal commissions assisted in enforcing iconoclasm and ousting clearly unreformed clergy. Relatively little of the courts' time, however, was devoted to cases of lay recusancy. This is not to say that Catholics suddenly disappeared from the English landscape, only that they quickly became a minority movement, remaining underground and eschewing active proselytization. When recusancy fines were imposed they generally fell on socially prominent or very outspoken Catholic critics; laity who kept a low profile were generally not targeted. For the surviving English Catholic community, however, this decade would prove to be the calm before the storm.

In 1569, things changed dramatically when Catholic nobility in the north rose in revolt. Six thousand strong, the rebels were intent on restoring Catholic worship. More politically alarming, they sought to release the Catholic Mary, Queen of Scots, the next best claimant to the English throne, from her English prison. The revolt was quickly quelled and its leaders executed, but the danger of continuing laxity towards Catholics was now clear. It became even more obvious in 1570 when the papal bull *Regnans in excelsis* excommunicated the heretic Queen of England, released her subjects from obedience and effectively legitimated efforts to depose her in favour of a Catholic ruler. Parliament responded to a threat now as much political as religious with a drastic increase in recusancy fines, levied with alacrity on Catholics who hitherto might have escaped attention. Recusancy nonetheless increased, particularly with the influx from 1574 of missionary priests trained at Continental seminaries like William Allen's foundation at Douai in the Spanish Netherlands. These missioners, hoping to stem the drift from occasional conformity into Protestant affiliation, insisted that English Catholics cease even token attendance of their parish churches. When the first Jesuit missionaries arrived in the country in 1580, therefore, the perceived threat had become such that the government responded with criminal prosecution and the executions began in earnest. Of about 600 identifiable missionary priests in Elizabethan England, nearly 300 were imprisoned and about 130 were eventually executed. More than 60 lay Catholics were added to their number after 1581, when a new statute made it treason to reconcile with Rome and raised recusancy fines from 12d. per offence to £20 per month.[4] Catholic laity anxious to dissociate themselves from Jesuit radicals announced their loyalty to the queen and rejection of plots for her deposition. But Elizabeth's government was not inclined to leniency in the face of real threats to the monarchy. In the end, the authorities may have executed nearly as many Catholics as Mary's government had Protestants, but with a crucial difference. Elizabethan Catholics were condemned not as heretics, but as traitors: they were ignominiously hanged as criminals, not burned as martyr-heroes. This queen would not be known as Bloody Elizabeth. By 1590, English Catholics had become a minority sect contained within a few seigneurial households and the priests they maintained had little effect beyond those family circles.

THE BUILDING OF PROTESTANT IDENTITY

The sinister political agenda now associated with Catholics provided a wonderful rallying point for Protestants intent on pushing for further reformation of the church. In forming a new cultural identity, it is extremely useful to have a despised or dangerous 'other' against whom to define oneself and, in Elizabethan England, Catholicism fitted the bill superbly. Opposition to 'papists' (the usual contemporary label for Catholics) may actually have done as much to establish Protestantism as foundational to English national identity as any number of Reformed doctrinal statements. From the beginning of the reign, Protestant propagandists made the most of the many ways in which Catholics had undermined England's best interests, put her legitimate ruler in jeopardy and committed violence against the most godly of the people of England. They drew attention to Catholic military failure in Mary's unwise participation in her Spanish husband's wars and specifically to the humiliating loss of Calais. They pointed to the disloyalty of the Northern Rising and they underlined Catholic cruelty to the best of English subjects by retelling the stories of the Marian martyrs. So effective was the propaganda machine that Protestantism (construed as anti-popery) became a defining element of Englishness.

The most successful in this genre was John Foxe's *Acts and Monuments*, soon abridged to the *Book of Martyrs*, first published in 1563 and destined to go through six English editions by 1596. It has been suggested that it was second only to the Bible in terms of influence and sales, and this is not hard to credit. Moreover, extant manuscript copies of large portions of the book increases our impression of very wide readership. Readers of Foxe's stories through the mid-seventeenth century copied their favourite passages into devotional journals and commonplace books, and godly householders recorded as a regular Sabbath observance the practice of gathering their children and servants to read to them from Foxe. Even the illiterate thus came to know the *Book of Martyrs* well. Nor did they have to wait for the stories to be read to get the point: Foxe lavishly illustrated his collection with woodcuts that made his message crystal clear. Recent research has found considerable evidence that many of these woodcuts, some of which were fold-outs easily removed from the book, were cut out, coloured and pasted on cottage walls for the edification of common viewers.

Foxe set the stories of the Marian martyrs in the larger historical context of ancient Roman persecution of the first Christians and mediæval Roman conspiracy to undermine monarchy and the gospel together. The popes and bishops responsible for the deaths of English believers from Wyclif to Tyndale to Cranmer were in this account heirs of the ancient tyrants who had killed the early Christians: enemies of the gospel and of England. The papal assault on Elizabeth was a continuation of mediæval pontiffs' usurpation of the authority of kings like John and emperors like Henry IV. The famous woodcut of John surrendering his crown to a papal legate sent a clear message even to the illiterate; so, more positively, did the picture of Henry VIII enthroned with the pope beneath his heel. 'Christ's enemy Anti-Christ', as Cranmer labelled the pope, provided on nearly every page of Foxe's work the 'other' against which English Christians could now define themselves. His agents, the persecuting Catholic churchmen, are consistently depicted in image and word as vicious, gratuitously cruel, even sadistic towards invariably patient, gentle, courageous professors of the Protestant gospel, with disproportionate attention given to English believers from Wyclif to the sixteenth-century martyrs. The narrative often draws attention to the foreignness of the persecutors (like the ubiquitous 'Spanish friar') and always to the foreign, Roman inspiration for all the persecutions, suggesting that to be English is to be Protestant or at least anti-popish. The dichotomy between truth and falsehood, Protestantism and popery, is built into pictures as well as stories, the title-page being the best example (see Figure 13.1, p. 232). Here true church and false church are placed on opposite sides of the woodcut and the visual story-line, from bottom to top, underpins the message of the text: popish 'superstition' in the lower and middle frames must result on Judgement Day in their expulsion from heaven. Popery is the wide path that leads to destruction, while the true worship of the good Protestants in the lowest frame on the opposite side ushers them through willing martyrdom in the middle frame into paradise at the top. There is no question which side represents godliness and which the enemy.

Developments later in the reign would serve to underpin the link between anti-popery and England's freedom from foreign tyranny. The identification of Catholicism with treason and foreign threat, so well established by the 1570s, was borne out by sundry plots in the next decade to assassinate the Protestant queen and replace her with the Catholic Mary Stuart. It became especially clear in 1588 when Philip II, with papal backing, sent his Armada to invade England, only to be turned back by a combination of English naval power and apparently providential storms. The ensuing ballad literature and popular celebration of England's divine deliverance reflected acceptance of the Foxeian theme of Protestant England in battle with the Romish Antichrist. Richard Rogers recognized in 'our late deliverance of the rage of Spain as memorable a work of God as ever was in any my remembrance'.[5] God would continue to be England's defender against popish conspiracy. In the next reign, the Catholic attempt in November 1605 to destroy

Parliament and king by exploding gunpowder stored in the cellars under West-minster Hall spawned a new national holiday devoted explicitly to anti-popery. Powder Plot sermons celebrated the providential deliverance of England and divine approbation of England's Protestantism, images of the pope were burned in street bonfires and even Puritans produced festal poetry, like John Wilson's *Song of Deliverance for the Lasting Remembrance of God's Wonderful Works*.[6] England's identity as a Protestant nation, protected by divine providence against Catholic assault, was confirmed by annual festival. To the official, statutory Reformation was thus added a powerful, if negative, reformation of national religious identity.

THE REFORMATION IN THE PARISHES

Foxe offered his readers more than mere anti-popery. His book also played its part in the doctrinal Reformation of England, begun under Edward but finally solidi-fied during the first decades of Elizabeth's reign. Built into both the pictures and the stories of the *Book of Martyrs* were the fundamental elements of Protestant teaching, set forth clearly and in a sufficiently dramatic way to indoctrinate and, indeed, excite a broad popular audience. Readers of the story of Tyndale's martyrdom were left in no doubt of the primary authority of scripture over mere human tradition. John Bradford's story made clear the doctrine of salvation by faith alone; Cranmer's interrogation clarified the spiritual rather than physical presence of Christ in the sacrament. A myriad of outspoken female martyrs like Anne Askew inculcated readers with the inclusive principle of the priesthood of all believers. Detailed criticism of the mass and auricular confession is central to many of the martyr stories. And the efficacy of good works for salvation was as roundly condemned by housewives and weavers as by Thomas Bilney's account of his conversion, when from scripture:

> I learned that all my travails, all my fasting and watching, all the redemption of masses and pardons, being done without trust in Christ, which only saveth his people from their sins, these, I say, I learned to be nothing else but ... a hasty and swift running out of the right way.[7]

For those who could not read the stories, the title-page woodcut not only told of the affiliation of papists with the Devil, as we have seen; it also identified specific erroneous doctrines and Protestant corrections. Here the prayer beads pictured in the Catholic worship scene are replaced in the parallel Protestant frame by Bibles; in the Protestant service, each believer, male and female, checks the claims of the preacher against the only real authority, Holy Writ. For the proces-sion of icons and adoration of the host by the superstitious (iconographically, in fact, the idolatrous) in the condemned corner, we find the logocentrism of Protestants in pictured veneration not of an image or object, but of the tetragram-maton, the Hebrew word for Yahweh himself. The message here is not just condemnatory of Catholicism; it is Protestant orthodoxy taught by image as well as story. Foxe's book thus stands not only as a monument to the martyrs, but also as a foundation for the doctrinal Reformation.

The book was a significant start on the Protestant didactic programme for England, but it had to be continued by a preaching ministry and a Bible-reading laity, neither of them hallmarks of traditional religion. Revisionist historians are surely correct that most English people in 1559 would have had a hard time declaiming the Protestant creed as cogently as Foxe's martyrs did. The slow progress of the doctrinal Reformation is hardly surprising in a nation largely illiterate and a church led by clergy who rarely did more for the assembled faithful than perform the mass and who were often not very well qualified to do even that. The discoveries of clerical ignorance on Bishop Hooper of Gloucester's 1551 visitation are notorious: of 312 clergy he examined that year, 172 could not repeat the Ten Commandments or could not identify the author of the Lord's Prayer.[8] This was not the failure of Protestantism, but the legacy of the Catholic past, and it would continue to hamper the Reformed cause in the next reign. Elizabeth's new Protestant bishops found it extremely difficult to fill with learned men the clerical vacancies left by the hundreds of deprivations of 1559–60. Certainly no significant reserve of university-trained Protestants was available. Of the 176 men ordained by Bishop Downham of Chester from 1562 to 1569, not one was a graduate. Trained preachers, able to produce sermons as well as to read the liturgy, were a rarity even among those who were graduates, so that a 1569 visitation of Chichester diocese reported that the 'whole diocese is very blind and superstitious for want of teaching'. Some parishes had not had a sermon in the past twelve years.[9] By the middle of the next decade, more than half of London ministers were preachers, but the figure for the nation was probably closer to 20 per cent.[10] Not until the Puritan drive to establish new seminaries for preachers – like Emmanuel (1584) and Sidney Sussex (1596) Colleges in Cambridge, or Trinity College (1596) in Dublin – would this situation change. And not until a new generation of trained preachers headed into the 'dark corners of the land' would the level of lay religious understanding change substantially.

Meanwhile, however, a second prong of the Protestant didactic campaign, the production and dissemination of catechisms, laid the parochial groundwork on which the preachers would build. More than 1,000 different catechisms poured off Elizabethan presses, many in multiple editions, so that there were well over 1,000,000 copies in circulation by 1600.[11] The attendant rise in literacy, especially in urban areas and the southeast, spurred the didactic progress of Protestantism, although it should be noted that the religion of the Word is aurally effective as well.[12] With catechism and sermons taken together, the foundational elements of Protestant doctrine would have been hard to escape by the latter half of Elizabeth's reign. They were reinforced by zealous Protestant bishops who enforced doctrinal standards for a renewed campaign of confirmation, in addition to demanding a higher level of theological competence from their clergy and themselves preaching actively throughout their dioceses. Toby Matthew, for instance, preached nearly 1,300 sermons as Dean and later Bishop of Durham.[13] In urban areas, especially where Puritans were influential, town corporations sponsored extra preaching by town 'lecturers'. The more zealous ministers sometimes organized 'exercises' or 'prophesyings', in which conferences of ministers gathered regularly to preach to each other and a lay audience, and after the departure of the laity to discuss the sermons delivered in a sort of continuing education programme for ministers in the field. By Elizabeth's death more than half of England's 9,244 parishes had preachers, and 40 per cent of ministers were graduates; by the 1620s, nearly all had university degrees.[14] A parallel development can be seen in Wales, where the advance of the Protestant gospel was ensured by the 1571 foundation for Welshmen of Jesus College, Oxford; the provision of a Welsh Bible in 1588; and the preaching activities of native Protestant ministers, including thirteen native bishops of a strongly pastoral bent. As a result, by the end of the century, the process of doctrinal Reformation can be said to have achieved remarkable success. As early as 1585 the literature of clerical complaint was countered by the Suffolk Puritan Oliver Pigg, who found that 'the Church of England is now in some sort flourishing'. By the reign of James (1603–25) the Reformation in England and Wales was indeed, as a recent historian has claimed, 'a runaway success'.[15] To an impressive extent, the religion of the Word had come to define the religious experience of the people.

PROTESTANT CRITICISM

For some Protestants, however, the Settlement was a halfway Reformation and the pace of further reform was too slow. Christened by their enemies in the 1560s 'Puritans' or 'Precisians', these Protestants preferred, with remarkable hubris, to identify themselves as the 'godly'. They opposed the remaining 'dregs of popery' in the service and in clerical dress as undermining the Protestant campaign against idolatry and superstition. Particularly targeted in the 1560s were clerical vestments, thought to retain a popish distinction between clergy and people at the expense of the priesthood of all believers. In the 1570s Puritans called on Parliament to abolish such popish vestiges as the ring in marriage, kneeling at communion, the sign of the cross in baptism and the use of communion wafers instead of table bread. Puritan M.P.s attempted to secure freedom for ministers of tender conscience to depart from the Prayer Book liturgy. In the 1570s and 1580s, a minority of Puritans led by Thomas Cartwright and John Field advocated replacement of episcopal church government with a classical or presbyterian form of polity that would effect a more comprehensive discipline of parishioners' behaviour, on the model of Geneva or Scotland. Their 1572 *Admonition to Parliament* comprised the presbyterian platform, elements of which were put forward in 1580s parliaments. At the same time, presbyterians did manage in a few localities to establish an embryonic system of *classes* exercising discipline and holding clerical conferences.

To each of these efforts, Elizabeth and her bishops responded firmly and negatively, suspending or depriving presbyterians and other ministers who refused to comply with the established ceremonial order. The episcopal hierarchy served the queen's interests well and, for opponents of Puritans, order and obedience stood a better chance of strengthening Protestantism than would continued and confusing change. Their fear of the radical sectarian wing of Protestantism contributed to their mounting campaigns against Puritans. They perceived separatist groups like the Anabaptist Family of Love and the anti-Trinitarian Socinians undermining the unity of the national church on one side, while popery threatened from the other. Their quite natural response was to cling more tenaciously to a *via media* or middle way, now graven in the Prayer Book liturgy and reformed episcopacy and not subject to amendment. In point of fact, separatist numbers were far too small to pose any threat and of course Puritans were as much enemies of separatists as conformists were. Some, like John Knewstub, won points with the establishment by actively combating Familists. But criticism of the state church could too easily lead in a separatist direction for it to be easily tolerated by authorities bent on order and conformity.

Accordingly, even the clerical education programme embodied in the Puritan 'exercises', which had won general episcopal approval, came by 1577 to be so feared by the queen that she quashed it and deprived Archbishop Grindal of his office for his support of such unsupervised and so potentially subversive activity. With the appearance in 1588–9 of the anonymous Marprelate Tracts – which made vicious use of biting humour and scurrility to attack bishops, the government and the new Archbishop of Canterbury – the vigorously anti-Puritan John Whitgift clamped down once and for all on the presbyterian movement. At the same time, John Bancroft, Bishop of London and after 1604 James's Archbishop of Canterbury, adopted and promoted a full-blown doctrine of episcopacy *jure divino*, that is, the notion that rule of the church by bishops was not merely a convenient form of church government, as Whitgift and his predecessors had held, but that God had instituted it as the only correct ecclesiastical polity. Henceforth, Puritans, most of whom were in any case moderate and supportive of episcopacy (of the older sort), prudently centred their complaint not on ecclesiastical polity, but on worship and lay conduct. Most Puritan preachers regarded retention of their pulpits as the highest priority and conformed to the external demands of the hierarchy as much as they needed to in order to keep preaching. Their criticism continued, but for the time being in a more muted and tolerable form.

Part of what enabled the coexistence of Puritan critics and conformist authorities within the same national body was the common ground they found in theology. Both held a Calvinist view of predestination. Much of Nowell's authorized catechism was in fact taken directly from Calvin's catechism and the 1579 statutes for Oxford University set as the basis of theological education both of those catechisms along with that of the Heidelberg theologians, to be followed by works of Bullinger and Jewel, and Calvin's *Institutes of the Christian Religion*. By 1600, ninety editions of Calvin's works had been published in English translation.[16] When, in the 1590s, Calvinist doctrine was questioned by two members of Cambridge University, William Barret and Peter Baro, Puritans and bishops happily joined in condemning both for their arguments favouring free will and the resistibility of grace. In formal response to the Cambridge problem, Archbishop Whitgift proceeded in the Lambeth Articles of 1595 to define an even more rigorously predestinarian doctrine than the Articles of Religion had included – one eminently satisfactory to Cambridge Puritans. Only the queen's objections to further doctrinal refinement prevented their inclusion with the Thirty-Nine Articles. The Lambeth document echoed the essentially Bezan view set forth by the Cambridge divine William Perkins (a sort of Puritan guru for his generation) in his very widely read *Foundation of Christian Religion* (1590). As his Table of Salvation and Damnation in that work makes very clear (see Figure 21.1), human will has no place whatsoever in determining whether one follows the white path of the elect or the black path of the reprobate. God's will alone establishes the end of every life, to his own glory. Those who held the opposing view, increasingly associated with the Dutch theologian Jacobus Arminius, would in the ensuing three decades be disciplined by bishops and university authorities, and their works would not pass episcopal censorship to publication.

Even with this theological consensus, though, Puritan zeal further to reform the church by transforming the believers who constituted it created a subtle distinction between the Calvinisms of the two groups. The credal Calvinism shared with conformists was expanded by the godly into an 'experimental' Calvinist variety, applied to the conscience of the individual believer. The challenge for believers who tried to apply the doctrine of predestination to their lives was to determine whether they had been chosen for election to life eternal or for reprobation to hell-fire. Puritans, following Calvin, taught that assurance of salvation can be achieved by the elect; however, collecting signs of election proved an agonizing task, for parishioners and pastors alike. Puritans were constantly taking their own spiritual temperatures, as their soul-searching diaries attest; they tested the depth of their sorrow for sin, the degree of their enthusiasm for sermons and scripture, the level of their commitment to performing good works in gratitude for salvation. The introduction of 'temporary faith' for the reprobate on Perkins' chart confronted them with an awful possibility, which they devoted much of their lives to eliminating by prayer, fasting, self-examination, penitence, Bible-reading and sermon repetition. Being godly was not easy.

The Reformation that Puritans aimed for was not limited, however, to this ongoing process of individual conversion. It extended to the whole community. What the godly sought for England was the last of our four possible definitions of Reformation. For them, the official Settlement, popular anti-popery, even the spread of Protestant doctrine, only went part of the way to true Reformation. These set the stage for true religion but did not finally achieve it. The godly understood that Reformation involved most fundamentally the internalization of new values; external conformity could never suffice and no auditor of a good Protestant sermon could ignore this. The church may have been a 'secret multitude of true professors' in the midst of an indifferent or hostile mass, but that multitude was driven to evangelism and the message they preached must have an impact on the masses. It undeniably did: the Essex preacher Richard Blackerby found that the ungodly among his parishioners 'would sometimes rise up against his preaching with rage and violence', a not atypical reaction. He recognized, though, that these were individuals 'whose consciences were scared' and in the end either they converted or 'the wrath of God did often most eminently take hold' and ruin them, often with sudden and gruesome death. Sales of lurid accounts of such providential judgements on the ungodly hint at a culture attuned to Protestant values and quite convinced of the judgement awaiting people who violated those values. Thus the same ministers who complained of persecution were also able to boast of the conversions they had effected. 'Multitudes of very

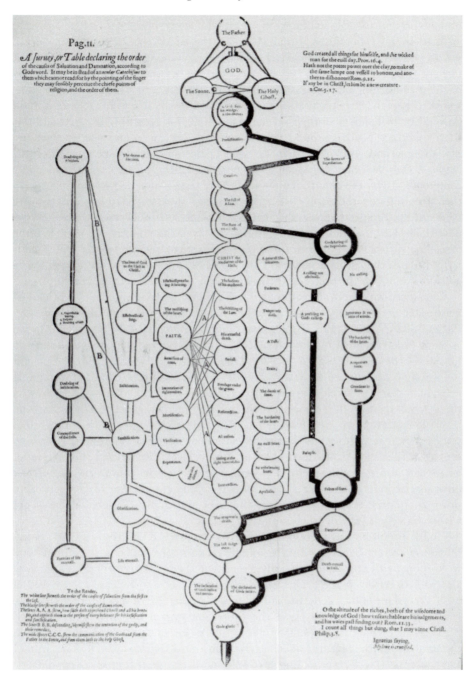

Figure 21.1 The Table of Salvation and Damnation from William Perkins, *Foundation of Christian Religion,* 1590. The table confronts anxious believers with the possibility of temporary faith in the reprobate, while 'despair' may assail the elect. Small wonder that the rigours of second generation Calvinism proved so unpalatable at parochial level. (London, British Library)

profane persons did fall under the power of the word' preached by Blackerby, we are told by his biographer, Samuel Clarke, who added that 'a society or club of young persons, who used to have their set times to meet, and dance, and frolic it in their youthful sports, sins and vanities, were by his preaching there, all or most of them converted, and became a company of gracious Christians, and used afterwards to join in prayer, as before they had done in sin and folly'. Clarke himself proved 'the instrument of the conversion of many'; his preaching brought auditors from six or seven miles around, 'both young and old, men and women, wet and dry, summer and winter, to their very great pains and labour, spending the time between the [two Sunday] sermons in repetition, singing of Psalms, and godly conference.' After the conversion of 'very many young men and women, who held their meetings on the Sabbaths in the evenings to repeat sermons and perform such duties', he could report that the town before called 'Drunken Alcester was now exemplary and eminent for religion all over the country'.[17] John White's preaching, in the wake of a fire that all but destroyed Dorchester in 1613, similarly made of that profane town a 'City on a Hill', the glory of the Dorset godly and a testimony to the power of the Reformation to effect a cultural revolution.[18]

Of course, not every dancing society turned into a prayer meeting and the next generation of Dorchester Puritans despaired of their own children's 'vanities'. Puritan divines like Thomas Young who urged stricter Sabbath observance found as many examples of the wrong behaviour as models of godliness, if the pictures on his well-balanced title-page are any indication (see Figure 21.2). But the Reformation had by the early seventeenth century set a new standard for correct behaviour that was as clearly recognized by those disinclined to its rigour as by those who espoused it. The descendants of the mediæval alehouse-haunters and maypole-dancers were well aware that their behaviour now flouted a religious standard designed to set a Reformed nation apart from its superstitious and profane neighbours. Sabbath-breakers and 'loose livers' recognized themselves for what their ministers told them they were: a scandal to the church and a source of providential judgement. The earnest preaching and catechizing of generations of increasingly well-trained Protestant ministers and godly householders was not without effect, at least in establishing the ideal.

Godly discipline was logocentric: the Word, preached and read, was the determinant of correct behaviour by the individual and good order in the community. In keeping with this fundamentally Protestant theme, the cultural Reformation also had its effect on the arts. Despite the success of the images in Foxe and of early Protestant efforts at Reformed religious drama, use of media other than the read or preached word to spread the Protestant gospel withered away in mid-Elizabethan England. Religious drama virtually ceased after John Bale's efforts in the mid-sixteenth century, and heavily illustrated works of religious history and doctrine like Foxe's became text-only, with the exception of a few didactic title-pages like Young's. Religious ballads gave way to a strictly scripture-based Psalter to fill the musical requirements of the new service.

Popular festivities followed the same track. While some traditional celebrations continued, they tended to be secular festivals like May Day. Old saints' days and religious celebrations like Corpus Christi Day, other than the seasons maintained

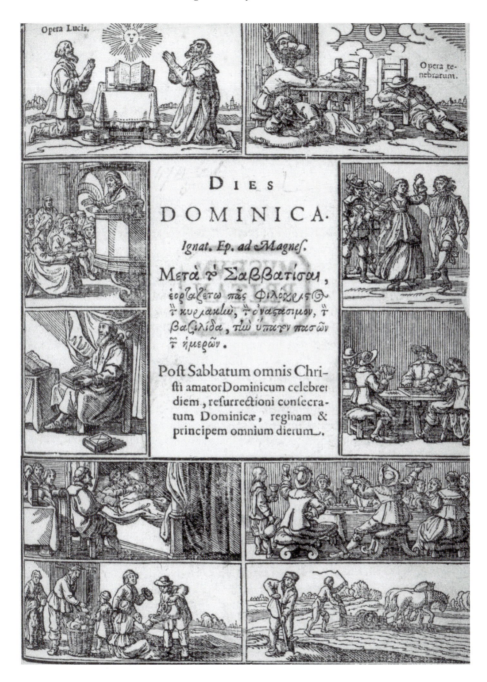

Figure 21.2 Thomas Young, *Treatise on Sabbath Observance*, 1639. The title-page of Thomas Young's treatise on Sabbath observance contrasts the Puritan pattern of piety with the frivolity of the unregenerate. The godly regarded good works as a possible sign of election; they pursued a 'reformation of manners' for the larger society to avert God's judgements on the whole community. (London, British Library)

by the new Prayer Book, fell away gradually, replaced by political celebrations like those associated with the defeat of the Armada or the Gunpowder Plot, or royal accession days. Conformists were as complicit in this campaign as Puritans, but the latter pushed for an even more austere calendar like that adopted by their northern neighbours. Only in the political disorder of the 1640s, though, did they finally manage to abolish Christmas.

THE RISE OF LAUDIANISM

The penchant of the godly to see England as fundamentally riven by the demands of Reformed piety ultimately created an impossible tension within the national church. For them, Foxe's old antithesis of papist and Protestant had become a division of English Protestants into 'mere' conformists and true professors. Puritan criticism and conformist repression of it could not coexist forever. One side or the other must inevitably become ascendant and upset the balance to such a degree that the unity of the church, and indeed the realm, would be destroyed.

The end of peaceful coexistence and compromise came after the 1625 ascension of Charles I and his promotion of a group of clergy anti-Calvinist in theology and ceremonialist in matters of worship. Associated from the 1620s with Bishops Richard Neile of Durham and William Laud of London (later Archbishops of York and Canterbury, respectively), the bishops among this group launched a campaign against the godly that drove many to Holland or New England, and others to political and finally military action. They also changed the grounds for judging conformity, specifically reintroducing into liturgical practice ceremonies and physical arrangements that had not been used since the Elizabethan Settlement – including bowing at the name of Jesus, replacing portable tables with altars in the east end of the church, railing the altars and elaborating ecclesiastical decoration with crucifixes and a proliferation of candles – and using the church courts to enforce them with a vengeance. They reversed the Protestant trend by emphasizing sacraments over the Word in worship and what Laud called the 'beauty of holiness' over Reformed simplicity. They crushed the 'lectures by combination' that had succeeded Elizabethan prophesyings. Laudian bishops like Matthew Wren engaged in particularly fierce prosecution of ministers who declined the new arrangements, escalating the exodus from the realm of godly preachers. As for the discipline of popular behaviour, they secured in 1633 the reissue of the 1618 *Book of Sports*, which reversed Puritan sabbatarianism by specifically authorizing Sunday recreations, and then prosecuted much more actively than their Jacobean predecessors the ministers who declined to read the *Book* to their congregations as ordered.

The same groups of divines held an Arminian theology, asserting that predestination is based on foreseen faith, that the human will is not completely bound by sin, that grace may be resisted and that even the elect may fall from grace. Late in the reign of James I, and again during his son's reign, they enforced royal directives banning preaching about predestination, lifted censorship on Arminian writings and made it more difficult to get Calvinist works published.

Finally, Laudians (to use the shorthand form for Arminian ceremonialists) upheld in no uncertain terms *jure divino* episcopacy, and many of them acknowledged the Bishop of Rome to be not Antichrist, as Elizabethan orthodoxy would have it, but a legitimate bishop of a true church simply troubled by error. With the king married to a French Catholic, Henrietta Maria, and toleration accorded to her Catholic courtiers, it is small wonder that Puritans by the 1630s were convinced that popery was about to be restored to England.

In the 1620s, the godly responded to this new threat to maintenance – let alone furtherance – of the Reformation in England with a mounting literature of complaint and with parliamentary action. Puritan members of both Houses, Lords and Commons, petitioned the king to suppress Arminianism and popery, but to no avail. Charles found ecclesiastical ceremonialism a useful underpinning for the sort of royal ceremony and spectacle that upheld his exalted notion of monarchy and, like Elizabeth and James before him, he abhorred criticism and dissent in the church of which he was head. Unlike his predecessors, however, he exercised scant political judgement. Rather than accede to parliamentary demands (which were fiscal and legal as well as religious), he chose after 1629 to dispense with parliament altogether. During the following eleven years of Personal Rule, he gave the Laudians free rein to persecute the godly and even extended their campaign to an ill-considered attempt in 1637 to force liturgy as well as episcopacy on his northern realm of Scotland. This proved a fatal political error. With the Scots' military response – invasion of England – Charles was forced in 1640 to summon a parliament in order to secure funds for an army. The parliament that gathered had spent more than a decade nursing their grievances, religious as well as political, and promptly demanded redress. The king refused and in 1642 the Civil War commenced.

The war and its mixture of causes is a complicated historical problem which has spawned a vast and even more complicated historiography. Fortunately, it need not be examined in detail here to make the point that needs to be drawn about England's later Reformation. For the godly who fought for Parliament against the Royalists, the conflict of the 1640s was nothing less than a war for the long-awaited true Reformation of England. It was their chance finally to get beyond the halfway Settlement, to reverse the backwards movement of the Caroline establishment and to achieve once and for all what the first Reformers had intended, to defeat the Romish Antichrist so long nestled within the formalism of the Church of England. The preachers summoned regularly to address Parliament naturally drew on apocalyptic images to spur the members on. The Long Parliament, which met from 1640 to 1653, produced increasingly radical Protestant legislation. From 1643, in part as the price of military aid from the presbyterian Scots, they legislated a fully presbyterian system for England, finally prohibiting use of the Book of Common Prayer and instituting Genevan ecclesiastical discipline by lay and clerical elders. In 1645 they went far beyond abolition of episcopacy and executed Archbishop Laud as a traitor to the realm and an enemy of the gospel. This, indeed, was a war of religion.

When at last the war was won (1648), the king also executed (1649) and a new English republic headed by Oliver Cromwell, a Puritan member of the House of Commons and commander-in-chief of the army, the godly had a blank slate upon which to inscribe the delayed Reformation. Unfortunately, while their commitment to that fourth and most demanding Reformation of heart and culture was as strong as ever, they found that they had scant notion of how, practically, to implement it and inadequate unity to develop a workable agenda. Presbyterianism having proved decidedly unpopular, it was replaced by a remarkably tolerant state church that encompassed congregationalism, presbyterianism and even a plethora of Baptist and millenarian groups. Ministerial candidates were examined by a committee of 'triers' and established clergy had to pass muster with committees of 'ejectors' charged to maintain a minimal Protestant orthodoxy within an unusually diverse church. Church and state then embarked on the construction of a disciplined social order. Parliament, which by the 1650s included radical sectarian as well as Puritan members, abolished the last of the religious festivals, banned stage plays and legislated the death penalty for blasphemy and adultery.

In parts of the country where Puritans had held sway for some time, much of this programme proved popular. The godly Richard Baxter reportedly had to construct five galleries in his parish church at Kidderminster to hold auditors of his sermons. But his example and those that Samuel Clarke collected in his *Lives of Eminent Divines* seem to have drawn comment because they were unusual. Much more of the population longed for a return to 'merry England' than flocked to sermons. The demands of 'heart religion' were more than most people were willing to meet and neither charismatic preaching nor stern statutes could compete with drama and dancing, Christmas and maypoles. Also, recent research on the popularity of the Prayer Book, which continued to be used for secret 'Anglican' conventicles throughout the war and Interregnum, makes the important point that the English liturgy had by now had several generations to become a comfortable tradition. It was not easily yielded by people now familiar with its language and dependent on its calendrical observances and rites of passage. Many people also quailed at the proliferation of radical, sometimes bizarre religious sects and feared that the new order was all too liable to lapse into disorder. Groups like Quakers and the antinomian Ranters threatened to turn topsy-turvy the social order, including the gender hierarchy, and militant Fifth Monarchists called for violent action against all obstacles to Christ's return to earth to establish his millennial kingdom. Together with the political and fiscal problems of the Cromwellian regime and the inability of Cromwell's son to carry on after his father's death in 1658, these factors sufficiently undermined what support there was for the government that in 1660 the king was invited to return to England. In the course of the subsequent Restoration, episcopacy and the liturgy would also be returned, Charles II being no more inclined than Elizabeth, James or Charles I towards zealous heart religion at the expense of order. By 1662 more than 2,000 ministers of the godly sort would be ejected from their pulpits, reduced to involuntary sectarianism. The final Reformation experiment had proved an abject failure.

CONCLUSION

Must we then modify that judgement of the English Reformation as a 'runaway success'? Surely not. In political terms, in achieving a fundamentally Protestant identity for the realm, it was an undeniable success. England from the mid-Elizabethan era onwards defined itself against an 'other' that combined popery with tyranny and military threat. Catholics survived, but were thin on the ground, especially after the 'providences' of 1588 and 1605. In cultural terms, in transforming a religion of image and sensuality into one of Word, again the Reformation looks like a success. Laudian efforts to revive ceremonies and images were, after all, one cause of the archbishop's (and indeed the king's) downfall. In broader cultural terms, in transforming a festal society into one of sabbatarian discipline and daily piety, the Reformation's success must be regarded as more qualified. Thomas Young's campaign to replace a frivolous, festal culture with one governed by a disciplined round of Bible-reading, prayer and sermon attendance would be an ongoing one. Finally, in spiritual terms – those most important to the Reformers – Protestantism as a transformation of 'worldlings' into 'saints' was no more successful than one would expect. Ultimately the achievements of the Reformation as the inculcation of heart religion must be judged at the level of the individual. A subculture of genuine Protestantism, stringently defined, certainly emerged from the long process of Reformation and would continue to goad the larger society to address the demands of biblical religion within the context of a basically Protestant superstructure of Word and sacrament. But after the failure of godly rule in the 1650s, the zealots would necessarily remain a subculture, in England as elsewhere. The language of conversion would no longer define a national agenda. In the end, however, it is probably unfair to demand success of the sternest demands to define Reformation. As the godly themselves would remind us, the elect are always a tiny remnant, equally besieged on the one hand by 'vicious and notorious evil livers, ... and all the prophane multitude' and on the other, within the visible church, by 'hypocrites, carnal Protestants, vain professors, back-sliders, decliners and cold Christians'. Thus Arthur Dent, whose *Plaine man's path-way to heaven* was not everyone's chosen path.[19] Reformation could not reasonably encompass the conversion of England, however dramatically it shaped the history and culture of the English people.

NOTES

1   George Gifford, *A Brief Discourse of Certaine Points of the Religion, Whiche is Among the Common Sort of Christians: Which may be Termed the Country Divinitie* (London, 1582), sig. A2–A2v; Philip Stubbes, *The Anatomie of Abuses* (London, 1583), sig. L2.
2   Eamon Duffy, *The Stripping of the Altars* (New Haven, 1992), p. 579.
3   Nicholas Tyacke (ed.), *England's Long Reformation* (London, 1998), p. 21.
4   P. McGrath, *Papists and Puritans under Elizabeth I* (London, 1967), pp. 177, 255–6.
5   M.M. Knappen (ed.), *Two Puritan Diaries* (2nd edn; Gloucester, MA, 1966), p. 81.
6   Written in England in the 1620s, published Boston, MA, 1680.
7   John Foxe, *Acts and Monuments of the Martyrs, with a general discourse of these latter Persecutions, horrible troubles and tumults, stirred up by Romish prelates* [even the title points to the Catholic enemy] (1st edn, London, 1563; quote from enlarged 1610 edn), p. 916.
8   Caroline Litzenberger, *The English Reformation and the Laity* (Cambridge, 1997), p. 71.
9   Christopher Haigh, *English Reformations* (Oxford, 1993), pp. 249, 250.
10 Patrick Collinson, *Godly People* (London, 1983), pp. 102–3.

11 Ian Green, *The Christian's ABC* (Oxford, 1996). Pages 580–751 list the catechisms; this book updates Green's ' "For children in yeares and children in understanding": The Emergence of the English Catechism under Elizabeth and the Early Stuarts', *Journal of Ecclesiastical History* 37 (1986), pp. 397–425.

12 By the middle of Elizabeth's reign, 65 per cent of Essex yeomen and 20 per cent of husbandmen were literate, rising to 77 and 34 per cent respectively by the 1620s, and figures for towns would be much higher: David Cressy, *Literacy and the Social Order* (Cambridge, 1984), pp. 150, 152.

13 Patrick Collinson, *The Religion of Protestants* (Oxford, 1983), pp. 48, 50.

14 Diarmaid MacCulloch, *The Later Reformation in England, 1547–1603* (London, 1990), p. 115; Haigh, *English Reformations*, pp. 271–2.

15 Diarmaid MacCulloch, *Building a Godly Realm* (London, 1992), pp. 19–21; Eamon Duffy, 'The Long Reformation: Catholicism, Protestantism and the Multitude', in Tyacke, *England's Long Reformation*, p. 36.

16 R.T. Kendall, *Calvin and English Calvinism to 1649* (Oxford, 1979), pp. 52–3.

17 Samuel Clarke, *Lives of Eminent Divines* (London, 1683), pp. 59–60, 4–5.

18 David Underdown, *Fire from Heaven* (New Haven, 1992).

19 Dent's extremely popular work was published in London in 1601; quote from pp. 285–6.

FURTHER READING

Diarmaid MacCulloch's *Later Reformation in England* (London, 1990) offers the best single-volume treatment of the Elizabethan Reformation, but it should be supplemented by Patrick Collinson's *Religion of Protestants* (Oxford, 1983) to take the story up to 1625. Nicholas Tyacke (ed.), *England's Long Reformation, 1500–1800* (London, 1998), takes the longest view of all. Christopher Haigh, *The English Reformation Revised* (Cambridge, 1987); the final sections of his *English Reformations* (Oxford, 1993), and Eamon Duffy's *Stripping of the Altars* (New Haven, 1992), offer the perspective of historians convinced that Protestantism met more resistance than welcome, though the focus of both is pre-Elizabethan. An antidote is provided by Margaret Spufford (ed.), *The World of Rural Dissenters, 1520–1725* (Cambridge, 1995), which traces popular rural Protestantism from Lollard antecedents to Restoration Quakers. Parochial religion is the subject of Katherine French (ed.), *The Parish in English Life, 1400–1600* (Manchester, 1997), and Susan Wright (ed.), *Parish, Church and People* (London, 1988). For Wales, see G. Williams, *Recovery, Reorientation and Reformation in Wales c. 1415–1642* (Oxford, 1987).

Reading on the later Reformation as a cultural shift should begin with Collinson's *Birthpangs of Protestant England* (Basingstoke, 1988). Important work on festivities includes Ronald Hutton's *The Rise and Fall of Merry England* (Oxford, 1994), and David Cressy's *Bonfires and Bells* (London, 1989) and *Birth, Marriage and Death* (Oxford, 1997). On popular print, see Tessa Watt, *Cheap Print and Popular Piety, 1550–1640* (Cambridge, 1991), and Margaret Spufford, *Small Books and Pleasant Histories* (Cambridge, 1982). New studies of Foxe's *Acts and Monuments* are collected in David Loades (ed.), *John Foxe and the English Reformation* (Aldershot, 1997), but the classic study remains William Haller, *Foxe's Book of Martyrs and the Elect Nation* (London, 1963). Other aspects of cultural Reformation are examined by Margaret Aston, *England's Iconoclasts* (Oxford, 1988) and *Faith and Fire* (London, 1993), and Keith Thomas, *Religion and the Decline of Magic* (London, 1971). Offering a cultural perspective on seventeenth-century religious division is David Underdown, *Revel, Riot and Rebellion* (Oxford, 1985), but also John Morrill's response, 'The Ecology of Allegiance', in his *Nature of the English Revolution* (London, 1993). Part I of this volume treats in six essays the Civil War as the last of the Wars of Religion.

Norman Jones, *Faith by Statute* (London, 1982), deals with political aspects of the Settlement. On the church courts, see Ralph Houlbrooke, *Church Courts and the People during the English Reformation 1520–1570* (Oxford, 1979); R.A. Marchant, *The Church under the Law* (Cambridge, 1969), and Martin Ingram, *Church Courts, Sex and Marriage in England, 1570–1642* (Cambridge, 1987). Marjorie McIntosh, *Controlling Misbehaviour in England, 1370–1600* (Cambridge, 1998), finds continuity in the activities the courts across the later mediæval period.

Catholic resistance and accommodation are treated by John Bossy, *The English Catholic Community* (London, 1975); Adrian Morey, *The Catholic Subjects of Elizabeth I* (Totowa, 1978); A. Dures, *English Catholicism, 1558–1642* (London, 1983), and J.H. Aveling, *The Handle and the Axe* (London, 1976). On the radical Protestant side, see M.R. Watts, *The Dissenters* (Oxford, 1978); B.R. White, *The English Separatist Tradition* (Oxford, 1971), and J.F. McGregor and Barry Reay (eds), *Radical Religion in the English Revolution* (Oxford, 1984).

A theological focus is offered by Peter Lake, 'Calvinism and the English Church, 1570–1635', *Past and Present* 114 (1987), pp. 32–76; R.T. Kendall, *Calvin and English Calvinism to 1649* (Oxford, 1979); C.M. Dent, *Protestant Reformers in Elizabethan Oxford* (Oxford, 1983), and Nicholas Tyacke, *Anti-Calvinists* (Oxford, 1987). For anti-Calvinist enforcement, see Julian Davies, *The Caroline Captivity of the Church* (Oxford, 1992). Questioning Calvinist consensus is Peter White, *Predestination, Policy and Polemic* (Cambridge, 1992).

On Elizabethan Puritans, the best places to start are Collinson's classic *Elizabethan Puritan Movement* (London, 1967), supplemented by essays in his *Godly People* (London, 1983), and Peter Lake's *Moderate Puritans and the Elizabethan Church* (Cambridge, 1983) and *Anglicans and Puritans?* (London, 1988). Recent work on early Stuart Puritans includes Tom Webster, *Godly Clergy in Early Stuart England* (Cambridge, 1997); C. Durston and J. Eales (eds.), *The Culture of English Puritanism, 1560–1700* (New York, 1996); Paul Seaver, *Wallington's World* (Stanford, 1985), and Jeremy Goring, *Godly Exercises or the Devil's Dance?* (London, 1983). Other historians stress consensualism in the English church: e.g. Kenneth Parker, *The English Sabbath* (Cambridge, 1987). Essays in Kenneth Fincham (ed.), *The Early Stuart Church* (London, 1993), represent both historiographical sides.

The status of post-Reformation clergy is treated by Rosemary O'Day, *The English Clergy* (Leicester, 1979); O'Day and F. Heal (eds), *Continuity and Change* (Leicester, 1976); Heal, *Of Prelates and Princes* (Cambridge, 1980), and Fincham, *Prelate as Pastor* (Oxford, 1990).

Local studies with a focus on religion include Peter Clark, *English Provincial Society from the Reformation to the Revolution* (Sussex, 1977); D. MacCulloch, *Suffolk and the Tudors* (Oxford, 1986); R.B. Manning, *Religion and Society in Elizabethan Sussex* (Leicester, 1969); Keith Wrightson and David Levine, *Poverty and Piety in an English Village* (New York, 1979); Marjorie MacIntosh, *A Community Transformed* (Cambridge, 1991), which questions Protestantism's impact, and Caroline Litzenberger, *The Reformation and the Laity* (Cambridge, 1998). Local studies of Puritan Revolution include Jacqueline Eales, *Puritans and Roundheads* (Cambridge, 1990); Anne Hughes, *Politics, Society and Civil War in Warwickshire, 1620–1660* (Cambridge, 1987), and William Hunt, *The Puritan Moment* (Cambridge, MA, 1983).

This last group of local studies offers the best view of religion and the Civil War, but see also J.T. Cliffe, *Puritans in Conflict* (London, 1988); Brian Manning, *The English People and the English Revolution* (London, 1976), and the essays in Richard Cust and Anne Hughes (eds), *Conflict in Early Stuart England* (London, 1985). On the outcome, consult essays in John Morrill (ed.), *Reactions to the English Civil War* (Basingstoke, 1982), and Derek Hirst, 'The Failure of Godly Rule in the English Republic', *Past and Present* 132 (1991), pp. 33–66. Judith Maltby, *Prayer Book and People in Elizabethan and Early Stuart*

England (Cambridge, 1998), examines the continued popularity of the liturgy during the years of conflict. For the Restoration, see Cliffe's *The Puritan Gentry Beseiged, 1650–1700* (London, 1993); W. Lamont, *Richard Baxter and the Millennium* (London, 1979); John Spurr, *The Restoration Church of England, 1646–1689* (New Haven, 1991), and G.H. Jenkins, *Protestant Dissenters in Wales, 1639–1689* (Cardiff, 1992).

GERMANY AFTER 1550

·•·

Bodo Nischan

The death of Martin Luther in 1546, followed shortly afterwards by the Protestant defeat in the Schmalkaldic War, marked the beginning of a lengthy period of strife among Germany's evangelicals. These conflicts exposed some of the unresolved tensions within Lutheranism and gave Calvinism, which up to then had barely caused a ripple in German lands, an opportunity to make major inroads. As was the case in the early years of the Reformation, religious developments were closely linked to politics in the late sixteenth century with the emergence of denominational churches coinciding with the rise of the early modern absolutist state. Scholars speak of 'confessionalization' to describe how these interrelated processes transformed society. Confessionalization entailed religious and political solidification, and polarization that led to conflict between Catholics and Protestants and also among Germany's evangelicals. Nowhere was this more evident than in those principalities that had first experienced a relatively conservative Lutheran reform in which many old usages had been retained and then, later in the century, a second Calvinist Reformation that aimed at eliminating what some perceived as 'leftover papal dung'. The way governments conducted their business and how people practised and experienced their religion was profoundly affected by these changes.

SEEDS OF CONTROVERSY

A clue for what was to come and how the confessional issue would dominate people's lives for the next three generations (well into the second decade of the seventeenth century) is provided by the reactions, both Protestant and Catholic, to the imperial victory in the Schmalkaldic War. Charles V's triumph allowed him to lay down the law. Determined to use his military advantage to restore the old church and to consolidate, as far as possible, his imperial position in Germany, he pressed the Protestant princes assembled at Augsburg to accept a religious compromise. This formula, popularly known as the Augsburg Interim (because it was intended as a temporary settlement until the Council of Trent had concluded its business) became imperial law on 30 May 1548. With the exception of the concessions of clerical marriage and communion in both kinds, the *interreligio imperialis* was little more than a thinly veiled reformulation of the old faith. It repudiated the very heart of evangelical doctrine, the gospel of Christ's all-sufficient sacrifice on the cross, restored the eucharistic canon, taught that the mass is a sacrifice, reinstated church usages which Protestants earlier had eliminated and ordered pastors to submit to the authority of bishops loyal to Rome.

The formula was instantaneously disliked by practically everybody. While it was enforced in some localities in the south where the presence of large contingents of Habsburg troops compelled the Protestants to lie low, it could make only little headway in the north. With the exception of Joachim II of Brandenburg, whose private chaplain Johann Agricola helped draft the document, most evangelicals, among them the new Elector Maurice, simply ignored Charles' directive. Maurice found himself in a particularly difficult situation. As Duke of Saxony-Dresden (Albertine Saxony) he had sided with the emperor against his co-religionists in the Schmalkaldic War and in return had been rewarded with his cousin John Frederick of Saxony-Wittenberg's electoral land and title. What he had not anticipated was that Charles also expected him to enforce in his lands the religious changes prescribed by the Interim. Philip Melanchthon and his colleagues at the University of Wittenberg, now part of Maurice's domain, were 'amazed that the elector of Brandenburg had accepted such an impossible arrangement'.[1] Maurice therefore reacted negatively at first but, pressured by Joachim and Charles, instructed Melanchthon to prepare a more palatable version of the formula which was to be introduced in northern Germany. This Philippistic compromise (soon dubbed the Leipzig Interim), while claiming to uphold the evangelical doctrine of justification by faith alone, actually presented a mixture of faith and works that most Lutherans found just as onerous as the Augsburg formulation. Melanchthon's use of the ancient Stoic concept of 'adiaphora' allowed him to embrace as 'indifferent' ceremonies which Protestants had repudiated earlier. Baptism, confirmation, penance, extreme unction, ordination, marriage and the Lord's Supper were lumped together as similar 'Christian ceremonies'; the Lord's Supper specifically was labelled a sacrament, thereby creating the impression that all were. The Leipzig Interim also restored the mass canon including the offertory, brought back the saints' days and dietary laws Protestants earlier had eliminated, and enjoined pastors to submit to the discipline and authority of papally appointed bishops.[2]

Even though the Leipzig formula had been trumpeted as a compromise that would allow Lutherans to remain loyal to the heart of evangelical doctrine while embracing as non-essential religious practices discarded earlier, the Interim became the catalyst for a series of acrimonious controversies among evangelicals. Not surprisingly, its leading backers were the two Protestant electors, Joachim and Maurice, both motivated less by genuine religious conviction than political expediency. Its chief theological advocates were Philip Melanchthon, the originator of the Leipzig Interim, and Johann Pfeffinger, the city's ecclesiastical superintendent. Their supporters, many on the Wittenberg faculty, became known as 'Philippists'. Those who opposed them – mostly because they professed to subscribe to a more genuine form of Lutheranism – were called 'Gnesio-Lutherans'. Both claimed to be faithful interpreters of Martin Luther yet, as the 'adiaphora controversy' quickly demonstrated, actually had markedly different views of religious externals and the princes' right to regulate them. The Philippists, Interim supporters, accepted much of the mediæval liturgical heritage as non-essential (adiaphoral) and recognized the government's authority to prescribe it; their opponents, the Gnesio-Lutherans, rejected both.

One of the first to inveigh against the Interim was Nikolaus Amsdorf. He had known Martin Luther personally and had served as Bishop of Naumburg in Saxony until ousted by Julius von Pflug, a Saxon Catholic who had helped draft the *inter-religio imperialis*. Amsdorf had found refuge in Magdeburg, the city that would become known as 'God's chancellery' because of the many hard-core Lutherans who gathered there, making it the leading centre of resistance. Amsdorf vigorously condemned the Interim for restoring old abuses, especially the sacrificial mass and the invocation of saints. His views were seconded by Matthias Flacius, a young Croat, who had studied under Melanchthon and had taught Hebrew at Wittenberg until a falling-out with his former mentor had forced him to leave the university in 1549. He too had fled to Magdeburg. Instead of making concessions to Catholics, even in seemingly unimportant 'adiaphoral' matters as Melanchthon claimed to have done, Flacius urged Protestants to take a firm stand in defence of their religious and political interests. 'When provocations demand an act of confession there is no such thing as an indifferent practice' (*in casu confessionis et scandali nihil est adiaphoron*), he asserted.[3] Nikolaus Gallus, a refugee from Regensburg who also had settled in Magdeburg, likewise objected to the 'Interimists' and in a treatise, published in Latin and German so that all could read it, cited seventy-eight reasons why old ceremonies should not be restored under the guise of adiaphora.[4] Similar objections were voiced in other north German cities, especially at Lübeck, Hamburg, Lüneburg and Brunswick. Doctrine and worship, critics charged, never can be separated. The formula's supporters disagreed, insisting not only that they could, but that governments had the right to regulate religious externals.

The Leipzig Interim caused other controversies that widened the gap between Philippists and Gnesio-Lutherans even further. The formula's ambiguous statement on justification, together with Melanchthon's increasing emphasis on the ethical implication of *sola fide*, set the stage for a series of acrimonious debates on the very heart of Reformation doctrine, justification by faith. Most famous among these was the 'Majorist controversy' that erupted in 1551 when Amsdorf accused Georg Major, a Wittenberg theologian and Melanchthon pupil, of teaching that good deeds are necessary for salvation. While Major had not taught that works are required as meritorious, he had referred to them as tokens of obedience, insisting that their absence was a sure sign that faith is dead, for as none are saved by evil works, none could be saved without good works. To Amsdorf this smacked of Pelagianism and a return to papal righteousness by works. The debate gained momentum when Melanchthon, who first had stayed aloof, entered the fray and defended Major, while Flacius and Gallus joined Amsdorf in attacking him.

This theological wrangle, arcane as it may sound to modern ears, had profound political implications. As Abdias Prätorius, a Philippist at the University of Frankfurt in Brandenburg, noted: 'if good works are dispensable, then taxes also need not be paid'.[5] Taken to its logical extreme, this line of argumentation would lead to antinomianism, the view that moral law is of no use because faith alone is necessary for salvation. This had been a point of controversy among the followers of the Wittenberg Reformation almost since its inception. With Johann Agricola, Brandenburg's antinomian superintendent-general, being one of the Interim's' chief supporters, it was no accident that the question should surface again in the 1550s.

These years also saw the renewal of the sacramentarian dispute, which quickly became part of the much broader Crypto-Calvinist controversy that would cast its long shadow over Germany's confessional history for the remainder of the century. The opening salvo in this debate was fired when the Hamburg pastor Joachim Westphal accused Melanchthon of surreptitiously subscribing to a Calvinist understanding of the Lord's Supper, thereby reviving an issue which had been a prominent source of division among Protestants of the first generation.

In these early debates Melanchthon had sided squarely with Luther, notably at the Marburg Colloquy (1529) where Swiss and German theologians, prompted by their governments' desire for closer political cooperation, attempted in vain to reach agreement on the Lord's Supper. Melanchthon reiterated this position in the Augsburg Confession of 1530. His humanist training, particularly his study of the church fathers, and political developments increasingly encouraged him to embrace a more spiritualized understanding of the Lord's Supper. By 1540, the year in which he published a new, slightly revised version of the Confession, the *Augustana Variata*, a significant shift had taken place in his thinking. The Confession no longer stated that the Body of Christ is '*in* the Supper', but 'with (*cum*) the bread and wine', not necessarily in the elements but certainly in the celebration of the Lord's Supper.[6]

Significantly, John Calvin, who participated in the religious colloquies of the early 1540s as a member of the Strasbourg delegation, accepted the *variata* version. While the conferences failed to heal the widening chasm between the old and new churches, Calvin, eager to overcome the legacy of the Marburg Colloquy, continued to promote closer links with the Lutherans through friendship and correspondence with Melanchthon. Calvin's esteem for Melanchthon aroused hope of the unification of Protestantism. His most immediate concern, however, became the union of the Swiss churches, a goal finally achieved in 1549 with the Zurich Consensus, a compromise formula that Calvin and Heinrich Bullinger, Zwingli's heir, had worked out in a series of intense negotiations. This consensus, which united the Protestants of German- and French-speaking Switzerland, combined Zwinglian and Calvinist views, defining the sacrament as both a sign and an instrument conveying spiritual gifts to communing believers. Second generation Lutherans distrusted Calvin's ecumenical advances in Switzerland, interpreting them as a move towards Zwinglianism away from Lutheranism.

The Consensus was not published until 1551. Its appearance set the stage for Joachim Westphal's strident attack on Calvin's doctrine. The Genevan reformer, supposing that Melanchthon's opinion would prevail among Lutherans and hoping that the Zurich agreement would provide a basis of understanding with them, publicly called upon the Wittenberg theologians for support. He was convinced that most agreed with him. They probably did, only by the early 1550s, with the other controversies over the Leipzig Interim raging and Philippists increasingly on the defensive, the Wittenbergers were hardly in a position to give Calvin the backing he was looking for.

THE PEACE OF AUGSBURG

The political situation in the empire was now rapidly deteriorating. The Gnesio-Lutherans of Magdeburg, fierce critics of Melanchthon, were actively promoting political resistance against the emperor. For Charles V, whose victory in the Schmalkaldic War had set into motion the series of events that produced the Leipzig Interim, the wheel of fortune again was turning, now against him. Just when he seemed to be in a position to impose his will on all of Germany, Maurice of Saxony, his erstwhile ally, turned against him.

In March 1552, the storm broke. Henry II of France (now in alliance with Maurice) invaded Lorraine, while the Saxon marched rapidly southward, almost capturing the emperor who barely managed to escape to Italy over the Brenner Pass. It was a disaster from which the Habsburg never recovered. Shortly afterwards, in the Peace of Passau, he agreed to free Philip of Hesse, as he had John Frederick earlier, and to refer the settlement of the religious question to the next imperial diet which would meet at Augsburg in 1555. The Religious Peace hammered out there was a compromise that subordinated religious principle to political expediency. It allowed secular princes and cities to choose between Lutheranism and Catholicism, but pointedly excluded all other Protestants, notably Zwinglians, Calvinists and Anabaptists. The *ius reformandi*, the right to order the religious affairs of a territory, became an attribute of princely sovereignty, a right later jurists would define with the phrase, *cuius regio eius religio* ('whose the rule, his the religion').[7]

Lutheranism thus had attained full legal establishment, yet (as the continued acrimonious debates demonstrated) was far from unified and, while officially sanctioned in the empire, hardly secure. The intra-Lutheran controversies, which increasingly took on the appearance of a referendum on Melanchthon's place within the evangelical movement, peaked in 1557 at the Worms Colloquy which Emperor Ferdinand I had initiated in yet another futile effort to bridge the chasm between Protestants and Catholics. Much to the delight of Roman Catholics, the Gnesio-Lutheran emissaries refused to participate unless Melanchthon and his supporters acknowledged their errors first.

While the Lutheran divisions continued, the feud over the Lord's Supper increasingly took centre stage in the broader Crypto-Calvinist Controversy. This debate became more heated as Calvinism assumed a wider European role (notably in France, Holland and Scotland) and, while legally excluded by the Peace of Augsburg, started to make major inroads in the empire as well. Calvinists generally regarded Lutherans as evangelical brethren who had not quite overcome certain mediæval superstitions, notably in their treatment of the sacraments. Where they gained a foothold in Germany, Calvinists quickly took aim at Lutheran piety, attacking religious practices which, they insisted, smacked of papism and therefore had to be eliminated. They called themselves 'the more reformed' or simply 'the Reformed', a label that stuck as the official designation of German Calvinists. Like the Genevan reformer, the Reformed looked to Philippists for support and readily accepted Melanchthon's 1540 revised edition of the Confession of Augsburg. This, they soon would argue, provided the legal basis for their faith in the empire where the 1555 Peace had recognized only Protestants who adhered to the Augsburg Confession.

THE EMERGENCE OF THE PALATINATE

The year 1559, which saw both the foundation of the Genevan Academy and publication of Calvin's final version of the *Institutes*, became a decisive juncture also in the history of German Calvinism. In this year Frederick III became Elector Palatine and shortly afterwards embarked on a confessional course that would make his principality the intellectual centre of the Reformed movement. Frederick succeeded the childless Otto Heinrich who had only recently completed the country's Lutheran Reformation, but who had left a potentially explosive legacy by indiscriminately hiring Lutherans, Philippists and Calvinists for his university. Frederick III reaped the trouble his predecessor had sown when a bitter controversy over the Lord's Supper erupted between Tilemann Hesshus, a strict Lutheran, and William Klebitz, a deacon who subscribed to a more Zwinglian view of the sacrament. As the Heidelberg faculty became involved in the dispute, Frederick tried in vain to mediate, but ended up dismissing both Hesshus and Klebitz. Philip Melanchthon, whose advice the elector had sought, approved wholeheartedly of his action. After intensive study of the issues, Frederick himself had come to the conclusion that the Reformed interpretation of the Lord's Supper was the correct one. Additional disputation at the university further increased his disenchantment with the Lutheran zealots. His conversion to the Reformed creed was sealed by the Naumburg Convention (1561), which had been called to unite Germany's Protestants but instead demonstrated anew the deep divisions among them.

Frederick now dismissed all Lutheran pastors and theology professors, and hired Calvinists in their stead. He named Caspar Olevianus, who replaced the deposed Hesshus in the chair of theology, and Zacharias Ursinus, a student of Peter Martyr Vermigli, to the Heidelberg faculty. He also ordered the removal of artworks, vestments, crucifixes, altars, baptismal fonts, organs and other 'papist idols' that had been retained in Otto Heinrich's moderate Lutheran reform. In the celebration of the Lord's Supper the *fractio panis* (bread breaking) rite, a sure mark of the Reformed communion, was introduced. The Heidelberg Catechism (1563), prepared by Ursinus and Olevianus, became the new norm of doctrine. It did not include the strict teaching on predestination characteristic of other Calvinist catechisms; but, on Frederick's insistence, it did contain a precise formulation of the difference between Protestant and Catholic views of the Lord's Supper that condemned the Roman mass as an 'accursed idolatry'. A new Church Order (1563), based on the Genevan and Zurich models, a Consistory Order and the introduction of strict church discipline in 1570 completed the Palatinate's Second Reformation.

While these changes found favour, especially among Calvinists abroad, they were adamantly opposed by Lutherans at home. The rulers of several neighbouring principalities, notably Christoph of Württemberg, Wolfgang of Zweibrücken and John Frederick of Saxony, expressed deep concern. The Colloquy of Maulbronn (1564), scheduled to defuse the issue, added further to the animosity between Lutherans and Reformed. Emperor Maximilian II accused Frederick of having violated the Peace of Augsburg and ordered him to annul the recent confessional changes. Frederick now was in serious trouble, for if it could be formally established that his religion did not agree with the Augsburg Confession, he was excluded from the Peace of 1555. The German princes meeting shortly afterwards at the Diet of Augsburg (1566) likewise demanded the revocation of all religious innovations but rebuffed the emperor's efforts to condemn Frederick for violating the peace treaty. Led by Elector August of Saxony, they refused to exclude the Heidelberger from the community of the Augsburg Confession. While August rejected the Palatines' understanding of the Lord's Supper, he wanted peace to consolidate recent political gains and therefore opposed any linkage of religion and politics that would have provoked yet another major crisis.

The fortuitous outcome of the 1566 diet not only convinced Frederick III of the truth of his faith but encouraged him to pursue his confessional interests even more vigorously. He now sided openly with his beleaguered co-religionists abroad, sending his sons to provide military assistance (Johann Casimir to the French Huguenots and Christoph to the Dutch Calvinists). In 1562 he gave Frankenthal as a place of refuge to Calvinists driven from the Netherlands. The elector's prestige reached its peak when he achieved the seemingly impossible by betrothing his son Johann Casimir to Elizabeth, daughter of August of Saxony (1570), thereby joining the empire's leading Lutheran and Reformed ruling families. The union assured Frederick of the continued goodwill of Germany's foremost Protestant prince and hinted at the possibility of further Reformed expansion into the very heartland of Lutheranism.

THE FORMULA OF CONCORD

This hope was not unjustified, for the supporters of Melanchthon, increasingly vilified as Crypto-Calvinist, continued to wield considerable influence in Albertine Saxony – in fact they had solidified their position there. This circle of Philippists included both theologians and laymen, among them Johann Pfeffinger of Leipzig, the court preacher Christian Schütz and electoral councillor Georg Cracow in Dresden, and at the University of Wittenberg, Melanchthon's son-in-law Caspar Peucer, a professor of medicine, and the theologian Christoph Pezel. They tried to harmonize the theologies of Wittenberg and Geneva and were conducting secret correspondence with Theodore Beza, Calvin's successor and rector of the Genevan Academy. Just how much influence the Philippists wielded became evident in 1571 when Pezel published a new catechism that clearly contained a Reformed view of the Lord's Supper. Gnesio-Lutherans condemned it, immediately renewing their charge that the Wittenberg theologians were, in fact, secret Calvinists.

The main point over which the two sides were arguing was the doctrine of the Real Presence, specifically the *communicatio idiomatum* which Lutherans cited to explain Christ's physical presence and Calvinists contemptuously dismissed as the doctrine of ubiquity. Accordingly, the divine attributes of Christ's nature – his omnipotence, omniscience and omnipresence – are communicated to his human nature so that, in the words of the later Formula of Concord, he 'can be and is present wherever he wills',[8] particularly in the bread and wine of Holy Communion. The Philippists, very much like the Reformed, emphasized Christ's presence in the celebration of the Lord's Supper, preferring to speak of his 'sacramental' rather then physical presence, 'in, with and under' the bread and wine.

The controversy became even more heated when the Palatinate theologians, eager to promote greater evangelical unity, insisted that they really saw no difference between the teachings of the Heidelberg Catechism and those of the Lutherans promoted by the Dresden court. Elector August, increasingly suspicious of the Philippists, finally became convinced of a Crypto-Calvinist conspiracy when in 1573 a Reformed tract on the Lord's Supper, written by the Silesian physician Joachim Curaeus, was anonymously published at Leipzig. Shortly afterwards, in the spring of 1574, he ordered the arrest of Peucer, Schütz and Cracow, and dismissed all Philippists from Wittenberg's theological faculty, among them Christoph Pezel who fled to Nassau-Dillenburg. While turning against those whom he suspected of conspiring to move Saxony into the Calvinist camp, August now became the powerful champion of a more orthodox and unified Lutheranism.

The Crypto-Calvinist crisis at the Saxon court, no doubt, was at least partly provoked by foreign political and religious developments. The threat of the Catholic Counter-Reformation, most discernible in the recent St. Bartholomew's Massacre in France and Spanish atrocities in Holland, had its impact on all of Protestant Germany. While Calvinists viewed these Catholic advances as a clarion call to greater Lutheran-Reformed cooperation against the ever growing papal menace, Lutherans, notably the rulers of Württemberg, Saxony, and Brandenburg, had come to a very different conclusion. Not stronger links with the Reformed, but a more unified Lutheran front was needed to counter what they perceived as the dual papal-sacramentarian threat. August, fearful that the French and Dutch conflicts, in which the Palatinate already was actively engaged, might spill over and involve Saxony in a war of unforeseen dimensions, therefore had turned against those whom he suspected of Crypto-Calvinism, to work instead for a confessionally more unified and stronger Lutheranism.

In promoting Lutheran unity, Elector August picked up a theme that also had the backing of other German princes, especially Elector Johann Georg of Brandenburg, and Dukes Ulrich of Württemberg and Julius of Brunswick-Wolfenbüttel. With their encouragement and the help of Germany's leading theologians, the pace towards unity now quickened. A series of drafts, the Swabian Concord (1574), the Swabian–Saxon Concord (1575) and Maulbronn Formula (1576), prepared by Nikolaus Selnecker of Saxony, Jakob Andreae of Württemberg, Martin Chemnitz of Brunswick and David Chytraeus of Rostock, laid the foundations for a meeting at Torgau in the late spring of 1576. Here these four theologians, joined by two Brandenburgers, Andreas Musculus and Christoph

Corner, drafted a union formula that was circulated among governments and theologians throughout Germany. A year later the group reconvened at Cloister Bergen near Magdeburg to revise the Torgau formula incorporating the comments garnered during circulation. The response of the Prussians, prepared by Tilemann Hesshus and Johann Wigand, had been most extreme, for they demanded an explicit condemnation of Melanchthon. The text that resulted from these deliberations, the Bergen Book, also called the 'Solid Declaration', together with Andreae's synopsis of the Torgau draft, the 'Epitome', came to constitute the definitive new confessional statement of Lutheranism. This Formula of Concord was presented on 28 May 1577 and signed immediately by Electors August of Saxony and Johann Georg of Brandenburg.

The initial plan, which August had promoted, called for submitting the confession to a vote at a general Lutheran synod. Johann Georg, fearing that this could result in a negative ballot, had strong misgivings about such a procedure; it would be much safer, he thought, to obtain separate subscriptions to the Formula in each territory. His divide-and-conquer strategy was endorsed by the six theologians at Bergen and in the end accepted by August. Accordingly, the two electorates – Brandenburg and Saxony, where ratification was reasonably certain – were to subscribe first, then the Palatinate where at the death of Frederick III in 1576 Lutheranism had been restored, followed by the other north German principalities and cities, and finally the remaining territories.

The Formula of Concord, which was to be the official and binding interpretation of the original Augsburg Confession, was incorporated with the three ancient ecumenical creeds (the Apostles', Nicene and Athanasian) and those Lutheran confessional statements generally recognized as definitive (the Augustana, its Apology, the Schmalkald Articles, the Treatise on the Pope and Luther's two catechisms) into the Book of Concord. It was ceremoniously presented on the fiftieth anniversary of the Augsburg Confession, on 25 June 1580. The majority of the Lutheran governments and clergy, 86 princes and about 8,500 pastors, signed the Book, but a significant minority refused. Duke Julius of Brunswick-Wolfenbüttel, initially one of the main promoters of Lutheran unity, decided for political reasons not to sign, even though one of his divines, Martin Chemnitz, had helped draft the Formula and most of his theologians supported the Book of Concord. Tactical reasons also kept Schleswig-Holstein (swayed by King Frederick II of Denmark) and most of the south German imperial cities (where the influence of the Helvetic reformers weighed heavily) outside the Formula. Hesse-Kassel, Anhalt, Pomerania, Danzig, Bremen, Magdeburg and Nordhausen objected for mostly religious reasons, either because they thought that the theology of Philip Melanchthon had been slighted, or because they had reservations about specific doctrinal formulations, particularly those dealing with Christology and the Lord's Supper.

The issues that had threatened to fragment Lutheranism had at long last been settled. Even those German Lutheran churches that refused to accept the Book of Concord generally avoided public condemnation of its teachings. But while the Formula of Concord healed the intra-Lutheran schism, it widened the gulf with those groups (notably the Reformed) that it excluded. The Formula destroyed any opportunity to occupy a middle ground and forced all theologians, especially

Philippists, to choose sides. Not surprisingly therefore, relations between the heirs of the Wittenberg and Genevan Reformations, its theologians and princely supporters, continued to be strained, in fact would reach new lows as they approached the end of the century.

THE SECOND REFORMATION

With the restoration of Lutheranism in the Rhine Palatinate under Ludwig VI (reigned 1576–83), only a small enclave about Neustadt that Frederick III had left to his youngest son, Johann Casimir, remained Calvinist. Many of Heidelberg's exiled Reformed pastors and professors, among them Zacharias Ursinus, found refuge there. The Casimirianum, a school Johann Casimir established at Neustadt, temporarily replaced Heidelberg as the centre of Calvinist learning in the Palatinate.

Another important hub for the German Reformed movement in the 1570s became the county of Nassau-Dillenburg where Count Johann VI (1536–1606), brother of William of Orange, the leader of the Dutch revolt, welcomed both Philippists (like the exiled Christoph Pezel from Saxony) and Calvinists (like Caspar Olevianus from the Palatinate). Their presence and collaboration in Nassau-Dillenburg encouraged what many Gnesio-Lutherans had feared for some time, the synthesis of Philippism and Calvinism, and resulted in 1578 in a princely decreed Second Reformation in Nassau-Dillenburg and neighbouring Wittgenstein. Pezel, author of the new Nassau Confession, declared that this reformation was needed to complete the earlier Wittenberg reform and to oppose more effectively the challenge posed by the Catholic Counter Reformation. Unlike the earlier Lutheran Reformation, which enjoyed considerable popular support, this new reformation was imposed from above, by princely fiat and, as evidenced by the people's reaction, encountered considerable opposition.

Johann VI played a prominent role in expanding the influence of the Reformed creed further into the neighbouring counties of the Wetterau princes and other territories – Solms-Braunfels (1582), Isenburg (1584), Bentheim-Tecklenburg (1587–8) and Wied (1589). His new university at Herborn, founded in 1584, with Caspar Olevianus, Johann Piscator and Johann Alsted its leading teachers, helped make Nassau-Dillenburg a major centre for the Reformed movement in northwestern Germany. Pezel, who had supervised the 'emendation' of the county's church, soon moved on to Bremen where in 1580–1 he would introduce a Second Reformation based on the Nassau model.

Meanwhile, the Protestant electorates continued to be an important battleground in the tug-of-war between Lutherans and Calvinists. In the Palatinate, the death of Ludwig VI in 1583 marked the end of the brief Lutheran interlude in which pastors and professors at the University of Heidelberg had been forced to sign the Formula of Concord. Johann Casimir (reigned 1583–92), regent for young Elector Frederick IV, restored the Reformed creed and embarked on a more active foreign policy. Educated at Nancy and Paris, and having fought on the side of the Huguenots, Johann Casimir was wont to emphasize the international political dimensions in the current confessional conflicts. He re-established Heidelberg as the leading centre of the German Reformed movement and, had it not been for the untimely death of its leading princely supporters, almost succeeded in uniting the German Protestants in a defensive alliance, the Union of Torgau (1591).

Developments in Albertine Saxony, where Elector August in 1574 had purged all Philippists, indicated that the Reformed influence had also spread there. August's son and successor, Christian I (reigned 1586–91), and his chancellor Nikolaus Krell not only favoured the very people August had banished, but actively encouraged and promoted Calvinism. Aided by a small cadre of like-minded pastors and professors, they planned the electorate's gradual transition from Lutheranism to Calvinism. They first dismissed, then exiled, Gnesio-Lutheran professors and superintendents like Nikolaus Selnecker and Polycarp Leyser, secretly suspended the obligatory oath of allegiance to the Formula of Concord, and prescribed a more humanistic and Melanchthonian curriculum for the universities. Catholic vestiges in the Lutheran liturgy, especially the exorcism rite in baptism, were eliminated to create a more clearly recognizable Protestant form of worship. An ecclesiastical commission, consisting of the elector's new court preachers Johann Salmuth and David Steinbach, and Urban Pierius, recently appointed to the Wittenberg faculty, produced a revised edition and commentary of Martin Luther's Bible translation which, though never completed, became known as the Krell Bible. The Reformed glosses in this text sought to explain the recent ceremonial and theological changes Christian and his chancellor had instituted. The electorate's confessional reorientation also manifested itself in a more active pro-Protestant foreign policy, particularly after 1589 as Christian I became involved in the negotiations that would lead to the Union of Torgau.

The Elector's untimely death in 1591 dashed both the alliance and Saxony's Second Reformation. As was the case in other German principalities where Calvinist reform from above was attempted in the waning decades of the sixteenth century, Christian's innovations lacked popular backing. The court's policies ran into stiff opposition from the nobility and the populace among whom Lutheranism had struck roots and who resented the ceremonial innovations, especially the elimination of the exorcism rite in baptism. The estates, indignant about the arbitrary and highhanded fashion in which Christian's government had promoted confessional change, had Krell arrested and tried for treason. He was found guilty, imprisoned for ten years and finally executed in 1601. The new regime, a regency led by Duke Friedrich Wilhelm I of Saxe-Weimar (reigned 1591–1601) on behalf of Christian II, a minor, ordered a visitation in 1592 in which all office holders were required to swear by the Formula of Concord and denounce Calvinism. Scores of suspected Calvinists were dismissed and sent into exile; their places were taken by individuals like Selnecker, Leyser and others whom Christian had fired earlier and who now returned as Electoral Saxony became a bastion of Lutheran orthodoxy.

Many of the displaced Calvinists found refuge in neighbouring Anhalt, the small principality sandwiched between Saxony and Brandenburg, where Philippism had remained strong even while it was being purged elsewhere. Under the guidance of the Zerbst superintendent-general Georg Amling, Anhalt's clergy had vigorously opposed the Formula of Concord. Instead they had formulated their own more Melanchthonian confession, the *Repetitio Anhaltina* (1581), and to ensure

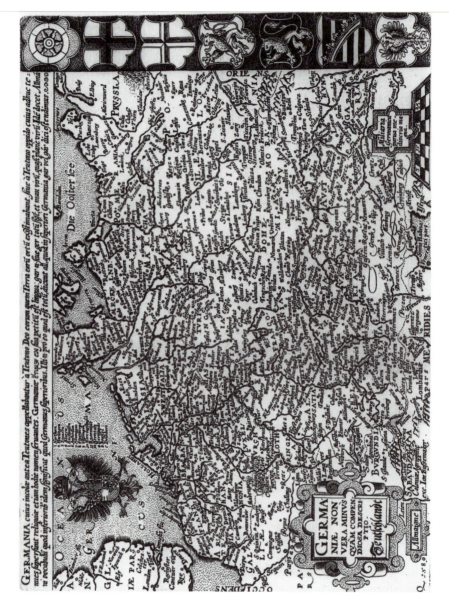

Figure 22.1 Germany in 1589. (Wolfenbüttel, Herzog August Bibliothek)

that the realm's clergy were educated accordingly Prince Joachim Ernst (reigned 1564–86) founded an academy at Zerbst. A new Confession of the Lord's Supper, to which all Anhalt pastors had to subscribe in 1585, sounded still Lutheran enough, but a much simplified communion rite hinted at a shift towards Helvetic Protestantism. This trend quickened under Johann Georg (1586–1603) who with Amsdorf's help initiated a number of reforms – most noticeable again, the elimination of exorcism in baptism (1589) – that confirmed the drift toward Calvinism. Shortly afterwards, in 1596, Johann Georg, related to the Heidelberg court through his second marriage, decreed the elimination of all remaining papal rituals and beliefs. Anhalt's Second Reformation was about to be fully implemented.

The Lutheran reaction came quickly as the state's nobility and townspeople, and many pastors, among them Johann Arndt, author of the famed *Wahres Christentum*, voiced strong opposition, charging that they had not been consulted and that their religious and political freedoms were being violated by these reforms. Their complaints were of little avail: Johann Georg refused to bend. He adamantly insisted that people conform to his instructions, particularly that the exorcism rite be abolished immediately. And he instructed Amling to produce a revised baptismal order without the onerous rite, and a defence of the theological and ceremonial changes that had taken place. In the ensuing propaganda war the superintendent was backed by the Heidelbergers while his local critics could count on support from Saxony and Brandenburg. Amling, the 'Zerbst poet', Lutheran propagandists declared, simply had 'ladled up the foul sewage of the Wittenberg Calvinists' and carried it into Anhalt.[9] These charges, of course, were partly true but could not prevent Amling from carrying out the confessional changes he had initiated.

The Second Reformation stuck, making Anhalt not only a popular place of refuge for displaced Philippists and Calvinists but another important centre whence the Reformed creed could be exported. During the next decade the Helvetic confession continued to make more inroads, especially in the Upper Palatinate (1596–8), Pfalz-Simmern (1598), Baden-Durlach (1599), Lippe (1604) and Hesse-Kassel (1605). Among these, the Hesse landgrave was of particular significance for it would become yet another important link in the expanding Calvinist network.

After the death of the legendary Philip of Hesse (in 1567), who had made his state a major player in the turbulent events of the early Reformation, the landgrave had been divided into four successor states which in 1604 were again consolidated into two, Hesse-Kassel and Hesse-Darmstadt. Succession disputes propelled the two in different confessional directions. When Darmstadt subscribed to the Book of Concord, Kassel (the larger and more powerful of the two) moved in the opposite direction, away from Lutheranism towards Calvinism. Landgrave Maurice of Hesse-Kassel (reigned 1592–1627), 'the Learned', strongly influenced by the humanistic learning associated with the theology of Philip Melanchthon, made his court a centre of late Renaissance culture, welcoming artists like the composer Heinrich Schütz and religious dissidents, including Calvinist refugees from France and the Netherlands. In 1597 Maurice founded an academy at Kassel, the Collegium Mauritianum, which quickly developed into a node of international

Calvinism and centre of political activism. Displaced Crypto-Calvinists from Saxony, among them Gregor Schönfeld and Georg Crucinger, taught here together with exiled academics from foreign countries. The Collegium Mauritianum thus had a decidedly international flavour and, judging by the composition of its student body, quickly became an important site whence the Reformed cause was being propagated to other German lands.

The Nassau princes, especially Johann VI of Dillenburg, who were looking for allies against the ever more menacing threat posed by the Spanish Habsburg, encouraged Maurice to declare himself publicly for the Reformed. Maurice's marriage to Juliane of Nassau and his close contacts with Christoph Pezel (who earlier had served the Dillenburg court) and Johann Piscator of Herborn University strengthened his inclination towards Calvinism. The landgrave's inheritance in 1604 of Hesse-Marburg with its noted university finally set the stage for the full introduction of the Second Reformation in Hesse-Kassel.

Within a year, Maurice proclaimed the 'perfection' and 'purification' of his church. An 'emendation decree', issued in July 1605, prohibited the teaching of 'ubiquity', enjoined the proper biblical numbering of the Ten Commandments and prescribed the fraction rite for all communion services. Gregor Schönfeld, the Crypto-Calvinist from Saxony whom Maurice had named superintendent at Kassel, and other Reformed pastors sought to explain the religious changes, assuring people in sermons and tracts that they were not introducing a new creed. Rather they were merely 'amending' the communion rite and removing surviving papal idols that posed a threat to the principality's evangelical heritage. 'His Princely Highness personally delivered ... a magnificent and lengthy Latin oration on the subject to a large audience of students and faculty at Marburg University.'[10]

Neither the people nor the academics were swayed. Maurice's innovations provoked massive public opposition. In Marburg, Lutheran burghers beat up the new Reformed pastors and professors the landgrave had brought in; at Eschwege and Hersfeld people simply stayed away from church when Reformed services were introduced; the nobility, especially in Upper Hesse and the Werra region, protested; meanwhile the displaced Lutheran divines initiated a massive propaganda campaign from nearby Gießen (in Hesse-Darmstadt) pouring more oil on the burning confessional fires. Maurice finally managed to gain control of the situation by creating, in 1610, a Palatinate-like consistory in Marburg that provided the central bureaucratic agency he needed to enforce his reforms; but even at this point problems remained.

THE DEFENCE OF POPULAR LUTHERANISM

The landgrave's experience in Hesse-Kassel points to a very central characteristic of the Second Reformation: the German Reformed movement, 'court Calvinism', rested on a most limited social basis. By the opening of the seventeenth century, the Lutheran confessionalization of the population had progressed to a point where it had become exceedingly difficult to impose, by simple princely fiat, a new confession from above. Just how difficult would become clear only a few years later when Elector Johann Sigismund of Brandenburg tried to reform the church in his domains.

As a child Johann Sigismund had received a strict Lutheran upbringing under the guidance of Simon Gedicke, the Hohenzollern's fanatically anti-Calvinist court preacher. Only instead of strengthening the young prince's faith, Gedicke managed to instil in him the first doubts about orthodox Lutheranism. These reservations became outright doubts a few years later when Johann Sigismund visited the court of the Palatinate Elector Frederick IV. At Heidelberg the young prince befriended the elector's family, especially his wife Louise Juliane, a daughter of William of Orange, and listened to Frederick's court preachers and theologians: David Pareus, the renowned Reformed irenicist, Bartholomäus Pitiscus and Abraham Scultetus. Here Johann Sigismund also was introduced to the work of the Swiss theologian Rudolph Hospinian, who sharply denounced the Formula of Concord as a *Concordia Discors*. It was at this time, in 1606, that Johann Sigismund became a secret Calvinist. But he waited another seven years, until Christmas Day 1613, before he made his conversion public by communion in the Reformed manner in the Berlin cathedral.

During the months leading up to this public confession Johann Sigismund strengthened his ties with well-known Calvinists. In the spring, Maurice of Hesse-Kassel and his court chaplain Hermann Fabronius visited the Hohenzollern court. The Hessians had lengthy discussions with the elector while Fabronius preached in the palace chapel. At the end of November, Stephen Lesieur (King James I of England's roving ambassador to the empire, and a Calvinist) had come to Berlin. He stayed for a month and attended the Reformed Christmas communion. Count Ernst Casimir of Nassau also was invited and came. In addition Johann Sigismund asked for and received advice and support from the Palatinate and Anhalt courts. Martin Füssel, the superintendent of Zerbst, officiated at the communion in the Berlin Dom which marked the beginning of Brandenburg's Second Reformation; Abraham Scultetus, the renowned Heidelberg theologian, came to Berlin in the spring of 1614 and helped draft the plan whereby it was to be implemented. However, the group that actually supported Johann Sigismund's reforms remained small. It included mostly members of his court: his two younger brothers, Margraves Ernst and Johann Georg; a few isolated aristocrats, like the Prussian Junker Abraham von Dohna who had served in the army of Maurice of Nassau. In addition there were Philippists like the principality's superintendent-general Christoph Pelargus and the elector's new Reformed court preachers, most of whom came from abroad.

All were convinced that the Second Reformation was simply a continuation and completion of the earlier Lutheran reform. While the elector and his advisors acted out of genuine religious concerns, political considerations were involved. Occurring at a time when the Hohenzollerns were about to acquire strategically important territories in Prussia and in the Rhineland, and while Europe was becoming increasingly divided along confessional lines and drifting towards war, the conversion of Brandenburg's ruling house was bound to have profound political and religious repercussions.

Internationally it placed the electorate in the most militant camp of Protestantism: Calvinism. Equally important, though, were the domestic consequences. Johann Sigismund's confessional innovations were met with widespread popular resistance. In Berlin a major riot erupted in the spring of 1615 when the government ordered the removal from the cathedral of all artworks and liturgical paraphernalia. The enraged mob ransacked and looted the homes of the elector's new Reformed preachers. Disturbances also occurred at Stendal, Küstrin and Beelitz; elsewhere people simply stayed away from church when the new Reformed services were introduced. 'The common man', observed one of the elector's councillors, 'was especially disturbed by the elimination of papal ceremonies in the Lord's Supper which up to now had been retained and tolerated in our churches.'[11] Such popular resistance was encouraged by the Lutheran clergy and reinforced by the nobility. In fact, the opposition of the Mark's Junkers, upon whose financial backing the elector depended, ultimately prevented him from imposing his creed on the principality. While he and his court worshipped as Calvinists, Johann Sigismund had to concede in 1615 that the rest of the country would remain Lutheran.

The Second Reformation had reached its limits in Brandenburg. While the Reformed continued to make a few more, though mostly insignificant, gains in northern Germany, in Silesia and temporarily in Mecklenburg (1619), confessionalization had advanced to the point where it had become increasingly difficult for a prince to impose, by fiat, a new creed; unless, of course, he was prepared to employ considerable force and violence to get his way.

Rulers supported the Second Reformation partly because they saw it as a means to enhance their own princely authority against powerful Lutheran estates at home and partly because they viewed it as an effective antidote to the threat of the Catholic Counter Reformation from abroad. Significantly, 1563 (the year in which Frederick III of the Palatinate publicly embraced the Reformed creed) also saw the conclusion of the Council of Trent and the beginning of Duke Albrecht V's aggressive policy of re-Catholization in Bavaria. Calvinist advances in the 1570s and 1580s occurred at a time when news about Catholic atrocities in the French and Dutch wars were sweeping Germany. In the Westphalian counties Bentheim, Tecklenburg and Steinfurt, the Second Reformation coincided with the aggressive re-Catholization of neighbouring Cologne and Münster. In 1588 (the year when Duke Ernst of Bavaria allowed Jesuits to settle in Münster) Count Arnold of Bentheim adopted Calvinism. The Second Reformation was introduced in Anhalt, Lippe and Hesse just when the Habsburg-supported Counter Reformation in Austria was peaking. And Johann Sigismund of Brandenburg tried to reform his principality's church at a time when supporters of the old church were challenging the Hohenzollern's dynastic interests in Prussia, the Rhineland and Silesia.

Calvinists were convinced that this Catholic threat was greatly aggravated by what they perceived as 'old papal superstitions' left in Lutheranism. These they identified as: the emphasis on the Real Presence in communion and the ceremonial equipage retained in the Lutheran liturgy (the outward form of the mass with altars, communion wafers, candles and liturgical vestments); the baptismal fonts and exorcism rite; the crucifixes, altar retables and other church art, and the traditional church calendar which retained the Marian festivals and in some localities even the Feast of Corpus Christi. To the Reformed these were not simply indifferent matters, adiaphora as the Lutherans claimed, but 'papal relics' that had to be eliminated. Such liturgical paraphernalia, they insisted, were confusing people by blurring Catholic/Protestant differences, a problem further aggravated by the fact that the Roman church was displaying renewed vigour and determination to regain territories earlier lost to the Reformation. To counter this offensive and make people less susceptible to Catholic subversion, the confessional lines of demarcation had to be sharpened. All superstitious ceremonies therefore had to be eliminated. These reforms 'were urgently needed because Your Highness' lands are surrounded by Catholic territories and today's papists use these very ceremonies to attract people back to their religion', Christoph Pezel had told Count Johann VI of Nassau-Dillenburg in 1578.[12]

As the Reformed continued to eliminate such links to the old church, Lutherans reacted by increasingly treating them as marks of genuine evangelical orthodoxy. And since the understanding of the Lord's Supper, specifically Christ's presence in the communion elements, remained the central point of controversy, the manner in which the sacrament was being celebrated – with or without the traditional ceremonial – became a decisive and divisive confessional issue. At the turn of the century, Lutheran–Reformed relations, which Philip Melanchthon only two generations earlier had hoped to bridge, had deteriorated to the point where Polycarp Leyser, the Saxon court preacher, dared to ask whether Lutherans shared more with Catholics than with Calvinists. Noting that the followers of Rome and Wittenberg both teach that holy baptism saves and that the true body and blood of Christ are distributed in communion, he concluded 'that Lutherans have more in common with Romanists than with Calvinists.'[13] Edwin Sandys, the English traveller who visited Germany early in the seventeenth century, found that many Lutherans 'professe openly, they will returne to the Papacy, rather than ever admitte that Sacramentarie and Predestinarie pestilence.'[14] The political corollary, of course, was that Lutheran princes became still more unwilling to cooperate with Reformed rulers, even as the Catholic Counter Reformation kept advancing. The Lutheran–Reformed confessional rivalry had escalated to the point where the future of both would be seriously jeopardized should their common foe, Roman Catholicism and its political backers – Austria, Spain and Bavaria – ever gain the upper hand in Germany.

THE DESCENT INTO WAR

That this indeed would happen within a few short years was largely the result of the militant and arrogant confessionalism of the Heidelberg court. Convinced that the wars in France and the Netherlands were not limited civil wars but the first phase of an all-out Catholic military campaign against Protestantism, the Palatines had pursued an increasingly aggressive anti-Habsburg policy. More than anything else it was the reckless behaviour of Elector Frederick V (reigned 1610–20) and his foreign policy adviser, Prince Christian von Anhalt, that turned a revolt in a remote corner of the empire into a major European conflagration.

The Thirty Years War, which grew out of the Bohemian rebellion (1618), at long last became a clarion call for Germany's Protestants to end, or at least to modify, their overheated confessional rhetoric. Frederick V of the Palatinate's

Figure 22.2 The Lutheran communion service. The officiates wear traditional eucharistic vestments, condemned by the Reformed as leftover 'papal dung'. The title-page of Andreas Musculus, *Vom Missbrauch … des Sacraments des Leibs und Bluts Christi*, 1561. (Wolfenbüttel, Herzog August Bibliothek)

defeat in the battle on the White Mountain (1620) glaringly exposed the disastrous consequences of the Calvinist extremism espoused by the Heidelbergers. But the continued progress of Habsburg arms in the Lower Saxon phase of the war, culminating in 1629 in Emperor Ferdinand II's Edict of Restitution, also exposed the folly of the belief that Lutherans were protected by the Peace of Augsburg. These events convinced even the most recalcitrant, Elector Johann Georg of Saxony and his powerful court preacher Matthias Hoe von Hoenegg, that the internecine Protestant feud was leading to disaster and that a way had to be found to resist further Habsburg military oppression and re-Catholization. As a political conservative, Johann Georg had supported the emperor, but the Edict of Restitution changed his tune. Hoe von Hoenegg, who in years past had distinguished himself by his vociferous anti-Calvinist polemics, now was advising armed resistance – if necessary jointly with the Reformed – against Ferdinand and his allies.

The Calvinist pastors at the court of Berlin in neighbouring Brandenburg welcomed such sentiments. For years they had urged, without much success, greater cooperation with the Lutherans and a more militant policy towards the emperor. But without the cooperation of Saxony the Brandenburg elector was too weak to strike out on his own. The more belligerent mood at the Berlin court received ideological support from Reformed irenicism, whose leading spokesman in the 1620s and 1630s was Johann Bergius, Hoe's counterpart in Berlin. Bergius' studies in Heidelberg, Strasbourg and Cambridge, and his visits to France and Holland, had brought him into contact with international Protestantism. As a theological moderate he was convinced that most of the Lutheran–Reformed disagreements could be overcome, since the two agreed on the 'fundamental articles' of the Christian faith. His views reflected the official confessional line of the Brandenburg court after the powerful Lutheran reaction earlier had forced Johann Sigismund to modify his Second Reformation.

The two north German electors met repeatedly to discuss the current crisis in the empire, a crisis further complicated by Sweden's intervention in the war in the summer of 1630. In spite of objections from his more conservative advisers, Johann Georg agreed to call a meeting of the Protestant rulers at Leipzig in the spring of 1631 to consider what counter-measures could be taken to meet the imperial–Catholic challenge. The response to this announcement was overwhelming. Of the 160 states invited to Leipzig, most sent representatives; except for the arch-conservative Lutheran Georg of Hesse-Darmstadt, every major Protestant prince attended and several imperial cities sent delegates as well.

While the politicians met, the theologians held their own colloquy. Hoe von Hoenegg and two of his Lutheran colleagues from Leipzig (Polycarp Leyser the Younger and Heinrich Höpfner) met with Bergius and two other Calvinists from Hesse-Kassel (Johann Crocius and Theophil Neuberger). Bergius' irenical spirit dominated these proceedings from beginning to end. Using the original Augsburg Confession of 1530 (a major concession from the Reformed) the six theologians spent the next three weeks going through the confession chapter by chapter. They easily concurred on twenty-six of the confession's twenty-eight articles but, not surprisingly, could not see eye-to-eye on the two articles dealing with Christology

Figure 22.3 A Lutheran anti-Reformed poster of 1590. The illustration shows John Calvin at the bedside of a dying man citing five articles of faith in which he is to find comfort. At the bottom, the text lists Bible passages to counter 'the above listed dreadful Calvinist articles'. (Wolfenbüttel, Herzog August Bibliothek)

and the Lord's Supper. As in the past, they were unable to reconcile their differences. However – and this was new – they did agree to consider these points further at a later meeting and promised 'to show each other Christian love in the future.'[15] The meeting thus concluded in an atmosphere of friendliness and good will. The Leipzig Protocol, the record of the proceedings, is noteworthy because here the term 'toleration' for the first time was used explicitly to describe Lutheran–Reformed relations.[16] The religious colloquy was important because it helped to create an atmosphere of good will and provided the ideological basis for the political and military cooperation to which the Protestant princes eventually agreed in their Leipzig Manifesto (1631). Significantly, Brandenburg's Reformed privy councillors, close friends of Bergius and strong supporters of irenicism, played a leading role in developing this Protestant defensive alliance.

The crisis precipitated by the Thirty Years War, specifically Emperor Ferdinand II's confessional absolutism, thus had driven Germany's Lutherans and Reformed to seek closer ties at Leipzig. An important breakthrough had been achieved at the height of the war. For Germany's two major Reformation churches and their princely spokesmen, Leipzig marked the beginning of the demise of confessional politics and the start of something akin to a common Protestant awareness. The intra-Protestant confessional rivalry was further diffused by the Peace of Westphalia (1648) which, largely due to the diplomatic efforts of Brandenburg's Reformed government, granted full recognition to Calvinism. The treaty provided that the Lutheran and Reformed members of the imperial diet henceforth meet together as a *corpus Evangelicorum* to resolve through peaceful negotiations any new confessional issues that might arise between them and the *corpus Catholicorum*. The flowering of pietism after the war, followed by rationalism at the end of the century, further helped diffuse the confessional barriers of the late Reformation, turning German Lutherans and Reformed into Protestants – or evangelicals, as they had called themselves in the heady days of the early Reformation, and would continue to do now that confessionalism had ceased to be an issue.

NOTES

1   'Caspar Crucinger and Philipp Melanchthon to Elector Maurice, Wittenberg, 17 June 1548', in Johannes Herrmann and Günther Wartenberg (eds), *Politische Korrespondenz des Herzogs und Kurfürsten Maurice von Sachsen* (4 vols; Berlin, 1900–92), vol. 4, pp. 60f.
2   'Leipziger Interim', in ibid., pp. 254–60.
3   Matthias Flacius, *Quod hoc tempore nulla penitus mutatio in religione sit in gratiam impiorum facienda* (Magdeburg, 1549), p. vi.
4   *Disputatio de adiophoris* and *Eine Disputation von Mitteldingen* (Magdeburg, 1550).
5   Cited in Gustav Kawerau, *Johann Agricola von Eisleben* (Berlin, 1881), p. 318.
6   The 'Augsburg Confession', Article X; for the 1530 edition, see EKD (ed.), *Die Bekenntnisschriften der Evangelisch-Lutherischen Kirche* (Göttingen, 1959); for the 1540 variata, see *Corpus Reformatorum*, XXVI, 357.
7   This formula was coined in 1576 by the Greifswald jurist Joachim Stephani.
8   Theodore G. Tappert (ed. and trans.), *The Book of Concord* (Philadelphia, 1959), pp. 606f.
9   Daniel Hofmann, *Beweis: Das M. Wolff Amlung vnd sein Anhang vnter den Anhaltischen Predigern/Caluinische Sacramentsschwermer … sein* (n.p., 1585), sig. Aiva.
10 *Historischer Bericht/Der Newlichen Monats Augusti zugetragenen Marpurgischen Kirchen Händel* (Marburg, 1605), sig. Biva.
11 Job Friederich, *Ein gar kurtzer Bericht von dem heutigen Religionsstreit und ärgerlichem Gezänck der Predicanten* (Frankfurt an der Oder, 1616), sig. Aiiia.
12 Christoph Pezel, *Auffrichtige Rechenschafft Von Lehr vn Ceremonien* (Bremen, 1592), sig. ava.
13 Polycarp Leyser, *Christianismus, Papismus & Calvinismus* (Dresden, 1602), sig. aiia.
14 Edwin Sandys, *A Relation of the State of Religion* (London, 1605), sig. Qiva.
15 'Colloquium Lipsiacum Anno 1631', in Wolfgang Gericke (ed.), *Glaubenszeugnisse und Konfessionspolitik der Brandenburgischen Herrscher bis zur Preussischen Union* (Bielefeld, 1977), p. 156.
16 Ibid., p. 152.

FURTHER READING

For general introductions to post-1550 Germany, see Thomas Brady, 'Settlements: The Holy Roman Empire', and Heinz Schilling, 'Confessional Europe', in Brady, Heiko A. Oberman and James D. Tracy (eds), *Handbook of European History, 1400–1600* (2 vols; Leiden, 1994–5), vol. 2. Harm Klueting, *Das konfessionelle Zeitalter, 1525–1648* (Stuttgart, 1989), and Heinrich Schmidt, *Konfessionalisierung im 16. Jahrhundert* (Munich, 1992), provide helpful encyclopedic surveys. The most sophisticated discussion of the concept of 'confessionalization' is Heinz Schilling, 'Die Konfessionalisierung im Reich: Religiöser und gesellschaftlicher Wandel in Deutschland zwischen 1555 und 1620', *Historische Zeitschrift* 246 (1988), pp. 1–45, accessible in English in Schilling, *Religion, Political Culture and the Emergence of Early Modern Society* (Leiden, 1992). A very helpful précis of research on the social and political implications of confessionalization is R. Po-Chia Hsia, *Social Discipline in the Reformation: Central Europe 1550–1750* (London and New York, 1989).

For a rich sampling of the current scholarship on Lutheran confessionalization, see Hans-Christoph Rublack (ed.), *Die lutherische Konfessionalisierung in Deutschland* (Gütersloh, 1992), an anthology of twenty papers from a 1988 symposium. The intra-Lutheran controversies are expertly treated by Robert Kolb, *Luther's Heirs Define His Legacy: Studies in Lutheran Confessionalization* (Aldershot, 1996), a collection of previously published essays, and *Confessing the Faith: Reformers Define the Church, 1530–1580* (St Louis, 1991), which traces the development of Lutheran confessionalism to the Book of Concord. On the intra-Protestant debates and their political implications, see also Bodo Nischan, *Lutherans and Calvinists in the Age of Confessionalism* (Aldershot, 1999), a compilation of published and unpublished articles. The 400th anniversary of the Formula of Concord yielded a number of studies on the formula's theological and historical setting: especially noteworthy are *The Formula of Concord: Quadricentennial Essays*, special issue of *Sixteenth Century Journal* 8, 4 (1977); Lewis Spitz and Wenzel Lohff (eds), *Discord, Dialogue and Concord* (Philadelphia, 1977), and Martin Brecht and Reinhard Schwarz (eds), *Bekenntnis und Einheit der Kirche* (Stuttgart, 1980). Theodore Jungkuntz, *Formulators of the Formula of Concord* (St Louis, 1977), provides brief biographical sketches of Andreae, Chemnitz, Chytraeus and Selnecker.

On Crypto-Calvinism and the origins of the German Reformed movement, see Thomas Klein, *Der Kampf um die Zweite Reformation in Kursachsen, 1586–1591* (Cologne, 1962), and Jürgen Moltmann, *Christoph Pezel (1539–1604) und der Calvinismus in Bremen* (Bremen, 1958). Moltmann introduced the much-debated label 'Second Reformation', now generally accepted as a synonym for 'Reformed confessionalization'. For this controversy, see the proceedings of the 1985 symposium of the German Verein für Reformationsgeschichte: Heinz Schilling (ed.), *Die reformierte Konfessionalisierung in Deutschland: Das Problem der 'Zweiten Reformation'* (Gütersloh, 1986), a collection of twenty topical and local studies. The Second Reformation in Germany still requires a definitive study. A succinct introduction to the subject is Henry Cohn, 'The Territorial Princes in Germany's Second Reformation, 1559–1622', in Menna Prestwich (ed.), *International Calvinism, 1541–1715* (Oxford, 1985). Several regional studies are available: Heinz Schilling's path-breaking analysis of the county of Lippe, *Konfessionskonflikt und Staatsbildung* (Gütersloh, 1981); Paul Münch, *Zucht und Ordnung: Reformierte Kirchenverfassungen im 16. und 17. Jahrhundert (Nassau-Dillenburg, Kurpfalz, Hessen-Kassel)* (Stuttgart, 1978); on Nassau-Dillenburg, Gerhard Menk, *Die Hohe Schule Herborn in ihrer Frühzeit (1584–1660)* (Wiesbaden, 1981); Menk, 'Absolutisches Wollen und verfremdete Wirklichkeit – der calvinistische Sonderweg Hessen-Kassels', in Meinrad Schaab (ed.), *Territorialstaat und Kalvinismus* (Stuttgart, 1993), and Bodo Nischan, *Prince, People and Confession: The Second Reformation in Brandenburg* (Philadelphia, 1994).

The Palatinate, Germany's foremost Reformed principality, continues to be the focus of scholarly attention. For a brief but concise introduction, consult Claus-Peter Clasen, *The Palatinate in European History, 1555–1618* (Oxford, 1966). The definitive politico-confessional account remains Volker Press, *Calvinismus und Territorialstaat: Regierung und*

Zentralbehörden der Kurpfalz, 1559–1619 (Stuttgart, 1970); the most comprehensive study of popular religion is Bernard Vogler, *Vie religieuse en pays rhénan dans la seconde moitié du XVIe siècle, 1556–1619* (3 vols; Lille, 1974). Note also Derk Visser's *Zacharias Ursinus: The Reluctant Reformer* (New York, 1983) and *Controversy and Conciliation: The Reformation and the Palatinate, 1559–1583* (Allison Park, 1986), the proceedings of a colloquium at the 400th anniversary of the death of Ursinus; W. Fred Graham (ed.), *Later Calvinism: International Calvinism* (Kirksville, 1994), sect. IV, on the theology of the Rhinelands, and Lyle Bierma, *German Calvinism in the Confessional Age: The Covenant Theology of Caspar Olevianus* (Grand Rapids, 1994).

SCOTLAND

Michael F. Graham

In the early sixteenth century, Scotland was home to a version of Catholicism not unlike its European counterparts, except that it was more subject to pressure from kings and noblemen than most, and its ties with the papacy were looser, due to distance and neglect. These characteristics made a crown-sponsored Reformation, like that of its neighbour England, unlikely. If papal power was generally imperceptible, it was little resented. But political pressures of another sort spurred the cause of reform and the agenda that eventually emerged was quite ambitious. By the time a Reformation became politically possible in Scotland, its backers had numerous Continental and English models to draw upon; theirs would be the last Protestant movement (before the eighteenth-century revivals) to achieve lasting success in any European kingdom. In 1643, when Scotland's ruling elite entered into the Solemn League and Covenant with England, they could invoke the ideal of the 'best reformed churches' with the confidence that all Calvinists would look to their own church (the kirk) as a prime example. This striking transformation took less than a century and has marked Scottish culture – even in its secularized, modern or post-modern permutations – ever since. How did it happen?

THE CHURCH BEFORE THE REFORMATION

Scotland's pre-Reformation kirk was subject to much lay participation and influence. Leading families (in rural areas) and guild or burgh officials (in towns) controlled the appointment to many clerical posts. They had in many cases endowed the kirk, and continued to support it and to exercise control over its buildings and furnishings. For example, the guilds of Dunfermline spent considerable sums before 1560 on items like wax candles and masses for the dead, despite trade links with the Low Countries which would have brought them into contact with Protestant ideas. Elsewhere, the burgh council of St Andrews held patronage rights over at least twelve altars in the burgh church of Holy Trinity.[1] Such officials were not likely to feel disenfranchized by the traditional church, although their regular participation in hiring decisions might have made them keen critics of pastoral care, quick to voice their opinions if clergy were not fulfilling their expected roles. The secular clergy of late mediæval Scotland's 1,000 parishes were

Figure 23.1 Scotland with major burghs. (Michael Graham)

under-funded, even by contemporary standards, due to the diversion of parish revenues to non-local ecclesiastical institutions such as monasteries, universities and cathedrals. Low-paying parochial posts did not attract the best or the brightest (indeed, many of them attracted no one, remaining vacant while absentees collected their pitiable salaries) and the poverty of underpaid priests made gifts and bribes attractive options.

Of course regular clergy (those belonging to orders) were less answerable than their parochial counterparts to the laity. Outside influence on them was more likely to come from the sons of landed families who were often imposed on religious foundations as abbots, priors or commendators. But the resulting possibilities for corruption should not be exaggerated. It is noteworthy that even commendators were forced to enter priestly orders in Scotland, although in the cases of minors this step could be delayed until adulthood. Nevertheless, one by-product of this influence was the tendency of leading families to gain control of a significant proportion of monastic lands. Having done so, neither they nor the Scottish crown had much need for anything akin to Henry VIII's dissolution of the monasteries. It was pointless for landed families to covet properties they already essentially possessed. In many cases they had endowed the monasteries and now they were gradually disendowing them, a process hastened by the widespread practice of feuing. This involved property owners (particularly administrators of church lands facing increased taxation from the crown) handing lands over to feuars in exchange for substantial one-time payments, followed by annual feu duties which became increasingly nominal due to inflation.[2] The feuing of church lands was Scotland's equivalent to the Henrician dissolution. It too led to a revolution in landholding, but it was a gradual one and it would have taken place whether or not there was a Reformation; indeed it was well underway decades before Scotland's 'Reformation Parliament' met in 1560. It meant that Scotland's pre-Reformation kirk had little economic power independent of the leading families with which it was inextricably linked.

The Scottish crown had also worked out cooperative arrangements with the papacy. The most important of these was the Indult of 1487, under which the pope promised to allow eight months after the death of any major benefice holder (including bishops and abbots) for the king to offer a nomination to the post. The pope would then approve the royal nominee while the crown collected any revenues accrued to the benefice during the vacancy. While the Indult lapsed temporarily from 1513–19, it was then reconfirmed by Leo X and in 1535 Paul III extended the vacancy window from eight months to a year. Scottish kings made use of these provisions to fatten their treasuries, reward supporters and establish lucrative careers for illegitimate offspring – James V (d.1542) was particularly notorious for the latter, appropriating the monasteries of Coldingham, Holyrood, Kelso, Melrose and the Priory of St Andrews for his natural sons. In addition, early sixteenth-century kings taxed the church freely, often with the explicit endorsement of a papacy determined to keep a foothold on the island of Britain after the English Reformation was underway.[3] Given all this, it is hardly surprising that the monarchy showed little interest in religious reform in the sixteenth century.

Why then, given such cosy relationships between the old church and the leading forces in Scottish society, did a Reformation eventually take place? Why did the elites whose support was essential to the success of any early modern political or religious movement conclude that change was needed? The answer is threefold. First, Scotland did have an indigenous reform movement, dating back to the fifteenth century. It was regionally based and not particularly strong, but could make itself felt at critical moments. Second, the close association between the church and secular notables made it impossible for the church to operate as an independent force: proposals for 'reform from within', however well-intentioned, often met stiff resistance from vested interests inside and outside the church. Third, during critical moments, political factors made it expedient for leading figures to champion the Protestant cause. Some were sincere believers, however recently converted; others simply saw the reform movement as a convenient stick with which to beat their opponents, given that the latter were closely associated with Catholicism. When churchmen, such as the cardinal-archbishop David Beaton of St Andrews in the mid-1540s, or his archiepiscopal successor John Hamilton in the late 1550s, held political power, attacking their religion was one way of undermining their political legitimacy as well. Such attacks drew on a discourse of criticism of clericalism and traditional Catholicism which was already circulating within Scotland's reform movement, however small the latter may have been.

GRASSROOTS DISSENT

Historians of England's Reformation, starting with the martyrologist John Foxe, saw Protestantism emerging from native sources, particularly the Lollards of the fourteenth and fifteenth centuries. Foxe's Scottish counterparts found themselves at a disadvantage in this regard. John Knox, not only a major participant in Scotland's Reformation but also its leading early historian (a conflict of interest often overlooked), sought the roots of reform in a Scottish version of Lollardy. But Knox was writing in the mid-1560s, searching for the elusive origins of a movement then in full bloom. As Arthur Williamson has noted, 'Knox quite evidently found that the Scottish past showed little indication of the progressive realization of sacred prophecy.'[4] In other words, there were not many martyrs. This might indicate there was scarcely any reform movement before the middle of the sixteenth century. Another possible explanation is that the authorities were not concerned with religious dissent, so it generated few records (the documentation of such movements usually being found in the registers of authorities who sought to suppress them).

Knox is the sole source for a group trial of 'Lollards' from Kyle (the central part of Ayrshire, south and west of Glasgow) in 1494. The trial was held in Glasgow with King James IV in attendance. Some thirty were charged with, among other things, denying transubstantiation, the usefulness of praying for the dead and papal authority (indeed, they allegedly associated the Roman pontiff with Antichrist), and advocating priestly marriage. In the end, all were acquitted. While the charges against them make them look like proto-Protestants, it must be remembered that Knox was writing from hindsight and with a polemical purpose. No other records of the trial survive. Nevertheless, the fact that Ayrshire was one of the first regions to embrace the Reformation suggests the existence of a regional dissenting tradition. It was kept alive by people like the laird Murdoch Nisbet, who translated the New Testament into Scots dialect in the 1520s, and John Lockart of Bar, another Ayrshire laird, an iconoclast in the 1530s and 1540s. In the east, Angus and the Mearns became a centre of reforming opinion, led by John Erskine, laird of Dun. There the case of David Straiton, taken to Edinburgh and burned in 1534 for a heresy originating in his refusal to pay teinds (tithes), became a *cause célèbre*.[5] By the 1520s the central government was concerned about Lutheran books entering the kingdom via its ports, and this led to an Act of Parliament proscribing such literature in 1525.

While Scotland's pre-Reformation history supplies relatively few examples of religious coercion, not all dissenters died in their beds. Patrick Hamilton, commendator of Fearn abbey, an academic who had adopted Lutheran ideas, died in flames in St Andrews in 1528. He had earlier studied on the Continent, meeting Luther and Melanchthon, and written a devotional work, before falling victim to heresy proceedings supervised by Archbishop James Beaton of St Andrews. The Beatons would supply ample villainy for Scottish Protestantism's black legend; when James Beaton died in 1539 he would be succeeded by his nephew David, already a cardinal and later (1543) chancellor of the realm. David Beaton would play a leading role in the heresy trial and execution of George Wishart in 1546. While Hamilton's views were Lutheran, Wishart had travelled in Zwinglian circles before returning to Scotland to preach in 1544. Among the assistants on his popular preaching tours was the Catholic priest and notary John Knox, and Wishart was reportedly welcomed in some of the lairdly homes of Angus, the Mearns, Fife and Ayrshire. In Ayrshire, enthusiasm for Wishart's message, with its emphasis on preaching the Word and cleansing Christianity of ritual accretions, led to outbreaks of iconoclasm. His eventual arrest and burning in St Andrews (March 1546) signified a clear line in the sand being drawn by Cardinal Beaton in the wake of the religious liberalization associated with 'Arran's Godly Fit' in 1543 (this brief political realignment will be discussed later). But it also galvanized Wishart's supporters, numbering among them the Fife lairds who murdered the cardinal in May 1546. Although the motives for this act were mostly personal and political, the killers' subsequent take-over of St Andrews Castle placed Knox on the public stage when he joined the besieged rebels as their preacher. They were only defeated after a year and with French assistance. In the aftermath, Knox and the others put in time as galley slaves in the French navy. This reinforced their hatred of France and helped alleviate the Scottish reformers' paucity of martyrs, even if these ones did not pay the ultimate price. But in the end, Beaton's effort to restore orthodoxy seemed successful, if fatal to him: Scottish Protestantism, still a minority movement, was politically marginalized. It would only resurface in the changed political circumstances of the late 1550s.

REFORM FROM WITHIN

Some of Scotland's leading churchmen were aware of the weaknesses of the old church and sought to rectify them. Cardinal Beaton, whose interests were primarily political, saw the overt Protestantism of the early 1540s as destabilizing and a potential embarrassment in the light of his Francophile leanings; he had been granted the French bishopric of Mirepoix two years before his elevation to St Andrews. Protestantism was associated with the cause of England (and a possible marriage between Mary, Queen of Scots, and Prince Edward of England); his response was to crack down on heresy, leaving little room for compromise.

But a different tack was taken by John Hamilton, Beaton's successor in the see of St Andrews and a scion of one of Scotland's leading families. The illegitimate son of the first Earl of Arran, he had been (as commendator of Paisley Abbey) involved in the reformist plans of his half-brother the second earl in 1543 and was probably the most competent representative of that ill-starred family. After becoming archbishop in 1547, he sought to balance Hamilton family interests with those of the church. For the next thirteen years he succeeded remarkably well in this nearly impossible task. The family had identified itself with the cause of moderate (essentially Lutheran-style) reform and Archbishop Hamilton pursued this through a series of Scottish church councils, in 1549, 1552 and 1559. These aimed primarily at reforming the lives and improving the educational standards of the clergy, and making visitations a regular aspect of episcopal responsibilities. Hamilton published a vernacular catechism in 1552, which described critical issues such as justification in terms broad enough to appeal to mild reformers as well as traditional Catholics, and failed to mention the pope at all. This was followed in 1559 by Hamilton's 'Twopenny Faith', a two-page leaflet of similar ambiguity. Hamilton also completed the foundation of St Mary's College at St Andrews, a project David Beaton had begun. At lower levels in the church, pressure for Catholic reform came from talented disputants like John Winram, subprior of St Andrews, who debated with Knox in 1547, may have had a hand in writing Hamilton's catechism and later served prominently in the Reformed kirk. Another Catholic reformer and close ally of Hamilton was Quentin Kennedy, commendator of Crossraguel Abbey, who became one of Knox's most vocal opponents. While Hamilton and Kennedy would remain loyal to the old church after the Reformation (Hamilton presiding at the Catholic baptism of Prince James in 1566 and sacrificing his life for his support of the deposed Queen Mary in 1571), others like Winram or the Bishops of Galloway and Orkney would make the switch and hold office in the Reformed kirk.

Thus Hamilton and other leading churchmen were not uniformly opposed to change. Some were in fact quite willing to make a commitment to improving discipline and oversight of the clergy, and making the essentials of faith more accessible to the laity. Some of these reforms could be carried out at little or no financial cost; that helps to explain their easy acceptance and highlights the central problem faced by the Scottish church both before and after the Reformation: money. Connected, like Hamilton himself, to leading families which controlled church lands, Scotland's highest-ranked churchmen were unable or unwilling to embark upon any course which might alter the financial structure of the church and shift revenue towards the parish clergy. Institutionally, the church was incapable of fundamental reform because it could not act independently of the family interests of its highest officials. As a result the population remained underserved and reformers could easily point to the disrepair of parish kirks in which sermons were seldom (if ever) heard, regardless of any doctrinal concessions from church councils. This supplied the old kirk's opponents with powerful rhetorical tools, but the prize for victory would include the inheritance of that nearly intractable financial problem.

THE POLITICS OF REFORMATION

Politics is discussed third in this Trinitarian explanation of Scotland's break with its Catholic past, but it is in many ways the critical factor. It determined the timing of the Reformation by creating a context in which the other two factors – the grassroots reform movement and the incapacities of the traditional church – could have significant effects. At the level of high politics, Scotland had not one Reformation but three. The first, an abortive Lutheran movement, achieved little. The second, a Catholic Reformation owing more to France than Rome, sowed the seeds of its own destruction, spurring a backlash against the French connection which made the Protestant cause the patriotic one even though it too was riddled with foreign influence. The third was the result of this backlash, and it eventually succeeded.

Scotland's unsuccessful Lutheran Reformation has been called 'Arran's Godly Fit'. The premature death of James V in December 1542 plunged the kingdom into another royal minority (James IV's death at Flodden in 1513 had created a similar predicament). The new monarch – Mary, Queen of Scots – was barely a week old. Her mother was the French noblewoman Mary of Guise. The governorship of the realm fell into the hands of James, 2nd Earl of Arran, the head of the house of Hamilton, who stood next in line for the throne due to his descent from a sister of James III. But James V's death had followed closely on the rout of the Scots army by the English at Solway Moss, and Henry VIII was aiming for a peace treaty involving marriage between his son Edward and the infant queen, a match which would pull Scotland away from its 'Auld Alliance' with France. Arran, despite his reversionary interest in the crown, was willing to listen to English offers; his rivals Mary of Guise and Cardinal Beaton, the latter made chancellor a week after Arran became governor, represented the French alternative, and the English had demonstrated their willingness to force the issue. In addition, English pensions began flowing into the pockets of the 'assured Scots', noblemen taken prisoner at Solway who had been freed and were now willing to encourage the English match. Some of the latter were also interested in religious reform and Arran himself began to express doubts about purgatory and papal authority.

So reformers like the Dominican John Rough and George Wishart (just returning from exile, most recently in Cambridge) received licence to preach, and the parliament of March 1543 approved a bill introduced by the assured Scot Lord Maxwell allowing the possession of vernacular scripture. This was despite protests from conservatives like Gavin Dunbar, Archbishop of Glasgow, that this was a theological question more appropriate for a church council. Iconoclastic riots in Perth and Dundee might have convinced Dunbar and others that the barbarians were indeed at the gates. Cardinal Beaton, despite a brief confinement in the spring, worked hard in alliance with the queen mother to frustrate negotiations for the English match. By the end of the year his efforts bore fruit; another parliament rejected the treaty terms and forced vernacular Bible reading back underground, while Arran publicly recanted his heresies. The obvious Anglophilia of the reformist party had discredited it in a kingdom wary of its powerful neighbour, and several leading noblemen, such as the Earl of Argyll, who controlled the western Highlands and islands, had never liked the idea of the English match in the first place. 'Arran's godly fit' was over, although the aftershocks would continue for a time, with English invasions of southern Scotland in 1544 and 1545 (the 'Rough Wooing' led by the Earl of Hertford) and the English defeat of a Scots army at Pinkie in September 1547. These invasions were devastating in some areas and strengthened anti-English feeling. Arran was now discredited and marginalized (he was eventually bought off with the French dukedom of Châtelherault in 1550), and in 1548 the young queen was shipped to the French court to be brought up and eventually married to the dauphin Francis.

The murder of Beaton in 1546 ended his campaign to enforce orthodoxy, but as a coup it failed. The pro-French orientation the cardinal had pursued was unaffected. Mary of Guise adroitly held the Francophile party together, in part by ensuring that the Hamiltons were kept on board. She used French influence with Rome to secure John Hamilton's appointment to the see of St Andrews and later that of James Hamilton, another illegitimate half-brother, to the archbishopric of Glasgow. John Hamilton was a religious moderate, as we have seen, and a large group of nobles, lairds and clerics who had displayed Protestant or pro-English tendencies accompanied Mary of Guise in 1550 on a visit to France, where they were showered with honours and pensions. Châtelherault retained prestige, but little real power, as governor. French troops arrived in Scotland to counter the English threat. But the succession of the Catholic Mary Tudor to the English throne in the summer of 1553 severed the tie between Scots Protestantism and English policy and further strengthened the queen mother's position; in 1554 Châtelherault was pushed aside and Mary of Guise became regent for her daughter. The combination of these political shifts and Hamilton's church councils looks like a Scottish Catholic Reformation, albeit one which owed nothing to the Council of Trent. But it owed too much to Paris, and the resentment of foreign influence which had stung the Anglophiles in the mid-1540s would eventually topple the French queen mother, bringing the old church down with her.

In 1557 a faction of four noblemen (the Earl of Argyll, his son and the Earls of Glencairn and Morton) and the reformist laird John Erskine of Dun adapted a traditional Scottish device to a revolutionary purpose. Ties of family alliance and patronage had often been formalized in Scotland through the practice of bonding – men pledging themselves in writing to unity, often in the face of perceived enemies. Bonds had helped create the alliances which sustained bloodfeuds, but they would now be turned to other purposes. Argyll and the others signed a bond pledging themselves

> before the Majestie of God, and his Congregatioune, that we (be his grace) s[h]all ... continewallie applie oure hoill power, substaunce, and oure very lyves to mentene sett forwarde and establische the MAIST BLISSED WORDE OF GOD, and his Congregatioune, and s[h]all lawboure, at oure possibilitie, to haif faithfull ministeres purelie and trewlie to minister Christed Evangell and Sacramentes to his Peopill.

The boldness of their programme was rivalled only by its initial unpopularity. These 'Lords of the Congregation' left plenty of room for signatures on their bond, but got none for the time being.[6] Their bond offered a religious agenda which implied criticism of the regent's government. The latter had been quite lenient towards religious dissent – reformers like Knox and John Willock, a former Dominican from Ayr, had been allowed to preach with impunity while visiting in

1554–5 – but it was clear Mary of Guise would not consider any fundamental alteration in the established kirk.

Others within the Scots political nation had become resentful of the regent's tendency to rely on Frenchmen for advice and now feared that the marriage between the teenage queen and the heir to the French throne would lead to Scotland's absorption by the larger and more powerful kingdom. French troops garrisoned Scottish fortresses and Scotland's foreign policy was dictated from abroad. The increased taxes the regent had to levy were blamed on France. But these two strains of dissent – Protestant and patriotic – were separate.

What brought them together was the death of Mary Tudor in November 1558. The succession of the Protestant Elizabeth to the English throne raised once again the possibility of foreign aid for Scots Protestants. In addition, the fact that Catholic powers refused to accept the validity of the marriage between Elizabeth's parents and thus the legitimacy of the new queen herself, gave Elizabeth sound political reasons for intervention. Mary, Queen of Scots, was the Catholic heir to the English throne, due to her descent from Margaret Tudor, eldest sister of Henry VIII. Upon Mary Tudor's death, the Scottish queen began styling herself Queen of England. These twists in dynastic politics forced the normally tolerant Mary of Guise to take a harsher attitude toward Protestant dissenters, since there were now clearly political dimensions to their movement. Religious exiles began flocking back to England. John Knox, who had spent time ministering to English congregations in Frankfurt and Geneva, sought to join in this domestic reconstitution of the British Protestant movement, although his return was delayed until May 1559 (and re-routed around England) by Elizabeth's disapproval of his poorly timed *First Blast of the Trumpet Against the Monstrous Regiment of Women*. The Genevan influence on Knox and many of the English exiles had changed the character of both British reform movements, pushing them well beyond what Archbishop John Hamilton would have found acceptable. But it would supply the Scottish Reformation with much of its ideological force and the English queen with many of her religious vexations.

While Knox has received much of the attention, one man does not a movement make. Willock, who had spent time in Edwardian England and then with the English Reformed congregation at Emden, actually returned to Scotland several months before Knox. In Edinburgh, he was reported to have been a leader in the burgh's 'privy kirk', a congregation which, according to Knox, met in 'secreit and privie conventiounis in houses, or in the fields', reading scripture and celebrating communion according to the 1552 English Book of Common Prayer in the late 1550s. Its members included several leading merchants and craftsmen. Privy kirks in Edinburgh and elsewhere may have functioned as revolutionary cells, but they left no records behind, so their role is difficult to assess. Nevertheless, the speed with which burghs such as Perth, Ayr and Dundee embraced the Reformation and established Reformed church structures suggests the prior existence of privy kirks.[7] We should not confuse mere existence with popularity, though; when Mary of Guise shrewdly suggested a plebiscite to determine the religious settlement of Edinburgh in the summer of 1559, the reformers declined, on the grounds that divine truth could not be subject to voting. They could also see that, while their views might not command majority assent, the tide was moving their way.

Indeed, 1559 proved to be a fateful year. It began with the 'Beggars Summons', an anonymous placard placed on the doors of friaries across the realm ordering friars to yield their places to the poor before Whitsunday. As that day approached, the burgh councils of Perth and Dundee declared themselves in favour of Reformation and Knox preached publicly in both burghs. At Perth, his sermon spurred a riot against the friaries and the Charterhouse, home to Perth's Carthusian monks. Shortly thereafter, authorities in Ayr in the west embraced reform also. Efforts by the regent to crack down on the preachers created a reaction among reformist (or anti-French) nobles and lairds, and the rejuvenated Lords of the Congregation gathered an army near Perth at the end of May. A temporary truce broke down when the regent insisted on restoring the mass in Perth, leading to an even larger muster by the Congregation at St Andrews in June, coinciding with the official Reformation of that town, complete with a Knox sermon. The army of the Congregation then recaptured Perth and marched on Edinburgh, reaching the capital at the beginning of July. Once the reformers had taken over Edinburgh's churches (and declined the regent's plebiscite offer), Mary of Guise hunkered down in the nearby port of Leith, easy both to defend and to reinforce. Hundreds of additional French troops arrived there in late summer, and the Congregation's forces (despite the addition of Châtelherault and his eldest son in September) began to dwindle. In November, the mass was restored in Edinburgh.

These setbacks for the Congregation spurred England to act more forcefully. English financial aid (due more to the efforts of William Cecil than Queen Elizabeth, ever wary of rebels), began arriving in the autumn and English troops crossed the border in March 1560. Burghs like Ayr, Perth and Dundee clearly favoured the reformist cause, but many others felt caught in the middle. On 30 November, members of Dunfermline's merchant guild divided up the silver from the Holy Blood altar, including the chalice, 'be caus of the trublus warld batht of the Congregatione and the Frenche men becaus we thowcht in nocht expedeante to put it all in ane hand ... '. The conservative burgh council of Aberdeen offered token support (forty men) to the Congregation in March 1560, but only with the proviso 'that it be nocht to interpryis ony porposs contrar the quenis grace and hir authorite'. It had earlier resisted attempts to reform the burgh's kirks.[8]

Edinburgh's magistrates leaned more toward reform, but they too were divided. In 1559 Edinburgh was captured twice by the Lords of the Congregation and retaken both times by the regent. In the spring of 1560, English troops helped recover the capital for the Congregation and the regent took refuge in Edinburgh Castle. Her death from illness there on 11 June cleared the way for a political solution to the crisis. The Treaty of Edinburgh, concluded in July between English and French diplomats, called for the removal of all foreign troops save two small French garrisons. Mary and her husband Francis (now, with the death of Henry II in July 1559, rulers of France as well as Scotland) would give up their claims to England. A council to govern Scotland would be named jointly by the sovereigns and the Scots estates, and a Scottish parliament would be summoned. It was this last concession which paved the way for the official institution of Protestantism.

The parliament which met in August 1560, including for the first time in Scottish history lairds below the status of 'lords of parliament', was explicitly

forbidden to consider religious matters. This restriction was ignored and the legislation it passed – outlawing papal authority, the mass and Catholic baptism, and
endorsing a Reformed confession of faith – was technically illegal, never receiving
the royal assent. Nevertheless, this 'Reformation Parliament' marks the beginning
of the Scottish Reformation in an official sense. The confession of faith, written by
a committee including Knox, Willock, John Winram and three others, was
Calvinist in theology, but went beyond Calvin in one significant respect. Like the
French Reformed Confession of 1559 and the Belgic Confession of 1561, the Scots
Confession insisted that congregational discipline was essential as the third mark
of the true church, in addition to preaching and the proper administration of the
Protestant sacraments of baptism and communion.

The parliamentary endorsement bestowed on the Scots Confession was conspic-
uously withheld from the Book of Discipline that followed several months later,
authored by the same group. This was a detailed blueprint for reform, proposing a
structure of authority for the new church and delineating the relationship between
it and Scotland's political institutions. Its most successful prescription was its
provision for the establishment of kirk sessions (consistories including ministers
and lay elders) in each parish to manage local ecclesiastical affairs and monitor
parishioners' behaviour. This Genevan concept had already been introduced in
Perth, Dundee and St Andrews in 1559, and may have been in use in 'privy kirks'
before then. Some Scots parishes would not see their first kirk sessions until the
seventeenth century, but this institution would critically shape Scots Protestantism.
The more controversial aspect of the Book of Discipline, and the reason it never
received any political endorsement (although some notables did sign in support),
was its claims on the full revenues of the old church to support the evangelical
mission of the new. Benefiting as they did from the diversion of much of this
wealth, Scotland's political leaders would not underwrite any such fundamental
redistribution. While some noblemen could accept Calvinist theology, they did
not see a Reformation as something they should have to pay for.

Indeed, Scotland's political leaders in 1560 do not seem to have regarded the
Reformation as the seismic historical shock that subsequent generations saw.
Death had removed the regent, but major political figures (even the unabashedly
Catholic Earl of Huntly) retained their offices and burgh oligarchies experienced
little upheaval. Parliament legislated religious matters without permission, but
otherwise the authority of the absentee Catholic monarchs was respected. Three
bishops accepted the new religious settlement, but the others did not and were
little bothered for it, at least as far as their revenues and social prestige were
concerned. This situation might have continued indefinitely had not the death of
Francis II in December 1560 paved the way for giving Scotland something it had
lacked for nearly two decades: an adult, resident monarch.

THE REIGN OF MARY STEWART

Mary Stewart saw few attractions in the French court after the death of her young
husband. She was a childless widow without power or influence. So she decided to
return to her native land, arriving in August 1561. The sudden appearance of an

adult monarch would cause some upheaval in any kingdom, but in addition Scotland was about to become the laboratory for an unusual experiment in the era of *cuius regio, eius religio*: this newly Protestant land would be ruled by a Catholic queen who disavowed any intention of re-Catholicizing her subjects. This is a testament both to her tolerance and her political realism. Huntly apparently offered her an army to nip the Reformation in the bud, but she chose instead to cooperate with her Protestant notables – particularly her illegitimate half-brother James Stewart, prior of St Andrews, to whom she gave the Earldom of Moray. Mary allowed the Reformation to proceed, provided she and her courtiers were allowed to attend their own Catholic mass (a concession deplored by Knox but prudently defended by Moray). Her suppression of a revolt by Huntly in 1562 clearly reinforced this moderate policy.

In that same year she offered the new kirk some financial support with the Thirds of Benefices scheme, under which holders of ecclesiastical benefices would surrender one-third of their revenues, which would then be split between the crown and the Reformed ministry. While two-thirds of the income of the old kirk could now freely be pocketed by benefice-holders without any pretence of pastoral care, this at least provided some financial basis for the Reformation. It was more tangible than anything the Protestant notables who had refused to accept the Book of Discipline had offered. Something else the queen gave the new kirk, if only by default, was the opportunity to develop independently from the crown. As a Catholic, she was unsuited for the role of 'godly magistrate'. Therefore the affairs of the kirk were largely left to the ministry and active laity, gathering (usually) twice a year in the General Assembly, with little royal interference. The General Assembly heard reports from superintendents and other ecclesiastical commissioners, petitioned parliament and the crown, arbitrated disputes within the kirk, and considered disciplinary questions too complex or sensitive to be handled locally. In the seven years between the Reformation Parliament and Mary's deposition, the General Assembly became accustomed to its role as head of the Reformed kirk. Its position would be tested throughout the reign of James VI (1567–1625), who was Protestant and therefore 'godly'.

It was not her religious policies that led to Queen Mary's undoing, but rather her mishandling of factional politics and the related matter of her matrimonial choices. The intrigues surrounding her 1565 marriage to her Protestant cousin Henry Stewart, Lord Darnley, which offended both Elizabeth of England (by moving Mary closer to the English succession) and the Hamiltons (by displacing them as the second family in the land in favour of Darnley's Lennox Stewarts) are well known both to students of sixteenth-century British history and afficionados of historical romance. The marriage soon offended Mary too; she found herself saddled with a husband she came to despise. Furthermore, it severed the successful political partnership she had forged with Moray, exiled after an abortive rebellion. After Darnley sired an heir, the future James VI, he was murdered in 1567 – a spectacular crime in which many of Scotland's political notables, including the queen herself, were implicated. Mary's subsequent hurried marriage to the rash and ambitious Earl of Bothwell, one of Darnley's murderers, only fanned the flames of outrage and led to her deposition by a Protestant faction. After military defeats at Carberry (June 1567) and Langside (May 1568), the queen fled to England and a genteel captivity which would only end with her 1587 execution for plotting against Elizabeth.

JAMES VI AND THE CHALLENGES OF 'GODLY' MAGISTRACY

Mary's deposition led to a six-year civil war between her supporters and the group which gathered around her infant son. The fact that the former contained many Protestant (such as Châtelherault and the Earl of Argyll) as well as Catholic nobles frustrates attempts to see this as a religious war, although the staunch Protestantism of most of James' party enabled it to couch its rhetoric in confessional terms. Edinburgh's kirk session, following an Act of Parliament passed early in 1573, forced the queen's former supporters in the capital to perform public repentance for their political sins in the aftermath.[9] Like the Lords of the Congregation ten years earlier, the king's partisans had English backing, for political and religious reasons. Moray, returned from his own short Genevan exile, led the king's faction and served as regent until his 1570 assassination (by a Hamilton laird). His successor was Matthew Stewart, Earl of Lennox, the young king's paternal grandfather and a long-time Anglophile who met an end similar to Moray's in September 1571. After another short-lived regency, James Douglas, Earl of Morton, emerged as head of the king's government until 1580 (regent until 1578).

Morton guided the kingdom out of civil war and placed the crown on a solid footing. He had long been a friend of England and took steps to bring the kirk under the wing of the royal government, along English lines. In this he met some resistance from the leadership in the General Assembly, who were now coming to see the disadvantages of having a Protestant king. There was little room for bishops in the structure of the Reformed kirk as envisioned by the Book of Discipline. The conforming bishops sometimes attended General Assembly meetings, but their role was seen as administrative, along the lines of the five regional superintendents appointed in the early 1560s. As the pre-Reformation bishops died off, the question of what to do about the bishoprics (and the revenues and parliamentary seats attached to them) remained unresolved. Morton wanted to maintain some form of episcopacy for political and fiscal reasons, and made a few episcopal appointments, but a vocal party within the Reformed kirk was coming to see episcopacy itself as anathema and to espouse a 'Two Kingdoms' theory, which saw civil and ecclesiastical jurisdictions as entirely separate. To this group, government by royally appointed bishops constituted an unacceptable mixture of the two. This battle would continue long after Morton's fall from power, becoming particularly intense in the late 1590s when the adult James VI began systematically to restore the episcopate.

This opposition came to be led by Andrew Melville, a laird's son from Angus who had studied under Pierro Ramus in Paris in the 1560s before spending several years in Geneva. He returned to Scotland in 1574 to take up the principalship of Glasgow University, moving on to St Mary's College in St Andrews in 1580. Melville found followers among the second generation of Reformed clergy, most of them university-educated, concentrated in the vicinity of Edinburgh and the eastern lowlands, particularly Fife. They probably were never a majority, but their geographical closeness to Edinburgh, where the General Assembly usually met, gave them influence out of proportion to their numbers, since they could attend meetings that their more distant colleagues (particularly in the conservative north) could not. Their party line was that no pure church could contain royally appointed bishops and that secular officials (including the king) had no jurisdiction over ecclesiastical matters, including statements clergy might make on any topic from the pulpit. Their manifesto was the Second Book of Discipline, drafted in the late 1570s by a large committee including Melville. Formally approved by the General Assembly in 1581, this book offered a new clericalism, with its insistence on a fully educated clergy policing its own ranks as well as the behaviour of its congregations. The lay elders who had assisted in the latter effort since the Scottish Reformation began were now to be elected for indefinite (even lifetime) terms rather than annually and were to be regarded as quasi-clergy themselves. The Second Book also called for the creation of district elderships, a new tier of authority between the kirk sessions and the provincial synods, which would review the qualifications of clergy and assist in discipline. They would include all the ministers and two elders from each parish in the district. The implementation of this idea began in 1581, when the General Assembly established thirteen presbyteries.

The presbyteries, and the presbyterian system of which they were characteristic, became central to the ecclesiastical politics of the late sixteenth century. They were outlawed by the crown from 1584–6 (when Melville and some of his allies were temporarily exiled to England) and only received parliamentary confirmation in 1592. By the end of the century they had spread throughout the Lowlands. Lay elders soon stopped attending their meetings, perhaps bored by the theological discussions which appear to have dominated many of them, as the qualifications of ministers were tested. The presbyteries were essential to the progress of the Reformation in the parishes, but some of them (particularly those of Edinburgh and St Andrews) came to be seen by the king as breeding grounds for sedition. His eventual solution to this problem was to pressure the General Assembly into accepting the idea that bishops should be permanent moderators of presbyteries, giving the Scots Reformed kirk of the early seventeenth century a hybrid presbyterian-episcopal structure. At the same time James revived the episcopate and found ways to control the frequency and locations of General Assembly meetings, thus bringing that body to heel as well. It met less regularly after James succeeded to the English throne in 1603. Melville, who once told the king to his face that in God's kingdom the King of Scots was but a 'sillie vassal', was permanently exiled in 1606, by then the relic of a movement which had been broken in the previous decade.[10]

THE WORK OF REFORMATION

Thus far this politically oriented discussion has largely ignored the Reformation as most people would have experienced it in their parishes. While the focus on politics explains much and provides a narrative thread, we must remember that each community experienced its own Reformation at its own pace and the changes which had reached some by 1570 were still unknown to others fifty years later. The ecclesiastical structure of the old church was not abolished; it was merely allowed to wither away while an alternative structure was devised. Many local elites used the Reformation to enhance their own positions and embraced only those ideas congenial to their interests. Burgh councils carefully safeguarded their independence and were wary of ministerial as well as royal or aristocratic influences. Those at the bottom of the social scale who had happily joined in the anticlerical riots of 1559 found their lives and behaviour subject to unprecedented scrutiny as the new authoritarianism of social discipline took root.

The first problem which faced the reformers in 1560 was finding clergy. Something like a quarter of the old Catholic clergy made the transition to serve in the Reformed kirk, but it quickly became clear that there were not nearly enough men with the educational and other qualifications necessary to serve as Reformed ministers. Even in the mid-1570s, only a quarter of parishes had them and, although leading towns such as Edinburgh, Dundee, Perth, St Andrews, Montrose, Stirling, Glasgow and Ayr acquired ministers (in some cases two) early on, the shortage was even more acute in rural areas. The temporary solution, proposed in the Book of Discipline, was the office of reader. Many a pre-Reformation priest or monk found himself retrained as a Reformed reader, authorized to read prayers and scriptural passages, and to deliver sermons prepared by qualified ministers. Some continued to perform sacraments in the traditional way, although this was officially forbidden, and over time there were efforts to root out these practices. Nevertheless, continuing compromises were necessary in some areas, as the Stirling Presbytery recognized as late as 1593 when it authorized the reader William Scot to minister baptism and marriage in four Highland parishes because he knew Gaelic. Without his services, the presbytery feared, the residents of those parishes would 'fall in ath[e]isme.'[11] Over time, as stipends improved and a second (and third) generation of ministers came into its own, virtually all of Scotland's lowland communities got their own ministers. But the expansive parishes of the Highlands would remain under-served well into the seventeenth century, due both to their sizes and a shortage of Gaelic-speaking Reformed clergy. In general, the Reformation took hold first in a swathe extending from Ayr in the west, across the central Lowlands and up the east coast as far as Montrose. From those regions it spread south into the Borders and far southwest, and north and east into the Highlands.

The burgh of Aberdeen provides a classic example of how the ideology of Reformed Christianity had to compromise with local interests. The lukewarm support Aberdeen offered the Lords of the Congregation in 1559–60 has already been noted. The most powerful family in the region was the Gordons, a conservative kin group whose chiefs, successive Earls of Huntly, wavered back and forth between open Catholicism and conservative Protestantism throughout the late sixteenth century. Their relative William Gordon, Bishop of Aberdeen and also Catholic, remained resident in Old Aberdeen (just north of the burgh) until his 1577 death. Aberdeen itself was dominated by the Menzies family, sometime Gordon clients who were more consistently Catholic than their aristocratic patrons. Burgh authorities did not get around to founding a permanent kirk session until 1573, although short-lived sessions were set up in 1562 and 1568 when outside pressures forced the Aberdonians to put on a show of commitment. Catholicism proved no impediment to eldership on any of these sessions and, unsurprisingly, Aberdeen's kirk session did not harass Catholics, except briefly in 1574 when the Earl of Morton paid a retributive visit in the aftermath of the civil war (he also saw to the removal of the organ and choir-stalls from the burgh church of St Nicholas). But Aberdeen's kirk session did go on the offensive against fornication and irregular marriage, practices Catholic and Protestant elders alike agreed should be eliminated. Even in these efforts, elders in the 1570s do not seem to have wanted to employ the sanctions of public repentance so common in communities which had adopted the Reformation more enthusiastically. Instead, they simply levied fines. The Reformation was not a popular cause in Aberdeen. But this does not mean that burgh populations opposed it everywhere. Perth, where craftsmen had much more power than in other burghs, took to it from the start, and Michael Lynch has discerned 'real Protestant populism' in burghs by the 1580s. The enthusiastic reception given to the Edinburgh minister John Durie in his return from exile in 1582 provides an example.[12]

This brief foray into disciplinary practices in Aberdeen highlights the aspect of the Reformation which many Scotsmen and women would have felt most keenly, and which had the most dramatic impact on popular culture. Scotland's reformers were in the vanguard of the widespread sixteenth- and seventeenth-century European movement to reshape behaviour through neighbourly oversight, using the sanctions of public admonition, repentance, suspension from the sacraments and, in extreme cases, excommunication. As kirk sessions spread in the wake of a full-fledged Reformed ministry, so did the work of social discipline.

The Books of Discipline laid out an ambitious programme of behavioural reform, although most first generation kirk sessions limited their efforts to punishing fornicators whose illicit unions resulted in illegitimate births. Offenders (male as well as female) were encouraged to marry and often forced to watch sermons while seated on the penitent stool, in plain view of other parishioners. In some communities, the penitent stool was used in tandem with the jougs (an iron brace similar to the stocks) or other forms of ritual humiliation involving special clothing, public apologies or fines (see Figure 23.2). In Scotland, where conceptions of personal and family honour were comparable to those of Mediterranean societies, such punishments would have been keenly felt, and their eventual extension to such offences as Sabbath-breaking, assault, slander, use of folk medicine or the observation of traditional festival days such as Yule was controversial. But many Scots found such actions subject to discipline by the end of the sixteenth century. In a similar vein, some kirk sessions required that couples demonstrate knowledge of the Lord's Prayer and the Ten Commandments before being allowed to marry. The celebration of communion, which the reformers proposed should take place four times a year in every parish, came to be preceded by communal reconciliation sessions. Those judged to be outside the pale of acceptable behaviour were denied communion tokens and thus could not gather with their fellow parishioners around the table. To some reformers, popular

Figure 23.2 The Bench of Repentance at St Andrews. (St Andrews University Library

culture seemed impervious to the civilizing mission of godliness and the successes of social discipline must not be exaggerated, as they were by the English separatist Robert Brown, who claimed that in Scotland, 'all men [are] made slaves to the preachers & their fellowe eldars.'[13] But kirk sessions did become the most effective local courts in some areas, arbitrating disputes and establishing community standards. They provided a forum for the extension of ministerial power as well as the authority of the lairds who served as elders in rural areas. The latter may have been the Scottish Reformation's prime beneficiaries.

THE REFORMED KIRK AND THE SCOTTISH REVOLUTION

The removal of the king and his court to England in 1603 took away the traditional focal point of Scotland's national identity – the Stewart monarchy. Scottish affairs were managed on James' behalf by a clique of noblemen. Many aristocrats also headed south, seeking their fortunes in English pensions and English marriages. King James' dream of a constitutionally united kingdom was dashed upon the rocks of English suspicion; many members of the English parliament saw only greedy foreigners in the king's entourage. Scotland's leaders, although more cooperative in the matter of union, had their own suspicions and these came to focus upon the role of Scotland's Reformed kirk within the union of crowns. This was in part because the ministry, wealthier and more educated than ever before, was now supplying some of the most articulate defenders of Scotland's identity.

Much of James' attention to his older kingdom after 1603 centred on his continuing efforts to strengthen episcopacy within the Reformed kirk. He blunted the criticisms of this strategy from the remains of the Melvillian left by appointing bishops who had good educational and preaching credentials. His major intervention into the practices (as opposed to the structure) of the kirk came during his only visit home after 1603, when in 1617 he introduced a set of guidelines known as the Five Articles of Perth. These required kneeling at communion, the observation of the traditional festivals of the Christian year and confirmation by bishops, and allowed for private baptism and communion. The first General Assembly to which they were proposed baulked at them, but an assembly meeting at Perth in 1618 under heavy royal pressure endorsed the articles. A parliament in 1621 approved them, giving them the force of law. The articles, which were in many cases disregarded, reflected James' growing interest in English religious practices, demonstrated the degree to which he had lost touch with opinion in his native kingdom and provided a taste of further interventions to come. To many Scots, even those who had no objection to episcopacy, the articles smacked of Catholicism. The Perth assembly was also a significant milestone in that it would prove to be the last meeting of that body (which habitually had met twice a year in the late sixteenth century) for twenty years.

While James' actions aroused some ire, those of his son spurred outrage, leading to a reorientation of Scottish politics. Historians in recent years have wisely shifted their attentions away from purely English issues and highlighted the ways in which 'British' problems helped to bring down the government of Charles I. His mismanagement of Scottish affairs provides a classic case-study. Most relevant to the history of the Scottish Reformation are the Act of Revocation (1625) and the introduction of the new prayer book (1637).

The Revocation was Charles' adaptation of a device commonly employed by Scottish kings upon reaching adulthood. Revocations would reclaim lands alienated during a royal minority, providing for redress against the rapacity and incompetence of those ruling in the name of a young monarch. But Charles was twenty-four when he inherited the throne and his Revocation extended claims to all church lands which had passed into secular hands since 1540. Charles was apparently trying to improve crown finances, rationalize landholding and provide better endowments for clergy, still trying to make ends meet under the provisions of the Thirds of Benefices and other *ad hoc* arrangements. But the Revocation was poorly explained and threatened the wealth of noblemen and others who had taken over church lands or whose abbacies or commendatorships had simply been converted into secular lordships in the late sixteenth century. Although finally accepted by a parliament in 1633, the Revocation was never really carried out. All it succeeded in doing was making Scotland's leading landholders profoundly suspicious of their absentee king, a suspicion which grew as the king adopted the habit of appointing bishops to his Scottish council in preference to noblemen, and sought to cut into the local powers of aristocrats.

The parliament of 1633 was lobbied personally by Charles, visiting Scotland for his formal coronation. He was accompanied north by William Laud, Archbishop of Canterbury, whose attempts to curb unlicensed Puritan preachers and redecorate churches were causing controversy in England. The king and the archbishop did not like what they saw of Scottish worship, regarding it as too simple and undignified. As a result Laud set out, with minimal input from the Scottish bishops, to devise a new Scottish prayer book more in keeping with English practices. The storm aroused by the introduction of this book (by royal proclamation, with no attempt to gain ratification from a general assembly) in 1637 is the stuff of Scottish national legend. Whether or (more likely) not an Edinburgh matron named Jenny Geddes stood up in St Giles Kirk and threw her stool at the Dean of Edinburgh as he conducted the first service using the new book, a well-orchestrated riot did greet its introduction. This popular opposition to the anglicization of Scottish worship (or 'popery', as it was pejoratively labelled) soon joined with the noble disaffection spurred by the Revocation and other issues to create a national movement. This was led by the nobility and the ministers in opposition to royal policy and, soon, episcopacy itself. Its manifesto was the National Covenant, signed by Scotland's disaffected notables in February 1638.

Once again adapting the device of the bond, the 'noblemen, barons, gentlemen, burgesses, ministers and commons' of Scotland reaffirmed the Negative Confession of 1581, written in response to an earlier Catholic scare at court. They then listed all anti-Catholic and pro-reform legislation passed by the Scots Parliament since 1560, suggesting that recent changes such as the Five Articles of Perth or the Prayer Book were illegal. The tone of the document was very constitutional. Episcopacy itself was not attacked explicitly, nor was the king. But the implication of statements such as 'with our whole hearts we agree ... to adhere unto, and to defend the foresaid true Religion ... forbearing the practice of all novations already introduced in the matters of the worship of God ... ' was clear. If the king would not preserve the true religion, his subjects would do it for him, in opposition to him if necessary.[14] Lay elders returned to the presbyteries in large numbers and the Reformed kirk became a vehicle for revolution. A General Assembly meeting at Glasgow later that year took what to many was the logical next step and abolished episcopacy. Sixteenth-century Scottish bishops tended to come from important families and thus had aristocratic defenders. The Scottish bishops of 1637–8, with good preaching credentials but humble social origins, found few friends in high places; the charge against them was led by noblemen resentful of their influence. The king who fought to defend them and his ecclesiastical directives had unwittingly revived the coalition (between noblemen and ministers) of 1559–60. Once again that coalition would find friends in England.

Archibald Johnston of Wariston, a lawyer and one of the authors of the Covenant, wondered at God's providence to have made him, 'the wickedest, wyldest, sinfullest, unworthiest, unaiblest servant, to be ane instrument in his hand of so great, so gracious, so glorious a work as is this renovation of that national oath of the whol land with our aeternal Lord the God of Glory.' He reckoned that the day the noblemen signed the Covenant was the 'glorious mariage day of the Kingdome with God.'[15] It would prove to be a rocky marriage. By so covenanting itself, the Scottish nation was starting a chain of events which would climax with the execution of Charles I by an English parliamentary faction and, soon thereafter, a devastating Cromwellian occupation of Scotland. Scotland had come to define itself in terms of religious reform, but would nearly destroy both itself and the British monarchy in service of that definition.

NOTES

1 Elizabeth Torrie (ed.), *The Guild Court Book of Dunfermline, 1433–1597* (Edinburgh, 1986), *passim*; W.E.K. Rankin, *The Parish Church of the Holy Trinity, St Andrews* (Edinburgh, 1955), p. 7.
2 It should be noted that feuing was not exclusive to ecclesiastical landlords – laymen also used it as a means to raise cash. For this practice, see Margaret H.B. Sanderson, *Scottish Rural Society in the Sixteenth Century* (Edinburgh, 1982), pp. 64–83, 135–52.
3 Gordon Donaldson, *The Scottish Reformation* (Cambridge, 1960), pp. 37–41; Mark Dilworth, *Scottish Monasteries in the Late Middle Ages* (Edinburgh, 1995), pp. 16–22.
4 Arthur H. Williamson, *Scottish National Consciousness in the Age of James VI* (Edinburgh, 1979), p. 4.
5 For an account which traces the genealogy of Ayrshire's reform movement back to the trial of 1494, see Margaret Sanderson, *Ayrshire and the Reformation* (East Linton, 1997), pp. 36–47. For Angus and the Mearns, see Frank Bardgett, *Scotland Reformed* (Edinburgh, 1989).
6 Gordon Donaldson (ed.), *Scottish Historical Documents* (Edinburgh, 1970), pp. 116–7.
7 David Laing (ed.), *The Works of John Knox* (6 vols; Edinburgh, 1846–64), vol. 2, pp. 151–2; Thomas Thomson (ed.), *The History of the Kirk of Scotland by Mr David Calderwood* (8 vols; Edinburgh, 1842–9), vol. 1, p. 304; James Kirk, *Patterns of Reform*, (Edinburgh, 1989), pp. 12–15.
8 Torrie, *Guild Court Book of Dunfermline*, pp. 99–100. John Stuart (ed.), *Extracts from the Council Register of the Burgh of Aberdeen, 1398–1625* (2 vols; Aberdeen, 1844–8), vol. 1, pp. 315–9, 321–2.
9 Scottish Record Office ms CH2/121/1, fols 1r–v, 3v–4r, 7v, 30v, 32v; *Acts of the Parliaments of Scotland* (12 vols; 1814–75), vol. 3, pp. 72–3.
10 Thomson, *History of the Kirk*, vol. 5, pp. 439–40.
11 Stirling Council Archives ms CH2/722/2, 21 August 1593.
12 Michael Lynch, 'Continuity and Change in Urban Society, 1500–1700', in R.A. Houston and I.D. Whyte (eds), *Scottish Society, 1500–1800* (Cambridge, 1989), p. 88.
13 Robert Brown, *A New Years Guift*, ed. Champlin Burrage (London, 1904), p. 26.
14 Donaldson, *Scottish Historical Documents*, pp. 194–201.
15 George Paul (ed.), *Diary of Sir Archibald Johnston of Wariston, 1632–1639* (Edinburgh, 1911), pp. 321–2.

FURTHER READING

For general histories of Scotland during the period, see Gordon Donaldson, *Scotland: James V–James VII* (Edinburgh, 1965); Jenny Wormald, *Court, Kirk and Community: Scotland 1470–1625* (Edinburgh, 1981), and Keith Brown, *Kingdom or Province? Scotland and the Regal Union, 1603–1715* (New York, 1992). The standard introductory work on the Scottish Reformation remains Gordon Donaldson, *The Scottish Reformation* (Cambridge, 1960), augmented (not replaced) by Ian Cowan, *The Scottish Reformation* (London, 1982), with the latter's strength in its discussion of regional variations. Several excellent urban and regional studies have followed, particularly Michael Lynch, *Edinburgh and the Reformation* (Edinburgh, 1981); Frank Bardgett, *Scotland Reformed: The Reformation in Angus and the Mearns* (Edinburgh, 1989); Margaret Sanderson, *Ayrshire and the Reformation* (East Linton,

1997), and various articles by Allan White on Aberdeen and Mary Verschuur on Perth. One of each can be found in Michael Lynch (ed.), *The Early Modern Town in Scotland* (London, 1987). The impact of social discipline in the regional spread of the Scottish Reformation is assessed in Michael Graham, *The Uses of Reform* (Leiden, 1996). James Kirk has long argued for an early and widespread reform movement which, in contrast to Donaldson, he sees as strongly Calvinist and anti-episcopal from 1560, if not before. The major collection of his work is *Patterns of Reform* (Edinburgh, 1989). The issue of episcopacy in the Scottish kirk is the subject of David Mullan, *Episcopacy in Scotland: The History of an Idea, 1560–1638* (Edinburgh, 1986). The early seventeenth-century kirk is described in Walter Foster's *The Church Before the Covenants* (Edinburgh, 1975), and its role in the Scottish Revolution is analyzed in Walter Makey's *The Church of the Covenant* (Edinburgh, 1979). Gordon Donaldson's *All the Queen's Men* (London, 1983) reconstructs factional politics in the mid-sixteenth century. The role of the kirk in Scotland's identity is explored in Arthur Williamson's brilliant but dense *Scottish National Consciousness in the Age of James VI* (Edinburgh, 1979).

PART V

THE REFORMATION AND SOCIETY

REFORMATION SOCIETY, WOMEN AND THE FAMILY

Susan C. Karant-Nunn

The Reformations of the sixteenth century were far more than an effort to correct doctrine that their leaders thought had become distorted after the period of the 'pristine' early Christian church. They were also a concerted attempt to reform people's behaviour. One of the ways in which the new churches sought to improve those brought under their sway was by focusing on the family, where, as they thought, good Christians were formed as children and best maintained as adults. The three main questions to be taken up here are these: how Protestants of ultimately mainline hues (Lutherans, Calvinists and Anglicans) envisioned the proper family, how those in authority strove to remake the families around them, and whether they enjoyed any measure of success.

THE REDUCTION OF MULTIPLE 'FAMILIES' TO THE NUCLEAR FAMILY

One of the findings of those historians who a generation ago began carrying out research on the history of the European family is that the nuclear or simple family, made up of mother, father and their children under one roof, had long prevailed. Certainly it did so during the Reformation era. Nevertheless, the Protestant Reformations put such heavy emphasis on the simple family at the same time as they eliminated other quasi-familial institutions, that they left an impression of having created the nuclear family. In the late Middle Ages, multiple organizations and corporations were conceived of in familial terms. Confraternities bound their constituents as brothers and, where women could join, as sisters too. Apprentices and journeymen addressed their superiors in the home as father and mother and their peers as brothers. Young men and women drawn or forced into the ordered religious life often (as in the case of Martin Luther's wife, Katharina von Bora) followed kin-based preferences in their selection of monasteries and so literally favoured the company of relatives, quite beside the well-known use of familial vocabulary within the convent. Less affluent beguines in northern European towns shared houses in the manner of family members, their intense common devotions binding them emotionally as well as geographically. Mediæval people saw the universe in terms of family bonds. They prayed for their dead, who in turn were to use whatever powers they had to benefit those left on earth. Cemeteries and ossuaries were at the centre of towns and villages, symbolizing the daily awareness of the deceased among the living. So indispensable were family connections that Christ without close kin on earth was unthinkable and Christians surrounded the Saviour with biblically condoned and some uncondoned relatives. Late mediæval people, even though they themselves 'hived out' when they wed and established separate residences to be inhabited by them and their offspring, shared a view of the cosmos that I shall call 'diffusely' familial, made up of shades and degrees of relatedness and levels of reciprocal obligation, stretching outwards even to encompass the dead. The Catholic church's 'trees of consanguinity', looked at not as documents that prohibited wedlock to relatives but as graphs of brethren, are evidence of this outlook.

The Protestant Reformations unwittingly tacitly redefined the family as nuclear by cropping off nearly every extraneous leaf and branch, every venue of 'diffuse' relatedness. Although guilds retained their lower echelons, the encroaching state weakened their internal governance and denatured 'parental' authority within them. In other spheres the role of the theologians is clearer. Confraternities with their socio-spiritual functions, altars and processions were shut down as idolatrous. Monastic houses were dissolved and their inhabitants urged to form families of the procreative type. Monastic vows were now odious as pious works designed to win God's special favour. The clerical landscape changed in that all the friars (brothers) disappeared and the number of priests (fathers, sometimes brothers) was radically reduced to half a dozen or fewer in the towns and their titles rendered impersonal; they were now called pastor or vicar or deacon or preacher rather than father. The superfluity of priests had sustained itself chiefly by the reading or singing of short-ened masses for the repose of relatives' souls; Protestant leaders rejected the efficacy of such rituals. Family-based endowments, whether of money or works of art, ceased and family identity with particular churches grew weaker.

Especially drastic was the curtailment of transactions between living and dead relatives. Against a background of burgeoning population and overflowing burial grounds, pastors and evangelically minded city fathers cooperated in creating new cemeteries at or beyond the periphery of settlement. This literally put distance between the quick and the dead, even as headstones and other markers were allowed more and more often to commemorate non-elite individuals. Perhaps the two developments are not unrelated: some additional aid was needed not to forget the dead entirely. In the course of the century, charnel houses were shut and their contents carted out to the fields for mass interment. Preachers urged their congregations to stop believing that the dead were accessible and could affect those who still breathed. The diffuse family made up of a network of the here and the here-after came to an end. God alone was powerful and His Son, through His crucifixion, was humankind's perpetual exclusive intercessor. The fate of the deceased was beyond negotiation.

Again, I doubt whether any of the Reformers detected that in reviving what they regarded as biblical Christianity they were altering the context of the family. And yet they were. By repeated implication, families were precisely those living individuals closely related by blood and intimately related by residence.

In the milieu of the liturgy, however, the reformers introduced changes which they might have understood as narrowing the definition of the family. While on the one hand limiting forbidden degrees of relatedness to three (as opposed to the official Catholic seven) and legitimating marital unions between godparents' and godchildren's kin, which would appear to broaden the pool of nuptial eligibility, they simultaneously tried to enforce other regulations that could have weakened kinship and concentrated more upon the immediate family. These processes varied from one emerging denomination to another, with the Anglican church evidently retaining more that was traditional than either the Lutheran or the Reformed (Calvinist) churches. In baptism, for example, the followers of Martin Luther insisted, like Catholics, on the necessity of baptism for salvation. Thus baptism was an urgent matter, not to be delayed. They imposed fines and other penalties on parents who postponed christening longer than about three days, which effectively terminated the practice of waiting to perform the rite until the local nobleman or noblewoman was available to serve as a godparent. Whether or not this was the practice in a given locale, authorities also made it difficult for parents to gather in relations who lived at some days' distance either to serve as baptismal sponsors or simply to lend their kinship-reinforcing presence to the occasion. The indulgence and reciprocity that lay at the heart of these festivities were interrupted, or at any rate continued despite increasing obstacles. Furthermore, every level of government attempted (probably in vain) to lessen people's expenditure on these familial rituals. They had no understanding of the socio-economic functions of popular culture but felt themselves to be guided strictly by the Bible.

The Calvinist emphasis on predestination could logically have produced an ecclesiastical polity within which baptism was not essential even though remaining a sacrament. In keeping with his conviction, John Calvin eliminated emergency baptism. Yet the threatening Anabaptist suspension of paedobaptism meant that the Reformed churches, like the Lutheran, treated baptism as essential, if not to the soul's eternal bliss than at least as a sign of the community's credal commitment. Infants were brought to the basin (not the font) promptly, with the same potential consequences for less immediate kinship ties. In Geneva, Calvin also interfered with the naming practices of generations, by which godparents had conferred their own names upon their tiny charges. Often these had been saints' names. These were now disapproved unless they were biblically or historically attested, further undermining the time-honoured methods of sealing friendships. Consistorial records would suggest that the Calvinists were the most successful of all the new churches in restricting those private celebrations that followed christenings and weddings. Demonstrations of generosity and the duty to respond in kind, both of which reaffirmed kinship, were concomitantly reduced.

The efforts of Catholic and Protestant governors alike to introduce restraint has rightly been seen as a facet of an age in which the state was bent on expansion and made use of every weapon, including 'social disciplining'. Virtually every creed lent its weight to this edifying enterprise. We have neglected to take into account the potential effects of this endeavour upon the family. To the extent that neighbourhoods and relations were no longer at liberty to act out their interdependence, immediate families were thrown back upon their own resources. They were to celebrate piously, modestly, frugally and within a small circle of intimates. This was the ideal.

Popular resistance to these restrictions and many more is most apparent along confessional boundaries, where the faiths lay in close proximity to one another and families were divided. Under these circumstances, blood and custom did prove to be at least as compelling as pastoral admonition. People on both sides of such a line passed quite freely back and forth in the furtherance of kinship obligations, not to mention the pursuit of pleasure.

Protestant lands, I am arguing, revised the context of the family, unconsciously paring it down to its core, scraping away what leaders of church and state saw as a surfeit of allegiances, occasions and gratifications. Although we have begun to perceive how similar Catholic and Protestant reforms were, in the restructuring of the familial world-view the Catholic church lagged far behind. Indeed, it did not aspire to abolish confraternities or monastic vows of marriage to Christ. Although Catholic reformers did strive to inculcate restraint upon their human flocks, they left the multi-metaphorical 'diffuse' family in place. In Protestant lands, the wedded pair, their children, their servants and their domicile now demarcated what we call the family, even though the word as we use it did not yet exist.

THE NEW MODEL: THE PASTORAL COUPLE

It is well known that every variety of the Reformation except the Catholic rejected vows of celibacy. Protestants did this on several grounds: that these oaths were founded upon the erroneous conviction that the performance of good works, including refraining from sex-tainted marriage, helped one to earn salvation; that the Bible approved of marriage as shown by the creation of Eve, by Christ's performance of his first miracle at a wedding and by the fact that some of the disciples had been and presumably remained married; that experience amply demonstrated that the sex-drive was so powerful that most people could not abstain and required the outlet of a sanctioned relationship in order to prevent fornication; that without marriage the human race would die out. The Reformers felt called upon to live up to their convictions and set an example for other Christians.

The most obvious early shift in official values, then, came when the leaders of the Reformation movement wed. Huldrych Zwingli married in 1522 but kept the fact secret for two years, whereas Luther held an open celebration of his nuptials (several days after the actual ceremony) in June 1525. Thomas Cranmer, whose first wife had died in childbed, found himself in the embarrassing and dangerous position of serving a monarch who decided in 1539 that the violation of vows of celibacy was a felony. He was forced to keep his second wife out of sight, even if he did not literally carry her around in a trunk as some people joked. Luther's own marriage to Katharina von Bora, because of his irrepressible and mostly happy references to it, itself became a model of connubial bliss and domestic propriety (see Figure 24.1).

More influential in the longer term was the post-Reformation parsonage with its duly wedded master and mistress and their legitimate children. This supplanted the ubiquitous priestly household presided over by a celibate but not chaste

Figure 24.1 The ideal Protestant family: Luther and his wife and children. Print of *c*.1750. (Wittenberg, Lutherhalle)

clergyman, his concubine (euphemistically referred to as his 'cook' or 'housekeeper') and their illegitimate offspring. Catholic society was evidently of two minds about the latter institution. The public could understand the irresistible nature of physical desire and tolerated these ties despite the hypocrisy that at one level they represented. Perhaps, indeed, the rampant non-marital housekeeping among the clergy helps to explain late mediæval preachers' positive utterances concerning women and marriage. At the same time, we see the populace's disapproval reflected in the lower social station of the concubines themselves. In addition, city fathers (and no doubt city mothers and city daughters in their homes) complained about priestly abuse of the confessional, alleging that lascivious clerics used their office to seduce citizens' wives and daughters. Lurking behind this grievance is the conviction that the priests' unblessed if often stable liaisons did not delineate moral limits as clearly as a properly consecrated marriage did.

The Catholic clergy were not, then, unacquainted with women. Rather, they had not been required to bring their lifestyle in line with the standards they and society professed. When the Reformation began and priests were virtually compelled to wed as a token of their theological conversion, they stepped into an arena that quickly came to be governed by local law. Clerical lives were henceforward under public scrutiny. We might anticipate that the populace would almost unanimously welcome the nuptials of their pastors, but it would appear that centuries of teaching the superiority of celibacy had taken root and that some souls would have preferred their spiritual leaders to adhere to the abstinent life. As priests began to wed, opinion was divided; but the laity soon became reconciled to the new principle.

The occupants of the reformed parsonage were different from their predecessors. The pastor's wife was likely now to come from the same socio-economic class as her husband. As post-Reformation authorities imposed a higher standard of doctrinal preparedness upon the pastors themselves, they became, in the course of the sixteenth century, not only better educated but they came from an urban background and were the bearers of urban attitudes into the countryside. England seems to provide an exception to the clergy's rising social station, for there even the nobility had sent their sons into the priesthood. Elsewhere the elevated ranks had thought the pastorate too lowly for their kin. In post-Reformation society, however, the pastor and his wife socialized with members of the magistracy and even with the nobility in the countryside. Even as a socio-economic separation between the pastorate and the ordinary laity grew, the parson and his wife were meant to present a paragon of piety and decorous behaviour. Even if other men might still rail at their wives or even beat them with impunity, this was now culpable in men of the cloth. They and their wives were tacitly expected to embody the more intense love that was finding favour by the end of the sixteenth century. While her husband visited the sick and wrote his sermons, the wife was to run a harmonious, smoothly functioning home, overseeing children and servants with Christian zeal. To produce a prodigal son or daughter could besmirch the reputation of a pastor and his wife, for this misfortune hinted at some fundamental flaw in the child-rearing practices of the parents, even if this had not been visible to their neighbours.

These were the official duties of the pastor's spouse, but her unofficial ones might be varied. Clerical wives were now often literate and saw the value of reading and writing for themselves and their daughters. Occasionally they played a part in teaching these skills to small children from the community. Informally they gave petty alms to their unfortunate neighbours and visited the sick. They stayed apprised of women's matters in their parishes, sometimes telling their husbands when a woman in labour invoked a saint, or if a midwife used 'superstitious' words or substances. Even though they held no office in the town or village, they were often, by virtue of their position, personages of some importance.

As post-Reformation pastors became the fathers of legitimate sons, they sometimes established veritable clerical dynasties. In northern Germany, the Spangenbergs were one such – a sequence of pastors which has been traced through six generations, beginning in the early sixteenth century. In the late Middle Ages, priests' masculine progeny had occasionally followed in their fathers' footsteps, were trained in the liturgy by them and sometimes took over their progenitors' very parishes. With the advent of the Reformation, this pattern gained society's blessing – though a prerequisite theological education for future clergymen was in place by the end of the century. The Electors of Saxony were among those princes who even earmarked university scholarships for the gifted sons of the clergy, in the hope that these would follow the religious calling and be ordained, or that they would enter the swelling territorial bureaucracy. The anecdotal evidence is plentiful of daughters marrying pastors.

ATTEMPTS AT REFINING THE FAMILY

Protestants and reform-minded Catholics had ample precedent for shaping the marital bond. If Luther and Calvin reduced marriage to a civil transaction and inveighed against the mediæval church for its departure from scripture, they also failed to see that within the twelfth- and thirteenth-century context the Catholic elevation of marriage (for the laity) to a new level of sacrality and the church's insistence upon consent in any valid nuptial probably provided a degree of protection, especially to brides, that they had not consistently enjoyed before.

We have been too inclined to notice the misogynist pronouncements of famous churchmen, such as those attributed to Albertus Magnus – these were the ones most readily recorded and disseminated, in any case – and to take them as the whole picture of ecclesiastical attitudes towards marriage. Curers of souls and preachers to lay audiences were much more realistic. It was the almost universal practice for late mediæval homileticians to take up the subject of marriage on the second Sunday after Epiphany (the third Sunday in England), often using the Wedding at Cana as their text. Extant sermons contain favourable themes very similar to those that will be taken up in their more plentiful Reformation counterparts: marriage is an honourable estate ordained by God; as a sign of his Father's approval, Christ performed his first miracle at a wedding; God created Eve and brought her to Adam, thereby establishing marriage as the divinely pleasing norm. Not every preacher reiterated St Jerome's derogation of marriage or attempted to persuade his audiences to enter a monastery or convent. Indeed, such a strategy would not have accorded with the elite nature of monastic life across Europe. The Catholic hierarchy desired most ordinary people to join the marital estate. This remained true of the Counter-Reformation church. This is not to deny the church's ambivalence as it simultaneously sought to perpetuate a celibate clergy and discourage uninhibited sexual expression. These two tendencies, the fostering of marriage and the praise of celibacy, existed side-by-side within clerical culture, though they were not wholly separate from misogynist lay conventions.

An evolution coinciding with and reinforcing the more negative view of women and marriage was the Renaissance revival of the classics. Even if humanists such as Desiderius Erasmus, Thomas More and Juan Luis Vives regarded women as educable, they shared with their contemporaries a generally negative assessment of the feminine nature. The reformers, along with other intellectuals of the day, were influenced by ancient letters, including their occasional vituperation of women. Nevertheless, the pagan ancients took marriage itself for granted.

Against this background, we can understand the reformers' positive estimation of marriage on the one hand and their ongoing mistrust of women on the other. These churchmen were innovative in certain respects and profoundly traditional in others. As seen above, they played a leading part in altering the familial landscape such that attention had ineluctably to focus on what was left, the simple family and its household. But their inherited ambivalence about women remained and found expression in sermons, prescriptive literature, rituals, art and judgements concerning marital problems. Undergirding their ideological inheritance was a disciplinary spirit that reached back at least to the mid-fifteenth century and that found earliest expression in rulers' efforts to increase their power at the church's, cities' and other corporations' expense. During the sixteenth century, these sporadic efforts became a veritable campaign, with which the Reformations shared a number of goals. Magistrates' and princes' ambitions were varied and far-reaching, and clergymen's vision coincided with only some of them. For a time, their differences notwithstanding, the reformers and their immediate successors found the state an indispensable partner in trying to rectify perceived religious and social ills. The state, genuinely pious in its conscious motivation, found credal and moral discipline a most useful tool. Churches and states cooperated in attempting to turn the family into a bastion of virtue.

The Reformation sermon as an instrument for the ordering of the early modern family is just beginning to be appreciated. Studies of the Reformation have rightly observed that with the abolition of the mass with its signal act of transubstantiation, the preached Word became the centrepiece and distinguishing feature of the evangelical service of worship. Luther and Calvin wrote of the Word of God as the means by which the Holy Spirit becomes active in the individual. In a still largely illiterate and financially ever-vulnerable populace, that Word was ordinarily heard rather than read. In Protestant lands, the sermon was probably the salient mass medium, another being pamphlets read aloud in public places.

The Lutheran churches in particular from the middle of the sixteenth century used the wedding homily as a principal means of shaping gender roles and the behaviour of husbands and wives. A secondary implement was the funeral sermon with its idealized summary of its subject's life. It quickly came to be incumbent on nearly every pastor or deacon who presided over weddings to deliver a carefully prepared excursus on one of a range of topics that, taken together, constituted the core of official definitions of suitable spousal and family life. Jean Bodin was by no means alone in regarding the family as the building block of any godly society, as the microcosm reflecting the higher orders of the state with the prince at its zenith and of the universe with God at the pinnacle. The Puritan Robert Cleaver called the household a 'little commonwealth'. The Venetian humanist Giovanni Caldiera took a similar view. Many other intellectuals and rulers were persuaded of this. Protestant leaders, then, were hardly alone in seeking to make this vision a reality, but it is noteworthy for our purposes that they made a very concerted effort from the pulpit (and uncounted thousands of their wedding sermons survive) to improve the family.

None of their topoi were unfamiliar. New, however, were the intensity, the frequency and the relentlessness of the clerical campaign, which lasted into the eighteenth century and sometimes beyond. Brides, grooms, their attendants and neighbours felt the full weight of most homileticians' divided heritage. The many printed collections of sermons, read in their entirety, range from high praise of the good of marriage and husbands' and wives' reciprocal esteem, to occasionally venomous attacks on the 'all-too-prevalent' bad woman. Much prescriptive matter lies between these extremes. Chief among their messages are the following:

First, they advocate marriage for all or nearly all people. Luther thought that only 1 in 100,000 men might have the gift of remaining chaste (that is, continent) while abstaining from marriage, but he did not envision even this small exception for women. Not all of his followers went quite this far, but they elevated marriage further than Catholic preachers either had or would.

Second, to the Catholic 'goods' of marriage, which were the begetting of children and the avoidance of sexual sin (*remedium ad peccatum*), they stressed more than their predecessors (who had not entirely overlooked this aspect) the mutual aid and companionship of marriage. By the end of the sixteenth century, and more obviously in the seventeenth, Lutheran preachers redefined the meaning of connubial love. To Luther's mind, love referred to passion, and husbands and wives ought more properly not to love in this sense with all the attendant dangers but rather to esteem one another. Whatever Luther's ideal, by the end of 1525 he was enamoured of his wife. He was irrepressible in expressing this sentiment to correspondents and visitors, which had the effect of presenting a frankly more affective image of marriage to his disciples. The privacy of men like Zwingli and Calvin (Cranmer was perforce a different case!) prevented their serving as similar exempla. During the late sixteenth and seventeenth centuries, preachers came to favour a more intimate and erotic devotion. At the core of the Christian household was the wedded couple, bound to one another in warm affection as well as in law. Steven Ozment's Magdalena and Balthazar Paumgartner were indeed very fond of one another.[1] Whether their emotions were affected by the post-Reformation clerical emphasis upon stronger feelings, or whether, like Katharina and Martin Luther, they were the selves that they would have been in any normal context, is impossible to know.

In his own writings, Luther redistributed the mediæval onus of sexuality, which had been placed chiefly upon women. Perhaps simply acknowledging his own unsuppressible longings, which ultimately found their release in the marriage bed, Luther consistently includes both genders in discussing the urges of the flesh. The reformer and Katharina continued their own intercourse until shortly before his death, after any further conception was possible. He saw marital sex (or as he sometimes called it, 'fleshly work') as an aspect of connubial life that did not merely forfend un-Christian forms of expression. In general, however, the Reformations remained suspicious of married sex. Many preachers reiterated couples' duty to shun lustful indulgence even with each other. Many churches prohibited weddings during the sacred seasons of Advent and Lent, on Sundays and on other holy occasions. Within Protestantism, the spirit and the flesh remained opposed, but less so than within Catholicism. Other, more permissive currents would mitigate this opposition in generations to come.

Third, sermonizers impressed upon women their almost complete subordination to their husbands as a result of Eve's part in causing the Fall of humankind. As before the Reformation, writers presented differing versions of Eve's status before her inveiglement by Satan, but nearly all agreed that in some measure she had had to submit herself in important matters to her husband owing to her inherent frailty as a woman. Eve had always been the weaker vessel. The degree of her subjection deepened markedly after the Fall, and she and all of subsequent womankind, the 'daughters of Eve', had to obey their mates in all things, including the domestic, except in those instances when an ungodly spouse commanded them to do something that was patently hateful to God – such as murder someone or abandon the true faith.

The corollary of these instructions to women was the prescription of men's behaviour. Throughout the longer Reformation era and beyond, preachers paid far and away more attention to wives' demeanour than to husbands', and yet the obverse (whether spoken or not) of every admonition to wives also defined the clerical ideal of the husband. The late mediæval laity had scorned, even imposed rituals of mockery upon, men who let themselves be dominated by their wives. The preachers and early modern society at large shared that bias. They enjoined upon husbands a proper mastery of their wives, which included directing their activities but above all supervising their character. Again, Protestants invented no new image of wifely obedience, but they advocated it and the masculine complement to it with a new determination. At the same time, they insisted that husbands should exercise restraint. Along with St Paul, they believed that men ought to love their wives as they loved themselves. The wedding pair was one flesh and no one hated their own body. While physical punishment might be necessary in extreme cases, the upright man should much prefer to deal rationally with his partner. This deprecation of violence grew such that in the seventeenth century, one Lutheran pastor could ask rhetorically,

> What does a husband do when he strikes his wife or behaves like a Tartar towards those who share his home? He who commits such a heathen act prostitutes himself, and he should not brag about it but on the contrary should be ashamed. No one who is able to use his reason behaves in this way. ...[2]

The Church of England officially disapproved of wife-beating. The 'Homily on Matrimony' declared, 'Let there be none so grievous fault to compel you to beat your wives'. A man who did so was 'a wild beast' and a 'Bedlam man'.[3] But on the Continent, among Catholics and Protestants opinion was divided and often reluctantly defended a husband's occasional resort to corporal punishment. It would seem that after the dissemination of Reformation values, men who abused their wives immoderately at least suffered greater injury to their reputations than husbands had earlier. For the most part, this loss of face remained a form of social pressure. It did not mean that wives necessarily enjoyed greater redress than before.

Fourth, wives were to abide exclusively in and around the home, an enjoinder that can have had no practical effect in the rural setting or among the urban poor. Moreover, they were not to earn their family's living. Men were to 'earn their [and their wives'] bread by the sweat of their brow' and preachers construed this to mean that they and they alone went out to labour in the public sphere. Men who let their wives support them either by wealth or by work not only lost prestige but their proper standing in the family. They were beholden to their spouses and had to 'dance to the tune' their wives played. Women were to devote their strength to bearing and raising Christian children and managing the home with whatever their men brought in. They should not dally around the windows and doors (such behaviour was associated with prostitutes), and they should not converse at length with other women. Not only was chatter a waste of time, but once their tongues were loosened, women were inclined to reveal their husbands' private affairs.

For their part, men were now assigned the almost exclusive responsibility for sustaining the family. We shall see at once that the division of labour of the countryside inevitably had its counterpart in the towns, for not even the housewives with servants could be idle. Even so, a new bourgeois ideal of the enclosed and apparently leisured 'lady of the house' is visible and it would develop more fully after the Reformation era. In reality, women worked just as hard as their feminine ancestors but received less credit for their trouble; they were increasingly subsumed under their husbands. The preachers were not oblivious to women's contributions. They praised the housewife of Proverbs 31:10–31:

Who can find a capable wife?
Her worth is far beyond coral.
Her husband's whole trust is in her,
and her children are not lacking.
She repays him with good, not evil,
all her life long.
She chooses wool and flax
and toils at her work.
Like a ship laden with merchandise,
she brings home food from far off.
She rises while it is still night
and sets meat before her household.[4]

They found such a one to be all too rare.

Fifth, brides and grooms ought to be alike in age, in the wealth and station of their parents, in religion, and in physical attractiveness. This bias in favour of sameness antedates the Reformation, but the preachers took it up – adding the issue of religious creed – with fervour. Artists, too, decried in their images the inappropriate pairing of young and old. Abbeys of misrule sometimes took violent action against such mismatches.

In neither the Calvinist and Anglican churches nor in the Catholic church were pastors compelled in the same systematic way to give wedding sermons or in other settings to expound so emphatically upon the marriage-bond. They did treat the subject, nevertheless, and in part by means of the nuptial homily, infrequent though the medium was compared to the Lutheran outpouring. More commonly they contented themselves with the pointed reading of the same scriptural passages that served the Lutherans as texts. Rituals as well as references within a greater diversity of sermons and commentaries, such as discussions of the Book of Genesis, reveal a striking similarity of perspective. In Lutheran and Calvinist churches, women continued to stand or, increasingly, to sit on the left and brides to stand on the grooms' left in their wedding ceremonies. Nuptial liturgies impressed upon brides their complete subordination to their husbands as a punishment for Eve's sin. In small churches, females received the eucharist after males and, in large urban churches, they partook on the left-hand (the inferior) side of the altar or table simultaneously with men and boys on the right-hand side.

A prominent genre across language areas for the shaping of the Christian family are the guides written for patresfamilias. The ancestors of such literature in classically sensitized circles were Aristotle's *Politics* and Xenophon's *Oeconomia*. Of more recent provenance were humanist works like Leon Battista Alberti's *On the Family* (1434–41), its stress being on the contributions of domestic propriety to the orderly state. Within Protestant regions, where Justus Menius is credited with writing the first handbook on marriage, patriarchs were to guide their households in spiritual as in practical matters.[5] Manuals for heads of households did not confine their attention to proper prayers, hymns and Bible verses for intramural devotions but variously took up the proper relations between husbands and wives (less thoroughly than collections of wedding sermons), between parents and children, and between masters and mistresses and their servants. In England, the treatise of William Goudge, *Domestical Duties*, was both exhaustive and very widely read.[6] It occurred to the authors, who were often clergymen, that the best place for conditioning the pious subject was the home. Although this genre flourished in the late sixteenth and seventeenth centuries, it is unlikely that it was widely encountered in the dwellings of the humble. Expenditure for such items was impossible for the ordinary laity and the prevalent illiteracy kept most husbands and fathers from consulting these treatises. Nevertheless, the number of surviving examples would suggest that the audience for such literature was not negligible. Literacy among the economically independent classes was growing in this period and the anecdotal evidence of the reading of printed sermons, tracts directed to housemasters, the Bible and other devotional works is considerable.

Works of art were another means both of depicting and of moulding the upright family. One of the most common types of family portraiture of the age (essentially a late mediæval tradition) is the placing of donors and their immediate families in religious scenes that the same donors presented to churches in the hope of improving their chances of going to heaven. Husbands and sons are usually lined up on one side (preferably the right) and wives and daughters in rank of age on the other (usually the left). When they are placed on the same side, the figures are arranged such that the husband and eldest sons occupy the position of honour. All are often shown kneeling with hands folded in prayer as they look to Christ or another holy person, who is the focal point of the scene. After the Reformation, such art enjoyed a new vogue in Lutheran churches as funeral painting (see Figure 25.8, p. 478).

Secular art flourished in those parts of Germany, England and the Low Countries where a general prejudice against images did not carry over from the church into the world. A favoured theme in the Low Countries were the pictures of domestic scenes that reveal, at one level, the Netherlanders' enjoyment of mundane activities; others suggest the widespread literacy among women and the preference that they peruse works of spiritual edification. At another level, however, we may see this genre as reinforcing the view that good Christian women stayed in the home and tended to homemaking and parenting. It would be impossible to claim that such works were products exclusively of the Reformation, and yet their content conforms very nicely to the ideals of both Protestant and Catholic leaders. It embodies the trans-credal masculine certitude that women were best kept in the house and at their traditional tasks. Only then could their families flourish.

Most common of the visual media disseminating uplifting images of family life were the cheaper prints that illustrated fliers, pamphlets and books. As a warning to others, many of these depict the unhappy family, such as Erhard Schön's woodcut, *Mrs Seldompeace*, of a woman wielding her distaff as a weapon and holding onto the tail of her husband's steed. The yapping dog leaping on her skirts conveys to us the stridency of her voice. As a social commentator, Schön was drawn to such scenes.

An allegorical portrait of 'the wise woman' is variously attributed to Anton Woensam and Wolfgang Resch and thought to have emerged from a Vienna printing press about 1525. It was very popular and was reprinted on into the seventeenth century (see Figure 24.2). One might at first think that this epitome of righteous womanhood, with horse's hooves, a serpent about her waist and a padlock through her lips, is detached from a family. However, one of the balloons explaining each symbol states about the dove on her blouse, 'I am constant like the turtledove toward him who is my companion in prayer; I shall never break my troth with him'. Sermons referred to spouses as being companions in prayer; the man referred to is her husband.

With the passage of time, more prints depict the ordinary family at its daily business. While the cautionary tales featuring husband- and child-murderesses and alleged fraternization with the Devil continued, viewers could also see, for example, Abraham Bach's *Proper Table Manners*, which shows a dinner table at which the adults and eldest son are seated as they say grace; a younger daughter

Figure 24.2 Anton Woensam or Wolfgang Resch, *Allegory of the Wise Woman*, *c.*1525. This complicated image is crammed with symbols instructing women how to behave. They should 'go on horses' feet in order to be firm in their honour'; they should gird themselves with serpents and avoid the poison of evil love; by contemplating Christ crucified they can learn to shun haughtiness. The padlock figuratively keeps their mouths closed.

stands at the table while smaller children pray in the foreground, and a little daughter tends an infant in its cradle (see Figure 24.3). A maidservant carries away a serving dish. This family is a community of faith presided over by the husband and father. It is also quite well-to-do, presenting a model to which the less well-off might aspire and thus wish to imitate.

In a frontispiece to a printed funeral oration published in 1669, we see the prosperous Lutheran family in another setting, as it attends the deathbed of the wife and mother, whose deceased new-born infant lies at her feet. In accord with Protestant advice, one was no longer to grieve wildly (as alleged of Catholics) at the passing of a loved one. In Jacob von Sandrart's print, only one little girl among the daughters lined up at one side of the bed gives way to tears, which the artist thought one might expect of girls. The sons stand in order of age on the other side of the bed, their hands folded in prayer. The husband decorously gives his hand to his dying wife and seems to bow to her in godly farewell. The woman's face is calm, and the balloon above her head indicates that she welcomes death, antici-pating a 'lovely crown of joy' in the presence of Jesus.[7]

In all its activities, the family envisioned by leaders of the reformed churches thought continually about God. In my judgement, whether or not historians can detect a growing secularization contemporaneous with the Reformation, the divines who launched it (and their successors too) intended to sacralize as much of life as they could. With the cooperation of the pious and self-serving state, theolo-gians, bishops, superintendents, parish inspectors and increasingly the better trained ordinary parsons attempted to impose discipline upon their human flocks. With rare exceptions (such as the Netherlands, where no church was, in the end, established), ecclesiastical governors did not draw a distinction between those who chose to attend services and receive communion, and those who chose not to, for in practical terms this choice did not exist. Penalties for dissent may have ranged widely but church overseers nevertheless meant to cast an inclusive net. Zwingli was persuaded that human beings had to reflect God's perfection. However evil the world might have remained as result of Satan's wiles, leaders saw their duty as relentlessly striving to subdue it.

This endeavour targeted the family. The rhetorical, liturgical and artistic models constructed for this societal building block were inadequate in that they alone did not cure all those ills to which the family, made up of corrupt mortals, was heir. Men and women secretly made and then reneged on promises of marriage. They engaged in premarital sex which, before and after the Reformation, many European societies did not categorically condemn (particularly between engaged couples). They committed adultery and abandoned their partners. Husbands (usually) and wives (sometimes) immoderately beat their spouses and their chil-dren, such that the health of the victims was undermined. They had incestuous sex. Reform-minded officials could not let these transgressions pass undetected and unpunished, and courts of various types seemed the suitable instruments of correction. With the dissolution of Catholic consistories, the responsibility for meting out justice in these and myriad other morals cases fell to several bodies: in Lutheran lands, especially appointed marriage courts (*Ehegerichte*) and also the consistories that in some places supplanted their diocesan predecessors; in

Figure 24.3 Abraham Bach, *Proper Table Manners* (17th century). This print shows an idealized family hierarchy arranged with the father seated in the place of honour. Mealtimes have become formal, structured occasions that begin with the father saying grace: part of his role as 'pastor' within the household.

Calvinist territories, those formidable consistories that kept an eye on all kinds of religious and moral infractions; and in an absolutist atmosphere, city councils and princes themselves, together with the civil courts under their direction, whenever a particular instance drew their attention.

A common modern misperception has been that the Reformation, in reducing marriage from a sacrament to a civil transaction, made divorce possible as it had not been before. If assessed for the sixteenth century alone, without regard to a gradual softening of the rule that occurred over a longer period, this perception needs correction on at least three points. First, in the late Middle Ages the Catholic church provided several avenues of relief, albeit probably more readily available to the privileged. These involved nullification and the formal separation of incompatible spouses from each other's 'bed and board'. In the former instance, the church declared that no valid marriage had existed and the parties were able to enter wedlock with another; in the latter case, the couple remained married but did not cohabit – the wife was assured of some support, as far as her dowry, marriage contract and her husband's means permitted. Second, informally, many peasant communities tolerated discordant husbands' and wives' living apart. We even hear of discontented husbands selling their wives in England. If they did not actually do so in Germany, some at least fantasized about it. Erhard Schön's print, *Wives' Market*, has men leading their wives as horses and perhaps dogs, the wives being on all fours with bit and bridle or muzzled, to a public market to be inspected by potential buyers.[8] Third, whatever the Reformers may have taught about the wedded estate being now merely a civil matter, they tried hard to render it holier than it had been before. This is clear in the close supervision to which they subjected it and it is visible in the liturgical alterations that the wedding ceremony underwent. Couples now were joined not outside but inside the sanctuary and before the altar. They no longer simply consented to their union but experienced elaborate religious instruction as part of the observances, taking oaths 'before God' that had not existed earlier. With the Reformation, the wedded twosome became even more of a sacral entity.

Although the Reformation permitted divorce in theory, during the first century it is more likely that opportunities for separating, whether the marital bond was terminated or not, actually declined. The increasingly sacred nature of marriage may be seen in the more thoroughgoing reluctance of churchmen to see separated those whom God had joined. In Lutheran areas, parish visitors pointedly enquired whether any couples were living apart and compelled them to live under the same roof again. The Genevan consistory tried to reconcile alienated spouses by reasoning with them and inducing them to compromise; it wished to restore broken marital bonds. Despite the differences between late mediæval Catholic and Protestant practice as regards marriage and divorce, it is noteworthy that Protestant lawyers adhered to much of canon law. For the most part, the number of divorces granted through official channels remained small. Nonetheless, a theological and a practical precedent was set for an increase in divorce in later times. England maintained a Catholic disinclination to allow divorce until the twentieth century.

Immoderate fighting between husband and wife always attracted the disapproval of neighbours. This did not change with the Reformation. In dealing with this misdemeanour, authorities tended to leave traditional forms of humiliation in place. In Zwickau such husbands were seated above a gate and their wives beneath it until they agreed to get along. In much of Germany, loud and quarrelsome wives had to wear as they walked around the marketplace heavy stones, which were painted or carved with the figures of similarly aberrant women, like medallions on a thick iron necklace. The public was happy to attend these events. Researchers on early modern England debate whether after 1550 scolds were more often dunked on ducking stools or otherwise punished. Whether they were or not, we cannot be certain that an increase in this punishment is related to the Reformation. This reminds us once again of the ambiguous causes of changes bearing on the family in this era.

Protestant courts were continually occupied with the issue of unattested promises to marry. Secret engagements had exercised late mediæval Catholic authorities too. If any child's secret oath could be considered binding, a flight of youthful fancy might cause parents' social and economic strategies to founder. Young people were expected to take their parents' wishes into account both before and after the Reformation, though we cannot be sure to what degree parents actually dictated their children's marital choices. Private preferences undoubtedly weighed heavily in any decision to wed. The trend in Protestant lands was to insist that engagements be generously, reliably witnessed and the Council of Trent wished to establish the same principle. Nor did consummation necessarily indicate a valid commitment but might be consigned to the category of illicit sex. Nevertheless, the seriousness with which authorities now regarded sexual relations meant that parents had to be on guard lest their children's dalliances have dire consequences for the family's economic future. Here the matter of class may have entered in. If young people had sex with partners considered unsuitable for them to marry, as with servants, courts may have been less intent on compelling marriage.

Before the Reformation, fornication between consenting and unmarried adults usually met with the normal consequences of sin: confession and penance. In addition, craft guilds and city councils had methods of dealing with such behaviour. The Reformation, as a salient current of an era that intended to bring human beings to order, took a dimmer view of moral lapses than the late mediæval Catholic church ordinarily had; civil rulers, too, adopted more rigorous policies. Elders in Calvinist towns watched closely for breach of the moral rules. Leaders everywhere tried to prevent sin. One method was to abolish get-togethers of young people – such as spinning bees. These occasions, despite their economic purpose, were rightly seen to facilitate pairing. Authorities now greatly feared that this pairing might be sexual and casual rather than abstinent and leading to wedlock. They interfered with traditional courtship as they simultaneously shut down the brothels that, if St Augustine had been correct, had saved many a respectable woman from being the target of men's lust. In many places, sin became criminalized and could bring fines, whippings, imprisonment or exile down upon its perpetrators. Even where it did not, the churches themselves imposed penalties of shaming, including public humiliation in the stocks or display in the manner of Hester Prynne in *The Scarlet Letter*, followed by Sabbath rituals of derogation, contrition and pardon. Punitive transactions by civil and church courts featuring the unhappy or contested marriage, implicitly provided the corollary – an image of decorous connubial behaviour – to the populace at large.

CHILDREN, THE 'FRUIT' OF MARRIAGE

If marriage and sexuality consumed most of Reformation leaders' attention as they tried to build the Christian family, children were not far behind. In the 1520s, as parish visitation got underway, Luther and his learned cohort in Wittenberg quickly realized that children would have to be the chief objects of their effort to convert the hearts and instruct the minds of most of the laity. Even after the two catechisms were available and pastors ordered to teach them, adults refused to attend special sessions. Instead, indoctrination had to be tailored to the youngsters of the parishes, including juvenile servants – although another device, the cate-chetical sermon, was directed to the entire congregation. Monetary penalties rose for neglecting to send all the children of the household to learn the basic precepts of the new creed. The reformers had perceived that the children were the hope for the future of evangelical Christianity. Children represented far more, then, than simply the next generation of the human species.

Childhood began in the birthing chamber, in the home. The reformers entered even here in the figurative sense that they imposed restrictions on what occurred there. Mothers and midwives could no longer invoke St Anne or St Margaret, those venerable patronesses of childbirth. They could not affix herbs to the bed or to the person of the parturient, or pronounce formulaic semi-magical blessings. Lutheran divines retained the Catholic emergency baptism out of their ongoing conviction that baptism was necessary to salvation, but they added the proviso that the infant had to be fully emerged from the birth canal before the sacrament could be administered. Baptism was, they said, the second birth; how could a child be born a second time if he had not been born a first? Calvin abolished emer-gency baptism on the premise that God had foreordained each soul's destination and this could not be affected by baptism. The threat of Anabaptism, however, rendered out of the question any serious consideration of postponing the rite. In Reformed parishes, baptism signalled the entry of the new-born into the Christian community on earth, the visible church.

Protestantism made of motherhood a holy work, women's calling from God. So persuaded was Luther of women's single vocation that he could advise in a way that seems cruel today,

> Think, dear Greta, that you are a woman and that this work of yours [giving birth] is pleasing to God. Console yourself happily by [thinking of] His will, and let Him do with you what is His right. Bring that child forth and do it with all your might! If you die in the process, so pass on over, good for you! For you actually die in a noble work and in obedience to God. Indeed, if you were not a woman, you should wish that you were for the sake of this work alone, so that in the course of this precious and godly task, you could suffer pain and die. For this is the Word of God, who has created you [and] implanted such pain in you. ... [9]

Women's role did not stop with giving birth. Luther saw that mothers bore the onus of raising their children as well. The ubiquitous late mediæval depictions of the Virgin Mary in loving interaction with her infant Son show us that this model of woman as mother was hardly new. Again, religious reformers merely pressed this ideal with new energy, unprecedentedly determined oversight and the support of a concurring state. They did this in an age that was persuaded of the malleability of children. Society's youngest members had to be carefully trained.

Philip Melanchthon's vision of nearly perfect mothering has come down to us in a seventeenth-century wedding sermon (for these sermons addressed proper parenting too):

> One time Philip Melanchthon went to Torgau, where the learned men were holding a synod. [On the way] he went past the house of a deacon, whose wife was sitting in the doorway. She had a nursing baby on her breast. Two others [little children] stood before her, for whom she prayed aloud the morning blessing. With her right hand, she cut bread to make into a pabulum or gruel for them. This pleased Herr Philip so much that he gazed for a long time. Afterward, when he reached the learned men, he praised this and told [them], 'I have just seen three holy deeds that a mother carried out at the same time. *O sanctos labores, & preces nubes coeli penetrantes!* O holy works! O powerful prayers that penetrate the clouds!'[10]

The three holy deeds that constituted prayer were that she nursed her own baby, which the Reformers favoured; that she taught the toddlers the morning blessing, instructing them in the rudiments of the faith; and that she prepared a meal for those who were already weaned. Her full-time occupation was caring for and educating her children.

Children were widely seen to be creatures of sin that required discipline whenever their bad proclivities showed themselves. In the Lutheran scheme, whereby before baptism infants were children of God's wrath, the sacramental washing did not preclude subsequent sin. For his part, Calvin more clearly anticipated upright behaviour as a fruit of God's election. Practical realities united both faiths in assigning to all parents the responsibility to watch their progeny closely so as to let no bad deed pass by. This was as true in Puritan New England as in Wittenberg. Parents everywhere accepted the adage that to spare the rod unduly meant to spoil the child. Yet in areas less acutely shaped by the Reformations, such as the southern colonies of North America, parental scrutiny might be more lax. Protestantism itself demanded a fresh commitment to the task of forming the Christian adult who would emerge at the end of years of rigorous conditioning. Some preachers regarded mothers as too inclined towards sympathy and over-indulgence. They urged fathers not to tolerate this softness but, at the least manifestation of the sinfulness inherited by all from the fallen Adam, to step in and deal sternly with their sons and daughters. Fatherhood meant caring, but that caring was to be shown in a strictness that, predestinarian theology aside, would ultimately help to save a child's soul. Love was not equated with petting and cozening but with unrelenting watchfulness and quick response. This was the theory. We may be sure that actual parents' interaction with their children varied widely.

The father's other official duty in the upbringing of his children and the guidance of his servants was, in presiding over devotions in the household 'church', to teach them right belief by means of the varied texts that conveyed it. The father was the 'abbot' in the tiny domestic monastery, seeing to the spiritual as well as the physical well-being of every inhabitant. The mother was sometimes described as his assistant, the 'prioress'. For certain purposes, not even Protestant divines could dispense with Catholic metaphors!

The Protestant encouragement of elementary education also had consequences for family life. We need to note that Luther could not have single-handedly provided the impetus to establish schools throughout Germany and beyond. In fact, at the time that he wrote his call to the magistrates of German cities to promote formal learning, literacy was already increasing in many parts of Europe in response to public demand. In the short term, the Reformation may even have curtailed learning, for it brought temporary chaos to many universities and parish inspectors attempted to eliminate the 'cranny' schools that were often led by literate women as well as men. In some territories, the visitors also discouraged vernacular learning for little boys, convinced, in this humanist heyday, that only classical letters were worth the trouble and tuition, and promised to make a greater pool of candidates available for clerical and bureaucratic posts. The populace everywhere preferred education in its mother tongue because it permitted ready application to practical problems. Or they rejected book learning in favour of using their offspring from a very tender age in the herding of animals and other labour.

Girls too, Luther said, ought to be taught to read and possibly write. The founding of girls' schools lagged far behind opportunities for boys on into the eighteenth century and beyond. There is some evidence that when basic tutelage became available in the hamlets of Saxony in the late sixteenth century, girls and boys took advantage of it in almost equal proportions. But in the cities, far more boys were educated. The substance of their learning was now very different because it was classically oriented and on a higher intellectual plane than that permitted to the girls. Girls were to learn to read simple vernacular prayers, hymns and Bible verses; and, if their parents could afford the extra tuition for writing, then they might be trained to write simple correspondence. This meant, in sum, that urban boys' and girls' mental worlds may have diverged, producing, eventually, husbands and wives with less in common than their counterparts in the countryside. In Calvin's Geneva it is not clear that a girls' school existed at all during the reformer's career there, or indeed until much later. Women there and elsewhere doubtless found ways to attain literacy, including scribal skills; but their achievement remained in general far below men's. Scotland and Sweden were apparently exceptions with their emphasis on reading the Bible and doctrinal mastery before admission to communion or, in the latter case, to matrimony. Otherwise, men's better education may have provided one more basis for the masculine predominance over women. The ideological content of girls' and boys' schooling was another means of inculcating upon the sexes, among other principles, the strict gender division sought by ecclesiastical leaders.

At the core of girls' education were those housewifely crafts that informed the feminine identity. The mother had the obligation to transmit these to her daughters. School curricula pointedly refer to their importance and sometimes include embroidery among the subjects to be taught. In the main, however, girls were to spend fewer hours in school than boys because of the need to be in the home receiving instruction in housekeeping from their mothers and being useful to them. Boys of the artisan class, on the other hand, were not compelled to learn practical skills from their fathers, for at the end of their grammar-school years, they might well enter an apprenticeship. Manuals on child-rearing are notably silent on the domestic responsibilities of boys.

The assertion that only in the early modern period parents developed affection for their children is generally rejected today. Mediævalists argue that there is ample evidence in the late Middle Ages of parents' concern for the physical, economic and social well-being of their offspring. These questions remain open and deserve further systematic treatment. An under-utilized source on attitudes towards children are the post-Reformation baptismal rites. Particularly in the southwest of Germany and in Protestant Switzerland, where communal identities were more pronounced than elsewhere, the reformers radically revised the old rubrics. They placed increased emphasis on the child's admission to the Christian community, a theme neglected in the late Middle Ages. Some of them began to employ language that made of the infant a treasure and divine gift. In the course of the later sixteenth and seventeenth centuries, such prayers and admonitions spread to other parts of Germany. The 1555 church ordinance of Kassel contains this prayer:

> Our faithful Father, grant the parents of these children, the godparents, and all of us who are gathered together, Your entire congregation, that in true faith we may receive this Your so gracious promise and work and take them up in right thankful spirit; that we may serve these children, who are supposed to be *Your* children and heirs, faithfully and enthusiastically [and] raise them in such a way that through them Your name is further hallowed. ... [11]

Beginning in the southwest, continuing in Geneva and, via the Genevan rubric, disseminated to all Reformed observances, fathers were required for the first time to attend their infants' baptisms. By itself this suggests an official vision of a bond between father and child. Mothers were, of course, confined and by convention could not leave their homes – not even in Geneva, where churching was abolished. Nevertheless, we see a growing persuasion that both mothers and fathers, as people of faith, conferred their good standing with God even upon their unfortunate babies who died before christening. After the Reformation, these came increasingly to be buried in the same cemeteries as other Christians and, in Lutheran lands, with full ceremonial. This, too, bespeaks an increased interest in the well-being of children, in the next life as well as this. That Catholic parents also cared is seen in mothers' taking the corpses of their deceased and unbaptized little ones to shrines where they could be 'brought back to life' long enough to receive sacramental initiation and be assured of entering heaven. Catholic theologians remained convinced that the unbaptized had to be consigned to peripheral and unconsecrated burial.

Even elite Protestant progenitors showed a growing concern for each and every one of their children, whether successors to their titles or not. Princely families brought disadvantage upon themselves rather than provide inadequately for any of their sons and daughters. In weighing this and all the other subtle indications of a qualitative shift in relations between parents and their children beginning in the sixteenth century, we might also ask whether the assertion concerning the rise of the individual in Renaissance Italy might have had geographically and socially broader applicability. Of course, the debate on the origins of Western individualism goes on, with mediævalists tending to see its foundations in, say, the establishment of auricular confession and the enumeration of sins in the thirteenth century; and early modernists dating its most visible evolution to the sixteenth through eighteenth centuries. The changing content of the liturgy as well as other evidence beg a reopening of the discussion on childhood in connection to individualism. Parents and spouses may have begun, if not necessarily to love more than before, to value the singularity of each member of their circle of intimates. Appreciating personality and not simply providing for the objective needs of a child or a marriage partner may have derived encouragement from the theologians' concentration upon every person's direct unique relationship with God the Father.

THE FATE OF SERVANTS AND THE WHOLE HOUSE

Parish visitation records, sermons and the prescriptive literature written for *patres-* and *matresfamilias* refer, as though in one breath, to 'children and servants'. They would make it seem as though the two did not constitute separate categories but were differentiated only by the technicality that some were the offspring of the master and mistress of the house while the others were not. Heads of households had the duty to feed and clothe both. They had to compel the attendance of both at worship services and catechism classes, and they were to supervise the maids' and menservants' deportment as closely as that of their own daughters and sons. Yet not all servants should be seen as having been members of the larger family, made up of all those dwelling together over the longer term.

Some servants were in fact day- or temporary labourers who were hired for the harvest season or some other specific task. Often these did not sleep on the premises of their employer but lived nearby. These hardly became members of the family in any convincing sense. Two other types, however, deserve closer consideration. Urban and rural domestic establishments of adequate means had servants who stayed for a number of years, even all their lives. They cannot have been children except in the beginning. Their dependence and lower station, plus their modest wages, kept them in a child-like status in the home regardless of how highly skilled in their masters' or mistresses' crafts they may have become; and some were indeed indispensable to the workshop. The conditions of their lives must have varied almost infinitely with the personalities and economic fluctuations in the household. Many families must have come to count these maids and menservants as virtual relatives, whether or not they were actually poorer kin.

Sometimes they were relatives, and hiring them was one link in the chain of reciprocity that bound the broader kinship.

A subset of this kind of servant were those who hired themselves out as children and remained until approximately their mid-twenties, when they had saved enough money to marry and found their own households. This is a most familiar pattern. Such servants could have begun service at around nine, which was regarded as a suitable age for going out to earn one's keep in this way, and ended at twenty-four or twenty-five, a sufficient time for them to become psychologically integrated into the family circle.

Finally, there were servants who worked for a year at a time. In sixteenth-century Saxony, such contracts spanned the year from New Year to New Year. Such temporary servants probably did not form close ties with their employers.

The phrase 'children and servants' refers, then, to the last two kinds of employees, to the extent that these were still youthful and malleable. If I am right about the greater concern that post-Reformation parents were developing for the individual formation of their immediate descendants, then a concomitant trend was the slow receding of servants as the focus of attention. They were still written of, and heads of households still had their Christian duties to fulfil towards them. But clerical opinion is more directed toward correcting maids' and menservants' misbehaviour – at making sure that they are honest, assiduous and chaste – than at seeing them to an honourable place in a godly universe. Books for fathers and mothers express concern that servants may learn family secrets, witness frays and convey this information to the public. They sometimes suggest that the physical punishment of male employees be left to fathers, but that mothers should similarly tend to fractious female servants. There is no talk of affection, nor worry that those in service may not be learning to read and write. Householders bore the expenses of formal education only for their own progeny. This was, we recall, a most hierarchical society. Servants stood or sat at the back of the church and their places of burial were among the least honourable in the cemetery. The receding of servants in psychological importance, though not in their presence, in the early modern period is one more change in the context of the family. Its effect was in yet another way to draw attention to the immediate or nuclear family, even though this type of family had been characteristic of European society for a long time.

We still know too little about the practice of wet-nursing in northern Europe. We have the image of Madame Bovary before us from the nineteenth century, but Emma Bovary was Catholic and also aspired to full membership in elite circles. Protestant preachers uniformly encourage mothers to nurse their own babies, but they do not harangue couples on this point and thus do not suggest that failing to breastfeed was common. Late mediæval clerical opinion, too, had favoured mothers' nourishing their own infants. The ubiquitous images of the Virgin with Jesus at her breast represent advocacy of this maternal activity, although they are much more as well. That such pictures all but disappeared with the Reformations, even in regions that retained some art, did not alter the official perspective on Christian motherhood. Lucas Cranach the Elder's frequent portrayals of Charity as a mother surrounded by tots and giving suck to a baby convey the same ideal but use a subject matter that was technically secular.

DID THE FAMILY HAVE A REFORMATION?

That change is inevitable is a platitude. We might conclude that the family would have been altered during the sixteenth and early seventeenth centuries in any case. After all, capitalism, with its need for specialized, low-wage, flexible labour, was gaining ground. This economic shift in combination with rapid demographic expansion and the growth of cities might well have helped to isolate the simple family from its more extended, folkish connections. The benefits that the state sought to gain by espousing the new economic system might underlie its determination to render docile every last subject. What role did religion need to play? Economic determinists could regard the credal campaigns of the Reformation and Counter Reformation as an ideological veneer glued upon a foundation made of statist and bourgeois self-interest.

I prefer to see this period as one in which religion, defined by performance rather than just theology, still lay at the heart of the predominant world-view. Society from top to bottom was concerned with knowing and fulfilling the divine will, and it feared the consequences for all of failing to do so. We should not dismiss the piety and idealism of the age. These strains emerged from within an established culture and resembled that matrix quite closely even as they departed from it in certain respects. In the eyes of its leaders, religious reform meant not just doctrinal rectification but also moral improvement. A return to scripture inevitably wrought the modification of late mediaeval ideas about, say, the sacraments; it also took note of the words of Jesus and His early followers on how one ought to live. These utterances touched on all aspects of life, not just on the family. The programmes of the Reformation and the Counter Reformation were encompassing. That Lutherans and Calvinists should have focused so much attention on the family was in keeping with their aims. The reformers implicitly recognized the family as the nexus between the public and private spheres. To concentrate on the occupants of the home was to strive to remake the personal as well as the collective. Public and private were not as compartmentalized as they are today. The idealists of the Reformation era instinctively addressed themselves to the domestic setting within which the two worlds came together as the best means of restoring the whole.

Initially optimistic that the power of the Word would effect the restoration of their imagined pristine early Christianity, they became discouraged as they found how deeply entrenched Satan was in the world. Acute social disciplining arose from their perception that the Devil could not be dealt with lightly but had to be hounded, along with his human cohorts, until he fled from human polity. Reformers used every means at their disposal to exorcize these demons even as they acknowledged that this could not finally happen until the end of the world. Yet in a practical sense, God – including the Calvinist God – allowed of no fatalism but required unceasing exertion in the interim. The family and its members were an eminently suitable target for thwarting the forces of darkness, for the pragmatic reality, in both Protestant and Catholic opinion, was that people consented to evil. No creed allowed miscreants to excuse themselves by casting blame at Lucifer and his minions.

The question remains of whether all the exertions of churches and states had a perceptible impact upon the dwelling and its inhabitants. It has been far easier to describe the agenda than its outcome. Can an enterprise shared to some degree by all the leading clerics and many statesmen of their day have completely missed its mark? Easiest to gain an impression of is people's gradual outward conformity in response to harsh penalties. Rates of bastardy declined in the seventeenth century, by which time the full weight of official disapproval could have been felt. There may have been a connection between suppressive measures and the rise of suicide rates. If social disciplining left its mark on behaviour, it may not have been without its destructive psychic cost. Whether attempts to restrain sexual expression also had psychological effects remains to be studied. One scholar has argued that the shift of authority over marriage from the local community to higher echelons of church and state drove a wedge between the neighbourhood and the married couple, who withdrew into their private domain and took solace in a more emotional bond with one another.[12]

We may speculate that the veritable campaign to order the family did succeed over the longer course in influencing opinion. Just as the visitation protocols reveal that by the second half of the sixteenth century, and certainly by its end, a majority of Christians conformed outwardly to the credal and participatory requirements of their governors, so we may assume that this cannot have been pure show, without any alteration of inner attitudes. The sermon was a medium imposed upon society at large, literate and illiterate alike. With the passing of generations, it must have had some effect. The well-off could read edifying books on family deportment, but it is unlikely that the poor majority did so. But these, too, were required to attend church. In the end, how greatly the resultant conformity or 'churchliness' corresponded to inner conviction is usually beyond our grasp. At least one Englishwoman of the mid-seventeenth century, Lucy Apsley Hutchinson, took her preachers' advice very seriously indeed. Lucy exerted herself to conform to the model wife depicted to her in 'Domestical' sermons that she had memorized.

> No 'pride and ambition' stiffened her against 'yeelding subjection' to her husband, against fashioning her 'minde and her will' to 'voluntary submission': happily, raptly even, she created John [her husband] king, priest, and prophet, to govern, pray with, teach, and instruct her.

John Hutchinson, her husband, likewise strove to be the spouse that God wished him to be.[13]

Later on, as a few women found their voices in writing about themselves, we hear of mothers who attempted to restrain their daughters' literary inclinations. Dorothea Friderika Baldinger's mother thought it was a mortal sin for her daughter to read anything other than the Bible and the hymnbook, and she sometimes closed Baldinger's books and nudged her towards the spinning wheel. Charlotte von Einem's mother had never had any book in her hands other than scripture, hymnal and sermons, and she reproached Charlotte's uncle for letting her daughter read storybooks.[14] Here for a moment attention must be directed towards the mothers instead of towards the ultimately distinguished daughters. The former had been shaped by Reformation and post-Reformation ideals of feminine decorum. Women were inscribed within the household, men within the world.

The Reformations, Protestant as well as Catholic, influenced the family but achieved their aims only gradually and in part. Their agenda was blunted in the encounter with families' very worldly, concrete desiderata. As the interests of states and churches diverged during the eighteenth century, the long-lingering aspirations of organized religion to oversee domestic life met with growing frustration. Without the enforcing might of secular authority, preachers could chiefly hold forth from the pulpit and hope to inspire some of their hearers. What one did at home, as long as it was not obtrusive, was increasingly one's own business.

NOTES

1 Steven Ozment, *Magdalena and Balthazar: An Intimate Portrait of Life in Sixteenth-Century Europe* (New York, 1986).
2 Hartmann Creide, *Nuptialia Continuata Oder Chrsitliche Hochzeit Sermonen, Ander Theyl sive Debitum Coniugale, Dat ist, Schuldige Pflicht der Eheleut* (Frankfurt, Johann Beyers Erbe, 1670), Sermon 28, p. 294.
3 Quoted by Margaret R. Sommerville, *Sex and Subjection: Attitudes to Women in Early Modern Society* (London, 1995), p. 94.
4 Quotation from *The New English Bible*.
5 Justus Menius, *Oeconomia Christiana* (Wittenberg, 1529).
6 London, 1622. The content of the leading English tracts paralleled almost precisely the ideas that prevailed on the Continent. See Patricia Crawford, *Women and Religion in English, 1500–1720* (London, 1993), esp. chap. 2, 'The Social Teachings of the Protestant Church: Women, Marriage and the Family'.
7 *Hollstein's German Engravings* (Roosendaal, 1994), vol. 39, p. 66, plate 349.
8 Max Geisberg, *The German Single-Leaf Woodcut, 1500–1550* (New York, 1974), vol. 3, G. 1182, p. 1129.
9 'Vom ehelichen Leben. 1522', *D. Martin Luthers Werke: Kritische Gesamtausgabe* (Weimar, 1883–1997), vol. 10, Part 2, p. 296. Cf. Merry E. Weisner, *Women and Gender in Early Modern Europe* (Cambridge, 1993), p. 9.
10 Hartman Creide, *Nuptilia Oder Fünffzig Christliche Hochzeit-Sermonen. Vber unterschiedliche Biblische Sprüch gehalten in der Evangelischen Pfarr-Kirchen bey St Anna in Augspurg* (Frankfurt, Johann Beyer, 1661), p. 15.
11 Emil Sehling, *Die evangelischen Kirchenordnungen des sechzehnten Jahrhunderts* (15 vols; Leipzig, 1902–13), vol. 7, part 2, p. 276. My emphasis added.
12 André Burguière, 'The Formation of the Couple', *Journal of Family History* 12 (1987), pp. 39–53, esp. pp. 44–5.
13 Described by Margaret George, *Women in the First Capitalist Society: Experiences in Seventeen-Century England* (Hassocks, 1988), pp. 20–1.
14 Magdalene Heuser, Ortrun Niethammer, Marion Roitzheim-Eisfeld and Petra Wulbusch (eds), *'Ich wünschte so gar gelehrt zu werden': Drei autobiographien von Frauen des 18. Jahrhunderts* (Göttingen, 1994), pp. 18–22, 46.

FURTHER READING

The majority of works treat the family during all or part of the early modern period without lengthy attention to the Reformations or the influence of religion. Of those that do take the Reformation into account, the following are a place to start. On England, see Patricia Crawford, *Women and Religion in England, 1500–1720* (London, 1993); Ralph Holbrooke, *The English Family, 1450–1700* (London, 1984); Martin Ingram, *Church Courts, Sex and Marriage in England, 1570–1640* (Cambridge, 1987); Alan Macfarlane, *Marriage and Love in England: Modes of Reproduction, 1300–1840* (Oxford, 1986); Lawrence Stone, *The Family, Sex and Marriage in England, 1500–1800* (New York, 1977).

On Geneva, which sets standards for Calvinism everywhere, see Robert M. Kingdon, *Adultery and Divorce in Calvin's Geneva* (Cambridge, MA, 1995), and William G. Naphy, 'Baptism, Church Riots and Social Unrest in Calvin's Geneva', *Sixteenth Century Journal* 26 (1995), pp. 87–97. On Calvinist (and non-Calvinist) child-rearing in North America, see Philip Greven, *The Protestant Temperament: Patterns of Child-Rearing, Religious Experience and the Self in Early America* (New York, 1977). On Calvinism in these and other regions, all the essays in Raymond A. Mentzer (ed.), *Sin and the Calvinists: Morals, Control and the Consistory in the Reformed Tradition* (Kirksville, 1994), are of high standard. On Calvinist Scotland, see Michael F. Graham, *The Uses of Reform: Godly Discipline and Popular Behaviour in Scotland and Beyond, 1560–1610* (Leiden, 1996).

On Germany and German-speaking Switzerland, see Joel F. Harrington, *Reordering Marriage and Society in Reformation Germany* (Cambridge, 1995); Lyndal Roper, *The Holy Household: Women and Morals in Reformation Augsburg* (Oxford, 1989); Thomas Max Safley, *Let No Man Put Asunder: The Control of Marriage in the German Southwest, a Comparative Study, 1550–1600* (Kirksville, 1984). Recently translated is Heide Wunder, *'He is the Sun, she is the Moon': Women in Early Modern Germany* (Cambridge, MA, 1998).

Of relevance to Protestant as well as Catholic Europe is Jean-Louis Flandrin's *Families in Former Times: Kinship, Household and Sexuality* (Cambridge, 1979).

ART

Andrew Pettegree

LUTHER AND THE ARTS

Luther was not personally hostile to the arts. Although prone to vulgarity in conversation and polemical writings, Luther was a man of highly developed artistic sensibility, as his original contribution to German hymnody would make clear. Added to which Luther was of a largely conservative and traditional disposition, entirely comfortable with large parts of the tradition of the Catholic church in which he had been raised and prospered. As he made clear on numerous occasions later in his life, Luther would have no sympathy for calls for root-and-branch reform which involved the destruction of much of what he cherished in the fabric of the old church.

Nevertheless, for Luther the question of religious imagery and representational art was fundamentally a theological rather than an aesthetic one. It was also an issue on which, as with many others, he moved in a steadily more conservative direction through his lifetime. His earlier utterances were somewhat sceptical of the value of religious images. In so far as they became an object of worship or evidence of works theology, devotional pictures and images might have been said to have been broadly encompassed in his critical utterances at the time of the indulgences controversy. In a sermon contemporary to the controversy, Luther urged that only after he had cared for the poor should the Christian expend his money on beautification of the churches.

However it was a long step from a pious admonition of this nature to arguing in favour of the removal of existing religious art. The turning point for Luther came with his forced intervention to quell the troubles which had arisen in Wittenberg in his absence in the winter of 1521, when, encouraged by Luther's more radical colleague Andreas Karlstadt, religious images in the parish church had twice been attacked. At this point Luther's innate conservatism asserted itself. The donation of works of art to churches could be an example of the works righteousness of which he disapproved, but abuse of images was not sufficient reason to remove them. Furthermore, as the evangelical movement moved from criticism of the Roman church to the building of a reformed church community, Luther came to have a much clearer appreciation of the pedagogic value of tangible things. He actively encouraged the inclusion of illustration in evangelical works and played a notable part, as we shall see, in the development of new Protestant iconographic traditions.

Luther's sympathetic perspective created a large space in the new Lutheran tradition for the visual arts. It helped, no doubt, that the new movement burst out at a period of extraordinary vitality in the artistic development of Germany. At a time when Dürer, Grünewald and the elder Holbein were taking painting into new heights of sensibility and technical accomplishment, Germany's sculptors and woodcarvers were producing artifacts of unprecedented beauty and sophistication.[1] In the battle for hearts and minds it would have been an act of extreme folly for Protestants to turn their backs on a tradition of such richness.

Nevertheless, as the sincere and heartfelt criticisms of images by Karlstadt and Thomas Müntzer were to show, there was scope for more than one view of the impact of the arts on the minds of the credulous populace. These critical voices were echoed by other influential figures outside Germany, notably the leaders of the principal non-German strand of the Reformation movement, Zwingli and Calvin. In the longer term, in its warm embrace of Reformation art, Lutheran Germany proved to be rather the exception within the Protestant tradition. Protestant artists throughout Europe therefore found themselves working in a variety of different environments and were forced to adapt their output to fit a wide variety of local conditions. Nothing illustrates this better than the contrasting careers of the three great painters of the Reformation: Dürer, Cranach and Holbein.

ALBRECHT DÜRER AND NUREMBERG

In some respects it is difficult to claim Dürer as a Reformation painter. On the one hand, of the three leading figures of German Protestant art, Dürer, Cranach and Holbein, it was Dürer who left the clearest evidence of personal commitment to the new faith; a conversion experience as complete, and almost as dramatic, as that of Luther himself. On the other hand, the Reformation movement occurred so late in Dürer's career that the proportion on his oeuvre which bore evidence of his new religious beliefs was comparatively slight. Had Dürer lived to the venerable age of Lucas Cranach, perhaps things might have been different. But his death in 1528 deprived the movement of its most distinguished and potentially innovative artistic supporter. Ultimately it would fall to others to find visual formulas to express the movement's new theological preoccupations.

It is arguable that in any case Dürer had given too much of his creative genius to the reinterpretation of an older artistic tradition to demand of him a further fundamental reorientation at this stage of his career. In artistic terms Dürer's work was already revolutionary and was widely recognized as such by contemporaries, who credited Dürer with bringing to German art the sophistication and poise of new technical discoveries of the Italian Renaissance. Dürer was widely acknowledged as the leading genius of German art, pampered and flattered by the powerful as Europe's leading patrons of art vied for his services. It says much for the peculiar charm of the emperor, Maximillian I, that despite his famously empty pockets he successfully commanded a disproportionate amount of Dürer's time and creative energies. But his successor, Charles V, was also a patron, as were the leading protagonists in the Luther controversies, Frederick the Wise and Albrecht of Brandenburg (Figures 9.1, p. 154, and 25.1). Dürer's work had a universal appeal which easily crossed the emerging confessional boundaries.

Albrecht Dürer was born in 1471, the son of a Nuremberg goldsmith. This was a fortunate heritage; Nuremberg, the largest city in the empire, was then at the height of its mediæval prosperity and the young Albrecht could have anticipated a prosperous career in his father's trade. Early evidence of the boy's precocious talent, however, dictated a change of direction and by 1494 Dürer had opened his new independent workshop as a painter and graphic artist. In the following years Dürer interspersed periods of intense creative activity with study trips to Switzerland and Italy, and it was the latter, inevitably, which had the greatest influence on his artistic style.

This was evident above all in his graphic art. Dürer was one of the first to comprehend the full possibilities of these relatively new artistic media, which in turn spread knowledge of his work far beyond the Nuremberg patriciate who were the major patrons of his portraits and religious painting. His two great woodcut series, the so-called 'Large' Passion and Life of Maria, were among the greatest artistic achievements of the opening years of the sixteenth century (see Figure 25.2).

Graphic art also brought Dürer considerable wealth and in his middle years the other educated members of the Nuremberg elite were proud to count him as a friend. It was in these circles, possibly through membership of the humanist *Soliditas*, that Dürer would have first heard of Luther. Dürer was profoundly affected by the new evangelical teachings. A letter of 1520 to the Wittenberg Chancellor George Spalatin expresses an unqualified admiration for Luther, who, he claimed, had helped him out of great spiritual anxiety. When, on a trip to the Netherlands in 1521, he heard rumour of Luther's incarceration and imminent death, his outpouring of anger and despair was heartfelt: 'Oh God, if Luther is dead, who will ever expound the gospel to us with such clarity?'[2]

Dürer was therefore a firm adherent of the evangelical party when in 1525 the Nuremberg city council formally adopted the Reformation. But he also very much approved the measured and restrained nature of this Reformation; he had little sympathy for the religious radicalism of those who sought to overturn the established political order – a radicalism which also often had such potentially serious consequences for the arts. These sentiments found considered expression in the last great work of his life, the pictures of the four apostles presented to the Nuremberg city council in October 1526 (Munich, Alte Pinakotek). The accompanying citations were taken from Luther's September Testament.

The innovative employment of text to enhance pedagogic impact became, indeed, a distinctive feature of Lutheran and other Protestant art over the whole Reformation century. This effectively reversed a trend evident in the High Renaissance, where the pursuit of realism and naturalistic style had seen the virtual elimination of the fragments of inscription often met with in early Renaissance painting. Protestant artists adopted a number of often rather awkward

ALBERTVS·MI·DI·SA·SANC·
ROMANAE·ECCLAE·TI·SAN·
CHRYSOGONI·PBR·CARDIN
MAGVN·AC·MAGDE·ARCH·
EPS·ELECTOR·IMPE·PRIMAS
ADMINI·HALBER·MARCHI·
BRANDENBVRGENSIS

SIC·OCVLOS·SIC·ILLE·GENAS·SIC·
ORA·FEREBAT
ANNO·ETATIS·SVE·XXIX
·M·D·XIX·

Figure 25.1 Albrecht Dürer, two portraits of a Renaissance prince: Albrecht of Brandenburg, 1519 and 1523. Is it possible to discern the shift of Dürer's own loyalties in the

contrast between the sensitive and sympathetic earlier portrait, and the proud prelate of the later version? (Wittenberg, Lutherhalle)

465

Figure 25.2 Albrecht Dürer, *Resurrection* from the 'Large' Passion, 1510; Lucas Cranach,

Resurrection, 1509. (Oxford, Ashmolean Museum)

strategies for the integration of text, ranging from verses painted (or sometimes printed on paper and then glued) at the bottom of a picture to the painting of text inscriptions into the composition itself.[3] The genre reached an early apogee in two new altarpieces commissioned by Duke Ulrich of Württemberg, one of which consists of 160 separate pictures, each with its painted inscription: in the ensemble it resembles nothing so much as a primitive strip cartoon.[4]

The choice of texts, however, was seldom other than carefully considered. In the case of Dürer's apostles the texts were those which warned against false prophets and sects.[5] The authorities were encouraged above all to uphold the established political order. 'All worldly powers should take good care that in these dangerous times they do not mistake human and erroneous teaching for God's Word.' The advice was timely, for the Nuremberg city fathers had recently had to take action to avert a challenge to their authority from supporters of a more radical Reformation. Among those disciplined were two prominent members of Nuremberg's artistic community: the brothers Sebald and Bartel Beham.

It is true to say that because Dürer was very comfortable with the policies of the Nuremberg elite his personal conversion to a measured support for the German evangelical movement required no great sacrifice. It was apparently otherwise for his two Nuremberg contemporaries (and possibly students), the brothers Beham. The Behams represented a different level of the Nuremberg art market: talented, but essentially artisan woodcut artists, who produced a variety of visual material for the established Nuremberg printers, illustrations for books, or increasingly, single-leaf broadsheets. Their careers remind us that, even in the medium of woodcut and engraving, there was a clear hierarchy of value and achievement. Contemporaries recognized a world of difference between the elegant print series of a Dürer, which might appropriately be offered as gifts to a prince or bishop,[6] and the journeyman work hawked on the streets and from booksellers' stalls: in Dürer's (descriptive rather than disparaging) phrase, *schlectes Holzwerk*.

What is clear is that Nuremberg was one of the principal centres of woodcut production in the early sixteenth century. Like printing itself, the art of woodcut manufacture had become emancipated from its monastic origins in the late fifteenth century. The capabilities of Nuremberg artists in the new medium were dramatically demonstrated with the publication in 1493 of Hartmann Schedel's *Liber Chronicarum* (the Nuremberg Chronicle), with its series of magnificent city views which provide the defining image of the sixteenth-century skyline (see Figure 25.3).

It was a matter of course that this new technical capacity was also at the disposal of the new religious movement. Among its principal exponents were the two brothers Beham. Born in 1500 and 1502, Bartel and Sebald were responsible for some of the most memorable of the single-sheet broadsheets denouncing the Roman church that appeared, often with accompanying text, on the Nuremberg market in the period 1521–5. These cheap mass-produced broadsheets also built on a pre-Reformation tradition, for printers already understood how to turn a quick penny through instant publications describing new and monstrous births, the passing of comets or the execution of a notorious criminal. Now the Catholic church hierarchy became the new target.

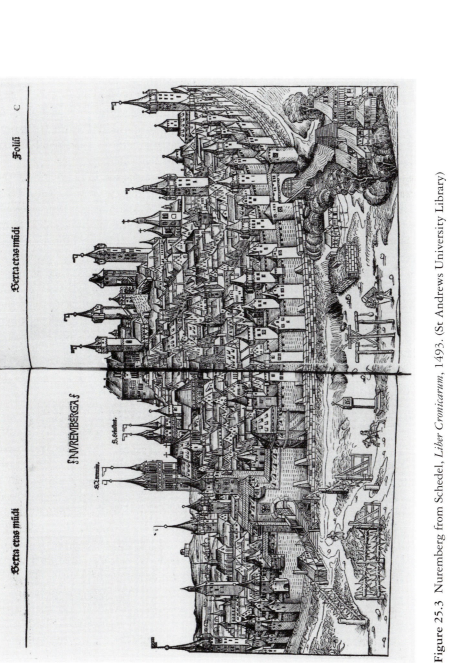

Figure 25.3 Nuremberg from Schedel, *Liber Cronicarum*, 1493. (St Andrews University Library)

The brothers Beham, already familiar to Nuremberg's printers for their illustrations of peasant weddings and soldiers in uniform, excelled in the new medium (see Figure 30.2, p. 553). In 1525, when the city council took action against signs of a worrying upsurge in religious radicalism, the Behams were arrested and interrogated. After giving answers which seemed to deny any belief in a divine being, they were both expelled from the city. On balance they were likely to have been followers of the spiritualist Hans Denck – also expelled from the city at this time – than atheists or revolutionaries. Nevertheless one would hesitate to see the brothers as martyrs for their religious convictions. The expulsion from Nuremberg was short-lived, less than a year, although both men soon moved on from Nuremberg permanently. For the remainder of their careers they found work predominantly with Catholic employers, in the case of Bartel the arch-conservative Dukes of Bavaria. Among Sebald's subsequent employers were Cardinal Albrecht of Brandenburg, a figure intimately associated with many of the church abuses that the Nuremberg artists had satirized so mercilessly.

The careers of the brothers Beham should warn against too modern an expectation that one should find in the work of a sixteenth-century artist a clear view of their artistic aesthetic or personal convictions. A Dürer, or to some extent a Cranach, might command or perhaps influence the market; but in the world of the more humble print artist, woodcuts were no more than, in Keith Moxey's phrase, 'components in the mechanised production of cultural commodities'. A recognition of their significance, or in many cases, their beauty, need not imply 'a romantic myth of the artists as autonomous creators who stamped their art with their personal beliefs, regardless of the political and social circumstances in which they operated.'[7] The best of them were successful because they recognized in the seismic changes in belief and religious behaviour at the beginning of the sixteenth century new market opportunities. None epitomize this trend better than the court artist of Wittenberg itself, Lucas Cranach.

LUCAS CRANACH: REFORMATION ART IN MASS PRODUCTION

Like Albrecht Dürer, Lucas Cranach had enjoyed a long and successful career before the Reformation. Born in 1572 in Kronach in Thuringia, Cranach migrated south to Vienna and the paintings of his early career clearly betray the influence of the flourishing Danube school, of which he became a leading exponent. Many art historians regard the work of these early years, as Cranach built his reputation, as the best of his long career. In 1505 Cranach moved to Wittenberg, to take up a position as court artist to the elector, Frederick the Wise, whose artist patronage had to this point extended to most of the leading painters of Germany. In Wittenberg, as opposed to the larger, more cosmopolitan centres of the southern empire, Cranach totally dominated the local artistic scene, a circumstance he clearly relished. In Wittenberg he turned out a whole series of distinguished and utterly conventional Catholic devotional pictures for his devout and conservative patron (see Figure 25.4). His expanding workshop also mastered the art of the woodcut print, and indeed brought the graphic arts to a level equal to that of the

Figure 25.4 Lucas Cranach, *Saints adoring the Sacred Heart of Jesus*, 1505. A typical example of Cranach's pre-Reformation woodcut art. (Oxford, Ashmolean Museum)

established Nuremberg masters. From these years date two print series, a Passion and the martyrdoms of the Twelve Apostles, that were as striking and dramatically successful as Dürer's familiar images (see Figure 25.2). Cranach also provided the illustrations for the richly decorated printed catalogue of Frederick's enormous collection of relics, the *Wittenberg Heiligsbuch* (1509). Cranach was well rewarded for his service. Already an astute businessmen, in 1520 he was awarded the Wittenberg monopoly of trade in spice, sugar and medicines for his apothecary business and it was this, as much as his artist's workshop, which laid the basis of his phenomenal prosperity.

Nevertheless there is no reason to doubt that Cranach was also powerfully and genuinely affected by the teaching of Martin Luther. Cranach became one of the most powerful and committed of Luther's local allies and his artist's workshop was soon at the disposal of the new movement. In 1520 Cranach issued a woodcut likeness of Luther as the young visionary monk, which became a powerful icon of the new movement. It was the beginning of a remarkable series of portraits emanating from Cranach's shop which chart both the career of the reformer and the growth of his movement. In 1521, when Luther returned briefly to Wittenberg against Frederick's instructions to quell the growing unrest in the city, it was in Cranach's house that he found refuge. It is from this period that dates Cranach's famous picture of Luther in his disguise as Jünker Jörg. Later images show the reformer in the years of his prosperity, along with images of his wife Katharina von Bora, parents and other close associates, such as Melanchthon and Bugenhagen. In 1546 it was Cranach's melancholy task to travel to Eisenach to make a last sketch of his old friend after Luther had passed away.

These pictures were more than a personal tribute to a long and enduring friendship. Such pictorial art also had a political and polemical purpose, to show the reformer as man of God and, later, as statesman of the church, in counterbalance to the hostile propaganda of his adversaries. With this in view Luther's image became one of the most widely disseminated of its time, as the best-known portraits of his mature years (particularly those of 1528 and 1533) were circulated in tens and perhaps even hundreds of copies. Cranach's workshop became a centre of an unprecedented, almost industrial production of such images, for which the precedent had been given by Frederick the Wise's conscious circulation of his own features, a tradition continued by his brother and successor John the Steadfast.[8]

Cranach's workshop also played its part in the new pictorial art of the Reformation. Cranach took a close interest in the business opportunities offered by the extraordinary demand for Luther's writings and the new translations of the Bible, and his workshop, with its established expertise in graphic art, was an important resource for Wittenberg's printers. Cranach's elegant title-page borders appear on literally hundreds of the editions which issued from Wittenberg's presses in these years, and played a large part in making possible Wittenberg's rise from a provincial backwater to one of the largest printing centres in Germany (see Chapter 7). Most influential of all were his dramatic illustrations for the Apocalyse in Luther's New Testament translation of 1522: an unacknowledged but no doubt profound homage to the influence of Cranach's great contemporary, Dürer. Cranach's workshop also played its part in the original polemical literature of the

Figure 25.5 The fruits of success. Lucas Cranach's superb Renaissance house, on the main square in Wittenberg, was tangible proof that the Reformation need not spell disaster for the enterprising artistic entrepreneur. (Wittenberg, Lucas-Cranach-Stiftung)

Reformation, not least with his design of twenty-six original illustrations for the influential and widely imitated *Passional Christi und Antichristi*. Issued with short pungent texts provided by Philip Melanchthon, Cranach's designs consisted of matching pairs which portrayed Christ's service to the poor contrasted with the lordly pomp of the pope (see Figure 25.6). Brilliant both in the simplicity of its construction and the clarity of its execution, the *Passional* became one of the greatest polemical creations of the Reformation.

There is little doubt that Cranach was a sincere supporter of Luther's movement. His devotion to Luther was heartfelt and lifelong; Cranach was one of those who supported Luther at his controversial wedding in 1525 and the two men were mutually godfathers of each others' children. Recently it has been questioned whether this personal fidelity amounts to a equal commitment to Protestantism. Cranach certainly did not regard a certain ruthlessness in his business dealings as inconsistent with personal piety, and one could argue that sound business sense would in any case have dictated his adherence to the Wittenberg movement. When occasion arose, Cranach was certainly not averse to accepting commissions

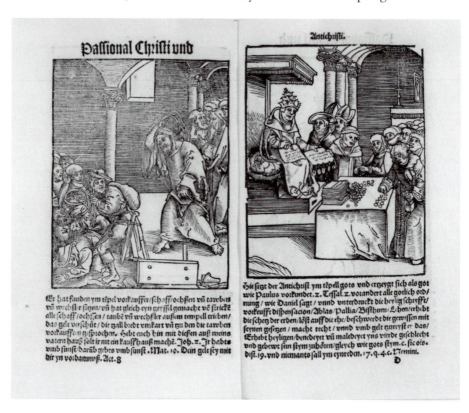

Figure 25.6 Lucas Cranach, *Passional Christi und Antichristi*, 1521. In one of thirteen paired illustrations Christ drives the money-changers from the Temple, while the pope sells indulgences. This is a fine example of close cooperation between the artists and the Reformers. In this case the text was provided by Philip Melanchthon while Luther assisted in the design. (Wittenberg, Lutherhalle)

from Catholic patrons, a circumstance which continued long after his own personal adherence to the Reformation.[9]

A picture of Cranach as a cynical opportunist would, however, be overdrawn. Whatever Cranach's personal convictions, contemporaries would have seen it as a matter of course that he continue to work for Catholic patrons. This indeed would have been the expectation of his employers, the electors, for whom diplomatic considerations demanded continued good relations with neighbouring princes and powerful magnates such as Albrecht of Brandenburg. The fact that until 1539 Ducal Saxony remained Catholic introduced another complication. Cranach and other local Wittenberg businessmen could not have functioned if denied access to the principal local market-centre at Leipzig, and this lay in the territory of Ducal Saxony. So Cranach made frequent journeys to the Leipzig fairs and retained close connections both with the ducal house and the local citizens who provided another market for his portraits and pictures.[10] Cranach's personal convictions are most eloquently expressed in his decision, at the advanced age of seventy-five, to join his master the elector in voluntary captivity after the Protestant defeat at Mühlberg. He died in the elector's new capital at Weimar six years later, without having returned to Wittenberg.

However this may be, Cranach's personal beliefs are in one respect irrelevant, for the fact remains that, through his established position in Wittenberg and close working relationship with the reformers, he was able to give the Reformation some of its most enduring and memorable images. To the extent that the Reformation found an authentic and original visual language for its new theological concerns, the debt to Cranach's Wittenberg workshop was profound. To some extent this was no more than a greater concentration on certain biblical themes – such as Christ and the Woman taken in Adultery, Christ the Good Shepherd – to replace the now redundant cults of the Virgin and saints. But Cranach also contributed at least one highly influential original design in his depiction of judgement and salvation known often as *Gesetz und Gnade* ('The Law and the Gospel'). This complicated image, which juxtaposes scenes from the Old Testament with the message of salvation and resurrection in the New, seems first to have been developed around 1526, possibly in collaboration with Melanchthon or Luther himself.[11] It appears in its fully developed form in two oil paintings of 1529–30 and a contemporary woodcut. The theme makes full use of the Protestant love of antithesis, here balancing the two contrasting faces of the Old and New Law round the central pivot of the Cross or Tree of Life. The theme had an extremely long life in Protestant iconography, not least since Cranach also provided an extremely influential reworking of the design for use as the title-page of a book. It was in this form that it became most familiar as the title-page of Bibles in German, Dutch and English (see Figure 25.7).

The lessons of the new Protestant theology were inevitably also applied to the focal point of Catholic artistic expression, the altar. Cranach had been an established master of the pre-Reformation altar and it says much for the endurance of his creative powers that he was able to contribute so successfully to a fundamental redesign of the altar in a Protestant form. His two most successful works in this form both date from the end of his career: the new altar for the Wittenberg parish

Figure 25.7 The Law and the Gospel: Cranach's famous exposition of Reformation doctrine recast as a book title-page. From Martin Luther, *Die Propheten alle Deutsch*, 1543. (Wittenberg, Lutherhalle)

church (1547) and the Weimar altar of 1555.[12] The Wittenberg altar built around a central depiction of the Last Supper (representing the eucharist) a didactic essay on the Protestant ministry, with the two wings and the predella representing respectively baptism and preaching, and the power of the keys. For the central panel Cranach amused himself by giving the disciples around the table with Christ features of Wittenberg contemporaries: Luther appears in familiar guise as Jünker Jörg. The Weimar altar, in contrast, was a celebration of the patronage for the Reformation of the Saxon ruling house. Here portraits of the Ernestine ducal house flank a central depiction of the crucifixion, representing the core Protestant doctrine of justification by faith. The blood spurting from the wound in Jesus's side alights on an open Bible, held by Martin Luther.

In these two great late commissions Cranach would have had the assistance of his son, Lucas Cranach the Younger, an established master and gifted painter in his own right. Born in 1515, Cranach the Younger was increasingly occupied with managing the business of his workshop, and with his father's departure from Wittenberg in 1547 the enterprise passed naturally into his hands. The younger Cranach continued to work in the traditions established by his father, producing a number of distinguished woodcut images of the now deceased Luther and Melanchthon, and several notable satirical prints on the old church.

Perhaps the most distinctive aspect of the younger Cranach's work was his development of the peculiarly Lutheran form of the epitaph picture. Hung in the church above the place of burial, these pictures included beneath the main picture a representation in miniature of the deceased and their family. The tradition seems once again to have been pioneered by the elder Cranach, who devised this scheme for moving the donor portraits from the side panels of a traditional Catholic altar into the main picture (see Figure 25.8). The epitaph picture allowed the continuing development of a number of typically Protestant themes, such as the baptism of Christ and the Vineyard of the Lord, as depicted in Cranach the Younger's epitaphs for Luther's loyal collaborators Johannes Bugenhagen and Paul Eber (both Wittenberg, Stadtkirche).

When one considers that this period also saw considerable innovation in the fields of church architecture and internal church decoration, one can see the later Lutheran tradition represented something of a golden age for sacred art. Once again the elder Cranach had shown the way, devoting a great deal of his personal energies to the new chapel in the electoral castle at Torgau, which for the first time reorganized sacred space around the central point of the pulpit (see Chapter 27). The creative energies of Lutheran arts were now lavished on providing a preaching space worthy of the calling, a tradition continued with the beautiful wooden pulpits of the northern Lutheran lands of Scandinavia.

NEW HORIZONS: HANS HOLBEIN IN ENGLAND

Hans Holbein was unique among the Reformation artists treated in this chapter in that he built a highly successful career in two centres: first in the established international metropolis of Basle; later in the comparatively virgin territory, in contemporary artistic terms, of England. Ironically the turning point in his life

Figure 25.8 Lucas Cranach the Younger, epitaph picture for the Ehepaar von Drachstedt. (Wittenberg, Stadtkirche)

came when he decided to abandon Basle as a result of the worsening climate for the graphic arts brought about by the onset of the Reformation; in this respect Holbein is a rather ambiguous hero of Reformation art. But Holbein's new orientation of his art in the fresh environment of Henry VIII's England was of the utmost consequence, for it was here, as painter to the Henrician court, that he brought the portrait art of the northern Renaissance to a new height. In this respect his career is an early and striking example of the cultural exchange brought about by the extraordinary movement of peoples caused by the religious upheavals of the sixteenth century.

Nevertheless there is a certain irony in celebrating Holbein as a great Protestant painter. Holbein's career was closely interwoven with the events of the Reformation. He was patronized by some of its leading figures and produced some fine examples of the new Protestant art. But personally he viewed Protestantism with some distaste, not least for its adverse effect on the artistic traditions in which he had been brought up.

Hans Holbein came from a family of artists. His father, Hans Holbein the Elder, was an accomplished painter of religious paintings who had made a distinguished career in the German city of Augsburg. His altarpiece for the city's Moritzkirche was one of the most important paintings recently commissioned by the city fathers. Holbein's two sons, Hans (b.1498) and Ambrosius (also a talented painter, though he would die tragically young), would have received their early training in their father's workshop, before the two boys moved together from Augsburg to Basle in 1514. For young men eager to make their way in the world, this was a shrewd choice. In the early decades of the sixteenth century Basle was one of the greatest cities of Europe, and certainly one of its most cultivated and cultured. Strategically placed on the crossroads of Europe's major trade routes, the city and its university were already famous through their association with Erasmus and the other leaders of the new intellectual movement of humanism.

Most importantly, Basle was also one of Europe's leading centres of book production and it is quite possibly this which attracted the young artists to the city. As we have seen, the new science of book publishing offered rich opportunities for the graphic arts, but it was only the richest and best established publishing houses which had the capital to embark on prestige projects which required elaborate illustrated title-pages, borders and text illustrations. In Basle, Holbein quickly made his name as one of the finest exponents of the new arts of the design of woodcuts and engravings. Among his work during this period was a superb series of illustrations for Bibles and Old Testaments published in 1522, 1524 and 1526, the years when the awakening interest in the new evangelical teachings of Martin Luther produced an almost insatiable demand for vernacular scripture. At this point, Holbein's designs had no particular confessional slant: he also provided the designs for illustrations of conventional devotional literature. But Holbein also used these years to cultivate contacts among Basle's ruling elite, particularly the humanism milieu which would provide some of the most outspoken exponents of religious change. His first portraits were of members of this artistic and civic elite, pictures which testify both to his growing skill as a portrait painter and to his established position in the city's artistic hierarchy.

In 1526 this prosperous and precociously successful career was rudely disturbed by contemporary political events. By this time the shockwaves unleashed by Luther's criticisms of the church hierarchy were making their effects known all over the German-speaking world, and even as cultivated a metropolis as Basle was not immune from its impact. As the Reformation movement gathered pace in Basle, Holbein decided the time had come to try his fortunes elsewhere. His passport to new opportunities was provided by his friends in Basle's humanist elite and Holbein left Basle with letters of recommendation to friends in Antwerp and England from no less a figure than Desiderius Erasmus. 'The arts are freezing here', wrote Erasmus to Pieter Gilles, in Antwerp; so 'he is on his way to England to pick up some angels [gold coins]'. Once again Holbein had chosen well. In England, Holbein was immediately assured of the patronage and friendship of Thomas More, Erasmus's familiar friend, who was at this point at the height of his powers and influence. It was More who provided Holbein with the crucial introductions to the king that enabled Holbein to be taken on as one of the king's salaried court painters.

Initially, Holbein's work as Henry's court painter was far from glamorous. The king had employed him largely to work on the new decorative schemes with which Henry was adorning his many newly constructed palaces (see Figure 25.9). But proximity to the great, in however humble a capacity, was what counted in sixteenth-century society, and it took little time for Holbein's exceptional gifts as a portrait painter to be widely known around the court. Soon he was once again in demand.

At this point in the sixteenth century, the native English artistic tradition lagged far behind the Continent. The artistic lessons of the Renaissance were yet to leave their mark on the few native painters who attempted the new art of portraiture and the English court elite eyed the portraits produced at the more sophisticated Continental courts with frank envy. It soon became obvious that even among these immigrant artists, Holbein was an exceptional talent. The painter soon established an extended clientele among the statesmen, courtiers and adventurers who flocked to Henry's court. His uncanny ability to capture the personality of an individual sitter makes his portraits some of the most lifelike and believable images of the sixteenth century. At Henry's court he was in a class of his own.

This was, of course, a talent which had to be used with discretion. Henry's court was a brutal place, where the struggle for the king's favour was fought with little mercy. Many of those who sat for Holbein were ruthless adventurers hardened by the cynical politics of the day. The extraordinarily revealing drawings Holbein made in preparation for his portraits often capture something of this hardness in his sitters, but the drawings were intended for Holbein's eyes only and the final portrait created a far more noble and flattering image. The full extent of Holbein's artistry is revealed only if one places the two side-by-side, as one can for instance with his portrait of the courtier Simon George. The portrait drawing, which survives in a superb collection of almost 100 similar preparatory sketches in the Royal Collection at Windsor, does not mask the brutal ambition of a young man on the make; the finished oil painting, on the other hand (all the sitter would see) was a masterpiece of studied elegance.

Figure 25.9 Hans Holbein's design for the gold Jane Seymour Cup. Holbein, like many artists, was employed on a wide variety of different projects by his royal patron, including designs for the decoration of the royal palaces and, as in this case, the fabrication of precious artifacts. (Oxford, Ashmolean Museum)

With his most important patron, the king himself, Holbein would risk no liberties. Henry employed Holbein both for conventional portraits and far more ambitious projects, such as the group portrait of the king with his parents and third wife, Jane Seymour, intended to proclaim and celebrate the new stability of the Tudor dynasty after the long-awaited birth of a male heir, the future Edward VI. For this monumental painting (again sadly lost), Holbein was able to draw on the design he had accomplished for another of his 'political' paintings: the famous full-length portrait of the two French ambassadors (London, National Gallery). Modern scholarship reveals this as one of the most subtle and innovative of all Holbein's English paintings, a design full of emblematic symbolism which perfectly evoked the intricate, understated world of European court diplomacy. The portrait is at once monumental and enigmatic, the impassive dignity of the ambassadors contrasting with the youthfulness of their faces, as the two men pose in rather uncomfortable formality around a table crammed with astronomical instruments and other impedimenta. At first sight these objects seem quite irrelevant to their mission, but to the educated eye all convey a subtle coded message. The astronomical instruments, the broken string on the lute on the lower table, the Lutheran hymnbook, all hint at a world out of joint and the perils of the religious disunity which would surely follow from Henry's new religious and matrimonial policies.

This was a form of emblematic representation with which Holbein was entirely comfortable from his long training in the polite humanist world of Basle, but in the turbulent world of English politics such elegant understatement was already increasingly irrelevant. In his later years in England Holbein was obliged to create images much more overtly partisan in character. His new patron, the Vicegerent in Spirituals, Thomas Cromwell, had now emerged as one of the leading spirits in the increasingly confident evangelical party and Holbein played his part in the new evangelical propaganda. Indeed it was for Cromwell that Holbein produced one of his most remarkable original designs, the title-page for Coverdale's new English translation of the Bible. This clearly drew its inspiration from Lucas Cranach's Law and the Gospel design, but in Holbein's rendition the theme is restated and stripped of much of its polemical intent. Panels of scenes of the Old and New Testament are (as with Cranach's design) ranged along the left- and right-hand borders, but the original central panel of man's redemption is replaced by an imposing representation of Henry VIII handing the vernacular scriptures to his assembled prelates and councillors. Nothing could more perfectly have captured the constraints which governed the reception of Continental evangelism in Henry's kingdom.

Subtle and pragmatic, Holbein seemed to have the perfect temperament to prosper in the maelstrom of Henry's court. On occasions, however, the painter's artistry could bring his patrons into unanticipated difficulties. In 1539 the king was in search of a new wife and Holbein was sent off to the Continent to take the portrait of the potential brides. Two of his pictures from this expedition survive: the full-length portrait of Christina of Denmark, now in the National Gallery in London, and his portrait of the successful candidate, Anne of Cleves. It is often asserted that Henry was only persuaded to marry Anne by seeing Holbein's flattering portrait, though there were also pressing diplomatic reasons for such a match. Whatever the reason, when Henry finally laid eyes on his new bride he conceived an instant aversion to her, which spelled the end of both the marriage and its architect, Thomas Cromwell.

Holbein, the painter, again emerged unscathed from this debacle, and it is interesting that whereas authors and printers often fell victim to the confessional politics of the age, painters were very seldom held accountable for the ideological content of their work. In this respect, contemporaries seem to have taken a very pragmatic view of the artist's role: their task was to do their patron's bidding, without their own personal convictions forming an important part of the equation. Such a climate suited a man like Holbein perfectly. For Holbein, while he cleverly accommodated his output to the changing demands for art in Protestant centres, does not seem to have been deeply touched by its religious messages.

Something of this is evident in his conduct of his personal affairs in his last years. Although after 1528 Holbein spent almost all of the remainder of his life in England, he never became an English citizen, preferring to keep open the option of a return to Basle. At one point he made to the Basle Council an undertaking to return within two years, if the council would in the meantime pay for the upkeep of his wife and children, who had remained in the city. Sadly, this seems to have been a bargain he never intended to keep. When Holbein died of the plague in London in 1544, he left behind debts and two illegitimate children, fathered during his English years.

Holbein's pragmatic adaptability indicates one face of the relationship between the Reformation and art. To a large extent artists still saw themselves as master craftsmen, fulfilling commissions according to the wishes of their patrons without large emotional involvement on their part. As educated men, the religious upheavals of the time could not but engage their attention, but one should not be surprised if by and large they conformed easily enough to the religious choices of their own locality.

Thus Hans Burgmaier of Augsburg and Hans Baldung Grien of Strasbourg adopted to the Protestantism of their home towns, whereas Albrecht Altdorfer remained with equal equanimity devoted to the Catholicism of his native Regensburg. A grateful city magistracy raised him to high honours, and Altdorfer would end his days as a respected member of the city council, as Cranach did in Lutheran Wittenberg. His brother Erhard, meanwhile, passed into the service of the Dukes of Mecklenberg and worked in the Lutheran tradition. The careers of these artists, sensible to the nuance of local allegiance and shifting market opportunity, are perhaps less extraordinary than the printers who did become entirely committed to the confessional orientation of the works they printed, to the extent of embracing exile and potential poverty rather than deny their religious beliefs (see Chapter 7).

THE CALVINIST ONSLAUGHT

All the great artists studied so far were fortunate in that they found a sympathetic context for their work: Dürer in Nuremberg, Holbein in England, and Cranach in

Wittenberg and Saxony. But it was not always neccessarily so. Holbein was driven out of Basle by the onset of religious radicalism that three years later would lead to the devastation of the city's greatest churches, prompting Erasmus to abandon the city for ever. Similar events were only averted in Wittenberg by Luther's precipitate return from the Wartburg in 1522. In Augsburg, the belated introduction of Protestantism in 1535 was accompanied by the destruction of many priceless works of art, including the only recently created altarpiece of the Moritzkirche of Hans Holbein the Elder, a terrible loss of one of the masterpieces of late fifteenth-century German art. These calculated acts of destruction, or iconoclasm, reflect the very ambiguous Protestant attitude to visual representation of sacred things, an issue which remained hotly debated and controversial throughout the Reformation century.

In Lutheran Europe the impact of Protestant hostility to religious art remained muted, a reflection of Luther's own conservatism on the issue. But further south the very different perspectives of the Swiss reformers, Huldrych Zwingli and John Calvin of Geneva, ensured that churches that fell under their influence would show a very different face. In Zurich, Huldrych Zwingli applied to Catholic decorative tradition the same remorseless logic that infused his developing eucharistic theology. In consequence, when Zurich made the decisive choice for the Reformation in 1524 the churches were immediately stripped bare for the new evangelical services. This unambiguous hostility was echoed by John Calvin, the young French exile who from 1541 was established as the leading minister of the independent city state of Geneva. Calvin took a strong line on the issue of images, to which he denied any merit, and considerable capacity to harm the weaker Christian consciences. In his most systematic exposition of his views, the *Institutes*, Calvin devoted a whole chapter to the issue, uncompromisingly entitled: 'It is unlawful to attribute a visible form to God, and generally whoever sets up idols revolts against the true God.' Images and pictures, he argued, were contrary to scripture, and he excoriated the false, perverted images of the papists in language which recalled the unrestrained polemic of one of his most violent (and funniest) tracts, *Against Relics* (1544).

Calvin was not advocating iconoclasm. He believed strongly that it was the duty of the magistrate to remove images from the church, not for Christian members of the community to take unilateral action. But the lands where Calvin's teachings made their greatest impact were on the whole places like France and the Netherlands, where the civil power remained uncooperative, and in these cases local members of the Calvinist churches were likely to be more impressed by the violence of Calvin's polemic against images than by his call for due order in their removal. Thus the first phase of the Calvinist advance in the lands of northern Europe was often accompanied by a direct and purposeful attack on the appurtenances of Catholic worship. A wave of iconoclasm swept the towns of France in 1560–1 and the Netherlands in 1566. In Scotland, the churches of St Andrews, cathedral city and mediæval shrine, were stripped bare in a single day after the congregations had been stirred by a sermon from John Knox.

The purpose of such action was relatively straightforward, to cleanse the churches and make them fit for Protestant worship. A subsidiary didactic intention was served by proving that the statues of saints in fact held no magical powers. For this reason statues and images were often subjected to ritual humiliation and ridicule as they were destroyed.[13] But the main purpose was to clear the churches and the Calvinist hierarchy were as anxious as their opponents to prevent this becoming the occasion for disorder. Thus in places where the magistrates would cooperate, church leaders often permitted the orderly removal and storage of the now superfluous religious art; on other occasions the families of donors were allowed to come and reclaim their family altars. Such considerations saved Jan van Eyck's great altarpiece of the Adoration of the Lamb in Ghent and the work of the Flemish Masters in Bruges. But an enormous amount was lost in the holocaust. The fact that so little is now known of fifteenth-century religious art in the northern Netherlands almost certainly owes less to any lack of a vibrant local tradition than to the scale of the sixteenth-century destruction.

With such profound hostility to the visual representation of holy things, it was by no means easy for these emerging Calvinist cultures to find a distinctive artistic voice. Calvinism was not hostile to all cultural expressions. A good deal of artistic energies were undoubtedly redeployed into other artistic media, most notably music (see Chapter 26). But the new Calvinist cultures were not wholly barren for the arts. Both England and (particularly) the Netherlands adopted with enthusiasm the Renaissance tradition of the commemorative medal, adapted here for polemical and political purposes. In the Netherlands the badges adopted by the rebellious nobles at the beginning of the revolt in 1566 (the so-called beggars or *Gueux*) stimulated a widespread adoption of the medal form, celebrating Protestant victories with appropriate symbols and scriptural texts. From the Netherlands the custom spread to England, most famously with the medals struck to celebrate the defeat of the Spanish Armada. In England the medal culture was closely related to the tradition of the painted miniature, which reached its high-point in this era in the work of Nicolas Hillyard and Isaac Oliver.

THE ARTISTIC DIASPORA

Even for the familiar media of painting and woodcut, perspectives were by no means wholly bleak. One accidental but wholly beneficial result of the religious turbulence was the diaspora of talent which accompanied the large-scale displacement of peoples in the era of the religious wars. Among those who took flight from the destruction and persecution of the wars of religion were many skilled craftsmen and artists.

The impact was most profound in England. There was no doubt that until this point England had lagged behind the Continent in artistic terms. Until the arrival of Holbein, it was widely believed that it was necessary to go to France to have one's portrait taken. But Holbein had no immediate successor and the English arts slipped back. Even in the first years of Elizabeth's reign, contempt for the culture of the island kingdom was a commonplace of Continental letters. The French philosopher, Pierre Ramus, confessed in 1563 that he could not name a single English scholar. His reply, when greetings were conveyed to him by Roger Ascham, gives a clear sense of England's cultural isolation: 'Who in Britain could possibly be such an admirer of me that he could take the trouble to forward good wishes across the very ocean and all the way to Paris?'[14]

The group of foreign artists who reached England during this decade thus provided a most necessary infusion of new life and talent. It was a French immigrant, Giles Godet, who imported from Paris the tradition of the woodcut religious broadsheet, sold as penny sheets to his London customers. Although a Protestant, Godet nevertheless made use of connections in the Paris publishing industry to obtain designs for his prints, shrewdly excluding the most offensively Catholic themes from his English repertoire.[15] The two most significant new arrivals were Marcus Gheeraerts and Lucas de Heere, both refugees from Alva's persecuting regime in the Netherlands. Both multi-talented artist/scholars, in London they found a sympathetic intellectual milieu among the merchant scholars who formed the elite of the immigrant community. Indeed, in the absence of a large number of fully authenticated paintings by these artists, it is sometimes in the 'friendship books' (*Alba Amicorum*) of members of this Anglo-Netherlandish community that some of the best examples of their work survive.

The *Album Amicorum* was another distinctive and revealing artistic manifestation of the age, a semi-private medium in which those with aspirations to scholarship collected proofs of their wide network of connections; much as in an earlier age a distant Eastern European humanist might have prized an autograph letter from Erasmus. It was an important feature of these collections that the connections revealed were not only international but also cross-confessional; evidence that many of those caught up in the confessional strife of the age deplored the consequent damage to the international community of letters. Sentiments of this sort found a more public expression in the emblem book. This was an important artistic genre which had its roots in the Erasmian milieu of wit and criticism, and the still older moralizing tradition of the *ars moriendi*. Holbein has himself produced a highly successful series of woodcut illustration on this theme (the Dance of Death), which were still being republished accompanied by appropriate verses long after his death. These later editions were published not in Basle, where Holbein had worked, but in Lyons, whose advanced publishing industry developed an important speciality in such literature. This can partly be explained by Lyons' prominence in the market for illustrated Bibles. Publishers who had invested in the expensive woodcut blocks often found ingenious ways to make the most of them, including a number of small volumes of *Images de la Bible* matching pictures to verse. The accompanying quadrain or octain drew the essential message from the text (see Figure 25.10). The emblem book moved beyond this to more abstract allegorical fancies which became increasingly fashionable in elite circles. The absence of direct confessional application was no doubt deliberate. It is as if the educated humanist circles in which emblems had their greatest vogue were offering an evocation of timeless and non-partisan virtues as a deliberate antithesis to the sharp polarities tearing apart the church. It is no surprise that emblem books, which went through many hundreds of editions in these years, enjoyed their greatest popularity in some of the centres of European culture where the destructive effects of religious division had been most keenly felt.

GENESE IIII.

Cain occit Abel, par grande offenſe,
N'ayant reſpect à ſon frere germain,
Duquel le ſang, en ſa pure innocence,
Crïa à Dieu, de ce meurtre inhumain.

GENESE VI. & VII.

Le grand deluge, à Noé Dieu predit,
Lui conſeillant ſa grande arche former:
Puis y entrer, & tout ce qu'il lui dit,
Ayant conclu toute chair conſommer.

B 3

Figure 25.10 Cain killing Abel and Noah's ark from *Images de la Bible* (Lyons), 1558. The Lyons presses specialized in fine editions which integrated verse and illustrations in this way. Printers welcomed the opportunity to re-use the fine (but expensive) woodcut designs commissioned for their Bibles. (Montauban, Bibliothèque Municipale)

WORD AND SYMBOL IN CALVINIST ART

The world of the emblem depended on an intricate relationship of word and image, often enigmatically disguised or deliberately obscure. That is not to say, however, that the literature of word and symbol could not be employed for straightforward confessional purposes. In rejecting the literal depictions of saints and the godhead, Calvinist churches were still sensible of the need for drastically simplified and visual representations of central religious truths. The result was the development of a genre of 'Godly Tables' – displays and designs which placed the teaching of the word prominently before the eye. These designs took several forms. Texts were often painted directly onto walls. In 1561 Queen Elizabeth gave orders for the painting of biblical texts onto the whitewashed walls of English churches, but such textual motifs were also common in private houses (which is where they have mostly survived).

These public and domestic inscriptions had their printed counterpart in the tables and charts included in many of books of this period, such as William Perkins' Table of Salvation and Damnation (see Figure 21.1, p. 377). Some might doubt that such constructions should be regarded as art in any meaningful sense; certainly they are austere and unappealing to the modern eye. But in one sense this was the most democratic of art forms. Such tables and particularly inscriptions had the widest possible exposure and an impact that went well beyond the literate. In the case of the text most widely adopted in all the Reformed traditions, the Ten Commandments, one may surmise that even those who could not read would have been powerfully aware of the central role in the life of the community implied by its privileged place behind the altar or communion table. Certainly such inscriptions would have been more accessible than many satirical woodcuts, which often required a high level of education and knowledge of contemporary debate to comprehend their allusions. This is a circumstance not always taken into account by scholars who regard pictorial representations as, by their very nature, more accessible than text.

CONCLUSION

Thus even the Reformed, the most iconophobic of the churches of the Reformation, found a place for art. But that is not to deny that for the greatest talents the religious arts hardly provided the same opportunities as in the pre-Reformation period. In consequence, in many Protestant traditions artistic energies were increasingly directed away from purely religious subjects. The church interiors depicted in the works of seventeenth-century Dutch artists such as Pieter Saenredam and Gerrit Berckheyde have a certain austere grace, but they indicate that the church buildings themselves allowed little other outlet for the talents of the Netherlands' teeming array of painters. The Dutch Republic continued to support a tradition of religious painting, but essentially as a branch of the wider school of history painting. The scriptures were quarried along with classical mythology for improving stories, and the resulting pictures were intended overwhelmingly for display in private houses or secular civic space.

The hungry army of painters in the Dutch Republic were forced to look elsewhere for employment. In this respect Hans Holbein was an early precursor of a more general trend, where the pressures of Protestant hostility to sacred art brought the redirection of his work towards the essentially secular field of portraiture. Perhaps it was in this respect, more than any other, that the artistic world was most indebted to Protestantism. For in the decades and century that followed, the energies which in Catholic countries were still directed towards religious art, were poured into developing new secular genres: alongside portraiture, the new art of landscape, the pictures of everyday life known as genre paintings and the still life. Within these ostensibly secular forms the artists of the Calvinistic Netherlands still found sufficient room for moralizing lessons and warnings against moral complacency. It is no accident that some of the greatest exponents of the new arts flourished in those parts of Europe where Protestantism had left the smallest scope for traditional religious art. And that, in a very important respect, is part of the artistic legacy of the Reformation.

NOTES

1   Michael Baxandall, *The Limewood Sculptors of Renaissance Germany* (New Haven, 1980).
2   Dürer had heard news of Luther's kidnapping and removal to the Wartburg by the agents of Frederick the Wise after his condemnation at the Diet of Worms. Since nothing was heard of Luther for some months, it was not immediately clear to contemporaries that this had been for Luther's own protection.
3   Example of the former in Cranach's Law and the Gospel at Gotha – see Max J. Friedländer and Jakob Rosenberg, *Lucas Cranach* (New York, 1978), no. 221 – and of the latter in Holbein's rendering of the same theme in the Edinburgh National Gallery.
4   The Gotha altarpiece illustrated in Sergiusz Michalski, 'Inscriptions in Protestant Paintings and in Protestant Churches', *Ars Ecclesiastica: The Church as a Context for Visual Arts* (Helsinki, 1996), pp. 34–47.
5   2 Peter 2:1–3; 1 John 4:1–3; 2 Timothy 3:1–7; Mark 12:38–40. When, at the height of Catholic success in the Thirty Years War, the pictures had to be surrendered to the Duke of Bavaria, the texts were removed and retained by the Nuremberg city council.
6   Cf. Dürer's diary of his journey to the Netherlands, where he records presenting the Bishop of Bamberg copies of his woodcut series of the Apocalypse and Life of Mary. He received in return hospitality and, more valuable still, a letter exempting him from tolls on his journey on from Bamberg. Albrecht Dürer, *Schriften und Briefen* (Leipzig, 1993), p. 21.
7   Keith Moxey, *Peasants, Warriors and Wives: Popular Imagery in the Reformation* (Chicago, 1989), pp. 33–4.
8   In 1532, for example, Elector John ordered from the Cranach workshop sixty pairs of a small matching portrait of the two electors. Carl C. Christensen, *Princes and Propaganda: Electoral Saxon Art of the Reformation* (Kirksville, 1992), p. 39.
9   As, for instance, in his involvement in the design of an elaborate cycle of devotional paintings for the new foundation of Albrecht of Brandenburg at Halle, executed by the Cranach student, Simon Franck. See Andreas Tacke, *Der katolische Cranach* (Mainz, 1992).
10 Jan Nicolaisen, 'Der Hofmaler in der Handelstadt: Aufträge und Auftraggeber Lucas Cranach in Leipzig', in *Vergessene Altdeutsche Gemälde: Catalogue of Exhibition in the Museum der bildenden Künste Leipzig* (Leipzig, 1997), pp. 100–11.
11 There is an ink sketch of 1526, apparently in Cranach's own hand and dated *c*.1526, which seems to be the first draft of a design for this theme. Illustrated in Friedländer and Rosenberg, *Lucas Cranach*, p. 24.
12 The Weimar altarpiece is illustrated in Friedländer and Rosenberg, *Lucas Cranach*, no. 434.

13 Natalie Zemon Davis, 'Rites of Violence', in *Society and Culture in Early Modern France* (London, 1975).

14 Quoted J.A. van Dorsten, *The Radical Arts: First Decade of an Elizabethan Renaissance* (Leiden, 1973), p. 12.

15 Tessa Watt, *Cheap Print and Popular Piety, 1550–1640* (Cambridge, 1991), pp. 182–90 (with examples).

FURTHER READING

The best work of introduction is Carl C. Christensen, *Art and the Reformation in Germany* (Athens, OH, 1979). On German art of the period more generally, see Otto Benesch, *German Painting from Dürer to Holbein* (Geneva, 1966). For a fine introduction to the woodcut art, see R.W. Scribner, *For the Sake of Simple Folk: Popular Propaganda for the German Reformation* (Cambridge, 1981); W.L. Strauss, *The German Illustrated Broadsheet, 1500–1550* (4 vols; New York, 1974) and *The German Single-Leaf Woodcut, 1550–1600* (3 vols; New York, 1975). David Landau and Peter Parshall, *The Renaissance Print, 1470–1550* (New Haven, 1994), provides an elegant and wide-ranging survey.

On Dürer, Erwin Panofsky's *The Life and Art of Albrecht Dürer* (1943; revised edn, Princeton, 1971) is still fresh and evocative; also Jane Campbell Hutchinson, *Albrecht Dürer, A Biography* (Princeton, 1990). On the brothers Beham, Keith Moxey, *Peasants, Warriors and Wives: Popular Imagery in the Reformation* (Chicago, 1989). On Cranach, the standard works are Max J. Friedländer and Jakob Rosenberg, *Lucas Cranach* (New York, 1978), and Werner Schade, *Cranach: A Family of Master Painters* (New York, 1980). The two-volume catalogue of the important centenary exhibition, Dieter Koepplin and Tilman Falk, *Lukas Cranach: Gemälde – Zeichnungen – Druckgraphik* (Basle, 1974), represented an important milestone in Cranach scholarship. Also of value are two more recent exhibition catalogues: Claus Grimm, Johannes Erichsen and Evamaria Brockhoff (eds), *Lucas Cranach: Ein Maler-Unternehmer aus Franken* (Regensburg, 1994) and *Gesetz und Genade: Cranach, Luther und die Bilder* (Torgau, Schloss Hartenfels, 1994). For the *Passional Christi und Antichristi*, Gerald Fleming, 'On the Origin of the *Passional Christi und Antichristi* and Lucas Cranach the Elder's contribution to Reformation Polemics', *Gutenberg Jahrbuch* (1973), pp. 351–68.

The Holbein anniversary of 1997–8 appears not to have inspired the expected rush of new studies. Derek Wilson's *Hans Holbein: Portrait of an Unknown Man* (Phoenix, 1996) is the more accessible; Oskar Bätschmann and Pascal Grenier's *Hans Holbein* (Reaktion, 1997) the more scholarly. John Rowlands, *Holbein* (Phaidon, 1985), remains the best survey of the paintings. Susan Foister, Ashok Roy and Martin Wyld's *Holbein's Ambassadors* (National Gallery/Yale, 1997) is the splendidly informative catalogue of an exhibition in London's National Gallery.

For the Calvinist attitude to images, see Carlos Eire, *The War Against the Idols* (Cambridge, 1986), and Sergiusz Michalski, *The Reformation and the Visual Arts: The Protestant Image Question in Western and Eastern Europe* (London, 1993). On iconoclasm in France and the Netherlands, see Olivier Christin, *Une Révolution symbolique: L'iconoclasme huguenot et la reconstruction catholique* (Paris, 1991). Examples of surviving (and desecrated) Netherlandish art can be found in W. Th. Kloek, W. Halsema-Kubes and R.J. Baarsen (eds), *Art before the Iconoclasm: Northern Netherlandish Art, 1525–1580* (Rijksmuseum Amsterdam, 1986). For the Anglo-Netherlandish art of the early Elizabethan era, see J.A. van Dorsten, *The Radical Arts* (Leiden, 1973); Roy Strong, *Tudor and Jacobean Portraits* (London, 1969). On *Alba Amicorum* and emblems, see Max Rosenheim, 'The Album Amicorum', *Archaeologia* 62 (1910); Alison Adams and Anthony J. Harper (eds), *The Emblem in Renaissance and Baroque Europe* (Leiden, 1992); Alison Saunders, *The Sixteenth-Century French Emblem Book: A Decorative and Useful Genre* (Geneva, 1988). The Puritan promotion of 'Godly Tables' is discussed by Tessa Watt, *Cheap Print and Popular Piety, 1550–1640* (Cambridge, 1991).

MUSIC

————◆•◆•◆————

Francis Higman

B etween 1450 and 1600 there was a rapid evolution in all aspects of the composition of music. In the middle of the fifteenth century, musical composition
and performance was a remarkably international affair. Musicians travelled widely
in order to broaden their experience, and even more in order to obtain a post in
one of the numerous courts or cathedrals of Europe. Although musical life in Italy
was particularly lively, the largest 'national' contingent of composers came from
the north – notably from Flanders. Secular music involved songs of various sorts
(for court performance or for popular consumption); instrumental music without
voices seems to have been confined to the dance. In the sphere of sacred music, the
major activity was the composition of masses (settings of the Kyrie, Gloria, Credo,
Sanctus and Agnus Dei, with extra sections for special occasions such as requiems)
and secondarily of motets (polyphonic pieces anticipating the modern anthem,
usually settings of scriptural or other sacred texts). Music was modal,[1] with infrequent use of accidentals. There was little attempt to relate the sense of the words
to the expressivity of the music.

By the end of the sixteenth century, all this had changed. Distinctive national
styles had evolved, with less interchange than before between countries. In secular
music, the years around 1600 mark the golden age of the madrigal (in Italy and in
England, notably); solo songs with musical accompaniment (whether by instrumental ensembles or by the lute or keyboard) were commonplace and gave rise to
the aria and to early forms of opera. Forms of music for instrumental ensembles,
without voices, had become far more varied than before. As regards sacred music,
the composition of masses and motets continued as before; but under the impact
of the Reformation, new forms of sacred music were introduced in Germany,
France, the Low Countries and England, and the Catholic Reformation responded
by developing its own characteristic music. Although musical theory continued to
think in modes, in fact only two modes were widely practised – those corresponding to the modern major and minor keys. Finally, throughout the period the
quest for ever greater expressivity and ever closer relationship between words and
music was a constant.

So a great deal was happening during the period 1450–1600 and much of this
was quite independent of the Protestant Reformation. On the other hand, the

Reformation made an important contribution to the broadening of musical experience – and not only in the strictly religious sphere. In what follows, we shall outline in turn the Roman Catholic musical scene, the contributions by the Lutheran, Calvinist and Anglican Reformations, and finally various interferences towards the end of the period, between Protestant and Catholic, and between sacred and secular music.

ROMAN CATHOLIC MUSIC

As regards the ongoing tradition of religious music since before the Reformation, it can best be summarized by the names of the four greatest practitioners of the sixteenth century: Josquin des Prés, Roland de Lassus, Tomás Luis de Victoria and Giovanni Pierluigi da Palestrina (we shall later mention William Byrd, also a contender for greatness).

Josquin des Prés (*c.*1440–*c.*1521) stands as a symbol of the early part of the period. Born in Picardy, northern France, he may have studied with the famous Johannes Ockeghem (a Fleming who spent most of his career in the service of the French throne) before being appointed to a post in the cathedral in Milan. He then spent some years as a singer in the papal chapel in Rome. After service in the French court under Louis XII, he worked briefly for the Duke of Ferrara and ended his career in a small town not far from his birthplace in Picardy. This illustrates vividly the international nature of the musical culture of the time.

Josquin's musical production was essentially religious: some twenty masses and over a hundred motets are known, as well as about seventy-five secular pieces. Characteristically, his masses are constructed around a melody borrowed from some other musical form, including quite often a secular or popular song. Thus he wrote two masses on the theme of the song 'L'Homme armé', another on the theme of 'L'Amy Baudichon madame' and so on: the technique is called (somewhat misleadingly) a 'parody mass'. The compositional principle which Josquin inherited from the past was based on the *cantus firmus*: the theme (tune) is carried, normally, by the tenor voice, in a slow rhythm, while the other voices embroider more decorative harmonizations around the theme. In Josquin's hands this principle begins that fundamental evolution which is the hallmark of the sixteenth century: the other voices, instead of being merely decorative additions to the theme, begin to imitate the theme at different moments. True polyphony is born. In his masses, and also in his numerous motets on biblical texts or paraphrases, Josquin also experiments in dialogue forms where some voices (e.g. treble and tenor) are answered by others (alto, bass). In his motets he also multiplies the number of parts (as many as eight in the most complicated case, his monumental *Lugebat David*).

Josquin was the great innovator of the Renaissance and his influence throughout Europe was immense. Martin Luther's admiring remark is frequently quoted: 'Musicians do what they can with notes; Josquin does what he wants.'[2]

Roland de Lassus (*c.*1532–94) continued the international tradition of the sixteenth-century musician. Born at Mons (Hainault, Belgium), he was early noted for his musicianship and his beautiful voice. He was several times kidnapped by ambitious choirmasters before being recruited into a choir specially formed for Emperor Charles V. This enabled him to travel widely, in particular to France and Milan (1546), each time broadening his musical experience. After his voice broke, he continued his career in Naples then in Rome, where he was director of the choir of St John Lateran. After brief stays in the England of Mary Tudor in 1554, then in France and in Antwerp, he entered the employ of Duke Albert V of Bavaria in 1556. He was still only twenty-four years old. Apart from a few visits to Italy to recruit singers, and one visit to Paris in 1571, he remained in the Munich court for the rest of his life. More than any other, Lassus embodied the encyclopedic musical culture of his time, embracing the musical experimentation of Italy (chromatism), France (*vers mesurés à l'antique*, of which more below), Germany (the folk-song or *Lied*) and mixtures of these various elements (as, for example, in the burlesque pseudo-Italian serenade of a German mercenary *Matona mia cara*). In England he was known as Rolandus Lassus, in Italy as Orlando Lasso or di Lasso. In character, Lassus seems to have suffered from a deep pessimism, against which he reacted by extravagant flippancy, bordering on mental instability. Percy Scholes says of him: 'through over-exercise of his intellectual faculties, he latterly fell into a settled melancholy.'[3]

Musically, all this translates into one of the most inventive and innovative creations of musical polyphony of all time. The key word is the quest for musical expressivity. Whereas the traditional *cantus firmus* provided simply a musical frame for the chant of the words, Lassus sought to model the musical language according to the sense of each phrase and each word. Thus his most fruitful field of expression was the motet (where the text is much freer than in the set pieces of the mass), of which he composed some 520, plus various cycles based on extracts from Job, the penitential psalms, the *Lamentationes Hieremiae prophetae* and the *Prophetiae Sybillarum*. He also composed some 50 masses, 101 *Magnificats* and numerous other religious pieces. In secular music, he produced 185 madrigals (of Italian inspiration), 141 French *chansons* and 90 *Lieder*. His music is characterized by its experimentation in unexpected modulations, chromatic progressions and startling dissonances, in which he brings to bear his vast amalgam of European musical techniques and experiences. It has been said of him that above all other musicians he embodied the Renaissance man.

Tomás Luis de Victoria (or Vittoria, as he is known in Italy) (*c.*1548–1611) marks the move away from the internationalism of the earlier Renaissance towards a more intensely national musical expression. Born and initially educated in Avila (Spain), he studied and worked in Rome between 1565 and 1587, including a period as student of Palestrina. He was ordained a priest in 1575. At the age of thirty-nine he returned to Madrid, where he remained for the rest of his life in the service of Empress Maria, widow of Maximilian II of Austria.

Unlike the vast majority of his contemporaries, Victoria appears never to have composed any form of secular music. His surviving works include twenty-one masses, forty-four motets and some fifty other religious pieces. While he used the technique of the 'parody mass', the themes he chose were those of religious motets, as for example in his mass based on the themes of his own motet *O Magnum Mysterium*. He sought to introduce into his music the intense expressivity which also characterized Lassus, but in a more specifically spiritual and devotional context. Among his greatest works are the cycles based on the liturgy of Holy Week, the *Officium hebdomadae sanctae* of 1585 in particular, in which he evokes musically the intense and varied emotions and experiences of the suffering Christ. He carried to its highest point the expressive techniques of polyphony in the service of a fervent religious emotion (his lifespan coincided with a great flowering of Spanish mysticism, including John of the Cross and Theresa of Avila).

Giovanni Pierluigi da Palestrina (*c.*1525–94) represents even more exclusively than Victoria the new nationalism. Although he studied the contrapuntal techniques of the Franco-Flemish school, his career was almost entirely centred on Rome, where he studied with French teachers as a teenager. He became organist and choirmaster in his native town of Palestrina (his family name was Pierluigi) at the age of nineteen, and married into the local bourgeoisie. But his bishop was elected pope in 1550, taking the name of Julius III, and Palestrina was summoned to Rome. He spent the rest of his life there, serving under eight successive popes. Among these, the most ephemeral, Marcellus II, was perhaps also the most influential: during the twenty-one days of his pontificate, he took exception to the musical offerings of the Sistine Chapel choir and commanded that henceforth 'what had to be recited should be recited, and what had to be sung should be sung, in such a way that the words should be both heard and understood'. Palestrina took the message to heart, for example in the *Missa Papae Marcelli* (1555–60). When the Council of Trent confirmed these recommendations and condemned the use of secular songs in parody masses, Palestrina had already established the new style and became the recognized leader of the Roman Catholic school of music.

Palestrina composed over 100 masses and over 500 motets and other hymns and compositions based on liturgical texts (35 *Magnificats*, for example), as well as nearly 100 secular madrigals. While his music is less adventurous and original than that of Lassus, it is characterized above all by its melodiousness and the delicacy of his harmonies. In keeping with the instructions of Pope Marcellus, the writing is frequently in 'vertical' chords which allow the words to be more easily perceived. He frequently used double or even triple choirs, enabling him to treat vocal music in an 'orchestral' form in which one choir replies antiphonally to another and a reduced number of voices alternates with the full choir.

Sir David Willcocks said of Palestrina that he produced 'the most perfect polyphonic music ever composed, its serene and supple lines combining to create beautifully spaced harmonic euphony.'[4]

LUTHERAN MUSIC

Martin Luther (1483–1546) was less radical liturgically than he was doctrinally. Luther himself was a competent musician – as a performer on lute and flute, and as a composer. His concern to engage the laity more directly in church worship led him to create new forms of religious music for use in the liturgy and also in private devotions. His most significant innovation was the chorale, involving German-language verse in stanza form, set to music similar to that of the German secular songs of the period and sung by the whole congregation during church services. Thus the well-known song 'Innsbruck ich muss dich lassen' was adapted for religious use by the modification of the words to 'O Welt ich muss dich lassen'. In 1524 he produced, together with Johann Walther (1496–1570), the first collection of Protestant music for congregational singing: the *Geystliche gesangk Buchleyn* (see Figure 26.1). In many of these 'hymns' (to use an anachronistic term) the words are by Luther, but the music is ascribed differently by various authorities either to Luther himself or to Walther. This includes the most famous of all Lutheran chorales, 'Ein feste Burg ist unser Gott', as well as the Christmas hymn 'Von Himmel hoch'. The tunes were harmonized in four parts, with the melody normally in the tenor. In 1526 he produced, again with Walther and also with Conrad Rupsch, a German-language mass (*Deutsche Messe*), adapting plainchant music to the German words. But Luther did not exclude texts in Latin from liturgical uses. The fifth edition of Walther's *Gesangk Buchleyn* (in 1551) included seventy-four German-language chorales and forty-seven Latin *Cantiones*. Some of the music is four-part 'vertical' harmony comparable to the modern hymn tune. In other cases – for domestic use rather than liturgical – more complicated polyphony is introduced, comparable to the motet tradition which culminated in Roland de Lassus.

Luther's church discipline allowed considerable latitude to individual congregations in liturgical matters, which led to the development of locally differentiated practices. Among these the development of versified psalm translations in the Strasbourg Reformation under the leadership of Martin Bucer, with music by Matthias Greiter, was to form the bridge to the Calvinist tradition of church music.

The Lutheran chorale has had a long and glorious tradition. At the end of the sixteenth century and the beginning of the seventeenth, Italian influences led to new developments. Hans Leo Hassler (1564–1612) studied in Venice and introduced into Germany the technique of setting off two choirs antiphonally or in combination. Michael Praetorius (1571–1621) added another Italian innovation, the intermingling of choral texts with solo passages and instrumental accompaniment: the chorale is evolving into the oratorio. Heinrich Schütz (1585–1672) dominated the seventeenth century by the variety of his musical forms (Italianate double-choir settings of psalms, three *Passions*, and a large number of motets and 'concerts'). The Lutheran tradition of the chorale culminates in its most famous practitioner, Johann Sebastian Bach (1685–1750), and his multiple settings, for example, of the Passion Chorale *O Haupt voll Blut und Wunden* – based on a melody composed by Hans Leo Hassler and words adapted by Paulus Gerhardt (1607–76) from a poem attributed to Bernard of Clairvaux. In Bach's hands the chorale definitively establishes the more complex form introduced by Praetorius, with solos, instruments and choral movements (the *St Matthew Passion*, for example).

THE REFORMED TRADITION

The Swiss-based reformation developed characteristics quite separate from those of the German Reformation. In Zurich, Huldrych Zwingli (1484–1531), although

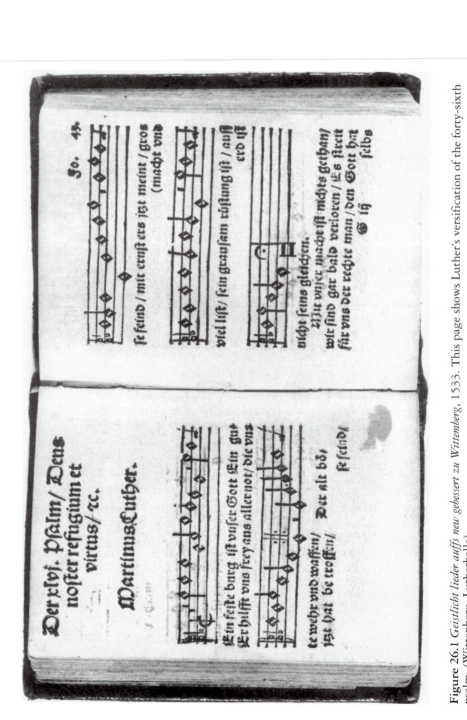

Figure 26.1 *Geistlicht lieder auffs new gebessert zu Wittemberg*, 1533. This page shows Luther's versification of the forty-sixth psalm. (Wittenberg, Lutherhalle)

himself a more accomplished musician than Luther, considered that music had no place at all in religious worship and banned it from all services.

The earliest French-language liturgy in western Switzerland, composed by Guillaume Farel (1489–1565) around 1529, did not allow for a musical component in worship. Farel's collaborators in Neuchâtel in the early 1530s, notably Matthieu (or Thomas) Malingre (d.1572), practised two forms of non-liturgical religious poetry: the *chanson spirituelle* or devotional poem and the satirical or polemical poem (collections first published in 1533–4). In both cases the poems were set to pre-existing secular tunes (at the head of each text there is simply the mention 'to the tune of … '). Thus, satirically, the words 'Paovres papistes retournez vous' are set to the tune of 'Dame d'Orleans ne plourez plus'; Clément Marot's love song 'Tant que vivray en eage florissant,/Je serviray Amour le dieu puissant … ' is modified into a devotional text: 'Tant que vivray, en eage florissant/Je serviray le seigneur tout puissant … '. Several augmented editions by other writers followed, in which the two genres were fused into a single series, and the collection became known as the *Chansonnier huguenot*.

John Calvin (1509–64) only arrived on the scene in 1536. In his draft ecclesiastical ordinances of 1537 he proposed that the liturgy should be enriched by congregational singing of psalms, but there is no surviving edition of suitable texts which could have served. In Strasbourg, however, where he worked as pastor from 1538 to 1541, he obtained a collection of a dozen or so psalms translated into French and versified – so-called metrical psalms – by Clément Marot. Calvin provided eight other versifications from his own pen and published the first collection of metrical psalms in French, *Aulcuns pseaulmes et cantiques mys en chant* (1539). Some of these twenty melodies are taken from the German-language Strasbourg psalter. The characteristics of Calvinist church music are already established in this collection. The texts are strictly limited to the versification in French of biblical texts (in the main the Psalms of David, with the addition of the Ten Commandments, song of Simeon, in later editions the Lord's Prayer, and – sole exception to the biblical rule – the Apostles' Creed). Each text is accompanied by a melody to be sung by the whole congregation: the idea of congregational participation, already present in Luther, is thus reaffirmed by Calvin. And, for liturgical use, the singing is in unison and unaccompanied (in contrast to Lutheran practice). We return below to these principles and their justification.

From the modest beginnings of the *Aulcuns pseaulmes*, the Genevan psalter developed. Clément Marot (1496–1544), court poet to King Francis I and known for his light and witty love poetry, as well as for his unorthodox religious views for which he had twice to go into exile from France, had already (1530) begun his series of metrical psalms. He continued the work of versification of the original text, notably during his stay in Geneva in 1542–3. By the time of his death in 1544 he had completed 52 of the 150 psalms. The remaining texts were versified by Theodore Beza between 1551 and 1562; by the latter date the psalter was complete. Successive editions of the psalms for use in worship (30 psalms in 1542, 50 in 1543, 52 in 1544, 83 in 1551 and so on) supplied the melody for each psalm. Little is known about the composers of these melodies. It seems that a series of *chantres* paid (stingily) by the Geneva Council – Guillaume Franc, Loys

Figure 26.2 Clément Marot, from Beza's portrait gallery of heroes of the Reformation, the *Icones*. (St Andrews University Library)

Bourgeois, Pierre Davantès being the most prominent – composed the melodies. The variety of stanza forms employed, particularly by Marot, meant that different music was necessary for the majority of the texts: a total of 125 different tunes are found in the 150 psalms of the full collection.

The first Genevan edition, *La Forme des prieres et chantz ecclesiastiques* (1542) included a preface by Calvin, which was extended in the 1543 edition. This fundamental text makes several important points. First, the power of the combination of words and music: following music theorists from Plato on, Calvin stresses that few things have a more profound influence on human emotions than the combined force of words and music. It is therefore essential that the words be comprehensible. Consequently, on the one hand, the words must be in a language comprehensible to the people: the vernacular, not Latin. On the other hand, the music must be a vehicle for the words, not a barrier to their appreciation. Hence the requirement that, in church, the psalms be sung in unison, without harmony or instrumental accompaniment. But the power of combined poetry and music to move the human spirit can be a good or a bad thing, it can uplift or lead to immorality. Spiritual music can therefore also serve as a bulwark against the 'lascivious madrigals' of the period. The poetry of the psalms 'of David', being divinely inspired, represents the highest possible spirituality (even though the name of Christ is absent from the psalter, the psalms are considered as referring throughout to the coming Messiah); they therefore have the greatest potential for spiritual uplift. Thus the psalms represent a repertoire of music for singing not only in church, but also 'at home and in the fields', and here (contrary to common belief) Calvin is not averse to harmonization.

The metrical psalms of Marot and Beza became a central feature of Calvinist (or Huguenot) spirituality. In periods when Protestant worship was illegal, the faithful found comfort in the shared musical experience of singing psalms. Several testimonies exist to the intense emotion of joy experienced by religious refugees arriving in Geneva, when they first heard the free congregational singing of psalms in church. During the French Wars of Religion (1562–98), the Huguenot armies marched into battle singing psalms. And many Calvinist martyrs died at the stake, singing psalms with their last breath.

The extension of the psalms to extra-liturgical use, domestic and popular, was rich in consequences. Almost every musician practising in France in the second half of the sixteenth century (some forty of them) tried their hand at harmonizing one or more of the austere and simple melodies of the psalms, usually placing the melody in the tenor line. Claude Goudimel harmonized the entire psalter twice (1564 and 1568) and in addition composed complicated polyphonic motets based on the melodies of a number of the psalms. Paschal de l'Estocart harmonized the entire collection (between four and eight parts, 1583). Claude Le Jeune did complete sets of harmonizations in three parts and in four, both published after his death in 1600. These three composers were, to say the least, sympathetic to the Protestant cause; but musicians of Roman Catholic convictions were equally touched by the fashion for harmonizing psalms, including Roland de Lassus, Clément Janequin and André Pevernage. We shall return below to the implications of these cross-confessional movements.

While at the beginning (harmonizations of the existing fifty versified psalms by Loys Bourgeois, 1547) the music remained strictly chordal (each of the four voices sings the same syllable at the same time) and thus retained the principle of comprehensibility laid down by Calvin, later versions became more and more

Figure 26.3 The Huguenot psalter. The psalter was the most remarkable publishing venture of the sixteenth century. More than thirty printers shared a joint edition which brought 35,000 copies of the book to the marketplace in one year. Considering the expense and technical difficulties involved with printing types of musical notation, this was a considerable achievement. (Grand Rapids, H. Henry Meeter Center for Calvin Research)

polyphonic. Examples of this development are provided by Goudimel's motets already mentioned, by Pevernage (Catholic organist in Antwerp) or Sweelinck (Calvinist organist in Amsterdam). The result, while being unfaithful to the original spirit of the *Psautier*, could and did on occasion provide spectacular results (e.g. the setting of Psalm 33 by Sweelinck).

In its poetry and its music, the Genevan psalter established an aesthetic which was opposed to the rich tapestry of the contemporary Pléiade poetics of Ronsard and his colleagues, and to contemporary Roman Catholic musical polyphony as it had developed by the time of Roland de Lassus. Based on simplicity and accessibility of language, structure and balance of form, the 'Calvinist aesthetic' was carried over on the one hand to other poetic and musical forms (the *Octonaires sur la vanité et inconstance du monde* by Antoine de la Roche-Chandieu, set to music by Paschal de l'Estocart and published in 1582) and on the other hand to Catholic 'replies' to the Marot/Beza psalter, notably the versified psalms of Philippe Desportes and others and their musical settings. The injunctions of the Council of Trent concerning comprehensibility of the words also indicate a move in the same direction.

ANGLICAN MUSIC

It has been said of the Anglican Reformation that it retained a Catholic style of liturgy while embracing a Reformed theology. The various Anglican services – matins, even-song, Holy Communion – are clearly derived from the offices of the mediæval church. The Communion service, for example, takes over the traditional elements of the mass (Kyrie, Gloria, Credo, Sanctus, Benedictus, Agnus Dei) and translates them into English. John Merbecke (died *c*.1585) set the English words to an adaptation of plain-chant, which has now been revived in many Anglican churches. Likewise 'Anglican chant' for the psalms is an adaptation of mediæval plainchant, unlike the metrical psalms of the Scottish Kirk, modelled on the Marot/Beza psalms. The major original contribution of the Anglican Reformation, however, is the 'anthem', which is neither the mediæval 'antienne' nor the contemporaneous 'motet'. Normally based on a scrip-tural text or paraphrase, it is a choral piece allocated a specific place after the collects in the liturgy of matins and evensong.

Thomas Tallis (*c*.1505–85) has been called 'the father of English cathedral music'. Before the Reformation he was organist in various abbeys (Dover, Waltham) and in Canterbury; in 1542 he became a Gentleman of Henry VIII's Chapel Royal. He served both the Catholic Mary Tudor and her successor Elizabeth I. He composed three Latin masses and over fifty motets, including the spectacular motet *Spem in alium* (1573), set for eight choirs of five voices each (possibly for the forty singers of the Chapel Royal). In English, he created nearly thirty settings of matins and evensong, and some twenty anthems. His techniques, especially in English, continue that trend already mentioned in other contexts towards simplicity and intelligibility of the text.

William Byrd (1543–1623) achieved a stature in English music comparable to that of Palestrina in Italy, Victoria in Spain and Lassus in the Franco-Flemish tradition. Although a convinced Roman Catholic, he served as Gentleman of the Chapel Royal (from 1570) under Elizabeth I and her successors. This makes a point particularly visible in the Anglican Reformation: musicians were peculiarly able to cross confessional divides barred to others. Together with Thomas Tallis, he was granted the monopoly of music printing for twenty-one years by Elizabeth I; in gratitude, the two musicians offered the queen a collection of thirty-four *Cantiones quae ab argumento sacrae vocantur* (1575), seventeen by each composer. Byrd later composed some 140 further Latin motets – entitled *Cantiones* or *Gradualia* – for five, six or eight voices, and three great masses (for three, four and five voices respectively); this was his 'Catholic' output. He also composed settings of the Anglican matins and evensong, and a vast number of English-language anthems, in which he introduced the idea of alternation between full choir and solo sections, full anthems and verse anthems, that was destined for a great future in the hands of Henry Purcell (1647–95) and George Frederick Handel (1685–1754). He also created a wide variety of madrigals and other secular part-songs, solo songs with string accompaniment and many innovative pieces of instrumental and keyboard music. Byrd's music is characterized by its rich harmony, its sheer melodic beauty and the close moulding of the music to express the sense of the text ('word-painting'). He established the forms of Anglican religious music for centuries to come and thus fixed, for England, that evolution away from internationalism towards national styles that is also seen in Palestrina and Victoria.

INTERFERENCES

Towards the end of the sixteenth century, a number of trends in the evolution of religious music (which we have mentioned in passing) converge on the central theme of cross-confessional exchanges or interferences. We have seen that the metrical psalms of Marot/Beza evoked the Catholic response from Philippe Desportes, whose metrical psalms, even more simple and 'accessible' than those of the Genevans, were set to music in the early seventeenth century in chordal arrangements as strict as those of the early harmonizers of the Geneva melodies. Desportes was not alone; his friend and colleague Jean-Antoine de Baïf also produced 'anti-Calvinist' metrical psalms – although, in this case, thanks to the strong views on spelling reform of the poet, Baïf's texts were not published until the twentieth century. Baïf's importance is elsewhere: in the *Académie* which he founded in 1570, the central concern of which was to put into practice the ancient doctrine of the power of combined words and music – just the same line of thought which lay at the basis of the Calvinist psalms. But Baïf's highly literary and learned approach led him to attempt to recreate the forms of Latin poetry (based on long and short vowels) in a form of verse in French (a language which does not have long and short vowels, so Baïf moved to stressed and unstressed syllables instead). These poems (secular, not at all religious, in content) were set to a music appropriate to the verse form, in particular by two composers closely associated with the *Académie*, Jacques Mauduit (a Catholic) and Claude Le Jeune (the same person as harmonized the Marot/Beza psalms). The rhythms of these *vers mesurés à l'antique*, as they were called, necessitated that all the voices pronounce the same syllables at the same time – the same chordal basis as in the earlier psalm settings. Inter-confessional influences thus led not only to the spread of the 'Calvinist aesthetic' to the Catholic psalm settings, but also to the junction between sacred and secular in the *Académie* (the aims of which were very moral).

We have already mentioned, in the case of William Byrd, that musicians (in particular composers) seemed to circulate across the religious divides of the sixteenth century with greater liberty than others. Composers were professionals and provided the music required of them by their employers, princely or ecclesiastical. While Byrd provided music for Queen Elizabeth, in Germany several eminent Protestant composers (Sixt Dietrich, Balthasar Resinarius) composed florid polyphonic music for the Catholic liturgy of their social context.

CONCLUSION

What were the major points at which the Reformation had an impact on the evolution of music? First and foremost, the new emphasis on congregational participation, among Lutherans, Calvinists and Anglicans alike, produced in the long run a musically cultured population far wider than that of pre-Reformation society, where the great majority of musical performances were provided by professionals, whether court musicians or cathedral choirs. By the end of the sixteenth century, a considerable tradition of domestic singing had developed – for example in the English madrigal, the French *chanson*, the German *Volkslied*; and a considerable part (though not the whole) of this evolution is related to the acclimatization to music-making provided by the Reformation.

This music-making was mainly in the vernacular languages – which encourages the divergence of national traditions by the end of the period. The English and the Italian madrigal are quite different in style; French and German songs are immediately distinguishable.

Finally, the evolving thinking about music in the Reformation led to a marked widening of the scope and variety of music, both religious and secular – the Anglican anthem being an obvious example, the vogue for part-songs being another. But this widening of scope was far from being entirely the result of religious factors. There are of course other, indeed more powerful influences which lead to the development of the solo accompanied song (hence the aria), to the *ballet de cour* (hence to the birth of the modern opera) and to the flowering in the seventeenth century of instrumental music without words to accompany it. Nonetheless, one might dare to make the generalization that the Reformation brought a considerable widening, even democratization, of musical culture, which can still be perceived in the popular musical culture of those countries which most generally embraced the ideas and the mind-set of the Reformation.

ACKNOWLEDGEMENT

With thanks to Fiona Kisby.

NOTE

1 The musical scale of eight notes consists of five intervals between notes of a whole tone and two of a semi-tone, the distribution of these intervals determining the difference in modern terms between major and minor keys: the major has semi-tones at the third and seventh intervals, the minor at the second and fifth intervals. A *mode* has the same principle, but the distribution of the semi-tones is more varied. Try playing a scale on the piano starting at each of the white notes, and playing only the white notes.
2 Howard M. Brown, *Music in the Renaissance* (Englewood Cliffs, 1976), p. 119.
3 Percy A. Scoles, *The Oxford Companion to Music* (10th edn; Oxford, 1970), art. Lassus.
4 Programme note on Decca CD of the *Alegri Misereri* and Palestrina *Stabat Mater* (Decca 421 147–2, 1988), p. 3.

FURTHER READING

The major reference work is of course Stanley Sadie (ed.), *The New Grove Dictionary of Music and Musicians* (20 vols; London, 1980). This contains articles on Luther, Calvin, Zwingli, the psalms and all the major composers. Shorter, lighter and more eccentric is Percy Scholes' *Oxford Companion to Music* (10th edn; Oxford, 1970). Hans J. Hillerbrand (ed.), *The Oxford Encyclopedia of the Reformation* (4 vols; New York, 1996), has an excellent article on music (by Bartlett R. Butler).

Of the many general works on music during this period, a number contain sections dealing specifically with Reformation issues. See G. Abrahams (ed.), *The New Oxford History of Music IV: The Age of Humanism, 1540–1630* (London, 1968); A. Leaver, 'The Lutheran Reformation', in I. Fenlon (ed.), *The Renaissance: From the 1470s to the End of the Sixteenth Century* (Basingstoke, 1989); L. Lockwood, 'Music and Religion in the High Renaissance and the Reformation', in C. Trinkhaus and H.A. Oberman (eds), *The Pursuit of Holiness in Late Mediaeval and Renaissance Religion*. For wider developments, a detailed but very technical treatment of the period is Howard M. Brown, *Music in the Renaissance* (Englewood Cliffs, 1976). See also Gustave Reese, *Music in the Renaissance* (revised edn; New York, 1959), still the basic work in English. On changing Catholic attitudes to the role of music, see Karl Gustav Fellerer, 'Church Music and the Council of Trent', *Musical Quarterly* 39 (1953), pp. 576–94.

The most comprehensive study of Protestant music (from the Reformation to the modern era) is Friedrich Blume and Ludwig Finscher (eds), *Protestant Church Music: A History* (New York, 1974). For Luther, see Carl Schalk, *Luther on Music: Paradigms of Praise* (Saint Louis, 1988); P. Nettl, *Luther and Music* (New York, 1967), and M.A. Egge, *Liturgy, Theology and Music in the Lutheran Church* (Northfield, 1989). Charles Garside, *Zwingli and the Arts* (New Haven, 1966) explains Zwingli's hostile attitude.

The richest vein of source documents for the Calvinist/Huguenot *Psautier* is Pierre Pidoux, *Le Psautier huguenot* (2 vols; Basle, 1959). For Continental material in general, E. Weber, *Le concile de Trente et la musique: de la Réforme à la Contre-Réforme* (Paris, 1982), is a broad-ranging study. Information on Dutch topics can be found in R. Leaver, '*Goostly Psalms and Spiritual Songes': English and Dutch Metrical Psalms from Coverdale to Utenhove, 1535–1566* (Oxford, 1991).

For England, Peter Le Huray's *Music and the Reformation in England, 1549–1660* (2nd edn; London, 1978) is still the standard work, supplemented by J. Caldwell, 'The Period of the Reformation', in *The Oxford History of English Music: From the Beginnings to 1715* (Oxford, 1991), pp. 174–266. See also Nicolas Temperley, *The Music of the English Parish Church* (2 vols; Cambridge, 1979); P. Phillips, *English Sacred Music, 1549–1659* (Oxford, 1992), and H. Benham, *Latin Church Music in England, 1460–1575* (New York, 1980).

To locate more detailed literature on specific topics, the most up-to-date and extensive bibliography for musicological research is the *Répertoire international de la littérature musicale* (New York, 1967–). Other bibliographies, together with a range of discographies, are listed in V.H. Duckles and M.A. Keller, *Music Reference and Research Materials: An Annotated Bibliography* (4th edn; New York, 1994).

ARCHITECTURE

Andrew Spicer

Historical studies of the Reformation controversies inevitably focus on the theological debates and doctrinal disputes which proved the major points of contention between the reformers and their adversaries. But there is little doubt that for many ordinary believers the Reformation would have been confronted primarily through liturgical and practical changes. Part of this was destructive, as with the ferocious attacks on the fabric of the church, both internal and external, which often accompanied the Protestant advances. But the Reformation also brought more positive innovation, and this too attracted widespread interest and curiosity. At the time of the first Calvinist Revolt in the Netherlands in 1566, the curious were attracted to visit the new buildings erected by the Reformed communities, as much to marvel at an entirely novel type of church building, as to hear the sermons preached. At Ghent, Marcus van Vaernewijk visited the temple outside the city walls 'not in order to hear the doctrines taught there but to view its interior design', while in Antwerp English merchants dispatched reports about the construction of Protestant churches. The dramatic contrast between the Protestant architecture and the existing churches excited immediate attention.

The Reformation not only resulted in the construction of new buildings for Protestant worship, it also meant in some states the radical alteration of existing churches where these were taken over and adapted by the Protestants. An impression of the radical contrast between the post-Tridentine Catholic church and a Protestant church, in this case Lutheran, is given in two polemical engravings of the early seventeenth century. The *True Image of a Papist Church* shows a long nave with the High Altar obscured by a rood screen; there are side altars along the length of the aisles and the nave at which priests in full vestments are saying mass (see Figure 27.1). There are triptychs behind the altars, statues above them with votive candles and stained glass in the windows. The engraving illustrates aspects of Catholic theology and teaching: the importance of the sacraments of baptism and marriage, the masses and prayers for the dead and the sanctity of the clergy. However, it is clear that the main focus of worship is the mass – although obscured the High Altar is the focal point for the building and the clerics' procession through the church adds to this sense of spectacle. The preaching of the Word of God from the pulpit in the nave is lost amongst a myriad of activities.

Figure 27.1 *The True Image of a Papist Church.* (Cliché, Bibliothèque nationale de France)

Figure 27.2 *The True Image of an Apostolic Church.* (Cliché, Bibliothèque nationale de France)

The True Image of an Apostolic Church provides a radically different view of the interior of a similar building (see Figure 27.2). The building is plain, stripped of images and seemingly with clear glass in the windows; the only decoration is the table of the Ten Commandments at the east end of the church. The side altars have been swept away leaving just two accessible altars at which communion is being administered in both kinds. However the main focus of this building is the preaching of the Word of God. The congregation is not engaged in a range of activities, a minority are participating in communion whereas the majority are ranged around the pulpit listening to the sermon. Therefore the pulpit in the nave has replaced the altar as the focal point in the adaptation of the building for Protestant worship.

Put simply, the engravings illustrate the fundamental architectural impact of the core doctrinal message of the Reformation, which was to emphasize the primacy of the Word of God. While there were certainly significant differences between Protestant churches, they all upheld the importance of preaching as a mark of the True Church. The Catholic church had, they argued, through corruption over time lost the marks of the True Church and was not based on *sola scriptura*. While the imagery of the engravings was clearly an attack upon Catholicism, the dramatic visual distinction between the Catholic and Protestant churches can also be seen in the seventeenth-century architectural paintings of the Low Countries. The portrayal of the interior of Catholic churches, such as the restored cathedral in Antwerp by Pieter Neeffs and Hendrick van Steenwyck, can be contrasted with the purged interiors of the churches of the United Provinces painted by Emanuel de Witte, Hendrick van Vliet, Gerrit Beckheyde and Gerrit Houckgeest (see Figure 27.3).

LUTHERAN CHURCH ARCHITECTURE

In the first years after the preaching of the Reformation message, the first priority in lands where the evangelicals gained control was inevitably to adapt existing ecclesiastical buildings for Protestant worship. These changes were often carried through by means of a violent assault on the fabric and decoration of the Catholic church. In Wittenberg itself, the preaching of Luther's colleague Andreas von Karlstadt resulted in a wave of iconoclasm between 1521 and January 1522. Returning hurriedly from his exile at the Wartburg, Luther quickly restored order and thereafter adopted a more conservative approach towards liturgical change. Although Luther did not actually express his views about church architecture, some insights come from his comments on the introduction of his reformed service of worship in 1525. The service was to honour God, but also to educate the ignorant through the preaching of the gospel. The involvement of the congregation in the service was increased dramatically, the significance of their role was reflected in the pastor facing the congregation during the reading of the lessons. As the pastor was obliged to face the altar when saying prayers, Luther did contemplate moving the altar so that the pastor could face the congregation, like Christ had done at the Last Supper. However Luther did not provide any clear guidelines about the layout of the church.

Figure 27.3 Emanuel de Witte, *Interior of the Oude Kerk in Delft*, 1651. (London, Wallace Collection)

The first building that attempted to express the new theological and pastoral priorities of the Reformation through radical innovation in church design was the new Electoral Schlosskapelle of Hartenfels, Torgau. The new construction, in which both Luther and Lucas Cranach had been closely involved, was inaugurated by a sermon preached by Luther on 5 August 1544. In his sermon Luther emphasized that 'the purpose of this new house may be such that nothing else may ever happen in it except that our dear Lord himself may speak to us through his Holy Word and we respond to him through prayer and praise.' The chapel was designed by Nickel Gromann (drawing upon the late fifteenth-century Schlosskapelle at Wittenberg with which Luther was closely associated) for the Elector John Frederick of Saxony and was built between 1540 and 1544. It is a simple rectangle with four bays, surrounded by a two-storey stone gallery. The focal point on entering the chapel from the courtyard is the elevated pulpit, placed centrally on the facing long northeast wall (see Figure 27.4). The pulpit is elaborately carved with polychromed reliefs of the Child Jesus in the Temple, Christ and the Woman taken in Adultery and of Christ driving the Money-Changers from the Temple. The altar at the east end is in comparison much simpler, a stone supported by four caryatids. The dominance of the pulpit in this layout emphasized the importance of preaching and the Word of God.

Torgau served as a model for a series of chapels built by the Lutheran Princes into the seventeenth century. These included Dresden (1548–55), built for Maurice of Saxony; Schwerin (early 1560s), for Duke John Albert I of Mecklenburg; Altes Schloss, Stuttgart (1560–2); Rotenburg (1570–81), for Landgrave William the Wise of Hesse; and the greatly enlarged version in the Friedrichsbau of the Heidelberg Schloss built for the Elector Palatine Frederick IV between 1601–7. Two of the most important examples were built at Augustusburg and Schmalkalden. The former, built for the Elector August of Saxony as part of his new palace between 1569 and 1572, abandoned the Gothic style of Torgau in favour of the Italianate style of decoration. The chapel at Schmalkalden was built for William the Wise of Hesse between 1585 and 1590. Here there was a significant alteration as the pulpit was positioned directly behind and overlooking the altar at the east end of the chapel, and above the pulpit was the organ. The altar at Schmalkalden was unique because it has a font incorporated into it. The building thereby clearly links the crucial elements of Lutheran worship: preaching the Word of God, the sacraments and hymn singing. This conjunction of altar and pulpit became a common feature in Lutheran churches, reaching its apogee in the theatrical churches of the eighteenth century, such as the Frauenkirche at Dresden.

Aside from the rarefied examples of the Schlosskapellen, new churches were mostly built to serve new communities. The earliest Lutheran churches were built in silver-mining towns: the first at Joachimstal in Bohemia, built between 1534 and 1540; the Marienkirche at Marienberg, built between 1558 and 1564. These churches however are of only limited architectural importance and do not seem to have greatly influenced the development of Protestant architecture. The church built at Klagenfurt in Carinthia between 1582 and 1591 seems to have followed the Torgau model but the building was much altered when it passed to the Jesuits in 1604. A more unusual church was designed as part of the model town of Freudenstadt laid out for Duke Frederick of Württemberg by the architect Heinrich Schickhardt. The church was built between 1601 and 1609, in the corner of the central square along two axes forming a 'L-shaped' plan. The church has galleries at the end of each axis and the siting of the altar, font and pulpit on

Figure 27.4 Interior of the Schlosskapelle, Hartenfels, Torgau. The raised and highly decorated pulpit (right) is placed halfway up the nave. (Bildarchiv Foto Marburg)

the outer angle ensured that the congregation had an unimpeded view during the service.

In the early seventeenth century, three more conventional and influential churches were built. They were the Marienkirche at Wolfenbüttel (begun 1608), Stadtkirche at Bückeburg (1610–15) and the Hofkirche at Neuberg-an-der-Donau (1607–18). The latter church began as a Protestant building, but it became a Catholic church in 1614 when it was handed over to the Jesuits. These churches were built as hall churches with a nave, tall aisles and a polygonal apse at the east end; Wolfenbüttel and Neuberg also had tribunes and a choir. The hall-church design, reminiscent of earlier Franciscan architecture, was ideally suited to preaching as it created a light and airy building with an unimpeded view. This longitudinal design was not adopted in the construction of the Stadtkirche zum Heiligen Geist built at Nidda around 1618. Here the church has a rectangular ground-plan with galleries along the sides of the nave and against the west end of the church. The design there is in stark contrast to those of Wolfenbüttel and Bückeburg, but provides another solution to the attempt to make the altar and the preaching of the Word visible but also audible.

The decoration of the Lutheran churches was influenced by the reformers' attitude towards religious images. Luther had reacted against the iconoclasm of Karlstadt in Wittenberg. For Luther images could perform an important educational role; they acted as a sign or a reminder of the Word of God. They were not the objects of devotion or adoration but were there to illustrate and, therefore, to support preaching. Therefore images of Christ, the Evangelists and the Apostles remained, whereas those of saints and also the Virgin Mary did not have a place in Lutheran churches. In fact there was a growth in the production of new altarpieces in northern Germany after the Reformation, particularly by Cranach. These altarpieces did, however, adopt Christo-centric and Protestant themes: the three principal scenes depicted the Last Supper, the Crucifixion and the Resurrection. Besides altarpieces, epitaphs and memorial monuments were another form of artistic expression which developed in Lutheran churches (see Figure 25.8, p. 478). These again served to educate the viewer but also provided a testament to the faith of the donor.

From the 1560s onwards pulpits were replaced in many churches in northern Germany by much larger and grander structures which served to emphasize the new primacy of the Word of God. As many as 200 were produced between 1595 and 1615 alone. One of the first such pulpits was commissioned by the cathedral chapter at Schleswig with seven carved panels. The common themes for such carvings were the Law and Gospel, the Crucifixion and Resurrection, the Evangelists and the Prophets.

THE SWISS REFORMERS

Such imagery and decoration of churches did not find favour with the Reformed. To Zwingli images broke the First Commandment and were seen to diminish God's glory. Even images of Christ or crucifixes were unacceptable as it was not possible to represent divinity. Images were a particularly contentious issue in the

Figure 27.5 Pulpit in Ratzeburg Cathedral with a contemporary portrait of the minister Georg Usler. (Bildarchiv Foto Marburg)

Zwinglian Reformation and at the end of June 1524 the city churches were stripped bare. The statues were removed together with their bases, murals chipped away and communion vessels melted down. The churches were purged of images and whitewashed. A further contrast between Lutheran and Zwinglian churches was the rejection of instrumental music by the Swiss reformer. Luther encouraged congregational singing and the organ had a prominent role in church services, but in Zurich the organs were destroyed in 1527.

In Geneva the Reformation had already purged the churches of images before the arrival of John Calvin. However, like Zwingli, Calvin rejected images on the grounds that it was not possible to represent the omnipotence of God and that to attempt to do so would belittle him. Furthermore, Calvin rejected the Lutheran argument that images could serve an educational role as God only revealed himself through his Word. The Calvinist rejection of images and church decoration was therefore reflected in the iconoclastic attacks made as the Calvinists attempted to take over the existing religious buildings for their worship, such as in France in 1562 and the Netherlands in 1566. However, the Genevans were not as zealous as their colleagues in Zurich; in Geneva the wall-paintings were not whitewashed over until 1543 and a cross remained, inaccessible, on the cathedral steeple until it was struck by lightning in 1556.

In Geneva, Scotland and eventually in the United Provinces, the Reformed took over the existing ecclesiastical structures, adapting them for their worship, as the Lutherans had done several decades earlier. While both the Lutherans and the Reformed emphasized the importance of preaching and the Word of God, their different theological positions on communion were reflected in their use of the church buildings. As the Lord's Supper was administered less frequently in the Reformed churches, it meant that the principal and sole focal point of the church was the pulpit; there was no place for an altar as in the Lutheran churches. Although initially chancels were used for the Lord's Supper in some Scottish churches (such as Crail, Culross and Perth), the chancel or choir had essentially become redundant. In some of the larger buildings (such as Aberdeen and Brechin Cathedrals), the choir was unroofed and abandoned, while the nave served as the parish church. In other churches the chancel was walled off from the nave and often served as a burial chamber for the local laird, sometimes with a loft constructed above for observing the services. A similar change in emphasis can be seen in the Netherlands. For example, while the Lord's Supper was administered in the choir of the Bavokerk at Haarlem, the new focal point was the pulpit in the nave with the seating ranged around it. In the Nieuwe Kerk in Delft, the choir was abandoned completely and became the mausoleum of William of Orange.

In the smaller Scottish churches, the placing of the pulpit in the nave (usually halfway along the south wall) was the main alteration of the Reformation. In some cases galleries were also built at the east and west ends to provide further seating and later the construction of a perpendicular aisle facing the pulpit transformed the ground-plan to a T-shape, providing either further seating accommodation or a 'laird's loft'. More dramatic alterations took place in the larger churches. Stone walls were erected inside St Giles' Church in Edinburgh in 1581 in order to divide the building into three separate churches. The construction of galleries ensured that the church had adequate seating but gave the impression of a theatre rather than a church. Although the building was restored in 1633 when it became a cathedral, it was again divided in 1639 and repartitioned several times until it was finally restored in 1882. Nor was this an isolated example: the church of St Nicholas in Aberdeen was another building which was divided into several churches at the Reformation.

Perhaps the clearest insight which can be gained into the architectural goals of the new Reformed churches are the buildings constructed by the Calvinists when they were unable to take over the existing religious structures. This was particularly true of France, but also of the Netherlands in the aftermath of the Iconoclastic Fury of 1566. Sadly, these buildings were also very obvious targets for Catholic revenge when the Calvinists lost power: few examples of buildings dating from this period survive today. The earliest surviving image of such a church is provided by Jean Perrissin's painting of the temple of Le Paradis in Lyons, an invaluable and exceptionally rare record of the interior of a sixteenth-century Huguenot temple. Le Paradis was built in 1564, but destroyed by rioters in 1567. It was a plain structure with an oval ground-plan; the pulpit, complete with hour-glass, is located in a central position facing the entrance. There is a first-floor gallery around the building and segregated benches before the pulpit, a catechizing bench and a more substantial bench for the consistory next to the pulpit. The interior is plain, apart from biblical texts on boards above the pulpit with Christ's summary of the Law (Matthew 22:37) and windows decorated with stained-glass *fleurs de lys* and coats-of-arms.

There are clear similarities between the interior of this temple and that constructed by the Calvinist community at Ghent in 1566, during the Reformed congregations' brief moment of religious freedom in that year. The Calvinist construction was visited and described in some detail by one curious Catholic observer:

> The temple was then octagonal and surrounded by a gallery, so that it was much broader at its base than at the top. It was largely built of wood, like the churches of Muscovy, except that the spaces between the posts had been filled with brickwork set in tanner's mortar. Both the lower and the upper storeys were lit by numerous windows. These were glazed with plain glass, except for the lower windows which bore inscriptions from the Ten Commandments of God and from other passages of Scripture. Looked at from both the outside and the inside, the temple resembled a lantern or riding school, only much larger ... the building measured 150 feet in length and 130 feet in width. ... Inside there was an enclosure, a good twenty feet wide, where men could stand or sit around. The women all sat in the middle separated by a partition or parapet against which they had put benches for the men to sit on and those outside, in the said enclosure, could use it as a balustrade on which to lean. The interior of the temple was supported by roof timbers, the work of some master craftsman. The pulpit, recently made of fir in the ancient style, stood at the far end. In the middle before the pulpit was the wide enclosure, mentioned above, where the women and girls

sat. ... A large number of fixed benches stood behind and on either side of the pulpit. ... The children and youth received their instruction in their sort of confession or catechism sitting on these benches. ... This temple had a very fine thatch while the roof of the surrounding covered way below (which we call the gallery or storey) was covered with planks from Magdeburg, the joints and seams of which were packed with linen cloth and pitch to prevent the rain from seeping through.[1]

Although the temples built at Lyons and Ghent were swept away soon after their construction, the vivid descriptions provide a clear insight into early Calvinist church architecture. The design and structure of these early buildings established the architectural principles which underpinned the temples built after the Edict of Nantes in 1598, most notably Grand Temple, La Rochelle (inaugurated 1603); Dieppe (1600); Quévilly, near Rouen (1601); Caen (1612), and Montauban (1615). This design was also employed by the exiles from the southern Netherlands at Hanau in the temples built between 1601 and 1608. There they built an octagonal structure for the smaller Walloon community which was attached to a twelve-sided building for the larger Flemish community. The pulpits were placed on the adjoining walls and the temples each had galleries. Although only the smaller octagonal church remains after the Second World War, it is a rare survivor of this form of Calvinist architecture.

These churches designed around a central plan reflected the importance of preaching the Word in Calvinist worship. The design ensured that the preacher could be heard and the provision of seating attempted to ensure a more attentive audience for the lengthy sermons. The buildings therefore were a complete contrast to Catholic churches and this contrast was further enhanced by the restrictions placed on the Huguenots in successive edicts.

The polygonal structure was not the only design adopted by the Huguenots. At Charenton on the outskirts of Paris, the temple was built by the leading architect Jacques II du Cerceau in 1607. Unfortunately it was razed to the ground by the Paris mob in 1621. A replacement was built by du Cerceau's nephew, the royal architect Salomon de Brosse. The temple resembled its predecessor but was a much larger and more innovative building. The design was based on Vitruvius' description of his basilica at Fano. There were four staircases, which gave access to a double gallery surrounding the building. The galleries cut across the tall windows, resulting in a light interior, and the pulpit was positioned centrally in front of benches of segregated seating. The Charenton temple proved to be an influential design, not only for other Protestant churches but also for the construction of synagogues.

The temple at Charenton was demolished in 1685 with the Revocation of the Edict of Nantes. Other temples had gradually been suppressed as the restrictions upon the Huguenots intensified from the mid-seventeenth century with the more rigorous enforcement of the edict; churches which could not prove their existence in 1596 or 1597 were destroyed. As a result most of these buildings are only known about from contemporary descriptions or illustrations, although the remains of a Calvinist temple were discovered in 1989 at the Château de Chamerolles near

Figure 27.6 *Interior of the Temple of Charenton, Paris*, 1648. (Copenhagen, Royal Library)

Orleans. A further survivor, although not strictly French, is the rectangular church at Montbéliard, which now lies within France. Montbéliard was built by Heinrich Schickardt for Duke Frederick of Württemburg between 1601–7.

The polygonal ground-plan also found favour elsewhere, although in Scotland and the United Provinces it was initially possible to take over the existing religious buildings. One of the first Calvinist temples in the Netherlands was built at Willemstad (a new town near Dordrecht) between 1597 and 1607 by Coenraat van Norenburch for Maurice of Nassau. The church built at IJzendijke in 1612 also probably had an octagonal ground-plan. The church has a diameter of 17.5 metres and the pulpit is in a central position, although the building lacks a gallery. Willemstad therefore reflects the earlier Reformed temples, but it was a design used elsewhere in the Netherlands, appealing to the architects of Dutch classicism. The Marekerk at Leiden was built between 1639 and 1649, by Arent van 's-Gravesande with the advice of Jacob van Campen. The church is a wide-based octagon, surmounted by a drum pierced by windows (ensuring a well-lit interior) which is in turn surmounted by a hemispherical dome topped by an open bell-tower. The whole church was built strictly observing classical principles. Further examples of this type of church were the Oostkerk in Middelburg (built 1647–67) by Bartholomeus Fransz. Drijfhout and Pieter Post; the Leidenschendam (1647–53) by van 's-Gravensande; and the Lutheran Church in Amsterdam (1668–71) by Adriaan Dortsman.

Other designs were also adopted in the construction of new churches in the Netherlands. In Amsterdam, three of the four new Reformed churches were built by the architect Hendrik de Keyser: the Zuiderkerk (1603–11), Westerkerk (1621–31) and Noorderkerk (1620–2). These buildings provide an interesting transition in architectural styles. The Zuiderkerk resembles the Gothic hall churches with a nave and two narrower side-aisles. However, the principal direction of the church was traversal rather than longitudinal, as the pulpit was placed against the middle pillar on the west side of the nave. The Westerkerk was a much larger structure, in fact the largest Protestant church in Europe at that time. The church is a fuller development of the Zuiderkerk with a clear rectangular ground-plan and the integration of the aisles into the main space of the building. Although the pulpit is again located in the centre of the nave, this is a much more centralized church. The design of the Noorderkerk is much more clearly based on classical principles, with a Greek cross as its ground-plan. The pulpit is located at the intersection of two arms of the cross, ensuring the maximum audibility and visibility of the minister. Variations on this Greek-cross plan appeared at Renswoude, Hooge Zwaluwe (1639–41), and the 's-Gravenland church (1657–8) built by Daniel Staelpaert. At the Nieuwe Kerk in Haarlem (1645–9), Jacob van Campen designed a church following the Greek-cross plan but inscribed within a square. The pulpit was located centrally at the aperture of the southernmost arm. All of these church designs served to combine the demands of Reformed worship for a centrally located pulpit with architectural fashion for classical principles. However, these demands were not always followed. The Nieuwe Kerk, The Hague (1645–9), was built by Pieter Noorwits and Bartholomeus van Bassen, who is also known for his paintings of fantastic church interiors. The church had a longitudinal axis which combines two centralized spaces, with the pulpit located on the middle wall linking these two areas. While the Baroque design conformed to architectural fashion, it was less successful as a place of worship because in some cases the congregation had their backs to the pulpit.

The exuberance and richness of the classical architecture in the United Provinces reflected the growing prosperity of the emergent state. In Scotland, while there was a growing need for new buildings, they do not on the whole reflect the richness of the Netherlands. The earliest churches were merely gabled rectangles adapted for the demands of Reformed worship and such structures continued to be built into the seventeenth century. Typical examples of this type of church were built at Dunnottar Castle in the 1580s, Greenock (1591), Durness (1619) and Nigg (1626). The church of Greyfriars in Edinburgh, built between 1602 and 1620, reflected this old-fashioned approach: an aisled nave with the pulpit placed against a pier on the south arcade. While Greyfriars perpetuated the Gothic style, the initially rectangular church at Dirleton (1612) was more sophisticated with a restrained classical style. A variation of this rectangular design was the T-shaped church, which was a common solution in adapting existing churches at the Reformation. The church at Kemback, Fife, is dated 1582 and has an asymmetrical aisle opening onto the south side. At Prestonpans, the church was built by the minister John Davidson after 1595 and has a rectangular ground-plan, a tower at the west end and the Hamilton aisle extending to the south forming the T-shape. Further examples of this style include Weem (1600) and Anstruther Easter, Fife (1634–44); in Ayrshire, the Auld Kirk, Ayr (1654–44), New

Figure 27.7 Interior of Burntisland Church with the Castle Pew and seventeenth-century gallery behind. (Edinburgh, Royal Commission on the Ancient and Historical Monuments of Scotland)

Cumnock (1657) and Sorn (1658). In the seventeenth century, the Greek cross ground-plan was also used at Cawdor in Nairn (1619), Portpatrick, Galloway (1622–9) and also Fenwick, Ayrshire (1643). In each of these examples, one of the arms of the Greek cross seems to have served as a laird's loft so that the actual interior of the church has a T-plan. All of these churches served to enhance the visibility and audibility of the preacher by ensuring a central position for the pulpit, but the development of laird's aisles and burial vaults emphasizes the dominance of the local landowners.

There are several particularly remarkable Scottish churches from the late sixteenth century. During the 1590s the burgesses of Burntisland built a new church overlooking the harbour which had a centralized plan (see Figure 27.7). The unusual design of the church has resulted in attempts by historians to seek precedents from the Continent, although these have not been always convincing or feasible. The square ground-plan again serves to emphasize the centrality of preaching and in the early seventeenth century galleries were built by the trade guilds; the Castle Pew, which faces the pulpit, dates from 1606. The radicalism of the design was reflected in Archbishop Laud's comments when he saw the church in 1633. He took it 'at first sight for a large pigeon-house; so free was it from any suspicion of being so much as built like an ancient church'. The homespun character of Burntisland contrasts markedly with the Chapel Royal, Stirling Castle, rebuilt at the same time (see Figure 27.8). This is a single-storey rectangular

Figure 27.8 Exterior of the Chapel Royal, Stirling Castle. (Edinburgh, Historic Scotland)

building, but was innovative in its use of classical forms – in particular with the entrance taking the form of a triumphal arch. However, this was a building which was intended to impress and was rebuilt for the baptism of Prince Henry in 1594. The influence of Dutch classicism, particularly from Henrik de Keyser's *Architectura Moderna*, was reflected in the design of the Tron Church in Edinburgh, built by John Mylne Jun. between 1637 and 1647. The T-shaped church had a pulpit centrally placed on the long wall opposite the projecting south aisle. Although the layout was a typically Scottish response to the demands of Reformed worship, its stylish decoration reflected the prevailing architectural fashion of the period.

The theological changes of the Reformation were therefore clearly expressed in the alterations to existing churches and in the layout and design of new buildings. While there were clear differences in attitudes towards the altar, the organ and the decoration of the churches, the importance of the pulpit and the preaching of the Word was recognized by all of the Reformers. Therefore the demands of preaching became the main concern in the design of new churches, although it was possible to combine this with the demands of architectural fashion.

NOTE

1   A. Duke, G. Lewis and A. Pettegree (eds), *Calvinism in Europe, 1540–1610: A Collection of Documents* (Manchester, 1992), pp. 153–5.

FURTHER READING

The only recent surveys of Protestant church architecture are provided by B. Reymond, *L'architecture religieuse des protestants* (Geneva, 1996), and an essay by Jeffrey Chipps Smith in the *Oxford Encyclopedia of the Reformation* (New York, 1996). In general, studies tend to focus on individual states and a longer time-period. Lutheran architecture is examined in its general context by H.-R. Hitchcock, *German Renaissance Architecture* (Princeton, 1981), and the interiors of the churches, pulpits and tombs is covered in J. Chipps Smith, *German Sculpture of the Later Renaissance, c.1520–1580* (Princeton, 1994). A useful essay is D. Grossmann, 'L'église à tribunes et les tribunes des églises en Allemagne au XVIe siècle', in J. Guillaume (ed.), *L'Eglise dans l'Architecture de la Renaissance* (Paris, 1995), pp. 257–66. For Scotland the main text remains G. Hay's *The Architecture of Scottish Post-Reformation Churches, 1560–1843* (Oxford, 1957), with more recent research assimilated by D. Howard, *Scottish Architecture from the Reformation to the Restoration, 1560–1660* (Edinburgh, 1995). On the Netherlands the most thorough examination of this subject is C.A. van Swigchem, T. Brouwer and W. van Os, *Een huis voor het Woord. Het Protestantse kerkinterieur in Nederland tot 1900* (The Hague, 1984); in English, the subject is discussed in the general context of Dutch architecture in W. Kuyper's *Dutch Classicist Architecture* (Delft, 1980). Only a limited amount has been published on the architecture of the Huguenots. An introduction to the subject is provided by D. Thomson, 'Protestant Temples in France c.1566–1623', in Guillaume, *L'Eglise dans l'Architecture*, pp. 245–56. A general work which includes a number of illustrations is H. Dubief and J. Poujol, *La France Protestante. Histoire et lieux de mémoire* (Montpellier, 1992). Much has been published on the subject of iconoclasm and the arts, but these works provide an introduction to the topic: C. Garside, *Zwingli and the Arts* (New Haven, 1966), and S. Michalski, *The Reformation and the Visual Arts* (London, 1993).

SCIENCE AND MEDICINE

Charlotte Methuen

It is often assumed that science and theology found themselves in a state of opposition during the sixteenth century, that the church was opposed to the pursuit of scientific knowledge and that religion tended to stifle new scientific developments. The condemnation of Galileo Galilei by the Italian Inquisition would be cited by many as evidence of this stance. Science, according to this interpretation, is the representative of 'modern' thinking, while the church and theology fight a rearguard action to defend their – fundamentally conservative – position. But a closer look at the sixteenth century demonstrates that such a picture is at best simplistic and at worst a profound misunderstanding of the complexity of the relationship between science, medicine and theology during the century of the Reformation.

Although I shall use it in the modern sense, the use of the term 'science' in discussions of the sixteenth century is really an anachronism, since science in the modern sense did not exist. The term *scientia* referred to knowledge which had been proved in a certain way, and was thus a term belonging to dialectics. In the sixteenth century, a systematically empirical science had not yet come into being and the origins of modern science can be traced back to a number of sources. Technological developments were beginning to influence what could be known about the natural world and to give rise to new theories. Science derived in part from knowledge about the natural world as it was taught in universities in the form of natural philosophy and astronomy; theological developments affected this teaching and the priority it was accorded. But the pursuit of knowledge was conducted not only in universities but in the courts of Europe; patronage could have a profound effect on the career of an astronomer or mathematician. Finally, the role of the practical sciences, including magic, in the rise of modern science should not be underestimated. In the sixteenth and seventeenth centuries, these elements were played out against the backdrop of the Reformation and of increasing confessionalization. The resulting theological beliefs influenced the way in which the world was seen and contributed to the development of new ways of looking.

LATE MEDIÆVAL WORLD-VIEWS

Educated people of the late Middle Ages were generally aware that the earth was approximately spherical. The dominant cosmology was based upon the theories of Aristotle and Ptolemy which argued for a spherical earth placed at the centre of a finite spherical universe (see Figure 28.1). The entire cosmology was based upon a system of nested spheres. The seven planets of the geocentric universe (that is, the moon, Mercury, Venus, the sun, Mars, Saturn and Jupiter) moved in concentric spheres around the earth and the universe was bounded by the sphere of the fixed stars. The status of these spheres – whether or not they were material – was

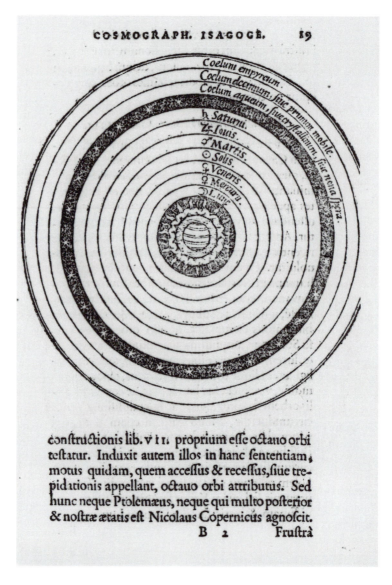

Figure 28.1 Aristotle's spherical cosmology. From Georg Peurbach, *Novae theoricae planetarum*, 1528. (Wolfenbüttel, Herzog August Bibliothek)

subject to debate, especially since Ptolemy's mathematical explanation of astronomical observation was difficult to reconcile with the Aristotelian theory of the spheres. Ptolemy postulated a complicated system of epicycles (circular motion around a centre which itself moves in a circle: see Figure 28.2) which allowed him to explain the motion of the planets, and to predict future movements and especially conjunctions with a degree of accuracy. Debates about the relationship between physical (Aristotelian) and mathematical or astronomical (Ptolemaic) explications of the universe continued well into the seventeenth century.

Figure 28.2 The theory of epicycles. From Georg Peurbach, *Novae theoricae planetarum*, 1528. (Wolfenbüttel, Herzog August Bibliothek)

Aristotle taught that the heavens – that is, the region above the moon – were of a different substance to the sublunar sphere. The latter was constituted from the elements, an ascending hierarchy of earth, water, air and fire, which were subject to change and decay. The heavens, on the other hand, were composed of a perfect 'quintessence' (fifth essence). Beyond the spheres no activity or motion existed, and so the cause of the uniform motion was understood to be the striving to imitate the unchanging perfection of a transcendent prime mover, which could be identified with God. Change could not take place in the supralunar regions; their shape (spherical) and the constant circular motion of the heavenly bodies were seen as a corollary of their perfection. Aristotelian science understood the unchanging motion of the heavens to be one of the causes of irregular motion and change in the sublunar elements. The heavens were thus understood to influence the sublunar sphere. Astrology and astrological interpretation were, therefore, integrated into physics. The close link between the heavens and the sublunar sphere, and particularly the frequently drawn analogy between the macrocosmos (the universe) and the microcosmos (the human body), meant that astrology also had a particular application in medicine.

Although other world-views were possible – in 1440 Nicholas of Cusa postulated a non-Aristotelian cosmology with an infinite universe – they were unusual. Aristotelian cosmology and Aristotelian theories of nature formed the basis for accepted theories about the nature of the universe and the world.

TECHNOLOGICAL DEVELOPMENTS

The most significant technological development for both the Reformation and the natural sciences was the invention of printing around 1450, together with improvement in the quality of paper. This removed control of the dissemination of information from the monasteries and massively increased the availability of standardized texts.

New forms of cannon, arising from improvements in the production of metals, brought new forms of war and saw an end to the culture of the knights of the Middle Ages. New forms of war resulted also in new needs for defence and these brought about changes in architecture. But a further effect of developments in refining and casting metals was better instrumentation. This affected many different areas of knowledge, notably astronomy, surveying and navigation. Refinements in optics and the production of glass led to the production of the first microscope by the Dutch brothers Janssen in 1590; Galileo and Kepler built the first telescopes around 1610. The production of more accurate clocks enabled more precise timekeeping and the natural day (with hours of different length by night and by day, in summer and in winter) began to give way to the artificial day, divided into twenty-four hours of equal length. There was growing criticism of the inaccuracies of the Julian calendar in dating Easter and in placing the solstices. In 1582 Pope Gregory XIII declared the introduction of the corrected, Gregorian calendar; however, many Protestant states refused to recognize his authority to do so and the Julian calendar remained in use in parts of Europe.

The development of instruments such as the astrolabe and the 'old quadrant', together with improved shipbuilding techniques also enabled better navigation, although it was still not possible to determine longitude accurately. Voyages of discovery of the fifteenth and sixteenth centuries led to the discovery of people living in the tropical regions, which Aristotle had deemed uninhabitable. Such discoveries raised serious questions about the validity of the mediæval world-view.

THE NATURAL WORLD AND THE UNIVERSITIES

The early sixteenth century found the teaching of philosophy in a crisis. Philosophy was taught in the arts faculty, often by students of one of the higher faculties – theology, law and medicine. Most arts faculties were affiliated either to the *via antiqua* or the *via moderna*, although some employed two sets of staff and taught both.[1] The onset of humanism with its new approach to philosophy rendered this pattern obsolete. Humanist faculties concentrated on teaching the seven *artes liberales*, the linguistic *trivium* (grammar, rhetoric and dialectics) and the mathematical *quadrivium* (arithmetic, geometry, astronomy and music), complemented by the study of natural and moral philosophy. Scholastic philosophy was deplored for its 'sophism' and 'playing with words', and focus was moved to the study of original texts, preferably in their original languages. Central to this approach was the assumption that human knowledge had been deteriorating steadily since the time of the Fall.[2]

NATURAL PHILOSOPHY

Despite the reorganization of the arts faculties under the influence of humanism, there was a good deal of continuity in the teaching of natural philosophy between the late Middle Ages and the Renaissance. Knowledge about the sensible natural world took the form of a largely theoretical or speculative study of the nature of sensible matter (that is, of 'material things as they appear to the senses'; these include the heavenly bodies) and of the causes of their motion. In most universities the curriculum was derived largely from a close study of Aristotle's *Physica*, *De coelo*, *De generatione et corruptione*, *De anima*, *Metereologica*, and other *libri naturales*, and sometimes considering also the *Metaphysica*. Natural philosophy was not studied as an empirical science, since Aristotle and other ancient philosophers were understood to have gathered all essential knowledge about the world. With the rediscovery of the works of Plato, a central concern became the reconciliation of the different theories laid down by the philosophers and their relationship to Christianity. Thus Marsilio Ficino attempted a Christian synthesis of Platonic and Aristotelian traditions, which was intended to demonstrate the continuity between pagan and Christian thought. Such speculative works remained largely divorced from empirical considerations.

There were exceptions to this rule. In Italy, the recovery of the pseudo-Aristotelian *Mechanica* encouraged natural philosophers to integrate the insights of technological developments into mechanical and physical theory. Similarly, the frequent practice of having natural philosophy taught by a student or professor of medicine encouraged the crossing of disciplinary boundaries and a closer relationship between the theory and practice of medicine. The reformer Philip Melanchthon was convinced that the study of natural philosophy should involve the study of God's created world, drawing upon medical and anatomical knowledge in his explication of the soul, appealing to Pliny's *Historia naturalis* and emphasizing the importance of observing the heavens and the motions of the planets for the study of physics. Here significant steps towards breaking down the boundaries between disciplines were being taken, but the incorporation of examples from the study of the natural world, especially from medicine, technology or astronomy, remained the exception rather than the rule among university natural philosophers of all confessions.

THE MATHEMATICAL SCIENCES

The mathematical sciences – arithmetic, geometry, astronomy and (to a lesser extent) music – also formed a part of the university curriculum. Astronomy had originally been included in the university curriculum because of the necessity of teaching priests to calculate the date of Easter. All the mathematical sciences were recognized as having practical applications, but they were taught also because their logical proofs offered a useful introduction to dialectics.

Arithmetic dealt largely with calculation techniques and included some algebraic work. The complexity of long arithmetical calculations and the lack of a clear general notation meant that algebra was not yet a more sophisticated science than arithmetic. Poor notation made the manipulation of algebraic expressions extremely difficult and algebraic problems were often solved either geometrically or by outlining a general method and giving specific examples.

Euclid formed the central text for the teaching of geometry. However, although the rediscovery of Arabic and Greek mathematical texts led to a renewed interest in mathematics for its own sake, in contrast to the other disciplines, mathematical sciences had no single text which could be regarded as a central authority. Indeed, by the beginning of the sixteenth century serious limitations to the ancient texts had been recognized and new disciplines and areas of work were being opened up. The work of mathematicians such as Regiomontanus (1436–76) and Rheticus (1514–76) not only established trigonometry as a new discipline, but moved the boundaries of the mathematical sciences. Their contribution was demonstrably superior to what had been discovered in classical works.

Astronomy included the teaching of geography, and professors of astronomy were often cartographers as well as practical astronomers. Celestial astronomy might be taught on the basis of Ptolemy's *Almagest* or Sacrobosco's *De sphaera*, but astronomy was plagued by the discrepancies between predictions made on the basis of these works and actual astronomical observations. Astronomical observations formed the basis for timekeeping (including the calendar); geographical position was calculated from the stars; analysis of the movements of planets and stars was essential in the practice of medicine; weather prediction also relied heavily on these observations. It was, therefore, essential that such observations should be accurate. Many sixteenth-century astronomers wrote their own textbooks seeking to correct these anomalies and these dealt to a greater or lesser extent with controversial observations or conclusions. The nature of the mathematical sciences, perhaps more than any others, was not conducive to a simple restriction to the humanist cry: *Ad fontes!*

The endeavour to improve observations was supported by theological considerations. Viewed as perfect, the heavens were understood to be closer to God than the sublunar sphere. Melanchthon believed that the study of the orderly movements of the heavenly bodies could reveal God's providence and care for the world and incite the observer to a godly life. Astronomy was important not only for its practical applications.

THEORETICAL MEDICINE

Like philosophy, law and theology, the teaching of medicine in the universities was in this period based on the study of ancient texts. Medical theory understood illness to be caused by a disturbance in the balance of the four humours: choler or bile, blood, phlegm and melancholer or black bile. The natural balance or temperament of each person was different, so that it was important to establish the individual's type before beginning to treat them. Since the stars were held to affect the humours, the position of the stars and planets at birth was important in understanding this basic make-up; celestial motions also affected the health. Horoscopes were, therefore, a necessary prerequisite to medical treatment.

The rediscovery of works by Hippocrates and especially Galen had made ancient anatomically based medical knowledge available, but this remained theoretical. Vesalius' criticism of the theoretical approach led him to include anatomical dissections as an essential part of the medical course and this practice became more common during the century. In Italy conflict arose between the followers of Galen and of Vesalius, while in northern Europe, the iatrochemical ideas of Paracelsus became influential, although they remained controversial.

Despite these conflicts, practical anatomy could be introduced as complementary to 'book anatomy'. This was the pattern in Wittenberg, under the influence of Melanchthon. Melanchthon believed that the study of the human body could illuminate the workings of the soul; moreover, knowledge of the workings of the human body would, according to Melanchthon, bring understanding of the orderly workings of the created universe and thus of the behaviour expected by God of human beings. The intention was to advance true religion through the understanding of humankind.

THE EFFECT OF THE REFORMATION

In Germany, in contrast to elsewhere in what was to become Protestant Europe, many universities had been established in the course of the fifteenth century, often with the stated intention of obviating the need for the sons of the local kingdom or duchy to 'go abroad' to study. German universities were thus bound up with understandings of national identity. After the Reformation, which also functioned as a cause to which princes and dukes could rally their people, universities became the obvious place to train loyal pastors, lawyers, teachers and clerks who had been versed in doctrine that had been approved by the local church. Arts faculty curricula were reformed to take account of the new status of the universities and to make the most of the fact that all students passed through the arts faculty before moving on to the higher faculties.

The content of the teaching of natural philosophy or astronomy was generally not much affected by these reforms. However, the institutional context in which such teaching took place changed significantly. The concern of the theologians that proper doctrine should be taught, combined with Luther's emphasis on theology and criticism of philosophy's theological aspirations, raised questions about the importance of both moral and natural philosophy. In Tübingen, a series of university visitation committees questioned the importance of natural philosophy and pleaded for the inclusion of more theology in the arts faculty. Natural philosophers responded that a proper understanding of physics formed a basis for the proper understanding of theological controversies; thus Jacob Schegk drew upon physics and his understanding of the nature of matter in his explication of the relation of the two natures of Christ. In a similar way, the theologian Jacob Heerbrand appealed to Aristotelian cometary theory in a sermon on the comet of 1577.

On the Catholic side, a move towards fixing the content of natural philosophical teaching can be observed from the time of the Council of Trent (1545–63) onwards. This gave rise to new strictures on natural philosophy and biblical interpretation which later played their part in the condemnation of Galileo (1633). While Lutheran princes and dukes also resorted to censorship and excommunication in an attempt to control what their people could know,[3] and natural philosophical and astronomical works also came under these rules, such censorship was local and banned Lutheran works could be published in other territories.[4]

ASTRONOMY AND THE CHURCH

Natural philosophy was concerned not only with nature, but with causes. It was largely free from mathematical analyses of motion, whether sub- or supralunar, for these were considered the preserve of the mathematical sciences. The distinction between astronomy and astrology reflected precisely this division of concerns. Although the two terms were often used interchangeably, technically speaking astronomy was concerned with the mathematical analysis of the motions of heavenly bodies, and with the prediction of celestial phenomena such as planetary conjunctions or eclipses. Astronomy did not concern itself with the nature of the heavenly bodies, although the fundamental assumption that their motion must be circular was drawn from physics (and astronomy was thus viewed as a mixed science). Astrology, on the other hand, was concerned with the effects of the motions of the stars and planets as observed and predicted by the astronomers. Not all astrological interpretations were admitted. Melanchthon, for instance, distinguished between superstition and astrology, defined to be 'the part of physics which teaches what effects the light of the stars has on simple and mixed bodies, and what kind of temperaments, what changes and what inclinations it induces'.[5] But most were convinced that a Christian astrology was possible. The star at Jesus' birth, the eclipse at his death and the gospels' apocalyptic warnings that heavenly signs would accompany the end of the world were cited as indicators that the stars could indeed relate God's intentions for the world.

The boundaries between astrology and astronomy were not always preserved, and most astronomers both made observations and offered astrological analyses. Indeed, such predictions and the production of almanacs and horoscopes in which they were distributed were economically essential to the livelihood of many astronomers and mathematicians. University astronomers were also expected to comment on celestial phenomena and such comments usually included astrological considerations. The role of the sixteenth-century astronomer was characterized by its position between court and university; princes were keen to understand the

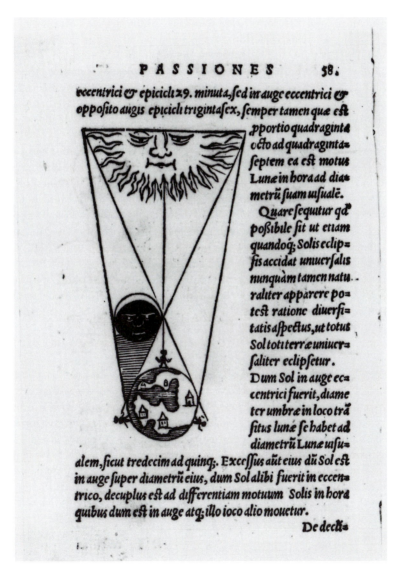

Figure 28.3 Observing an eclipse of the sun. From Georg Peurbach, *Novae theoricae planetarum*, 1528. (Wolfenbüttel, Herzog August Bibliothek)

implications of the heavens for themselves and a patron could offer the serious astronomer the instruments he needed for his observations.

THEOLOGY AND THE STUDY OF THE HEAVENS

The need for accurate observations had not only a scientific background, but a theological basis. The understanding that God had created the world led swiftly to the conviction that the created world should be studied in order to yield a better understanding of God. This was particularly important in a period in which traditional doctrines and theology were coming under attack. Moreover, within Lutheran circles, Luther's rejection of the theology of works left a need for an ethical authority. It is no coincidence that when Melanchthon called for the study of the natural world, he emphasized the orderly aspects of nature, the way in which the human body represented in microcosm the macrocosm of the universe, and the regular motions of the heavenly bodies. Melanchthon offered this order as a model for the order which he believed God intended to be present in society. The study of the natural world provides a model for human behaviour.

Melanchthon's integration of philosophy (both natural and moral) and theology was rooted in Aristotelian and Platonic cosmology: God's mind and will were expressed in the form of creation and were transmitted through the medium of the heavens to earth. His Aristotelian conviction that the heavens were made from perfect matter allowed him to teach that they represented God's will and God's mind more closely than could the sublunar sphere. Had the Fall not taken place, Melanchthon believed, human beings would have been able to understand the will of God directly from the stars. After the Fall, the human mind needed training (in the form of philosophy) to understand God's message. But philosophy and the natural world belonged to the law, and could never make known the gospel, the salvific work of God in Jesus Christ. Nonetheless, the study of the heavens could lead to a proper appreciation of God's creative work in the world. More accurate observations, in theory at least, were to be desired since they increased this knowledge.

The conviction that the natural world, and in particular the heavens, could reveal God as creator and could demonstrate God's providence was shared by most sixteenth-century theologians, natural philosophers and astronomers. A number of other justifications were offered for this view. Michael Maestlin, astronomer in Tübingen in the later sixteenth century, drew upon the Old Testament wisdom tradition for his own justification of his astronomical work. Jacob Heerbrand, a student of Melanchthon, later professor of theology in Tübingen, understood the natural world to constitute the *liber naturae*, a source of revelation in some ways parallel to the *liber scripturae*, the Bible. This 'two books' theology, derived from Augustine, was an important element in the thought of Johannes Kepler and was also used by hermeticists and alchemists, among others, to justify their study of the natural world. The emphasis on the book of nature is not, however, necessarily indicative of an interest in the natural world. Matthias Hafenreffer, Heerbrand's younger colleague at Tübingen, also cited the *liber naturae*, but did so on the basis of biblical texts alone, without any reference to the natural world.

COMETS AND THE CRITICISM OF ARISTOTLE

Such theological justifications could be useful to astronomers, especially when their observations contradicted accepted theories. In the course of the sixteenth century, with better accuracy of observation made possible by technological advances, this was increasingly the case. The close study of the comet of 1530–1 led the German astronomer Peter Apian and the Italian Girolamo Fracastoro to conclude that a comet's tail always pointed away from the sun, and Jean Pena in France proposed a new theory of comets, which included the anti-Aristotelian thesis that not all comets were sublunar.

The possibility that comets might be supralunar was confirmed by observations of the comet of 1577–8. Astronomers including John Dee in England, Maestlin in Germany and Tycho Brahe in Denmark observed that the comet was further away from the earth than the moon. Maestlin's observations of a further comet in 1580 confirmed this finding. Observing that his conclusions were opposed to Aristotelian theory, Maestlin offered a detailed theological justification for his work, arguing that the heavens should be observed and accurately interpreted since they had been created by God.

But theology did not appear only as a justification for precise observation. The conviction, grounded in the doctrine of special providence, that God could intervene in the normal running of the world, allowed the interpretation of phenomena which contradicted physical theory. When the nova of 1572 was recognized by Wilhelm of Hesse and Casper Peucer to be above the moon (in fact it was a star), they were able to cite this supernatural (to them) phenomenon as an example of God's intervention in the natural running of the world. In this way they could explain a phenomenon which the terms of Aristotelian physics made impossible.

THE GREGORIAN CALENDAR

Astronomy in the sixteenth century was central for the measurement of time and place. Until the development of accurate clocks, the heavens were the only way of determining the length of days and years. By 1500 the calendar had become divorced from the actual year. Calendar reform was a feature of the century. The Gregorian calendar, which corrected the old calendar by ten days, was eventually introduced by Pope Gregory XIII in 1582. Although this reform was supported by many astronomers, including John Dee in England, the pope's support for it raised suspicion in many Protestant quarters. In Lutheran Tübingen, both theologians and astronomers rejected the calendar and in England the opposition of the bishops delayed its introduction by 170 years.

COPERNICUS AND THE HELIOCENTRIC UNIVERSE

Concern for the accuracy of the calendar was one of the reasons which prompted Copernicus to develop his heliocentric theory of the universe. *De revolutionibus*, in which this theory was propounded, was published in 1543. Its reception was mixed.

The publication had been supported by Rheticus, mathematician in Wittenberg, who remained a convinced Copernican. More typical, however, was the reaction of Rheticus's colleague, the reformer Melanchthon, who welcomed Copernicus's contribution to the calculation of more accurate observations, exemplified in the Prutenic tables, but who did not himself espouse heliocentric theory, believing that only the traditional theories should be taught to students. Tycho Brahe developed a modified heliocentric theory, in which the sun orbited the stationary earth and the other planets orbited the sun. From 1616, when the Catholic church ruled against the Copernican theory, this became the accepted cosmological model for Jesuit teaching of astronomy. In Tübingen, Maestlin taught the Copernican theory to his more able students, including Johannes Kepler, who in turn developed more precise laws to describe heliocentric planetary motion. Thomas Digges in England and Galileo in Italy accepted the theory, and in the seventeenth century Galileo's observations of the satellites of Jupiter did much to further its cause.

Emphasis on literal exegesis of the Bible, a feature of Protestant theology, but present also in Catholicism, brought criticism of the heliocentric principle. (How could 'the sun stand still' if it did not move?) In response astronomers indicated other biblical passages in which God's Word had rephrased a deeper truth to make it accessible to human understanding.

Discussion of the heliocentric theory was not the priority for sixteenth-century astronomers. Challenges to Aristotelian cometary theory and natural philosophy, corrections to the calendar and the status of astrology were much more burning questions.

PRACTICAL SCIENCES

All the theoretical sciences described above had a practical side and, as has been seen, it was the meeting of practical and theoretical which led to developments in theory. Within universities, astronomers and physicians were particularly subject to this interaction, but the tensions between theory and practice manifested themselves clearly outside university life and in the practical sciences.

Paracelsus had introduced new medicines into the pharmacopoeias which were based on mineral preparations, rather than being exclusively herbal.[6] These and other practical investigations concerned the hidden properties of natural materials and could thus loosely be termed magic. Since only God could act beyond nature (supernaturally), all magic, whether good or demonic, was held to be natural. Demonic magic occurred when the magus sought to transcend the limitations of human knowledge and sought to call up a demon and exploit its perfect knowledge of natural properties. It was condemned, not because it was magic, but because of the traffic with demons.

The investigation of magical properties, whether of plants, the planets, metals or other materials, brought about fundamental changes in the way the world was seen. Thus, improvements to compass design during the fifteenth and sixteenth centuries raised questions about the nature of magnetism and the magnetic properties of the earth which Aristotelian physics could do nothing to answer. Similarly, alchemical attempts to produce gold revealed properties of materials which conflicted with Aristotle's theory of the elements. Increasingly the examination of 'magical' or 'occult' properties of bodies which could not be explained in Aristotelian terms gave rise to a major shift in theories of matter, in which the newly rediscovered theories of the ancient atomists were revived to provide the basis of the so-called 'mechanical philosophy' of the seventeenth century.

THEOLOGY AND THE DEVELOPMENT OF MODERN SCIENCE

During the sixteenth century the combined forces of humanism and Reformation shook scholastic theology and philosophy to their foundations. The consequent discrediting of accepted systems of thought rendered the search for new sources of authority necessary. In part these were sought in the natural, created world. The search was aided by technological developments and magical investigations, for these raised questions about the natural world which were unanswerable from the teachings of Aristotle and other ancient texts.

Although Catholics also became empirical observers, it is probably fair to argue that the Protestant emphasis on the priesthood of all believers encouraged believers to interpret both the book of the scriptures and the book of nature for themselves. Within Protestantism it is not possible to distinguish confessional influences in the content of sciences in the sixteenth century. An interest in the study of the book of nature is normally, although not always, related to the conviction that God tends to act according to general providence rather than intervening arbitrarily in the world (special providence). Those theologians who emphasized that knowledge of God could be attained through precise observation of the created world were generally prepared, at least to some extent, to integrate the findings of such observations into natural philosophical or cosmological works.

ACKNOWLEDGEMENT

With thanks to John Henry for his comments and suggestions.

NOTES

1   At the university of Tübingen, the two *viae* were housed in the same building, but separated from one another by a wall down the middle.
2   The idea that human knowledge might develop from a pre-lapsarian innocence appears first with the early Enlightenment.
3   In 1612, Johannes Kepler was excluded from communion by a pastor in the Church of Würrtemberg on account of his theological views and his refusal to sign the Formula of Concord.
4   Nicodemus Frischlin's astronomical work, rejected for publication in Württemberg, was published in Frankfurt.
5   Philip Melanchthon, *De dignitate astrologiae*, in *Corpus Reformatorum*, vol. 11, p. 263. This view was shared by Calvin and to a lesser extent Luther; the latter was in general more critical of astrology than was Melanchthon.
6   Paracelsus developed the 'weapon salve', which involved 'treating' the weapon which had caused the wound rather than the wound itself, while simply keeping the wound clean and dry. This was a great improvement on the previous practice of packing

wounds with irritating ointments – such as ground up eggshells – in the (empirically based) belief that wounds needed to form pus to heal. He also introduced laudanum and the use of mercury in the treatment of syphilis.

FURTHER READING

For the historical relationship between science and theology, see John Hedley Brooke, *Science and Religion: Some Historical Perspectives* (Cambridge, 1991), and Amos Funkenstein, *Theology and the Scientific Imagination from the Middle Ages to the Seventeenth Century* (Princeton, 1986). On the relationship between scientific revolution and the Reformation, see essays in David C. Lindberg and Robert S. Westman (eds), *Reappraisals of the Scientific Revolution* (Cambridge 1990); David C. Lindberg and Ronald L. Numbers (eds), *God and Nature: Historical Essays on the Encounter Between Christianity and Science* (Berkeley, Los Angeles and London, 1986), and Stephen Pumfrey, Paolo L. Rossi and Maurice Slawinski (eds), *Science, Culture and Popular Belief in Renaissance Europe* (Manchester and New York, 1991). Mikulás Teich and Roy Porter (eds), *The Scientific Revolution in National Context* (Cambridge, 1992), also offers some useful insights. For magic and occultism, see Keith Hutchison, 'What Happened to Occult Qualities in the Scientific Revolution?', *Isis* 73 (1982), pp. 233–53, and William Eamon, 'Technology as Magic in the Late Middle Ages and the Renaissance', *Janus* 70 (1983), pp. 171–212. Keith Thomas, *Religion and the Decline of Magic* (Harmondsworth, 1973), deals with important issues from another perspective. Much scientific development took place in the century after the Reformation; thus Reijer Hooykaas, *Religion and the Rise of Modern Science* (Grand Rapids, 1972), and Eugene M. Klaaren, *Religious Origins of Modern Science: Belief in Creation in Seventeenth-Century Thought* (Grand Rapids, 1977) – these works focus primarily on the seventeenth-century. Natural philosophy in the Renaissance is discussed in Charles Schmitt, Quentin Skinner and Eckhard Kessler (eds), *The Cambridge History of Renaissance Philosophy* (Cambridge, 1988). Specific studies of the influence of the German Reformation on aspects of science are Sachiko Kusukawa's *The Transformation of Natural Philosophy: The Case of Philip Melanchthon* (Cambridge, 1995) and Charlotte Methuen's *Kepler's Tübingen: Stimulus to a Theological Mathematics* (Aldershot, 1998). For medicine, see Ole Peter Grell and Andrew Cunningham (eds), *Medicine and the Reformation* (London and New York, 1993). Technology is discussed by Lynn White, Jr, *Medieval Technology and Social Change* (Oxford, 1962), and Donald R. Hill, *A History of Engineering in Classical and Medieval Times* (London and La Salle, 1984). Also of relevance are Jim Tester's *A History of Western Astrology* (Woodbridge and Wolfeboro, 1987) and David M. Burton's *The History of Mathematics: An Introduction* (Boston, 1985).

CHAPTER TWENTY-NINE

EDUCATION AND LITERACY

◆•◆

Karin Maag

A survey of the twin themes of education and literacy in the world of the Protestant Reformation raises a number of fundamental questions about the Reformation and its impact on the society of sixteenth-century Europe. The first are ones of terminology, as scholars are faced with the problem of defining terms such as literacy in the context of the sixteenth century. The second set of questions bring up the problem of unity of purpose among the reformers: in other words, can one claim that there was one consistent Reformation attitude towards education? Indeed, more fundamentally, can one claim that the Reformation was in fact the determining factor in the expansion of educational provision in Protestant areas in the sixteenth century? In answering these questions, the most fruitful approach may be to distinguish both between the aims of ecclesiastical and political leaders, and between the leaders' educational aspirations for the elite versus their aspirations for the main body of the population. Thus one must begin with an overview of the assumptions and goals of the reformers and their civil counterparts, and then examine the process by which education was provided, before finally analyzing the impact that the Reformation had (or failed to have) on the literacy and education levels of the populations of Protestant Europe.

THE REFORMERS AND EDUCATION

The debate over the reformers' impact on the education and literacy levels of the populations of Europe in the sixteenth century has been long running, fuelled by the lack of unanimity in defining its key terms. Scholars agree that one cannot apply twentieth-century standards of literacy to the sixteenth century, but uncertainty still persists as to its characteristics, compounded by the meagreness of surviving data in helping to establish who could or could not read and write. Literacy rates for the sixteenth century have generally been based on statistics taken from the proportion of the population able to sign their names in official documents. One should be clear, however, that in the sixteenth century reading and writing were two different skills, acquired at different times, and that the ability to do the one did not necessarily imply mastery of the other.[1] Furthermore, given that reading was taught first in school, and was more generally applicable, the trend of current scholarship suggests that the number of those who could read was higher than the number of those who left evidence of any ability to write. For the purposes of this article, and in order to encompass as broad a field as possible, the most basic form of literacy shall be understood as the ability to decipher a text in one's mother tongue sufficiently to be able to read it aloud and impart its meaning to others. Higher levels of literacy include those who could read silently to themselves, those who could write and those capable of reading texts in other languages than their mother tongue, including Latin.

Establishing what constituted education in the Reformation is equally complex, not so much because of the absence of data as because of an over-abundance of varieties of formal and informal education being provided at the time. For those living in Protestant Europe in the sixteenth century, education could include training at home by one's parents or by tutors, elementary vernacular schooling, Latin schooling, higher education at university level and catechetical instruction. Obtaining access to these different levels of education was dependent on factors such as social origins, gender and intended occupation as much as (if not more so than) on talent. As stated above, there was little uniformity of educational provision across the board in the Protestant areas of early modern Europe.

Part of the reason for the lack of uniformity was the corresponding lack of complete consensus among ecclesiastical and civil leaders as to the ultimate purpose of education for their populations. Furthermore, the leading reformers themselves were not necessarily consistent in their views throughout their lifetime, largely in response to evolving circumstances in their movement. The prime example of such changing views was Martin Luther. Up until the early 1520s, Luther believed that the most effective form of education was one combining religious training in the home, led by the head of the household, and academic study in schools, which were to be supported and funded by parents and the magistrates. However, after the shock of the German Peasants' War and the increasing realization that appealing to the voluntary support of parents and civil authorities was not producing any concrete results, Luther's views changed. By the late 1520s and early 1530s, he argued vigorously for compulsory schooling, to be organized and overseen by the secular authorities. Yet even this form of education did not touch the entire population: children whose education ended when they completed the curriculum of their local vernacular school, youngsters (particularly in rural areas) with no access to schooling on a regular basis, and of course older people, were left out of this educational scheme. Hence Luther and other German reformers, such as Johannes Bugenhagen, also strongly urged the importance of catechetical instruction to provide basic doctrinal education for a broader range of people. Works such as Luther's Small Catechism of 1529 were designed to help the general population in rural as well as urban areas to learn the basics about their faith through a question-and-answer format to be memorized and learned by rote. Indeed, there are signs that the reformers favoured catechetical instruction over unlimited access of the population to the Bible, because the catechism did not raise the spectre of multiple interpretations. In other words, the advocacy of catechetical study by the reformers was motivated in part by their perception of the catechism as a safe learning tool in the hands of otherwise ignorant populations.

Luther's two main approaches to the question of education, namely the provision of schools under civil control and the establishment of obligatory weekly catechism sessions, at least for the young, was a pattern adopted by other reformers and civil leaders across Europe. In many cases, the civil authorities took over schools previously controlled by the Catholic church, as in Zurich, where there were two Latin schools centred around each of the two main churches. The city fathers of Zurich also emphasized the importance of education at a more basic level by creating one main German vernacular school, organized and overseen by the city. Geneva, under the influence of John Calvin and Theodore Beza, created its Latin school together with the Academy in 1559. The reformers also organized the provision of catechetical works and, with the help of their civil counterparts, made attendance at catechism sessions mandatory, as did the Bernese authorities in the Pays de Vaud in 1545, for instance. It is clear therefore that the church and state powers did cooperate in many of these attempts to provide different forms of education for the people.

Both the ecclesiastical and civil authorities shared a belief in education as the means to a goal, rather than an end in itself, and the goal of that education depended on the social status of those being taught. For those boys and girls whose schooling was limited to what the vernacular schools offered, namely a basic knowledge of reading, counting and memorization of the catechism, the goal was to teach them to be good Christians and keep them off the streets. The authorities' aim in providing Latin schools and access to academies or universities was very different: in this case, the goal was to train up an elite to serve as the next generation of leaders, whether in the church, the law courts or the halls of government. The establishment of Latin schools, academies and universities in Protestant areas took the lion's share of educational resources, both human and financial. The magistrates of the French city of Toulouse, for instance, spent over 5,000 livres over the course of five years on the construction of their Latin school building. This was a significant sum of money, especially coupled with the principal's yearly salary of between 200 and 800 livres a year from the city to cover his wages and those of the regents.[2] This high level of investment was understandable given that, in doing so, the church and state leaders were fostering the development of those who would succeed them. Insofar as the civil and church authorities shared these goals in the Reformation period, they worked together to achieve the desired results.

However, this collaboration did not always imply that the reformers and the secular authorities were in total agreement over the aims of their educational programmes. The main tensions between the civil and ecclesiastical leaders in Protestant areas were ones of control and oversight. The secularization of the property and benefices of the Catholic church had brought increased income to the civil powers and part of the income gained was used to pay the salaries of the teachers and professors in the newly Protestant educational institutions. Yet allowing the civil authorities to have full control over educational provision on the strength of their financial support was not always to the liking of the reformers and their successors in the church. The ministers felt that they too should have oversight of the educational process, especially in terms of the doctrinal suitability of those teaching. This problem was particularly acute in areas where the clergy and secular authorities were already in conflict, as in the United Provinces after 1581. There, the synod meetings record the ongoing struggle of the ministers to maintain their right to examine the schoolteachers' orthodoxy, in the face of the magistrates' unwillingness to have the clergy involved. For instance, the Synod of Dordrecht, meeting in 1574 urged, 'The ministers shall see that the schoolmasters subscribe to the Confession of Faith, submit to the discipline and also instruct the youth in the Catechism and other useful things'.[3] In some cities, such as Geneva, the tensions between the two powers extended to criticism by the ministers regarding the inadequacy of the magistrates' financial support for the Academy and to warning of the dangers of broadening the curriculum of the Genevan Academy to include non-theology-related subjects such as civil law. In general, the Genevan Company of Pastors preferred to keep the Academy focused on what they perceived as its main goal, namely the training of ministers for Calvinist areas across Europe.

Yet in spite of these and other jurisdictional conflicts between the ecclesiastical and civil leaders, the curriculum in Latin schools and centres of higher learning rapidly acquired a relatively similar character across Protestant Europe. This similarity extended to the textbooks used in the Latin schools, the subjects taught in the academies and universities, and the overall teaching approach, which was one emphasizing grammar and memorization as the cornerstones of learning. Indeed, these features were common to all schools of that level, regardless of confessional orientation. Yet Protestant educational institutions highlighted their common identity more specifically through the provision of religious studies in the curriculum, based on the catechism and biblical studies. It remains to be seen whether the overall development and general uniformity of the curriculum in the period were due to impulses coming from the Reformation itself, or to other factors.

As noted above, the foundation level of the formal education system was the vernacular school, either run under the direct supervision of the civil authorities (as in Zurich) or with a minimum of intervention (as was the case in Geneva and for vernacular schools in England and the German lands). The authorities' involvement in the latter cases was limited to requiring teachers to seek permission from the authorities to run a school, and in many instances the schools received no official sanction whatsoever. These schools, where girls and boys were taught together in some places, and separately in others, provided the only opportunity for many to acquire any form of education. This was particularly true for the majority of girls, who could not attend the more advanced Latin schools and thus had little hope of advancing further in their studies. Girls who came from a wealthy or noble background were the only ones who could hope to accede to higher levels of learning, as they could sometimes share their brothers' private lessons. The vernacular schoolteachers did not generally have much schooling themselves and, in rural areas in particular, only offered their classes during the winter season, when the children were not needed in the fields. Private vernacular schools required pupils to pay a small fee, either in money or in kind, while official schools such as the one in Zurich were free for local children.

THE LATIN SCHOOLS

The next educational tier, the Latin school, was an institution with strong links both to the Renaissance and the Reformation. Usually located in cities, these schools offered a curriculum geared to boys from the ages of seven or eight to their mid-teens, and focused primarily on Latin grammar and composition, together with an introduction to Greek and Hebrew, alongside study of scripture and the catechism. Based on models provided by the Collège de Guyenne in Bordeaux and Jean Sturm's Latin school in Strasbourg, these schools evolved a system of successive classes, where pupils advanced from one level to the next by successfully passing yearly or semi-yearly examinations. These Latin schools are often seen as by-products of the Renaissance and northern humanism, particularly in France, where the pre-Reformation *Collèges* (as the Latin schools were known) served to reinforce and heighten French cities' pride in their accomplishments. The *Collèges*, organized and funded by the city authorities, represented both their new-found pride in the lay powers' control over higher education – a domain previously run solely by the Catholic church – and their desire to train the sons of the elite at a regional level, rather than in large and distant cities like Paris. England also saw a significant growth in the number of its Latin schools, known as grammar schools, which benefited from significant endowments provided by benefactors. By the mid-seventeenth century, England had over 400 schools open to the laity, most of these being grammar schools. This figure compares with only slightly over 30 schools open to the laity in England in 1480.[4] In France, the teachers in the Latin schools (known as regents) were usually products of this form of education themselves and in most cases also had university or academy training. Across Europe, the Latin schools generally provided education for free to local boys. Only those coming from outside the city at times had to pay a fee to the school over and above their boarding fees.

In other areas, such as the Holy Roman Empire and the Swiss lands, the creation or re-establishment of Latin schools by the secular authorities coincided with the adoption of the Reformation. Indeed, Luther's call for compulsory education found its response much more in the creation of municipal Latin schools than in the foundation of vernacular schools. The reasons for the civil authorities' support of Latin versus vernacular schools are clear. On the one hand, the Latin schools provided a much higher level of prestige for cities and principalities than did the vernacular establishments. On the other hand, the Latin schools were intended primarily to attract and educate the offspring of the secular leaders, rather than the sons of the poor artisans.

The greater involvement of the civil authorities in the Latin school took many forms. As well as paying the regents' and principals' salaries, the magistrates and princes also at times erected or renovated buildings to serve as the school and, in cities like Zurich, offered a programme of scholarships to attract worthy recipients to study there. Those attending the Latin schools had to conform to a code of discipline and attested daily to their allegiance to Protestantism through mandatory church attendance and daily school-wide reciting of psalms and prayers.

UNIVERSITIES

Students who continued their studies beyond the Latin school were usually destined for careers for which a certain amount of university-level education was increasingly seen as necessary. This included members of the clergy, lawyers, medical doctors and professors, in short, those who would later occupy significant positions in their society. Although the expansion in the number of universities in particular largely pre-dated the Reformation, especially in the German lands, the increasing Reformation emphasis on university-level training, especially for the clergy, fed the growth of higher study. Prior to the Reformation, there were around fifty universities across Europe. By 1600, Protestant powers had founded another twenty universities and academies. Once again, the significant investment in higher education by the civil authorities reflects their perception of universities and academies as prestige institutions, which would attract both students and world-famous scholars to their city or principality. The magistrates of the Dutch city of Leiden, for instance, competed fiercely for the privilege of having a university set up in their city and worked at recruiting top-level professors. By 1600, only twenty-five years after its foundation, the university already had twenty professors.

The impact of the Reformation on these institutions was also quite strong, particularly at times of confessional change. The Universities of Basle and Heidelberg, for example, which pre-dated the Reformation, saw their theology curriculum and overall statutes transformed once the secular authorities in these territories accepted the Reformation. This was equally true when territories changed their allegiances from one Protestant confession to another. For instance, when the strongly Lutheran Ludwig VI of the Palatinate succeeded his moderate Calvinist father Frederick III in 1576, the University of Heidelberg was rapidly affected: the Calvinist professors were dismissed – first in theology and then in humanities, law and medicine – and replaced with Lutheran professors. Simultaneously, the statutes governing the faculty of theology were altered to allow only Lutherans to teach there. Overall, throughout the sixteenth century, universities played a significant role in training ministers: by the end of the sixteenth century, 85 per cent of the clergy in the Electoral Palatinate were alumni of Heidelberg University.[5]

Areas which could not or would not create a university because of the absence of the necessary papal or imperial charter, established academies instead, similar in curriculum and academic reputation to the universities, but often smaller-scale both in the number of professors and range of subjects on offer. This was the case both in Geneva and in Zurich, as well as in France, where eight academies were set up between 1560 and 1604. These academies focused primarily on the most urgent task confronting them, namely the training of ministers. Over 160 students, mainly from France, enrolled in the Genevan Academy during the first three years of its existence and the majority of those whose career is known went on to become ministers in France. Indeed, the Genevan Company of Pastors fostered the close relations between the academy and churches elsewhere, by encouraging congregations to provide scholarships for young men who would return to serve those churches as pastors after their studies in Geneva were over.

The links between the Reformation and university-level education were clear, not only in the use of these institutions to prepare future Protestant clergy, but in the high level of involvement of the Protestant ecclesiastical authorities in the operations of these universities and academies. In Zurich, for instance, the day-to-day affairs of the Zurich academy were run by the *Verordneten zur Leer* – an educational committee in which the ministers of the city held the majority – together with the professors of the academy, who were in most cases also ordained. Although financial decisions remained the prerogative of the civic authorities, it was the educational committee that oversaw teaching, discipline and the progress of young men through the Latin colleges and the academy. The same held true for Geneva, where the day-to-day activities of the Academy were overseen by the Company of Pastors, though here too, the magistrates retained overall financial control.

IMPACT

The main difficulty in assessing the impact of the Reformation on educational provision in Protestant areas during the sixteenth century lies in establishing whether the developments which occurred were due solely or in part to the Reformation itself, or to other factors. Indeed, one line of argument suggests that it was the increased availability and participation in education that led to more general acceptance of the Reformation, especially in cities, and not the other way around. In this perspective, the development of education is tied much more to humanism and growing urban self-confidence than to religious change. And yet one cannot ignore the major increase in the number of Latin schools, academies and universities across Europe in the Reformation period. Leading reformers and their successors saw the creation of schools at all levels as part of their more general plan to transform society. The schools were instruments to train the young, and through them, it was hoped, older generations too would come to a fuller knowledge of Lutheran or Reformed doctrine. Increasingly as the decades wore on, however, both the ecclesiastical and civic authorities concentrated their attention and their resources on the education of the elite, both in an attempt to train up worthy successors to themselves and in response to the seemingly muted impact of the Reformation and its teachings on the population at large. For instance, visitation records from the second half of the sixteenth century in the German lands suggest that few people were able to give a satisfactory account of the faith in their own words to the visitors. Even those who had memorized and could recite the catechism could not necessarily explain the meaning of what they had learned.

What impact did the various forms of education provided in Protestant areas have on the people who were its recipients? Those who argue for the failure of the reformers' broader educational initiatives may be taking the reformers' own complaints too much at face value. The first years of the Reformation in the German lands were ones of heady hopes, not only in the realm of education. Once it was clear that the Reformation was establishing itself for the long-haul, rather than as a short-term radical movement culminating in Christ's return, the reformers' own attitudes were also transformed. By the time Zwingli and Calvin set up schools and academies together with the magistrates in their respective cities, the reformers' educational objectives had changed from a scheme in which all children would voluntarily be sent to school by their parents to a more selective process. The key question is therefore not whether the reformers' original objectives were met, but whether their more limited aims over the longer term were attained.

For their part, those sending students to Protestant centres of learning seemed convinced of the important spiritual and intellectual dimension of the education these students received. On 8 January 1565, for instance, the church of Aubeterre in France wrote to Geneva, asking the Company of Pastors to oversee the studies of Jean Boutellant, 'so that he may study and benefit not only from learning the ancient languages and doctrine of the Word of God, but also from church practice and polity, which is needed for ecclesiastical discipline.'[6] This church and others saw the Genevan Academy's role as a combination of intellectual and vocational training designed for the future leaders of the church.

The same confidence in the value of education in a Protestant context is clear from the letter sent on 21 March 1572 by the pastor Josue Finsler to the Zurich minister Burckhardt Leemann. Finsler recommended his fourteen-year-old son, Samuel, stressing the boy's preparatory work in Latin and Greek, and asking Leemann and Heinrich Bullinger to encourage his future studies in Zurich and to help him win a scholarship from the city.[7] Finsler's interest in having his son go to Zurich to study, in spite of the family's lack of necessary funds, highlights the importance attached by contemporaries to this training.

LITERACY

One of the chief ways in which historians attempt to measure the success of educational programmes is by examining their effect on literacy rates. As noted above, this presents particular difficulties for the Reformation period. Furthermore, the correlation between formal education and literacy is not necessarily complete, in that people could and did learn how to read by being taught informally by others, rather than attending school. A striking example of this is in Sweden, where the size of the territory and sparse population made it more effective for parents to teach their children at home, rather than to create formal schools except in the cities. By 1700, thanks to this approach, nearly 90 per cent of Sweden's population, both male and female, were literate.[8] Yet in spite of the variation in rates and differences in ways of measuring literacy, certain observations can be made.

The traditional approach to the question of literacy in Protestant areas has been to link the increase in the number of people, particularly among the laity, who were able to read, to the Reformation emphasis on generalized access to the Bible. The reformers' encouragement of Bible-reading by the laity, it is argued, led to a growth in the number of those actually able to decipher the scriptures and other texts. Some scholars point to the large number of Bibles or parts of the Bible being printed in the sixteenth century as evidence of an increasingly wide readership: the printers would not have been producing such large numbers of copies unless there were equally large numbers of purchasers. However, others suggest that the churches purchased these primarily for use as pulpit Bibles. Yet such an explanation fails to account for the production of small-format Bibles, unsuitable for use in the pulpit. Indeed, basing one's argument on the volume of works being printed in the years following the Reformation, it is clear that, at the very least, the idea of book ownership was spreading to a wider section of the community. In the French city of Amiens, for instance, 887 out of 4,443 after-death inventories recorded between 1503 and 1575 included lists of books, mainly religious works such as Books of Hours, Psalters and Bibles, but also works of law, literature and science.[9] However, the fact of owning a work does not necessarily imply the ability to read it.

Estimates of literacy rates for the early modern period vary greatly. One such estimate suggests that approximately 5 to 10 per cent of the population in the Holy Roman Empire was literate by 1600, rising to around 30 per cent of men in the cities of the German lands. This compares with a literacy rate of around 3 to 4 per cent in the German lands in the early sixteenth century.[10] The figure for women was consistently lower, though women in the cities had a greater chance of being literate than their sisters in rural areas. Literacy rates also grew as one progressed up the social scale, not surprisingly since (as described above) the sons of those at the upper end of society had a much better chance to benefit from both longer and higher calibre schooling. Estimates for England at Elizabeth's accession in 1558 were that 20 per cent of men and 5 per cent of women were literate.[11]

Having established that literacy rates did increase in the Reformation era, the question remains as to the impact of the Reformation on this trend. In the end, while the Reformation emphasis on Protestants reading the scriptures was one factor in the development of literacy, the impact of printing itself, the wider availability of printed works at a cheaper price, and the increasing focus on education and learning as key factors in obtaining a lucrative post, were also significant contributory factors. Indeed, the ferment of new ideas in the early years of the sixteenth century, coupled with the development of printing, may have been more significant than Protestantism in and of itself in making literacy attractive to a wider group. The advantages of literacy and education went beyond the goal of reading the scriptures. Those who saw the benefits of education and took part in the process of learning may well have had other, more pragmatic reasons for wanting to study. Yet the reformers' commitment to foster literacy and education as part of their overall programme cannot be doubted. In the end, it may be most accurate to consider the Reformation as one of the impulses towards increased education and literacy, but to move away from any mono-causal explanation of these complex phenomena.

NOTES

1   Jean-François Gilmont (ed.), *The Reformation and the Book* (St Andrews Studies in Reformation History; Aldershot, 1998), pp. 15–16.
2   George Huppert, *Public Schools in Renaissance France* (Urbana, 1984), pp. 24, 34.
3   From the minutes of the Synod of Dordrecht (1574), in A. Duke, G. Lewis and A. Pettegree (eds), *Calvinism in Europe, 1540–1610* (Manchester, 1992), p. 172.

4   Lawrence Stone, 'The Educational Revolution in England, 1560–1640', *Past and Present* 28 (1964), p. 44.
5   Bernard Vogler, *Le clergé protestant rhénan au siècle de la Réforme* (Paris, 1976), p. 57.
6   *Registres de la Compagnie des Pasteurs* (Geneva, 1969), vol. 3, p. 165.
7   Zurich Staatsarchiv, E II 344, fol. 33r.
8   Geoffrey Parker, 'An Educational Revolution? The Growth of Literacy and Schooling in Early Modern Europe', *Tijdschrift voor Geschiedenis* 93 (1980), p. 218.
9   Henri-Jean Martin, *The History and Power of Writing* (Chicago, 1994), pp. 347–8.
10 John Flood, 'The Book in Reformation Germany', in Gilmont, *The Reformation and the Book*, p. 85.
11 Paul F. Grendler, 'Schooling in Western Europe', *Renaissance Quarterly* 43 (1990), p. 779.

FURTHER READING

Apart from a few general studies, most of the works on education and literacy in the Reformation period have focused on a particular geographical area. An older work whose conclusions are still debated is Gerald Strauss's *Luther's House of Learning* (Baltimore, 1978). Strauss and his students have restated the conclusions of that work in various scholarly articles, including R. Gawthrop and G. Strauss, 'Protestantism and Literacy in Early Modern Europe', *Past and Present* 104 (1984). For France, the leading work in English remains George Huppert, *Public Schools in Renaissance France* (Urbana, 1984), though both Henri-Jean Martin, *The History and Power of Writing* (Chicago, 1994), and Roger Chartier, *The Cultural Uses of Print in Early Modern France* (Princeton, 1987), have made recent French scholarship available to English-speaking audiences. For developments in England, see Geoffrey Parker, 'An Educational Revolution? The Growth of Literacy and Schooling in Early Modern Europe', *Tijdschrift voor Geschiedenis* 93 (1980), pp. 210–220 and Tessa Watt's in-depth study of printing in England, *Cheap Print and Popular Piety, 1550–1640* (Cambridge, 1991). General works focusing on aspects of literacy, particularly printing, include the detailed survey by Elizabeth Eisenstein, *The Printing Press as an Agent of Change* (2 vols; Cambridge, 1979), and Jean-François Gilmont (ed.), *The Reformation and the Book* (St Andrews Studies in Reformation History; Aldershot, 1998). Useful overviews of recent work in a more condensed form include Paul Grendler (ed.) 'Education in the Renaissance and Reformation', *Renaissance Quarterly* 43 (1990), pp. 774–824 and Francis Higman, 'Quelques livres récents sur la réforme et le livre', *Bibliothèque d'humanisme et renaissance* 53 (1991), pp. 131–40.

THE REFORMATION AND POPULAR CULTURE

Trevor Johnston

Acommonplace assumption about the Reformation is that its relationship with popular culture was largely antagonistic. For Protestants, the reform or suppression of substantial elements of the culture of the people was vital to the creation of a genuinely Christian society. The attainment of godliness required the stark separation of religious from profane matters, the abolition of holidays and festivals, the disciplining of sexual relations, the restriction of recreation, the eradication of drunkenness and swearing, and the elimination of superstition. In short, it represented an assault on the bedrock of the culture of the masses in the pre-industrial period. However, while such campaigns were indeed important to the Reformation, recent scholarship has tended to stress the complexity and ambivalence of the relationship between the Protestant movements and popular culture. Peter Burke's *Popular Culture in Early Modern Europe* (1978), which inspired a resurgence of academic interest in the theme, presented a nuanced view of the process of reform, an approach reflected in the immense body of work by many scholars appearing since. Although it is impossible to speak of a consensus on this question, historians now are much less eager than were their predecessors to present the relationship between Protestantism and popular culture simply as one of antagonism and conflict. Important instances can be cited where the historical relationship was friendlier, where the Reformation did not seek to make (rather than merely ineffectually attempting) inroads, where Protestantism used and appropriated popular cultural forms rather than simply attacking them, or where the evangelical movement could be said to have developed a distinctive popular culture of its own.

Any approach to this topic confronts particular theoretical as well as methodological difficulties. Popular culture is not a given entity but a relatively modern construct, invented by theorists in the early nineteenth century and constantly subject to debate and refinement. However, the period in question, whilst admittedly not articulating a notion of popular culture (or of its corollary 'elite culture') did employ a system of binary classification of society and culture which could produce, or at least recognize, analogous categories, including such paired opposites as learned–unlearned, clerical–lay, powerful–disempowered, privileged–unprivileged, elites–masses, rich–poor, male–female, orthodox–heterodox and religious–superstitious.[1] Stuart Clark, in a recent study of early modern theories of witchcraft, has particularly emphasized the centrality to early modern culture, logic and rationality of such binary oppositions or 'contrarities'.[2] But, anachronism aside, conceptual difficulties remain – above all that of defining what popular culture is. Any definition must be dependent upon how one thinks of *culture* itself. Again there is no consensus, but theorists have tended to define the word broadly, arguing that it denotes a collective way of life as well as the works and practices of intellectual and artistic activity which reflect it. From this perspective, practices and texts become the raw material of any analysis aiming to uncover the underlying principles on which any society is founded. In the generous definition favoured by Peter Burke, culture is a system of shared meanings, attitudes and values, and the symbolic forms in which they are expressed or embodied. Defining 'popular' is, if anything, even more problematic. Modern cultural theory has expended much ink on whether popular culture is simply a reflection of cultural quantification (the culture of the majority), a residual category of elements left over after elite or 'high' culture has been defined, a populist 'mass' culture imposed from above, an authentic expression of 'the people' (generally conceived as the economically and politically subordinate strata of society), or, in terms redolent of the approach of the Italian Marxist theorist Antonio Gramsci, as the terrain of exchange, of resistance, incorporation, negotiation or ideological struggle between dominant and subordinate classes and groups.

If we take the 'residual' categorization as possibly the least problematic for our purpose of investigating early modern popular culture, it is clear that even this is not without its complications. Elite culture, the 'great' tradition as it has been called, might be defined as the exclusive culture of the literate minority of pre-industrial Europe (some 20 per cent of the population at most), popular culture (the 'little' tradition) as that of the remainder. Even here the boundaries are not hard and fast; there is substantial evidence that members of the elite themselves engaged in what one might regard as popular cultural activity. Whilst elites could be culturally amphibious in this way, however, the non-elite could not. Within the residual popular culture, there was, moreover, great differentiation. As historians have insisted, popular culture was *structured*. Cultural contrasts can be, and have been, pointed out between the different regions of Europe, between urban and rural communities (artisan and peasant), between diverse occupations and between groups of differing social status and wealth. Sex and age were also key variables. Popular culture embraced a variety of subcultures. Given this, the French historian Roger Chartier has preferred the analysis of 'cultural appropriation' to that of an essentialized popular culture, arguing for a focus on the varieties of engagement with shared cultural forms and products.[3] Such conceptual problems are compounded by empirical difficulties arising from the attempt to reconstruct a largely oral culture from surviving documentary sources. These were composed in the main by the period's elite, who had no interest in recording popular culture for its own sake and little interest in recording it at all, except perhaps when they were attempting to suppress it.

POPULAR CULTURE BEFORE THE REFORMATION

A prime feature of early modern popular culture, as noted above, was its orality. Folk stories, ballads and songs were transmitted orally from generation to generation. Tales, legends and proverbs helped to define and pass on practical knowledge of the natural world or provide guidelines to popular ethics, defining codes of conduct and perpetuating collective wisdom. The formulaic nature of much of this material (throughout Christian Europe the shared inheritance of Biblical phrases was important), backed by a strong auditory memory, facilitated its retention. As literacy gradually spread, partly as a consequence of the Reformation, some of this communication was also committed to text in the form of newsbooks, chapbooks, jest-books, almanacs, ballads, single-sheet broadsides and other printed ephemera. The relationship between orality and literacy is a complex one and given the nature of its production such cheap print cannot be taken as a direct reflection of popular culture, although it did enjoy a popular readership, if never exclusively so.

A further characteristic of popular culture was its visual sensitivity, one might even say its visual literacy. Distinctions of dress, the symbolism of colours, the devotional iconography of the pre-Reformation church, the brilliance of the night sky, were all supercharged with meanings and invitations to interpretation. Cheap print often reflected this visual acuity through its use of striking woodcut images. The corresponding texts would most likely have been read aloud (or sung) in company, oral and textual forms of communication thus neatly combining with the visual. Popular culture was moreover a ritual culture, dependent upon a repertoire of repeated, symbolically charged communal performances, gestures and patterns of speech. Alongside collective recreations and sports, parodies of church services, insults and even ritualized protest and rebellion were its stock ingredients. In the everyday life of the craft guilds of mediæval Europe, for example, economic processes were regulated, at least in part, by symbolic and ritualistic activities, including secret initiation ceremonies such as journeyman 'baptisms'. Ritual helped to define time as well as group identity. Popular festivals like May Day, Midsummer and Carnival shadowed the regular rhythms of the mediæval Catholic liturgical year, itself aligned to the agricultural cycle. Throughout Europe, particular trades celebrated the annual feast days of their patron saints, while each parish held an annual feast on its saint's day, a moment of great celebration and conviviality. Ecclesiastical holidays, and Sundays generally, offered the occasion not just for special religious celebrations, but also for collective recreation, providing opportunities for dancing, gambling and sports. A further link with ecclesiastical culture can be seen in the fact that many games were played in churchyards.

Since the liturgical year was closely allied to the seasons, the festive year followed suit and took its symbolic ingredients from its association with fertility and fecundity, with ploughing, sowing and harvesting. May Day, Whitsun, Midsummer and, above all, Carnival, the period immediately preceding the Lenten season of prescribed sexual as well as alimentary abstinence, were periods of licence in which human sexuality was both represented symbolically and expressed practically. Furthermore, such festivals (and Carnival in particular) gloried in taboo-breaking rituals of inversion, whereby the world was symbolically turned upside down through cross-dressing, elections of ordinary folk, fools or children to the *ersatz* status of kings, queens or bishops, or the storming of town halls and the creation of 'courts' to dispense popular justice. The social and political functions and significance of such ritualized behaviour in general, and of the element of inversion to be seen in festivals like Carnival in particular, have been much debated. There is indeed an obvious paradox in the apparent institutionalization of a ritual of disorder. Did festive inversion present a challenge to authority? Was it socially and politically subversive, or did it rather serve to uphold the existing order? Did the licence of Carnival actually work as a 'safety valve', as a canalization of dissatisfaction, allowing the oppressed to let off steam and express their frustration in ways which did not threaten the elite? Was it genuinely revolutionary, or did it instead express a rebelliousness that had become so institutionalized as to lose its potency? Such questions are more easily posed than answered, but, if we look beyond licensed misrule and its attendant inversions and parodies of the existing order, certain aspects of popular culture appear conservative. One could cite the use of shaming rituals such as the 'charivari' (in England sometimes known as 'rough music' or the 'Skimmington') to maintain a traditional patriarchal moral economy.

Historians have coined the rather nebulous term 'popular religion' to describe a particular subcategory of popular culture. In addition to dramatized accretions to the official liturgy, this has been taken to include customs that were more ominous to the ecclesiastical authorities because they were not restricted to the precincts of the church and were therefore less easily monitored by the clergy. The popular predilection for sacramentals – the sacerdotally consecrated water, herbs, palms and other objects which were given to the laity to be used for their own ends – is a case in point. Whilst theologians debated the status of sacramentals, they were popularly regarded as automatically efficacious and were used as talismans to protect people, property, livestock and crops from accident or disease. They thereby blended with a wider world of popular 'magic' which more transparently exceeded the limits of canonical orthodoxy. Along with officially sanctioned rituals, such as pilgrimages and the veneration of thaumaturgic relics and images, the widespread recourse to such practices demonstrates an instrumentalist approach to religion, whereby the sacred is harnessed for material gain.

Although many features of pre-Reformation popular culture appear universal, we must not forget its structural differentiation. There were, for example, significant contrasts between urban and rural cultural environments. While the inhabitants of the countryside might have been restricted to a few days of festivity in the course of the annual cycle, cities (particularly the largest like London, Venice or Paris) boasted a concentration of cultural activity, from bear-baiting to the theatre, to fill the gaps between holidays. The sexes also experienced popular culture differently, with women often cast as victims. Throughout Europe, women, generally educated to a lesser level of literacy than men, were often alienated from the textual forms of popular cultural transmission. They were also excluded from many cultural points of contact: the apprentice's workshop and the tavern remained male-dominated milieux and many leisure activities were male-oriented. Women did, however, participate in popular festivals and agrarian labour

Figure 30.1 Palm ass. The wooden ass was traditionally paraded round the village on Palm Sunday. (Colmar, Musée d'Unterlinden)

and furthermore enjoyed their own sites of sociability and cultural space. One early seventeenth-century illustrated English misogynist broadsheet attacking gossip or 'tittle-tattle' included the alehouse in such stereotypically 'female' locations as the childbed, the hothouse, the bakehouse, the well, the church, the market and the river.[4]

THE REFORMATION OF POPULAR CULTURE

Given the intimacy between popular culture and official religion, it was inevitable that the transformations wrought by the Reformation would have consequences for the relationship between the two. It was indeed the very intimacy of the relationship, which appeared to imply the entanglement of religion in secular culture, that so alarmed many reformers. To varying degrees all sought to open up a divide between the two, to liberate the faith from its enslavement to carnal profanity. Like the culture it assaulted, this campaign was far from uniform, being waged with differing intensity, at different times and in different places within the Reformation world. Between and among Lutherans, Calvinists, Anglicans and sectaries separate emphases emerged. As self-conscious a Calvinist as James I of England could promulgate the *Book of Sports* (1618), tolerating certain sports on Sundays after church, which in turn attracted the ire of equally self-conscious English Puritans. The example further underlines the fundamental political problem faced by reformers: the potential effectiveness of godly preaching, publishing and catechizing was one thing, that of enlisting the state and its policing powers (however underdeveloped these might have been in the period) was another. Still, certain generalizations about a 'Protestant' attitude towards popular culture can be made.

In the first instance, we find an assault on the popular cultural 'spaces' and 'moments' linked to the festivals of mediæval Catholicism. As Protestantism attacked the extravagant profusion of the mediæval liturgical year, eliminating holidays, saints' days and festivals such as Corpus Christi, so the secular or quasi-liturgical celebrations which had accrued around them were also eliminated. The reformers had no interest in appeals to tradition as a defence of such customs. Miracle and mystery plays and pilgrimage festivals were obvious early victims. The abolition of Catholic feasts also removed the symbolic utility or necessity of rituals parodying, or in other senses parasitic upon, the liturgical calendar. Carnival excess, for example, lost its symbolic power once the nature of Lent as a period of compulsory abstinence was diminished.

Carnival was attacked anyway, since its many-layered rituals and symbolism represented a microcosm of the disordered, carnal, immoral, inverted, pagan and, ultimately, demonic nature of popular culture in the eyes of the godly. Peter Burke, indeed, has referred to the reform of popular culture as the 'triumph of Lent', borrowing the metaphor from Brueghel's well-known mid-sixteenth-century painting of the 'Combat between Carnival and Lent'. The great Nuremberg *Schembartlauf*, for example, an especially elaborate Carnival procession dominated by the butchers' guild, was suppressed by the Lutheran town council in 1524. It was revived thereafter only once, in 1539, when its key feature was, appropriately enough, a satirical attack on the city's leading Lutheran reformer and the Carnival's most vocal critic, Andreas Osiander.[5]

In part to refute charges of antinomianism prompted by their advocacy of justification by faith, in part as a consequence of their staunch biblicism, Protestants stressed more than their Catholic predecessors had done a reformation of the morals of society. Popular culture and its array of recreations appeared to offer a host of opportunities for immorality: dancing, for example, being seen as a clear incitement to carnal lust. Games and festivals were associated in the reformers' eyes with idleness (and the sins which resulted from it), competition, jealousy, inebriation and violence. The young in particular were seen as both vulnerable and pernicious. Structures of youth sociability were often targeted. So-called 'abbeys of youth' were suppressed in Geneva in 1538 and Lausanne in 1544, where the youth had openly mocked the discipline of the Calvinist consistory. While the Protestant state was enlisted in the collective crusade to reform public recreations, individual rejection of such pastimes became a key theme of the spiritual conversions of the godly. Like many of his Reformed peers, the early eighteenth-century Yorkshire Quaker, Josiah Langdale, regretted a youth misspent in wrestling, playing football, going to the races and joining in the dancing which 'took much with the young people of our town'.[6] With alcohol a major lubricant of popular (especially masculine) culture, drunkenness became a special target. Godly preachers and writers focused on the evils of drink, inebriation leading to loss of control over one's passions and appetites, to lechery, swearing and other sins. Particular emphasis was duly placed on the alehouse as a prime location of popular culture to be disciplined and reformed. In his *God's Judgements upon Drunkards* (1659), the English moralist Samuel Hammond went so far as to describe the campaign against alehouses as the 'foundation of reformation'.[7]

In the place of recreation and its attendant disorder and mischief, reformers stressed sobriety, decency and order as the essential marks of godliness for the individual, the community and the state. For many Protestants, strict and decorous Sabbath-observance became a benchmark. The Lord's Day, they argued, should no longer be profaned by post-devotional recreation. Besides attending church, Sundays were to be spent reading the scriptures or learning the catechism. Divine worship itself was to express order and control, while preaching was to be untainted by excessive emotion, humour or coarse colloquialism. Sabbatarian strictures were a reflection of the complete disentanglement of the religious from the secular, of the sacred from the profane, which lay at the heart of Protestantism's approach to popular culture and which constituted perhaps the most ambitious element of the entire Reformation programme. It was an objective which brought immense psychological as well as social tension, not least to the godly themselves. The late seventeenth-century Saxon pastor, Christian Gerber, who attacked journeyman culture with its 'baptisms' and Shrove Tuesday 'sermons' as a blasphemous inversion of the Christian liturgy, still found it personally so pervasive and internalized that he feared for his own salvation. 'I myself worry', he wrote, 'that these insulting and blasphemous phrases will come into my mind and will entangle me, when I shall speak with God seriously and piously.'[8]

The assault on popular culture was moreover an attempt to replace bad religion by good. The reformers saw little distinction between orthodox pre-Reformation religion and its popular variants: all had to be reformed. Once the mass, the formal liturgy and such hitherto accepted practices as saints' holidays and pilgrimages had been disposed of, the godly could turn their attention to popular religious culture, to the non-canonical, magical or 'superstitious' practices of the laity. Such operations were denounced as blasphemous, idolatrous, vain and, implicitly if not explicitly, demonic in inspiration. The campaign, which found its most extreme expression in the witchcraze, was pursued across Protestant Europe, although with varying degrees of intensity. Zealous reformers could find superstition almost anywhere, for example in popular attitudes towards time and place, which were held to echo Catholic notions that some seasons or sites were more sacred than others. John Knox even suggested that all mediæval churches might have to be destroyed because of their superstitious associations.[9]

The campaign met with varying degrees of success. Recent scholarship has tended to question and qualify its practical impact. Against a background of traditional triumphalism regarding the Reformation's impact in Germany, Gerald Strauss has offered a valuable corrective, stressing the limitations of reform during its first century and the failure of Protestantism to reduce the rural areas to anything beyond the most superficial conformity. This failure occurred despite the mobilization of the resources and policing functions of the territorial state behind the reformers' cause. Strauss attributes this failure to the crude and hasty techniques of indoctrination themselves, but also to the surprisingly stubborn resilience of popular religious culture. State-appointed inspectors and godly pastors railed against the ignorance, 'superstition' and loose-living of their congregations, who in turn seem to have reacted with bored apathy towards prescriptions which they saw as irrelevant and prohibitions which they interpreted as threats to their material existence. Attacks on popular festive culture hit at established vehicles of socialization and communal cohesion, while Protestant advocacy of prayer and resignation to the divine will offered scant replacement for the array of sacramentals and instrumentalist magic tolerated by the pre-Reformation church. It was not unknown, for example, for the populations of officially Lutheran parishes to browbeat their pastors into continuing the ancient practice of ringing church bells during thunderstorms to ward off the devils responsible for the weather. At the risk of alarming the most vocal and zealous of their theologians and moralists, or of co-religionists elsewhere, many Protestant regimes indeed seem to have found that measure of compromise with popular traditions in the long run made for better social control. Such toleration also extended to popular recreational culture. In England, to Puritan consternation but in part through explicit royal protection, many popular diversions survived the Reformation era. In 1720 a commentator could still note that, in London, 'the more common sort divert themselves at Foot-ball, Wrestling, Cudgels, Ninepins, Shovelboard, Cricket, Stow-ball, Ringing of Bells, Quoits, pitching the Bar, Bull and Bear baiting, throwing at Cocks, and lying at Alehouses.'[10]

Nevertheless, the reformers did make inroads, even if these were slower, more uneven and less irrevocable than they themselves had anticipated. One example of Protestantism's impact on popular culture is the growth of literacy, a product and aim of the educational expansion of the sixteenth and seventeenth centuries. For the godly, literacy was a key to the advance of the Reformation, implanting knowledge of the Word, fostering faith and in turn salvation. One seventeenth-century Zurich schoolmaster even claimed that those who could not read or write would go to hell.[11] However limited, a gradual expansion of literacy enabled a text-based popular culture to develop and prosper alongside the oral and visual

Figure 30.2 Hans Sebald Beham, *The Dance of the Noses*, 1520. Evangelical ministers of all confessions set their face against popular revelries, often the occasion for wild and prolonged debauchery. But their strictures usually fell on stony ground. (Oxford, Ashmolean Museum)

modes of transmission. In England by the 1660s up to 400,000 almanacs were being sold annually, although the largest area of growth, it has been argued, was specifically that of vernacular religious literature.[12]

Despite the implacability of the language used by godly reformers in their attack on popular culture, despite the apparent centrality of the campaign to the core objectives of the Reformation and their invocation of it as a barometer of the movement's success or failure, Protestantism was not the sole motor for cultural reform. Indeed, such reform long pre-dated the Reformation. In Strasbourg, Sebastian Brandt attacked the 'folly' of Carnival as a useless waste of time and money in the second edition of his *Narrenschiff* (1495), while the following year Savonarola lambasted the Florentine festival in almost identical terms. This was itself a long tradition and, as Peter Burke has recalled, churchmen had condemned popular culture along such lines since the beginnings of Christianity, although arguably there was a difference between sporadic mediæval reform and the concerted campaigns of the Reformation period, driven by sharper ideological motivations.

It must further be remembered that post-Tridentine Catholicism generated its own campaign against popular culture, both as a continuation of older drives and in response to the Protestant challenge. Space prohibits a detailed discussion here of the Catholic reform movement, but, as historians of confessionalization have demonstrated, in many respects Catholic campaigns closely mirrored those of Protestantism in their objectives, methods and degree of success: an interesting example of convergent evolution. In the Catholic world, popular festivals were abolished or restructured to encompass a more explicitly spiritual message, while greater clerical control over confraternities was intended to spiritualize their energies and activities. A traditional culture of courtship was attacked through the Tridentine prohibition of clandestine marriage, while harsher attitudes towards pre- and extra-marital sex, blasphemy, drunkenness and 'superstition' can be observed. Like their Protestant counterparts, Catholic ecclesiastical and secular authorities desired, as one Bavarian diocesan decree put it, that 'little by little the common folk of both sexes should be led from dances, plays and other games and spectacles to piety and the observance of divine mandates'. Nevertheless, and again like many of their evangelical counterparts, Catholic elites often plumped for a *modus vivendi* with much of popular culture in preference to constant confrontation. Often, too, more subtle techniques of substitution were employed in preference to crude suppression. In Germany, Jesuits staged their own Carnival plays to lure their flocks away from the 'scandalous' versions, or extended the range of sacramentals offered to the laity in order to obviate their recourse to non-canonical magical techniques. The seventeenth-century Jesuit Georg Vogler set hymns to popular melodies and published a catechism for people to read at home or in their spinning-bees, those sites of youth sociability which other reformers were simultaneously lambasting as dens of lechery.[13]

Moreover, it would be wrong to attribute all reform of popular culture to religious impulses alone and to ignore its secular motivations. Naturally it is difficult to distinguish the two, since profane concerns were habitually given a window-dressing of religious language. The expansion of literacy already noted arguably owed as much to humanist ideals of social well-being and good citizenship as to narrower evangelical concerns. Similarly the creation and maintenance of an orderly, disciplined, thrifty population of obedient subjects, workers and taxpayers was a ubiquitous aim of the increasingly centralized municipal and dynastic regimes of late mediæval and early modern Europe. The Reformation might well have accelerated the process, but it did not initiate it. The regulation of Carnival in German cities, for example, had already gathered pace during the fifteenth century (the earliest recorded ban on mumming, or Carnival masking, was in Cologne in 1403). This owed much to the concerns of urban patriciates to preserve public order and their own authority in a period of intensified economic, political and social competition between guilds. Hans-Ulrich Thamer has observed a

LOCATION	QTY	ISBN	AUTHOR/TITLE
Y-13A-003-73	1	0-415-26859-1	PETTEGREE, ANDREW REFORMATION WORLD

strongly secular and utilitarian concern with economic efficiency, as well as a religious motivation, behind the reform of handicraft culture in Germany as early as the start of the sixteenth century, although the heyday of utilitarian regulation would come in the seventeenth and eighteenth centuries.[14] Practical concerns of a different kind underlie an attack on sports by the authorities in mediæval England: too much recreation of the wrong kind distracted folk from more useful activities, such as archery practice. For early modern England, it has been suggested that population growth and price-inflation exacerbated a social polarization between the 'middling sort' of parish elites and their poorer neighbours, provoking a steady withdrawal of local elites from more popular recreations. This was a fissure which, in so far as it figured at all, the advent of Puritanism merely intensified.

THE REFORMATION AS POPULAR CULTURE

Thus far, the relationship between the Reformation and popular culture has been presented as largely adversarial. However, much recent historical work has pointed to a more dynamic and positive relationship and to ways in which Protestantism was shaped by and accommodated itself to popular culture. Indeed a description of the Reformation as itself, in part at least, a form of popular culture is not too extreme.

In the first instance there is the striking propagandistic use of popular cultural forms to advance the cause of the Reformation, especially at its inception when the new movement lacked the backing of the state. Indeed the speedy response to and grass-roots appeal of reform is scarcely explicable without this medium. One can speak here of a Reformation *through* popular culture. Much of the research on this theme to date has focused on the evangelical movement's German heartland. There, Protestantism made an appeal to the people through the cultural forms with which they were familiar, above all the oral medium of preaching and the combined textual and visual medium of the printed broadside. A popular medium was accompanied by a popular message, for the content revealed an effort on the part of the Reformation's clerical and lay leaders to meet the concerns of ordinary folk and to couch the delicate nuances of Protestant theology in simple terms. The result was an unprecedented wave of popular propaganda, both undermining the authority of the church by unmasking its corruption, arrogance and blasphemy, and at the same time positively announcing the new reformed message. In German broadsheets, images of 'Karsthans', a kind of Piers Ploughman figure – a sturdy, honest and upright peasant – acted as the visual embodiment of the 'simple' folk whom the Reformation leaders were inviting to embrace the gospel. The crude, often scatological content of the imagery, as in Luther's series of lampoons of the papacy which were accompanied by woodcuts showing, among other activities, peasants defecating into the pope's inverted tiara, was firmly anchored in the coarse, flatulent and topsy-turvy world of Carnival.

Beside such printed propaganda, attention has been drawn to the role of ritual in the inception of the Reformation and in particular to the stock popular cultural mode of festive inversion as a powerful weapon of reform. In the context of the religious tensions of the early Reformation, carnivalesque mockery of the clergy could easily become a trigger for the expression of serious, even violent anticlericalism. Popular festivals thus constituted privileged sites for the introduction of the Reformation. Rituals of inversion acquired novel and radicalized significance in this climate of evangelical expectation. In 1524, for example, revellers in the Ernestine Saxon town of Bucholz parodied the exhumation in the ducal Saxon city of Meissen of the relics of the newly canonized St Benno with a procession featuring horse- and cattle-bones. They had doubtless been influenced by Luther's own published critique of the canonization, *Against the New Idol and Old Devil who is to be Elevated in Meissen*, which itself constituted a deployment of rhetorical inversion. By 1536 the real relics at Meissen were themselves in danger from iconoclasm.

Iconoclasm, which was almost everywhere a feature of the onset of reform, was a phenomenon which despite its novelty appears to have often exhibited structural similarities to pre-Reformation festal inversion. Such a homology would account for the ways in which many Catholic devotional images were assaulted, often being subjected to a range of verbal and physical insults, to imitations of early modern rituals of capital punishment or to parodies of their original rites of consecration. Such images could be subjected to alarming abuse, as when a man defecated into the mouth of a crucifix in Ulm in 1534 or when crucifixes were smashed, dismembered and decapitated in Augsburg in 1529, Cologne in 1536 and in other German cities in the same period. 'With such actions', Natalie Davis has written of parallel events in France during the Wars of Religion, 'the crowds seem to be moving back and forth between the rites of violence and the realm of comedy'. Such events have prompted some historians to describe the Reformation as a 'ritual process', as a collective rite of passage for entire congregations and communities which drew in turn on the stock performances and gestures of traditional popular culture. Ritual, one might speculate, was a necessary psychological facilitator for the shocking transition from one, hitherto accepted, culture and sacred system to another.

This paradoxical Reformation through ritual and the deployment of festive inversion to further evangelical objectives is most marked in the early period of the reform, when there was clearly an overlap, if not a conscious alliance, between a subversive religious ideology and the latent rebellious streak within popular culture. In a second phase, which saw the consolidation of Protestantism and the formation of territorial or state churches, one can observe popular cultural forms still associated with religious reform, but with their content adapted to the maintenance of a new religious order. In Lutheran Nuremberg, for example, traditional Carnival plays were retained, but their style and content were adapted to communicate a message more in tune with the values of the city's newly reformed elite. The plays of the cobbler Hans Sachs were moralizing, post-Reformation versions of their obscene and scatological predecessors. Elsewhere, though, the ambivalence inherent in the use of popular cultural forms to convey a message of religious renewal could lead to a repudiation of them by the radicals. For England, Patrick Collinson has written of a 'Protestant cultural revolution' as in the late sixteenth century an accommodation of popular cultural forms such as plays, songs and images for propagandistic purposes gave way to their rejection as an acceptable tool of reform by the godly. Nevertheless, this repudiation was nowhere total, even in England, where the 'pulp press' of the seventeenth century featured works which, although crude and salacious in style, nevertheless contained moralizing critiques of sinful behaviour which echoed the strictures of godly ministers. Peter Lake has argued that a common literary subgenre, the 'murder pamphlet', which overdosed on schlock, horror and titillation, nevertheless contained an almost subliminal message that was Protestant and even Puritan, concentrating on the catastrophic consequences of any abuse or loss of patriarchal control and authority, on the ubiquitous activity of the Devil and on the awesome power of divine providence.[15]

Protestantism could appropriate aspects of traditional popular culture, but it could also develop a distinctive popular culture of its own. England provides the setting for the growth of a culture which combined a strong sense of Protestant identity (grounded not least on anti-Catholicism) and a secular patriotism which at times could express itself in violent xenophobia. David Cressy and others have explored the way in which a new, Protestant and uniquely English festal calendar came to supplement the pre-Reformation festive round in the Elizabethan and Stuart periods, providing for a novel form of 'national memory'. Highlights of this new year, celebrated with bonfires and bells, were the dates of 5 and 17 November, commemorating respectively the deliverance of the monarchy from the popish conspirators of the Gunpowder Plot of 1605 and the accession of Elizabeth I, the champion of Protestant England against Catholic Spain. The latter festival, 'Crownation Day', was the first annual concert of bells in England that was not tied to the traditional Christian year.

Harder to discern, although the subject of recent scholarly research, is the development of a distinctively Protestant popular religion and magical culture. This must be distinguished from vestiges of Catholic practices, which were everywhere difficult to eradicate. Whilst repudiating Catholic notions of sanctity, for example, otherwise orthodox Lutheran officials simultaneously fostered the development of a Luther-cult, attached to the person, the 'relics', portraits and even the house of the reformer, to which quasi-miraculous powers of incombustibility were attributed. This stance was echoed at the popular level, where Luther (as a Jesuit reported from Lower Bavaria in 1564) was called 'holy Dr Martin and noble man of God'.[16] By contrast German Protestants could retain the festive processions marking the onset of winter which had formerly been dedicated to St Nicholas by simply demoting the Catholic saint into a mere holy man. Meanwhile, the martyrologies composed in the sixteenth century by Anglicans, Huguenots and Anabaptists also helped to ensure a continued focus in popular consciousness on the heroic spirituality of individuals rather than on abstract soteriological concepts.

In the formal absence of miracles, prodigies (which were more easily accommodated within a reformed providential framework) assumed greater significance within Protestant popular culture, and not only in the early years of the Reformation when religious renewal was associated with a heightened sense of apocalyptic expectation. Harder to accommodate were the lay prophets, visionaries and even thaumaturgists who gained prominence, above all in Lutheran Germany and Scandinavia. Their popular resonance could not be ignored by Lutheran elites, even if their experiences did not always appear to fit within the prescribed parameters of belief. Authors, often pastors, tried to gloss such experience in orthodox terms in a subgenre of popular pamphlet literature, the stock ingredient of which became the encounter between ordinary folk and angels announcing the doom through plague, war or famine of communities which failed to repent.[17] Besides an expanded angelology, popular Protestantism in Germany and elsewhere also developed its own 'magical' traditions, exemplified by the sacrality attributed to such objects as Bibles, hymnbooks, catechisms or other religious books, which were employed for divination, healing or protective magic. One might also cite popular evangelical burial practices, such as the laying of wreaths in the grave or hanging them up in church as a memorial to the deceased, a custom which developed in Reformation Germany and was defended by ordinary folk against the ecclesiastical authorities when elite attitudes towards it hardened in the eighteenth century. Such practices are evidence of the continuing role of ritual and of an instrumentalist approach to religion in Protestant culture, and a reminder that the popular division of the world between sacred and profane did not always match the official template designed by the godly.[18] In a flagrant act of apotropaic magic, recounted by the historian David Sabean, the villagers of Beutelsbach in Lutheran Württemberg were discovered by the ducal authorities to have buried a live bull as a defence of their cattle against an outbreak of foot-and-mouth disease; perhaps the most astonishing aspect of this case is that it occurred as late as 1796.

CONCLUSION

The relationship between the Reformation and popular culture, however one defines the latter term, was complex and multi-faceted, making neat generalizations impossible. If the attitude of reformers towards the most central popular customs was usually negative, the degree of hostility, the mechanisms employed to implement change and the effects of such assaults varied enormously. They were determined not only by formal theological positions (although Calvinists were generally less compromising than, say, Lutherans) but also by contingent factors, by each reforming instance's particular dynamic. The result was that much popular culture remained intact, much established custom survived in a partially reformed guise and 'new' popular traditions arose, which while recognizably Protestant were nonetheless at odds with elite attitudes. Ironically perhaps, a significant effect was that increasingly the godly seem to have given up on their initial attempt to reform popular culture into a simulacrum of their own and to have concentrated instead on putting distance between them. This cultural divergence, which can be seen throughout Protestant Europe, owed much to secular factors, to broader social and economic trends, as well as to religion. It represented, nevertheless, one of the most lasting legacies of the Reformation world.

NOTES

1   Bob Scribner, 'Introduction', in Bob Scribner and Trevor Johnston (eds), *Popular Religion in Germany and Central Europe, 1400–1800* (Houndmills, 1996), p. 3.

2   Stuart Clark, *Thinking with Demons: The Idea of Witchcraft in Early Modern Europe* (Oxford, 1997), pp. 31–68.

3   Roger Chartier, 'Culture as Appropriation: Popular Cultural Uses in Early Modern France', in Steven L. Kaplan (ed.), *Understanding Popular Culture* (Berlin, New York and Amsterdam, 1984), pp. 229–53. A similarly 'dynamic' view of cultural exchange underpins the work of Natalie Zemon Davis. See, for example, 'From "Popular Religion" to Religious Cultures', in Steven Ozment (ed.), *Reformation Europe: A Guide to Research* (St Louis, 1982), pp. 321–41.

4   Martin Ingram, ' "Scolding women cucked or washed": A Crisis in Gender Relations in Early Modern England?', in Jenny Kermode and Garthine Walker (eds), *Women, Crime and the Courts in Early Modern England* (London, 1994), pp. 48–80. A reproduction of the broadsheet appears facing p. 88.

5   Keith Moxey, *Peasants, Warriors and Wives: Popular Imagery in the Reformation* (Chicago and London, 1989), pp. 14–15.

6   Barry Reay, 'Introduction: Popular Culture in Early Modern England', in *Popular Culture in Seventeenth-Century England* (London and Sydney, 1985), pp. 1–30, here p.2.

7   Keith Wrightson and David Levine, *Poverty and Piety in an English Village: Terling, 1525–1700* (2nd edn; Oxford, 1995), p. 136.

8   Hans-Ulrich Thamer, 'On the Use and Abuse of Handicraft: Journeyman Culture and Enlightened Public Opinion in 18th and 19th Century Germany', in Kaplan, *Understanding Popular Culture*, pp. 275–300, here pp. 282–3.

9   C. John Sommerville, *The Secularization of Early Modern England: From Religious Culture to Religious Faith* (New York and Oxford, 1992), p. 28.

10 Robert W. Malcolmson, *Popular Recreations in English Society, 1700–1850* (Cambridge, 1973), p. 34.

11 Kaspar von Greyerz, 'Switzerland', in Bob Scribner, Roy Porter and Mikuláš Teich (eds), *The Reformation in National Context* (Cambridge, 1994), pp. 30–46, here p. 42.

12 Keith Wrightson, *English Society, 1580–1680* (London, 1982), pp. 197–8.

13 *Constitutiones et decreta ... per dioecesim Ratisbonensem observanda* (Ingolstadt, 1588), p. 9. On Vogler, J.M. Valentin, 'Jesuiten-Literatur als gegenreformatorische Propaganda', in H. Glaser (ed.), *Deutsche Literatur. Eine Sozialgeschichte* (Reinbek, 1985), vol. 3, pp. 172–205.

14 Harry Kühnel, 'Die städtische Fasnacht im 15. Jahrhundert', in Peter Dinzelbacher and Hans-Dieter Mück (eds), *Volkskultur des Europäischen Spätmittelalters* (Stuttgart, 1987), pp. 109–27. Thamer, 'Use and Abuse of Handicraft'.

15 Peter Lake, 'Deeds against Nature: Cheap Print, Protestantism and Murder in Early Seventeenth-Century England', in Kevin Sharpe and Peter Lake (eds), *Culture and Politics in Early Stuart England* (Houndmills, 1994), pp. 257–83.

16 Benno Hubensteiner, *Vom Geist des Barock* (2nd edn; Munich, 1978), p. 62.

17 Jürgen Beyer, 'Wahrhafte Wundergeschichte von neuen propheten, die aller Welt zu rechtschaffener Busse und besserung aufrufen: Lutherske folkelige profeter i 1500- og 1600-tallet', Magister Dissertation, University of Copenhagen, 1990.

18 Robert W. Scribner, 'The Reformation, Popular Magic and the "Disenchantment of the World" ', *Journal of Interdisciplinary History* 23 (1993), pp. 475–94; 'The Impact of the Reformation on Daily Life', in *Mensch und Object im Mittelalter und in der frühen Neuzeit. Leben–Alltag–Kultur* (Vienna, 1990), pp. 315–43.

FURTHER READING

The indispensable point of departure remains Peter Burke, *Popular Culture in Early Modern Europe* (London and New York, 1978), still the only work on the subject to encompass the whole of Europe. A revised reprint, with an updated bibliography and introduction discussing the major recent debates on the subject, appeared in 1994. See also Burke's summary of recent historiographical trends: 'Revolution in Popular Culture', in Roy Porter and Mikuláš Teich (eds), *Revolution in History* (Cambridge, 1986), pp. 206–25. The theoretical and methodological problems associated with the topic are also addressed in an essay by the late Bob Scribner, 'Is a History of Popular Culture Possible?', *History of European Ideas* 10 (1989), pp. 175–91. John Storney, *An Introductory Guide to Cultural Theory and Popular Culture* (New York, 1993), summarizes the debates of modern cultural theorists. Considerable conceptual as well as empirical work on pre-modern popular culture has been undertaken by French historians, much of it now available in English. Their approaches are reviewed by Stuart Clark in 'French Historians and Early Modern Popular Culture', *Past and Present* 100 (1983), pp. 62–99. A separate theoretical lineage is that of the Italian micro-historians, whose leading exponent Carlo Ginzburg has written a classic of popular cultural history with *The Cheese and the Worms: The Cosmos of a Sixteenth-Century Miller*, trans. John and Anne Tedeschi (London, 1980). Anthropological and sociological theories of ritual and their application to early modern culture are discussed in a valuable synthesis by Edward Muir, *Ritual in Early Modern Europe* (Cambridge, 1997). The earthy, flatulent, inverted world of pre-Reformation Carnival is vividly evoked in Richard Wunderli, *Peasant Fires: The Drummer of Niklashausen* (Bloomington and Indianapolis, 1992).

In contrast to Peter Burke's geographically wide-ranging approach, most discussion has been rooted in national contexts. For England, a set of essays edited by Barry Reay, *Popular Culture in Seventeenth-Century England* (London and Sydney, 1985), provides a starting point. The relationship between popular culture and the Reformation in England is explored in a subtle analysis by Martin Ingram, 'Ridings, Rough Music and the "Reform of Popular Culture" in Early Modern England', *Past and Present* 105 (1984), pp. 79–113. Much debate has centred on the role of print, a medium traditionally regarded as having revolutionized popular culture. A superbly nuanced study, emphasizing cultural continuities and the ambiguous nature of 'reform', is presented by Tessa Watt in her *Cheap Print and Popular Piety, 1550–1640* (Cambridge, 1991). The growth of a distinctively Protestant festal culture is documented in David Cressy's lively *Bonfires and Bells: National Memory and the Protestant Calendar in Elizabethan and Stuart England* (London, 1989). Still highly suggestive on 'popular religion' is the classic study by Keith Thomas, *Religion and the Decline of Magic* (London, 1971).

For France, the collection of essays by Natalie Zemon Davis, *Society and Culture in Early Modern France* (Cambridge and Oxford, 1987), explores the relationship between Protestantism and cultural conflict, while a classic case-study of slippage from festive inversion to violent social protest in the context of the French religious wars is Emmanuel Le Roy Ladurie's *Carnival in Romans: A People's Uprising at Romans, 1579–1580*, trans. Mary Feeney (Harmondsworth, 1981).

For Germany, the work of Bob Scribner has been pioneering in relating Reformation studies to early modern popular culture and in developing an original approach to the subject, stressing the paradox of a popular Protestantism still wedded to images, ritual and magic. His extensive research on this theme can be approached through his *For the Sake of Simple Folk: Popular Propaganda for the German Reformation* (2nd edn; Oxford, 1994) and *Popular Culture and Popular Movements in Reformation Germany* (London, 1987). The story of the Beutelsbach bull is recounted in David Sabean, *Power in the Blood: Popular Culture and Village Discourse in Early Modern Germany* (Cambridge, 1984). Gerald Strauss has questioned the extent of the reformers' impact on popular religious culture in his *Luther's House of Learning: Indoctrination of the Young in the German Reformation* (Baltimore and London, 1978).

INDEX